T0300799

The Franklin Scandal

A Story of Powerbrokers, Child Abuse and Betrayal

Nick Bryant

Published by:
Trine Day LLC
PO Box 577
Walterville, OR 97489
1-800-556-2012
www.TrineDay.com
publisher@TrineDay.net

Library of Congress Control Number: 2012944884

Bryant, Nick
The Franklin Scandal: A Story of Powerbrokers, Child Abuse & Betrayal—1st ed.
 p. cm.
Includes references and index.
(ISBN-13) 978-1936296-07-1 (ISBN-10) 1936296-07-1
1. Political corruption—Nebraska—Douglas County—Investigative Case Studies. 2. Political corruption—United States—Washington DC—Investigative Case
Studies 3. Child Abuse—United States—Nebraska—Investigative Case Studies.
4. Child Abuse—Pedophilia—Pandering—Investigative Case Studies. 5. Franklin Scandal—Mechanics of cover-up—Nebraska—Douglas County—Investigative
Case Studies. 1. Title

FIRST EDITION (REVISED FOR SOFTCOVER)
10 9 8 7

Printed in the USA
Distribution to the Trade by:
Independent Publishers Group (IPG)
814 North Franklin Street
Chicago, Illinois 60610
312.337.0747
www.ipgbook.com

All that is necessary for the triumph of evil is that good men do nothing.
—attributed to Edmund Burke

Foreword

The Franklin Scandal

As a psychiatrist, I have observed numerous times the extremes to which some individuals go to control, exploit, sexually abuse, and physically damage vulnerable children (who are frequently their own offspring). The ability to maintain an enduring silence is an essential feature of the abuser's power. Remove that silence, and you make him powerless. Any system of government that does not have built in checks and balances, credible appeal processes, and access to truly independent review will inevitably become corrupt. Non-accountability, allied with ignorance, self-interest and/or certainty of belief, is very troubling, whether the institution is the police, intelligence services, child safety services, the church, state orphanages, cults, or the family.

Yet the forces within society that silence the open reporting of trauma have been tenaciously powerful, generally taking a global stand that, of course, child abuse is to be deplored, and then setting out to discredit the veracity of reports and the motivations and credibility of those who make such claims or those who support them. Threat, intimidation and even the manipulation of the legal and political system may occur. Human rights abuses are only able to be investigated and documented where there is an accessible police and justice system, and enough political awareness and resolve to recognize that all of society generally benefits when such abuse and exploitation is publicly reported via a free press.

One might conceptualize the human condition as an enduring struggle between the dynamics of selflessness and the dynamics of narcissism. The selfless dynamic sees individuals bonded into family groups. It encompasses empathic connection, mutual support, and brings with it a capacity to love and to grieve. The narcissistic dynamic is in many ways the opposite. People and resources are used: personal priorities and personal gratifications (frequently involving power, sex, and money) are paramount. Narcissistic individuals are not encumbered by empathy, and some highly talented and intelligent narcissists can be very persuasive and attain prominent and powerful positions.

An expanded reporting of abuse and exploitation scandals—involving churches, church schools, state institutions, politicians, police, therapists, cults, the military, human traffickers, and families—does not indicate that mankind has fallen into an abyss. But rather, as painful as it sometimes is, it demonstrates that we have begun to acknowledge much more publicly those sorts of abuses that have always been endemic in our society.

As an example of courageous and thorough reporting about a powerfully connected child sexual exploitation ring, Nick Bryant's seven-year investigation of the Franklin saga is unsurpassed. What makes Nick's account so powerful and credible is that he amassed so many witnesses and so much documentary evidence as to establish his case beyond reasonable doubt. At the same time, he is at pains not to make pronouncements of apparent fact that go beyond the verifiable data. He also leaves the reader an unwritten challenge to be a member of a society who is not seduced or threatened into accepting the proposition that it is somehow in our best interests not to know.

Professor Warwick Middleton MB BS, FRANZCP, MD
Director, Trauma and Dissociation Unit, Belmont Hospital, Brisbane, Australia
Chairman, The Cannan Institute
Fellow, International Society for the Study of Trauma and Dissociation

Dedicated to Jerrold Ballinger and also to the Voiceless...

Author's Preface

The 2012 child abuse scandals that erupted at Penn State and Syra-cuse universities, Brooklyn's Poly Prep Country Day School, Fenway Park, and the Amateur Athletic Union, along with the intimations of possible cover-ups, have shocked and outraged Americans. Unfortunately, these recent scandals are only the latest variations on a theme of abuse and cover-ups by churches and respected organizations like the Boy Scouts.

Although witch-hunt hysteria is to be avoided when these accusations come to light, it is important to consider that the cover-up of child abuse may be rife in our society. Sexual-abuse victims are often very reluctant to come forward, because they are frequently branded as liars, opportunists, and gold diggers. Such denunciations were quickly leveled against the victims of Penn State's Jerry Sandusky and Syracuse University's Bernie Fine.

Many specialists in the field of child sexual abuse have concluded that it is highly improbable for individuals to fabricate accusations of these crimes. In 2002, the *New York Times* interviewed Patrick Schiltz, former associate dean of the University of St Thomas law school in Minnesota and now a Federal judge, who had defended Catholic dioceses against sexual-abuse lawsuits in more than 500 cases. Judge Schiltz expressed the belief that "fewer than 10" of those cases were based on false accusations.

Likewise, I have spoken with scores of men and women who claim to have been sexually abused as children. And I have concluded that the overwhelming majority are telling me the truth, but I am not aware of a single perpetrator who has been indicted for their respective alleged abuses.

I spent seven years researching and writing *The Franklin Scandal*. With access to thousands of documents that were sealed by two grand juries, as well as the sealed testimony of one, I demonstrated that state and federal grand jury processes in Nebraska played an integral role in covering up the interstate transportation and sexual exploitation of numerous children.

Instead of indicting the alleged perpetrators, these grand juries indicted the victims who would not recant their accounts of abuse on charges of perjury. In one case, a 21-year-old who had been abused since adolescence was indicted on eight counts of perjury by both state and federal grand juries. Facing more than 300 years in prison, she still refused to recant her abuse. Her travesty of a trial resulted in a prison sentence of nine to fifteen years. She spent nearly two years in solitary confinement.

This young woman was released from prison in 2000, and she has become a model citizen: she is happily married and gainfully employed. Conversely, one of the pedophilic pimps singled out by *The Franklin Scandal* was not charged with a single count of child abuse. By 2009, he had enmeshed himself among a new brood of economically disadvantaged children.

Before *The Franklin Scandal* was published, I attempted to publish an article on the subject matter. After I felt I had collected clear proof of an extremely organized child-pandering network and its cover-up, I distilled the information into an article and submitted it to numerous mainstream magazines, but none would go with it. The magazine editors rejected the article without even looking at the thousands of pages of corroborating law enforcement and social services documentation I had collected. Although I was put off by the editors' apparent callousness, or perhaps fear for their careers, I thought the primary problem may have been that I shoehorned such a sprawling story into an article.

Undeterred, I wrote a rather lengthy book proposal and gave it to the major literary agency representing me. Within weeks, I was dumped as a client. Still determined, I found a second agent who tried to sell the book proposal, but he found no takers. I did meet with one publisher, however; his primary concern was potential libel lawsuits, not the destruction of numerous children. Finally, I found a small publisher on the West Coast who had the fortitude to publish *The Franklin Scandal,* which, in addition to nearly 500 pages of narrative, provides 100 pages of documentation, but no one in the mainstream media would review or even mention it. I managed to dispense copies of the book to the producers for television personalities who are child-welfare advocates, and they would not touch the story.

When the child abuse allegations documented in *The Franklin Scandal* originally surfaced, corrupt entities within state and federal law enforcement perpetrated the cover-up, and the media, by either commission or omission, helped facilitate it. Since *The Franklin Scandal* has been published, the mainstream media has perpetuated the cover-up through omission.

Possibly, most media are scared off by the fact that two grand juries declared that the perpetrators had not abused a single child and a jury had found the young woman guilty of fabricating her story and convicted her of perjury. Juries, after all, are the finders of fact in our system, but it is also true that her charges and those of the other victims implicated some very powerful figures. So I believe that many in the media looking at a summary of *The Franklin Scandal* concluded that my tale could not possibly be true, and there was no reason to even read the book. Throughout my odyssey over the last nine years, I've found that people's denial is one of the most potent weapons in the arsenal of affluent and/ or seemingly well-adjusted perpetrators. Many people will choose denial over cognitive dissonance until the evidence becomes overwhelming and incontrovertible.

In *The Franklin Scandal*, acceptance of the victims' allegations had the potential to necessitate felony indictments of a chief of police, a sitting judge, affluent businessmen, a newspaper publisher, etc. These men also would have been under pressure to reveal their pedophilic association with even more powerful individuals who were alleged perpetrators within the same network. That leverage doomed a powerless victim to long years in prison for simply telling her "inconvenient" truth.

I freely concede that the facts that comprise *The Franklin Scandal* are quite different from the facts that have emerged from Penn State thus far. As I write this Preface, the genesis of the cover-up surrounding Sandusky appears to be his potential to besmirch the reputations of Penn State and his coaching associates. Penn State has prestige, and rightly so—it has done a lot of good. Institutions, however, are made up of individuals, whose primary concerns are their reputations and the reputations of their institutions, and those concerns can trump the welfare of children in their charge. The mandate of such institutions must be to protect children, and to put that imperative ahead of the protection of their own reputations, because pedophilic predators are attracted to environments full of prey: schools, churches, youth groups, etc.

In addition to denial and the preservation of the reputations, a third factor that dooms many child abuse investigations, and abets corrupt ones, is that the victims are often from disadvantaged backgrounds, and the adult luring the child frequently introduces the underage victim to drugs or alcohol, further eroding his or her credibility. Moreover, the abuser can have powerful allies in law enforcement, government, and the media, who decide that the sordid details are too hot to handle. Add into the mix the public's understandable squeamishness toward the entire subject of pedophilia, and we arrive at the perfect recipe for a cover-up.

The reality is that many perpetrators are not shady men in dirty, threadbare trench coats living in seedy hotels, but are, in fact, so-called pillars of our community. Until our society addresses these facts and its institutions are willing to face embarrassment, instead of heaping more abuse upon victims, our national shame of widespread child abuse and its cover-up is unlikely to end.

Nick Bryant July 24, 2012

Acknowledgements

The vast majority of this book's narrative was derived from official records and from the interviews I personally conducted over the course of years. Given that many of the interviewees are identified within the text, I feel it would be redundant to name them here, but I am extremely indebted to their contributions. I would also like to thank those persons I interviewed whose names didn't make it into the text, either because they wished to remain anonymous or because I omitted their names for the sake of simplifying the narrative. I would especially like to thank John DeCamp for providing me with my initial foothold and continued support, and Dirk Gillespie for providing me with shelter during my numerous trips to Nebraska. Scores of people have given me encouragement and feedback over the years, but I would explicitly like to thank Mark Connor, Michael Rhodes, Phil Kronzer, Jim Rothstein, Charles Young, David Beilinson, Ann McNamee, Mathew Pritchard, Daniel O'Brien, Marta Curro, and Shelley Stenhouse. Finally, I thank TrineDay's Kris Millegan, who had the courage and fortitude to embrace this project after several publishers passed on it, and also TrineDay's Russ Becker for his editorial acumen.

Table of Contents

Introduction

As I sat in the reception area of a prominent national magazine headquartered in Manhattan, I had a nasty secret I was about to tell its editor. The secret wasn't my secret—it was a national secret that had been buried for nearly two decades. I had previously let other magazine editors in on the secret, but it was so divorced from day-to-day reality that I encountered only dismissive skepticism. I was acutely aware that my upcoming meeting would mark my last face-to-face stab at pitching the story to the editor of a major national magazine, and I wanted it to count. The reception area was a beehive of activity—magazine employees and delivery men flitted in and out—but I tried to remain focused on the task at hand.

A friend of mine worked at the magazine, and he had been instrumental in arranging the meeting. While I waited for the editor to summon me, my friend gave me a few last-minute words of encouragement, even though he conceded my prospects were bleak—I would essentially be attempting to scale Mt. Everest without a rope. The receptionist eventually gave me a nod, and I stood up and walked to the door that granted me entry to the magazine's inner sanctum.

The editor stepped out of his office to greet me. He was in his late thirties or early forties, medium height, and lean. His long face was crowned by thick brown hair, and he wore wire-rimmed glasses. His overall appearance gave him an academic look that had vestiges of a high school wonk. My friend had given the editor a terse overview of the story, and as we shook hands, he seemed less than enthusiastic to meet me.

I had the article I had written, supporting documentation, and also a DVD that was a montage of footage, newspaper clippings, and interviews ten minutes in length—I was prepared. After we sat down at a circular desk in his office, I suggested that he play the DVD, because it provided tangible, audio-visual corroboration of an absolutely implausible story.

I watched him as he watched the DVD. The DVD told the tale of a national pedophile network that pandered children to America's power elite and also of its cover-up by state and federal law enforcement. The story was shocking and surreal, and it ran counter to everything that the editor had been taught to believe about America.

I could see that the DVD piqued his interest. But when it concluded, he quickly reverted to indifference. I handed him a list of victims that had been compiled by an investigator who was hired by Nebraska's state legislature. The list contained the names of approximately sixty victims. He sighed, a sigh of both disbelief and distress, as he paged through the list—then he shut down and denial set in.

I had witnessed other editors have similar responses when I unveiled the secret to them, so I wasn't taken aback by his surge of incredulity. He didn't even want to consider the story's validity, mechanically tossing out that it wasn't current enough. I expected that response, and I had a rebuttal: I said some stories are just too far-fetched and their cover-up is so exquisite that only a post-mortem is possible. I mentioned J. Edgar Hoover's being a closet homosexual and his FBI sending Martin Luther King, Jr., a recording of King having an extra-marital affair along with a letter that attempted to blackmail King into suicide. My rebuttal fell on deaf ears.

My meeting with the editor lasted approximately half an hour. I left him the article, some supporting documentation, and the DVD. But I knew it was all for naught. The magazine in question has since published numerous stories reporting on events older than my article—one story reported on an event that took place over 100 years ago. Not wanting my friend to find himself unemployed, I've refrained from mentioning the magazine.

By that time, I had been working on the story for over four years, and no mainstream magazine would flirt with it. When I gave the story to the literary agency that represented me, I was summarily and unceremoniously discarded as a client. I acquired a second literary agent who attempted to sell the story, but he found no takers. Though I had no qualms acknowledging that the story was bizarre and improbable, I was nonetheless deeply troubled by the way publishers reacted to a story entailing the destruction and ruin of untold numbers of children.

America, unfortunately, is a society that pays great lip service to children as its most precious resource, but, in actuality, it is unwilling to put its money where its mouth is concerning their plight. Prior to my current incarnation as a freelance writer in Manhattan, I was employed by the University of Minnesota to write about the obstacles facing disadvantaged children, and I co-authored several academic papers and a book on the subject.

The book, *America's Children: Triumph or Tragedy*, documented the deplorable state of children in our society. The book pointed out that nearly 22% of America's children lived below the poverty threshold, and roughly ten million children were uninsured. As of 2007, those figures had declined slightly: 18% of America's children lived below the poverty threshold and nearly nine million were uninsured. *America's Children: Triumph or Tragedy* also noted that at least 100,000 American children fell asleep homeless every night, and that children accounted for 63% of homeless families. Moreover, 5.5 million American children under the age of twelve suffered from malnutrition and hunger.

When these trends are superimposed on each other, or their developmental consequences are considered, they become quite startling. For example, low-income children are at a twofold greater risk of being born at a low birth weight, and researchers at the University of Michigan have shown that infants born at low birth weights who are subjected to continuous poverty throughout their first five years of life have I.Q.s 9.1 points lower than children never subjected to persistent poverty. Researchers have also demonstrated that learning disabilities are approximately 40% higher for children living in the lowest socioeconomic strata.

America's Children: Triumph or Tragedy also commented extensively on the plight of uninsured children in the United States, and their elevated vulnerability to numerous diseases and adverse health conditions. The infant mortality rate in the US is currently 6.9 deaths per 1,000 births, ranking it 29th in the world—behind even Cuba. The infant mortality rate for African Americans is 13.6, which ranks behind several third-world countries.

Families with children are the fastest growing homeless subpopulation in the US, and the physical and developmental consequences for homeless children can be severely devastating. One study found that homeless children have a sevenfold increased risk of seizure disorders, a nearly thirtyfold frequency of malnutrition, and are at a thirty-fivefold greater risk of having lice. Studies have also found that 54% of homeless children had at least one major developmental delay, and 54% were in need of psychiatric intervention.

America's Children: Triumph or Tragedy discussed the wholesale destruction of America's children, and *The Franklin Scandal* elucidates their retail destruction. My personal involvement with the bewildering secrets of organized child trafficking in America began in 2002, while I was working up an article on another shadowy subject. Unknown to me, I had been launched on a journey to a parallel universe, one that coexists with the universe of Little League, Boy Scouts, Disneyland, and the other hallmarks of wholesome, youthful Americana—a universe where lies masquerade as truth, where shadows reflect light, where innocence is condemned.

I initially embarked on my dark odyssey skeptical and bold, and it left me utterly anguished. I wasn't so much anguished by the threats and intimidation I endured delving into the arcane mysteries of this universe, but, rather, by the realization of its very existence: a universe that encompasses the refined, industrial destruction of children and its cover-up by the very state and federal authorities who have pledged to protect children from the depravity of evil men. The children, and our society as a whole, have been betrayed.

—Prologue—

The Finders of Lost Children

I was in rural Nebraska charging up Highway 81 in a rented GMC Envoy—our destination was Madison, Nebraska, ten miles due north. An early evening August sun cascaded shafts of sunlight onto seemingly infinite tracts of cornfields, and a faint breeze tugged gently on the tall shafts of corn. The temperature was an ideal 75° Fahrenheit and no clouds blemished the azure sky. The speed limit was 65 MPH—my speedometer read 70. A sensible person in my shoes would have second thoughts about even slightly breaking the speed limit, but I felt a sense of urgency.

Gazing into my rearview mirror, I noticed the flashing red and amber lights of a Nebraska state trooper. My fight-or-flight response flared—I felt a burst of adrenaline and I was also smacked by a swell of anxiety. I abruptly swerved onto the shoulder, ripped my New York driver's license from my wallet, and dredged the rental paperwork from the Envoy's glove compartment. The trooper wore opaque sunglasses, and a smirk creased his well-tanned, square face. I handed him my license and rental agreement before he said a word.

After he gave my documentation a cursory glance, he inexplicably escorted me to his "cruiser." He called in for priors—I came up clean. I was also clean-shaven, and my hair was neatly trimmed above my ears. I wore an immaculate Joe Boxer T-shirt, beige khaki shorts, and new Nike running shoes—Air Max. I looked like the Platonic ideal of an upstanding citizen.

He was unimpressed with my pristine record and appearance; so I tossed out a few polysyllabic words—smirk intact, he remained unimpressed. When he pulled out a pencil and a pocket-size notebook and started asking questions, I had a bad feeling—a really bad feeling. He wanted to know my whereabouts for the past week. I told him I'd been "mountaineering" in Colorado. The trooper seemed to have little concern for my Constitutional rights, but I felt the predicament dictated that I refrain from ACLU buzzwords and comply. He jotted down my answers and left the car.

The trooper talked to my passenger for ten minutes or so before returning. He scribbled my passenger's name—Rusty Nelson—in his notebook. As he furnished Nelson's name to the dispatcher, I sensed that the situation was on the verge of becoming ugly—seriously ugly. The dispatcher reported that Nelson was a "registered sex offender," and then she barked out a flurry of numbers. Though I had no idea what the numbers meant, I felt confident they weren't nice numbers. A second state patrolman pulled up behind us in a gray SUV.

The trooper twisted to his right and gesticulated like a football referee indicating a bobbled reception: He said Nelson's story and mine didn't "match up." He then exited the car and spoke to the other trooper for a few minutes. Returning to the car, he opened the passenger's door, poked his head into the vehicle, and again remarked that our stories didn't "match up"—once more making the gesture of a football referee. He slammed the door shut and trotted over to my vehicle.

His backup ran over to the Envoy with a shaggy brown mongrel of a dog, and they took two or three laps around the vehicle. The dog sniffed at the tires and every little crevice. After the dog started to appear bored, the first trooper escorted Nelson from the Envoy. Nelson's facial expression was taut with fear—his eyes repeatedly darted back and forth. The trooper deposited him between the cruiser and State Patrol SUV to keep us separated.

The trooper then made me an offer I couldn't refuse: He said they could arrest us, impound the vehicle, and search it or they could simply search it on the spot. I gestured to the Envoy, grimaced, and said, "Knock yourselves out." The troopers then meticulously searched every inch of the vehicle and ripped apart all of our possessions—I think it probably took them about thirty minutes to completely scour the Envoy, but it seemed interminable as I watched and waited.

Sitting in the cruiser, flooded with fear, I had difficulty imagining how our stories didn't "match up," even though Nelson has a habit of speaking in ambiguities and asides. We weren't exactly "mountaineering" in Colorado; nevertheless, I was absolutely certain that Nelson hadn't told the trooper the motives behind our trek—he's definitely not stupid. I've heard a number of unbecoming adjectives applied to Nelson but "stupid" wasn't one of them.

Nelson was the admitted former "photographer" of a nationwide pedophile network I'd been investigating for over three years at that time. The ring pandered children to the rich and powerful and had access to the highest levels of our government. Before we made our trip to Colorado, I thought I could prove the network's existence, its cover-up by federal and state authorities, and make a case for CIA involvement and blackmail. However, I felt it would be next to impossible to name names without pictures, because of the pedophiles' lofty social status. I was confident that society would never take the word of damaged victims, who had themselves become predators and felons, over the word of seemingly well-adjusted politicians and affluent businessmen. Nelson told me he had blackmail pictures stashed in the mountains of Colorado. I was incredulous, but had to give it a shot.

As I watched the troopers rip apart the Envoy, I glanced at Nelson— he looked quite nervous too. I even felt a begrudging kinship with him, which was rooted in a mutation of the Stockholm Syndrome—we were both under siege. I then recalled the various tribulations I'd endured since I started investigating this story: My life had been threatened, I'd been followed, I'd received ominous, anonymous phone calls, menacing emails, and Nebraska law enforcement had taken a keen interest in me.

Nelson was my second "on record" interview when I was first cutting my teeth on the story. During our initial meeting, he alluded to having "pictures in the mountains," and over the course of our subsequent conversations he occasionally mentioned the pictures. I had no illusions about Nelson's being a paragon of morality: He confessed that his former vocation consisted of taking pictures of adults in sexually compromising positions with children; therefore I viewed his revelations with skepticism until they were confirmed. But he provided me with considerable information that I ultimately corroborated. I caught him lying to me too.

Over the course of three years I cultivated Nelson's trust, and he eventually agreed to accompany me to southwestern Colorado, where he said the pictures were stashed. Nelson warned me that the mountain terrain was treacherous and required a 4-wheel drive, so I rented an Envoy. I drove the brawny SUV from Minneapolis to Nebraska, and met up with Nelson at his girlfriend's house on the outskirts of Madison, Nebraska. The next morning we loaded up the Envoy with enough gear and provisions to explore Antarctica for a month, and after a visit to Omaha we set out for Colorado. We grabbed some shut-eye in a motel near Denver and arrived in the mountainous Uncompahgre River Valley the following day.

After two days of tortuous driving and strenuous hiking yielded only three "dry wells," and Nelson's elaborate excuses, I had no interest in looking for a supposed fourth stash spot. Nelson has a tenuous relationship with truth, and had made no guarantees of recovering the blackmail pictures; I had made the sojourn to Colorado knowing full well that it might be a wild goose chase. Moreover, given Nelson's nature, I decided at the onset of the trip that I wouldn't take a "goose egg" personally. After all, I was grateful for the vast amounts of information he provided me that I ultimately corroborated.

I have to admit, though, I have a tendency to be optimistic, and there was a vestige of it in me that hoped to retrieve pictures. During our odyssey, I had held onto a slight shred of hope that Nelson might possibly be sizing me up simply to see if I was on the level—he suffered from extreme paranoia and rightfully so: The pedophiles were men of extravagant wealth and power, and a number of individuals associated with the network and its cover-up had died under mysterious circumstances. For every person who went "on record" with me, I found seven, eight, or nine people who refused to even talk about talking.

Nelson and I had a chilly and silent drive to Denver, and the next morning we had an equally chilly and silent drive to Nebraska, which brings us to Highway 81. When the troopers' search came up empty, they were kind enough to cut us loose. As Nelson and I drove away, he turned to me and said, "Do you know how lucky you are?" In a nutshell, Nelson was implying that the troopers' harassment had been a set-up, and they were looking for blackmail pictures. If we, in fact, possessed pictures, the troopers' search would have been catastrophic.

I've never subscribed to sprawling conspiracy theories: I've always thought that the Warren Commission's "magic bullet" conclusion was a bit suspect, but never devoted a great deal of time to the various scenarios debunking it.

The improbable prime mover in my nexus with the state troopers on Highway 81 was a conversation I had in July 2002 with a magazine editor, who said he was looking for "very dark" stories. Never having shied away from dancing in the dark, I pitched him a flurry of stories whose themes included Satanism and Nazism. He resonated with the Satanism angle. I had a simple plan: ferret out Satanists, attend a black mass, and write an article. Over the next month or so, I talked to a gamut of Satanists—not surprisingly, I found them a rather unsavory lot. I quickly discovered that they were either very, very smart or cognitively challenged. Punk rockers are the only other group I've encountered with such a marked gray-matter polarization, which I discovered while working as a bouncer at a club in the early eighties.

I eventually drifted toward a "sect" of intelligent Satanists—I've always preferred intelligent and unsavory to slow and unsavory. Anthony was the first of the cerebral Satanists I met. He was fond of black: black blazer, black shirt, black pants, and even black socks and tennis shoes. He, like the other Satanists I came across, was a Republican. It struck me as ironic that Satanists and fundamentalist Christians—groups embracing antithetical religious doctrines—generally share political affiliations.

I evidently impressed Anthony with my knowledge of metaphysics: I studied philosophy in college, I lived on the ashram of a genuine Indian guru, and, over the years, I've attended groups dedicated to Gurdjieff, Krishnamurti, Zen, and Sufism. Our philosophical and metaphysical conversations ranged from Nietzsche to Eastern mysticism.

After Anthony and I talked four or five times, he consented to take me to his sect's version of a black mass, which is patterned after the mass of Roman Catholicism. He only had one condition, and it was non-negotiable: he insisted I partake of the "host." The host, in Anthony's sect, is a floury wafer that contains the high priest's semen and the high priestess' menstruation. Anthony and I parted ways.

While I was courting Anthony in the hopes of attending a black mass, I continued to troll the Internet for stories pertaining to Satanism. The Net was replete with stories of Satanists abducting children, and also of clandestine bonds between Satanists and the CIA. Given my inherent skepticism of conspiracies, I initially dismissed the tales. Eventually, I came across a number of stories about a cult called the "Finders" that weren't rooted in fringe paranoia, but, according to the sources, in a US Customs report.

The existence of tangible evidence intrigued me, and I phoned a "conspiracy theorist" who claimed to have the authentic US Customs report on the Finders. We spoke for maybe twenty minutes, and he discussed the Finders, the "Illuminati," and a cavalcade of far-reaching speculation, convincing me that he wasn't of sound mind. A week or so after our conversation, however, I did in fact receive a package from him that contained the US Customs report on the Finders and also a *US News & World Report* article on the Finders that quoted the report.

The Customs report, written by Special Agent Ramon Martinez, recounted a sordid, horrific cluster of events. On February 4, 1987, a concerned citizen notified the Tallahassee Police Department—he had observed six white children, "poorly dressed, bruised, dirty, and behaving like wild animals," in a Tallahassee park. The children were accompanied by two well-dressed white males driving a white 1979 Dodge van with Virginia plates.

The Tallahassee police responded to the call and took the children and adults into custody. The adults refused to cooperate, and one produced a business card that stated he planned to exercise his Constitutional right to remain silent. Police officers noted that the children, whose ages ranged from three to six, could not adequately identify themselves or their custodians and were "unaware of the function and purpose of telephones, televisions, and toilets." The children also said that they were not allowed to live indoors and were given food only as a reward. The Tallahassee police charged the two adults with felony child abuse, and they were held on a $100,000 bond. The children were placed in protective custody.

Police officers found documents in the van that enabled them to tentatively identify the two adults and partially identify the children. They also found documents containing two Washington, DC addresses.

The Tallahassee police suspected child pornography; they contacted the US Customs Service (USCS), which has a Child Pornography and Protection Unit. Shortly thereafter, Detective James Bradley of the Washington, DC Metropolitan Police Department (MPD) contacted Special Agent Ramon Martinez of the USCS. Detective Bradley indicated that the Tallahassee arrests were probably linked to a case that he was investigating in the DC area, involving a "cult" called the Finders. An informant had told Bradley that the Finders operated various businesses out of a warehouse in DC and housed children at a second warehouse.

"The information was specific in describing 'blood rituals' and sexual orgies involving children, and an as yet unsolved murder in which the Finders may be involved," wrote Martinez in his report.

Bradley told Martinez that the Tallahassee arrests of the two adults for child abuse were the critical mass he needed for warrants to search the two warehouses. And on February 6, the MPD, accompanied by the USCS, executed search warrants on the warehouses. Rummaging through the first warehouse, they found jars of feces and urine and also a room equipped with several computers and printers and a cache of documents.

"Cursory examination of the documents revealed detailed instructions for obtaining children for unspecified purposes," wrote Martinez. "The instructions included the impregnation of female members of ... the Finders, purchasing children, trading, and kidnapping. There were telex messages using MCI account numbers between a computer terminal believed to be located in the same room, and others located across the country and in foreign locations. One such telex specifically ordered the purchase of two children in Hong Kong to be arranged through a contact in the Chinese Embassy."

The investigators also discovered documents that discussed "bank secrecy," "high-tech transfers," "terrorism," and "explosives." To their astonishment, they even found a detailed summary of the events surrounding the arrests in Tallahassee the previous night and instructions that were broadcast via a computer network. The instructions advised the "participants" to move the "children" through different police jurisdictions, and "how to avoid police attention."

Martinez and the MPD officers also found a large collection of photographs. A number of the photos were of nude children, and one appeared to be a child "on display" in a way that accented the "child's genitals." An MPD officer then presented Martinez with a photo album. The album contained photos of adults and children dressed in white sheets slaughtering two goats. The photos portrayed the slaughter, disembowelment, skinning, and dismemberment of the goats by the children. The photos showed the removal of the male goat's testes and the removal of "baby goats" from the female goat's "womb," and the presentation of a goat's head to one of the children.

"Not observed by me but related by an MPD officer were intelligence files on private families not related to the Finders," Martinez continued in his report. "The process undertaken appears to be have been a systematic response to local newspaper advertisements for baby-sitters, tutors, etc. A member of the Finders would respond and gather as much information as possible about the habits, identity, occupation, etc., of the family. The use to which this information was to be put is still unknown. There was also a large amount of data collected on various child care organizations."

Approximately a month after the MPD executed the warrant, Agent Martinez set up an appointment with Detective Bradley to review the documents that had been seized at the two warehouses. His report stated that he was to meet with Bradley in early April. On April 2, 1987, Agent Martinez arrived at MPD headquarters at approximately 9:00 A.M., and he was in for a shock. Detective Bradley was unavailable, but he spoke to a "third party" who was willing to discuss the Finders only on a "strictly off the record basis."

"The individual further advised me of circumstances which indicated that the investigation into the activity of the Finders had become a CIA internal matter," Agent Martinez concluded in his report. "The MPD report has been classified secret and was not available for review. I was advised that the FBI had withdrawn from the investigation several weeks prior and that the FBI Foreign Counter Intelligence Division had directed MPD not to advise the FBI Washington Field Office of anything that had transpired. No further information will be available. No further action will be taken."

Wow! After I finished reading the USCS report, Buffalo Springfield's "For What It's Worth" came to mind: "There's something happenin' here. What it is ain't exactly clear." The USCS report certainly triggered a paradigm shift within me—I suddenly became willing to entertain ideas that I previously would have discarded with dismissive skepticism.

Though I was intrigued by the USCS report, I attempted not to jump to conclusions—I've met many people over the years whose only aerobic regimen is jumping to conclusions. But I felt that the Finders definitely merited a LexisNexis search of all newspaper articles relating to the cult. I went online and collected over twenty articles on the Finders from a hodgepodge of daily newspapers, ranging from the *New York Times* and *Washington Post* to the *Orange County Register*.

Almost all of the articles pertained to the investigations launched by the Tallahassee police, MPD, and USCS. The earliest articles discussed the Finders' probable involvement in "Satanism," and a spokesman for the Tallahassee police said that one of the children "showed signs of sexual abuse." An FBI spokesman also announced that the Finders were being investigated for "the transportation of children across state lines for immoral purposes or kidnapping."

A February 10, 1987 article in the *Washington Post* reported on a news conference kicked off by MPD Chief Maurice Turner, Jr. This news conference occurred after the CIA intervention, and at it Chief Turner backpedaled with ferocity, rejecting allegations that the Finders were involved in satanic rituals or child abuse. The chief also elevated the Finders from a cult to a "communal group." He neglected to mention that the Finders were a communal group that reportedly had an interest in "purchasing children, trading, and kidnapping," and also an interest in "terrorism" and "explosives." He omitted discussing the jars of feces and urine as well.

Two days after Chief Turner's press conference, an FBI spokesman said that their investigation of the Finders was "winding down," because the Bureau hadn't "uncovered any evidence of federal violations." The two adult Finders taken into custody by Tallahassee police had their felony child-abuse charges reduced to misdemeanors. Six weeks later the abuse charges were dropped altogether, and the children were eventually returned to the Finders.

That was seemingly the end of the Finders saga. But almost seven years later, the grisly USCS report was leaked to the media, because a cadre of Customs agents were aghast that law enforcement hadn't followed up on the Finders. A December 27, 1993 *US News & World Report* article, "Through a Glass, Very Darkly: Cops, Spies and a Very Odd Investigation," discussed the efforts of Democratic Representative Charlie Rose of North Carolina and Florida Representative Tom Lewis, a Republican, to expose the government's ties to the Finders.

"Could our own government have had something to do with this Finders organization and turned their backs on these children?" asked Representative Lewis in the article. "That's what all the evidence points to. And there is a lot of evidence. I can tell you this: We've got a lot of people scrambling, and that wouldn't be happening if there was nothing here."

The MPD declined to comment on the Finders to *US News & World Report*, but an anonymous investigator for the Tallahassee Police Department criticized the MPD's handling of the matter: "They dropped this case like a hot rock." The article also quoted "ranking officials" from the CIA who described accusations linking the CIA to the Finders as "hogwash." The efforts of Representatives Rose and Lewis to hold a hearing on the Finders/CIA connection ultimately came to naught.

My LexisNexis post-mortem on the Finders and the subsequent *US News* article left me perplexed and whetted my curiosity. The LexisNexis articles provided me with the names of a dozen or so people enmeshed in the Finders saga, and I decided to start making phone calls.

The first *Washington Post* article on the Finders interviewed a psychologist "who works with cult members." In the article, the psychologist said that he had "tracked" the Finders for five years. I really wanted the skinny on the Finders, and the psychologist's remarks had the academic perspective of a zoologist commenting on a rare species for a *National Geographic* documentary. I thought he could offer me deep, anthropologic insights into the Finders' mating habits, rituals, and mores—so I called him first.

Our conversation lasted all of five or six seconds. I said, "My name is Nick Bryant, and I'm a freelance writer researching the Finders," and he stammered: "I don't know what you're talking about! N-n-n-o comment! N-n-n-o comment!" Click. The word "Finders" elicited such a negative response that I immediately thought of Pavlovian conditioning, à la *A Clockwork Orange*, or, perhaps, a threat to life or limb.

I phoned the mother of a Finder: "No comment!"

I phoned a former Finder: "No comment!"

I phoned law enforcement: "No comment!"

Freelance writing has largely immunized me to rejection: Being barraged by "No comment!" didn't dent my resolve. But I found it nearly impossible to garner information about the Finders and why the CIA might quash an investigation into the group's seemingly sinister activities.

As I attempted to crack the enigma of the Finders and the CIA, I found the Internet to be rife with accounts of another "conspiracy" involving Satanist and CIA collusion. The tale was rooted in a book, *The Franklin Cover-Up*, written and self-published by John DeCamp (a former Republican Nebraska state senator), and also in a documentary, *Conspiracy of Silence*, produced by Britain's Yorkshire Television for airing in 1994. On the Internet, the bizarre, implausible confluence of events I would spend the next seven years investigating is simply called "Franklin," because of its association with Omaha's Franklin Credit Union.

I ordered a copy of *The Franklin Cover-Up* from Amazon and a VHS of *Conspiracy of Silence* from the conspiracy theorist who had sent me the Customs report. As I talked to the conspiracy theorist a second time, I conceded a Finders/CIA connection that appeared ominous, even though I was reluctant to draw definitive conclusions about their relationship. The conspiracy theorist adamantly maintained that the Finders were a Satanic/CIA "factory" for sex slavery and mind control, but he offered absolutely no proof for his assertions. I still felt he wasn't of sound mind.

Conspiracy of Silence arrived before *The Franklin Cover-Up*, and I popped it into my VCR. The fifty-minute film told the tale of an interstate pedophile ring that plundered Boys Town for under-age prostitutes, and pandered children to a cabal of powerful pedophiles in Washington, DC. The film included footage of alleged victims recounting chilling experiences of sadism. *Conspiracy of Silence* also described the fruitless efforts of Nebraska legislators to expose the ring amidst the juggernaut of a massive cover-up that included murder, media manipulation, and a full-court press by federal law enforcement.

I found *Conspiracy of Silence* extremely disturbing. As I watched it a second time, I was even more disturbed. Wanting to assure myself that

I wasn't free-falling into an abyss of conjecture, I invited friends to my apartment and gave screenings of the documentary. They, too, found it chilling.

Conspiracy of Silence had a fairly coherent narrative, but it was an unfinished rough-cut devoid of titles and credits. The documentary proper was preceded by a scrolling preamble, stating that *Conspiracy of Silence* was to be shown on the Discovery Channel, but "influential members of Congress" had prevented the program from airing and "ordered all copies destroyed." The preamble ended on an Orwellian note: "This is the program they didn't want you to see!"

I phoned Yorkshire Television and eventually managed to contact Tim Tate, who had directed *Conspiracy of Silence*. After we discussed Franklin, I asked him about the veracity of the preamble. He said that Yorkshire Television wasn't responsible for it, and his account of the documentary's cancellation lacked the preamble's drama. Tate maintained that the Discovery Channel commissioned the documentary and then pulled the plug on the production, offering the same nebulous rejection journalists have eaten for years: It's just not right for us.

Tate's clarification regarding the preamble was an important first lesson as I entered the Franklin wormhole. In my quest for truth, I would have to be extremely cautious. An edifice of lies could easily obscure a foundation of truth—an edifice built by overzealous conspiracy buffs going a bridge too far or, perhaps, a deliberate attempt at misinformation. I would find that even individuals who were directly enmeshed in Franklin had embraced Web-based accounts and anecdotes that I concluded were apocryphal.

DeCamp's *The Franklin Cover-Up* arrived shortly after *Conspiracy of Silence*. The book had inspired *Conspiracy of Silence*, and interviews with DeCamp played a central role in the documentary. *The Franklin Cover-Up* was primarily an amalgam of documents that were collected and subpoenaed by the Franklin Committee, a subcommittee of the Nebraska legislature, which was formed to investigate crimes related to Omaha's failed Franklin Credit Union. DeCamp acted as legal counsel to the Franklin Committee's chairman, and the Committee's documents made a strong case for the pedophile ring's existence, even though state and federal grand juries had ruled that rumors of its existence were a "hoax."

The Franklin Cover-Up made two major assertions that were absent from *Conspiracy of Silence*: The book cited victim debriefings stating that the ring was enmeshed in Satanism, and it also *implied* that the ring was connected to the CIA. DeCamp, a seasoned lawyer, presented tidbits of compelling evidence here and there, and I was intrigued.

Both *Conspiracy of Silence* and *The Franklin Cover-Up* implicated one Lawrence E. (Larry) King, Jr., of Omaha, as the primary pimp of the nationwide pedophile ring.

Throughout the 1980s, the middle-aged King, tall and corpulent, had been described as a "GOP high-roller" and "the fastest rising African-American star" in the Republican Party. He was Vice Chairman for Finance of the National Black Republican Council, a sanctioned affiliate of the Republican National Committee. King also ardently campaigned for the 1988 presidential bid of his "personal friend" George H.W. Bush. In a 1988 flurry of name-dropping, King told a reporter for Omaha's weekly *Metropolitan* of his lofty connections atop the political food chain: "I know some of the people I admire aren't very popular. Ed Meese. The late Bill Casey of the CIA. And I love former Chief Justice Burger. Those are the people I really like to talk to. Bill Casey ... I thought so very highly of him."

Though King emerged from humble Nebraska origins, his highfalutin persona had the colossal dimensions of a signature balloon floating above the Macy's Thanksgiving Day parade. He had a special affinity for flowers, and his life was a bouquet of finely tailored suits, limos, chartered jets, and glistening jewelry. He had an array of diverse business ventures, but his primary day job was manager of an Omaha credit union, created to provide loans for Omaha's underserved black community. The full name of the firm was the Franklin Community Federal Credit Union.

On November 4, 1988, federal agents descended on the Franklin Credit Union, and the National Credit Union Administration (NCUA) would ultimately conclude that $39.4 million had been stolen. King would be indicted on 40 counts that included conspiracy, fraud, and embezzlement. Federal law required annual audits of federally regulated credit unions, but King had possessed the political juice to stave off audits for years.

After reading about the exploits of Larry King in *The Franklin Cover-Up*, I phoned John DeCamp at his law office in Lincoln, Nebraska. I left two or three messages before catching him. DeCamp's life, I would learn, was a non-stop montage of multitasking: He politely cut the call short, but gave me his home phone number and suggested that I call him over the weekend.

When I phoned him on Saturday afternoon, he said that a University of Nebraska football game had just started, and he asked me to call later. DeCamp remarked that life in Nebraska had scant recreational diversions, and Cornhusker football was the unofficial state religion. Investigation of child sexual abuse, with all its sinister foreboding, and the archetypical Americana of "Husker" football initially struck me as strange bedfellows.

I called DeCamp in the early evening, and we talked for half an hour or so. I had a list of questions that were kindled by *Conspiracy of Silence* and *The Franklin Cover-Up*. DeCamp couldn't provide answers to the majority of my questions, and he wasn't willing to voice crazed conjectures, which impressed me. He lived in a small town forty miles south of Lincoln, and he invited me to spend the night. The holidays were near; I decided to visit my grandmother in Minneapolis, rent a car, and then drive to Nebraska.

I sent an email to the magazine editor who had conscripted me to write an article on Satanism, noting my new direction. He wasn't particularly enthusiastic about backing a fact-finding junket to Nebraska, so I decided to make the trek without his blessing. I then phoned an old friend who lives in Omaha, explained my mission, and requested the use of his couch. He welcomed my visit.

The five-hour drive from my grandmother's to Omaha gave me time to ponder the story. Though *The Franklin Cover-Up* offered compelling evidence for the existence of King's pedophile ring and its cover-up by law enforcement, it lacked substantive proof for the ring's connection to Washington, DC, blackmail and the CIA, and also the pandering of Boys Town kids. The latter I found especially jarring in the context of the saintly mythology of Father Flanagan's Boys Town.

Crossing over the Missouri River on Interstate 80, I entered "The Good Life State" and quickly made my way to Omaha. My friend, Dirk, greeted me at the door of his apartment. I hadn't seen him in eight years. His look was still indelibly counterculture: bib overalls, shoulder-length black hair, and a graying beard; an earring—a silver half-moon—dangled from his left earlobe. He was a potter and also worked at a natural foods emporium.

I had first met Dirk on the ashram of an Indian guru, His Holiness Sri Swami Rama, over two decades earlier: I was nineteen and he was twenty-four. I lived on the ashram, in Honesdale, Pennsylvania, for five months before Rama tapped me to work at his New York City bookstore. While in New York, I discovered things that made me believe that Rama, a professed celibate, had an insatiable appetite for young women, and I edified my bookstore coworkers about our beloved guru's lower chakra predilections. Word of my insubordination quickly reached Rama, and he gave me "24 hours to leave the city or else." I interpreted his "or else" as a death threat—I had no idea that I was flirting with a second death threat during my visit to Nebraska.

Dirk split with Rama shortly after my departure and moved back to Omaha. Over the years, we kept in touch and periodically visited each other. After Dirk and I reminisced a bit, we grabbed a bite at a restaurant near his apartment. As we ate, I asked him if he remembered the scandal surrounding King and Franklin twelve years earlier. All he recalled was the Nebraska media reporting that three or four kids alleged they had been molested. They recanted, and a grand jury ultimately declared their allegations had been fabricated.

As Dirk and I later sat in his living room, digesting our dinners and talking, I showed him the USCS report on the Finders and also *Conspiracy of Silence*. His initial reaction was similar to mine: "There's something happening here. What it is ain't exactly clear."

The next night, Friday, at 7:00 P.M., I was slated to meet John De-Camp at the Coyote Den in Claytonia, Nebraska—population 296. The Coyote Den was wedged in among the dozen or so buildings that formed Claytonia's main drag. The bar had a musty scent, and a cloud of blue smoke hovered near the ceiling. The bar's wood-paneled walls were decked out with the festive posters and signs provided by beer distributors, and fifteen or twenty men, most of them farmers, sat around wooden tables, drinking and swapping yarns. The wooden counter, to the left of the entrance, stretched for approximately twenty feet, and featured a big glass crock of pickled pigs' feet. Though I've lived an adventurous life, I had somehow never come face-to-face with pickled pigs' feet before, and they looked indescribably repulsive and daunting.

John DeCamp was one of three men huddled around a corner table. His face poked upwards when we made eye contact—he had brown hair parted to the side, a round face, and tinted glasses. He wore a black turtleneck and slacks, and sipped from a brown bottle of Budweiser. Though he appeared perfectly innocuous in the humble confines of the Coyote Den, his self-published *The Franklin Cover-Up* had evolved into a fountainhead of fertile and ubiquitous Internet gossip. A highly decorated Vietnam vet and former sixteen-year Nebraska state senator, DeCamp had projected an imposing persona in *Conspiracy of Silence*. In person, his stature was more akin to Edward G. Robinson than John Wayne.

I walked over to his table, shook his hand, and introduced myself—he seemed less than enthusiastic to meet me. Since DeCamp first published his book in 1992, he's been a living, breathing mecca for conspiracy theorists—he cautiously scrutinized my soundness of mind and motives. After nonchalantly strafing me with a fifteen-minute Q & A, he must have concluded I was sufficiently benign. We then hopped into his car, picked up his teenage son, and drove to a nearby Chinese buffet.

I felt reluctant to discuss this material in front of DeCamp's son. According to *Conspiracy of Silence*, DeCamp's family had been terrorized for his efforts to expose the pedophile ring. After dinner, we drove back to DeCamp's sprawling Claytonia home, which had an indoor pool and plenty of space for his wife and four children.

DeCamp and I talked for about half an hour before we crashed. I gave him a list of people I wanted to interview and asked if he would help facilitate the interviews. He said he would give it a shot, but his resolve seemed lukewarm. DeCamp's revelations in *The Franklin Cover-Up* had never managed to pierce the mainstream national media, and he was legitimately skeptical of its ever happening.

The following morning, after a night of insomnia, I followed DeCamp to his Lincoln law office in pursuit of documentation. He directed me to an upstairs room, pointed to a mountain of white cardboard boxes, and departed. I spent hours digging through the boxes, but retrieved only one or two documents that I thought would be useful.

By mid-afternoon, DeCamp had already left the office, and I emerged from the upstairs room tired and despondent: I'd sifted through hundreds of documents and hadn't found any of the tantalizing tidbits De-Camp cited in his book. Jan, the office manager, and I converged at the coffeemaker—I explained to her that my five-hour search for documents had essentially resulted in zilch. She then told me that the documents excerpted and alluded to in *The Franklin Cover-Up* were in the basement. We walked down two flights of stairs, and she pointed to the Franklin mother lode—a wall of large, brown boxes.

The boxes yielded Omaha Police Department (OPD) reports and internal memos, Nebraska State Patrol (NSP) reports, Nebraska Department of Social Services (DSS) reports, internal Boys Town reports, victim debriefings, hundreds of the ring's flight receipts, etc. The cache of documents was a research junkie's nirvana, and I filtered through three or four boxes before Jan concluded the workday.

I made copies of the documents that I thought were relevant, stapled them back together, and fastidiously returned them to their respective boxes. I sensed that Jan was fond of order, and that my being a conscientious citizen scored major points with her. Over the next two weeks, she often griped that media personnel—including Yorkshire Television and ABC—had haphazardly rummaged through the boxes and left a wake of disarray.

I spent Saturday night and Sunday at Dirk's and returned to DeCamp's office on Monday morning. A brief conversation with DeCamp, who was in the midst of frenetic multitasking, provided me with a few phone numbers and a caution to be careful. Though DeCamp dispensed the warning with uncharacteristic gravitas, I'm generally not prone to paranoia and didn't take it too seriously.

One of the numbers was for Monsignor Hupp, the Director of Boys Town from 1973 to 1984. The eighty-eight-year-old Hupp had just moved from Omaha to Necedah, Wisconsin. In *Conspiracy of Silence*, Hupp was evasive and vague, but when I interviewed him, he made a number of truly scandalous allegations about Boys Town. I asked Hupp about Larry King's association with Boys Town: He said that after he had left Boys Town, he heard a staff member was allegedly taking Boys Town kids off campus to a restaurant owned by King.

But he confessed that he wasn't able to fully explore the rumors because, according to Hupp, his successor, Father Valentine Peter, ordered that the Boys Town Police Department arrest Hupp if he was ever seen on campus, which prompted him to discuss the matter with Omaha's archbishop. Hupp said that the archbishop ordered him to walk away from Boys Town and not look back. He also told me that he didn't trust Father Peter or the archbishop. Hupp's accusations were the first crack in my preconceived notion of Boys Town as a utopia for troubled youth.

The next person on the list I contacted was Rusty Nelson. In *The Franklin Cover-Up*, DeCamp discussed Nelson's involvement in "child pornography," referencing an Omaha Police Department report and a victim debriefing that painted a rather sordid picture of Nelson as King's "photographer," and their association perplexed me. DeCamp told me that he had offered Nelson legal assistance after the latter was pinched for child pornography. Nelson ultimately did time for the charges, but maintains that he had been set up to undermine his credibility.

After Nelson and I played phone tag for a couple of days, he voiced his reluctance to be interviewed, but he ultimately relented. He lived with his girlfriend and her two teenage children in a rural Columbus, Nebraska trailer park. Shortly after I pulled into the driveway—before I had a chance to ring the doorbell—Nelson opened the front door. I was struck by his dark brown eyes, which were glazed and a little spooky.

I talked to Nelson for ten or fifteen minutes, easing his reluctance before I plucked a tape recorder from my backpack. Over the course of the next two hours, he related an improbable tale of Larry King's nation-wide network. He alleged the ring pandered or outright sold children to the rich and powerful, employed blackmail, and had ties to US "intelligence." He maintained that King had attended satanic rituals, and had routinely plundered Boys Town for underage prostitutes. Nelson also named eminent politicians as pedophiles.

"King hired me to take pictures of adults and children in compromising positions," Nelson told me. "The pictures showed who the adults were and who the kids were. I gathered that the purpose was blackmail, and it was political. The content of the pictures, and the events surrounding them, would be an instant end to a politician's career."

Nelson claimed that King attempted to pressure him into making "snuff films," causing their relationship to fissure. After Nelson severed his ties to King, he alleged, he was harassed by the FBI. Nelson claimed that the crux of the FBI's threats wasn't designed to force disclosures about King's pedophile ring, but rather to silence him.

Nelson's allegations were jarring, but his shifty personality severely detracted from his credibility. After the interview, I returned to my friend Dirk's apartment and let him listen to the tape. "If even half of this interview is true," I told Dirk, "this story is one of America's worst nightmares."

The next day I drove to DeCamp's office and continued to sift through the basement boxes. I also contacted, or attempted to contact, individuals who had granted interviews to Yorkshire Television and appeared in *Conspiracy of Silence*. A number of people ignored my repeated phone calls, but I met with a woman who works within Nebraska's foster care system and also with a former state legislator.

Neither would grant an "on record" interview, citing the welfare of their families. Though they wouldn't talk "on record," they both alluded to the Franklin activities as a malignancy that was vast and seemingly omnipotent. Their fear was palpable—DeCamp's book mentioned the mysterious deaths or suicides of numerous people affiliated with the investigation into King's alleged child-pandering network.

Both my contacts had thought *Conspiracy of Silence* would break Franklin wide open. But when the documentary was shelved, they lost all hope of the story's ever being exposed, and both voiced the same concern: An unheralded journalist like myself wouldn't have a snowball's chance in hell to land the story: Why jeopardize the welfare of their families for a fruitless effort? After all, major newspapers, including the *New York Times* and *Washington Post*, had reported on a federal grand jury that refuted the existence of an interstate pedophile network.

I also contacted numerous people who weren't interviewed by Yorkshire Television, but whose names surfaced in *The Franklin Cover-Up*, and they recoiled from meeting with me. After a week or so of constant rebuffs, I remarked to DeCamp, "It's like these people are living in Stalinist Russia." Nodding his head, he added, "And they don't even know it."

A couple of days after I spoke to the woman working in Nebraska's foster care system, an investigator for the Nebraska State Patrol started to phone me every day, leaving voice mails that pertained to my conversation with her. I had mentioned to her that Monsignor Hupp had uttered a number of damning statements about Boys Town. The NSP investigator wanted to know the exact nature of Hupp's statements. I attempted to reach the woman to discuss her statements to the investigator, but she wouldn't return my calls. Three years after my initial visit to Nebraska, she finally took one of my calls—she told me that she'd never talked to the NSP investigator.

My friend Dirk was quite intrigued by *Conspiracy of Silence*, and then by my interviews with Monsignor Hupp and Rusty Nelson: He started phoning friends and acquaintances in an attempt to nurture my budding inquiry. He spoke to the friend of a friend whose name appeared in *The Franklin Cover-Up*, but the man wouldn't meet with me.

Dirk also had a rather unorthodox phone conversation with an acquaintance, who had an acquaintance who claimed to have been a drug courier for the ring. The courier wouldn't speak directly to Dirk and used his buddy as a conduit. He apparently recounted a few incidents of murder and mayhem, breaking down in tears, and said I was in great danger: The conversation seemed to blind-side Dirk like an unanticipated left hook—I was a little freaked out too.

The sum total of Rusty Nelson's disclosures (even if only partly true), people's intense apprehension to talk, daily calls from the NSP investigator, and the courier's warning were whittling away at my cavalier attitude. I also had the feeling that I was being followed, but I was unsure if I should chalk it up to a bona fide intuition or an evolving uneasiness—either way, I kept one eye on the rearview mirror.

Though I had the willies, I phoned two purported victims who appeared in *Conspiracy of Silence*. The first victim wouldn't return my calls, but I eventually talked to Paul Bonacci. Yorkshire Television had filmed him in Washington, DC, discussing his life as a child prostitute molested by the power elite. The thirty-three-year-old Bonacci, married and the father of two little girls, had an extremely troublesome history. He'd been diagnosed with multiple personality disorder, and at the age of twenty-two served time for the sexual assault of a minor.

Bonacci, too, was averse to being interviewed. So I invited him and his family to lunch, mentioning that we would merely chat, and he accepted my offer. On a brutally cold Wednesday, Bonacci, his wife, and their two preschool daughters trudged into the restaurant like they'd just finished the Iditarod—his daughters were bundled up in hooded snowmobile suits, snowmobile boots, thick scarves and mittens.

Bonacci's smile was brimming with white teeth. He appeared relatively conventional at first sight, but the indelible black grooves under his troubled brown eyes conveyed a nightmarish past. He and his wife spent ten minutes peeling off the multiple layers of their children's winter garb, wiping the girls' runny noses, and situating them around the table.

As we ate lunch, I noticed two men in their late fifties, burly and casually dressed, periodically peering at our table—they had the menacing look of KGB apparatchiks. I struggled not to comment on their undue attention, because it was possibly a figment of my increasing wariness, and Bonacci's wife was already visibly agitated. After a lunch of spaghetti, smiles, and small talk, Bonacci consented to an interview the following afternoon at 2:00 and gave me directions to his house.

The next morning Bonacci didn't answer my phone calls, but I decided to pay him a visit nonetheless. He and his family lived in Valley, Nebraska, twenty miles west of Omaha. Once I made it to Valley, I navigated a series of twists and turns before taking a left onto a dirt road, which I followed for a block or two before coming to a triple fork.

Swerving sharply to the right, I instantly realized that I should have veered left. I abruptly stopped and, preparing to back up, glanced in my rearview mirror: A nondescript brown sedan had just turned onto the dirt road and also stopped. I drove on, stopping just before the main dirt road was out of sight. The brown sedan started and then stopped again. I felt a flight-or-fight adrenal boost and made a squealing U-turn, waiting for the car to catch up and pass. The car never passed me, and I concluded it must have turned around on the dirt road.

After collecting myself, I proceeded to the far left fork. The Bonaccis lived in a rural area that was an odd smattering of trailers, shotgun shacks, and middle-class houses. The dwellings were spread out on a grid of dirt roads that had the contours of a maze. I eventually found the Bonaccis' modest, single story, brown home—no one was there. I pulled into his driveway and hung out for an hour or so, constantly craning to the left and right, but there were no signs of the Bonacci family or the brown sedan.

Driving back to Omaha, I thought that I probably hadn't been followed after all; the driver of the brown sedan had most likely turned onto the dirt road by mistake and realized his mistake precisely when I looked into my rearview mirror. Just as I convinced myself that I'd been beguiled by paranoia, a brown sedan with civilian license plates began tailgating me—a tinted windshield obscured the driver's face. I sped up, the brown sedan sped up; I slowed down, the brown sedan slowed down. I hit my brakes and then sped up. The brown sedan backed off briefly, and then began tailgating me again.

I abruptly swerved onto an exit ramp and slammed to a halt at a stop sign. The brown sedan followed, pulling up behind me. I looked into my rearview mirror, but the tinted windshield continued to obscure the driver. When I took a quick right, the brown sedan streaked past me. I pulled into a gas station, caught my breath, and bought an ice cream sandwich—ice cream sandwiches have a way of alleviating my stress. I ate the ice cream sandwich and mulled over my options. I then made a beeline back to the Bonaccis'.

Prowling down the dirt road to the Bonaccis', repeatedly glancing in the rearview mirror, I noticed Paul Bonacci's white van in his driveway. I parked on the dirt road, walked over to the house and knocked on the door. Bonacci and his wife answered the door. I invited myself into their house and appealed to Bonacci for a half-hour interview; he begrudgingly consented, against his wife's objections. I sat on a couch in their cluttered living room, attempting to allay Mrs. Bonacci's marked agitation as she bundled up their children. She then hustled them off to her parents' house a few blocks away. Twilight was yielding to night as they departed.

Bonacci had a history of psychiatric illness, and I hoped to calm him down before I started the interview. According to *The Franklin Cover-Up*, Bonacci had been a victim of extreme sadism and had even witnessed murder. I lobbed a few softballs at him before broaching the horrors he'd reportedly endured. Just as I started hurling fastballs, Bonacci's wife opened the front door. She reacted to my last question by demanding that I stop the interview—she feared that their children would be endangered if Bonacci talked.

The day had been fraught with too many difficulties for me to abandon the interview, and I backed away from the darker questions. Though

I attempted to placate Bonacci's wife, her agitation was having an adverse effect on her husband's psychological state. I found myself constantly comforting both of them, though I repeatedly thought of men in black—driving nondescript brown sedans—kicking down the house's front door and raking us all with machine-gun fire.

After several stops and starts, Bonacci related a tale that was eerily similar to Nelson's. In fact, he named the same "intelligence" officer as had Nelson. He also said that Larry King had been the ringleader of a nationwide pandering network, had attended satanic rituals, and had pillaged Boys Town for victims.

Though child-abuse charges were never brought against King, Paul Bonacci and John DeCamp pursued federal civil lawsuits against King and other alleged pedophiles Bonacci named as his assailants. US District Court Judge Warren Urbom declared Bonacci's accusations of Satanism and sadism to be unsubstantiated and "bizarre," and he dismissed all but one of the lawsuits filed by DeCamp—Larry King was incarcerated for looting the Franklin Credit Union when Bonacci's lawsuits were initiated, and he didn't bother to respond to the court's summons.

Judge Urbom therefore granted Bonacci a default judgment against King. DeCamp then requested a hearing on the single issue of damages, and called Bonacci to the stand along with other witnesses who corroborated his "bizarre" accusations. After Judge Urbom listened to the testimony, he awarded Paul Bonacci a *one million dollar* judgment. The ruling was based upon *some* of the horrific events that Bonacci related to me.

Judge Urbom wrote in his decision, "Between December 1980 and 1988, the complaint alleges, the defendant King continually subjected the plaintiff to repeated sexual assaults, false imprisonments, infliction of extreme emotional distress, organized and directed satanic rituals, forced the plaintiff to 'scavenge' for children to be a part of the defendant King's sexual abuse and pornography ring, forced the plaintiff to engage in numerous sexual contacts with the defendant King and others and participate in deviate sexual games and masochistic orgies with other minor children. The defendant King's default has made those allegations true as to him. The issue now is the relief to be granted monetarily.

"The now uncontradicted evidence is that the plaintiff has suffered much. He has suffered burns, broken fingers, beatings of the head and face and other indignities by the wrongful actions of the defendant King. In addition to the misery of going through the experiences just related over a period of eight years, the plaintiff has suffered the lingering results to the present time. He is a victim of multiple personality disorder, involving as many as fourteen distinct personalities aside from his primary personality. He has given up a desired military career and received threats on his life. He suffers from sleeplessness, has bad dreams, has difficulty in holding a job, is fearful that others are following him, fears getting killed, has depressing flashbacks, and is verbally violent on occasion, all in connection with the multiple personality disorder and caused by the wrongful activities of the defendant King."

"I don't think the judge would have given Paul a million dollar award if he didn't think he was telling the truth," DeCamp said of the ruling. King appealed the judgment but then withdrew his appeal. DeCamp told me that King retracted his appeal following "actions for depositions." The award for damages, however, remains uncollected.

I left the Bonaccis' stressed and exhausted. As I entered Dirk's apartment, he gave me a concerned look. I told him about the nondescript brown sedan and the Bonacci interview, and red-alert registered in his eyes. I eventually rolled into bed, tossing and turning for an hour or two before falling asleep. The following morning, Friday, I drove to DeCamp's office and finished sifting through his documentation, thanking Jan for all her help.

I made it back to Dirk's by early evening, and he wasn't home. I'd been sitting on the couch, channel-surfing for about five minutes, when I heard a knock on the front door. I cautiously crossed the living room and peered through the peephole, focusing on the convex image of a woman in her late twenties or early thirties. She had a mane of unkempt, long red hair, a full, freckled face, and wore thick-lensed glasses. I asked if I could help her, and she held up a book and said she wanted to give it to me. Her speech and mannerisms had the somnolence of someone in a hypnotic trance.

After the brown sedan incident, there was no way in hell I was opening the door: I wasn't sure if she was alone, and I didn't want her potentially incriminating fingerprints in Dirk's apartment or my prints on her book. I wish I'd had the presence of mind to grab my tape recorder, but I was too tired and freaked out to think straight.

Though I repeatedly asked her to leave, she wouldn't, insisting that I take the book. I eventually walked back to the couch, resumed channel-surfing, and she finally left. Within minutes of her departure, Dirk came home, carrying a sack of groceries. I mentioned that we'd had a visitor bearing a gift. Dirk said that he'd passed her on his way into the building. Taken aback by her freaky appearance, he couldn't help himself from turning to watch her walk into the night. He remarked that he'd never seen her before.

As Dirk toiled away in the kitchen, making dinner, and I settled on the History Channel, I again heard a knock on the front door—she was back, bearing the same gift. I motioned Dirk over to the door, and he gazed into the peephole. The events of the preceding twenty-four hours had depleted my adrenal reserves, but her reappearance gave Dirk a major adrenaline jolt. His facial expressions cycled through dread, foreboding, and bewilderment as she relentlessly knocked on the door.

Dirk and I huddled five feet from the door, discussing possible responses while she continued to knock. We agreed that under no circumstances should she enter the apartment, because there were just too many unknown factors. Stunned and perplexed, Dirk walked back into the kitchen as I implored her to leave. Before she left, she said, "You're in danger—they're going to kill you."

Though our dinner was delicious, neither Dirk nor I slept well that night.

Eulice Washington — 2007

Eulice & Tasha —1979

Tasha Washington — 2007

—Chapter One—

Webs of Corruption

I left Nebraska utterly devastated. I was beginning to believe that Franklin had been a killing field for the souls of innumerable children. The documentation I garnered revealed scores of victims and the harassment I encountered reinforced my burgeoning beliefs. Over the years, I've wavered on several investigative stories in the face of doubt—I wasn't convinced the stories were noble enough to stalk with reckless abandon. But the evil represented by Franklin unshackled me from any fetters of doubt.

I wouldn't be able to return to Nebraska for eight months, but in the meantime I started digging into the background of one Larry King. King's father, Lawrence King, Sr., grew up in Omaha and was tagged with the nickname of "Poncho" as a youngster. The nickname followed him into adulthood, and, as Poncho King came of age in the 1920s and 1930s, Omaha, the county seat of Douglas County, was on its way to becoming the world's leading livestock market—it overtook Chicago in 1955.

In Poncho King's later teens, he found employment in the meatpacking plants of the Omaha stockyards—like thousands of young men hailing from Omaha. Poncho King went to work in Omaha's Swift meatpacking plant; the Swift Company would employ him for over forty years. He started at Swift on the bottom rung, skinning hogs, but gradually worked his way into a supervisory position.

The founder of the Swift Company, Gustavas Swift, had revolutionized the meatpacking industry in the 1880s by using refrigerated rail cars to transport dressed livestock east. Swift's little trick was to harvest ice from the Great Lakes each winter and then build ice stations along the route. The sprawling Union Pacific Railroad was also headquartered in Omaha, and it was integral to providing the infrastructure for Omaha's booming meat industry.

Poncho King married his teenage sweetheart, Vineta Swancey, in 1942, and they ultimately settled into a clapboard house that was flanked by the roar of the Union Pacific Railroad and the wafting tang of the stockyards on the periphery of Omaha's economically depressed North Side. Poncho and Vineta King had six children; Lawrence Jr. was their second child and oldest son—he was born September 7, 1944. The Kings were devout Presbyterians, and they attended North Omaha's Calvin Presbyterian Church every Sunday. Larry Jr. was a tall, husky kid who was an excellent student and talented singer. King's parents encouraged him to take singing lessons as a youth, and he was a notable fixture in the church's choir.

As a student at Omaha's Central High School, King worked as a waiter at the ritzy Blackstone Hotel. The downtown hotel was a "symbol of elegance" and kept a small fleet of limousines for visiting dignitaries. The Blackstone Hotel offered the teenage, working-class King his first portal into the dazzling world of the rich. King went on to graduate from Central High School in 1962 and then enrolled at Omaha University, where he eventually took up pre-med studies. Becoming disillusioned with pre-med, he signed up for a four-year hitch in the Air Force in 1965, rising to the rank of sergeant. During his stint in the Air Force, King married Alice Ploche, whom he met in Chicago.

A 1973 article in the *Omaha Sun* was the first media mention I found of Larry King. According to the article, the Air Force sent King to Thailand to be an "information specialist" as the Vietnam War was raging, and he handled "top secret" military communications. King also told the reporter that after his honorable discharge from the Air Force, he took classes at the American Banking Institute in Omaha. King's résumé states that he was a 1972 graduate of the University of Nebraska with a Bachelor's in Business Administration, but the 1973 article made no mention of his degree.

At the age of twenty-five, King entered the "management training program" of First National Bank in downtown Omaha. The *Omaha Sun* reported that King, working in the bank's "computer section," and a janitor were the bank's only African-American employees. "I was dissatisfied with my advancement there," King said in the article. So in August of 1970, King left his job at First National Bank with no employment prospects in sight.

Later that year, a key organizer of the faltering, two-year-old Franklin Community Federal Credit Union asked Poncho King if he wanted to take it over—Poncho King had successfully headed the employees' credit union at the Swift Company. Poncho declined, but suggested that the Franklin Credit Union hire his son as its manager. Larry King was interviewed and given the job.

One of King's first moves as Franklin manager was conscripting the fair-haired Tom Harvey to manage the books. Harvey was a former high school teacher, and it was rumored among Franklin employees that he had been fired from his teaching job for fondling a male student. King had reportedly met Harvey at Omaha University, and both were ostensibly Presbyterians. Harvey's mother, Mary Jane, a Presbyterian Church bigwig, also came aboard at Franklin. She would eventually lend a hand to her son and King in the plundering of Franklin, and would likewise be convicted on related charges.

The 1973 *Omaha Sun* article lauded King for his diligence and industriousness as he worked "eighteen-hour" days to single-handedly save the sinking credit union. Interestingly, Warren Buffet owned the now-defunct *Omaha Sun*, and his wife, Suzie, was a benefactor of the Franklin Credit Union.

The *Omaha Sun* article was clearly written to puff up King's image, but the article contained a pair of peculiarities as it described up-and-comer Larry King. The peculiarities revolved around the Kings' relocation from North Omaha to a large, rambling home in the affluent Omaha suburb of Ponca Hills. The paper reported that "King renewed FBI acquaintances recently" when a heroin trafficker who lived in King's neighborhood was busted—FBI agents suggested to King that he move out of North Omaha. If the FBI "renewed" its "acquaintances" with King, that would imply that they already had a relationship. As this story unfolds, it will become all too apparent that the FBI had a vested interest in protecting Larry King ... and his dirty deeds.

The second peculiarity involved the Kings' relocating to a lavish house in an opulent suburb inhabited by millionaires. At the time of the article, the Franklin Credit Union's total assets hovered around $100,000, and

Larry King reportedly never received more than $17,000 a year from the credit union.

Four years after taking the helm of Franklin, King created the Consumer Service Organization (CSO) as an affiliate of the credit union. The CSO became an en masse receiver of welfare, disability, and social security checks for many residents of North Omaha. CSO officers set up Franklin accounts for the entitlement recipients and offered financial counseling. King vociferously extolled the virtues of the CSO for providing "a hand up and not a hand-out," and Franklin's coffers soon swelled with not only the entitlement monies but with grant monies too. The grants were given to Franklin for its good works in the community.

King and his Franklin underlings also started to peddle certificates of deposit around the country, offering interest rates 2% to 3% above the market rate—a Franklin executive raked in a cool $1 million in just one day by vending Franklin's high interest CDs. The Franklin CD con was a Ponzi scheme—Franklin perpetually pushed CDs so it could cover maturing ones.

Corporate powerhouses like Mutual of Omaha, Union Pacific, and the Kiewit Corporation (a Fortune 500 Omaha-based contractor) and several religious organizations, including Boys Town and the American Baptist Church, lined up to give Franklin grants or purchase its CDs. King also cultivated a relationship with President Ronald Reagan's Secretary of Housing and Urban Development, Samuel Pierce, whose political favoritism would later be exposed and give rise to scandal. Under Pierce, HUD would chip in many thousands of dollars to the Franklin Credit Union—Franklin solicited $1 million in HUD grants in 1981. The US Department of Health, Education, and Welfare also gave Franklin thousands. So King was ultimately glomming onto millions via his massive Ponzi scam and also via grants for all his good works.

Omaha World-Herald publisher, Harold Andersen, seemed to be a stalwart ally of King and the Franklin Credit Union. In addition to the *World-Herald* depositing thousands in the credit union, Andersen was Chairman of Franklin's Advisory Board. The tall, fair-haired Andersen attended Franklin's annual meetings, dispensing smiles and handshakes. In fact, Andersen headed a 1984 Franklin fund drive that raised $672,170, enabling King to build a bedroom in the credit union's basement.

The bedroom would be furnished with a brass bed, fluffy white comforter, a stereo, and a television. King told a Franklin employee that the bedroom served two functions—it allowed him to "unwind" and it also housed a live-in security guard. I talked to one of the "security guards" who briefly inhabited Franklin's basement bedroom—he alleged one of his first official duties as a Franklin security guard was performing oral sex on Larry King in the basement bedroom.

King referred to the credit union as "my baby," and his baby quickly became his personal, bottomless ATM. King flaunted his newfound wealth with all the pomp and garishness appropriate to a nouveau-riche vulgarian. He moved into a second Ponca Hill home, a mansion that overlooked the Missouri River. He eschewed his Corvette in favor of a sleek Mercedes, and sported several diamond rings and a bejeweled $65,000 watch. King's lifestyle was soon a succession of Lear Jets, limos, and five-star restaurants. He also had his hand in a diverse array of business ventures, including restaurants and bars. He bought Omaha's Showcase Lounge, which I'm told was a favored destination of pimps and prostitutes.

King's conspicuous consumption was certainly eyebrow-raising for those taking notice: In a thirteen-month period prior to Franklin's closing, money gushed from Franklin's coffers into King's hands. He racked up $1,131,229 on six different credit cards—$1,033,975 on American Express alone. He spent $186,395 on limos, $45,806 on chartered planes, $45,166 on jewelry, and various florists billed him a total of $145,057.

Though the National Credit Union Administration required federally insured credit unions to be audited every year, Franklin hadn't been audited during its last four years of operation. According to a former Franklin executive, when auditors would show up every now and then, King would holler, "Phone Washington!" After King talked to "Washington," the auditors begrudgingly made a hasty retreat. In December of 1988, a *Des Moines Register* article quoted an NCUA investigator discussing King and the Franklin Credit Union: "We'd sit around while having a beer in Omaha 10 years ago and wonder where he was getting all the money to pay for his lifestyle." So NCUA officials were apparently cognizant of the fact that King had been looting Franklin for years. But King got by with a little help from his friends—his friends in DC.

Early in 1984, a Franklin employee wrote a memo that documented King's embezzlement of funds. After the employee wrote the memo, he was summarily fired. The former Franklin employee then met with the Director of Nebraska's Department of Banking and Financing and even talked to a representative of the NCUA, but his tale fell on deaf ears.

In the 1980s, King started translating his ill-gotten wealth into political power. In his twenties, King had been a Democrat and die-hard supporter of Democratic Presidential candidate George McGovern, who was walloped by Richard Nixon in the 1972 presidential race. But as King's personal fortunes took a vertical trajectory, he switched his political alliances to the Republicans in 1981.

King was the founder and Chairman of the Nebraska Frederick Douglas Republican Council, which threw a 1983 reception honoring none other than Larry King for his "service to the Republican Party both locally and nationally." The reception, held at Omaha's upscale Regency Hotel, had presenters form ranks to praise and venerate King and impart plaques of recognition. The function had so many individuals extolling the virtues of Larry King that presentations were limited to a mere ninety seconds.

Hobnobbing with Nebraska's Republican elite was just an appetizer for King—he also started to become a force in Republican politics at the national level. His entrée into big-time Republican politics was through the National Black Republican Council. King reportedly wore several hats for the Council—he was Vice Chairman for Finance and also participated with its Nominating Committee and Development Committee. King also reportedly served as an advisor to its Youth Committee. King seemed to be particularly interested in children—his résumé acknowledged that he was on Head Start's Board of Directors, Regional President of the Girls Club, and on the Executive Committee of the Camp Fire Girls. King's résumé also mentioned that he was "Secretary/Treasurer" of the Planned Parenthood Federation of America.

As King became a fixture of Republican politics at the national level, he rented a swanky Washington, DC townhouse on California Street NW, near Embassy Row, and started to throw fabulous parties. A 1987 guest list from one of his DC parties boasted such luminaries as Supreme Court Justice Clarence Thomas, then Chairman of the Equal Opportunity Commission; United States Ambassador to the United Nations Jeanne Kirkpatrick; New York Congressman Jack Kemp; and Nebraska Congressman Hal Daub. Congressman Daub, like *Omaha World-Herald* publisher Harold Andersen, had a stint on Franklin's Advisory Board.

King also started to make hefty contributions to Republicans and their causes and sponsored Republican fundraisers. He shelled out $23,500 to Citizens for America, a conservative group run by the infamous lobbyist Jack Abramoff that assisted Oliver North in garnering support for the Nicaraguan Contras. King held a fundraiser for Congressman Hal Daub that was attended by HUD Secretary Samuel Pierce. King also gave a generous donation to Republican Kay Orr in her successful 1986 bid to become Nebraska's governor—he even sang the national anthem at her inaugural ceremony.

King's early musical training gave him a niche among Republicans when it came to belting out the "Star Spangled Banner." His national anthem debut for a Republican audience came in 1982 at a National Black Republican Council dinner. President Reagan and his wife were in attendance, and they were quite impressed with King's booming baritone. King then opened the 1984 GOP convention in Dallas with a spectacular rendition of the national anthem.

King had a busy time at that convention in Dallas. In addition to singing, he threw his biggest bash ever. He rented the Southfork Ranch—the fictitious lair of *Dallas* patriarch J.R. Ewing. Southfork's sprawling white mansion and grazing horses gave the six hundred people who attended King's party a hearty Texas welcome. Teenage cowgirls—wearing navy satin tights, vests, and cowboys hats—handed out yellow roses. A resplendent King, attired in white, sporting a thick gold chain, served the partygoers ribs, baked beans, coleslaw, and pecan pie.

HUD Secretary Samuel Pierce attended the shindig as did Reagan's daughter, Maureen, who was photographed with King in a very admiring embrace. Two months after Reagan's landslide victory over Walter Mondale in the 1984 presidential race, the *Washington Post* published an op-ed by King, "Why Blacks Should be Republican," wherein King touted the "substantial gains" made by African Americans under Republican policies.

As the Reagan administration was in its waning days, King apparently had high hopes for the presidential aspirations of New York

Congressman Jack Kemp: the *New York Post* reported that King made his party rounds in New York City and DC proudly displaying a "Jack Kemp for President" button. King kicked in cash to Kemp's 1988 presidential bid and to a Kemp political action committee. King also planned to host a Kemp fundraiser at his home—his florist said no expenses were spared for the Kemp fundraiser. Floral arrangements were scattered throughout the house and outside—King even had the florist float flower arrangements in the pool. Kemp, however, cancelled the fundraiser at the last minute.

Kemp's abrupt cancellation of the fundraiser didn't seem to put a damper on their association. King and Kemp would team up at the 1988 Republican Convention in New Orleans. Two months before the Convention, King formed the Council of Minority Americans, which sponsored a $100,000 gala in New Orleans—Jack Kemp, Alexander Haig and former President Gerald Ford were on the Council's "host committee." A ten-minute video, featuring King and Kemp, urged African Americans to vote for George H.W. Bush in the upcoming election. The *Washington Post* reported that a "child singer," whose "hair was pulled back in an 'Alice in Wonderland' hairdo," belted out "Dixie" at the gala. At the time, King was reportedly lobbying for an ambassadorship to Jamaica, where his wife's family was said to be from.

When the Franklin Credit Union was raided later that year, Republican VIPs started distancing themselves from King like rats fleeing a sinking ship. A spokeswoman for the Republican National Committee initially denied that King was involved in Republican politics at the national level, but a few days later she acknowledged that King had a role with the National Black Republican Council, whose chairman exclaimed, "Of course they knew!" A spokesman for Jack Kemp said of King and Kemp, "They met at a fundraiser, but King was not a personal friend."

Kemp was a former National Football League quarterback, and a golden boy of the Republican Party. President George H.W. Bush appointed Kemp the Secretary of HUD, and Kemp would be Bob Dole's running mate when the latter made his 1996 presidential bid. But rumors of homosexuality plagued Kemp for decades. In fact, Kemp was asked about his purported homosexuality during a 1986 interview on NBC's *Today Show*. He "categorically" denied the rumors.

Kemp, who died in 2009, insisted that the genesis of the rumors dated back to the 1960s when he was a part-time aide to then-California Governor Ronald Reagan and also a quarterback for the Buffalo Bills. At the time, Kemp co-owned a Lake Tahoe ski lodge with a second Reagan aide, who threw "homosexual parties" at the lodge. The latter Reagan aide resigned amidst contentions of his homosexuality, but Kemp said he purchased the lodge as an investment and never visited it. Kemp maintained that his co-ownership of the lodge was the sole wellspring of the homosexuality rumors that stalked him for decades.

Surprisingly, Clarence Thomas was one Republican big shot who didn't disavow knowing King; instead, he called King's legal travails "unfortunate." Though Thomas' name appears on the invitation list of a 1987 DC party hosted by King, Thomas said he first met King in 1988 at the New Orleans Convention. Like King, Thomas' wife had grown up in Omaha. She was a protégé of Nebraska's Congressman Hal Daub and accompanied Daub to DC as an aide, the very same Hal Daub who sat on Franklin's Advisory Board and was also the beneficiary of a King fundraiser and campaign contributions.

Thomas' 1991 appearance before the Senate Judiciary Committee hearing, which decided his fate as a Supreme Court Justice, held millions of Americans spellbound before their televisions. Law professor Anita Hill had been a subordinate of Thomas when he headed the Equal Opportunity Commission, and Hill testified that Thomas was lewd, talked of bestiality, and kept abreast of porno stars. Thomas called the proceedings a "high-tech lynching" and absolutely denied Hill's allegations.

The hearing was ultimately a "he said, she said" affair, and Thomas became a Supreme Court Justice, but very few Americans were aware of the fact that a second female subordinate of Thomas' had been subpoenaed to appear before the hearing who could have corroborated Anita Hill: Angela Wright had been employed by the Equal Opportunity Commission during Thomas' reign as Chairman, and she too alleged lewd conduct and sexual harassment by Thomas.

Though Wright had flown from North Carolina to Washington to testify at the hearing, the Senate Judiciary Committee never called her. Senate Judiciary Committee Chairman Joseph Biden said Wright's subpoena had been lifted because of the wishes of Wright and her attorney.

But Wright's attorney adamantly denied Biden's claim and stressed that Wright never asked for the subpoena to be lifted.

Because Biden and the Senate Judiciary Committee didn't call Wright to testify, the hearing came down to Thomas' word against Hill's, and Thomas subsequently eked out a razor-thin majority in the US Senate—52 to 48—to be confirmed as a Supreme Court Justice. However, if Biden had called Wright to testify, it's certainly possible that the Senate wouldn't have confirmed Thomas. A book about Thomas, *Strange Justice: The Selling of Clarence Thomas*, supported Hill's allegations that he had a penchant for pornography, and several women have since come forward to corroborate Hill's other allegations.

America is a society that predominantly believes that an individual's sexual predispositions or preferences shouldn't be illegal insofar as they involve consenting adults, and I'm of that opinion too. But the import of Franklin is the age-old story of sexual blackmail. *If*, in fact, Jack Kemp had homosexual liaisons or Clarence Thomas had an interest in bestiality or lascivious pornography, their preferences would make them susceptible to being compromised and controlled. Given Kemp's former positions as a US Congressman and Secretary of HUD, and Thomas' status as a US Supreme Court Justice, they have made decisions that affect every American. Their potential to be blackmailed thus makes them vastly different from John Q. Citizen.

Before the fall of Franklin, Larry King seemed to be exempt from bad press, even though just below the surface of his lavish lifestyle lurked very dark shadows. In addition to allegations of King being a pimp, rumor and innuendo would connect his name to several suspicious suicides or outright murders. As the story of Franklin unfolds, it will become evident that the media and law enforcement were hands-off concerning King, and I've found it nearly impossible to link him to the various suicides and murders that Franklin lore attributes to him. I've also located people who might have had information to offer on the deaths, but they've obstinately refused to talk to me.

An FBI debriefing of an alleged victim of King's pandering network discussed a relationship between Larry King and a drug dealer named Bill Baker, who also reportedly dealt in child pornography—he was found murdered near downtown Omaha: An unknown party had put a bullet in the back of his head. The alleged victim told the FBI that Baker had molested her at King's behest. She also related to FBI agents that she was in Baker's apartment when Baker and King were screening child pornography to determine its marketability. She informed the FBI that Baker's murder had been a "contract killing," but I couldn't find any evidence that the FBI conducted a follow-up investigation.

The "suicide" of twenty-nine-year-old Charlie Rogers is highly suspicious, and I found substantial corroboration connecting Rogers and King. Rogers' fully clothed body was found on November 10, 1986 in his west Omaha apartment with a fatal shotgun wound to the head: The stock of his twelve-gauge shotgun rested between his legs, and the barrel of the gun was pointed at his head. His television was on, and there was no suicide note—his apartment's front door was locked, but the door to his third-floor deck was unlocked. Though Rogers' death was ruled a suicide, his relatives and friends were dubious of the official pronouncement. He was very close to his mother and younger sister, and both told law enforcement that he surely would have left a suicide note.

Rogers, a body-builder, was six feet tall and tipped the scales at around 180 pounds. He had a thick head of brown hair, brown eyes, and ruggedly handsome features. He owned a lawn service and also worked as a bouncer at The Max, Omaha's popular gay bar, frequented by Larry King. But the interactions between Rogers and King weren't limited to The Max. In addition to finding Rogers' body on November 10, law enforcement found a gold deerskin coat in his apartment—a receipt in the coat's pocket showed that Larry King had purchased the coat for $2,810. King also sent Rogers "dozens of flowers" and bought him a "closet full of clothes." A lover of Rogers had an 18-karat gold bracelet King purchased for Rogers: "Charlie" was engraved on the bracelet's topside and "From the Boss" was engraved on the underside. In Rogers' pocketbook of telephone numbers, the name "King" was accompanied by five different numbers.

Approximately three weeks before Rogers' death, he stopped by his mother's house for a roast beef dinner, a routine ritual in his life. He told her that he had a plane ticket to Washington, DC, but he decided not to use it and asked her if she wanted to fly to DC. His mother declined her son's offer and abruptly cut short their conversation about the ticket. In retrospect, she felt Rogers was attempting to explain the ticket to her; therefore she deeply regretted interrupting him.

After Rogers' death, his mother found the plane ticket while sorting through his possessions—the Franklin Credit Union had purchased the ticket for Rogers. He was slated to fly out of Omaha at 11:25 A.M., make a stopover in Minneapolis, and arrive in Washington, DC at 4:35 P.M. On the same day, he would leave DC at 8:00 P.M, and after a stopover in Minneapolis, return to Omaha at 10:57 P.M. She felt it was very strange that someone at the Franklin Credit Union, presumably King, wanted her son to be in DC for just three-and-a-half hours.

A week or so after Rogers' conversation with his mother about the DC ticket, he visited his twenty-six-year-old younger sister and her husband— he had about two weeks to live. Rogers showed up at their place around 10:00 P.M. on a Sunday night. Rogers and his kid sister were very close, and she immediately noticed that Rogers, who was usually effervescent and a prankster, appeared extremely tense and paranoid. Rogers had a lot on his mind, and he would spend the next four or five hours talking to his sister and brother-in-law. Rogers had nicknamed his little sister Crunch, and he piped, "Crunch, I think I'm in trouble."

Rogers then alluded to the fact that he was living a double life but, he said, for the physical welfare of his sister and her husband he wouldn't divulge many of its specifics—he told them that he was attempting to extricate himself from an endeavor that was seemingly ominous. Though he wouldn't specifically state the particulars of the endeavor, he said it was connected to a very powerful individual whose name was "Larry King." His sister had never heard of Larry King before, and she didn't have the foggiest clue about King or the Franklin Credit Union.

Rogers disclosed to his sister that he had been enmeshed with King for a couple of months, and he took several trips with him, primarily to Washington, DC—he said he'd received approximately $50,000 from King. Rogers revealed that King was connected to people who harnessed unbelievable power—he mentioned four or five times that he was merely a bug on the floor, and these powerbrokers had the ability to squash him at will. Rogers then conveyed to his sister and brother-in-law a rather mind-boggling account of that power—the powerbrokers had the "juice" to completely erase people's backgrounds and insert them into high-ranking political positions.

Rogers told his sister that he wanted out of King's sphere, because he had renewed a relationship with a former boyfriend who disapproved of King's activities. Before Rogers left his sister's house at approximately 3:00 A.M. the following morning, he gave his sister a pair of letters King had written to him. Rogers also gave his sister a small stationery card that had "Larry King" inscribed on the front.

Rogers departed his sister's house in the wee hours, and she would never see him alive again. Though the three had talked for hours, Rogers' fear for his life hadn't abated in the least. Shortly before his departure, he told his sister and brother-in-law that if something happened to him or he went missing, they should contact Douglas County Deputy Attorney Bob Sigler—he said Sigler would be fully cognizant of his situation.

Rogers' mother phoned her son two days before his death, and he was in good spirits—her call found him catching up on his lawn service's bookkeeping. The night of Rogers' death, he was bouncing at The Max, and he seemed to be quite agitated—he and his boyfriend had a physical altercation on the sidewalk outside the bar. He punched his lover, who fell onto the sidewalk and hit his head. The fall resulted in a minor laceration that required him to be taken to the emergency room for stitches. After work, Rogers stopped by the hospital to see his boyfriend. And then Rogers supposedly went home and blew his brains out.

The day Rogers' body was found, his mother received a call from the Douglas County Sheriff's Office. The officer phoning Rogers' mother insisted he stop by her place of employment, but he wouldn't tell her why. Officers from the Sheriff's Office then showed up at her work around 1:00 P.M. and informed her that her son was dead. She has said that she felt as if every drum in the world was being pounded, every bell in the world was being rung, and the building was crashing down upon her.

The son-in-law who had been privy to Rogers' startling revelations two weeks earlier picked up Rogers' mother and they drove to her daughter's home—it was a cold, sleeting day. When they arrived, Rogers' sister and her husband told Rogers' mother of his confessions and that he feared for his life. They also told her that he'd said if anything happened to him, they should contact Douglas County Deputy Attorney Bob Sigler. Later in the day, Rogers' father phoned Sigler.

Sigler maintained that he had no idea why Rogers insisted that he be contacted if Rogers turned up dead or went missing—Sigler would say that their only connection was that Sigler had handled a few misdemeanor cases for Rogers when he was in private practice.

Rogers' mother, sister, and brother-in-law were perplexed by Sigler's reaction and quickly swept away by dread—they developed a rapid-onset fear of Larry King. Shortly after Rogers' death, his mother received a letter from King requesting that she return a pager King had given to her son: "Please accept my sincere sympathy on Charlie's death. After having Charlie as an employee, I was very sad to read about your loss. Unfortunately, I must ask a favor of you at this time. Charlie had a paging beeper provided by us that he used when he worked."

Omaha World-Herald reporter James Allen Flanery talked to Rogers' kin, and started delving into Rogers' mysterious death. (Flanery would also tell the Nebraska Attorney General's Office that the "suicide" of a former Boys Town student might also be connected to King.) Flanery made a visit to the Douglas County Sheriff's Office, requesting Rogers' autopsy report. The Sheriff's Office generally dispensed autopsy reports without much ado, but the Sheriff's Office phoned Douglas County Deputy Attorney Bob Sigler, and he refused permission to cough up Rogers' autopsy report.

A puzzled Flanery then wandered over to Sigler's office—he had a few questions for Sigler: Flanery wanted to know why Sigler wouldn't give him Rogers' autopsy report, and he also wondered why Rogers had told his sister and brother-in-law that they needed to contact Sigler if Rogers suffered an unexpected death. Flanery walked into Sigler's office and plied him with questions.

Sigler wasn't receptive to Flanery's queries and exploded: "There's no interview here!" barked Sigler. "I don't affirm, I don't deny. I don't have any comment." Sigler then made a comment that struck Flanery as especially strange: He asked Flanery if *Omaha World-Herald* publisher Harold Andersen knew that Flanery was poking around into Rogers' death.

Flanery would eventually publish an article on Rogers' death in the *World-Herald* linking Rogers to King, but the newspaper only published the article after the fall of Franklin, and *over two years after* Rogers' death. The article also neglected to mention that Flanery had come by Rogers' little black book during the course of his investigation into Rogers' death. Flanery had phoned one of the numbers in the little black book and left his name and number on a man's answering machine. Shortly thereafter, Flanery received a call from the man's sister—she and Flanery were acquainted. The sister told Flanery that he had stumbled onto a national prostitution ring.

Upon my return to Nebraska, I started looking for Larry King's alleged victims, now young adults. I was particularly interested in interviewing Eulice Washington, because she had been the first of the purported victims to come forward. I eventually found Washington's grandmother, Opal Washington, whom I talked to for twenty or thirty minutes. I told Opal of my intentions, and she seemed genuinely pleased that a journalist had taken an interest in the "horrible things" her granddaughters had endured.

She said that she would contact Eulice on my behalf, and I gave her my cell phone number—Eulice Washington phoned me later in the afternoon. She was suspicious of my motives but, after we conversed for half an hour or so, I quelled her concerns and she invited me to her home. Washington's white, split-level house was located in a western suburb of Omaha. Shortly after I knocked on the front door, she greeted me and invited me into her home. She wore a denim shirt and blue jeans—her complexion was unblemished and she had lucid, bronze eyes.

Washington was gracious, yet guarded, as she directed me to a living room sofa. Her living room was decorated with the trophies and ribbons that commemorated the many academic and athletic achievements of her four teenage children. We talked for maybe an additional hour when she consented to be interviewed. Before I pressed "RECORD" on my tape recorder, she ushered her four children down the hallway, directing the two older ones into a bedroom to the right of the hallway and her two younger kids into a bedroom to the left, gently closing the doors. Almost immediately, her two older children switched on their stereo and her two younger children launched into video games. A muffled mix of Sade's crooning and PlayStation machine-gun fire wafted down the hallway as Eulice returned to the living room and sank into the couch, leaning her head on her right hand.

In 1977, Nebraska authorities found that Washington's biological mother was unfit to raise her three daughters—Eulice, Tracy, and Tasha—due to her heroin addiction. The sisters subsequently became wards of the state and were placed in the home of Jarrett and Barbara Webb. Eight-year-old Eulice was the eldest of the Washington sisters—Tracy and Tasha were six and two. The Webbs ultimately adopted the Washington sisters, and they were stamped with the Webb surname. The Webbs also adopted two other children, Wally and Robert, and three additional foster siblings were placed in their home.

The forty-one-year-old Jarrett Webb was a twenty-year employee of the Omaha Public Power District, a utility company that supplied electricity to the greater Omaha area, and he also sat on the Franklin Credit Union's Board of Directors for two years. Barbara was thirty-nine years old and a cousin of Larry King. Jarrett was tall, thin, and withdrawn, and Barbara was short, large, and outgoing.

The Webbs lived in a lovely blue and white ranch house that was surrounded by rolling acreage and shrouded by oak trees—their home was approximately twenty miles north of Omaha in Washington County. The property had been in Barbara Webb's family for three generations. Her grandparents founded Nebraska's first orphanage for African-American boys, Oakview Home for Boys, near the site where the Webbs resided. Up to twenty children lived at the Oakview Home for Boys at any given time. "My grandmother never made a difference between all the children she raised," Barbara once remarked to a reporter. "To her, a child was a child. Being with her and my grandfather taught me so much about love." Barbara Webb would publicly declare that it was her calling to continue the good works of her grandparents.

The Washington sisters quickly discovered that the Webbs' house was not as it appeared. "I was in third grade when my sisters, Tracy and Tasha, and I were adopted by the Webbs," began Eulice, born in June of 1969. "The first night we were scared. Tracy and Tasha were crying. Tasha peed on herself, and Mrs. Webb tied her to a doorknob. Then she beat her and left her there all night."

Washington would tell me that she and her sisters suffered repeated beatings for the next eight years. Her accusations are not only corroborated by her sisters, but by a trove of documents from Nebraska's Department of Social Services (DSS).

The DSS documents pointed out that the Webbs' other adopted and foster children received repeated beatings too. The Webbs introduced the children to an extension cord, bullwhip, rubber hose, and a black strap dubbed the "railroad prop," a two-foot strip of black rubber perforated with holes. "They beat us all the time," said Washington. "I took most of the abuse so they wouldn't beat Tracy and Tasha."

Indeed, in separate interviews, the Webbs' adopted and foster children flooded DSS personnel with bone-chilling anecdotes of horrific physical abuse. A myriad of infractions incited the beatings: The grade of a "C" or lower, using the telephone without permission, or even having the temerity to have friends call the Webb home. During the beatings, the children were generally required to remove all their clothes—the beatings could last for five minutes or persist for well over an hour.

DSS records detailed that the Webbs, as a punishment, consistently denied the children food too. A DSS document related that Tracy Washington was deprived of food for four days—she was only allowed to eat school lunches. In the summertime, the children were tasked with mowing and manicuring the acreage around the Webb's house: The chore would usually take them two days, and they were deprived of food until the task was completed to the Webbs' satisfaction. "They starved us as a regular punishment," Eulice Washington told me. "After dinner, we would clean off the table and eat the scraps from the Webbs' plates, because we were so hungry." Tasha Washington would later tell me that the Webbs forced her adoptive brothers to eat dog food from a bowl on the floor.

The children were also subjected to mental cruelty and mind games, and they were brainwashed into believing that being welcomed into the Webb fold was their good fortune. One of the adopted boys, who had a deformed leg, was warned by Barbara Webb that because of his handicap the Webbs were the only family willing to ever provide him with a home. A DSS document noted the following: "All of the children have frequently been told by the Webbs that 'no one else would want you.'"

Like Orwell's Big Brother, the Webbs also sought to either eradicate the Washington sisters' past or reframe it—they burned the girls' family pictures and recurrently told them that their biological mother was "no good" and a "slut."

Jarrett and Barbara had an unorthodox arrangement with the DSS—they received state subsidies for all eight adopted and foster children living in their home. The rationale of the Webbs' receiving state subsidies for even their adopted children was that they came from extremely troubled backgrounds and required extensive counseling. But the Webbs never voluntarily provided the children with counseling—Barbara Webb's preferred form of "counseling" was to simply tell the children to "forget" their past.

Barbara Webb attended Omaha's Seventh Day Adventist Church almost every Saturday, and she sang in the choir—she had a honey-coated voice, just like her cousin Larry King. Her entrance into the church would be a wondrous spectacle: She would be adorned in a mink coat, designer clothing, and expensive jewelry—her hair was perfectly done. The children would be immaculately dressed and silently follow in her wake. The children, wearing their Sunday best, sat in the church's pews like little cherubs. They never acted up or made the slightest peep. But the Webbs' fellow churchgoers found them aloof and occasionally intimidating, because Barbara's hair-trigger temper periodically erupted.

The Webbs also dressed up the children and took them to the lush home of "Uncle Larry" King and to soirées hosted by King. The Webbs made Eulice attend functions at the North Omaha Girls Club, where Larry King served as president. Eulice said that these gatherings gave her the creeps: She said the functions included approximately fifteen "older men," and they seemed to salivate over the twenty or so teenage girls who were present.

In addition to being kin, Eulice found out that Larry King and Barbara Webb shared more sinister bonds. Eulice claimed that she was at King's home, watching television, when King and Barbara Webb entered the room—King unlocked one of the room's cabinets and handed Barbara Webb a number of videotape cassettes, which she slipped into a large handbag. Shortly afterward, the Webbs were out on the town and they forgot to lock their bedroom door. According to Eulice, she and the other children found the videotapes and popped them into the Webbs' VCR—one of the tapes explicitly showed "teenagers" engaged in sex. The children also discovered pornographic pictures tucked away in the Webbs' dresser.

Unfortunately, the Webb children would find out that even their school wasn't a safe refuge, because the Webbs cultivated friendships with some of the school district's administrators—Tracy said they periodically visited the Webb home and Barbara often dropped by the kids' school to talk with them.

DSS documents reported on one occasion Tasha showed up at school with "marks all over her body" and her "eyes were swollen"—she revealed to a friend that she had been beaten by the Webbs. Tasha's DSS caseworker contacted a school district administrator who was reportedly a friend of the Webbs, and he claimed that no one informed him about the marks on Tasha's body—he felt that Tasha was put up to her wild fabrication by Eulice and Tracy. The same administrator said he asked Tasha's adopted brother, Robert, if the Webbs hit Tasha, and Robert replied that the Webbs had never hit her. The administrator then told the caseworker that Robert said the Webb household was the "best place he's ever lived."

The Webbs managed to cultivate the public image of ideal parents. In 1983, the *Omaha World-Herald* ran an article—"Making the Best of it ... a House full of Kids"—about the Webb household, and it depicted Barbara and Jarrett as the wellspring of love and compassion, including a Norman Rockwell-esque photograph of the "family." A beaming Barbara was seated on a sofa, and the Washington sisters were draped around her as if she was the physical embodiment of heavenly compassion. The two adopted boys, with ear-to-ear smiles, stood next to Jarrett in the background.

The article's author was enamored with Barbara Webb's good-natured mirth and "deep, hearty" chuckle as she tossed out thoughtful, maternal quips about smothering her adopted children with "the love that I think they need." The article talked about the Webbs' "love" producing a truly miraculous transformation in the lives of the Washington sisters. Barbara Webb said that when the sisters arrived at their home, their threadbare clothes were "so bad you couldn't even give them to the Goodwill." She pointed out that the girls were malnourished too—they didn't even know the difference between an orange and a peach—and two had learning disabilities. But under the compassionate guidance of the Webbs, she said, the sisters were now happy and flourishing.

The article also stressed the financial sacrifices that the Webbs had made to meet all the needs of their adopted children. The author discussed Barbara Webb "gardening, canning, and cooking a lot of casseroles—things that will stretch," and Barbara Webb chimed in on the economic tribulations of spreading her love among so many children: "Financially, things get tight sometimes, but we just draw in our strings and go around another way to see that the children have everything they need."

The article in the *Omaha World-Herald* would be part and parcel of a propaganda campaign that culminated in Barbara Webb being named Nebraska's foster care mother of the year! The award was presented to Barbara Webb by then-Nebraska Governor Bob Kerry. The Washington sisters distinctly remember donning their Sunday best and driving with the Webbs to Lincoln, where Kerry bestowed the award. The girls were utterly baffled by the afternoon's festivities.

In a testament to the resilience of the human spirit, the children started to doubt their perceptions of the Webbs' omnipotence, and the psychological levies that held back their fear and anguish ultimately started to crumble. The incident that precipitated the first breach was the grave offense of a ripped jacket.

According to a Washington County Sheriff's report, Jarrett and Barbara Webb suddenly awoke adoptive son Wally and foster charge Kevin, who slept in the basement. The Webbs mercilessly beat both boys, because Kevin had accidently ripped his jacket.

Approximately ten days later, in June of 1985, Wally and Kevin fled to their neighbors' house and talked to their son. They divulged to him that they planned to run away because the Webbs habitually and mercilessly beat all their children. Kevin lifted up his T-shirt and showed the neighbors' son the numerous welts that covered his back. The neighbors' son told his mother about the incident, and she phoned the Washington County Sheriff's Office.

After a deputy sheriff talked to the neighbors, he paid a visit to the Webbs. When the deputy sheriff met with Kevin and Wally, they voiced their reluctance to utter a word about the Webbs' abuse, because they would surely receive a severe beating if they talked. But they eventually opened up to the deputy sheriff and told him of repeated floggings—Kevin also showed the deputy sheriff the welts on his back.

Barbara Webb dismissed Kevin and Wally's allegations by telling the deputy sheriff that the welts on Kevin's back were merely the result of a spanking. The deputy sheriff didn't buy her explanation and took Kevin and Wally into custody. Kevin was taken to a local hospital and examined by a doctor whose report stated that the welts on Kevin's back were "most likely caused by something similar to a heavy rubber hose." A Washington County Sheriff's report noted that law enforcement, accompanied by Child Protective Services, returned to the Webb household the following day.

After authorities talked to the other foster children in the Webb household, they took the three foster children and Wally out of the Webb home. The foster children would be placed in a new foster home, but the Webbs wouldn't be charged with a single count of child abuse—they also retained custody of their other adopted children. In Wally's case, the Webbs denied the child-abuse allegations: He was ruled "uncontrollable" and eventually became a ward of the state.

According to DSS documents, the Webbs changed their punishment regimen after the DSS intervention and started beating the remaining children on the bottoms of their feet, as if they were POW's at the Hanoi Hilton. But liberation of the four children had an effect on the others; roughly two months after the foster children and Wally escaped, Tracy and Robert ran away to a second neighbor's house, alleging physical abuse. This time the Webbs convinced the children to return home before law enforcement and DSS personnel arrived. DSS caseworkers converged on the Webb home the following day, but Tracy and Robert recanted their allegations of abuse, saying they "ran away" to avoid being disciplined for "wrongdoing"—DSS workers noted that Barbara Webb was in earshot of the conversation.

In November of 1985, Eulice managed to find her biological grandmother, Opal Washington—despite the Webbs' concerted efforts to disavow the sisters' family of origin—and she fled to Opal's house in Omaha. Eulice phoned the Webbs from her grandmother's and said she would only return to the Webb's house if her sisters were allowed to visit their grandmother. The Webbs consented to let Tracy and Tasha visit, and the sisters stayed with their grandmother for a few days.

The children then opened up to their grandmother about the physical abuse in the Webb household. Opal reportedly placed a call to the Omaha Police Department, and the responding officer told her that the Washington sisters were legally adopted by the Webbs and lived in Washington County: the matter was out of OPD's jurisdiction.

At the conclusion of the girls' visit with their grandmother, she drove them to the rendezvous location designated by the Webbs, but the Webbs were nowhere to be found—Opal Washington and the girls then returned to Opal's home. Following their arrival back at Opal's, the OPD showed up—the Webbs had phoned the OPD alleging Opal had kidnapped the children!

The Webbs in concert with the OPD picked up the Washington sisters at their grandmother's. Upon their return to the Webb home, DSS documents reported, the three sisters were pushed into chairs, and the Webbs barked, "You are dead to us!" The sisters were also derided as "whores" and "bitches." The Webbs made the sisters clean and scrub their house the entire night and into the morning. The ten-year-old Tasha became too exhausted to continue scrubbing; so the Webbs heaved her onto the kitchen's counter and shook her every time she appeared to be falling asleep.

The following day, the Webbs' attorney notified DSS personnel that the Webbs wanted to relinquish their custody of Eulice and Tracy. Later in the day, in near blizzard conditions, a Washington County Deputy Sheriff and three DSS caseworkers descended upon the Webb household. Though Jarrett and Barbara answered the door, they wouldn't let the deputy sheriff or the caseworkers into their home. One of the caseworkers had a heated exchange with Barbara Webb, and she slammed the door on his hand. The Webbs finally consented to allow Eulice and Tracy to leave with DSS personnel. As snow cascaded to the ground, Eulice and Tracy were driven away from their eight-year nightmare. The girls were rapturous to see the Webb home recede into the background, but they expressed tremendous concern for Tasha's safety.

Roughly a month after Eulice and Tracy were removed from the Webbs' home, Washington County filed a petition to make the girls wards of the state, and a December hearing was held to determine the Webbs' parental rights regarding Eulice and Tracy. But the girls had yet to be assigned a guardian ad litem—someone, usually a lawyer, appointed by the court to represent minors in litigation. So the judge appointed the girls a guardian ad litem and postponed the hearing.

In front of the judge, Eulice voiced her concerns for the welfare of Tasha and insisted that she and Tracy be allowed to visit their little sister, but the judge ruled that Eulice and Tracy wouldn't be granted visitations to the Webb home, prompting Eulice to break down in tears. Inexplicably, that judge told Washington County Attorney Patrick Tripp that he wanted nothing more to do with the case, and the county imported a judge from a neighboring district to adjudicate the predicament.

Eulice and Tracy were ultimately placed in the foster home of Ronald and Kathleen Sorenson. The Sorensons had temporarily taken in Wally and Kevin right after they were liberated from the Webbs—Kathleen Sorenson had witnessed firsthand the "walnut-sized bruises" on both boys' backs.

After Eulice and Tracy had been in the Sorenson home for a month or so, Eulice started to seem very distressed. The Sorensons discovered that she slept in the closet one night, and then she started to talk about a friend who had been raped by her adoptive father and also of orgies. Kathleen Sorenson gradually earned Eulice's trust, and Eulice eventually said that Jarrett Webb had repeatedly molested her—Sorenson notified DSS personnel of Eulice's allegations.

On January 2, 1986, shortly after Eulice's disclosures to Kathleen Sorenson, the sisters met their guardian ad litem, Patricia Flocken, for the first time. Flocken had a private practice in Fort Calhoun and served as a guardian ad litem for several children, including the girls' adoptive brother Wally. Flocken remembered showing up at the Sorensons' house in a yellow jogging suit, which was a recent Christmas present, and being teased for not looking very lawyerly. Shortly after her arrival, though, the atmosphere became dreadfully serious.

Kathleen Sorenson watched as Eulice and Tracy discussed the physical abuse in the Webb household—their allegations of physical abuse corresponded closely with the allegations Wally had made to Flocken. The girls also talked about being terrified of the Webbs' lawyer, and then they started to mention Barbara Webb's cousin. They said he was powerful and politically connected, and they were terrified of him—Flocken had never heard of Larry King before. After Eulice started to feel comfortable with Flocken, she brought up her molestations at the hands of Jarrett Webb. Tears streamed down her face as she discussed being violated by Webb. Flocken left the Sorenson home that day troubled and concerned.

As Flocken familiarized herself with the girls' case, DSS personnel began to pursue Eulice's allegations of sexual abuse. A DSS caseworker contacted the Washington County Deputy Sheriff who had originally taken Wally and Kevin into custody and had also accompanied DSS caseworkers to the Webb home when Eulice and Tracy were removed from the home. He made arrangements for Eulice and Tracy to be interviewed by a Nebraska State Patrol (NSP) investigator at the Washington County Sheriff's Office.

Approximately two weeks later, Kathleen Sorenson drove Eulice and Tracy to the Sheriff's Office, where a female NSP officer interviewed them separately. Eulice stated to the investigating officer that she was initially molested by Jarrett Webb after living in the Webbs' home for approximately a year—the first molestation occurred towards the end of her ninth year or in the beginning of her tenth year. Jarrett Webb made Eulice take a "nap" with him, and he "played with all parts" of her body.

According to Eulice, over the next three years, when Barbara wasn't home, Jarrett Webb would threaten her with a "whipping" if she didn't accompany him into the Webbs' bedroom. Eulice somehow gathered enough gumption to start threatening to tell Barbara Webb—Jarrett Webb said he would hurt her if she uttered a word about the molestations.

Eulice told the NSP officer that Webb didn't molest her from her twelfth to her fifteenth year, because of her threats to tell Barbara. But when Eulice was sixteen years old, Jarrett Webb walked into her bedroom and ordered her to take her clothes off; and as she lay face down on the bed, he pelted her on the back with the railroad prop and then molested her. In addition to providing the NSP investigator with considerable detail about her molestations, Eulice said she was willing to take a polygraph on her statements.

A DSS caseworker of Eulice's met with Washington County Attorney Tripp and discussed the sexual abuse allegations with him. Tripp told the caseworker that since Eulice had consented to take a polygraph, he felt that she should follow through with it. After talking to Tripp, Eulice's caseworker inferred that if Eulice passed the polygraph, a petition to emancipate Tasha and Robert from the Webb home would be forthcoming, and Tripp might "possibly" bring criminal charges against Jarrett Webb. At the end of January, Eulice was driven to NSP headquarters by Kathleen Sorenson to be polygraphed. In fact, over the course of a few hours, she took four series of polygraphs or polygrams on her previous statements to the NSP investigator. The polygraph examiner concluded that Eulice was telling the truth.

Flocken then had a meeting with two DSS caseworkers, the NSP officer who originally interviewed Eulice, and County Attorney Tripp concerning Eulice's allegations. Flocken said that everyone at the meeting believed Eulice about the sexual abuse allegations with the important exception of Patrick Tripp. According to Flocken, Tripp had talked to the Webbs' attorney, and he felt that Eulice had so intently rehearsed the allegations that she actually believed them—Tripp opted not to file abuse charges against Jarrett Webb.

In February, Eulice and Tracy had their relinquishment hearing. The Webbs' lawyer attended the hearing, but the Webbs were conspicuously absent. In a rather bizarre twist, the presiding judge ruled that Eulice and Tracy were "uncontrollable," so the Webbs were *voluntarily* relinquishing their parental rights. The judgment made absolutely no mention of the inhumane abuse and torment, even though DSS documents are replete with seemingly countless incidents of abuse.

Right after the relinquishment hearing, Flocken was shocked: Eulice told her that Tripp and the Webbs' attorney had informed her that she and Tracy were immediately scheduled for a deposition. Flocken later said she approached Tripp and inquired why she hadn't been notified of the girls' forthcoming deposition—Tripp responded that since the girls' parental rights were terminated, she was no longer their guardian ad litem. Flocken replied that she would accompany Eulice and Tracy to the deposition and represent the sisters pro bono. A major feature of the deposition was the Webb's attorney grilling Eulice about her allegations of sexual abuse, but she refused to recant the allegations.

Later in February, Washington County filed a "Juvenile Petition" to have Tasha and Robert removed from the Webb household. A week later, Tasha and Robert were taken out of school and placed in a foster home. Unfortunately, Tasha couldn't be placed with the Sorensons since the family had the maximum number of foster children under the terms of their licensure.

Tasha and Robert were placed in the home of a foster family who lived a few blocks from the Sorensons'. DSS reports noted that Tasha and Robert had difficulties sleeping, and they initially had a habit of hoarding and hiding food. Both Tasha and Robert told their new foster parents that they no longer wanted to live in the Webb household—they were terribly frightened that the beatings would continue.

When a counselor asked Tasha about the prospect of returning to the Webb home, she started to cry and replied, "God wouldn't let this happen to me—He wouldn't make me go back to the Webbs." Tasha also confided to her foster mother that she had been forced to perform oral sex on an "uncle" who visited the Webbs. Tasha said that though Barbara Webb knew about her being molested, she did "nothing." Her foster mother immediately reported her allegations to Tasha's DSS caseworkers.

To the utter shock of DSS personnel, in March of 1986, a judge ruled that Tasha and Robert would be returned to the Webb household with a "rehabilitation plan." A DSS document mentioned that Tasha's allegations of sexual abuse hadn't been properly investigated. Tasha grasped her foster mother's leg and screamed, "Please don't make me go back!" She refused to let go of her foster mother, and the judge ordered Tasha's foster mother to leave the courtroom. Robert said nothing, cocked his head downward, and looked at the floor.

The judge ordered that Tasha, Robert, and the Webbs undergo psychotherapy and family counseling. Though the judge essentially sentenced Tasha to a second stretch of unremitting torment and agony, he conceded that she should be allowed to have supervised visits with her sisters.

At the conclusion of the hearing, Barbara Webb allegedly charged at a pregnant DSS caseworker of Tasha's, poking her in the stomach and saying, "I hope your baby dies."

After the hearing, the Webb's lawyer threatened the DSS with a lawsuit if the Webbs' casework wasn't transferred out of Washington County's jurisdiction. At first, DSS personnel refused to accommodate the Webb's and their attorney, but they eventually knuckled under, and the Webbs' casework was assigned to a Douglas County branch of the DSS. The Webbs' new Douglas County caseworker noted that Tasha's contact with her two sisters was "thwarting" her relationship with the Webbs, and she suggested that her visits with Eulice and Tracy be "discontinued." Strangely enough, the psychologist would find that the children's social isolation stemmed from depression instead of the Webbs' oppression!

Despite the Webbs finding a kinder, gentler social services milieu, Tasha and Robert were ultimately removed from their home in August of 1986, and the Webbs relinquished their parental rights to the two children approximately a month later. As was the case with the previous children, the Webbs denied allegations of abuse; Tasha and Robert were deemed "uncontrollable."

It's astounding that Jarrett and Barbara Webb evaded child-abuse charges over the years. If the authorities weren't cognizant of the Webbs' cruelty and malice, their failure to press child-abuse charges would be understandable, but they had pages and pages of documented corroboration regarding the abuse, and Eulice passed a polygraph on her repeated molestations by Jarrett Webb. Yet even after the abuse became all too apparent, the Webbs still meted out cruel and inhumane punishment with impunity.

Social service documents identified various agencies that facilitated the Webbs' abuse through willful neglect, but the FBI may have pro-actively abetted the Webbs. According to documents I possess, a DSS social worker who made home visits to families renewing their foster care licenses had a very bad feeling about the Webbs, and she took it upon herself to make inquiries. She wrote a letter to her superiors explaining her suspicions about the Webbs; she also found that many of the DSS files pertaining to the Webb children were missing. The social worker said that FBI agents contacted her, and they told her it would be in her best interests to "forget this information."

I interviewed the Washington sisters' guardian ad litem Patricia Flock-en, and she said that her representation of the Washington sisters was the most stressful period of her life: Flocken told me that she was routinely followed by unidentified individuals when representing the Washington sisters, and she also told an investigator employed by the Nebraska legislature that she felt her phones were tapped or her office was bugged during this period. Flocken later became a Deputy Attorney for Washington County after Tripp left his position as County Attorney.

Could FBI intervention possibly account for the authorities not investigating the Webb household? If so, the next logical question is: "Why?"

As I've previously mentioned, a month or so after Eulice arrived at the Sorenson home, shortly before her first meeting with Flocken, she talked of a "friend" who had been molested by her adoptive father. At the time, Kathleen Sorenson was perplexed by her disclosures, but then she realized that Eulice was attempting to gauge her reaction to determine if it was safe for her to divulge that Jarrett Webb had molested Eulice herself. She talked of orgies too, again perplexing Kathleen Sorenson.

As Eulice grew more and more comfortable with Sorenson, she tentatively asserted that the Webbs' powerful cousin, Larry King, had flown her and other children, via a charter plane, to Chicago in the fall of 1984 and to New York in the spring of 1985. Eulice said that King forced her to wear negligees and attend orgies. She told Sorenson that Boys Town students were on the flights, and she recognized a nationally prominent politician, who procured a kid at the orgy in Chicago and quickly slipped out.

Kathleen Sorenson was initially dumbfounded by Eulice's revelations, but everything that Eulice had previously mentioned had panned out: Sorenson had also witnessed Eulice pass four polygrams, yet Jarrett Webb wasn't charged with a single count of molestation. Because the Webbs had completely escaped child-abuse charges, Sorenson began to feel that the system's traditional checks and balances that safeguarded children had been corrupted in the Webbs' case. So she relayed Eulice's allegations about Larry King and Boys Town students to Julie Walters, a friend of hers who worked at Boys Town.

Walters then approached the Director of Boys Town, Father Valentine Peter, and told him about Eulice's allegations—Peter said she should check them out. Walters interviewed Eulice and Kathleen Sorenson on three occasions in March of 1986—Tracy and a friend of Sorenson's, Kirstin Hallberg, were also present. Eulice gave Walters details of the abuse in the Webb household and also accounts of her trips with Larry

King. Eulice and Tracy also discussed seeing Boys Town students at parties hosted by King in Omaha. Walters brought Boys Town yearbooks to the second interview, and Eulice and Tracy identified former students who they alleged were involved with King. Walters penned a forty-three page, handwritten "report" on Eulice and Tracy's information.

Walters then began to ask around about King's affiliation with Boys Town and Boys Town employees—she quickly discovered that the Franklin Credit Union employed a Boys Town teacher. She also heard additional rumors that a yellow, limited edition Tojan sports car leased by King had repeatedly prowled the Boys Town campus, and three Boys Town teachers had been spotted driving the car. Walters mentioned the rumors to Father Peter, who said he would look into it. Walters eventually learned that a Boys Town administrator whom she didn't trust was tasked with investigating the rumors.

Within a week of transcribing Eulice Washington's allegations, Julie Walters contacted Eulice's former guardian ad litem, Patricia Flocken, and introduced herself. Walters said she was investigating Eulice's allegations on behalf of Boys Town and requested a meeting with Flocken. At this point, Flocken had fallen under the scrutiny of the nameless and faceless, and she had become a bit wary about her involvement with the Washington sisters. She made a few calls to confirm Walters' identity.

She then phoned Walters back and they agreed to meet at Boys Town's campus. Shortly after Walters greeted Flocken in her office, she handed Flocken a photocopy of her report, and they reviewed it together. As they leafed through the report, Flocken noticed parallel after parallel between the confessions she had heard and Eulice's disclosures to Walters. If Flocken had any doubts about Eulice's allegations, they seemed to have been dispelled after her two-hour meeting with Walters.

In the following days, Flocken struggled with the enormity of Eulice's revelations: a network that pandered children to a cabal of America's highest political strata. She also struggled with the ethical quandaries involved in divulging information garnered from juveniles. She discussed the latter quandary with the Washington County Judge who had inexplicably removed himself from the Webbs' relinquishment hearing of Eulice and Tracy Washington. She opted to confer with him due to the fact that he was partially cognizant of the Webb predicament—he suggested that she back away from further involvement in the matter. Flocken phoned Walters and said she was extricating herself from the Boys Town "investigation." Julie Walters would eventually leave Boys Town, and the content of her report would essentially lie dormant for almost three years.

Kirstin Hallberg was a close friend of Kathleen Sorenson, and she'd been present while Eulice Washington made her initial confessions to Julie Walters about Larry King in March 1986. Two months later, in May 1986, Hallberg went back to work for Uta Halee, a residential psychiatric facility in Omaha for adolescent girls. She had previously worked there in 1981, but a pair of pregnancies punctuated her first and second stints. She was now a thirty-six-year-old mother of two.

Hallberg was a "resident advisor" on the 3:00 P.M. to 11:00 P.M. shift at Uta Halee, and her duties included admitting the girls, administering their treatment plans, one-on-ones, overseeing their conduct, and driving them to activities. In June 1986, she was tasked with the intake duties for twelve-year-old Shawneta Moore. The facility's Intake Unit consisted of a cozy one-bedroom apartment, and, as Moore sat in a chair, crocheting a potholder, Hallberg reclined on the couch and interviewed her. Though Moore was thin and slightly undersized for her age, Hallberg immediately noticed that she had an exceptional precocity.

Moore grew up in North Omaha, and her parents had two children. Moore's parents had a rocky four-year marriage that ended in divorce when Shawneta was two years old—her brother was four years old. Two years after the divorce, Moore's mother and her two children moved in with her boyfriend. Moore developed a tight, nurturing relationship with her mother's boyfriend, but she and her mother had a tumultuous and troubled relationship. Moore was ten years old when her mother and her boyfriend split up—Moore then started staying out late, and some nights she didn't even bother to come home. Moore's mother had no idea how her ten-year-old daughter had the means and wherewithal to disappear for such periods. Moore's mother ultimately found her daughter to be incorrigible—Moore became a ward of the state and was placed at the Uta Halee facility.

Hallberg inquired if Moore had any hobbies or pastimes, and Moore replied that she once frequented the North Omaha Girls Club. Hallberg was aware of King's affliation with the Girls Club, and she asked Moore if she knew the Webb girls. Moore said that she was acquainted with Eulice and Tracy—Hallberg then posed a question or two about the Girls Club. Moore became acutely distressed, started to crochet in a staccato whirlwind, and suddenly blurted out that she had been involved in a prostitution and pornography "ring." Moore said she had attempted to break away from the ring, and her mother was raped in reprisal. After Moore's startling revelation, she became withdrawn and extremely frightened.

Moore's account of her mother's rape is corroborated by an OPD report. At around 3:00 A.M. on June 15, 1986, Moore's mother was in bed sleeping when a short, thin African-American man, wearing a nylon stocking over his face, slipped into her bedroom, put a butcher knife to her throat, and in a high-pitched voice said, "Where's Shawneta?" He then raped her. The assailant was never apprehended.

After Moore discussed her mother's rape, Hallberg attempted to probe for specific information, but Moore said the ring had too much power, and if she made further disclosures to Hallberg they would both be in danger. Moore then shut down emotionally and refused to discuss the ring any further. Though Moore didn't specifically mention Larry King's name, Hallberg was mindful of King's affiliation with the Girls Club from Eulice and Tracy Webb.

Hallberg charted Moore's allegations about her involvement in a pornography and prostitution ring, and then she approached her supervisor about the allegations. Hallberg told her supervisor that she knew of a girl who had also attended the Girls Club and made similar allegations—she suggested they contact the Nebraska State Patrol. Hallberg recalled that her supervisor became very agitated at the suggestion, replying that Hallberg would be breaching confidentiality statutes if she single-handedly contacted the authorities—Hallberg assumed her supervisor contacted the authorities and also Moore's mother.

During Hallberg's tenure at the Uta Halee facility, she attempted to coax Moore into providing additional details about her abuse, but was repeatedly rebuffed. Hallberg worked with a second girl there who also made allegations of being in a child prostitution and pornography ring. A third girl also alluded to organized abuse, even though she too declined to be specific. Hallberg usually wasn't assigned to the unit where these three girls resided. Nevertheless, when they were in the midst of emotional turmoil or a crisis, they had a tendency to reach out specifically to her.

Hallberg gradually began to have gnawing suspicions that Uta Halee personnel might be covering up malfeasance, and her reservations produced a mounting discomfort: She wasn't absolutely certain her suspicions were well founded, and there were times when she felt terrible about even having these suspicions. However, her supervisor's reaction to Moore's allegations made her extremely uneasy, and she heard unsubstantiated rumors that girls were sneaking off campus in the middle of the night—she voiced her concerns to a co-worker. Hallberg's concerns quickly ricocheted back to her supervisor, who informed her that "everything was fine."

Hallberg's supervisor also seemed to be overly concerned with the relative ease with which certain residents confided in Hallberg—her supervisor suggested that she interrupt the girls who confided in her to ask, "Are you sure you can trust me with this information?" Hallberg's suspicions were further intensified by the fact that an Uta Halee employee was a friend of Barbara Webb, and that Alice King actually sat on Uta Halee's Board of Directors.

Shortly after Hallberg's supervisor expressed concerns about the residents confiding in her, a co-worker of Hallberg's was suspended for harboring one of the residents—Douglas County Sheriff deputies then converged on Uta Halee to make inquiries about the co-worker and her relationship to the resident. Hallberg then found herself summoned by her supervisor's supervisor. According to Hallberg, her superiors informed her that she had jeopardized her job by preemptively phoning the Douglas County Sheriff. She was then grilled about whom she "knew" at the Douglas County Sheriff's Office—Hallberg replied that she hadn't blown the whistle.

The next day Hallberg phoned the Douglas County Sheriff's Department to request that it notify her superiors that she didn't make the call in question. Strangely enough, the deputy who spoke to Hallberg said that he had talked to Uta Halee personnel the previous morning, and he was asked if Hallberg had, in fact, phoned the Sheriff's Department—he responded that she hadn't. Later that day, Hallberg's supervisor approached her and said she was in "deeper trouble" for requesting that the Sheriff phone her superiors to reiterate that Hallberg hadn't made the initial call.

Shortly thereafter, the Douglas County Sheriff's Department conducted a pornography investigation at Uta Halee—the Sheriff's Department ultimately cleared the facility of any illicit activity. During the investigation, however, Hallberg noticed that Moore was "extremely fearful"—Hallberg again attempted to talk to Moore, but she refused to open up. Hallberg asked Moore if her trepidations were associated with Uta Halee—Moore replied "it" was too big, and if Hallberg continued to pry she would "get hurt."

On March 5, 1987, Hallberg's supervisor and two administrators summoned her to a meeting and informed her that Uta Halee was suspending her for five days. They said Hallberg had been "over-involved" with the residents "beyond a therapeutic level." Hallberg assumed that her superiors were referring to Moore and the two other girls who disclosed to her that they had been involved in organized child exploitation. At the meeting, Hallberg voiced her concerns about Alice King sitting on Uta Halee's Board, and, according to Hallberg, her supervisor's boss exploded and started screaming at Hallberg. On March 10, Hallberg would be given the option of resigning from Uta Halee—she refused to resign and was fired.

After Uta Halee terminated Hallberg, she eventually landed a job at Richard Young Hospital, a psychiatric facility in Omaha. While Hallberg was employed at Richard Young, Moore was discharged from Uta Halee—she returned to her mother's home and enrolled in an alternative high school. In June 1988, Moore phoned Hallberg and said she had been confiding in her school counselor, who wanted to confer with Hallberg. The three agreed to meet on June 27, but on the eve of their meeting, Moore phoned Hallberg and sounded suicidal. Hallberg placed a frantic call to the school counselor, and asked for his advice since he had been working closely with Moore. The counselor suggested that Hallberg pick up Moore and take her home for the night.

Hallberg picked up a friend, also a former Uta Halee employee, and drove to Moore's mother's house. When they pulled up to the house,

Moore was sitting on the front steps of the house, wearing a white sweater and blue shorts—she was crying. Hallberg talked to Moore's mother, and she was given permission to harbor Moore for the night. After Hallberg and Moore made it back to Hallberg's home, Moore became very despondent and started to bawl. Moore said she wanted to end her life, because it would be far less painful than if "they" decided to murder her. "If they find out I've talked," Moore cried, "they will torture other kids in my name." Moore gradually calmed down and fell asleep around 2:30 A.M.

The next morning Hallberg drove Moore to see her school counselor. While they sat in the counselor's office, Moore seemed to be smothered by hopelessness—she had great difficulties articulating words and expressing herself. The counselor turned to Hallberg and revealed that Moore had told him "everything about Larry King," and he asked if Hallberg knew about King—she recounted what Eulice had conveyed to Kathleen Sorenson and Julie Walters. As the counselor and Hallberg talked, Moore sounded increasingly suicidal. She refused to promise the counselor and Hallberg that she wouldn't hurt herself, so the counselor decided she needed to be hospitalized.

The counselor opted to hospitalize Moore at Richard Young Hospital, but said he required the consent of Moore's mother. He also told Hallberg that it was important that Moore's mother be apprised of her daughter's allegations. Hallberg was stunned by his disclosure, because she assumed that Uta Halee personnel had contacted Moore's mother about the allegations two years earlier—Moore's mother would later confirm that Uta Halee hadn't notified her about the allegations.

Later in the day, Moore was admitted to Richard Young's adolescent unit where Hallberg worked. Shortly after her hospitalization, Moore's attending psychiatrist gave her a physical and mental health evaluation. The psychiatrist found that Moore's hypothetical judgment was "good" and she was "orientated to person, place, and time." In other words, Moore wasn't psychotic or delusional. Moore also confessed to her psychiatrist that she had been entangled in an underage pornography and prostitution ring.

Richard Young's July "Nurses' Notes" on Moore depict a truly troubled adolescent. One morning in July she was found sitting in a chair and sobbing inconsolably—she eventually covered herself in a blanket and silently rocked back and forth. She seemed to be harboring horrific nightmares—yet she was unwilling to share them with hospital personnel. She told staff that her past was too "painful to think about," and she couldn't possibly forgive herself.

In the middle of August, Moore evidently began to trust her caregivers, because she started to open up about deeds of unfathomable evil. In the winter of 1983, Moore said, when she was nine years old, she started attending the North Omaha Girls Club, where she met an older man named "Ray," who also befriended four or five other girls at the Girls Club. Moore thought Ray was a volunteer at the Girls Club and described him as an overweight forty-year-old African-American male, standing 5'7" to 5'8".

Shawneta Moore indicated that Ray transported the girls to various locations in a white van, but whenever he drove the girls he would blindfold them. Ray originally took the girls to an abandoned building and broke out a joint. After Ray and the girls smoked the joint, they sat around the building and talked for a while, and then he returned them to the Girls Club. Ray spent three or four weeks driving the girls to the abandoned building, and smoking marijuana with them, before he brought them to a "party."

The men at the party were in their mid-thirties—they initially sat around and talked to the girls about their "problems." They then started to drink and take drugs with the girls, and, after the girls were "wasted," the men started having sex with them. The girls didn't have a choice of who would have sex with them.

Moore said she attended parties for approximately six months before she was taken to her first "power meeting" in the summer of 1982. The meeting was held in an abandoned shack, and Moore told hospital personnel that "candles and other weird stuff" were at the power meetings. Moore identified the men by pseudonyms—Ace, King's Horses, Jerry Lucifer, and Mike. The men were dressed in robes adorned with upside-down crosses, and the leader wore a long black cape and gold skull-head rings on his fingers. Moore and the other girls were told that the room would start spinning; and after the room started to whirl around Moore, she realized she'd been drugged. Moore then told Richard Young personnel that she witnessed the murder of a child, and she was locked in small room with the remains of the child. While Moore sat in the locked room with the dead child, she heard the men whipping and beating one of the girls.

Moore told hospital personnel that as she sat in the locked room, she felt that the girl who was whipped and beaten had it much easier than she did. Shortly after the men stopped assaulting the girl, they unlocked the door of the small room and informed Moore she passed the test. The men then drove Moore to a park near her house and dropped her off. Moore said she felt dazed as she wandered home. Moore said the next time she saw the men was at a party, where the girls were again forced to "sleep around." She identified Larry King as attending this party.

Moore also told Richard Young staff about four additional "sacrifices." She said that a little boy was ritualistically murdered because he threatened to notify authorities of the sacrifices. She also named one of the girls who had been slaughtered. As Moore continued to describe the various sacrifices, Richard Young's "Nurses' Notes" detail that Moore started to have dreams about the cult murdering Richard Young staff, she wrote a suicide letter, and also conveyed to staff that she could not "forgive herself." In September, Moore told the staff that she harbored no more secrets, but she was convinced that she was "going to hell." In October, a nurse walked into Moore's darkened room and found her curled into a fetal position.

In the spring of 1988, Larry King's name made its first *documented* echoes throughout the OPD concerning the exploitation of children. In May of that year, a twenty-four-year-old man with dishwater blond hair and a moustache, standing 5'11", weighing 150 pounds, approached a seventeen-year-old girl working at an Omaha supermarket. The man introduced himself as Rusty Nelson and informed the girl that he was a photographer. He told the red-haired girl that he was taking pictures for Easter Seals, and he just happened to be looking for red-haired models—he gave her his card and proposed that she stop by his studio for a photo shoot.

The seventeen-year-old girl no doubt brimmed with enthusiasm as she made her way home that afternoon. She announced to her mother that she had bumped into a photographer at the supermarket, and he was very interested in photographing her. The girl phoned Nelson and left a message on his answering machine—Nelson called her back almost immediately, and they set up an appointment. The girl requested that her mother accompany her—Nelson said that would be all right.

Nelson's "studio" was located in the Twin Towers, a pair of luxury apartment buildings near downtown Omaha. The apartment's extravagant furnishings and plush interior instantly impressed the mother and daughter. After they seated themselves on a living room settee, Nelson placed a large bowl of strawberries in front of them and also offered both flutes of champagne. The mother's first red flag shot up when Nelson disclosed that his "boss" kept the apartment well stocked, because he had initially said to her that he was self-employed. Nelson attempted to allay her concerns by boasting that he worked for the city's top modeling agencies and also for an upscale mall in Omaha.

Prior to the shoot commencing, Nelson had the mother and daughter sign a minor-release form. The mother and daughter spent the next five hours with Nelson, and they became increasingly uncomfortable—Nelson made repeated references to photographing the girl in her "birthday suit." Though he never specifically asked her to pose in the nude, he attempted to have her bare more and more skin and also slip on lingerie—she and her mother declined his overtures.

As Nelson was in the midst of a shooting frenzy, the girl's mother started to peek at photographs scattered throughout the apartment. To the mother's shock, she spotted several pornographic pictures of girls who appeared as young as twelve years old. The mother had seen enough, and she told her daughter that it was time to leave. Nelson invited the girl back to his studio, but he insisted that her mother not accompany her—he felt that the mother made the girl nervous.

The mother ultimately decided to phone the OPD and report Nelson. The officer who fielded her call jotted down the mother's information and directed the complaint to the OPD's Robbery and Sexual Assault Unit. The case landed on the desk of Officer Irl Carmean a few days later. The thirty-eight-year-old Carmean was married and the father of two. A scar descended from his right ear to his chin—a female suspect had slashed him across the face with a knife nine years earlier.

Carmean graduated from Ohio State University with a Bachelor's in Journalism in 1974–he had been the news director of a Lincoln, Nebraska radio station for three years before deciding to join the OPD in 1977. Carmean left the OPD in September of 1982 to study law at Omaha's Creighton Law School. After attending law school for a year, he returned to the OPD in 1983 and pursued his law degree part-time. Carmean graduated from Creighton Law School in 1985, but continued to serve as an OPD officer. Among his fellow officers, Carmean had a reputation for having a sharp mind and being a top-notch investigator.

On May 9, 1988, Carmean contacted the girl and her mother–he took their statement and wrote up a report. The following day, a superior of Carmean's, Officer Michael Hoch, talked to the owner of the Twin Towers in an effort to gain background information on Nelson. The owner of the Twin Towers told him that Nelson resided in an apartment that was sublet to him by Larry King.

On May 11, Carmean drove through the Twin Towers parking lot, and spotted a Ford van registered to Nelson. He radioed in for priors on Nelson: With the exception of a speeding ticket the previous year, his record was clean. Carmean also spoke to a professional photographer familiar with Nelson. The photographer had placed an ad for "test photographers" approximately six months earlier, and Nelson had replied. The photographer told Carmean that Nelson's portfolio confirmed he was a talented photographer, even though it included pictures of an inordinate number of nude females. The photographer said he hired Nelson to assist him in a photographic shoot; Nelson, however, had an altercation with a male model. The employer found Nelson to be "rude, excessive, and unprofessional," and was sufficiently appalled by Nelson's behavior not to give him a second chance.

The initial reports filed by Carmean and Hoch on the incident listed "child pornography" or "possible child pornography" in the reports' "Offense" headers, but none of the reports listed a name in the "Suspect" header. Approximately two weeks later, Hoch filed a "Supplemental Report" on the "child pornography" investigation, and Larry King's name showed up in the "Suspect" header. The report detailed a conversation Hoch had with the property manager of a second luxury apartment building in Omaha. She informed Hoch that King's one-year-lease on an apartment had expired four months earlier—he had paid the entire year's rent in advance. King's concurrently renting a luxury apartment at the Twin Towers struck Hoch as "very strange," and he asked the property manager if she was privy to any scuttlebutt on King. She relayed rumors of King being a "drug dealer" and also of his penchant for "young men or boys."

The following day, Hoch drove to the Twin Towers and talked to the owner once more. He told Hoch that in addition to renting the apartment where Nelson resided, King also rented a penthouse apartment. The owner also reported that King rented three parking spots in the basement garage, and he had at least five cars, including a Mercedes-Benz and a Cadillac. He expressed bafflement about King's newfound wealth too, because a realtor informed him that King had attempted to buy a home five years earlier and had difficulties making the down payment.

The owner of the Twin Towers also gave Officer Hoch the name of King's cleaning lady. Hoch never had a documented contact with her, but two FBI agents would interview her. She disclosed to the agents that she cleaned both the apartment where Nelson resided and also the penthouse apartment. Though she hadn't personally observed child pornography in either apartment, she said that a Twin Towers security guard alerted her to the fact that Nelson photographed "young boys."

By the end of June, Shawneta Moore's initial confessions at Richard Young Hospital had prompted her psychiatrist to phone the OPD, and Officer Carmean visited the hospital to interview Moore, who had recently turned fifteen. Officer Carmean, like Kirstin Hallberg, found that Moore "spoke and acted rather maturely for her years." Moore told Carmean that at the age of nine she and a handful of other girls had been transported from the Girls Club to a studio and photographed in the nude. Moore said that the adults who participated in photographing the children were the "leaders" of the Girls Club. She also indicated that other prominent individuals were involved, "including doctors and lawyers."

Moore informed Carmean that the adults used threats against the girls to ensure their participation in the kiddy porn. If the girls refused to participate, the adults warned, they and their entire families would be murdered. In addition to discussing child pornography, Moore disclosed that she had also attended "devil-worship rituals." Carmean noted that Moore's descriptions lacked the names of the participating adults and the specific locations where the child pornography and rituals had occurred.

On June 30, Officer Carmean's supervisor phoned Moore's psychiatrist to discuss Moore's disclosures to Carmean. She informed him that Moore had been intentionally ambiguous with Carmean to test the waters, but she said Moore had "no problem" continuing her dialogue with Carmean. Carmean's supervisor replied that he would assign Carmean to revisit Moore the following week. Apparently, Moore had begun to feel comfortable with Carmean relatively quickly, because she phoned him at OPD headquarters later that day.

During the course of their conversation, Moore divulged to Carmean that she believed Larry King to be a "supporter and participant" of both the child pornography and the devil worship. She also talked about a "sex and drug" party at one of King's residences, where she witnessed three or four teenage boys performing oral sex on each other. Moore said the residence was on Wirt Street in North Omaha, but she couldn't provide the exact address. In Carmean's report on the conversation, he wrote down that Moore became evasive and lacked "specificity" when she talked about King, making it evident to him that she was reluctant to provide further "detail."

Six days later, Moore called Carmean and disclosed the exact address and phone number of King's residence on Wirt Street. After Carmean hung up the phone, he dialed the number provided by Moore: "King Company," said the man who answered the phone—Carmean told him that he had the wrong number and hung up. Carmean then drove by the address provided by Moore and noticed a large two-story, gray frame house with a gray awning.

Officers Carmean and Hoch expended a considerable number of hours investigating King's possible link to child pornography. They uncovered financial irregularities and potential leads concerning the exploitation of children, but their probe hit a wall, which is evidenced by the fact that they stopped generating reports on the subject.

As the OPD was uncovering leads on King's exploitation of children, and seemingly not pursuing them, officials who oversaw the state's foster care system were starting to hear murmurs about King too. Nebraska's Foster Care Review Board is a state agency that reviews the plans, services, and placements of children in foster care to ensure their optimum welfare. The Executive Director of the Foster Care Review Board was the then-thirty-four-year-old Carol Stitt.

Born in 1954, and raised in the western Nebraska town of Minatare, Stitt ventured east after high school to attend the University of Nebraska at Omaha. The industrious Stitt usually worked a couple of jobs as she put herself through college, earning a Bachelor's and Master's degree in social work. Stitt started her career in social work as an employee of Child Protective Services and then transferred to the Foster Care Review Board. Stitt quickly developed a reputation as conscientious, sharp and diligent, and she was appointed Executive Director of the Board in 1983.

Roughly four years after Stitt became the Board's Executive Director, she had her first encounter with the name of Larry King. In December 1987, the vestiges of Tasha Washington's DSS files belatedly made their way to Stitt and the Board. After officials at the Board scrutinized Tasha's perilous odyssey, they were absolutely dumbfounded by the universal failure to safeguard her. The Board started to make inquiries about the "system breakdown" concerning Tasha Washington, and her former guardian ad litem, Patricia Flocken, quickly received a letter from the Board.

Flocken might have decided to disengage from further pursuit of Eulice Washington's allegations relating to Larry King, but the allegations continued to pursue her. Before the Board contacted Flocken, she received a call from the Washington County Deputy Sheriff who had previously assisted DSS personnel in confronting the Webbs. He informed Flocken that the Washington County Sheriff's Department was conducting an investigation into illicit pornography, and he asked if Eulice had been enmeshed in pornography. Flocken told him about Julie Walters' report, and he stopped by her house the next day and picked it up—he returned it to Flocken the following day. She never heard another peep from the Sheriff's Department concerning its investigation or the report.

When Flocken received the Board's letter about Tasha, she phoned Stitt. Flocken and Stitt weren't strangers—Flocken had served as guardian ad litem for a number of children whose out-of-home placement had been evaluated by the Board. After Flocken and Stitt exchanged a few phone calls concerning Tasha and the other children placed in the Webb household, Flocken dropped a bombshell on Stitt—she disclosed the sum total of Eulice's allegations and informed her about the existence of Julie Walters' report. Stitt pressed Flocken for the report, but Flocken felt ethical conflicts—she told Stitt that she would mull it over.

At the end of January 1988, Stitt called an Executive Committee meeting of the Board to discuss Flocken's revelations. In addition to Stitt, the Executive Committee included Dennis Carlson and Burrell Williams. Stitt's position as the Board's Executive Director was full-time and permanent, but Carlson and Williams served the Board in a voluntary capacity. The Nebraska Bar Association employed Carlson, and Williams earned his livelihood as a junior high school assistant principal. Though the three kicked around Eulice's allegations, they had scant information to make sound decisions. So they decided that Stitt would direct Board personnel to review the case histories of all the children who had the misfortune of falling into the Webbs' clutches.

Within months of the Board's Executive Committee meeting in January, additional accounts of Larry King's exploitation of children started filtering into Stitt. In early May, a DSS employee approached Stitt and asked her, "Are you aware of Larry King and his activities with our children?" The question "came out of the blue" and shocked Stitt like a thunderbolt. A few weeks later, Kirstin Hallberg and Stitt exchanged phone calls that intensified Stitt's concerns. Hallberg told Stitt about the girls at Uta Halee who reported being enmeshed in a child exploitation ring. Hallberg also said that a young man hospitalized at Richard Young hospital made allegations of sexual abuse against King to hospital personnel. Hallberg wasn't willing to breach their confidentiality, and wouldn't provide their names to Stitt.

Hallberg disclosed to Stitt that she had recently attended a child exploitation conference in Kansas City. At the conference, a Kansas City Police Department detective approached her and inquired if and when Nebraska authorities were willing to address Larry King's use and abuse of children. Hallberg gave Stitt the detective's name, and Stitt phoned her. The detective informed Stitt that King had been in the Kansas City area donating money to a boys' group home, and shortly afterwards three boys came forward with allegations of sexual abuse against him. The detective would repeat the same story to the Board's Dennis Carlson.

As Stitt became increasingly alarmed about the accusations swirling around King, she continued to press Flocken for Julie Walters' report—Flocken finally relented in July. The two met at Flocken's office, and Flocken handed her a copy of the report. A week or so later, Hallberg phoned Stitt once more. At this point, Shawneta Moore was hospitalized at Richard Young, and she was detailing allegations about her sexual exploitation and the sacrifices she had witnessed. Hallberg updated Stitt on Moore's grisly disclosures, but, again, confidentiality protocols prevented her from disclosing Moore's name.

The Board's Executive Committee, particularly Stitt and Carlson, had a very hectic July. On July 13, 1988, Stitt met with Nebraska governor Kay Orr, and Orr directed her to take the "necessary" measures to investigate the allegations. Stitt and Carlson set up a second meeting with the governor to discuss the allegations, but Orr inexplicably cancelled the meeting. The governor's response would become an all-too-familiar pattern as Stitt and Carlson pushed to have officials address the allegations.

Stitt also compiled the various documents that the Board had collected, including Julie Walters' report, and wrote a letter to Nebraska's Attorney General Robert Spire. Her letter to Spire, dated July 20, 1988, discussed evidence of a "child exploitation ring" and "respectfully requests an investigation." After Stitt's opening salvo to Nebraska's Attorney General, Dennis Carlson would help her navigate the shoals of Nebraska's judiciary and law enforcement.

Carlson was a 1974 graduate of the University of Nebraska College of Law, and from 1974 to 1981 he served as a deputy public defender for Nebraska's Lancaster County. In 1981, Carlson was appointed Counsel for Discipline of Nebraska's Bar Association, which required him to supervise a staff of attorneys who investigated and prosecuted grievances against Nebraska lawyers. As the Nebraska Bar's Counsel for Discipline, Carlson had steadfast connections to just about every stratum of Nebraska's legal community.

The day Stitt sent a letter and accompanying documentation to Attorney General Spire, Carlson phoned Spire and also discussed the child-abuse allegations with him. Carlson and Spire had cultivated an amicable rapport over the years, and Spire assured Carlson of a prompt response. Shortly after Carlson contacted Spire, he talked to Stitt—she had recently found out that OPD Officer Carmean interviewed a girl at Richard Young Hospital who had made allegations of sexual exploitation regarding King. Though Stitt was referring to Moore, Board personnel weren't privy to her name as of yet. According to Carlson's notes, he phoned Officer Carmean at OPD headquarters that afternoon and left a message for him—Carmean returned his call later in the day.

Carmean and Carlson had never met face to face, but Carmean told Carlson that he had graduated from law school three years earlier and that he was familiar with Carlson's status as the Nebraska Bar's Counsel for Discipline. Carmean confirmed that he interviewed the girl at Richard Young, and she did make allegations against Larry King. Carmean then informed Carlson that the OPD had investigated additional allegations of child abuse related to King, but he wasn't aware of Julie Walters' report and Eulice Washington's allegations. Carlson updated Carmean on the Board's documentation relating to King, and he asked Carmean if the OPD would be interested in the Board's information. Carlson wrote that Carmean was "very interested" in obtaining the Board's documentation, and the two scheduled a meeting for the following week at Carlson's Lincoln office.

Carmean then made a stunning disclosure to Carlson: He confided that the investigation of King was "super sensitive," and being concealed from OPD Chief Robert Wadman, because of rumors that Chief Wadman and King were friends. Carmean said that the officers conducting the investigation weren't submitting their reports on King to the OPD's stenography pool to be typed so they wouldn't be accessible to Wadman. Carmean also told Carlson that an assistant to Wadman had asked officers in the Robbery and Sexual Assault Unit if they were looking into King, and the officers lied to him, replying that King wasn't under investigation.

The following day, Nebraska's Assistant Attorney General, William Howland, made a jaunt to Carlson's office. Carlson gave Howland a run-down of the Board's information regarding King, and he voiced his reservations about OPD Chief Wadman. Carlson said that he felt it was necessary for the Attorney General's Office to oversee an investigation into King's activities, because the OPD might be too compromised to adequately investigate King—Howland assured Carlson that the Attorney General's Office would act decisively on the Board's behalf.

On July 25, OPD officers Carmean and Hoch made the forty-five minute drive from Omaha to Lincoln to meet with Carlson. At the meeting, Carlson handed Carmean and Hoch the packet of documents compiled by the Board, and they talked for roughly an hour. Carlson felt that Carmean and Hoch were extremely enthusiastic about pursuing the Board's information as they left his office. Carlson described Carmean as a "horse at the starting blocks, raring to go."

Carmean, however, later claimed that he never had a chance to look over the Board's documentation—he said that Hoch reviewed the materials and concluded that the allegations were out of the OPD's jurisdiction and also had statute-of-limitations impediments.

On the same day Carmean and Hoch stopped by Carlson's office, Carlson met with an investigator from the Attorney General's Office. Carlson gave the investigator a packet of the Board's materials too, and he guaranteed Carlson that the Attorney General's Office would investigate the allegations.

Both Carlson and Stitt experienced a collective relief after fielding assurances from the OPD and the Attorney General's Office that Nebraska's law enforcement was finally embarking on a long overdue investigation of Larry King. But the optimism of Stitt and Carlson would be short-lived: On September 21, Stitt received a frantic call from Moore's Richard Young social worker—she reported that Moore hadn't been revisited by the OPD. Throughout September and October, additional phone calls from Richard Young personnel trickled into the Board, reporting that Moore still hadn't been reinterviewed by law enforcement. On October 17, an infuriated Carlson phoned Assistant Attorney General Howland. He told Howland that the girl at Richard Young hospital was giving intricate details about several homicides, and nobody from law enforcement had revisited her. Howland declared that he was "on top of it," and he assured Carlson that there was a "good reason" for state law enforcement's paralysis concerning King. Although Howland said he wasn't at liberty to discuss the particulars of the paralysis, Carlson sensed an implication that the feds were taking over the investigation.

Carlson's interpretation of Howland's response is consistent with an OPD "Inter-Office Communication" from Carmean to Chief Wadman: Carmean wrote that the head of the Robbery and Sexual Assault Unit assembled the Unit's officers and told them that the feds had ordered the OPD to "slow down or back off" from its "Larry King investigation." Wadman, however, would assert that such a meeting never went down. In a later Inter-Office Communication, Wadman noted that he spoke to one of the officers whom Carmean identified as attending the meeting, and the officer said that no such meeting ever took place.

The story initially offered by OPD personnel for Carmean not revisiting Moore was that he had voluntarily transferred from the OPD's Robbery and Sexual Assault Unit to its Research and Planning Section before he had an opportunity to reconnect with Moore. But Carmean didn't make the transfer until early September—he had well over a month from the time he met with Carlson until his transfer to drop by Richard Young Hospital.

The OPD's cover story also flies in the face of Carmean's prior pursuit of the investigation. Six days after he originally interviewed Moore, she phoned him and provided a phone number and address for King, and that same day Carmean called the number and hopped into a squad car and drove past King's Wirt Street residence. Carlson also noted that Carmean was "very enthusiastic" about pursuing the Board's information, and Carmean phoned him after their meeting and said he would definitely be revisiting Moore. Moreover, Carmean himself would say that he found Moore to be credible. So, given Carmean's earlier eagerness to investigate King and the fact that he thought Moore was credible, it seems highly unlikely that he wouldn't have reconnected with Moore unless he had been ordered to "back off."

On November 22, Carlson talked with OPD officer Hoch, who said that the OPD had undergone reorganization—Hoch said he was no longer involved with the investigation, but that it was still active. Hoch also told Carlson that Moore's social worker had not come forward with additional information and "could not verify anything." From this conversation, Carlson inferred that the social worker had been reinterviewed by the OPD. When Carlson phoned her, however, she claimed to have had only one conversation with law enforcement, and that was her initial interview with Carmean.

Carlson's November notes are unclear about whether or not Carlson explicitly asked Officer Hoch if Wadman was now aware of the investigation or if Hoch volunteered the information: But Hoch did disclose that the Chief had been apprised of the Larry King investigation.

By November 1988, various state and local agencies had been alerted to King's alleged exploitation of children: The OPD had cultivated its own leads on King and also received the allegations compiled by the Foster Care Review Board, the Attorney General's Office had been given the Board's material, and Patricia Flocken handed Julie Walters' report to a Washington County Deputy Sheriff. Despite various sources alleging King's use and abuse of children, and Julie Walters' report being circulated among at least three branches of the state's law enforcement, Eulice Washington had yet to be interviewed.

It seems highly unlikely that Larry King—by himself—would have the clout to immobilize state law enforcement, but the feds certainly possess the juice to shut down a state investigation. And, to this point in the story, the feds had purportedly intervened on King's or the Webbs' behalf on three occasions. The FBI threatened a DSS employee who took it upon herself to investigate the Webbs. The feds also reportedly told Nebraska's Attorney General's Office that they were taking over the King investigation, and they also ordered the OPD to "back off." If the feds had interviewed Eulice Washington or Shawneta Moore, their intervention would surely have been justified, because, after all, Larry King was accused of being an interstate pimp. But by early November neither the US Department of Justice nor the FBI had interviewed either girl.

The feds shut down the Franklin Credit Union on Friday, November 4, 1988, and shortly thereafter a foul stench arose from the credit union's remains and drifted westward from Omaha to the state's legislature in Lincoln. Unique in the United States, Nebraska has a single-chamber system—an amendment passed in the 1930s discarded the state's House of Representatives and created the "Unicameral," consisting of forty-nine senators from forty-nine legislative districts that today contain approximately 35,000 people.

Early accounts of Franklin's monetary woes led senators to believe that they were dealing with something akin to a staph infection that could be treated with a course of antibiotics. "We will take immediate action to determine the facts and to decide on the appropriate response," King had declared at a press conference the day after Franklin was closed.

A week after Franklin's closing, the credit union's treatable infirmities had turned terminal—the feds acknowledged that $30 million had vanished, and Franklin had been hawking high-interest CDs from coast to coast and racking up millions and million of dollars. The little, home-grown credit union in North Omaha was much more than a nickel-and-dime boiler room—it was a nuclear reactor.

"I've talked to my staff, and they've told me that there are no unrecorded CDs," said King of the latest revelations. Shortly after the feds announced the missing $30 million, they said that King kept a second set of books. The feds then announced King had looted $34 million—and counting.

On November 18, during the Unicameral's year-ending special session, senators had seen enough Franklin press about missing millions and cooked books to conclude that something was seriously awry. The senators unanimously approved Legislative Resolution 5, which called for a Unicameral subcommittee to investigate the credit union's failure. Senator Loran Schmit, who chaired the Unicameral's Banking Committee, drafted Resolution 5. Schmit was a third-generation corn farmer from rural Bellwood and a twenty-one-year veteran of the Unicameral.

The sixty-year-old Schmit was Nebraska's version of a rural Renaissance man: He had earned a B.S. in Agriculture from the University of Nebraska, juggled various business ventures, and was a licensed pilot. Schmit was a devout Catholic and staunch Republican, and he wore conservative suits that were occasionally accentuated by Stetsons and cowboy boots. Over his years of public service, Schmit had cultivated respect and admiration among both his Republican and Democratic peers in the Unicameral. He had a reputation for being a shrewd politician, but projected a benign, grandfatherly presence. In fact, he had ten children and numerous grandchildren.

As chair of the Unicameral's Banking Committee, Schmit had witnessed major improprieties with three Nebraska savings and loans during the 1980s. Though these savings and loans were federally regulated, Schmit perceived endemic corruption within the state's banking community that needed to be fixed. He initially thought Franklin was merely one more example of Nebraska's banking industry chicanery. "You can't get rid of that much money without someone knowing about it," said Schmit the day he introduced Resolution 5.

Shortly after Schmit introduced Resolution 5, he received an anonymous phone call that foreshadowed the forces that the Committee would be challenging: The caller urged Schmit not to pursue the investigation into Franklin, under the auspices of being a "good Republican," because he said it would "reach to the highest levels of the Republican Party."

This was not likely to deter Ernie Chambers, the fifty-two-year-old Democrat representing North Omaha, who immediately jumped on the Resolution 5 bandwagon. Chambers was a nineteen-year veteran of the Unicameral and its only African-American senator. Chambers, a firebrand liberal, wore T-shirts and khakis to the floor of the Unicameral and repeatedly infuriated his fellow senators with protracted filibusters. Chambers graduated from Creighton University School of Law, but had opted not to take the bar exam, citing the bar's racist bias—he earned his livelihood as a barber in North Omaha.

The national spotlight shone on Chambers when he appeared in the 1966 Oscar-nominated documentary *A Time for Burning*. The film depicted the instrumental role he played that year in quelling Omaha's race riots by negotiating concessions from Omaha's power structure on behalf of disenfranchised African-American youths in North Omaha. "There might be some prominent toes in the path we will have to walk," Chambers quipped of Resolution 5.

The vast majority of senators voting for an investigation into the financial collapse of Franklin Credit Union weren't aware of the child-abuse allegations regarding King, but the streetwise Chambers was fully cognizant of King's alleged pedophile network. Carol Stitt had briefed Chambers on the child-abuse allegations, and Chambers had put heat on the Attorney General's Office for stonewalling the Foster Care Review Board. Chambers also brought the concerns of Stitt and Dennis Carlson to the attention of the Unicameral's Executive Board, a nine-member committee that functions as Nebraska's legislative body when the Unicameral is between sessions.

On December 12, the Unicameral's Executive Board had a "closed-door meeting," where Chambers brought up the Foster Care Review

Board's information and discussed how law enforcement had neglected to investigate the child abuse allegations. Prior to the Executive Board retreating into a closed session, Chambers dispensed a few remarks that were intended for public consumption. He talked about receiving reports of "sexual and physical abuse" of children in connection with Franklin and said he suspected a "cover-up."

A December 19 *World-Herald* article, bylined James Allen Flanery, made mention of the Executive Board meeting—and also of Franklin-related child abuse. The article reported that a second Executive Board meeting was slated for the next day, and that "three people with state foster care" had been subpoenaed to testify at the meeting. The article then quoted the FBI's Special Agent in Charge of Nebraska and Iowa, Nick O'Hara, who said the feds were investigating the allegations, because federal statutes make it a felony to transport children "across state lines for immoral or illegal purposes."

Stitt, Carlson, and Williams made a December appearance before the Unicameral's Executive Board. Over the course of two hours, they reiterated Chambers' account and provided additional details. "The information brought tears to my eyes," said Senator Schmit. "I do not cry easily, and I was not the only person that was moved." After Stitt, Carlson, and Williams addressed the Unicameral's Executive Board and fielded questions, its members decided on the senators who would complete the special subcommittee investigating Franklin.

In the upcoming days, the *World-Herald* and *Lincoln Journal* ran articles on Franklin-related child abuse that quoted Attorney General Spire and OPD Chief Wadman. "We did receive some sensitive information in July," said Spire. "My office acted promptly and professionally and nothing was sat on." Wadman spoke of a thoroughly conducted investigation and denied a lack of action by the OPD: "Every step that should have been taken was taken."

The remarks of Attorney General Spire and Chief Wadman were all the more remarkable, considering that Shawneta Moore had been interviewed only once by law enforcement, and Eulice Washington had *never* been interviewed. Wadman also said the "information and evidence" were so scant that he wasn't apprised of the investigation until Chambers shepherded the allegations into the public spotlight in December—

Carlson's notes, however, explicitly state that Hoch informed Carlson in November that Wadman was cognizant of the King investigation.

The Unicameral went into regular session on January 7, and Schmit's Legislative Resolution 5 was again ratified on January 10. The Franklin Committee would have a sweeping mandate to determine "what happened," "how it happened," "who was involved," and "what could or should have been done, and by whom, to prevent it." To carry out its mandate, the Committee would scrutinize both state and federal agencies, including the DSS, Child Protective Services, and the Foster Care Review Board. In other words, the Committee was going to take a long, hard look at the child-abuse allegations.

Schmit was named the subcommittee's chair and Chambers its vice chair. The conservative corn farmer Schmit and the liberal urbanite Chambers were the yin and yang of the Unicameral, but they were tasked with taking the helm of the Franklin Committee. The Committee members quickly realized that they would be navigating through perfidious waters; so their first major order of business was to appoint a chief legal counsel.

The Committee members kicked around a number of names for a week or so, and at the suggestion of Schmit they voted to invite former CIA Director William Colby to apply for chief counsel. "I felt after some of the comments I heard that the scope is broader than just Nebraska, and I thought that Mr. Colby might be able to handle that," Schmit said. Since the credit union's demise, several rumors were wafting around Lincoln and Omaha that Franklin monies had been covertly diverted to the CIA in its efforts to support the Nicaraguan Contras' fight against the Communist Sandinistas. The *Lincoln Journal* even mentioned the murmurs in an article, but then it reported "there is no evidence to support the rumors."

Colby had taken up the practice of law in Washington, DC after being fired from the CIA in 1975—Colby and Schmit had a mutual friend: John DeCamp. Colby directed the CIA's Phoenix program in South Vietnam from 1968 to 1971, and then-Captain John DeCamp had been one of Colby's Phoenix subordinates. Colby developed a paternal affection for the brash, young Nebraskan, and over the years they remained very close—DeCamp had introduced Schmit and Colby in 1983. Colby flew to Nebraska to be interviewed by the Committee.

Colby told the Nebraska media that his knowledge of the case came primarily from newspaper reportage, but the "paper trail" presumably left by the missing money was enough to capture his interest: "You've got $35 million that is unaccounted for," said Colby. "You start on these trails, and it frequently goes into some startling areas. It's not just used up on fancy cars or something. You've got to have some kind of bigger activity in mind."

Schmit lobbied intensely for Colby to be named as the Committee's chief counsel, but his fellow Committee members shot down Colby's appointment by a narrow margin—four to three. The dissenting Committee members felt that Colby's $250-an-hour rate would quickly exhaust the Committee's $100,000 budget, even though Colby made it clear that he was willing to lower his standard hourly rates. A second reason cited for rejecting Colby was his "political baggage." Committee members were worried—"once CIA, always CIA"—and Colby flew back to Washington without the appointment.

After interviewing a handful of candidates, in early February the Committee eventually voted in the forty-two-year-old, Lincoln-based attorney Kirk Naylor as its chief counsel. Naylor had grown up in Omaha, where his father served as the president of Omaha University and oversaw its merger into the University of Nebraska system. Naylor graduated in 1971 from the University of Nebraska's College of Law and specialized in criminal defense. He was tall, always impeccably dressed, and urbane.

Senator Chambers had encouraged Naylor to apply as the Committee's chief counselor, but after applying for the job he had withdrawn his name—Naylor claimed that he initially didn't think the Committee would grant him the authority to properly pursue the allegations. He said a couple of factors played a role in his reconsideration: First, the Committee's senators assured him he would have the requisite authority to adequately address the allegations. The second factor was a conversation he had with Dennis Carlson, who told him that the allegations were legitimate and touched on the failure of government agencies to tackle the accusations.

Naylor had feathered his cap roughly five years earlier by successfully prosecuting a Nebraska Attorney General for perjury in connection with a looted savings and loan. But at least one senator on the Committee thought Naylor's prosecution of the former Attorney General was little more than a cover-up—he felt that the inner circle of Nebraska's former governor Bob Kerrey had been instrumental in plundering the savings and loan, and the Attorney General was merely a convenient scapegoat. So Naylor didn't have the unanimous backing of all the Committee members.

Naylor quickly conscripted Lincoln Police Department officer Jerry Lowe to serve as the Committee's primary investigator. Lowe was a nine-year veteran of the LPD, and he had acted as Naylor's principal investigator when Naylor previously prosecuted the looted savings and loan. Lowe took a leave of absence from the LPD, and initially commenced his work for the Committee at Naylor's law office in Lincoln. Lowe's initial forays into Franklin involved collecting all the newspaper articles about Larry King and the credit union, and reading the materials compiled by the Foster Care Review Board.

After reviewing the Board's information, an apparently dumbfounded Lowe sent a February memo to the Committee's members. "What appears to be documented cases of child abuse and sexual abuse dating back several years with no enforcement action taken by the appropriate agencies is ... mind boggling," he wrote. "The information that became public in 1988 relative to Larry King's family connection with one of the principals ... is cause for further concern."

The Committee's formation and its early questions about whether or not Franklin-related child exploitation had been properly investigated made it impossible for state and federal law enforcement to take refuge behind claims that the allegations had "no substance." The Nebraska State Patrol and the FBI were now forced to actually conduct an investigation.

A *World-Herald* article, by James Allen Flanery, discussed federal and state investigations into Franklin-related child abuse. The article quoted the FBI's Nick O'Hara, who said that the FBI had maybe "one or two follow-up interviews to conduct," but after "dozens of interviews" he concluded that there was no "substance to the initial allegations," even though the FBI had yet to interview the initial victims to come forward— Eulice Washington and Shawneta Moore! The article also quoted two beacons of truth—Larry King and Barbara Webb. "It's all hearsay and it's all garbage," said King of the allegations. His beloved cousin then had her say about the Washington sisters: "They are not telling the truth—we don't know anything about this." In the article, Flanery wrote that Chief Wadman reiterated that the OPD immediately "followed up" on the Foster Care Review Board's July report and concluded there was "no substance."

Shawneta Moore was the first victim to be interviewed by the FBI and NSP, and their tactics were questionable. Moore had spent five months at Richard Young Hospital before being discharged to the care of her mother. At the time, Moore's mother was staying with her grandmother in North Omaha, a few blocks from King's Wirt Street residence. A handful of Moore's caregivers at the hospital decided that she was potentially too vulnerable at her grandmother's house; so they decided to shuffle her around to their respective homes until she had official placement. I've talked to one of the caregivers who gave Moore refuge, and she acknowledged that harboring Moore was counter to standard professionalism, but her caregivers were overwhelmed and perplexed by the extraordinary circumstances: Moore was making horrific allegations and law enforcement was ignoring her—they felt a humane obligation to protect her despite the ethical quandaries.

In December, Hallberg met with the investigator from the Nebraska Attorney General's Office who was investigating the child abuse allegations at the NSP office in Omaha. He informed Hallberg that he would be stepping away from the "investigation" and told her that Chuck Phillips of the NSP would be the state's primary investigator into the child-abuse allegations. The investigator said that it was the intention of the FBI and NSP to re-hospitalize Moore and question her about the allegations she made at the Richard Young facility and to Officer Carmean. He apparently felt that Moore's re-hospitalization would offer her protection and the same support system she had prior to her discharge.

Hallberg's notes state that the investigator originally said a Douglas County Deputy Sheriff would pick up Moore at the address where she was staying, but later he phoned Hallberg and instructed her to deliver Moore to the Douglas County Sheriff—a deputy would then give her a ride to the hospital and she would be committed. Moore, however, balked at a second stretch at the Richard Young facility and refused to accompany Hallberg to the Sheriff's Office. So, Hallberg abandoned her ill-fated attempt to deliver Moore to the Sheriff's Office, made a dentist's appointment, and eventually drove to Richard Young Hospital, where she was scheduled to work the second shift that day.

While there, Hallberg contacted one of Moore's caregivers and told him of her troubles with Moore. The caregiver harbored second thoughts about law enforcement's motives in Moore's case and opposed the idea of recommitting Moore. He suggested that Moore spend the weekend at his girlfriend's house, but the Attorney General's Office reportedly vetoed his offer. Hallberg's co-worker grudgingly agreed to gather up Moore and phone her mother. Moore became hysterical when the caregiver informed her about the commitment petition, and it took a number of hours for him and Moore's mother to calm her down and deliver her to the hospital.

Hallberg was in for the first of many shocks when she talked to Moore's new case nurse at Richard Young Hospital—she told Hallberg that the Douglas County commitment petition stated that Moore was suicidal and living on the streets, which the Douglas County Attorney's Office knew was untrue. The petition also specifically directed that Moore have absolutely no contact with her mother—nor was the hospital to give her mother any information on her hospitalization. The psychiatrist who admitted Moore then ordered that Moore was to have no contact with her previous caregivers, including Hallberg and the caregiver who coaxed Moore back into the hospital—Hallberg later learned that the Douglas County Attorney's Office issued the latter order. Law enforcement had succeeded in having Moore committed under false pretenses and severing her from her support network, and she was then subjected to FBI agents whom she found to be extremely hostile.

The day of Moore's initial interview by the FBI and NSP, Hallberg met with the thirty-two-year-old Chuck Phillips at Omaha's NSP office later that night. Phillips seemed to wear an omnipresent scowl, and Hallberg found him to be very overbearing and hostile. She felt that Phillips would only accept statements that had absolute, irrefutable proof, and she brought their meeting to an abrupt close. After Hallberg met Phillips at the NSP office, she wrote the following about him: "My impression at the time was that if I, as an adult, could be so easily intimidated by him, I wonder how kids will react if he is the one to question them."

Phillips had been with the NSP since 1978—he had spent three years in the Army's military police prior to signing on with the NSP. Phillips started out with the NSP in rural western Nebraska, assigned to the traffic division, working as a uniformed trooper. After a year or so, he was transferred to Omaha, where he continued to work as a uniformed trooper. In 1981, Phillips took a big career leap to the NSP's Drug Investigations Division, and approximately six years later he was assigned to the Criminal Investigations Division. At the onset of the NSP's Franklin "investigation," Phillips worked in close conjunction with FBI agents Peter Brady and Jerry Tucker, but the FBI would eventually undergo a changing of the guard concerning Franklin. Though Brady and Tucker receded into the background, Phillips would aid the FBI's second crew of agents tasked with investigating Franklin. Phillips would ultimately see Franklin through to the bitter end.

Phillips and FBI agents knocked on Opal Washington's front door on December 28, looking for Eulice, Tracy, and Tasha. The children's grandmother also felt intimidated by the investigators, and she initially wouldn't let them into her house. Opal says they ultimately wedged themselves through her front door and pressed her to provide them with the whereabouts of her granddaughters, but she refused to acquiesce. She told the investigators that she wanted her granddaughters to meet with Senator Chambers before they talked with them.

The NSP and FBI weren't willing to accommodate the grandmother's wishes—they tracked down Eulice the following day, and, according to Eulice, grilled her for three to four hours. They then had her come to Omaha's FBI Field Office the next day where they grilled her for an additional three or four hours. Though Eulice found the ordeal to be extremely grueling, she didn't divert from many of the details about her trips to Chicago and New York as she had related them to Julie Walters.

After the NSP and FBI "interviewed" Eulice, they set their sights on Tracy—she was subjected to the same harsh treatment as her sister. A long-lost relative of the Washington sisters who became reacquainted with them after their removal from the Webb household gave a quote to the *Lincoln Journal* about Eulice and Tracy's ordeal at the hands of the FBI: "The FBI has accomplished what it set out to accomplish–to make the girls seem as though all this were a fabrication." The FBI interviewed Patricia Flocken in January 1989–Flocken too found the FBI to be extremely hostile. In fact, she told investigator Lowe that the agent questioning her "seemed pissed" and repeatedly snapped that Flocken's information was only "hearsay."

Earlier, I cited a February 5 article in the *World-Herald* that quoted the FBI's Nick O'Hara, stating that the FBI carried out "dozens" of interviews, and maybe had "one or two follow-up interviews to conduct," but he was convinced that the allegations were without "substance." O'Hara made that declaration even before FBI agents interviewed their prime suspect in the investigation–Larry King!

FBI agents and NSP Investigator Phillips would, in fact, finally interview King at his Wirt Street residence on February 10. After they gave King his Miranda rights, a seemingly benign chat ensued, where King was tossed a succession of softballs. He denied everything: the pandering of children, kiddy porn, drug involvement, and even homosexuality. He talked extensively about his participation in the Presbyterian Church and of his piety. King adamantly maintained that he never had "nasty" parties at the Twin Towers–he said the closest one of his soirées ever came to depravity was when he had hired a couple of belly dancers for his birthday party two years earlier.

King disclosed to FBI agents that he was a good friend of *World-Herald* publisher Harold Andersen, OPD Chief Wadman, and Nebraska Attorney General Spire–all three show up on King's party invitation lists. But, because of the unsavory rumors, nobody wanted to acknowledge their friendship with him or to admit that they attended his fabulous parties. He said that even FBI agents had frequented his parties in the past–he then looked at one of the FBI agents questioning him and contended that he had attended one of his parties.

King concluded the interview by saying that he never lied, and that he would be more than willing to take a polygraph. Investigator Phillips was later called before a grand jury and said that King was never given a polygraph, even though he consented to take one. Under oath, Phillips maintained that the NSP or FBI didn't polygraph King because they hadn't finished their investigation—he stated that the NSP and FBI were still in the process of culling facts and interviewing additional witnesses when they interviewed King, even though the FBI's O'Hara stated publicly the investigation was winding down.

The FBI and NSP interviews documented in this chapter reveal that investigators approached all interviews with unbridled skepticism and hostility. Eulice and Tracy Washington and Shawneta Moore alleged that the investigators who interviewed them were extremely antagonistic, and Kirstin Hallberg and Patricia Flocken support their accounts. The FBI's starting maxim seems to have been: the allegations are bogus, and we will prove that they're bogus.

The backdrop for the Franklin Committee commencing its long day's journey into night was the OPD's Wadman and the FBI's O'Hara proclaiming that the child-abuse allegations had no substance, but the Committee's members decided early on that law enforcement's viewpoint would not deter their investigation. "We'll pursue our investigation without regard to what the chief or the FBI says," Chambers told the *World-Herald*. Indeed, Lowe started to kick out memos and reports, and the Committee commenced to orchestrate hearings.

Lowe would backtrack on the accounts gathered by the Foster Care Review Board and essentially conduct an investigation of the state and federal investigations. Some of the individuals who played an instrumental role in the Board's inquiry—including Dennis Carlson and Kirstin Hallberg—gave him meticulous blow-by-blow accounts of their tribulations, and he conducted protracted interviews with others.

The FBI and NSP had been caustic with Shawneta Moore and Eulice Washington; so they weren't particularly enamored with the prospect of being reinterviewed about their respective abuses, but Senator Chambers facilitated Lowe's interviews with both. Eulice Washington told me that she didn't find Lowe to be particularly gracious either.

When Lowe first met Shawneta Moore at her mother's home, her mother and Senator Chambers were also present. Lowe and Moore initially discussed the latter's contacts with the OPD. Moore told Lowe that Carmean interviewed her once in person, and they talked twice over the phone, corroborating the OPD reports.

Moore then discussed her second stay at Richard Young Hospital and the FBI interviews. Moore disclosed that a Douglas County attorney and an individual on the hospital's staff made it clear to her that she wouldn't be released from the hospital if she didn't talk to the FBI agents. Moore felt the agents who questioned her were hostile and incredulous. She maintained that the agents made a concerted effort to keep her off balance and trip her up. Lowe asked her to cite an example of the FBI's tactics: She responded that FBI agents simply told her to relate her story from the beginning to the end, implying that they wouldn't interrupt her. But after she commenced telling her story, they repeatedly interrupted her and demanded that she provide additional details.

Lowe scheduled a second meeting with Moore the following week. During their second meeting, Lowe questioned Moore about the two parties she said Larry King attended. The details she initially provided Carmean and then the FBI regarding the parties are consistent with the details she provided Lowe.

Moore also talked of being transported from the Girls Club at the age of nine to a studio and photographed in the nude—she claimed four other girls accompanied her. Lowe asked her if the African-American man she identified as "Ray," who shuttled her to the parties and power meetings, delivered her to the studio where she had been photographed. At first she indicated that Ray had not brought her to the studio, and then she said she couldn't remember. Lowe suggested the use of hypnosis to jog her memory—she started to cry, replying she didn't want to be hypnotized.

Moore initially described five homicides to Richard Young Hospital personnel, but she only described three homicides to the FBI. Lowe pointed out the discrepancy to her, and she said that she felt hurried and badgered by the FBI. Lowe noted that the information provided by Moore to the hospital staff, the FBI, and Lowe about the names of the men attending the sacrifices and the descriptions of the locations were consistent. Lowe also noted that Moore's hospital accounts of the sacrifices' aftermaths were consistent with the aftermaths she conveyed to him, including her being dropped off in a park following the first sacrifice. According to all of Moore's interviews, Larry King was never present at any of the sacrifices, and Lowe "pressed" her regarding her contention that King was an alleged participant in the devil worship. Lowe wrote that Moore disclosed to him that a specific individual said that King was involved, but she later told Lowe that the individual in question hadn't made such a disclosure.

Though Moore previously disclosed to Richard Young Hospital personnel that she had been blindfolded when she was driven to parties or power meetings, she told Lowe that she might be able to identify one of the buildings in Omaha and also a building in Fort Calhoun. Lowe drove Moore past various locations in Omaha and Fort Calhoun, and she wasn't able to identify any buildings in Omaha. However, she tentatively identified a building in Fort Calhoun—she asked Lowe if the building in Fort Calhoun recently had an addition built onto it, and he replied in the affirmative. Lowe later found out that the building identified by Moore was in close proximity to the home of a school administrator whom Moore said had attended the child-sex parties and power meetings. The building's owner had also employed Barbara Webb.

After Lowe's three interviews with Moore, he was ambivalent concerning her veracity: "At this point I don't really have a firm read on the information which Shawneta has provided, other than the opinion that if she has fabricated or imagined the information ... she is indeed a young individual in desperate need of counseling. If the information that she has given has any validity, it's my opinion that she has succeeded in blocking the information out of her mind and will not share it with anyone."

Lowe met with Eulice Washington twice the following month. His first interview with her primarily centered on her upbringing by the Webbs, and the second interview focused on her trips with Larry King. Washington's depiction of her abuse and the abuse suffered by the other children in the Webb household were consistent with the Board's information. Lowe questioned her with regard to the North Omaha Girls Club, and she admitted to hearing stories of older men connected with the Girls Club having sex with the young girls who frequented it—she emphasized, though, that her information was "second hand."

Washington and Lowe then discussed the sex parties that she was flown to in Chicago and New York. She initially discussed her Chicago trip, which occurred in September or October of 1984. She gave Lowe a general description of the chartered plane, and, after exiting the plane, she said, they took a limousine to a fancy hotel in Chicago, but she couldn't remember the hotel's name. She told Lowe that the party occurred in the same hotel, recalling it was on a different floor because she had to take an elevator from her room to the party. Prior to the party, Larry King came to her room and gave her a black negligee to wear. He then escorted her to the party, and ordered her to sit, like a mannequin, on a little "pedestal." When King and Washington initially arrived at the party, the young men who had been on the plane were already in the room, and hors d'oeuvres were being served.

Washington indicated that two African-American men, stationed at the door, scrutinized the older men as they started rolling into the party—she said the two men had been on the chartered plane. Once the party was in full swing, she noticed the older men giving money to King and leaving with the boys. Though she didn't see any explicit sexual acts between the boys and the men, she observed the older men hugging and kissing the boys.

Approximately forty-five minutes into the party, Washington said, she recognized a nationally prominent politician enter the gathering—he was greeted by Larry King and accompanied by a pair of Caucasian bodyguards. She related that the politician left with a former Boys Town student named "Brant." Lowe asked her how she was able to positively identify the politician, and she responded that his political campaigns gave him widespread visibility—she had also seen a picture of him and Larry King in King's home.

Washington specified that the flight to New York occurred in February or March of 1985. She left school early on a Friday and was driven to King's home. A limousine then collected her and King and drove them to the airport—she told Lowe that King chartered the same plane that delivered her to Chicago. She said that some of the boys who were on the plane to Chicago accompanied King to New York. Washington informed Lowe that two older female "hookers" and two young girls, no older than seven years of age, were on the plane too—she described the young girls as "fast" and was startled by their streetwise lingo. She also stated that King's son was on the plane.

Washington said that a limo drove them from the airport to a hotel in Manhattan, but, again, she couldn't recall the name of the hotel. As in Chicago, she stayed in a hotel room by herself. Lowe asked her where the little girls lodged, and she replied she didn't know. Once more she was forced to wear a negligee without underpants and sit on a pedestal poised like a mannequin—she pointed out that it was a different negligee than the one she wore in Chicago. She recounted that the party in New York had considerably more sexual activity than the party in Chicago. At one point, she was surrounded by men who were masturbating in front of her. Washington said she missed school the following Monday and Tuesday and later found out that a secretary from the school phoned the Webbs about her absence. She presumed the Webbs told school personnel she was sick.

For Lowe, his interviews of Moore and Washington seem to have been a tale of two victims: He noticed inconsistencies between Moore's accounts of her abuse as she related them to the FBI and to him, but he noted that the accounts Washington furnished to the FBI and to him were "consistent."

I've spent numerous hours with Eulice Washington, and she's never wavered in her accounts of the two trips. I've also spent considerable time with her two sisters, Tracy and Tasha, particularly Tasha, and they definitely don't doubt her accounts of the trips with King. Indeed, Tasha disclosed to me that she felt Barbara Webb was grooming her for out-of-town flights with King—Webb informed Tasha about the possibility of her flying to New York for "dancing lessons."

As the Franklin Committee began its work, and Lowe started pumping out reports, the local press, namely the *World-Herald* and the *Lincoln Journal*, escalated their reportage on the burgeoning scandal. But the local press was by no means the only media taking an interest in Franklin. During December 1988, the nation's paper of record, the *New York Times*, ran a pair of articles on the "lurid, mysterious scandal shaping up in Omaha." The articles discussed King's theft of millions from the credit union and also the nascent "reports of sex abuse." A February 1989 *Village Voice* article also commented on the "sexual abuse of children." But the allegations trickling out of Omaha were so bizarre and divorced from conventional perceptions of the heartland that many major media outlets apparently took a wait-and-see attitude.

In March, a *World-Herald* article by Flanery and a *Lincoln Journal-Star* article featured the Foster Care Review Board's Dennis Carlson and OPD Chief Wadman sparring over the abuse allegations. Both newspapers quoted a nonplussed Dennis Carlson publicly jabbing at law enforcement: "I'm still concerned as to whether the allegations have been thoroughly investigated." Carlson said that the Board enlisted the Nebraska Attorney General's Office to investigate the allegations because it had grave concerns about the OPD. In the articles, Carlson revealed that Officer Carmean told him that OPD officers lied to Wadman in an effort to ensure that the OPD's investigation into King remained a secret from the chief. Wadman responded to Carlson with a flurry of counterpunches: He said that an officer, presumably Carmean, made "a mistake in judgment," and he produced reports from five officers stating that he hadn't been kept in the dark concerning an investigation into King. The *World-Herald* article attributed the following quote to Wadman: "The genesis of most of these allegations comes from uncredible sources."

Needless to say, Lowe was quite interested in talking to Carmean, but he didn't want to contact him at the OPD. He staked out Carmean's residence for a few days, but their paths never crossed, and Lowe eventually contacted him at the OPD. Lowe felt it was optimal not to talk to Carmean at his workplace; Carmean consented to be interviewed at Naylor's Lincoln office. Lowe, Naylor, and Carmean met for two and a half hours on Sunday, March 12. During the initial stages of their meeting, Carmean expressed a great deal of consternation over his conversations with Dennis Carlson being made public—he had assumed they were confidential. He told Lowe and Naylor that having his exchanges with Carlson hit the papers had heaped anxiety and embarrassment upon him.

Carmean said he had acquired a copy of Carlson's notes and related that he didn't tell Carlson that the investigation of King was "super sensitive," but, rather, he conveyed to him the investigation was merely "sensitive."

Though Carmean would fault Carlson for making their conversations public, he extensively corroborated Carlson's notes. He confirmed to Lowe and Naylor that the OPD swelled with rumors of a friendship between King and Wadman and of rumors about Wadman staying at King's DC residence. Carmean also said that he bypassed the OPD's standard stenography pool when he investigated King to ensure that word of the investigation didn't leak out of the Robbery and Sexual Assault Unit. Carmean informed Lowe and Naylor that he thought Shawneta Moore was a credible witness, and he mentioned a meeting where it was stated that a federal agency told the OPD to "back off" from its investigation of King.

Four days after Lowe and Naylor interviewed Carmean, Lowe was contacted by the OPD's Internal Affairs Unit. The IA officer said he was calling on behalf of Chief Wadman and inquired why Lowe hadn't used the OPD's customary channels to contact Carmean—Lowe responded that he and Naylor had decided to circumvent those channels when lining up their meeting with Carmean. The IA officer then told Lowe that Wadman wished to talk to Lowe and gave him Wadman's number. Lowe phoned Wadman, and they agreed to meet at OPD headquarters the following week.

When Lowe and Naylor showed up at the OPD, Wadman commenced the meeting by saying that he felt that the OPD had conducted an adequate investigation of the child-abuse allegations and that the NSP and FBI validated its findings. He stressed that he didn't have a friendship with King, and the extent of their social contact was the three parties of King's he had attended. He maintained that he had been invited to additional parties, but he declined the invitations. According to Lowe, Wadman also made a point of questioning Carmean's stability—Wadman stated that Carmean was receiving mental-health counseling.

Interestingly, Wadman's comments to Lowe and Naylor about Carmean's mental health proved to be a self-fulfilling prophecy: Three months later, Wadman sent an Inter-Office Communication to Omaha's Public Safety Director, the city's overseer of the fire and police departments, requesting a psychological referral for Carmean. Wadman wrote that Carmean's symptoms "seemed to fall into two areas." The first class of symptoms consisted of Carmean feeling that the OPD hadn't adequately investigated the allegations of child exploitation pertaining to King. Carmean's second area of symptoms revolved around his thinking that Wadman "intentionally hindered" the OPD's investigation into

King's activities because of the latter's "influence and association" with Wadman. The Public Safety Director concurred with Wadman's assessment and referred Carmean to a psychologist. The Public Safety Director just happened to be a cousin of Larry King.

After Wadman interceded on behalf of Carmean's mental health, the *Lincoln Journal* ran a rather shocking story about a phone call between Chief Wadman and Senator Schmit: The paper reported on a meeting that Schmit had with three citizens who were concerned about law enforcement's approach to the child-abuse investigation, and Schmit stated to them that Wadman threatened him. The *Lincoln Journal* reported that Schmit told the concerned citizens that Wadman had said the activities of Committee members could be monitored: "He said, 'We can get something on anybody' or something of that nature," the paper quoted Schmit. Schmit also told the group that he did, in fact, feel that his activities were being monitored, and that he was being followed. At this point, Schmit had also become the target of threatening, anonymous phone calls.

In addition to the threats dispensed to Schmit, the members of the Franklin Committee found themselves navigating upstream against a strong current of opposition by the OPD, NSP, and FBI.

The Committee was also hindered by the Nebraska Attorney General's Office. The Attorney General's Office allowed Naylor to look over its investigative reports on King, but at least one member of the Committee distrusted Naylor, and other Committee members wanted to see the reports for themselves. So in June, the Committee issued a subpoena that required Assistant Attorney General Howland and the Office's investigator to cough up the reports, but the Attorney General's Office refused to honor the subpoena. The ludicrous response initially provided for not surrendering the reports was that someone else in the Attorney General's Office was actually in possession of them! The Franklin Committee was probing the sexual abuse of children, the most heinous of crimes, and the Office of Nebraska's Attorney General was seemingly hindering their investigation.

As the Attorney General's Office stonewalled the Committee, and the OPD, NSP, and FBI declared that the King-related child-abuse allegations had "no substance," a number of Omaha's citizenry looked on with shock and disbelief, because talk of King-related child abuse had drifted throughout their community for years, and the closing of Franklin only served to intensify the innuendo. By the summer of 1989, eddies of Nebraska's populace who had lost faith in their local, state, and federal institutions of government's ability to protect the community's children took it upon themselves to form a group called Concerned Parents. Initially, Concerned Parents met at an Omaha church, and it attracted only a trickle of members. But as the cover-up of King's activities intensified, its ranks started to swell.

Bonnie Cosentino was a co-founder of Concerned Parents. The forty-five-year-old Cosentino was the soft-spoken single mother of a twelve-year-old boy. Cosentino designed and constructed team mascots for a living—the life-sized mascots that are spotted running around college and professional sporting events, enthusing fans. She had heard of King's harem of boys since the early 1970s, so the allegations didn't surprise her, but she was sickened and dismayed by law enforcement's response.

"We had heard on numerous occasions about young people who had dared to go to law enforcement with the allegations, and they would simply be laughed at," Cosentino told me. "If you're fourteen years old and you can't trust law enforcement, who can you trust—it's like the fire extinguisher was on fire."

Concerned Parents sought to provide a "constructive" voice for the victims and to investigate their allegations, because of law enforcement's unwillingness to act. Concerned Parents also acted as a support network for adults who had become bewildered and furious that the child-abuse allegations were receiving such scant attention from the authorities.

Cosentino's role as an organizer for the disenchanted singled her out for a campaign of terror. One day she and her son were crossing the street when an approaching car sped up and sideswiped them—a bomb was also detonated in her backyard. She, too, started to receive life-threatening phone calls.

"There were several people who ran Concerned Parents so one person wasn't on the front lines all the time," said Cosentino, "because it was clear that whoever took a stand would be subjected to retaliation, or their families would be subjected to retaliation. Our lives were turned upside down by fear. We felt that our phones were tapped, so just ordinary day-to-day routines like talking on the phone took on a new meaning."

On June 22, 1989, the Franklin Committee held public hearings, and it subpoenaed the Foster Care Review Board's Carol Stitt and Dennis Carlson, Officer Carmean, Attorney General Spire, Assistant Attorney General Howland, and investigator Vlahoulis. Officer Hoch was also subpoenaed to appear before the Committee, but he claimed a scheduling conflict, and the Committee let it slide. The witnesses were sworn in before their testimony, and then Naylor and members of the Committee questioned them.

Stitt and Carlson testified together, and they basically rehashed their repeated rebuffs by law enforcement. Prior to the hearing, Stitt had cultivated excellent relationships with some of the Committee's members—Senator Chambers had turned up the heat on the Attorney General's Office after it reacted to the Board's allegations with mere apathy at best, and she found Schmit to be very receptive to the Board's concerns when the Committee was forming in December. But the day before Stitt testified in front of the Committee, Naylor threatened her with a perjury charge concerning her account of the conversation she had with the detective from Kansas City, who was reportedly privy to King's abuse of children. The detective had told Hallberg, Stitt and Carlson in three separate conversations about King exploiting children in Kansas City, but she had completely denied having the foggiest idea of King's abuses when questioned by the FBI and then by investigator Lowe. Stitt also received a life-threatening phone call the night before she testified in front of the Committee.

Carmean was the next witness called before the Committee, and he essentially reiterated the statements he had made to investigator Lowe. Carmean, however, was making these statements in a public forum: A TV camera caught him saying that he heard rumors of an "association" between Wadman and King and also of his belief that Shawneta Moore was credible. Within two weeks of Carmean's testimony before the Committee, Wadman requested that King's cousin refer Carmean to a psychologist.

After Carmean, members of the Nebraska Attorney General's Office were called to face the Committee. Assistant Attorney General Howland and the Attorney General's investigator were subjected to the wrath of the Committee members, particularly Chambers, not only for their failure to adequately investigate the Board's allegations in a timely manner, but also for refusing to honor the Committee's subpoena. Though Howland and the investigator did their best to soft-shoe away from the accusations that they "sat on" the Board's materials, they couldn't dance fast enough to belie the grim reality. The investigator confessed that he had not interviewed a single victim.

But as Howland and the investigator dipped and dodged, they couldn't help themselves from making relevant disclosures. Howland initially testified that the Attorney General's Office wanted to oversee the OPD's investigation of the abuse allegations and requested updates from the OPD. Howland said he received no reports from the OPD on its investigation of the abuse allegations until he met with Chief Wadman in late October or early November, even though Wadman told the media that December marked his first inkling of the investigation because the evidence was so scant.

Howland also testified that the US Attorney for Nebraska had informed him that the FBI was investigating King not only for his financial improprieties but also for child exploitation and drug dealing. Howland said he was told about the federal investigation by the middle of October, but the feds later claimed they were only investigating King's financial crimes at the time.

By the time Attorney General Spire testified, the Committee had decisively established that the Attorney General's Office had, in fact, sat on the allegations, and Chambers used a number of adjectives to characterize its investigation—"slipshod," "superficial," and "incompetent." Chambers also inquired of Spire why the Attorney General's Office hadn't honored the Committee's subpoena. After considerable circumlocution, Attorney General Spire replied that it wouldn't be "legally appropriate" for his office to turn over its reports to the Committee.

Shortly after the Committee's initial hearings on June 22, Committee members held a meeting to discuss its Interim Report—Resolution 5 mandated that the Committee submit a progress report to the Unicameral by July 1. Naylor would be tasked with writing the Interim Report, and he submitted a draft of it to the Committee members before the July 1 deadline.

Schmit read Naylor's draft of the Interim Report, and he was outraged, because Naylor seemed to focus on a lack of response primarily by the Attorney General's Office. Naylor's draft of the Interim Report also said that the Committee's investigation of the King-related child-abuse allegations was "intensive and ongoing," but it would be wrapping up at the end of August. Schmit absolutely wouldn't sign off on the Committee discontinuing its investigation of the child-abuse allegations by the end of August.

Schmit then wrote a three-page addendum to the Committee's Interim Report. His addendum conceded that the Committee hadn't uncovered prosecutable offenses relating to child abuse; he believed that it needed to change its investigative tactics and follow the money in order to ferret out improprieties, including child abuse. Schmit's addendum provoked Naylor, Lowe, and also Chambers to resign from the Committee.

A *World-Herald* article, "Sen. Schmit Told of Pressure to Halt Probe," written by Flanery, reported on the Committee's rupture. The article quoted Lowe, who said Schmit had remarked to him that there was "pressure to stop the investigation." In the article, Schmit confirmed the pressures: "I have gotten phone calls threatening me," he said. "I've been told to leave it alone or my kids were going to be orphans."

The article also reported on comments made by Chambers about Schmit's addendum and his own resignation. Chambers said that Schmit's change of direction "dried up possible avenues of information" and "de-emphasized the investigation of child abuse"—he felt that the Committee's probe was becoming a "sham" and "might intentionally or inadvertently be a cover-up." Chambers added that it would be impossible for the Committee to follow the money trail, because the NCUA and other federal entities wouldn't grant the Committee access to the credit union's records.

Schmit responded to Chambers' comments: "I resent the implication I'm not concerned about the children and determining whether or not the allegations of child abuse are true." He retorted that he hadn't changed his mind about the child-abuse allegations, but the prior tactics of Naylor and Lowe hadn't yielded prosecutable offenses. "Find out where the money went, and you'll find the rest," said Schmit, and then he cited a $2,800 credit card receipt that showed King purchased a coat for Charlie Rogers, whose death had unconvincingly been ruled a suicide.

The distrust and apprehension that caused the Franklin Committee to rupture would become a salient characteristic of this story. Those who were touched by its shadow learned to mete out trust carefully and cautiously—if at all. In addition to anonymous, life-threatening phone calls, the narrative is brimming with examples of people who trusted law enforcement and were burned. When citizens come to believe that both state and federal law enforcement are covering up crimes against children, their trust in all government institutions quickly evaporates. Moreover, as this tale unfolds, suspicious suicides and mysterious deaths will multiply.

The Caradori Family — 1987

—Chapter Two—

Caradori

After the resignations of Kirk Naylor and Jerry Lowe in July of 1989, Senator Schmit and the Franklin Committee conscripted Lincoln attorney John Stevens Berry and his law firm to replace Naylor as the Committee's counsel. In addition to reviewing the Committee's previous reports and testimony, Berry and his law firm quickly negotiated the Committee's access to the previously withheld Nebraska Attorney General's reports, and to the financial records of Larry King and the credit union impounded by the NCUA.

At the behest of Berry, Schmit and the Committee looked to Gary Caradori as the Committee's next investigator—Berry described Caradori as "the finest private investigator in this part of the country." The forty-year-old Caradori was the CEO of the Lincoln-based Caracorp Inc., which provided a wide array of security and investigative services, numbering 120 employees in eight states.

Though Caradori was the CEO of a large security and investigative agency, he was a seasoned, relentless, and hands-on gumshoe, and his passion was finding missing persons, particularly abducted children and teenage girls enmeshed in drugs and prostitution. Over the years, the *Lincoln Journal* and *Lincoln Journal-Star* had published a number of articles on Caradori's daring exploits. One article, "Lincoln Private Detective Walks Nation's Mean Streets," described Caradori's stealthy feats on the gritty streets of New York, Los Angeles, and Las Vegas. The article reported that Caradori posed in the undercover disguises of a priest or a plumber to infiltrate brothels and the inner sanctums of Mafiosi to find and retrieve young women ensnared in prostitution. "If I didn't have to make a living, I'd track them down for free," Caradori said in the article. In another article, the *Lincoln Journal* showered him with accolades: "When the police tell you their hands are tied.... When your only witness has skipped town and when the justice system seems like it's breaking apart, people call Gary Caradori."

Born April 15, 1949, Caradori was the second of Leno and Mary Caradori's five sons and two daughters. The Caradori family lived in a split-level house in the small township of Ralston, southwest of Omaha. The Caradoris were an archetypal Midwestern family from the 1950s: Leno was a teacher at Boys Town and Mary a homemaker. In 1964, Gary Caradori attended Ralston High School as a freshman. At the onset of his freshman year, as Caradori entered the school building, he held the door open for Sandi Anderson, also a freshman—it was love at first sight. They were married in 1969. The couple had two sons—Sean was born in 1974 and Andrew James (A.J.) in 1981.

Shortly after graduating from high school in 1967, Caradori was drafted into the United States Coast Guard, and, following basic training at Cape May, New Jersey, he was transferred to Alaska, where his duties included handling teletype messages and directing aircraft. In 1969, the Coast Guard sent the nineteen-year-old Caradori to study anti-submarine warfare at Radarman School on Governors Island, New York.

Caradori spent the next two years abroad on the Coast Guard Cutter *Mellon*, serving one year in Vietnam. As a 2nd Class Radarman on the *Mellon*, Caradori demonstrated innate leadership skills, supervising eight men.

After receiving an honorable discharge from the Coast Guard in 1971, Caradori joined the Nebraska State Patrol. He impressed his NSP supervisors with his leadership qualities and instinctive investigative talents, and they promptly placed him in charge of one of the state's six Mobile Crime Evidence Vans. At the age of 23, Caradori transferred to the NSP's Criminal Division, one of the youngest men ever to have been appointed an NSP Investigator. There he refined his investigative skills by enrolling in numerous FBI-sponsored training curricula, including Snipers, Bomb Threats and Hostage School, Criminal Investigation Photo Lab School, and Sex Crime Investigation.

Caradori possessed a strong entrepreneurial spirit, and he left the NSP in "good standing" in March 1977 to become the co-proprietor of JC Security and Detective Agency. Four years later, he formed a second partnership: Caradori/Weatherl Investigations. In February 1989, the industrious Caradori underwent a final entrepreneurial incarnation, becoming the founder of Caracorp, which landed investigative contracts from a number of corporate powerhouses—ConAgra, Cargill, and Archer Daniels Midland. Caradori was clearly a man on the escalator of upward mobility.

According to Caradori, Senator Loran Schmit made an unannounced visit to the offices of Caracorp on an August afternoon in 1989. Caradori felt that the senator was "lucky" to catch him, because stationary days at the office were a rarity for him: He was usually in perpetual motion, traveling in excess of 150,000 miles a year. Caradori assumed his usual seat behind his cherry wood roll-top desk, and Schmit seated himself in one of the well-padded leather chairs facing it. Both men were licensed pilots, and Caradori later said that Schmit broke the ice by discussing airplanes and other generalities before broaching the subject of Franklin. Caradori had spent nine of the previous twelve months working around the country, and he wasn't familiar with the particulars of Franklin—Caradori initially thought that the Franklin Credit Union was just "another bank that went under."

At the conclusion of Schmit and Caradori's initial meeting, Caradori was invited to meet with the entire Franklin Committee the following week at the statehouse. After the Committee members interviewed Caradori for two hours, he left the room while they voted on his appointment. He was then ushered back before the Committee, and they informed him that he had been retained as their new investigator. Though Caradori had the razor-sharp street smarts of an extraordinary detective, it would take him weeks before he realized the full scope and malevolence of the corruption he was investigating.

On August 21, Caradori plunged into the Franklin investigation with his usual tenacity and zeal. His initial foray included devouring the reports and memos generated by Jerry Lowe and all the previous documentation and testimony collected by the Franklin Committee. Whereas Lowe had conducted an investigation of the federal and state investigations, Caradori was committed to carrying out *his own* investigation. Early on, Caradori received a call from a friend who was an OPD lieutenant—his friend cautioned him of the looming danger ahead, saying that the sexual component of Franklin had been covered up from the start.

Caradori assigned Karen Ormiston to be his principal assistant in the investigation. A trusted employee of Caradori's for over six years, she was Caracorp's office coordinator and business manager. Together they had complementary investigative styles that paralleled the choreography of Fred Astaire and Ginger Rogers: Caradori would lead, gathering extensive evidence in a whirlwind of intensity; Ormiston would follow up, collating and processing the evidence.

From the onset of the investigation, several obstacles confronted Caradori and his staff. Many of Caradori's "Investigative Reports" from August and September note that he faced the formidable barriers of "distrust" and a pall of fear as he attempted to cultivate confidential informants or simply interview individuals who had previously volunteered information—they suspected that the Franklin Committee was merely serving the function of a continuing cover-up. They also feared that divulging specific or personal information would be a surefire way to blow their anonymity, because their disclosures would inevitably be published in the *World-Herald*. Caradori quickly came to the realization that it was imperative to nurture the withering civic trust; so he sent a September memo to the Franklin Committee, insisting it was "crucial" that nothing be published implicating specific individuals until his investigation was completed.

In addition to widespread distrust, Caradori also encountered enemies he hadn't anticipated. Caradori's wife, Sandi, a middle school English teacher, informed me that a family friend confirmed a troubling hunch of her husband's. "An old friend of ours who used to work for Lincoln Telephone came to our house and told us that our phones were tapped," she said. "Gary already suspected it was the FBI, because when he arranged meetings over the phone FBI agents would already be at the designated place when he arrived."

Ormiston also felt that her phones were tapped, prompting Caradori to send a letter to Lincoln Telephone, requesting that the company provide him with information concerning their lines being tapped or monitored. After a Lincoln Telephone representative received the letter, he phoned Caradori and relayed that the information he requested required a court order or a subpoena. According to Ormiston, a subpoena was served on Lincoln Telephone, but the company refused to honor it.

The vast majority of today's US telephone exchanges employ digital technology, which enables telephone monitoring to be conducted from remote distances. In 1989, however, the monitoring connection generally had to be applied directly to the line of the phone being tapped, and the wiretaps occasionally resulted in telephonic glitches for the monitored individual—Ormiston related an anecdote about a telephone snafu at Caracorp.

"When our office phones started malfunctioning," she commented, "Gary contacted his friend at Lincoln Telephone who stopped by our office. After he fidgeted with our jacks for a few minutes, he electronically zeroed in on a room where we heard people talking. They eventually realized that their jack was open and suddenly cut it off."

In addition to tapped phones, Caradori had to start dealing with home intruders. On September 14, 1989, while Caradori and his wife were out with friends and their two sons were at home sleeping, someone entered their home around 10:00 P.M. The Caradori's oldest son was alerted to the trespasser by the family's dogs, and then he heard a door being opened and closed. Caradori filed a trespassing report with the Lincoln Police Department—the intruder was never apprehended.

In newspaper reportage of Caradori's derring-do adventures, he discussed the investigative necessity of nurturing a network of contacts and informants, and he quickly incorporated that modus operandi into his Franklin investigation. Within weeks of commencing the investigation, his records confirm that he had several meetings with "confidential informants." He also started zigzagging the streets and bars of Omaha to cultivate additional informants. The street buzz was rife with rumors corroborating Larry King's abuse of children and enabled Caradori to identify other perpetrators. At this point in the investigation, it wasn't uncommon for Caradori to log over one-hundred-hour weeks, talking to scores of unsavory individuals in sordid, nocturnal haunts. Sandi Caradori told me that her husband started taking long, hot showers to relax physically, and seemingly cleanse the investigation's dark residue from his soul.

Caradori scrambled for leads on the streets and from informants, and also adhered to the Watergate refrain of following the money—two investigative techniques that are not mutually exclusive. To follow the money, Caradori originally received help from the NCUA. After Franklin was closed, the NCUA had set up a "reconstruction office" in Omaha to decipher the whereabouts of the missing $40 million. The stacked boxes there contained thousands of checks, invoices, receipts, etc.

The NCUA initially granted Caradori and Ormiston access to the reconstruction office during normal business hours Monday through Friday, and they were allowed to make copies of documentation they deemed relevant to their investigation. A ranking NCUA official in Washington, DC also provided Caradori with leads.

At the NCUA reconstruction office, Caradori and Ormiston managed to find boxes containing scores of receipts from various air charter services. The flight receipts rarely listed passengers, or would merely list "Larry King." The receipts also revealed that King chartered Lear jets on an almost weekly basis. Though King jetted to numerous locations throughout the country, his favored destination was Washington, DC.

The flight receipts presented Caradori with a fresh avenue of investigation that he maneuvered with his customary doggedness. A September Investigative Report indicated that Caradori contacted a charter service in Columbus, Ohio repeatedly used by King, but the company's lawyer rebuffed his request for flight records, demanding a subpoena. Unfortunately, the Franklin Committee's subpoena power had no standing outside the borders of Nebraska.

In October 1989, Caradori made contact with the pilot of a second charter service frequented by King. The pilot informed Caradori that he had piloted King, two teenage boys, and a teenage girl to Los Angeles. Caradori phoned another pilot from the same charter service who acknowledged that minors accompanied King on flights.

In a later Investigative Report, Caradori described his meeting with a former employee of a third charter service used by King. Though the woman was apprehensive about having her name connected to the "Franklin investigation," she disclosed that King used her charter service on a weekly basis. She said he routinely traveled with a number of young men: "very good looking," dressed in fancy suits, and "clean cut and clean shaven." The young men, she remarked, never spoke, which she found strange.

Caradori and Ormiston called on a fourth charter service patronized by King located in Sioux City, Iowa. They met with the company's chief executive, who instructed his secretary to direct them to a basement room where their records were stored—Caradori and Ormiston then began to burrow through the company's countless records. Caradori must have felt like a miner striking gold when he found Franklin Credit Union itineraries listing children whose names had surfaced during his investigation. As Caradori continued to burrow, Ormiston snatched the itineraries and darted to a nearby copy machine. While Caradori scanned the itineraries, he came across one that had a sticker on it denoting a previous FBI inquiry.

When Caradori and Ormiston were on the verge of leaving the charter service with their newfound cache, the company's chief executive barged into the room and demanded that they leave without the copied itineraries. Caradori grudgingly acquiesced to abandoning the itineraries, but they were a sterling lead that his tenacious disposition was disinclined to relinquish without a fight. Because the Franklin Committee's subpoenas lacked authority in Iowa, he phoned his NCUA contact in DC and implored him to authorize a federal subpoena for the company's flight itineraries. The NCUA official consented to subpoena the charter service's records.

As Caradori awaited the prized itineraries, he was slapped with a federal subpoena that demanded he surrender Franklin evidence to the FBI. Caradori found the subpoena to be particularly vexing, because the Committee routinely surrendered its evidence to state and federal authorities. He nonetheless complied with the subpoena and delivered a bundle of files to Omaha's FBI headquarters.

He glanced at the desk of the FBI agent receiving the files, and he noticed a stack of documents from the charter service in Sioux City, Iowa. Weeks later, Caradori walked into Senator Schmit's office at the statehouse—Schmit was talking on the phone but handed him a large envelope containing the subpoenaed itineraries. Caradori leafed through the itineraries and quickly realized that they had been altered—all the incriminating information relating to the interstate transportation of children had been deleted.

At the onset of an investigation, first-rate investigators make few, if any, assumptions as they're stalking their initial leads. And Caradori's earliest forays into Franklin resulted in his treading metaphorical avenues and alleyways that were fruitful, fallow, or downright bizarre, and his interactions with Michael Casey would encompass all three. In the role of a "freelance journalist," Casey had been delving into Franklin for months, scouring Omaha's seedy underside, accruing contacts and tantalizing tidbits. In fact, he co-authored that early, relatively superficial article about Franklin in the *Village Voice* in February 1989.

Casey had a talent for blarney and drinking vast quantities of liquor, two talents that often accompany and complement each other. In a testament to Casey's gift of blarney, he reportedly convinced the *Los Angeles Times* that he had the underworld connections to locate then-fugitive Patty Hearst, and the paper bankrolled his ill-fated high jinks. Casey also had a talent for absconding with the money of concerned Nebraska citizens and compelling them to give him shelter. He even talked the NSP into footing the bill for a motel, where he freely availed himself of movie rentals. According to the NSP, Casey had a long rap sheet, which included forgery, credit card fraud, and alcohol-related driving infractions, resulting in various convictions and incarcerations.

Caradori first became aware of Casey from one of Jerry Lowe's reports, and he found Casey crashing at the home of an Omaha talk radio personality. Caradori and Ormiston visited the latter's home and talked to both Casey and his host—Casey's Franklin materials were displayed throughout the living room. The radio personality would become disillusioned with Casey after a month or so and give him the boot. After Casey's departure, an employee of the phone company visited the radio personality's home and told him his home phones had been tapped, too.

Because of Casey's ability to spin convincing yet contradictory yarns, his sketchy history is a complex tapestry of truth and falsehoods and, perhaps, grand intentions yet destructive actions. In 1974, after a stint in prison, Casey briefly served as Boys Town's "special projects director," but according to the *World-Herald* he was fired for taking the confidential case histories of residents and sending the files to MGM in an effort to sell a television series based on the orphanage. Though Casey claimed that Boys Town had given him permission to take the files, Father Hupp emphatically stated that permission was never granted. Hupp said Casey picketed the main gate at Boys Town to protest his termination.

Given Casey's dodgy history, Caradori's cultivation of him as a source may seem questionable, but Casey allegedly had information to offer: Casey initially told Caradori that he had access to a videotape showing Larry King engaged in sexual acts with children and had also conducted an audiotape interview with a former Boys Town student who discussed being molested by Peter Citron, an *Omaha World-Herald* columnist and one of the prominent Nebraskans whom Caradori's early sources had tied to King's pandering network. Caradori concluded that the videotape never existed, but he quickly acquired the audiotape of the Boys Town student.

In the interview, the Boys Town student, who was then a senior, told Casey that he met Citron on the Boys Town campus, where Citron was reporting on the filming of a movie about Boys Town—*Miracle of the Heart.* The Boys Town student said that he was fifteen years old when Citron molested him. He maintained that their association lasted three months and that he visited Citron's home on numerous occasions. The student said he initially didn't report Citron to Boys Town staff, but came forward a year later when he became aware that Citron was preying on a second Boys Town student. Though the student talked to Boys Town staff and an OPD officer regarding the molestation, nothing ever came of his allegations. In fact, he spotted Citron on the Boys Town campus even after he had given his information to Boys Town staff.

Caradori's Investigative Reports noted that he made an assiduous effort to talk to the former Boys Town student whom Casey interviewed. After they exchanged a number of phone calls, he finally agreed to meet Caradori. When Caradori and Ormiston showed up at his apartment at the agreed upon time, he was nowhere to be found. But four days later Caradori finally managed to have a face-to-face meeting with the former student.

The young man was ambivalent about granting Caradori a formal interview, because he didn't want his name in the newspaper, and, strangely enough, he was concerned about his disclosures sullying Boys Town's reputation. He told Caradori and Ormiston that he had to give some thought to making a formal statement. Approximately two weeks later he consented to meet with Caradori and Ormiston, but, again, he stood them up. Caradori would eventually receive a phone call from the young man's sister—she relayed to him that her brother was "extremely scared" to talk because the FBI and NSP had been "harassing" him.

In addition to acquiring Casey's interview, Caradori spent a handful of nights rummaging the streets and bars with Casey, but he wrote he found Casey's drunkenness counterproductive to forging further leads. In the second week of September, Caradori made his final throw of the dice with Casey, and it revolved around Franklin's Rosetta Stone: pictures of King and company engaged in sexual acts with children. Casey had fostered a tenuous relationship with one of the photographers employed by King, and Casey claimed he could score illicit pictures for $300. Though Caradori was dubious, his notes make clear he felt risking $300 for the possibility, albeit scant, of acquiring visual proof of King's illicit acts would be acceptable. Casey never came through with the photographs, and Caradori completely disengaged from him. Nebraska law enforcement later accused Caradori of naïveté and of being "duped" by Casey, but the NSP had accommodated Casey in a hotel for three nights and four days, and it hadn't even acquired his audiotape of the Boys Town student.

Caradori had a final, curt encounter with Casey at the Cornhusker Hotel in Lincoln on the morning of November 25, 1989. Caradori received a message from a man lodging at the Cornhusker—he returned the call and the man requested to meet with Caradori concerning a prospective assignment. Caradori told him that he would be driving from Lincoln to Omaha that morning and consented to stop by the Cornhusker at 8:00 A.M. When Caradori arrived at the hotel, he was directed to a suite. The man answering the suite's door introduced himself, and then disclosed that he was a Hollywood producer who was working with Casey on a cinematic treatment of the Franklin story. Following their cursory introduction, Casey walked into the room from an adjoining room. Caradori expressed his irritation to Casey over the $300-picture fiasco and brought the meeting to an abrupt conclusion.

Caradori's contract with the Committee forbade him to discuss the Franklin investigation with publishers and producers, and shortly after his impasse at the Cornhusker, he phoned Committee counsel Berry and explained the circumstances surrounding his "meeting" with the Hollywood producer and Casey. If this had been a typical investigation,

Michael Casey would be merely a handful of footnotes in Caradori's efforts, because Caradori labored incessantly for a year, amassing thousands of leads and interviewing hundreds of individuals. But this wasn't a typical investigation, and Casey's role in the "official" account of the affair would significantly eclipse Caradori's.

On September 22, 1989, a Douglas County judge had imposed a three-to-four-year sentence on the twenty-one-year-old Alisha Owen for two "bad check" convictions: The respective amounts of the two checks were $378.04 and $358.92. A sentence of three to four years for checks totaling $736.96 would only be the beginning of Owen's bizarre odyssey through the Douglas County judiciary—an odyssey that is perhaps unparalleled in American history.

Casey had met Owen earlier, when both were patients at Omaha's St. Joseph Hospital's psychiatric ward. Owen had been admitted for "depression" in September 1988—Casey later boasted to a friend that he feigned a psychiatric illness to cultivate a friendship with Owen at St. Joseph's. Casey, however, had a long history of alcohol abuse, and individuals who abuse alcohol and other substances frequently opt to dry out in psychiatric hospitals. If Casey had admitted himself to St. Joseph's solely for the purpose of developing a friendship with Owen, it's rather odd that he didn't leave until about a week after Owen's discharge from St. Joseph's.

Psychiatric patients who aren't in the throes of psychosis, like Owen and Casey, have a tendency to congregate, forming bonds that last throughout the course of their hospitalization and perhaps afterward, but Owen contends that her interactions with Casey were limited. Upon her discharge, though, she did give Casey the phone number of her parents' home in Omaha.

Owen was harboring secrets, and she thought that revealing those secrets would jeopardize the welfare of herself and her family—she was resolved to divulge her secrets to no one, including Casey and St. Joseph's personnel. But Owen's secrets were severely straining her emotional well-being, and she attempted suicide two weeks after her psychiatric discharge, landing in St. Joseph's for a second time.

In addition to being extremely troubled, Owen had a bench warrant pending for bad-check charges. Law enforcement initially requested a hold on Owen, but then inexplicably dropped the arrest warrant, per-plexing St. Joseph's personnel. After Owen's second discharge from St. Joseph's, she continued to live at her parents' house, even though she felt her secrets were imperiling her family.

Casey phoned Owen at her parents' home following her second hos-pitalization. He was freeloading at a friend's house and offered her its vacant studio apartment. She accepted his offer but only slept in the apartment for a handful of nights. Owen quickly concluded that residing in the studio would be potentially hazardous to her health—the home-owner was an associate of Alan Baer, a prominent Omaha millionaire whom Caradori would link to King's pandering network.

Since Casey initially met Owen at St. Joseph's, the Franklin Credit Union had been raided and sordid insinuations were surfacing—Casey had taken a budding interest in the Franklin scandal and questioned Owen because of her evident familiarity with Omaha's gay community. Owen told me that her brief stay with Casey was the first and only time they ever discussed Franklin, emphasizing that she never revealed her involvement to him.

However, she felt grateful to Casey for providing her with shelter and tossed out two names—Troy Boner and Danny King—stating that they were enmeshed in Franklin. Owen felt confident that Casey would never find Boner or King, and she was right: Casey never made contact with either one.

Within two or three weeks of departing Casey's friend's digs, Owen and a young man she met at St. Joseph's would fall in love and flee Nebraska. He wrote a slew of bad checks, purchased a car, and they em-barked on a cross-country trek. Their love fest came to a screeching halt in Greeley, Colorado.

They had run out of money and started writing bad checks. The couple then had a domestic spat, and Owen landed in Weld County Jail. As Alisha Owen languished in the Colorado jail, she would be arraigned for six bad checks, totaling $582.63. The twenty-year-old Owen, overwhelmed and demoralized, phoned her parents. Owen's mother, Donna, then contacted the OPD and informed an officer about her daughter's circumstances in Colorado, but, to her utter astonishment, the officer phoned a week later and said Nebraska

wouldn't extradite her daughter, even though Colorado had consented to her extradition.

When Owen was released from the Weld County Jail in the middle
of May, her parents provided her with a one-way bus ticket to Omaha. Owen chose not to reside at her parents' home when she arrived
in Omaha, perplexing them. She decided to take refuge with a grade
school friend—the two had limited contact in recent years, and Owen
thought she might have a measure of invisibility at her friend's. In early
July, Owen's mother received a call from the OPD—she was instructed
to transport her daughter to OPD headquarters. Because Nebraska had
elected earlier not to extradite Owen, her mother was confounded when
Douglas County opted to incarcerate her.

By July 1989, Douglas County's law enforcement and its judiciary had
already started to display a puzzling schizophrenia concerning Owen.
When she was hospitalized at St. Joseph's, law enforcement requested a
hold on her because of outstanding warrants but later dropped the hold.
In May, Owen's mother was informed that she wouldn't be extradited to
Nebraska; yet after she voluntarily returned to Omaha, a judge's directive
that gave her the option of making bail was disregarded. Moreover, she
would eventually receive three to fours years in prison for bouncing two
checks that totaled a whopping $736.96.

Caradori later said that "Alisha Owen" was just one of numerous names
he had scribbled on a "scratch pad" while talking with Michael Casey,
and he had no idea whether she was a hot lead or a dead end. His Investigative Reports indicate that he initially contacted personnel at the
Nebraska Facility for Women at York on October 11, 1989, but nearly
three weeks elapsed before he made the trek to York, which illustrates
that he consigned Owen to the status of a low priority lead. If Caradori
had thought Owen was a surefire lead, he likely would have made a beeline to York.

On Monday, October 30, Caradori and Ormiston arrived at York
around 7:00 P.M. Earlier that afternoon, Caradori had phoned the
Associate Warden and requested to meet Owen in a location that offered a modicum of privacy, and prison personnel escorted Caradori
and Ormiston to a conference room in the prison basement. Their

day had been consumed chasing charter-service leads, and they were exhausted.

A pair of guards then ushered Owen into the room, and Caradori and Ormiston introduced themselves to her. Owen stood 5'4" and weighed 150 pounds in her brown state-issued prison garb. She had a thick mane of curly brown hair and hazel eyes. Her rounded face, tentative voice, and mannerisms had the qualities of a timid teenager, even though she had turned twenty-one the month before, and her adolescence had been a detour to her own private hell.

Though Caradori was gracious to Owen, he quickly cut to the chase. She was initially hesitant to discuss her past, but Caradori and Ormiston conveyed an integrity that allayed her suspicions and fears. Over the course of the next three hours, she confessed to her involvement in illicit acts, and specified perpetrators whose names had repeatedly surfaced throughout Caradori's investigation. At the conclusion of the interview, Caradori asked Owen if she would be willing to make a formal statement the following week. Owen said she needed to sound out her parents, because she felt that her cooperation would potentially endanger members of her family.

After Owen discussed her past with Caradori and Ormiston on Monday night, she was plagued by nightmares for two nights. On Wednesday, she requested a psychiatric consult—she felt that patient confidentiality statutes permitted her to safely disclose her Franklin participation to the prison's psychiatrist. When she entered the psychiatrist's office, she insisted that he turn off his tape recorder and not take notes. Once he acquiesced to her requests, and assured her of his confidentiality, she opened up. The psychiatrist, taken aback, insisted that Owen discuss her situation with the warden. Owen subsequently set out for the warden's office, and, after the warden granted her the same assurances as the psychiatrist, she told him about her history and her dilemma of whether or not she should grant Caradori a formal interview.

A memo from York's warden to the Nebraska Attorney General's Office corroborated Owen's account of her visit to the prison's psychiatrist and then to the warden. The warden wrote that on the morning of November 1, 1989, he was "advised" by York's psychiatrist that he "needed" to talk to inmate Owen. The warden inquired about the nature of the psychiatrist's concerns, but he wouldn't disclose the content of their conversation.

Owen, the warden continued, explained to him "she had been a witness and victim of child abuse and numerous other illegal activities by ... suspects in the Franklin Credit Union investigation." Owen told the warden that the suspects in the investigation had "considerable power and influence," and she had anxiety about her safety at the prison—she also said their authority might "extend into the prison and possibly affect" the warden. The warden assured Owen that he was "not at all inclined to be receptive to bribes," and he noted that Owen "seemed to be accepting of that sentiment and expressed relief that she had talked with me about her problems."

Later in the week, Owen's mother and father visited her at York—Owen and her mother then took a walk in the prison's yard. Owen told her mother that she was personally mixed up in sordid events now coming to light. Her mother inquired if she had direct knowledge of child abuse, and she replied that she had been one of the abused. Though Owen's mother was dumbfounded by her daughter's disclosures, she finally had an explanation of her daughter's peculiar behavior, starting at the age of fourteen. As Owen and her mother cried, her mother asked her daughter why she hadn't come to her parents for help. Owen said that even though the perpetrators were too powerful for her parents to challenge, she knew they would never have backed down—she was convinced her parents would have been murdered.

Alisha Owen phoned Caradori on November 4 and consented to be interviewed. Caradori copied a myriad of pictures, including those of the alleged perpetrators, and a lawyer from Berry's law firm drafted a "waiver" to be signed by Owen and Caradori and notarized by Ormiston, a notary public. The waiver clearly stated that Owen's statements were made freely and voluntarily without promises or threats, and she was under oath during her statement and would be subject to prosecution for perjured statements. The waiver also denoted that Caradori did not have the authority to grant immunity. On the morning of November 7, Caradori and Ormiston arrived at York and started videotaping Owen's statement around 11:30 A.M. After a series of respites and breaks, they finished at 10:00 P.M.

Owen came from a deeply religious family. Her parents, Al and Donna, had been married nearly twenty-five years, and Al was the proprietor of a modest construction company. Al and Donna had four kids—Alisha was the second oldest. Owen's parents enrolled her in a strict parochial school, which she attended from kindergarten through the sixth grade—she entered public school in seventh grade. At the age of thirteen or so Owen started developing a rebellious streak. It's not uncommon for teenagers from religious homes to rebel and run with the "wrong crowd," but unfortunately Owen wasn't streetwise enough to distinguish the wrong crowd from an evil horde.

Owen told Caradori and Ormiston that she was fourteen years old when she allegedly met a group of Boys Town students, including Jeff Hubbell, at an outdoor dance in August of 1983—Hubbell invited Owen to a party the following Friday night. She said Hubbell declared that the party would be a flood of alcohol and a blizzard of cocaine. On Friday night, Hubbell and a "friend" picked up Owen and drove her to the Twin Towers. They arrived at the party between 9:30 P.M. and 10:00 P.M.

The Twin Towers apartment and the party were a world removed from Owen's working-class background and prior life experiences. The living room had a fully stocked bar, plush furniture, and a big screen television—a pornographic movie, featuring two adolescent males, spilled from the television. Lines of cocaine were splayed on a mirrored table next to a maroon couch, and the living room's large windows offered a spectacular nightscape of downtown Omaha. The party consisted of six adults and twenty minors. At the time, Owen said, she didn't have a clue about the identities of the adults—she would later learn they included Larry King and Alan Baer. She was also introduced to an older man named "Rob."

Though Owen felt uncomfortable, she also said she felt a sense of exhilaration and sophistication. She did cocaine for the first time and was even allowed to "play bartender"—she became increasingly intoxicated. The adults then watched the minors play the "501 game," which involved the minors unbuttoning each other's jeans with their teeth and toes. Owen made it clear to Caradori and Ormiston that she didn't partake in explicit sexual acts at the first party, even though she observed adults fondling minors and noticed some of the adults and minors shuffling in and out of the bedrooms. Owen didn't make it home until 1:30

A.M.–her curfew was 12:30 A.M. She received a scolding from her mother but wasn't grounded.

Over the next three or four days, Owen attempted to sort out her Friday night at the Twin Towers. She had previously fooled around with alcohol here and there, and also fooled around with guys to the point of heavy petting, but the party at the Twin Towers was far afield from her previous acts of rebellion, and she felt conflicted. As Owen struggled to make sense of this new reality, Troy Boner, a boy she met at the party, phoned her and talked about the great time they had.

His call ultimately convinced her to attend her second Twin Towers party the following Friday night. She asked her parents if she could spend Friday night at a girlfriend's house and they consented—Owen's parents would later discover that her friend's mother was very lax about curfews. In addition to King, Baer, and Rob, she said *World-Herald* columnist Peter Citron attended the party. Owen became extremely intoxicated, drinking champagne and shots of cognac, as the kids played the "501 game." She stood up and stumbled to the bathroom—she said she accidentally entered one of the bedrooms and saw a pubescent boy performing oral sex on Larry King.

At one point, Owen alleges, Rob asked her to undo his pants zipper with her teeth. Owen balked at Rob's request, and she was teased and taunted for being a "little girl." After succumbing to the taunts, she knelt before Rob, who placed a cushion under her knees so she could reach his groin. Owen told Caradori and Ormiston that quiet fell over the room as everyone watched to see if she could unzip Rob's fly with her teeth. As she managed to unzip Rob's pants, he ran his fingers through her hair. Owen said that Rob then sat in a chair, holding a glass of cognac, and invited her to sit on his lap. She sat on his lap, and he caressed her breasts and thighs—Owen thought Rob was "really nice." After Rob left the party, an inebriated Owen lost her virginity to Troy Boner. In retrospect, Owen thought she was "supposed" to lose her virginity that night so she would then be sexually accessible to the group.

Owen told Caradori and Ormiston that she attended her third party at the Twin Towers three weeks later, and Rob showed up about an hour after she arrived—she felt that Rob had probably been called when she arrived. The gathering that night was sparse—adults and kids trickled into the bedrooms, leaving Owen and Rob alone in the living room. Owen was wearing a leather jumpsuit that was "ten years too old" for her, and Rob maneuvered her onto his lap. He said that she was pretty and indicated to Owen that he knew she had lost her virginity; he felt her breasts and genitalia. Rob asked Owen if her parents knew she was no longer a virgin—she felt mortified by his question because she thought that he might tell her parents about her promiscuity.

Owen said that Rob started unzipping her jumpsuit, and she implored him to stop, but he clenched her wrist and twisted it. As Rob removed her clothing, he continued talking—he whispered that she had a "pretty" mouth and then inquired if she knew the meaning of "fellatio." After Rob had her repeatedly say "fellatio," he said he would teach her the word's meaning. When she was nude, he stood up, put a cushion under her knees, and told her to unzip his pants. She unzipped his fly, and then he grabbed her head and had her perform oral sex on him—he also pinched her breasts. After the act, she ran to the bathroom, vomited, and began to cry.

She emerged from the bathroom crying, and Rob gave her a gentle hug and expressed to her that he was sorry. As Rob comforted her, he said that he would take her to lunch on Wednesday afternoon. He also instructed her to pick out a dress at the downtown department store owned by Alan Baer on Monday and put it on "hold." Owen was given a ride home that night by a couple of the party's attendees, and one stated that Rob was the Chief of the Omaha Police Department—she instantly feared that Rob would tell her parents about their encounter.

As Owen talked about her "relationship" with OPD Chief Robert Wadman to Caradori and Ormiston, she occasionally stared at the floor and also broke down in tears. At one point, she burst out crying and Caradori briefly stopped the interview. When the interview proceeded, Owen said that on the following Monday, after school, she had wandered to Alan Baer's department store and found a dress that she liked, filled out a receipt, and gave it to the clerk, whom she described as a fifty-year-old woman with glasses and dyed auburn hair. Caradori asked her a number of questions about the dress: She replied that it was a size ten, "black, lace dress" and cost $115.

Owen told Caradori and Ormiston that Wadman picked her up across the street from Central High School on Wednesday at 1:00 P.M. in a brown compact car. He drove her to the chic French Café in downtown Omaha—Owen disclosed that the Café's owners and hostess frequented King's parties. She said that the French Café was generally closed in the afternoons, but the hostess guided her and Wadman to one of the Café's small side rooms. Once they were seated at a table, she said, Wadman handed her a wrapped package that contained the dress she had picked out on Monday, and then they ordered lunch.

Owen ordered a crepe dish that she didn't like and just picked at it. After lunch, Owen said, Wadman offered to show her the café's wine cellar, and she followed him through the kitchen and down a stairway to the left—she told Caradori and Ormiston that the basement was "rickety and yucky" and there wasn't a wine cellar. Owen uttered that she was afraid of being raped—she "tried to think of anything else but what was happening" as she gazed at the basement ceiling's molding.

Wadman, Owen continued, requested that she put the dress on in front of him. She initially balked at undressing, but he said that she had a beautiful body and she didn't have to be ashamed. She also felt like a "heel" for not immediately acquiescing to his request, because the dress was so expensive. As she disrobed and started slipping into the dress, she recalled, Wadman caressed her breasts, pulled down his pants and started to masturbate. Owen told Caradori and Ormiston that Wadman wanted to ejaculate on her, but she jumped back—Wadman was incensed that she had recoiled.

Owen said that she attended a Twin Towers party two weeks later and Wadman eventually showed up. She was afraid of him and started to leave, but Larry King's enforcer, also named Larry, a muscular African American in his early twenties, said, "You're not leaving!"—Owen didn't know his last name and called him "Larry the Kid."

Owen quickly found herself in over her head—she worried about retribution against her family, and she understandably felt she couldn't turn to the police for help. Larry the Kid and Larry King repeatedly terrorized Owen by threatening her life and the lives of her family members—Larry the Kid occasionally slapped Owen around and raped her. She stressed that her fear of retribution was very real—she had heard of kids who were either sold or murdered. The threats were counterbalanced by financial rewards: Owen regularly received funds as a drug courier.

Owen said she began to meet Wadman on sporadic Wednesday afternoons, engage in group sexual encounters, and also flew with King to Los Angeles and Kansas City to be pandered as an underage prostitute—Owen described extremely sadistic abuse on the out-of-town trips.

Owen also discussed the circumstances of her incarceration with Caradori and Ormiston. Shortly before the Franklin Credit Union was raided, she said, Larry King and Alan Baer insisted that Owen and Troy Boner relocate to California—Owen and Boner had become lovers and were living together. They were now too old to be pandered to King's pedophilic clientele, and their detailed knowledge of the network posed a significant risk with the potential heat that might follow the Franklin raid.

Boner had Owen write a flurry of checks to feed his cocaine habit, and Baer agreed to cover the checks when they left for California. Owen, however, began to distrust Boner, and she worried that a trip to California might be the pretext for her ending up in a body bag. She decided not to leave Nebraska; so Baer pulled the plug on his financial support, resulting in an avalanche of bounced checks. Her intuition not to trust Boner would prove to be well founded.

Caradori and Ormiston interviewed Owen on two other occasions. After Caradori videotaped Owen for a second time on November 21, he started to search for Troy Boner. On November 24, Caradori located Boner's mother, who was living in Council Bluffs, Iowa, a short jaunt from Omaha across the Missouri River. She worked nights as a nurse, and Caradori and Ormiston waited until roughly 8:00 P.M. before they knocked on her front door. They introduced themselves, and Boner's mother eventually invited them into her kitchen, where an hour-long discussion ensued. She said that her son routinely bounced between California and Omaha, and she would contact him on Caradori's behalf. She also mentioned that she felt her son was "carrying a great weight on his shoulders" that he refused to discuss with her.

Later that night, Caradori met with a confidential informant in Omaha who disclosed the names of Boys Town students who were allegedly involved with Larry King. After their meeting, he drove home to Lincoln, arriving early Sunday morning. At 4:40 A.M., Caracorp's answering service directed a call from Troy Boner to Caradori's home. An exhausted Caradori and Boner spoke for nearly an hour. A seemingly paranoid Boner fired questions at Caradori non-stop.

He initially asked if Caradori had any affiliations with law enforcement—Caradori replied that he was employed by the Franklin Committee and that he had no affiliations with state or federal law enforcement. Boner inquired who had informed Caradori about him—Caradori replied that he received the information from an inmate in a correctional facility, but didn't reveal his source to be Alisha Owen. Boner then divulged to Caradori that he had, in fact, suffered abuse, and it had left him deeply scarred emotionally. Caradori insisted that they not discuss his circumstances over the phone, and Boner consented to meet Caradori at Boner's mother's house in Council Bluffs the following night at 6:00 P.M.

Boner called Caradori back approximately ten minutes after their initial conversation. He had phoned the Lincoln Police Department, and the officer fielding his call stated that the department didn't employ Caradori. Boner said he felt "satisfied" that Caradori wasn't a cop and, again, consented to their meeting. Boner then phoned Caradori at 8:00 A.M. and indicated they could meet that morning—they agreed to meet at a Denny's Restaurant in Bellevue, Nebraska at 10:30 A.M.

As Caradori and Ormiston waited for Boner in the Denny's parking lot, he pulled up in a green Gran Torino that was driven by his mother's boyfriend. The twenty-two-year-old Boner cautiously emerged from the car and shook hands with Caradori and Ormiston. Boner, 6'3", weighing 200 pounds, wore a patent leather jacket, a T-shirt, and designer jeans—his T-shirt had a silk-screen of The Cure's *Love Song* album.

Boner was noticeably agitated, and the restaurant was too congested to confer a feeling of privacy, so Caradori suggested one nearby. Boner rode with Caradori and Ormiston, but he had his mother's boyfriend tail them. His mother's boyfriend hung out in the parking lot as Boner, Caradori, and Ormiston entered the second restaurant. The three situated themselves around a table and talked in "generalities" for five or ten minutes before Caradori dropped a succession of details that were designed to convey that his information was "on target." After half an hour, Boner decided to grant Caradori a formal, videotaped statement.

When they departed the restaurant, they proceeded to the home of Boner's mother's boyfriend, where Boner and his fiancée were living.

Boner packed a week's worth of clothes, and told his fiancée and his mother's boyfriend that he was accompanying Caradori and Ormiston to Lincoln. Boner's fiancée seemed to understand the import of his decision, but his mother's boyfriend was uncomfortable. Caradori pledged that Boner would be safe, and he handed his mother's boyfriend a business card, assuring him that either he or Boner's mother could phone him anytime.

Driving to Lincoln, Caradori would find out that Boner and Owen came from very different backgrounds: Boner's father had spent years in prison for various offenses, and he didn't have the intact nuclear family of Owen. Though Boner's father had been absent from the family for years, his mother and grandmother still managed to impart a sense of family to Boner and his siblings. Troy was the oldest of four children.

Caradori, Ormiston, and Boner made the hour trek from Omaha to Lincoln and stopped at a Residence Inn. Caradori left Ormiston and Boner in the hotel room and made a foray to pick up pizza and videotapes. After eating, Ormiston read the waiver prepared by Berry's law firm—it was then signed by Boner and Caradori and notarized by Ormiston. Caradori and Ormiston interviewed Boner from 3:35 P.M. until 10:22 P.M., taking breaks and respites. The next morning Boner was interviewed for an additional two hours.

During Boner's videotaped statements, he corroborated Owen's information on numerous perpetrators and many events. Caradori also noted a number of discrepancies concerning the dates and precise locations of the events they mentioned. Owen had admitted to drug and alcohol abuse during her teenage years, and Boner was a self-confessed drug addict. Caradori felt that their years of incessant sexual abuse and their drug-addled memories made it extremely difficult for them to recall the precise dates and locations of events that had transpired years earlier, whereas the events themselves would have been easier to remember.

Among King's crew, Troy Boner's nickname was "Mr. Hollywood" because of his movie-star good looks and fashionably cool persona. But as Caradori started to interview Boner, his cool demeanor began to crack. Caradori's questions required a degree of introspection, and as Boner was confronted with the horrors of his life, he became increasingly uncomfortable. At certain points in the interview, Boner seemed to look back on the carnage of his life with shock and dismay.

Boner recalled that a friend of his introduced him to Alan Baer in August of 1983. He said he was seventeen years old when he first met Baer, but his date of birth was January 16, 1967; so in actuality he would have been sixteen years old in August of 1983. Boner related that he had a number of paid sexual encounters with Baer at his Twin Towers apartment before meeting Larry King.

Boner said that Baer had given pictures of him (Boner) to King prior to Boner's initially meeting King at a gay bar. Boner claimed that King, who introduced himself as "Chuck," approached him and tucked a $100 bill in his shirt pocket. King then took him to dinner, and they drove to a Red Lion Inn—Boner alleged that King performed oral sex on him, and gave him an additional $50.

After their initial sexual encounter, King put up Boner at a Travel Lodge Inn for three weeks. Boner said that King would routinely stop by in the afternoons to have anal sex with him. He also alleged that King was fond of being urinated on. Boner said King eventually provided him with a furnished apartment in Omaha—King regularly visited the apartment to have sex with Boner or for sexual liaisons with other minors.

Boner also spoke about his relationship with Owen: He confessed that he had taken Owen's virginity and also stated he had introduced her to Chief Wadman, but he recalled that their introduction occurred at a party in the Woodman Tower, rather than the Twin Towers. Boner confirmed Owen's alleged Wednesday afternoon trysts with Wadman and even named the same hotels that she specified. Boner said that Owen was often threatened and even "slapped around" by one of King's henchmen to ensure her compliance with Wadman and others in King's network.

Boner, like Owen, discussed being on interstate flights to be pandered as an underage prostitute and being used as a drug courier. Boner and Owen both mentioned making a joint drug run to Los Angeles on United Airlines for Larry King. Regarding a second drug run, Boner backed Owen's account, saying they flew to Los Angeles on a commercial flight to make a drug buy for Alan Baer—both Boner and Owen mentioned that they scored "$4,000 worth of cocaine" for him.

Boner, again corroborating Owen's allegations, discussed a private charter flight to California that included Larry King, Owen, Danny King (no relation to Larry King), two prepubescent boys, and himself. Boner and Owen remembered a stopover in Denver and then flying to Southern California. Owen, who admitted to be being "bombed," recalled Larry King departing at a "small airport in California" with one of the prepubescent boys as the others proceeded to an airport near Pasadena—Owen speculated that the boy had been either sold or murdered.

Boner, who confessed he was "flying on coke," told a slightly different tale: Everyone departed the plane at the airport near Pasadena, and he said that Owen and Danny King were picked up by a fat, older white male. He told Caradori and Ormiston that he then accompanied Larry King in a rental car as King dropped off each of the little boys at two different locations. As Caradori questioned Boner about the two little boys, he had great difficulty elaborating—he repeatedly turned his head to the right, sighed loudly, and made a number of nervous gestures. Boner ultimately said he believed the two younger kids had been "sold."

In Southern California, Boner alleged, Larry King pandered Owen and Danny King to a pair of sadistic pedophiles, again corroborating Owen—she had said that she and Danny King had been served to a couple of sadistic pedophiles in Pasadena. Boner related that he and Larry King picked up Owen and Danny King following their nightmarish ordeal. According to Boner, Owen "looked and smelled" terrible and Danny King wanted to "go back and kill the guy." On the return flight to Omaha, Owen refused to talk to him. Boner said he felt like reporting Larry King after the trip, but he was afraid to contact law enforcement.

Boner also described taking commercial flights to Los Angeles: On one Los Angeles trip, he said, King arranged for him to have a tryst with a prominent producer, whose name he mentioned. On a second trip to Los Angeles, he was driven to the Hollywood home of a man named "Henry," who tied him up and played various "sexual games" with him. In addition, Boner discussed extremely sadistic child-sex orgies that corresponded to the sadistic abuse endured by Owen. He talked about a party at the Woodman Tower, and alleged that he was forced to have oral sex with his "best friend" Danny King and that Larry King then had anal sex with him and put out a cigarette on his buttocks.

Boner confessed to Caradori that he had trepidations about returning to the Omaha area, so Caradori rented a small apartment in Lincoln for him. Caradori later said that Boner was accustomed to living the high life, even though his mindset often resembled that of a confused adolescent. Boner boasted of $1,000 suits and $500 shoes, but he had never washed his own clothes. When Caradori took Boner out to eat, Caradori typically ordered a cheeseburger; Boner would order a T-bone steak.

After Boner's second interview, Caradori visited Berry's office later that morning to give him an update—Berry told Caradori to stick around because Senator Schmit wanted to talk to him. When Schmit arrived, he expressed his concerns to Caradori and Berry about the FBI starting to scrutinize his businesses. They also discussed whether or not they should "go public" with Caradori's evidence or proceed directly to Washington, DC, because they felt that influential agencies of both state and federal law enforcement in Nebraska were corrupt and antagonistic to their objectives. Caradori's Investigative Report recorded that the meeting yielded only uncertainty regarding their next move.

The next day, Caradori and Boner drove to Omaha and proceeded to Danny King's apartment. Boner knocked on the front door as Caradori stood next to him. Danny King let Boner into the apartment, and Boner briefly explained Caradori's intentions to King—Caradori noted that Boner and Danny King were alone for "two minutes" before he entered the residence. Both the apartment and King were in a state of disarray. King was admittedly recovering from an LSD spree, and the sudden arrival of Boner and then Caradori had shocked him like a stun gun—he was paranoid and frightened.

The twenty-year-old King—short, frail, and skinny—had a blanched, boyish face, and, because of a congenital throat condition, he spoke in a guttural rasp. Danny King had a single, nomadic mother, and he grew up as a wild child with very little supervision, whereas Owen came from an intact nuclear family and Boner came from a semi-intact family. King also lacked the native intelligence and even nominal self-esteem of Owen and Boner.

King was unemployed and in the process of being evicted—Caradori had him pack up all of his belongings, which fit into a bulging vinyl suitcase. As the three climbed into Caradori's car, King started volunteering details about his abuse, but Caradori politely asked him to refrain from discussing the subject. During the drive back to Lincoln, King sat silently in the front seat, and Boner, sitting in the back seat, occasionally reassured him: "Everything is going to be alright. Nobody is going to hurt us anymore...."

Caradori, Boner and King arrived at the offices of Caracorp at approximately 11:30 P.M. Caradori then "indicated" that Boner should return to his apartment, a few blocks from Caracorp. Before Caradori drove King to the Residence Inn, he asked Boner if he and King had discussed any details of their experiences during that day, and Boner replied that they hadn't. King then asked Boner, "Did you tell them everything?" and Boner responded, "Yes, I told them everything."

Caradori met Ormiston at the Residence Inn the following morning. After breakfast with Danny King, they proceeded to King's room. As King seated himself in front of the video camera, he became visibly frightened and agitated. He told Caradori and Ormiston that the statements of Owen and Boner were fabricated, and he wanted to leave. Caradori talked to King, attempting to assuage his concerns, and King confessed that he was afraid of retribution, disclosing that he had been threatened just three and a half weeks earlier. After King's acute fears abated and he relaxed, Ormiston read the waiver, and it was then signed by King and Caradori and notarized by Ormiston.

King said Boner initially introduced him to Alan Baer in the fall of 1983, when he was fourteen years old—he maintained that he accompanied Boner to Baer's Twin Towers apartment, and the three drank schnapps. King claimed that he didn't have sex with Baer at their first meeting—Boner also said that Danny King and Baer didn't have sex on that occasion. King disclosed that he took the bus to Baer's Twin Towers apartment approximately two weeks later. He and Baer again knocked back schnapps, and Baer performed oral sex on Danny King—afterward Baer gave him fifty dollars. King said he then started having sexual liaisons with Baer on a weekly basis.

Danny King recalled meeting Larry King at Baer's apartment around April 1984, when Larry King took him into Baer's bedroom and allegedly had anal sex with him. Danny King said that he pleaded with Larry King to stop, since it was hurting him; so Larry King had Danny King perform oral sex on him. Danny King spit out Larry King's semen, he said, prompting Larry King to smack him on the side of the head with his shoe. Danny King also discussed the party at Woodman Tower where Larry King forced him and Boner to have sex together, corroborating Boner.

Danny King, Troy Boner, and Alisha Owen all reported accompanying Larry King and the two little boys on a private flight to Southern California. But Danny King remembered being delivered to a party at a house where he was required to perform oral sex on a man, instead of the hotel mentioned by Owen. King corroborated Owen on a flight to Kansas City, even though his description of the events differed slightly from Owen's. He confirmed that Larry King delivered him and Owen to a hotel with a waterfall. Danny King described three men initially showing up at their room, and Owen said a third man turned up later. A second discrepancy noted by Caradori was that Owen said one man molested her and two men molested King, whereas King claimed that two men molested Owen and one man molested him. Danny King also corroborated Owen's claim that Larry King's primary henchman was named Larry.

Caradori noted that Danny King was very disoriented and had difficulties remembering that January followed December—I would eventually locate Danny King, and I, too, would find him extremely confused, befuddled, and possessed of a flawed recollection on even relatively straightforward events.

Caradori videotaped Danny King for approximately six hours with periodic breaks, and then drove him to the apartment he rented for Boner. Caradori was a meticulous investigator, and he realized the importance of corroborating their videotaped statements. So he spent the next two days shuttling King to Omaha and Council Bluffs to identify the numerous locations he had mentioned throughout his statement. As Caradori and King navigated a major Omaha thoroughfare, King identified the Twin Towers and pinpointed Baer's apartment balcony. Caradori also had an associate shuttle Boner to Omaha and Council Bluffs for the same purpose—they subsequently photographed the locations named by Boner and Danny King. After accruing scores of photos, Caradori had Boner and King separately identify them, and they consistently corroborated each other on the photographed locations.

Interestingly, the allegations of Owen and Danny King corroborated Shawneta Moore on one perpetrator, even though they had never met her. Moore had told Irl Carmean that an administrator for the Fort Calhoun school system accompanied Larry King to one of the child-sex parties she attended, and both Owen and Danny King identified the same individual as frequenting King's sex parties. Moreover, Owen, Boner, and Danny King corroborated Eulice Washington on the chartered flights. Owen and Boner also corroborated Washington on the entanglement of Boys Town's students in King's pandering network.

By mid-December of 1989, Caradori had accrued approximately twenty-one hours of victim testimony from Owen, Boner, and King. His Investigative Reports noted that the evidence he was amassing had begun to create dissonance between him and the Committee and also spark confusion within the Committee itself. As the Committee members were confronted with Caradori's mounting evidence, they became increasingly perplexed about where to turn because of their distrust of state and federal law enforcement. Unrequited overtures to the US Attorney General's Office further confounded the Committee members. Caradori's Investigative Reports also indicated that he was extremely concerned for the welfare of Owen, Boner, and King. In addition to renting an apartment for Boner and King, he purchased food and various toiletry articles for them.

In a letter to Berry, he acknowledged that the victims he videotaped represented a "small portion" of the case, but he felt that the Committee had a responsibility to look out for their welfare. He requested that they receive physicals, counseling, and "secured living arrangements." Caradori mentioned that Owen was particularly vulnerable and emphasized that her cooperation should not be made public until she was in a safe environment that met both the needs of the Committee and also her obligations to the State of Nebraska. He stressed that the victims had never communicated their experiences before, and, therefore, he had established a trusting bond with them that needed to be nurtured and free of "surprises." Caradori concluded the letter by stating that his "requests may seem unusual," but the financial resources of the perpetrators and the "possible political ramifications" made it necessary for the Committee's moves to be "cautious, well planned, and expedient."

Caradori's investigation was quickly sideswiped by one of the surprises he had feared in his letter to Committee counsel Berry. Two NSP investigators made a visit to Owen at York on December 15, and their visit elicited an alarming phone call from her. Caradori immediately phoned York's warden, who confirmed that two NSP investigators had interviewed Owen throughout the afternoon. After Caradori spoke to both Schmit and Berry, he drove to York that night, but he arrived too late in the evening for York personnel to grant him entry into the prison.

Caradori drove to York again the following day and talked to Owen. She said that the investigators had arrived at York in the morning, conspicuously ate lunch in the cafeteria with the inmates, and then interviewed Owen in the warden's office. According to Owen, the NSP investigators were menacing to her, and they degraded Caradori. She told Caradori the investigators declared that the Franklin Committee didn't exist.

Caradori checked the prison's logs and noticed that two NSP investigators signed in at 9:29 A.M. and signed out at 3:15 P.M. The Committee had yet to hand over the videotaped statements of the victims to state and federal law enforcement; Caradori surmised that Owen's whereabouts had been gleaned through wiretaps. For Caradori, the NSP's sandbagging of Owen would be merely the first of many "surprises."

Caradori feared that the NSP investigators' salient presence at York and their interrogation of Owen in the warden's office would set off rumors of her being a jailhouse snitch—six weeks later three inmates attacked her in the prison's shower room. The State Ombudsman's Office, which investigates citizens' complaints against state administrative agencies, conducted an inquiry into the assault on Owen, and it concluded that the attack "was motivated, in part, because some of her fellow inmates thought that she might be an informant against the women at York."

The Ombudsman investigators wrote the following about Owen: "We did not find, in our dealings with her in this matter, that she engaged in any exaggeration or magnification of the facts; nor did we detect any attempt on her part to stretch the truth or to falsely color the facts surrounding the assault upon her." Shortly after the assault, Owen was placed in "24 hour lock up" segregation for her own "protection"—she would remain in solitary for nearly two years.

Three days after the NSP investigators harassed Owen at York, the Committee held a press conference in Lincoln, announcing that it would hand over its twenty-one hours of videotaped testimony to Nebraska's Attorney General and the US Attorney for Nebraska. The Committee also publicized a letter that would accompany the tapes. The *Lincoln Journal* quoted Berry commenting on the letter: "Our letter was to show that we're keeping a lot of options open," he said. "The fact of turning this information over is not our swan song. We're not removing ourselves from the quest."

The letter itself stated, "It is the opinion of committee members that the activities described and the personalities involved scream out for action whether the statute of limitations problems are involved or not." The letter also alluded to the possibility of others covering up crimes: "The members of the committee are dismayed by the fact that no state or federal investigative bodies interviewed any of the witnesses we have, even though they were discovered by our investigative efforts after a fairly short time and with a very small budget."

Perhaps Attorney General Robert Spire forgot that his office initially refused to honor the Committee's subpoenas when he responded to the letter: "There has been a high degree of cooperation all along between the Franklin Committee and the Attorney General's Office, and I'm sure that will continue." Spire then criticized the Committee for implying a cover-up and defended the efforts of state and federal law enforcement. "The letter in effect is saying that the FBI and State Patrol have not done a good job," he said. "I do not think that's fair.... They've been very thorough." He then promised that the State Patrol would "get right on it." He neglected to mention that the NSP had jumped "right on it" three days earlier, harassing Owen at York.

After the Committee held its press conference, it directed Caradori to condense the statements of Alisha Owen, Troy Boner, and Danny King into a five-hour video, which it showed to select officials within Nebraska's judiciary and law enforcement. The officials included Assistant Attorney General William Howland, an NSP official, the Sheriffs of Douglas and Butler counties, and a Douglas County judge. The Committee hoped to marshal support from the officials before surrendering the tapes to state and federal law enforcement. The Sheriff of Douglas

County would, in fact, tell the *Lincoln Journal-Star* that he found the victims' testimony on the videotapes to be credible.

The Committee submitted its twenty-one hours of videotaped statements to the offices of Nebraska's Attorney General and the US Attorney on December 27, 1989. Spire and US Attorney Ronald Lahners were now forced to act—the toothpaste had managed to squirt out of the tube. They no longer had the luxury of defaulting to the canard that the child-abuse allegations didn't "bear up." In addition to pledging immediate action by the NSP, Spire called upon the Douglas County judges to impanel a grand jury to probe the child-abuse allegations.

Caradori had strong misgivings when the Committee relinquished its videotaped statements to state and federal law enforcement: His primary concerns were FBI or NSP harassment of victims, as Owen had already endured, and also leaks to the press. He realized that Owen, Boner, and Danny King were fragile, and he felt that heat from the FBI or NSP would melt their cooperation. His videotaped statements also contained the names of several additional victims who would be subjected to harassment before he even had an opportunity to contact them—Caradori had made contact with several victims who refused to talk to him for fear of publicity and reprisal.

The collective reverberations of Caradori's investigation, and the impending Douglas County grand jury coincided with a pair of major "surprises." The first occurred when President George H.W. Bush rolled into town—Bush would speak at a February 7, 1990, fundraiser for Governor Orr, a fellow Republican. Larry King considered the president a personal "friend" and proudly displayed a picture of himself and Bush, looking like the best of friends, at the Franklin Credit Union. You will recall that King hosted a $100,000 gala for the newly-nominated Bush at the 1988 Republican Convention in New Orleans.

A source informed Caradori that King had purchased a ticket to attend the "$1,000-a-couple" fundraiser, even though the event's organizers later denied it. The source also disclosed to Caradori that when the Secret Service discovered King's plan to grace the fundraiser, they either ushered him to the federal courthouse or demanded that he make haste thereto. Either way, King made an impromptu appearance at the federal courthouse in the early afternoon of February 7, before US Magistrate Richard Kopf. (In the US federal court system, a magistrate judge is a judge appointed to assist a US District Court judge in the performance of his or her duties. Magistrate judges serve terms of eight years if full-time, or four years if part-time, and may be reappointed. They conduct a wide range of judicial proceedings to expedite the disposition of cases in United States District Courts.)

Magistrate Kopf ordered King to undergo a "mental health evaluation" at the US Medical Center for Federal Prisoners in Springfield, Missouri—"with no delay." King waived a hearing on Kopf's ruling and immediately found himself en route to Springfield in the custody of two US marshals. Kopf's preemptive decision on King's "mental health," made without a motion from anyone, was extremely odd, but the magistrate didn't feel inclined to defend his ruling. When questioned about his decree, Kopf stated, "The decision speaks for itself!"

The outspoken Senator Chambers, who had resigned from the Committee the previous July, chimed in on King's sudden psychiatric woes. In a *World-Herald* article, Chambers is quoted as having "reason to believe" King planned to attend the fundraiser. "Powerful people at the national level," Chambers surmised, "have more to gain by Larry King being eliminated than standing trial, people of sufficient power to cause him to be sent to Springfield in the first place." Chambers quipped that he would elaborate on his allegations if King "should die or his mind should be destroyed." Senator Schmit wasn't buying King's mental maladies either—he said that he was "very suspicious" about the circumstances surrounding King's mental-health exodus.

Meanwhile, personnel at the Springfield medical facility were evidently taking King's newfound "condition" rather seriously. An administrator at Springfield assured the *Lincoln Journal* that King's mental health evaluation commenced "the minute he walked through the door." The administrator mentioned that the evaluation would include assessments by psychiatrists and psychologists, including a battery of mental-health tests.

Though Springfield personnel were purportedly determined to probe the depths of Larry King's psyche, his friends and family were left scratching their heads about this unexpected turn of events. King had ostensibly found employment with an Omaha florist as he awaited his upcoming trial, and the owner of the floral shop told the *Lincoln Journal* that King hadn't shown any signs of mental problems, nor had he undergone abrupt behavioral changes—he even said that King was an above-average employee. King's pastor concurred with the employer. "He is a man under stress and is coping with it the best he can," said the pastor. "I thought under the circumstances he was doing pretty well." In a *World-Herald* interview, King's pastor speculated that he would be surprised if King was found to be psychologically unsound: "I didn't see any indications of mental problems."

But Springfield's chief psychiatrist disagreed and diagnosed King with a "probable delusional paranoid disorder, grandiose type." King was returned to Omaha on March 18, and roughly two weeks later he was again marched before Magistrate Kopf. Kopf embraced the diagnosis of Springfield's chief psychiatrist and ruled that King's "intellectual system of grandiosity leads to disorganization of thought processes which gravely impairs the ability of Mr. King to withstand a lengthy trial." In other words, he declared King unfit for trial—he also sealed his psychiatric report.

US District Judge William Cambridge, who was slated to be King's trial judge for his financial charges, adopted Kopf's findings and recommendations and found King incompetent to stand trial. He ordered that King be taken "forthwith" to the US Medical Facility in Rochester, Minnesota. Cambridge instructed Rochester personnel to determine if King had the "capacity to permit the trial to proceed" in the foreseeable future. US Attorney Lahners didn't object to Cambridge's maneuver and actually seemed rather pleased by this chain of events because of his foremost concern for King's mental health. "It's in the best interest of the defendant to get back into treatment," remarked Lahners. Kopf's bizarre and preemptive whisking of King to Springfield, Cambridge's cosigning Kopf's ruling, and Lahner's kowtowing ensured that King would be safely tucked away from both wayward subpoenas and the press.

King's extraordinary treatment by the federal judiciary begs a rather troubling question: Were federal judges bending over backwards to provide a legal sanctuary for an alleged child molester?

King would have a five-month sabbatical in Minnesota as a "pretrial detainee." The US Medical Facility in Rochester is considered to be the

"Club Fed" in the federal prison system, and King's stay at Rochester would overlap with those of evangelical charlatan Jim Baker, political agitator Lyndon LaRouche, and Joey Aiuppa, the former capo of the Chicago mafia. I interviewed a former federal prisoner who served time at Rochester with King—he told me that King didn't display the slightest signs of mental instability. He also said that Rochester's other high-profile criminals made an effort to steer clear of him.

While psychiatrists in Springfield were diagnosing King as "delusional," *Omaha World-Herald* columnist Peter Citron would be at the epicenter of a second surprise. At approximately 6:00 P.M. on February 22, 1990, OPD officers converged on the fifty-year-old Citron at Omaha's Ak-Sar-Ben horse track, and he was arrested for the felonious sexual assault of two children. Citron's charges stemmed from his sexual molestation of two boys, ages 11 and 13, who lived in his neighborhood and did "chores" for him. The "rumors" of Citron's perversity had wafted to the mother of one of the boys, and she asked her son if Citron had acted inappropriately with him. The boy confessed to Citron's abuse, and his mother phoned the OPD—her son also knew of a second boy who had been molested by Citron.

On the night of Citron's arrest, the OPD executed a search warrant at his home. The OPD officers who raided Citron's house found a sordid assortment of 8-millimeter films, videos, pictures, and magazines. Citron's prized kiddy porn collection included the following magazines: *Young Boys & Masturbation; Chicken Little; Naked Boyhood; Boyland; Young and Ready; Boy Heat; Like Young; Young Boys and Fellatio; Teenage Masturbation; Young Boys and Sex Play; Oh Boy; Kids; Naked Boyhood; Boys, Boys, Boys;* and *Young Boys and Sodomy.*

Citron spent the night in jail, and the next day he and his lawyer, prominent Omaha attorney James Martin Davis, appeared in Douglas County District Court. Standing before the judge in a rumpled sports shirt, blue jeans, and loafers, the diminutive Citron entered a plea of "not guilty" to the charges. Douglas County Deputy Attorney Bob Sigler requested that the judge forgo requiring Citron to post bail, and he skipped out of the courthouse without coughing up a penny or saying a word to a swarm of reporters.

Though Citron didn't feel inclined to talk, his attorney wasn't shying away from the press. Davis emphasized that the charges against Citron weren't Franklin-related, but he said he would have to withdraw from Citron's case due to the fact that he had previously advised Senator Schmit on the Committee's investigative direction. Davis then gave an impassioned soliloquy on how "Omaha is going to be the first city to gossip itself to death" as he condemned the city's rampant rumor-mongering: "We're suffering here in Omaha under a firestorm of suspicion, and we have hurricane-force rumors. Peter Citron and so many others are suffering as a result of that."

The viewpoint that Peter Citron's "suffering" would be the byproduct of rumors is a bit peculiar, especially after he was arrested for molesting two children, but the *World-Herald* seemed to sprinkle sympathy on Citron too. In an article published two days after his arrest, "Citron: Rumors Have Ruined Journalism Career in Omaha," the *World-Herald* reported that an indignant Citron felt that "the rumors about his involvement in Franklin" had destroyed his career, even though the *World-Herald* had suspended him only *after his arrest*. Citron also thoroughly denied his purported association with Franklin. "If I have any connection with the Franklin case," said Citron, "so does anyone who's ever eaten at a Larry King restaurant, because that's the only connection I've had with him." Citron maintained that he had three interactions with King—"twice in person and once by phone," and only in the capacity of a journalist.

Within days of Citron's arrest, the Committee requested that Douglas County law enforcement provide the Committee with the evidence it had collected from its investigation of Citron. But Douglas County Attorney Ronald Staskiewicz refused to assist the Committee—he contended that imparting information to the Committee would "jeopardize" the Douglas County investigation of Citron and also the upcoming "grand jury investigation." Schmit responded by saying that he considered Citron to be a "small fry" in the Franklin hierarchy of perpetrators, and he was annoyed by law enforcement's chasing of "straw men."

Citron would be allowed to plead "no contest" to two counts of felony child molestation. His lawyer said the plea meant "we do not wish to contest the charges, and we do not admit to the charges." The cover story for Citron opting to plead no contest was that he decided not to subject himself and the two boys to the trauma of trial. But under the terms of Citron's plea agreement, he would be absolved of additional charges stemming from the OPD's seizure of his cache of child pornography. So, ultimately, Citron never had to face the music for his kiddy porn collection. In addition to the magazines, Citron had a considerable ensemble of Polaroid pictures, videos, and 8-millimeter films. Citron's two counts of child molestation each carried a maximum penalty of five years in prison and a $10,000 fine; but if he were charged on the many counts of child pornography that his colossal collection of kiddy porn potentially entailed, he would have been staring at decades in prison.

Following his plea of no contest, Citron was sentenced to between three and eight years in prison for two counts of child molestation. The sentencing judge said that Citron was a "convicted child molester with repeat offenses over the past twenty-five years." Though Citron had never been charged with child abuse during his years in Omaha, he had been charged with molestation twenty-five years earlier in his native New York. Moreover, additional victims of Citron stepped forward after his arrest. But the statute of limitations had expired on their alleged abuses, and Citron skated on those charges too.

Shortly after Citron's arrest, a police spokesman said that the OPD and the Douglas County Attorney were the only "agencies" involved in investigating the molestation charges leveled against Citron. However, an NSP memo dated the day of Citron's arrest referred to a prior FBI memo, which stated that US Postal Inspectors had the name and address of Peter Citron on a list "of individuals who are known to have received child pornographic material." Thus, Citron had a history of child molestation, his name turned up on a list of individuals receiving kiddy porn through the mail, but federal and state law enforcement had ignored him until his name surfaced in connection with Franklin, but they nonetheless vowed that Citron was not actually connected to the scandal.

Though Douglas County Attorney Ronald Staskiewicz and Assistant Douglas County Attorney Bob Sigler continued to insist the charges against Citron weren't Franklin-related, they never allowed the Committee to scrutinize the evidence impounded from Citron's home—even after he was sentenced and the state's grand jury had been dismissed. In fact, Citron's profuse stock of kiddy porn would be conveniently sealed when he was sentenced.

By the time of the arrest, Gary Caradori had been on Citron's heels for quite some time. Caradori wrote a letter to Citron on January 31, 1990, requesting an interview, and his Investigative Report on the day of Citron's arrest stated, "It is my opinion now that Peter Citron could be a very helpful reference in this case if the proper arrangements were made." Besides street buzz linking Citron and King as perpetrators, Owen said that she had seen Citron at a Twin Towers sex party. Caradori would also videotape a fourth victim in May, who also linked Citron to the Twin Towers sex parties.

I also possess interviews conducted by Caradori where Citron's name springs up. In the first interview, Caradori questioned a "confidential informant" who did consulting for King and the Franklin Credit Union—she remarked that she and King had a meeting in his office where King specifically instructed his secretary "to get Citron on the phone." The second interview was with a Nebraska Department of Social Services supervisor. Caradori asked him about Citron, and he replied that it was common to see Citron in the company of "little boys." Caradori inquired why nobody in Social Services scrutinized Citron's activities—the interviewee responded that it wasn't his "responsibility." Caradori then pressed him for an explanation for Social Services' steering clear of Citron, and he responded, "I don't have a good answer for that."

Citron's arrest was in the wake of a major metamorphosis at the *World-Herald*: Larry King booster Harold Andersen stepped down as the *World-Herald*'s CEO after over two decades, and became a contributing editor. Shortly before Andersen relinquished his lofty status at the *World-Herald*, he and his wife were honored by the Nebraska Society of Washington, DC with its annual Distinguished Nebraskan award—it was the first time the Society honored a couple with the award. Nebraska Senator J.J. Exon presented the award to Harold Andersen, and Governor Kay Orr presented the award to his wife. The ceremony even included a tribute letter from President George H.W. Bush, who bestowed praise on Andersen for his "efforts to improve the quality of life in his community." Bush also described the *World-Herald* as "an example of journalistic integrity."

By the time of Larry King's hospitalization and Citron's arrest, Caradori found himself treading a treacherous minefield that required him to navigate tapped phones, repeated intimidation, and harassment of victims and witnesses. To circumvent the scrutiny and surveillance, he started using pay phones and taking other covert measures to ensure the integrity of his investigation. Though Caradori took measures to nimbly sidestep a gauntlet of potential hazards, he couldn't dodge criticism as his investigation became the focal point of "leaks" and media bias, led by the *World-Herald*.

James Allen Flanery's *World-Herald* reportage on Franklin had been unprejudiced and attentive, but he took a leave of absence from the newspaper for a year in August of 1989 to teach journalism at the University of Kansas. The *World-Herald* ultimately replaced Flanery with reporters who were seemingly hostile to the Franklin Committee and its investigation, and they started churning out articles that were clearly slanted. The Committee mandated that Caradori refrain from media interaction, and he was forced to be a bystander as a hostile media started dismantling his investigation—and the victims he had interviewed.

Caradori also started to take considerable heat from the local media for the expenses Caracorp was accruing. The media inquiries prompted Nebraska's Secretary of State to scrutinize Caracorp's billing. Under the terms of Caracorp's contract with the Committee, Caracorp charged the Committee a whopping $24.00 an hour for investigative services and $7.00 an hour for clerical support.

In a comeback letter to the Secretary of State, Caradori wrote that it was unfortunate he was forced "to respond to questions from unnamed sources arising out of Caracorp's role in the Franklin Credit Union Investigation," but he nonetheless "appreciated the opportunity to clarify" his handling and billing of the investigation. "Please understand that if I were billing this directly, as a private investigator, my billing rate would be anywhere from two to four times higher," Caradori wrote in the letter.

After Caradori politely explained Caracorp's charges, he turned his attention to the "unnamed sources" provoking the Secretary of State's inquiry: "This infatuation with my billing and their scrutiny of my abilities and integrity can only be construed as something similar to a 'witch hunt.' Why? Am I too close to something they do not want to become public?" Caradori also touched on the peril he and his employees had faced throughout the investigation: "I must reiterate that we—my employees and myself—have been followed and questionable situations have arisen during this investigation. Threatening situations have resulted numerous times."

In February, Caracorp was slapped with its first federal subpoena, requiring it to surrender Franklin evidence. Inexplicably, Omaha's KMTV Channel 3 obtained a copy of the subpoena and broadcast excerpts of it. The subpoena would be the first of many leaks that state and federal law enforcement would pin on Caradori and the Committee. In a *World-Herald* article, First Assistant US Attorney Thomas Thalken exclaimed that leaking the subpoena was a "deplorable" act, and he "assumed" it was provided by someone affiliated with Caracorp or the Committee.

Thalken's allegation made Caradori's blood simmer, and he was quick to fire off a memo to the US Attorney's Office. In the first paragraph of the memo, Caradori commented on the risks of making assumptions: "To 'assume' in the investigative business is as dangerous as ignoring evidence and supportive evidence, when evidence is presented. It is appalling, and certainly disquieting, when the US Attorney's Office makes public assumptions on any matter." Later in the memo Caradori pointed out Thalken's double standards and demanded proof for his statements to the media: "For you, Mr. Thalken, to 'assume' that information regarding the subpoena came from me or my office puts you in the same rumor mill as the people you are criticizing.... Also, it is recommended that you verify your sources before you 'assume' anything publicly or otherwise about matters related to this investigation." Thalken never provided the proof Caradori requested.

A February article published in the *World-Herald*, "One Accuser was Guilty of a Felony," reported that a twenty-one-year-old victim videotaped by the Committee was incarcerated at York for a bad check "felony." The article didn't directly name Alisha Owen, but it essentially marked a red bull's-eye on her forehead. The article also detailed that a second videotaped victim had been the "subject of legal proceedings" in the Douglas County juvenile court. A second February *World-Herald* article concerning Owen, approximately a week later, discussed the accuser's "run-ins with the law in 1988 and 1989," and mentioned she had been treated for "mental problems."

Later in February, the *World-Herald* assaulted Owen's motives for giving Caradori a formal statement: The article quoted Nebraska's outgoing Corrections Director discussing the "21-one-year-old inmate" who "has given videotaped testimony to a legislative committee"—the article appeared two days before he bowed out of Nebraska to become Colorado's Corrections Director. Showing remarkable disregard for Owen's confidentiality, he said the inmate told prison officials that investigators involved in the child-abuse probe promised to have her sentence reduced. His statements, however, were at odds with the waiver signed by Caradori and Owen, which explicitly stated that no "promises" were made to Owen. The Director also said that Caradori and Ormiston were the inmate's only regular visitors, even though York's Visitor's Register showed that family members visited Owen on a regular basis.

Since Owen had granted Caradori an interview, her quality of life had severely diminished: She had been harassed by the NSP, attacked by fellow inmates, confined to segregation, and the *World-Herald* had maligned her character. But those were only opening salvos: On the night of March 8, FBI agents and the NSP, executing a *federal* search warrant signed by Magistrate Kopf, raided Owen's cell and seized a number of her personal belongings, even though York's warden confirmed to a reporter that prison officials had the authority to search her cell and confiscate items at their whim. Committee Chairman, Senator Schmit, was shocked by the actions of the FBI and NSP: "I'm speechless," he said about the search. "It would seem to me that they would have enough leads from the stuff we dumped into their laps."

A March *World-Herald* article reported that Caradori hadn't used lie-detector tests on the three victims. Shortly thereafter, a *Lincoln Journal* article, citing an "anonymous source," reported that the two young men videotaped by Caradori flunked FBI polygraphs. The source said that the young men fabricated their stories because they were seeking riches via movie and book deals and also to help their friend dodge prison time.

The *World-Herald*, chronicling the earlier *Lincoln Journal* story, had a catchy front-page article: "Paper: 2 Franklin Witnesses Flunked Lie Detector Tests." The FBI refused comment on the leak, but a state senator who wasn't affiliated with the Committee denounced the leaks as a violation of federal law and expressed his disgust over law enforcement's response to the child-abuse allegations: "I've been around a lot of investigations in my 53 years, and I've never seen one like this in my life."

Members of Concerned Parents and other citizens who were deeply disturbed by the *World-Herald*'s depiction of the victims repeatedly picketed the newspaper. The protesters passed out literature and touted signs—"Lie Detector Tests for Victims? Lie Detection for Suspects," "Reporting or Fabricating," "Pravda of Plains," etc. A spokesperson for Concerned Parents was interviewed by a local television station, and she said that Nebraska's "Bar-Press Guidelines"—voluntary principles that the Nebraska Bar Association and the media have agreed upon to provide fair trials for defendants—forbade the newspaper from attacking the credibility of the victims.

In response to the criticism, the *World-Herald* released an outlandish statement that justified its declaring open season on the victims. The newspaper put forward that the Bar-Press Guidelines were "designed to protect the rights of defendants not their accusers," and because there are no defendants, "the Bar-Press Guidelines haven't kicked in." The Bar-Press Guidelines also discouraged publication of a defendant's prior criminal record, but, again, the newspaper replied that this didn't apply to the victims since they were not "defendants."

As leaks and newspaper coverage chipped away at the victims' credibility like a jackhammer, Caradori wasn't prepared for his investigation's next ambush: His twenty-one hours of victim testimony inexplicably ended up at an Omaha TV station! By the end of March, KETV had acquired Caradori's videotapes. At first, the station allowed J. William Gallup, an Omaha defense attorney, to screen excerpts of the tapes—Gallup exclaimed that he was "shocked" by Caradori's questioning methods, and accused Caradori of leading the victims. Gallup didn't seem to be particularly fond of the victims either—he later called Alisha Owen a "short, fat, ugly girl" during a speech he delivered to Omaha's Rotary Club, and the *World-Herald* quoted him.

Gallup would quickly become a media darling for his outspoken criticism of the Committee and its investigation, and he routinely provided

TV sound bites and *World-Herald* jibes—Gallup's law firm actually represented Franklin's financial mastermind Thomas Harvey! Shortly after Gallup's Franklin debut, KETV started to broadcast almost nightly excerpts of the tapes with the victims' faces scrambled.

The other stations in Omaha also acquired Caradori's tapes, and they became quite a spectacle on Omaha's nightly news. The leaked tapes sent a resounding message to victims who might have the temerity to step forward: In addition to being crucified in the print media, they would also be telling their deepest and darkest secrets to the greater Omaha area. The leaked tapes were a gushing catastrophe for Caradori, because he now found it nearly impossible to coax victims from the shadows.

A March *World-Herald* article, "2 Officials Disagree on Source of Leaks," quoted Senator Schmit and Assistant Attorney General Howland sparring over the source of the leaks. Schmit stressed that the leaks occurred after the Committee relinquished the tapes on December 27 and implicated state or federal law enforcement: "There were no leaks as long as I had full possession of the tapes," he said. Howland, who spearheaded the Attorney General's early investigation into the abuse allegations—an investigation that hadn't interviewed a single victim—teed off on Schmit: "This is ridiculous, just farcical," retorted Howland. "It's unfortunate that the senator feels obliged to make accusations against law enforcement.... Now they've got a hot potato, and they don't know what to do with it."

In a subsequent *World-Herald* article, "Schmit: Abuse Victims Fear Scrutiny," Schmit commented on the seemingly insurmountable difficulties that Caradori faced: "If you were an abused child and you heard the reports about the original three witnesses who came forward and then you saw what happened to those witnesses, would you come forward now? Or would you just hunker down and say, 'I've taken all the abuse I'm going to take'? You'd say, 'The hell with it. There's no point talking to anybody because they're going to cover it up.'"

By April of 1990, Alisha Owen had taken a beating in the press, and, like Gary Caradori, she was acutely interested in finding out who exactly had leaked the tapes to the TV stations. Unlike Caradori, however, Owen had an ace to play in discovering the source of the leak: For a media personality she would have been the hottest ticket in town—her scrambled silhouette saturated the Omaha airwaves, and she resolutely shunned media attention and requests for interviews.

But in the second week of April, Owen phoned KETV's on-air personality Mike McKnight and consented to an "off the record" meeting—York's Visitor's Register confirms that McKnight visited her on April 12. In a quid pro quo, Owen offered to make particular disclosures if McKnight revealed who had leaked the tapes. According to Owen, McKnight said that FBI personnel hadn't actually *leaked* the tapes to the TV station—they had *sold* them! Though McKnight would eventually be subpoenaed to give an account of how he acquired the tapes, the subpoena would be quashed.

In Franklin, the perception of reality intended for public consumption was basically a byproduct of the media, and the imperceptible reality generating that perception was primarily law enforcement—the wizard behind the curtain. Law enforcement's Byzantine machinations were generally devised in stealthy conclaves, and in January, shortly after the Committee surrendered its video tapes to state and federal law enforcement, the top brass from the US Attorney's Office, Nebraska Attorney General's Office, FBI, NSP and OPD met to discuss the Franklin "investigation." At that meeting, the FBI played its federal trump card: The FBI would conduct the impending investigation and interview the victims on "FBI terms."

Though Caradori wasn't cognizant of the January conclave, he by now knew the meaning of "FBI terms": the FBI would subject Alisha Owen, Troy Boner, and Danny King to an inhumane pressure cooker until they melted. Caradori steadfastly hoped that their attorney, Pamela Vuchetich, had the wherewithal to abate their upcoming trial by fire.

Caradori had investigated a child sexual abuse case for Vuchetich, and he introduced her to Troy Boner in November 1989. In December, Vuchetich consented to represent Owen, Boner, and King in litigation that might arise from their alleged abuse. The attractive thirty-five-year-old was married and the mother of two young children. Vuchetich was born in Topeka, Kansas, where her father had been a psychiatric resident at Topeka's Menninger Institute.

Her family then moved to Lincoln, Nebraska, and she graduated from Lincoln's Southeast High School. She studied modern dance at the University of Utah and upon her graduation took a shot at a dance career in New York. Four years later, she aborted her theatrical aspirations, returned to Nebraska, and enrolled at the University of Nebraska Law School. The self-employed Vuchetich shared a Lincoln office with her father, a practicing psychiatrist.

Initially, Vuchetich sounded dedicated to saving the children—a veritable catcher in the rye. A February 1990 *World-Herald* article quoted her saying that her three clients were entangled in a teenage prostitution and pornography ring centered in Omaha that included "at least 100" victims. The article reported that Vuchetich had inferred the scope of the ring from the videotaped statements of her three clients. Attorney General Spire responded that he had watched "significant excerpts" of the twenty-one hours of videotaped interviews provided by the Committee, but he had no knowledge of whether or not 100 youngsters were involved. "If she has information of that kind," Spire said, "she should report it to authorities." Both the US Attorney for Nebraska and the NSP declined to comment on Vuchetich's statements.

A week after Vuchetich commented on the scope of the Omaha ring, she asserted that the *World-Herald* had misquoted her. Vuchetich told a *Lincoln Journal* reporter that she spoke in generalities when estimating the scope of the Omaha ring, because large child prostitution rings typically number 100 or more victims. In the *Lincoln Journal* article, she maintained that a "legal code of ethics" prevented her from discussing the facts of the case, and therefore, she didn't make those comments. Vuchetich also suggested that the *World-Herald's* misquotes corresponded to a pattern of sullying the Committee's investigation. "I feel like they've tried to discredit the Committee and they've tried to discredit the investigator ... and now they're trying to discredit me," she said. The *World-Herald*, though, wouldn't budge, and its managing editor issued a statement that the newspaper had "full confidence" in the reporter and stood behind the story.

Vuchetich demanded that federal and state law enforcement give Owen, Boner, and King immunity agreements before she made them accessible for interviews. Vuchetich said the immunity agreements would enable her clients to discuss "any criminal activity" they committed as a consequence of their association with the ring without fear of prosecution. In the February *World-Herald* article where Vuchetich reportedly commented on the scope of the ring that had ensnared her clients, she also announced that FBI investigators had interviewed her clients because she and US Attorney Lahners had negotiated written immunity agreements.

Though I'm agnostic concerning whether or not the *World-Herald* misquoted Vuchetich about the scope of the "ring," her statements about *all* her clients receiving federal immunity are false. By the time of that article, Alisha Owen had signed a federal immunity agreement, but neither Troy Boner nor Danny King had received federal immunity.

Vuchetich arranged for the FBI to have a go at Boner and King long before they signed federal immunity agreements: An "FBI Memorandum" remarked that FBI Supervising Special Agent John Pankonin, FBI Special Agent William Culver, and two NSP investigators met with Vuchetich at her Lincoln office, and Vuchetich consented to let the agents interview Boner the following day.

Evidently, the date to interview Boner was pushed back because a later "FBI Memorandum" stated that Culver and NSP Investigator Charles Phillips returned to Vuchetich's office a week later to question Boner, who was nowhere to be found. The memo said that Vuchetich had been "working" with Boner for several days, "preparing him for the interview," but the streetwise Boner must have had a bad feeling about the meeting—he bolted to whereabouts unknown in the middle of the night because his immunity deal wasn't worked out and he feared arrest.

Vuchetich, however, was considerate enough to ensure that the FBI hadn't made the jaunt from Omaha to Lincoln in vain—after Boner fled she fetched Danny King. An FBI memo related that though Vuchetich said King "was not emotionally prepared to be interviewed," he would be willing to meet with Culver and Phillips on an "informal basis in order to begin the interview process." The "informal," introductory meeting lasted two and a half hours, and agent Culver wrote a formal FBI debriefing on the interview.

The debriefing stated that "King was told that he would not be subjected to marathon interview sessions, but instead would be interviewed throughout several sessions over a period of time." Culver and Phillips also "stressed to King that he should not feel that he must relate the exact same story to the criminal investigators that he told Caradori on the videotape." The above excerpts from Danny King's initial FBI debriefing contain a falsehood and a truth: The falsehood is that King wouldn't be subjected to "marathon interview sessions," and the truth is that the FBI "stressed" to King that he need not stick to the story he told Caradori.

The FBI debriefings of Danny King commenced in earnest on March 1 in a hotel room. FBI Special Agents Michael Mott and William Culver interviewed King, who was accompanied by Vuchetich. The first interview lasted approximately three hours, and King basically reiterated the events as they were spelled out to Caradori. The next day, the FBI interviewed King for approximately five hours, and, once more, he relayed the events as they were given to Caradori.

On March 5, however, Danny King started to recant his story: He said the stories about the two interstate flights to Los Angeles and Kansas City where Larry King pandered him and Alisha Owen were fabricated. The debriefing stated, "King said that he has decided to be totally honest with the interviewing Agents. He realized that the telling of fabricated stories would only hinder the investigation into any abuse that had actually occurred." So after King "decided to be totally honest," he told the FBI agents about his sexual trysts with Alan Baer at the Twin Towers. King vowed that he and Baer had sex about twice a month for three years.

According to the March 5 FBI debriefing of Danny King, Boner made a visit to King in Omaha the night before Boner and Caradori rolled up at King's front door. Boner, however, was lodging in Lincoln without a car. During the alleged nocturnal visit, Boner supposedly described his upcoming visit with Caradori the next day, and stated that King needed to make up stories about the two interstate plane trips with Larry King. The FBI debriefing stated that the motives behind Boner's actions were to "sue" Larry King and Alan Baer so Boner and Danny King would "get a lot of money." Though Danny King was initially unsure about why the fabrication included Owen, the FBI debriefing later explained that King said Owen's motive for the fabrication was to "get herself out of jail."

The March 5 debriefing also mentioned that "King said Alisha Owen told him to tell the investigators about an old man named Rob picking her up at her apartment on several occasions for dates." In King's statement to Caradori, he said that in April or May of 1986 he answered the door to Owen's apartment to find an older man named "Bob," who drove a blue car equipped with a spotlight. King's March 5 FBI statement about what "Owen told him" is in glaring contradiction to the fact that Danny King hadn't talked to Owen since her incarceration at York.

A March 6 "FBI Memorandum" is extremely bizarre indeed: The memorandum discussed Vuchetich visiting the FBI's Omaha Field Office and meeting with Supervising Special Agent John Pankonin and Special Agents Mott and Culver, and it detailed a conversation Vuchetich had with the boyfriend of Danny King's mother. Vuchetich said the boyfriend related that Boner, 6'3" weighing 200 pounds, requested that the frail King, 5'6" and maybe 140 pounds soaking wet, act as Boner's bodyguard that night, which would be like Hulk Hogan conscripting Pee-wee Herman to be his muscle.

Vuchetich also maintained that the boyfriend informed her that Danny King suggested to Boner they recruit "another victim," but Boner vetoed the idea because "millions and millions of dollars" were at stake, and additional witnesses "would cut up the pie into smaller pieces." Special Agent Mott purportedly phoned the boyfriend, but he "refused to be interviewed and terminated the telephone call."

By early March, Pamela Vuchetich definitely seemed to be molting her save-the-children persona, bringing Danny King to FBI agents again on March 8. Though King pledged "to be totally honest" on March 5, he evidently wasn't able to seamlessly assemble the opus of lies that was now required of him. For example, after he turned over a new leaf on March 5, he said that Boner imparted the fabricated stories to him on the eve of his meeting with Caradori, but on March 8 he said Boner imparted the fabricated stories as Caradori filled his tank with gas. These contradictions didn't seem to trouble the FBI agents.

On March 8, FBI agents apparently felt that King's singing lessons had been sufficiently honed for a recital, because they invited US Attorney Lahners and 1st Assistant US Attorney Thalken to his debriefing, and King sang the following tune: "King also told Caradori that Troy Boner had fabricated several of the incidents Boner had told him about, and

Alisha Owen was not involved in any incidents at all. King said he did not wish to fabricate stories and wanted to tell the truth. Caradori kept pressuring King to tell the whole story and not be afraid. After some amount of time, King decided that if Caradori wanted to hear the story so bad, he would go ahead and tell him, at which time King participated in the videotaped interview. King included in his taped interview all the fabricated stories that Boner had told him to."

Danny King had a final debriefing on March 21, and by then he had recanted just about everything but his name, including his recurrent molestations at the hands of Baer. The March 21 debriefing is basically a cut-and-paste of the debriefings after King became "totally honest" on March 5, but it contained a new, innovative twist: King disavowed Boner's visiting him on the eve of his initial contact with Caradori and also disavowed Boner's explaining the fabrications to him as Caradori filled his gas tank: "Caradori and Ormiston left Danny King and Troy Boner in King's room while they returned to Caradori's room. Boner told Caradori that he and King were going to take a swim for about an hour. After Caradori and Ormiston left the room, Boner and King went to the bar in the hotel where they drank alcohol and talked for approximately one hour. It was during this hour-long meeting at the bar in the Residence Inn that Troy Boner first told Danny King what he (Boner) wanted King to tell Caradori."

The FBI debriefing's new, innovative twist is in glaring contradiction to Caradori's Investigative Report on the day he initially met Danny King. The Investigative Report explicitly stated that Boner didn't accompany King to the Residence Inn—Caradori drove Boner and King to Caracorp and, as Boner walked back to his apartment, Caradori deposited King at the Residence Inn.

The final paragraph of King's March 21 debriefing ends on a serious note: "King told the interviewing Agent and Investigator that the facts as he is now relating them on today's date is the truth and full truth and that he was not leaving any details out or fabricating anything that did not happen. He also understood fully that he would be taking a polygraph examination later in the day and would be asked about the truthfulness of this statement. He stated that this was the truth, and he had nothing to worry about from the polygraph." And, lo and behold, Danny King passed the FBI's polygraph.

Troy Boner had bouts of being AWOL after his attorney Vuchetich informed him that the FBI and NSP wanted to interview him. However, Caradori's Investigative Report from March 5 indicated that Boner phoned him that day: Boner disclosed that he had a "hard time" communicating with Vuchetich and had retained a new attorney, but he wouldn't disclose how he initially made contact with his new attorney. He also mentioned that a "friend of his" had recognized a high-ranking official from the US Attorney's Office on TV because that official regularly cruised an adult bookstore in Council Bluffs. Though Boner wouldn't reveal his friend's name over the phone, he consented to meet with Caradori the following afternoon in Council Bluffs. The next day, Caradori drove to the designated location of their meeting—he waited around for an hour. Boner never showed up.

Caradori's Investigative Report from March 9 mentioned that Boner phoned him at approximately 1:00 A.M. that morning. Boner had signed his federal immunity agreement the previous day, and he was tormented and ambivalent. Boner said that the high-ranking official in the US Attorney's Office who frequented the adult bookstore in Council Bluffs had threatened him with perjury charges, and he was "very scared"—Boner also told Caradori that this individual had a sexual penchant for "young kids." Boner then informed Caradori that his videotaped statement was true, but Danny King's was false. Boner maintained that he imparted the fabrication to King the day he and Caradori buttonholed King at his apartment, contradicting King's final account of Boner's imparting the fabrication. Caradori nonchalantly stated that he was "sorry to hear" that Boner had changed his story, and he reminded Boner that he and King were alone for a "minute and a half" and there was "no way in hell" they "could have concocted that story" in such a short time frame.

During the March 9 phone call, a terrified Boner requested that Caradori accompany him to Omaha's FBI Field Office later that morning. Caradori consented but insisted Boner clear it with his new attorney—Boner replied that he would immediately phone his attorney. Ten minutes later, Caradori received a call from Boner's attorney, who conveyed that he didn't have a problem with Caradori accompanying him and Boner to the FBI—Caradori said that he would adjust his schedule accordingly. But Caradori received a call later in the morning that specified he "would not be accepted at the FBI office in Omaha."

FBI agents had good reason not to have Caradori accompany Boner to the FBI—Boner was being put through the wringer and would soon recant his videotaped statement. According to a 1993 affidavit of Boner's, FBI agents subjected him to a torrent of threats, and he ultimately concluded that he must either "lie or die"—Boner's notion of "lie or die" may sound overly dramatic but, certainly by 1993, he had rationales for such a conclusion.

For Danny King, I possess the battery of FBI debriefings that show how his original statement was methodically whittled away, but, unfortunately, I don't have a series of FBI debriefings that show how Boner was methodically broken down. Rather, I have a nine-page, handwritten statement he composed on March 20, 1990, at the FBI's Omaha Field Office. Boner's statement is nearly a categorical recantation of his videotaped statements to Caradori and also in stark contrast to Caradori's Investigative Reports, even though strands of truth are woven into it.

He jotted down that Caradori initially approached his mother, and he also confessed to his initial late night phone call to Caracorp's answering service that patched him through to Caradori's residence. Boner wrote that Caradori said he was an investigator for a "Special Committee" and was aware of Boner's being enmeshed in a pandering network because of information garnered from Owen, but Boner replied that he didn't know a Larry King and hung up the phone. The next twist in Boner's statement is peculiar though: He claimed he phoned the Lincoln Police Department and talked to an officer who said that Caradori was a former State Trooper and a private detective, and then he made a second call to Caradori. If Boner knew "nothing" about Larry King, why would he have bothered with phoning the LPD and then Caradori once more?

When Boner phoned Caradori a second time, his statement continued, he told Caradori that Owen was "lying." Caradori threatened to subpoena him however, so Boner begrudgingly agreed to meet Caradori later in the morning. Caradori and Ormiston initially met Boner at an overcrowded Denny's, and they ultimately decided on a less crowded restaurant. As Caradori, Ormiston, and Boner drove to the next restaurant,

Boner said he reiterated that "this whole thing was bullshit." Caradori, though, zealously insisted it had to be true.

After their arrival at the second restaurant, Caradori gave Boner the following pitch: Larry King and company are terrible men, and Caradori would help Boner sue them for millions of dollars and also help get a friend out of jail—Boner bought the pitch and decided to give Caradori a "statement." Boner maintained that they returned to the house where he lived, he packed a suitcase, and told his fiancée he would be home in approximately "six months." Upon arriving at Caracorp, Caradori described an event to Boner where Larry King, Owen, Danny King, and Boner took a trip to California and "Larry King dropped off the two little boys." Shortly thereafter, Boner related, Caradori went into an employee's office, phoned Owen, and handed the phone to Boner: "I got on the phone and said what in the hell is going on? She said sit down and relax—she will explain. She told me to cooperate with Gary. He will help us, and we will all be rich. She told me there were very important issues I needed to remember."

Over the next twenty minutes, Boner's drug-addled memory supposedly downloaded all the places, locations, people, dates, times, and parties that corroborated Owen's videotaped statements. Caradori then talked to Boner and showed him pictures for the next three hours—Boner asserted that he didn't "recognize" a picture of Larry King until Caradori "told me who he was." Boner then supposedly gave his six-hour videotaped statement to Caradori. The FBI then polygraphed Boner regarding his hand-written statement and found that he passed with "excellent results."

That's the "official" story of how a great "hoax" was hatched, but Boner's account obviously contains an assortment of problematic details. Boner claimed he didn't meet Owen until 1988, when they started dating as boyfriend and girlfriend. Yet he involved himself in a dangerous scheme with a former girlfriend he had known less than two years, even after they split up and he was engaged to be married to another woman. And so on.

Another problem pertains to Karen Ormiston: Boner's statement mentioned that she was constantly at Caradori's side throughout the entire day of their initial meeting. And after both the state and federal grand juries had besmirched Caradori's methodology, Ormiston flew to Los Angeles in October of 1990 to undergo a polygraph assessing if Caradori had acted duplicitously concerning the victims he videotaped. She would be polygraphed by Hollywood-based Professional Security Consultants, and her examiner was the then-President of the National Polygraph Association. As the examiner questioned Ormiston, he monitored her blood pressure, pulse, upper and lower respiration, electrodermal skin resistance changes, and her blood volume responses. In addition to control questions, she was asked if Caradori threatened the victims, coached the victims, or advised the victims to fabricate their stories. She answered "No" to these questions, and the examiner concluded "that Ms. Ormiston answered all of the above relevant questions truthfully."

Though it is hard not to conclude that Boner's recantation was a tissue of lies, I freely concede that these inconsistencies aren't irrefutable proof. However, I have the phone records for Caracorp on November 25, 1989, the day the hoax was supposedly hatched. The records clearly show that no Caracorp phone calls were placed to York, Nebraska or received from York, Nebraska on that date; Caradori, like the vast majority of Americans, did not have a cell phone in 1989. Further, I possess the log of all the phone calls Owen made from York in November and December of 1989, and it shows she didn't place a single call on November 25.

The fact that the flight to California, which entailed the sale and/or murder of a little boy or boys, according to Owen and Boner, was the first recantation of both Danny King and Troy Boner indicates that FBI agents felt it imperative to dispel that story immediately. Such a deed is so evil and divorced from everyday reality that it defies imagination, but Caracorp's phone records prove that Boner is lying about his purported conversation with Owen, and, if Caradori didn't coach or advise the victims, as Ormiston's polygraph implies and Boner later confessed, Boner and Owen either conjured up this seemingly implausible story independently or they were actually privy to the horrendous event.

The FBI started making forays to York in early February 1990—York's Visitor's Register shows that the FBI descended upon Owen for ten "interviews" in February but, surprisingly, Owen wouldn't give an inch, even though she was confined to segregation and isolated.

Though Owen refused to recant her videotaped statement, the forces arrayed against Caradori and the Franklin Committee must have been rather pleased as the Douglas County grand jury began its deliberations. The leaks, abetted by the media, had effectively accomplished a meticulous hatchet job on Caradori's investigation and the victims he videotaped, and the FBI had coerced Troy Boner and Danny King into recanting their accounts of the Franklin pandering network. Moreover, the leaked videotapes of the victims, which were now ubiquitous on Omaha's airwaves, coupled with intimidation, had terrified additional victims from stepping forward, and the US Department of Justice had ensured that Larry King was safely tucked away in a federal psychiatric facility.

Caradori realized that he had stepped into the ring with the feds, albeit a corrupt subgenus of the federal government, but his innate moral barometer wouldn't permit him to throw in the towel. And by May of 1990, Caradori compiled a "Leads List" of 271 people who may have been the victims, perpetrators, or witnesses of child abuse. The Leads List included the names of approximately sixty underage victims of alleged abuse.

Also in May, Caradori managed to videotape a fourth victim—Paul Bonacci—whose name he had gleaned from a member of Concerned Parents. The twenty-two-year-old Bonacci was incarcerated at the Lincoln Correctional Center. In November, within weeks of Franklin's fall, he had been charged with two counts of sexual assault on a child—his victims were two boys, thirteen and nine years old. Bonacci, like Alisha Owen, claims that shortly before his incarceration he was warned to make himself scarce and to talk to nobody.

After Bonacci's arrest the court appointed a psychiatrist, Dr. Beverley Mead, to determine if Bonacci was a "mentally disordered sex offender"— Mead would interview Bonacci six times and conclude in an April 1990 report that Bonacci wasn't a mentally disordered sex offender, but, rather, that he suffered from Multiple Personality Disorder or MPD. Mead wrote that Bonacci has "20 or more alternates, several of them well-formed, as much or more so, than Paul himself...." Bonacci's alternates, Mead discovered, had an "individual identity, a different name, and certain individual characteristics." Mead found that various alternates had heterosexual orientations and others homosexual orientations; some alternates were even color blind. Mead felt the "principal personality Paul has no wish to molest children, is quite religious, and is not inclined to have homosexual interests."

Mead's April report stated that Bonacci wasn't cognizant of his MPD prior to Mead's interviews, and "he is still mystified by the situation and finds it difficult to accept." According to Mead, MPD is associated with a "very disorganized childhood," where the child undergoes "severe and often repeated abuse," and this was "quite true" in Bonacci's case.

Born in the Omaha area, Bonacci was the second youngest of six children. His parents divorced when he was a toddler, and he had minimal contact with his biological father during his formative years. His mother's second husband repeatedly pummeled Bonacci and his siblings—he told Mead that he remembered his stepfather chopping up the kids' toys with an axe. Bonacci's mother and her second husband divorced after he severely battered her.

She remarried shortly thereafter—her third husband didn't subject Bonacci to physical abuse but simply ignored him. At the age of six, Bonacci told Mead, a neighbor repeatedly molested him. Bonacci maintained that he informed his mother and stepfather about the abuse, but they disregarded his pleas for help. In third grade, Mead noted, Bonacci began to "lose time," i.e., have blackouts of previous activities; Mead inferred that "these were the first experiences of having an alternate personality takeover." At the age of nine or ten, Bonacci was turned on to drugs and child prostitution—his "friends" showed him a park where pedophiles cruised for children. Bonacci would perform sexual favors for money, but he never derived pleasure from these experiences "as Paul."

By the age of twelve, Mead wrote, Bonacci was heavily enmeshed in drugs, child prostitution, and Satanism. He attended "a lot of parties where he served as a young male prostitute." Mead's report on Bonacci ended on a perplexing note: "Without treatment, it is conceivable (and this is probably what happened in the contact with the little boy) that if placed in an unusual circumstance, an alternate personality might temporarily take over and commit such an act of fondling, although it is also true that such behavior will be stopped, or at least quickly checked, by another alternate personality which would disapprove of such behavior. It all gets quite complicated."

Gary Caradori and Karen Ormiston would videotape Bonacci for approximately seven hours at the Lincoln Correctional Center. By the time they interviewed Bonacci, Caradori and Ormiston had been on an extremely dark excursion for eight months, negotiating threats and dangers and edging into maybe the darkest crevice of the human condition. Still, they weren't prepared for Paul Bonacci, who had spent much of his life entangled in a sinister web of child prostitution, kiddy porn, Satanism, and "scavenging" for vulnerable children.

The clean-shaven, well-mannered Bonacci had thick, dark brown hair, parted to the side, and a youthful face, but his eyes revealed a horrific anguish. When Caradori and Ormiston interviewed Bonacci, he had yet to receive psychiatric treatment for his MPD—he appeared to be devoid of emotion and almost autistic throughout most of the interview as he recounted tales of unfathomable abuse.

Bonacci named the same abusers as Owen, Boner, and Danny King, and he identified the same settings of pedophilic activity—the Twin Towers, French Café, and the Run Bar. Bonacci affirmed that he met the three at the Twin Towers in late 1983 or early 1984, but added that he had several sexual encounters with Citron, Baer, and Larry King before meeting the other three.

Bonacci maintained that he first met Citron at an Omaha area amusement park when he was around eleven years old. He discussed numerous sexual encounters with Citron from 1979 to 1987, and also group-sex encounters that Citron would photograph. Bonacci was aware that Citron had lived and worked in California from 1981 to 1984, and he mentioned that Citron would occasionally fly him to the West Coast during that time. Bonacci talked about being at Citron's house when Citron molested a number of children—Citron was charged with sexually assaulting one of the children Bonacci named. His name had never been released to the media.

Bonacci told Caradori and Ormiston that he met Baer when he was approximately eleven years old as well, and he had hundreds of sexual encounters with Baer between 1979 and 1988—Baer would lavish him with money, jewelry, and drugs for their trysts. In 1981, Bonacci said he attended his first of approximately one hundred parties at the Twin Towers. Bonacci then named several children who attended the Twin Towers parties, including Jeff Hubbell, the Boys Town student who purportedly introduced Alisha Owen to Larry King's pandering network. Bonacci, like Owen, named Rusty Nelson as a photographer who photographed the orgies.

Bonacci also spoke of the same sadistic abuse that had been described by Owen, Boner, and Danny King. He discussed being repeatedly tied up, whipped, cut by knives, and burned by cigarettes. Bonacci showed Caradori a scar that was left by a knife wound and also cigarette burns on his arms—he claimed to have cigarette burns on his genitals, too. He recalled a party at the Twin Towers, in Baer's apartment, where he was forced to perform oral sex in rapid succession on five adult males.

In addition to recurring molestations at the hands of Citron and Baer, Bonacci would name Larry King as both a perpetrator and a pedophilic pimp. Bonacci disclosed that King took him on possibly three hundred flights around the country as an underage prostitute, and he mentioned several nuances about Larry King or his network that were also mentioned by Owen, Boner, and Danny King. For example, he stated that Larry King was fond of kids urinating on him, corroborating Boner. Bonacci also told Caradori and Ormiston that he had personally witnessed Owen and Chief Wadman having sexual relations.

He corroborated Owen about Larry King's African-American henchman named "Larry"—Owen gave him the impromptu moniker of "Larry the Kid," and Bonacci called him "Larry the Enforcer." They both described him as a muscular black male in his twenties—Owen confessed to being molested and slapped around by "Larry the Kid," and Bonacci said that "Larry the Enforcer" had assaulted him on three occasions. Their descriptions and accounts of him were strikingly similar.

Bonacci was almost catatonic as he detailed the countless molestations he endured and the flights with King, but he actually broke down and bawled when he talked about a trip to Sacramento, California in 1985. According to Bonacci, Larry King chartered a plane that departed from Eppley Airfield, near Omaha. The plane made a stop in Grand Island, Nebraska, where King picked up camera equipment, and then they stopped in Aurora, Colorado to pick up a boy named Nicholas, who was approximately thirteen years old. The plane refueled in Las Vegas, Nevada before landing at Sacramento.

In Sacramento, Bonacci said, they rendezvoused with a "little Italian guy" whom he identified as the "producer." The producer subsequently drove Bonacci, Nicholas, King and the pilot of the plane to a remote wooded area, where they met a few additional men, who comprised the "camera crew," and also a young boy named "Jeremy"—the producer said that Jeremy had been kidnapped. Jeremy was jostled into a small cage, and after he was let loose from the cage, Bonacci and Nicholas were ordered to run him down and drag him back to the older men. Bonacci stated that Jeremy divulged to him that he was from Idaho—he described Jeremy as roughly twelve years old, having braces on his teeth, with blond hair and brown eyes. Bonacci sobbed when he told Caradori and Ormiston that he and Nicholas were forced to have sex with Jeremy while members of the camera crew kicked and beat the three of them—an adult male then kicked Jeremy in the face, molested him, and, as Jeremy screamed, shot him in the head with a handgun.

Following the filming of Jeremy's murder, Bonacci said, he was transported to the hotel, where he had sex with the pilot. He described the pilot as having brownish blonde hair, a brown eye and a blue eye, a scar on his left arm, and an eagle tattoo on his chest. After having sex with the pilot, Bonacci slit his wrists in the hotel room.

Bonacci's account of his trip to Sacramento and its aftermath was given to Caradori and Ormiston with great detail and profuse emotion. His description of Jeremy's murder is comparable to Shawneta Moore's account of the sacrificed children and also to Owen's and Boner's account of the little boy or boys in California who were either sold or murdered, a realm of evil that places absolutely no value on a child's life. The narratives of Moore, Owen, Boner, and Bonacci beg an extremely disturbing question: Are they making up these implausible stories *independently*, or did they actually witness these events?

Bonacci discussed trips to Washington, DC with Larry King that also sounded improbable. Bonacci implicated King in a DC blackmail operation and said that he made numerous trips to DC with King to be used as a boy-toy for politicians and other powerbrokers who in turn were then "compromised." Caradori asked Bonacci to name the compromised politicians, but Bonacci could only identify one by name—he was in the US Congress.

Before Caradori found Bonacci, OPD detectives had conducted a series of interviews with him earlier in 1990. According to Bonacci, he made many of the same disclosures to the OPD detectives that he made to Caradori—Bonacci said he gave the OPD a diary that contained detailed accounts of his abuse, named his abusers, and even contained a pornographic picture of him and Alan Baer.

But the OPD said they investigated Bonacci's allegations about Larry King, Baer, and Citron and couldn't corroborate the allegations. The OPD also gave Bonacci a lie detector test, which was "inconclusive," but the investigating detectives dismissed him as a pathological liar nonetheless. Bonacci told Caradori and Ormiston that the OPD didn't take his allegations seriously and made threats to ensure he recanted them. Indeed, Caradori was subjected to ridicule within the OPD for even interviewing Bonacci—the OPD asserted that Bonacci garnered all of his information through the "jailhouse grapevine."

Throughout Caradori's interview of Bonacci, he made a number of contradictory statements that Caradori duly noted. Conversely, Bonacci provided Caradori with a number of fine details that would be extremely difficult to ascribe to the jailhouse grapevine. It's conceivable that the names of Larry King, Alan Baer, Peter Citron, and Robert Wadman could have coursed through jailhouse scuttlebutt because of Franklin's intense media exposure and notoriety. It's also conceivable, though less likely, that the names of Alisha Owen, Troy Boner, and Danny King could have been gleaned this way. But how would Bonacci have known about photographer Rusty Nelson, and how could he corroborate Alisha Owen on the name of Jeff Hubbell, or name one of Citron's victims? If Bonacci wasn't involved with Larry King, it's exceedingly improbable he would have been able to corroborate Boner's account of King's penchant for "golden showers."

In my interviews with Rusty Nelson, Alisha Owen, and Danny King, they all confirm that Bonacci attended child-sex parties at the Twin Towers—Troy Boner's 1993 affidavit confirms this fact too. Moreover, it would have been next to impossible for Bonacci to know about Larry

King's DC activities if he wasn't thoroughly enmeshed with Larry King—Owen, Boner, and Danny King were unaware of Larry King's DC deeds.

Though Bonacci provided Caradori with several details that led him to believe Bonacci had been a child prostitute in the Franklin pandering network, he couldn't account for many of his contradictory statements. On a veracity scale of one to ten, where ten represented absolute veracity, Caradori gave Bonacci a seven and a half.

Dr. Mead was called to testify before the Committee because its members wanted to understand Bonacci's disorder and determine his credibility. Mead told the Committee that Bonacci's contradictory statements didn't necessarily mean he was "lying," but, rather, they were the outward manifestation of Bonacci's assuming completely different personalities. In other words, over the course of an interview with Bonacci the interviewer might be interacting with several different personalities, who would have different perspectives on any given event; some alternate personalities wouldn't even be able to recall a given event, whereas others would be able to describe it in precise detail.

I've watched Caradori and Ormiston's videotaped interview of Bonacci in its entirety, and his lack of emotion is consistent with untreated MPD: If he approached details that were uncomfortable or painful, he would merely switch to an alternate personality to evade those feelings. I realize that this explanation for Bonacci's emotionless deportment may sound like voodoo psychiatry, but it is supported by extensive psychiatric literature.

On June 22, 1990, the Franklin Committee and Caradori assembled at the statehouse to discuss a number of disconcerting events and numerous frustrations. A transcript of the closed-door meeting conveys that the Committee members were shell-shocked from a flurry of media barrages and law enforcement affronts, but they were resolved to talk through their qualms and suspicions to avert descending into a collective bunker mentality.

By then, state and federal grand juries were in the process of investigating child exploitation allegations related to Franklin. During the June meeting, Caradori voiced his reluctance to furnish the evidence he was amassing to state and federal law enforcement, since he believed they were using it to sabotage his investigation. He explicitly warned the Committee that "various people in the FBI" and the NSP were deliberately hijacking the state grand jury. According to Sandi Caradori, Gary felt true heartbreak when he first realized that NSP investigators were colluding with the FBI to crush his investigation, because he had treasured his years in the NSP.

The Committee members also conversed about a strange, recurring phenomenon that plagued their prospective witnesses—they would earnestly consent to testify before the Committee, and then they would "disappear" or "refuse to show up." A second recurring problem that the Committee discussed was that individuals who assisted the Committee suddenly found themselves clobbered by the federal government. Senator Schmit commented on the latter phenomenon: "There seems to be a tendency for those who cooperate with this Committee to suffer harsh penalties before the law."

Though Franklin was jigsaw puzzle with many peripheral pieces, Gary Caradori applied his customary tenacity to the larger, inner pieces—like Alan Baer. Whereas Larry King emanated the gaudy aura of the nouveau riche, Baer descended from old money. His great, great uncle, Jonas L. Brandeis, founded the Omaha-based Brandeis Department Store chain in the late 1880s. Jonas Brandeis built up the chain with his three sons—Arthur, Hugo and Emil—and formed J.L. Brandeis & Sons; Jonas died in 1903 and left the company to his sons. The Brandeis brothers had a regrettable 1912—Emil Brandeis accompanied the *Titanic* to Davy Jones' Locker and Hugo died of surgical complications—leaving Arthur the sole proprietor of J.L. Brandeis & Sons. Arthur died in 1916, and his son E. John Brandeis assumed the mantle of the flourishing Brandeis empire.

E. John quickly added two stories and a penthouse atop the Brandeis Building, the chain's flagship store in downtown Omaha, and "the largest department store west of Chicago." E. John, perched in his lofty penthouse overseeing his empire, was a high-flying symbol of the American dream, but he had a dark side. After only four years of marriage, his first wife divorced him in 1921 on the grounds of "extreme cruelty"—she was awarded a $400,000 alimony settlement. The next year, a railroad clerk sued E. John for absconding with his wife and whisking her off to the bright lights of New York. Later in the year he married again—his second wife divorced him on the grounds of "indignities and cruelty" after only a year of marriage, and she would be awarded $250,000. In three short years, E. John's indignities and cruelties had enabled his two former wives to acquire $650,000 of his beloved wealth, a staggering sum in the 1920s, and he decisively renounced future matrimony. Bizarre occurrences were also purportedly unfolding in his penthouse, including bouts of sexual debauchery with female employees and rumors of a murder.

Though E. John had a long, fabled history of frolicking, he hadn't produced a legitimate heir to the family fortune; so he tapped his sister's son, Alan Baer, as successor to the Brandeis fortune. Baer was born and raised in San Francisco, and, ironically, he majored in "child psychology" at Stanford University before serving in World War II. After Baer's stint in the service, he journeyed to Omaha, where his uncle welcomed him into the Brandeis fold. Whereas the robust and swashbuckling E. John had a reputation of inveterate womanizing, globetrotting, and hunting big game in Africa, his nephew was short, scrawny, and cerebral.

Following the death of E. John in 1974, Alan Baer would prove to have the cunning of Octavian in the aftermath of Caesar's assassination. He deftly maneuvered through protracted legal wrangling and emerged as the Brandeis potentate—he then purged Brandeis of executives who weren't comfortable with his lifestyle. Baer would hold the purse strings of the Brandeis fortune until his death. He eschewed the pomp and circumstance of his uncle, and he seldom showed his face on the retail floors, preferring to summon floor managers to his office. On Saturdays, Brandeis employees would catch a rare glimpse of the casually dressed Baer as he made halfhearted attempts at customer relations.

E. John and his nephew had numerous dissimilarities, but they shared a runaway libido. Baer, unlike his uncle, enjoyed a long-term marriage, but the Brandeis rumor mills repeatedly churned out innuendo of Baer's insatiable appetite for young men and even boys. Baer would ultimately earn a reputation as Omaha's blueblood reprobate, and his plausible denials concerning homosexual trysts with minors were in short supply as Caradori's investigation bore down upon him.

One Investigative Report mentioned that a Caracorp employee interviewed a former Brandeis executive who maintained that Baer was mortified about the "criminal aspect" of the matter, as opposed to "public knowledge" of his lifestyle or a "civil suit." In other words, Baer coveted his gilded life, and his fear of being thrown in prison considerably outweighed any concern about his name being further besmirched. In an October 1989 Investigative Report, Caradori remarked that he had phoned Baer for the first time. Caradori later noted that the call stirred Baer to make inquiries about the investigation—inquiries that quickly ricocheted back to Caradori. Baer wanted to know if Caradori had dirt on him, and he was willing to shell out cash for worthwhile info.

After a flurry of phone calls in December, Baer and his lawyer consented to meet Caradori at an Omaha restaurant. Caradori's Investigative Report related that they "discussed child abuse, transporting minors across state lines for sexual purposes, and drug trafficking." Caradori advised Baer and his lawyer that he was aware of "times, dates, and locations," and he indicated that it would be in "Mr. Baer's best interest to contact committee counsel, Steve Berry, in order to possibly set up an interview."

Baer's wealth and connections had afforded him an exquisite sanctuary from the legal consequences of his depraved lifestyle, but he also realized that Caradori was a hard-charging investigator, and Franklin was unraveling with a velocity that even a law-enforcement cover-up had difficulties outpacing. Fearing a long stretch in prison, Baer hedged his bets, and contacted the Franklin Committee to inquire about the prospect of immunity.

According to an affidavit from Senator Schmit, Baer's queries about immunity provoked a response by the FBI that is almost inconceivable even within the context of Franklin. Schmit's affidavit asserted that two attorneys representing Baer visited Schmit and two other individuals affiliated with the Committee in Schmit's Lincoln office. The affidavit stated that the "two attorneys advised us with everybody present that the FBI officials dealing with them and with Alan Baer had warned Mr. Baer to 'Keep your head down, or you'll get it blown off, your mouth shut and talk to no one.'"

If the events described in Schmit's affidavit are true, FBI agents were not above administering death threats to silence prospective witnesses. Schmit's affidavit begs an extremely shocking question: If FBI agents were, in fact, threatening to murder prospective witnesses to cover up evidence, perchance were they actually willing to follow through on their threats?

By June 1990, Caradori had been immersed in the nightmare of Franklin for nearly a year. The nightmare included uncovering organized child abuse of a horrific nature, persistent media assaults, harassment and intimidation, and a seemingly concerted effort by state and federal law enforcement to sabotage his investigation. But Caradori realized that the nightmare also had a trap door: Federal and state authorities were possibly in the process of framing him to take the fall for scripting the child-abuse allegations.

An Investigative Report mentioned that Committee Counsel Berry received a phone call from a fellow attorney who warned him to "get out" of the Franklin investigation before he lost his license to practice law—Berry said the attorney "hinted" that Caradori had deceived the Committee by writing scripts for the victims he videotaped. A later Investigative Report noted that Caradori received a call from Owen, who made a similar claim: "She talked about the FBI hinting to her that if she changed her story ... they would 'go after' this writer [Caradori] and Mike Casey for 'fabricating' the investigation."

Gary Caradori had witnessed the FBI make short work of Danny King and Boner, fluently spinning truth into lies and vice versa. So Caradori had no illusions about the truth being his ultimate sanctuary. He was also unsure if Owen and Bonacci would have the mettle to continue enduring their respective crucibles with state and federal law enforcement.

Caradori requested that the Committee defend him from the false charges that he surmised were stirring on the horizon, but the Committee declined to provide legal assistance. The following excerpt from a letter written by Berry to Caradori stated the Committee's position: "I believe that the Committee has been very supportive of you throughout, but I do not believe that it is the function of the Committee to devote its energy to defending you." Caradori and the Committee had butted heads before, but he felt that the Committee should have provided him with counsel, because his work for the Committee had transformed him from the hunter into the hunted.

Caradori wrote a letter to renowned defense attorney Gerry Spence, requesting his representation. After mentioning an attorney who had approached Spence on his behalf, Caradori stated his problem: "The legal counsel for the Legislative Committee has come to me privately and informed me ... I am being 'set up' for an arrest because of the evidence which I had discovered." Caradori then gave a terse rundown of his investigation thus far: "In short, what we have discovered is only a small part of a nationwide child exploitation network. It is obvious that the people behind this organization are powerful and ruthless, and are going to great lengths to keep this matter contained." He further stated that the network extended "to the highest levels of the United States," which echoes the anonymous phone call received by Senator Schmit as the Committee was forming.

Caradori's letter to Gerry Spence elucidated his foreboding at the might of his perceived foes, but his moral hardwiring evidently made him constitutionally incapable of conceding defeat and consigning further children to inevitable destruction. Caradori would now have to use his razor-sharp investigative skills to save his reputation and business, and, perhaps, his freedom. He needed pictures of the orgies—Alisha Owen, Troy Boner, Danny King, and Paul Bonacci all said they had been photographed.

Early on, Caradori had made a halfhearted attempt to obtain pictures through Michael Casey, but now he focused upon that goal. His search for pictures would be undertaken in extreme secrecy, and his Investigative Reports make scant mention of this quest. Caradori had agonizingly learned through trial and error that trust had to be meted out cautiously and carefully—his confidants had become few and far between.

A reporter for the *Washington Times*, Paul Rodriguez, had evolved into one of Caradori's trusted confidants. King's financial records had directed Caradori's attention to Washington, DC, because the majority of King's flight receipts listed DC as his destination and he also rented a DC townhouse. Caradori would discover that he wasn't the only person investigating Larry King's activities in our nation's capital.

"One of the angles I was pursuing in our Washington, DC prostitution investigation were allegations that children were involved," Rodriguez told me. "One of the names that crossed our radar was Larry King, which very quickly led us to Caradori's investigation. Caradori's investigation initially focused on the homegrown abuse of minors, but he said the underground network that he had been investigating was far larger than he ever anticipated."

Following leads that might yield pictures, Caradori trolled milieus on the West Coast and developed contacts within the occult fraternity. Paul Bonacci informed me that one of his final conversations with Caradori revolved around pictures—Bonacci told Caradori that Rusty Nelson was his best bet for pictures. Alisha Owen had also singled out Nelson as a photographer for Larry King during her videotaped interviews. Caradori commenced a hunt for Rusty Nelson.

Nelson, as I've noted, was my second formal interview after I leapt into the Franklin rabbit-hole. John DeCamp had arranged the interview. At first, I found DeCamp and Nelson to be rather strange allies, because DeCamp's *The Franklin Cover-Up* painted an unsavory picture of Nelson: DeCamp discussed the OPD child pornography investigation into Nelson, depicting him as a "pervert," and he also provided Caradori's synopsis of Alisha Owen's interview, which gave an account of Nelson photographing "group sex encounters" of minors and photographing Owen while "her hands were handcuffed and her feet were tied up."

I talked to both DeCamp and Nelson to try to grasp their improbable association. Following the fall of Franklin, Nelson claims, FBI harassment and threats forced him to flee his native Nebraska, and he embarked on an odyssey throughout the southwest, Rocky Mountains, and California, working odd jobs and washing windows to make ends meet. Nelson eventually drifted to Oregon, where his van was pulled over and searched, resulting in an arrest and incarceration for possessing child pornography.

The "Oregon authorities" were groping for information on Nelson, and John DeCamp was the recipient of a rather astonishing phone call from Oregon law enforcement. In a 1997 affidavit, DeCamp said the following: "I, John DeCamp, received a phone call from Oregon authorities advising that they had arrested an individual named Rusty Nelson who had in his possession pornographic pictures and also a copy of *The Franklin Cover-Up*, which I had authored some years earlier." DeCamp's affidavit further stated that Nelson's "family" phoned him and requested his legal assistance, even though Nelson had previously cautioned his family "to never let John DeCamp know where he was or how to contact him." Nelson maintains that the FBI explicitly warned him not to talk to DeCamp.

DeCamp traveled to Oregon to determine if it would be possible to assist Nelson legally and also to peruse the pictures seized from Nelson's van. Nelson sought clemency based upon his cooperation, but the State of Oregon put the kibosh on his request. DeCamp, however, with an Oregon detective at his side, was allowed to sift through some of Nelson's pictures. DeCamp's 1997 affidavit further stated that if Nelson's pictures were "properly identified and validated," they would "almost certainly prove the truth of the children's stories." DeCamp's quest to preserve the pictures proved to be of no avail, and they were destroyed.

When I first interviewed Nelson in January of 2003, he was living in a rural Nebraska trailer park with his girlfriend. Their relationship would rupture, and Nelson would then crash at a succession of places, including his parents' home, before he moved to the rural Nebraska trailer of a second girlfriend.

Approximately three years elapsed between Nelson's breakup and his second romance, and I made a concerted effort to stay in touch with him throughout his various relocations. I even spent a night at his parents' home, which was a very strange experience. Nelson's parents are truly Ozzie and Harriet, salt-of-the-earth Nebraskans, and their son's involvement in Franklin has brought them considerable anguish and heartache. They were acutely aware of my motives for associating with their son, but they nonetheless invited me to dinner and graciously accommodated me for the night. As the four of us had a pleasant dinner, we politely avoided discussing the topic of Franklin, even though it seemed to linger over the table like a dark cloud.

The first time I interviewed Nelson, I found him to ooze an unctuous, spooky vibe, and the story he outlined was so divorced from day-to-day Americana that it would have been next to impossible for me to listen to him without a filter of skepticism. But he came across as quite candid, and his deportment was very matter-of-fact—he didn't feel compelled to convince me of the implausible events he discussed, which included allegations of pedophile politicians at the pinnacle of national power, Larry King's CIA connections, blackmail, and the auctioning of children.

The events Nelson described and the politicians he fingered were explosive—I was determined to ferret out the truth. I spent numerous hours talking to him face to face and over the phone. I would buy him dinners and talk to him until the wee hours. I would put him at ease and then push him to fatigue, mentioning his previous statements, seeking additional details. To my utter astonishment, I encountered occasional discrepancies, but I didn't catch him in any outright lies—despite Nelson's conviction for child pornography, his history of psychiatric illness, and my earnest efforts to test his veracity.

However, another "surprise" suddenly transpired that changed my perspective on Nelson. He has an undying love of photography, and his girlfriend footed the bill for him to open a photography studio in Norfolk, Nebraska. Shortly after the studio opened for business, it was raided by law enforcement—Nelson was arrested for not registering as a "sex offender" and all of his photography equipment and computers were seized and impounded. Predictably, this event put an irrevocable strain on his romance. Once more, Nelson found himself without a girlfriend, homeless, and with absolutely no prospects of partaking in his beloved photography. He apparently lost his mind.

Prior to the raid, Nelson had largely shunned Internet "conspiracy theorists" who sought to interview him about Franklin, but now he seemed to grant interviews to all comers. As I read the articles and listened to the interviews, I was aghast—it was clear that his rage was redlined: He felt that Franklin had yet again decimated his life, and he began spewing what I knew to be lie after lie after lie. Many of the statements he made were in direct contradiction to the statements he made to me; others, I concluded, were outright fabrications. I've come to believe that Nelson was never a paragon of sanity, and his involvement in these events and their repercussions had left him living on a very narrow psychological precipice—the raid on his studio served the function of pushing him over the edge.

Nelson epitomizes the problem of discerning Franklin's truths from falsehoods: The credibility of those who extensively participated in its dark underside, and who are actually willing to talk, has been compromised by themselves and/or with a helping hand from law enforcement. That said, Nelson maintains that Gary Caradori contacted him through a "family member" when he was in New Mexico, and he agreed to meet Caradori in Chicago and slip him incriminating pictures that would blow the case wide open. Nelson gave that account to DeCamp in 1997—I have the transcripts of their preliminary telephone contacts—and he also delivered the same account to me in 2003. He's never wavered about his Chicago rendezvous with Caradori.

On July 9, 1990, Caradori, accompanied by his eight-year-old son Andrew James (A.J.), flew his 1984 single-engine Piper Saratoga from Lincoln to Chicago. Caradori ostensibly made the jaunt to attend the July 10 Major League Baseball All-Star Game with A.J., a die-hard baseball fan, whose Mets cap and baseball mitt were his most prized possessions. In a July 13 Investigative Report, Karen Ormiston remarked that Caradori made "several attempts" to contact her just prior to his Chicago jaunt, but they were unable to have a face-to-face connection—Ormiston felt Caradori had something of extreme importance to tell her that he didn't feel comfortable discussing over the phone. Though Caradori didn't meet with Ormiston before his departure to Chicago, his wife said he explicitly told her he would be meeting "Rusty Nelson" in Chicago before attending the All-Star Game.

After Caradori and A.J. landed at Chicago's Midway Airport, Caradori's hour-by-hour activities are unclear prior to the game, but four sources—Paul Rodriguez, Sandi Caradori, Loren Schmit, and Donna Owen—say they received phone calls from him. His conversation with Rodriguez, who was in DC, was quite candid—Caradori unequivocally told Rodriguez that he was on the verge of acquiring pictures and other materials that would corroborate the victims' stories. The calls Caradori placed to his wife, Schmit, and Owen didn't overtly mention pictures; he undoubtedly thought their phones were tapped.

Caradori's call to his wife cryptically conveyed to her that his Chicago trip had been a success. He also had a pithy conversation with Schmit that the latter relayed to a reporter: "Loran, we got them by the shorthairs." Caradori, having talked to Alisha Owen's parents on various occasions since initially interviewing their daughter, felt terrible about the horrors that had befallen her, and he told Donna Owen that she would be "the happiest mother in the world" upon his return from Chicago.

Nelson claims that he had left the Albuquerque area the previous day and drove through the night to meet Caradori in Chicago. "I met with Caradori briefly," Nelson told me. "I gave him the pictures, and I got out of there." In 2003, when I originally interviewed Nelson, he actually broke down and started to bawl as he described his rendezvous with Caradori. Prior to our first meeting, my only background on Nelson was from *The Franklin Cover-Up*, which cast him as a minion of darkness; I was absolutely stunned by his intense emotional outburst.

On the night of July 10, Caradori and his son A.J. attended the All-Star Game, which ended around 11:45 P.M., and they flew out of Chicago's Midway Airport at 1:51 A.M. on July 11. Approximately an hour later, Caradori's plane crashed in the cornfield of Harold Cameron, who lived near Ashton, Illinois. After Cameron heard the sound of a plane and then an explosion, he drove around his property, looking for the crash site. But it was dark, and the four-foot-high corn obscured the wreckage. The plane was spotted at daybreak by a medical helicopter, and deputies from the Lee County Sheriff's Department were the first responders to the crash site, where they found the remains of Gary and A.J. Caradori.

Parts of the plane were scattered up to 1,800 feet from the fuselage, and the National Transportation Safety Board stated almost immediately that Caradori's plane "broke up" in flight, because it was strewn over such a vast area, but the "exact mechanism" for the plane's breakup was "unknown." On July 12, the *World-Herald* originally reported that the Federal Aviation Administration's regional air traffic control center lost radio and radar contact with Caradori's plane at approximately 2:40 A.M., and the plane crashed between 2:40 A.M. and 2:57 A.M. The next day, however, the *World-Herald* reported that Cameron heard the plane explode around 2:30 A.M., and then an FAA spokesperson said that the crash occurred at 2:30 A.M.

Caradori's crash has been the focal point of profuse speculation—both on and off the Internet. *The Franklin Cover-Up* only cited the call Caradori made to Schmit from Chicago—DeCamp's book doesn't discuss Cara-

171

dori's purported rendezvous with Nelson or the calls Caradori placed to his wife, Rodriguez, or Donna Owen. Given Nelson's propensity to spin tall tales, it's difficult to take his word at face value, but Caradori explicitly told his wife that he would be meeting Nelson in Chicago—I've known Sandi Caradori for over six years, and I find her credibility to be unimpeachable.

But even if Sandi Caradori is mistaken about her husband's mentioning "Rusty Nelson" shortly before his departure to the airport, Caradori phoned Paul Rodriguez from Chicago and said he was on the threshold of acquiring pictures, and he also phoned his wife, Senator Schmit, and Donna Owen and cryptically conveyed that he had accomplished his Chicago objective. So if, in fact, Nelson is lying, there's still considerable corroboration that Caradori most likely came by pictures in Chicago. Moreover, the day after Caradori's death, Schmit told the Associated Press that Caradori had been in the process of trying to obtain pornographic pictures of the alleged victims.

The Internet is rife with accounts stating that the Lee County Deputy Sheriff who first responded to the crash site encountered a team of FBI agents, and a cornfield that was littered with pornographic pictures. I eventually tracked down the Lee County Deputy Sheriff in question, and he informed me that he was indeed the first official to respond to the crash site—he said he didn't see a single FBI agent or pornographic picture when he initially responded to the crash.

Farmer Cameron, however, was huddled around the fuselage with local law enforcement after the plane was located, and he says one officer stated, "We better get the FBI involved in it." The Lee County Coroner said that the FBI would only investigate the crash if there were signs of sabotage, and two days after the crash, the National Transportation Safety Board (NTSB) and the Lee County Sheriff announced that the crash entailed no signs of foul play. So it's rather baffling that local law enforcement apparently discussed FBI involvement at the crash site.

In the July 12 article on Caradori's crash, the *World-Herald* quoted the Lee County Sheriff saying there were "indications" that Caradori called in a "Mayday" before his plane crashed to the ground—a newscaster on an Omaha TV station also said that Caradori had radioed a Mayday prior to the crash. A spokesman for the NTSB wouldn't confirm or deny a

Mayday, but he said the FAA "tape" of Caradori's radio transmissions was sent to Washington, DC to be analyzed. The NTSB ultimately announced that Caradori hadn't issued a Mayday.

The Lee County Coroner held an inquest into the deaths of Caradori and his son. The *World-Herald* reported that the Chicago-based investigator for the NTSB testified that he "saw no evidence of an on-board explosion." The inquest failed to find a reason for Caradori's plane breaking apart in midair ... but it nonetheless excluded sabotage. The Lee County Coroner also stated that toxicology tests conducted by the NTSB found no evidence of "drugs or foreign substances" in Caradori's system.

I eventually acquired the toxicology report on Caradori and his son—I found that "no evidence of drugs or foreign substances" isn't exactly false. Yet it is somewhat misleading. Carbon monoxide and cyanide testing are customary in the aftermath of a plane crash, but the toxicology report of the NTSB stated that a "carbon monoxide analysis" and "cyanide analysis" were "not performed" on Caradori and his son because of "insufficient" amounts of "tissue." Moreover, the lab typically used by the NTSB for its toxicology analysis had certain "analytical procedures" and it wasn't "presently operational." So the analysis was performed by the Armed Forces Institute of Pathology in Washington, DC.

Caradori's last statement to Senator Schmit was "We got them by the shorthairs," and Schmit never bought the explanation that Caradori's plane mysteriously "broke up" in flight. After the crash, Schmit said in an affidavit that he had been warned that Caradori's life was in danger. He also wrote a letter to the NTSB regarding the backseats of Caradori's plane that were never recovered: "I do not know anything about sabotage, but I have been told that a phosphorous type bomb would, in fact, vaporize metal and any other material with which it came in contact and that unless someone knew what they were looking for, it would be difficult, if not impossible, to detect.... I am sure there will be those who will scoff at such a suggestion, but there have been entirely too many violent deaths associated with this investigation."

The NTSB released its final report on the crash two years after the fact. The report determined that the crash occurred at 2:21 A.M., contradicting the original statement by the FAA, and also its later statement. The report concluded that Caradori lost control of the plane "for an unknown reason," but it cited "pilot fatigue and probable spatial disorientation of the pilot and/or an instrument malfunction" as likely "causes" for Caradori's loss of control. As Caradori attempted to recover from "uncontrolled flight," the report continued, the wings on his Piper Saratoga snapped off due to an "overload" of stress.

The personal effects of Caradori and his son salvaged by the NTSB were eventually returned to Sandi Caradori. A.J.'s little backpack and Caradori's 35-millimeter camera were relatively undamaged, but the film in Caradori's camera had been taken out and returned inexplicably developed. Caradori's sturdy leather briefcase, a birthday present from his wife, was never returned. Ormiston told me that the briefcase was virtually an extension of Caradori—it almost "never" left his side throughout the Franklin investigation. If Caradori had scored pictures in Chicago, she felt, they definitely would have been in his briefcase.

The sudden demise of Caradori created a truly bizarre and macabre circus. Unbelievably, even in death, the World-Herald's assault on Caradori's credibility was unabated. A July 12 article, "Caradori Faced Criticism of Probe, Utah Firm" reported that the Utah division of his security company had committed the grave offense of employing an "unlicensed" security guard. In response to criticism for publishing a disparaging article on Caradori the day after his death, an Omaha newscaster gave the World-Herald's rather disingenuous rebuttal: "The World-Herald defended the story saying there are people who allege foul play in the crash of Caradori's plane ... for that reason the paper is looking at all those who were critical of the private investigator." The World-Herald reporter who bylined the article would later say that her source for the story was Pamela Vuchetich.

On the day of Caradori's crash, several of his family and friends gathered at the Caradori home to comfort his grieving wife and son. Caradori's death would again launch Troy Boner into the throes of tormented ambivalence, and, in the early evening, he made a stream of phone calls to the Caradori household. But Sandi Caradori was either talking to visitors or "in no shape" to talk to Boner. Later in the evening, Sandi Caradori finally took one of Boner's calls—a tearful Boner told Sandi Caradori that her husband hadn't dictated instructions to him during his videotaped statement. He said that threats had coerced him into recanting his videotaped testimony.

Boner then voiced the same account to Sandi Caradori's sixteen-year-old son. Boner eventually handed the phone to his mother, who also talked to Sandi Caradori—Boner's mother reiterated to Sandi Caradori that her son had been threatened into recanting his prior statements.

After Boner's mother expressed her condolences to Sandi Caradori, she handed the phone back to her son—Boner promised Sandi Caradori that the following day he would march into the FBI and also approach the media to set the record straight. Not hearing a peep about Boner on the radio or the television the next day, Sandi Caradori felt that his sudden surge of courage had been quelled by fear. He phoned her later in the evening, though, and said that he had, in fact, visited the Omaha FBI and told the truth, but he claimed the FBI agents he spoke to only laughed in his face. Boner also said that he talked to a television reporter who didn't want to deal with him.

The following day, July 13, both Sandi Caradori and Karen Ormiston were subjected to a campaign of shock and awe. Ormiston found "handfuls of nails" behind the tires of a pick-up she frequently drove that was parked in Caracorp's parking lot. Sandi Caradori somehow summoned the gumption to drive to Caracorp and assure her husband's employees that the business wouldn't be folding. When Sandi Caradori arrived at Caracorp, to her utter dismay, she found FBI agents standing in Ormiston's office—her written account of that morning states that an FBI agent sporting a "smirk" introduced himself as "Mickey Mott."

The agents descended upon Caracorp that morning and served it with a federal subpoena. The subpoena was issued on July 12, and it ordered Caracorp to surrender "any and all" of its Franklin evidence to federal authorities. In addition to Franklin evidence, the subpoena demanded a litany of additional documents—Caradori's expenses, Caracorp's payroll records, invoices for services billed, telephone records, checkbooks, receipts for billed and unbilled expenses, tax statements, etc. It's interesting that the subpoena included "location of safe deposit boxes or offsite business documents storage facilities." Perhaps the feds thought that Caradori might have squirreled away a few pictures? In response to criticism of the subpoena's timing, US Attorney Lahners replied that it's not always possible "to be polite." The feds claimed they were building a "corruption" case against Caradori as a rationale for issuing the subpoena to Caracorp.

Sandi Caradori asked the FBI agents serving the subpoena if Troy Boner had contacted Omaha's Field Office the previous day, and they initially responded that they couldn't "confirm or deny" that information. Sandi Caradori then said that she had just lost her husband and son and deserved an answer. Her written account related that Agent Mott bent his head downward and said, "Yeah, he came to the office. But we can't waste our time on him. He has lost all credibility." If this is an accurate quote, it is indeed ironic that Boner would ultimately become the FBI's star witness.

Though the FBI purportedly rebuffed Boner, he still couldn't shake his torment. According to Senator Schmit and six other individuals affiliated with the Franklin Committee or Caracorp, Boner paid a visit to Schmit's office on July 16 and recanted his recantation. Schmit held a press conference announcing that Boner had stopped by Schmit's office to "set the record straight." Shortly thereafter, however, Boner snapped back into line—he denied visiting Schmit's office and refuted accounts that he had come clean with the FBI. In a *World-Herald* article, Charles Lontor, who had replaced Nick O'Hara as the Omaha FBI's special agent in charge, even went to bat for Boner, stating that Boner never recanted his recantation to the FBI.

But Boner would learn that to whom much is given ... much is expected. In the same *World-Herald* article where Boner was backed up by the FBI's top man in Nebraska and Iowa, Boner declared that Owen made up the story about being assaulted by three York inmates. "I helped her make that up. I said, 'Why don't you say that someone hit you.'" Boner then elaborated how Owen "banged her head against the wall and hit herself on the lip." York's warden was incredulous of Boner's account, because he said that Owen didn't need to inflict bruises upon herself to land in segregation—she merely had to tell him she didn't feel safe in the general population. You will also recall that the state Ombudsman's office had previously refuted Boner's charges.

The media would paint Gary Caradori as "delusional" and a "Keystone cop," but his funeral wasn't the funeral of a marginal character. Approximately five hundred people attended the memorial service for Caradori and A.J., and Caradori had twenty-four honorary pallbearers, including

US Senator J.J. Exon and former Omaha Mayor Mike Boyle. The US Coast Guard also conducted a military tribute at the cemetery where Caradori's body was interred.

Though the Franklin Committee hobbled along after Caradori's demise, his death would prove to be the final coffin nail in its investigation for a couple of reasons. First, Caradori was an extraordinary investigator whose diverse talents were practically irreplaceable. Second, very few people who were affiliated with the Committee, Caracorp, Concerned Citizens, etc. felt that Caradori's crash was an accident—they viewed it as a public assassination designed to send a message: None of you or your children are immune. According to a Chinese proverb: "Kill one man and silence one hundred." In Caradori's case, it was kill one man and his child and silence hundreds.

After Caradori's death, the Franklin Committee hired former CIA Director William Colby to investigate Caradori's plane crash. Schmit had lobbied for Colby to be appointed as the Committee's initial counsel, but his fellow senators on the Committee overruled Colby's appointment by a narrow margin because of Colby's "political baggage." By the time of Caradori's demise, however, some of the more influential members on the Committee suspected that King's pandering enterprise was connected to the CIA, and they felt that Colby might be able shed light on the crash.

In 1975, then-CIA Director Colby appeared before the US Senate's Select Committee to Study Governmental Operations with Respect to Intelligence Activities, commonly called the Church Committee after its Chairman, Democratic Senator Frank Church of Idaho. Colby proved that he wasn't averse to publicizing the Agency's nasty secrets or "family jewels." In front of a national television audience, he candidly confessed to assassination initiatives and mind-control programs that had been shrouded from the American public. Colby didn't receive accolades for his candor, but, rather, incurred the wrath of ranking intelligence officials and President Gerald Ford—Ford fired him as CIA Director, and Colby was replaced by then-envoy to China, George H.W. Bush. Colby later wrote that he found solace in his disclosures before the Church Hearing, because he believed the CIA must be accountable to Congress and the public under the Constitution—he felt he had done the right thing, not only for his country but also for his conscience.

Given Colby's prior candor on the CIA's abuses of power, members of the Franklin Committee hoped he would have the means and mettle to provide a definitive explanation of Caradori's death. But Colby wouldn't say that Caradori's death was a consequence of foul play—at least publicly. Writing to Senator Schmit about his investigation into Caradori's crash, Colby stated, "I only regret that we were not able to penetrate more effectively the clouds of confusion and contradiction that have surrounded this whole case." Though Colby wouldn't publicly declare that Caradori had been murdered, I have been told that he apprised at least three people who were affiliated with either the Franklin Committee or Caracorp that Caradori's death was an assassination.

In 1993, Colby also consented to be interviewed by the makers of *Conspiracy of Silence*, but he didn't discuss Caradori's death with Yorkshire Television. However, he did comment on the advice he dispensed to John DeCamp concerning his publishing of *The Franklin Cover-Up*: "I said you have to consider the possibility of some danger not only to your reputation but to your person." Colby also promised to submit the Franklin Committee's findings to the US Attorney General.

Approximately three years after Colby granted Yorkshire Television that interview, his body washed up on the banks of Maryland's Wicomico River—he had been missing for nine days. The Maryland medical examiner's office in Baltimore concluded that the seventy-six-year-old Colby had fallen out of his canoe as the result of a heart attack or stroke, suffered hypothermia, and drowned. On the surface, the medical examiner's conclusions may seem rational, but Colby's death is chock-full of enigmas.

Colby had a summer home in Rock Point, Maryland on the banks of the Wicomico River, a tributary of the Potomac. On the cold, blustery night of April 27, 1996, the septuagenarian Colby reportedly went canoeing in the Wicomico River—the winds were gusting at twenty-five miles per hour. "I don't see why a man his age would be out there," said a Rock Point neighbor. "If I went out there it would be in a 16- to 20-foot boat—not a canoe."

Colby's canoe was spotted the next day on a sand bar, but Colby was nowhere to be found. The US Coast Guard was summoned, and one of its investigators said that Colby had left his radio and computer on when he went canoeing. The investigator also said, "There were dinner items on the table." It was later reported that Colby's meal was half eaten, but I'm unsure if that was mere conjecture based upon the Coast Guard investigator's saying that "dinner items" were on the table.

Colby had phoned his wife earlier in the evening—she was in Texas visiting her mother. I've found differing accounts of their conversation: The Associated Press reported that Colby told her he didn't feel well, but was going canoeing anyway. The *Guardian* reported that he phoned his wife to say he was going to eat dinner, take a hot shower, and hit the sack. A third newspaper account stated that Colby told his wife he wasn't feeling well, but it did not state whether or not Colby told his wife he was going canoeing.

The day Colby's canoe was found, Coast Guard crews started to search the Wicomico for his body. The Coast Guard ultimately scoured the river and banks for eight days with divers, sonar equipment, draglines, and dogs—Colby's body was not recovered. Then, on May 6, Colby's body washed ashore close to where his canoe had originally been spotted—it's odd that Colby's body materialized so close to the canoe even though the Coast Guard had scoured the vicinity.

The Associated Press reported that Colby's body was clad in khaki pants, a blue and white shirt, and a red windbreaker, but he wasn't wearing shoes. So, if the Associated Press account of Colby's canoeing apparel was accurate, Colby went canoeing on a cold, blustery night without shoes: It was cold enough for him to wear a windbreaker, and yet he opted not to wear shoes.

I've discussed Colby's enigmatic death simply because it is an integral facet of Franklin lore. According to John DeCamp, Colby disclosed to him shortly before his death that he had become disillusioned with the CIA's use of children for sinister agendas and was determined to make the Agency accountable for its abuses. Colby, a devout Catholic, had certainly bared a number of the CIA's abuses to the Senate. But he had balked at publicly stating that Caradori's death was a murder. Ultimately, I am unable to provide a satisfactory explanation for William Colby's very strange demise.

Todd Rivers — 2007

Rue Fox — 2007

Boys Town — 2007

Tony Harris — 2007

—Chapter Three—

Boys Town

Initially, I had tremendous skepticism about the likelihood of Larry King's plundering of Boys Town for underage prostitutes, because of the orphanage's fabled history as a sanctuary for troubled youth. But as I burrowed deeper and deeper into Franklin, I started to accumulate considerable corroboration that Boys Town students had been involved with Larry King. Eulice Washington's was the first documented account that Larry King had pandered Boys Town students—Alisha Owen, Troy Boner, and Paul Bonacci also told Gary Caradori and Karen Ormiston that Larry King had exploited Boys Town students. Caradori's father, Leno, had been employed as a teacher at Boys Town for years—Caradori revered Boys Town. So as he started stripping off the outer veneers of Franklin, like he was peeling an onion, repeated references to Boys Town broke his heart—perhaps even more than the NSP aiding and abetting the FBI.

Boys Town, founded in 1917 by Father Edward Flanagan, is probably the world's most famous "orphanage," and it has certainly become an icon of the American experience. A 1938 movie, *Boys Town*, starring Spencer Tracy as Father Flanagan and Mickey Rooney as a lovable, rascally delinquent, branded the orphanage into the national consciousness. The film garnered an Oscar nomination for Best Picture, and Tracy's portrayal of Father Flanagan won him the Academy Award for Best Actor. Over the years, three additional movies about Boys Town would follow.

Boys Town arose from humble origins near downtown Omaha to eventually become an incorporated "village" ten miles west of the city. The village of Boys Town, Nebraska has its very own zip code, post office, and police force. Boys Town, according to their June 2009 website, "provides direct care to more than 400,000 children and families each year through its youth care and health care programs at sites in a dozen states and the District of Columbia."

Boys Town founder, Father Edward Flanagan, was born in rural Ireland in 1886—his foreign roots made him an unlikely candidate to start America's most famous and prosperous orphanage. Flanagan initially came to the US in 1904, studying at a seminary in New York, but he was sent back to Ireland in 1906 after a bout of pneumonia. The next year he enrolled at Gregorian University in Rome—he lasted a year in Rome before returning to Ireland because of a recurrence of pneumonia. He finally ended up at Jesuit University of Innsbruck, Austria. He was ordained a priest in 1912.

The Bishop of Omaha sponsored Flanagan's studies, and, after his ordination, he served several parishes in Nebraska from 1912 to 1915. In 1916, he opened Workingmen's Hotel for homeless and jobless men. Father Flanagan noticed young, homeless boys hanging around Workingmen's Hotel, and a year later he turned his boundless energies to helping indigent children. The lore is that Flanagan borrowed $90 to rent a rundown Victorian mansion near downtown Omaha, Father Flanagan's Boys' Home, where he initially provided shelter to five young boys that the court assigned to him.

The media-savvy Flanagan printed his first issue of *Father Flanagan's Boys' Home Journal* in 1918, and then he started sending letters to residents of eastern Nebraska and western Iowa, appealing for donations, which enabled him to purchase a farm ten miles west of Omaha—Boys Town's present location. In 1926, Flanagan kicked off a weekly radio show and instituted a student government for the village of Boys Town— its mayor was elected from the student body.

In the aftermath of World War II, Father Flanagan became a globe-trotter: The War Department called upon him to tour Japan and Korea and assess the needs of children orphaned by the war. President Truman then requested that Father Flanagan travel to Europe and attend discussions about orphaned children in the European theater of war. He accepted Truman's assignment and made a journey to war-torn Berlin, Germany, where he died of a heart attack in 1948. He was entombed on the grounds of Boys Town, and President Truman even laid a wreath on his tomb.

Monsignor Nicholas Wegner, a native of Nebraska, sat at the helm of Boys Town from the time of Father Flanagan's death until 1973. Under

Father Wegner, Boys Town doubled in residents, and expanded its educational, vocational, athletic and arts programs. But it was also rocked by a financial scandal: In 1972, the *Omaha Sun* found that Boys Town was hoarding vast assets, reporting it had a net worth of $209 million. At the time of the scandal, Boys Town only had approximately 900 residents; so the enormous wealth amassed by the orphanage was rather jarring to the newspaper's readership. The *Omaha Sun*'s exposé on Boys Town would be awarded a 1973 Pulitzer Prize.

The scandal marked the end of Wegner's tenure at Boys Town, and Father Robert Hupp replaced him. Hupp made a pair of sweeping reforms during his twelve-year reign as Boys Town's Executive Director: He replaced Boys Town's dormitories with the Family Home Program, where residents lived in homes supervised by married couples called "Family-Teachers," and the orphanage also began admitting girls.

Various sources have informed me that Hupp was a heavy drinker and actually only the titular head of Boys Town. While Hupp sat at Boys Town's helm, I've been told that he delegated wide-ranging responsibilities to those administering the sweeping changes of the Family Home Program.

When Hupp appeared in *Conspiracy of Silence*, he had the red, bulbous nose indicative of a heavy, heavy drinker. As the makers of *Conspiracy of Silence* questioned Hupp about Larry King's ties to Boys Town, he was vague and evasive. But documentation collected by Gary Caradori demonstrated that King forged ties to Boys Town during Hupp's tenure. Caradori interviewed a former paramour of King's who had been a Franklin executive, and he provided Caradori with a July 20, 1980 letter written by Boys Town's Director of Finance and Administration. The letter was in response to a proposal by King whereby the Franklin Credit Union would "provide counseling services" for people being displaced by Boys Town building an alternative school near the site of their dwellings.

A second document provided by the former executive, "Deposit Update," was handwritten and dated April 21, 1981. The document listed various corporations that either made deposits in the Franklin Credit Union or the credit union anticipated their deposits: The document stated that the credit union "anticipated" a $1 million deposit by "Boys Town, Fr. Hupp." The former executive didn't tell Caradori whether or not Boys Town, in fact, put up the money. I attempted to interview the former Franklin executive, and our conversation lasted perhaps twenty seconds before he hung up the phone.

When I interviewed Father Hupp, he said that Boys Town had "some money" in the Franklin Credit Union, but, being told that the investment was potentially risky, he ultimately pulled out the funds. So there's a discrepancy between the former executive's paperwork and Hupp's recollection. A former Franklin executive told both Yorkshire Television and me that Boys Town had more than one account at Franklin. Father Valentine Peter would later say that Boys Town had $31,000 in the credit union that Hupp was responsible for depositing, again contradicting Hupp's recollection. Ultimately, the financial relationship between the Franklin Credit Union and Boys Town is quite fuzzy.

Hupp essentially described a coup d'état orchestrated by Omaha's Archbishop that deposed him as Boys Town's Executive Director. Hupp told me that Boys Town's Board of Trustees had pledged that he would be allowed to spend the balance of his days living on the Boys Town campus after his retirement, but the Bishop reneged on that agreement.

After Father Peter replaced him, Hupp told me, he eventually became *persona non grata* at Boys Town, and the Boys Town police were actually ordered to arrest him if he was spotted on campus. He also told me that Boys Town employees who were seen talking to him were summarily fired. "I found out later that anybody who associated with me lost their job," he said. "Everybody was scared to death to say one word to me. Father Peter didn't want me around period, so I didn't trust the whole situation after I left. I told the Bishop that something's going on out there, but I reached a point where I didn't trust the Bishop either. I was told by the Bishop to mind my own business and stay out of it." I found Hupp's disclosures disconcerting.

I interviewed Hupp within a week of his move from Omaha to a little cabin in Necedah, Wisconsin. He felt as though he had been exiled, and he sounded extremely bitter, which I believe provoked his unprecedented candor and his disparaging comments about Father Peter. I phoned Hupp a number of times after our initial conversation—I left messages for him, but he never returned my calls. In a *World-Herald* article, published on August 23, 2003, Father Hupp declared that he and Father Peter had "ironed everything out." Given my interview with Hupp earlier in the year, I was extremely surprised by his conciliatory statements. Two days after the article appeared, Hupp died at the age of 88, reportedly of a viral infection.

I acquired Gary Caradori's "Leads List" on my first trip to Nebraska, and it contained the names of several former Boys Town students who were the alleged victims of abuse. Upon my return to Nebraska, I commenced a search for additional victims. By my standards as a freelance writer, the previous year had been lucrative for me, and I had the resources to spend a couple of months on the road without fear of ending up with financial worries.

Before I revisited Nebraska, I phoned Dirk and broached the subject of a second visit. Though we were old friends, I was unsure of his response because of the bizarre death threat I received on my initial visit. He had become a believer in "Franklin," and offered to put me up without reservation. I was very grateful for his hospitality.

Prior to returning to Nebraska, I performed database searches on many of the alleged Boys Town victims, generally gleaning a number or addresses for each. When I returned, I quickly discovered that the alleged victims were extremely nomadic: All the addresses I had collected were obsolete. Most of the addresses were also far more Skid Row than Park Avenue.

The first former Boys Town student on the Leads List I managed to locate was David Hill. Caradori's own investigation hadn't identified Hill as a victim of abuse, but, rather, his name had come up in the Julie Walters report. Tracy Washington had picked out Hill's picture in a Boys Town yearbook—she identified Hill as a Boys Town youth she claimed she had seen at Larry King's home—and Caradori incorporated that information into his Leads List.

One of the addresses I had for Hill was the home of his mother and stepfather in North Omaha. It was a blistering hot day in late August when I knocked on the porch door of his mother's wood frame, ramshackle house. I knocked on it a few times without a response before circling the house and knocking on the back door.

His mother came to the door—I introduced myself and told her that I was a journalist looking for her son. She was middle-aged, African American, and wearing a maroon housedress. Hill's mother looked me up and down—she was extremely suspicious and brimming with questions. I told her that I was writing a story that pertained to Boys Town and that I would like to talk to her son. I attempted to ease her suspicions by superfluous small talk before giving her the number of my cell phone.

Though I was uncertain if I had managed to abate her suspicions, David Hill phoned me the next day, late in the morning, with a swarm of questions—I told him about the story and offered to buy him lunch. He took me up on the offer and gave me the address of his girlfriend's apartment, where he was residing. His deep voice and the fact that he lived with a woman took me by surprise. At that point, I had a synopsis of Jerry Lowe's synopsis of the FBI interviews of alleged victims. And though the synopsis of the synopsis didn't note an interview with Hill, it contained an interview of a classmate who was an alleged victim of Larry King. Hill's classmate denied all connections to Larry King, but he told FBI agents that he "recalled a young man by the name of David Hill from Omaha being the 'Number one drag queen on campus.'" The classmate also described Hill as "swishy." Given the classmate's depiction of Hill to the FBI, I anticipated meeting a Rupaul clone that day.

I found Hill waiting for me when I pulled up to his girlfriend's apartment, and he appeared to share no similarities with Rupaul other than being African American. He was approximately 6'1" and weighed a stout 235 pounds. He wore a faded blue T-shirt, silvery jogging pants, and beat-up Nike high-tops. I rolled down the window, poked my head outside, and said, "David?" He nodded, walked around to the passenger's door, and climbed into the car.

Initially, Hill wasn't very talkative and seemed somewhat hostile. I asked him where he wanted to eat, and he suggested a fast food restaurant in North Omaha. As we ate, I posed a few questions to him, but he was unwilling to answer any. I sensed that Hill had a big-time problem with drugs, and his street ethos made him apprehensive about answering questions. In addition to having a crack addiction, he was unemployed and had also served a prison stint for robbery.

After lunch, I suggested that we drive over to Boys Town, and he consented. I had never been to Boys Town before, and, as we drove around the campus, its handsome brick buildings and impeccably manicured lawns impressed me—Hill had me park next to an administrative building. We walked over to the Alumni Center in the Hall of History, where the yearbooks were stored. Hill paged through the yearbooks from the early and mid-eighties when he was a Boys Town student.

He had been a football player for Boys Town, and one of the yearbooks singled him out for an outstanding game where he scored two touchdowns. He had completely forgotten about the game, and as he read about his athletic feats he was infused with fond memories—it was the first time that he smiled and showed the slightest signs of mirth. With the yearbook in his hands, he recounted the game aloud to me. A big smile creased his face, and he repeatedly flashed his gold incisor.

He said he was a second stringer at the time; but the first stringer fumbled the football one or two times early in the game, and the coach pulled him out and put Hill in the game. I almost broke out laughing when Hill mentioned the name of the benched first stringer—he had been the very same student who made the disparaging remarks about Hill to the FBI. I opted not to tell Hill that his former teammate still harbored a major grudge against him that had been unleashed during an FBI interview.

After Hill paged through a few yearbooks and relived his bygone gridiron glory, we walked over to the football field—his chilliness was starting to thaw. The Boys Town football team was practicing, and we watched them for a while. I spotted a cluster of footballs piled up; so I walked over to the coach and asked him if Hill and I could toss one of the balls around, and he said, "Sure." I have little impulse control when it comes to footballs: I love to throw footballs around, despite rotator cuff surgery years ago.

Hill was up to the task, and we played catch for about fifteen minutes. It was stifling hot though, and Hill tired out relatively quickly. I thanked the coach for lending us a football, and then we walked back to my car. After we climbed into my car, Hill said that he needed to run back to the Alumni Center real quick, and I told him to go for it. I thought that he wanted to inquire about getting a copy of the yearbook that featured his gridiron exploits.

He returned to the car maybe ten minutes later. He held up an alumni book, smiled, and asked, "What are you willing to pay for this?" "Let me think about it," I said, backing up the car. I really grew to like Hill, but he took every conceivable opportunity to extract money from me.

Hill suggested that we stop at a park, and we walked to a park bench. After our jaunt to Boys Town, Hill started to open up with me, but he refused to talk about his sexual exploitation unless I paid him $500. As we sat on the park bench, he repeatedly attempted to have me shell out $500, but I absolutely refused to pay him for an interview: I had hopes of selling the story to a magazine, and I didn't want to taint the interviews by the slightest suggestion that I had swayed interviewees with cash.

After maybe an hour on the park bench, we came to a stalemate on the interview, and we eventually drove to a Chinese restaurant and had dinner. I then drove him to his mother's house, where he consented to be interviewed—without charge. As twilight retreated to night and the sound of crickets, I interviewed Hill on the front porch's threadbare couch. Hill told me that he had two stints at Boys Town: His first stay was from 1979 to 1981, and his second was from 1983 to 1985. Hill said he was kicked out of Boys Town in 1985 due to his use of drugs.

Though Hill denied being molested by Larry King or anyone affiliated with King, he did tell me that an older student molested him during his first year at Boys Town, when he was thirteen years old. The older student had a managerial position in the Boys Town house where Hill lived, and Hill had sex with him on a handful of occasions. Hill maintained that his liaisons with the older student enabled him to have privileges that weren't afforded to other students. But the molestations by the older student caused Hill considerable inner turmoil, and he eventually approached his Family-Teachers about the matter. His Family-Teachers referred Hill to a Boys Town priest named Father James Kelly—Hill said Father Kelly then molested him.

During the interview, I doubled back on Hill and asked him a number of questions about Larry King. He continued to deny any affiliation with King, but he recalled a Boys Town student working for King off campus. After I interviewed Hill, I offered to give him a ride to his girlfriend's apartment, but he opted to stay at his parents' house. The day had been very taxing, and I was exhausted, so I drove back to Dirk's apartment and crashed.

Hill phoned me in the middle of the night, but I had turned off my phone. He left a voicemail telling me that he had buried his molestations at Boys Town in the distant recesses of his mind, and the turbulent emotions that were let loose by our interview prevented him from sleeping that night. I phoned him the next morning, agreeing to pick him up later in the afternoon.

He had made it to his girlfriend's, and I picked him up at her place. He was hungry and wanted me to stop at a Burger King. After I bought him lunch, we proceeded to a supermarket, where I bought apples and oranges. The thought of fast food on back-to-back days was extremely disagreeable to me—Hill couldn't get over the fact that I would choose fresh fruits over a Whopper.

As we ate a late lunch, he talked to me about the abuse he had suppressed for years. I found Hill to be very sharp, articulate, and outgoing, but the suppressed molestations were a ball and chain that he lugged everywhere—he lugged them into crack addiction and also into a prison sentence for robbing a pizza delivery man. No matter how much crack he smoked, he couldn't shake the ball and chain. His early familial circumstances, drug addiction, incarceration, and the molestations had wrecked his enormous potential. If Hill hadn't been subjected to so many factors that gave him a ground-level glass ceiling, I think the sky could have been the limit for him.

I also realize that people have free will and the ability to create their own destiny, but Hill's sexual abuse and drug addiction had forged a steel-trap denial. I've talked to other people engulfed by horrendous childhood misfortunes and drug addiction, and their denial is so pervasive that it's practically a psychosis. They can be living in a cardboard box, scavenging for crack every day, and yet they think self-respecting people living in the workaday world are absolutely crazy or mere chumps. Such is the power of denial.

As Hill and I talked, I pulled out Caradori's Leads List and let him give it a gander. He was familiar with most of the former Boys Town students on the list. Hill also spotted an individual on the Leads List who wasn't a Boys Town student, but who worked at a bar in North Omaha—so off we went. The bar had red shag carpeting and wood paneling, and, as I looked around the place, I felt like I had entered a time warp to the 1970s—Hill and I took a seat at the counter. I was the only white guy in the establishment, and I thought I probably reeked of cop.

Hill and I parked at the bar for a few hours, and he eventually started to chat up the bartender, who was a woman in her late twenties or early thirties—he certainly had the gift of gab. Hill and the bartender had a few common acquaintances, and she warmed up to him rather quickly. She told Hill that the individual we were looking for would be in the following day.

When we departed, I left a sizeable tip for the bartender, hopefully ensuring she wouldn't forget me. I planned on returning to the bar the following night with Hill. But the next night he was nowhere to be found—I went to the bar by myself. It was a Friday night, and the place was hopping. I was the only white guy in the crowd, but I noticed a couple of white women—the bartender had little difficulty recognizing me. I sat at the end of the bar, and, unbeknownst to me, I had pulled up a barstool next to one of the bar's proprietors.

In that environment I must have appeared to be a walking and breathing non sequitur; so the co-proprietor took an interest in me, and we started to talk. After I told him I lived in New York, his interest in me ascended an octave or two. He was a retired New Jersey Transit bus driver, who had moved to Omaha a few years earlier and parleyed his nest egg into co-ownership of the bar. One of his routes had been from New Jersey to the City of New York's Port Authority, and he quizzed me a bit about certain nooks and crannies of the City to test my veracity—he quickly concluded that I was being truthful, and we talked for an hour or so. I learned that the individual I was looking for had just been fired.

Though I established a rapport with the bar's co-owner, I didn't feel comfortable with abruptly hitting him up for his former employee's number—I intuited it would backfire on me. Moreover, the bartender was very busy, and I didn't want to interrupt her. So, again, I left the bartender a sizeable tip and planned to return the following night. The next day I phoned David Hill at his girlfriend's, but he hadn't come home the previous night and she was very upset with him. I listened to her vent a litany of frustrations about him, and I concluded that he wasn't long for his current relationship.

On Saturday night the bar was again hopping. I sat at the counter and watched the bartender skirt back and forth. I didn't spot the co-owner, and the bartender was in the midst of mixing drinks in staccato flurries—she looked way too busy for me to bother her. Just as it seemed I would burn another night at the bar with no results, the bartender dashed by me—she smiled and dropped a piece of paper in front of me. It was the phone number I sought. I left a third sizeable tip before leaving.

The individual whose number I garnered was one of three brothers linked to Larry King. I even noticed his name on a few of King's chartered planes' passenger manifests—it was rare to see a name other than King's on a passenger manifest. King had also leased a sports car for one of the brothers—the same sports car that had reportedly been seen on the Boys Town campus and driven by Boys Town Family-Teachers. I phoned the individual the next day—I think he may have felt violated because I had managed to glean his cell phone number. We had a very brief conversation, and he was exceptionally caustic—I quickly concluded that Antarctica would melt before he gave me an interview. I had spent three nights in a bar for a one-minute conversation—such is the nature of this story.

Hill and I eventually managed to converge—I bought him dinner, and he looked the worse for wear. I assiduously try not to give advice: As the Greek playwright Aeschylus wrote, "It is easy when we are in prosperity to give advice to the afflicted." But I told Hill that his addiction was like wrestling with an alligator—the wrestling is only over when the alligator decides it's over, and that's usually after you've been devoured. He didn't react with hostility and actually agreed with me, even though changing his ways wasn't yet in his repertoire.

I also told him that I had returned to the bar on two subsequent occasions, and managed to acquire the former employee's number. I said I phoned him and quickly got nowhere. Hill was disappointed with me for reaching out to the individual without his help, but I replied that he was MIA, and I didn't have time to wait around in pursuit of leads—I had to seize the moment.

After dinner, we walked back to my car, and I pulled out the Leads List again. A second person that jumped out at Hill was Fred Carter—he had been a roommate of Hill's at Boys Town, and his name and number were in the alumni book that Hill provided me. I handed my phone to Hill, and he gave Carter a call—Carter was a 1983 graduate of Boys Town, and hadn't talked to Hill in twenty years. Needless to say, Carter was quite shocked to hear from him, but they spent about ten minutes getting caught up with each other. Hill eventually informed Carter about me and then handed the phone over to me. I talked to Carter for a few minutes—he had a number of questions for me. After I answered his questions, I asked him if I could phone him in the next couple of days—he said that was no problem.

I passed the phone back to Hill, and he wrapped up his conversation with Carter. Hill said that Carter had successfully campaigned to be the "mayor" of Boys Town, and he knew "where all the bodies are buried." I contacted Carter after our introductory conversation, phoning him on a landline so I could record the conversation. He had attended a prestigious college after Boys Town, currently resided in Ohio, and had a lucrative day job. Carter inquired if I had a vendetta against Boys Town, and I replied absolutely not—I had a vendetta against child abuse.

My answer seemed to satisfy him, and he gave me an interview. Carter said that he was cognizant of Larry King's plundering of Boys Town while he was its mayor.

"It would surprise me if a lot of the kids participating in this Larry King situation would say anything against him to this day, but back then, they would never have said anything," Carter told me. "There were certain kids that had the look and marketability, and it was about the money. These were generally the tough kids, and they knew what they wanted and what they wanted to do. They didn't care about the rules and what Boys Town was trying to do, or, I should say, what their individual Family-Teachers were trying to do. These were the type of kids that bucked the system every chance they could, and King capitalized on them."

Carter didn't know about King flying kids out of the state, but he knew about King's "parties" in Omaha and said that Boys Town students recruited other Boys Town students for King. He told me that allowances were a principal means for Family-Teachers to control the kids in their charge, but the funds that the Boys Town students received from King severely crippled any ability to control the kids.

"There were instances where a Family-Teacher would say that you haven't done what you were supposed to do, and you get no allowance," recalled Carter. "To some of the kids it didn't mean anything, because they knew they could get a few dollars doing other things. A lot of Family-Teachers lost control of certain kids because there was nothing to hold over their heads about getting money or privileges."

Like Hill, Carter also alleged to me that Father James Kelly molested him. He said he had a solid support group that enabled him to put it "aside" and move on. "If you don't put it aside, it'll destroy you." Carter didn't directly implicate Father Kelly as being in collusion with King, but he said Kelly would give kids privileges they didn't deserve. "Father Kelly was very instrumental in getting the Family-Teachers to give kids certain privileges—whether they earned them or not. Family-Teachers are not going to deny a priest or the ministers out there pretty much anything—if they call and put in a good word for you, you can pretty much bet that you're out of whatever trouble you had got into."

I asked Carter if he thought Father Hupp knew about King's preying on Boys Town students, and he reinforced the view that Hupp was a "figurehead" or titular frontman for the organization: "Father Hupp primarily allocated funds and raised funds for Boys Town, but Dr. Lonnie Phillips was the man where the buck stopped. If Dr. Phillips didn't want an issue to make it to Father Hupp, it didn't go further than Phillips, and you better not take it further." Phillips was the architect for Boys Town's facelift in the 1970s, and Carter told me that he called a lot of the behind-the-scenes shots at Boys Town. I eventually attempted to contact Phillips, but he was deceased.

I also asked Carter if he was aware of Boys Town students informing the administration about King—he replied that he knew of kids approaching the administration about molestations, but not pertaining to King. Though Carter told me he knew nothing of Boys Town kids being on interstate flights, he corroborated Eulice Washington, Alisha Owen, Troy Boner, and Paul Bonacci concerning Larry King's plundering of Boys Town.

A second Boys Town student on the Leads List that Hill had befriended was Tony Harris, who was a 1981 graduate of Boys Town—a former Boys Town employee provided Gary Caradori with the names of both Carter and Harris. Harris had been an all-star running back for Boys Town's football team and also shone as a sprinter for the track team. Harris was four or five years older than Hill, and Hill looked upon Harris as an "idol." Hill gave me an awestruck description of Harris' athletic feats and his physical attributes, and he was surprised to see his name on the Leads List.

Hill and Harris had actually "partied together" several times after both left Boys Town, but they had gradually lost touch with each other. Before my return to Nebraska, Harris had been one of the alleged victims I had performed a database search on. The most recent contact info I had for Harris was in Kansas City. While in New York, I had phoned the number and reached an elderly woman who was quite curt—she said there was no Tony Harris at the number and hung up on me.

Hill told me that Harris had a couple of children by a former lover who lived in Omaha—we set out to find her. Hill eventually learned that she worked at a fast food restaurant in downtown Omaha. We popped in a few times and, over the course of two days, finally managed to catch her—she gave Hill a phone number for Harris. I was a bit nonplussed when I realized that the phone number she gave Hill was the same phone number I had retrieved from the database search.

I handed Hill my cell phone, and he phoned the number nonetheless. It turned out that the number belonged to Harris' grandmother. Hill and Harris' grandmother had a protracted conversation—Hill once again exhibited his gift of gab. Harris' grandmother would tell Hill that Harris lived somewhere in Kansas City—she said that he checked in with her every now and then. Hill gave Harris' grandmother the phone number of Hill's girlfriend, but we hadn't heard from Harris by the time I ventured back to New York.

Before I left Omaha, I bought Hill a phone card, and we worked out a financial arrangement. For every name on the Leads List that he arranged for me to interview, I would give him $100. I felt $100 was the right amount, because it was enough to provide an incentive, but not enough for him to enlist accomplices for some scheme.

After I returned to New York, Hill kept in touch with me. He called me periodically to tell me about his rocky relationship. Once he left a voicemail and, when I returned the call, I talked to his girlfriend because he wasn't home. She said she had major concerns about his drug abuse, but she loved him dearly and didn't want to end their relationship.

A month or so after my departure, Hill phoned me and said that he had just heard from Harris. Hill talked to Harris about me, and Harris consented to be interviewed. I asked Hill whether or not Harris had disclosed to him that he had been affiliated with King—Hill replied that Harris didn't give him a yes or no; he just said he was willing to talk. I was in the midst of various writing assignments—I told Hill that I couldn't possibly break away until late December or early January.

After I completed the assignments, I spent Christmas with my grandmother in Minneapolis; shortly after Christmas, I drove a rental car to Omaha. By then, Hill's girlfriend had reluctantly booted him out of her apartment, and he was flip-flopping between a homeless shelter near downtown Omaha and the couch in his mother and stepfather's living room. Upon my arrival in Omaha, I initially stopped by their house, but they hadn't seen him in three or four days—I drove to the shelter and looked for him. The shelter's personnel couldn't provide me with his whereabouts either, so I made inquiries among the shelter's residents.

Hill's street name was "Squeaky," and one of the residents gave me a probable location for him: It was a fleabag motel near the shelter. Actually, a fleabag motel is being charitable—the place was a decrepit crackhouse. After I walked over to the "hotel," I took a deep breath, opened the door, and walked inside. I was immediately accosted by a rather foul stench and three crackheads who weren't very gracious—a woman flanked by two guys. They ordered me out—I inferred that they were managerial types. Crack addiction was carved on their faces like twenty miles of bad road. The three were emaciated and wearing T-shirts, even though it was relatively cold outside. I quickly discerned that they didn't have weapons, and I felt I could take my time.

I initially asked them, very politely, if "Squeaky" was about, but they hollered at me to leave. Apparently, they felt my fashion statement was out of place. I glanced around and yelled Hill's first name and also his street name a few times as the trio moved within four feet of me. I then realized that the situation was on the verge of escalating to violence and decided to split.

I left messages for Hill with his parents and the shelter personnel, and he phoned me the following day. We agreed to meet at his parents' house and then embark for Kansas City. When we met, he looked fatigued and depleted—it was disheartening to see him in such rough shape. I felt that Hill, addiction and character defects aside, was a decent guy, and his potential was vast if he cleaned up.

We stopped at a McDonalds before hitting the Interstate, and I bought Hill "lunch." Harris didn't have a phone, so Hill called his grandmother, and she gave us directions to his place. When we arrived in Kansas City, we became hopelessly lost. Hill phoned Harris' grandmother and she met us in a beat-up blue Chevy—we followed her to Harris' house. Harris and his girlfriend lived in a two-story, brick house that was in a poorer neighborhood. Harris' girlfriend had a second-shift job, and Harris was unemployed. After being a star athlete at Boys Town, he had floundered, spending time in the army and also in prison for robbery.

We thanked Harris' grandmother and said good-bye—Hill knocked on the door and Harris quickly stepped outside. The forty-year-old Harris was a trim 6'2"; he wore a white T-shirt tucked into his blue jeans. Harris had the looks and physique of a top-notch male model who had aged gracefully. He and Hill hugged, and then Hill introduced me; we followed Harris into the house's living room. The house was well-kept, and pictures of Harris' children adorned a corner of the living room. Harris pointed out the pictures like any proud father. After Hill and I studied the pictures, we sat on the couch, and Harris seated himself in a facing chair.

Hill and Harris bantered back and forth—small talk mostly. They eventually touched on an event that transpired years earlier in Omaha. They were relatively cryptic, but I discerned someone had snitched on someone—I was never able to find out who snitched on whom or what the event entailed. After they discussed the event, a long silence descended upon the room, and they both looked at me—it was my cue. I told Harris about my investigation and myself. Maybe I touted my bona fides a bit too strongly, because Hill said, "If you weren't righteous, you wouldn't be here."

I told Hill and Harris that my questions to Harris might be awkward, and I suggested that Hill go upstairs and play games on Harris' computer. They agreed with me—Harris accompanied Hill upstairs before returning to the living room. He then sank into the chair next to the couch, leaning forward and folding his hands into his lap.

Harris said he had attended Boys Town for three and half years, and in his junior year a fellow student conscripted him for King's pedophile network.

"The only place I flew was to Washington, DC, but I had opportunities to fly to other places," he told me. "I would say that there were five to ten kids on a flight and about half the kids were Boys Town students. The gatherings would be in people's houses or hotel suites. The men there would want things done to them sexually or they would want to do things to me sexually. The minimum I would get is $100, but I could get up to $500."

Harris said that he was "baited" and "reeled" into participating with King. On his first junket to DC, he recalled that King and the student who conscripted him stated that his participation was optional, and he didn't perform any sexual acts. Though he didn't participate in the sexual activities, King gave him some money nonetheless. Harris maintained that King promised him far more money if he participated. On the next junket he did participate, and he continued for the next two years.

"Appearances can be deceiving, but these men appeared to be well-distinguished gentleman of the upper echelon, very prominent types," Harris remarked about the men at the parties. "They wore jewelry and had nice tailor-made suits, leading me to believe that they were high-society type men. They would pick and choose the kids by mingling over to you and starting a conversation. I was under the impression that Larry King had already set it up. The men and King had their little arrangement, and anything beyond that was on the gentleman. Depending on how you performed, they sometimes offered you an additional gratuity."

Harris claimed he flew to DC about once a month while he was a Boys Town student. He told me he declined several junkets, because of athletics and also because he only participated when he needed cash—"If I needed money, I knew where to go." He said the trips with King really didn't bother some of the Boys Town students, and they became frequent flyers. "Some of the kids who liked it did it all the time, and then there were other kids like me who were only in it for the money. Some kids did it one time and that was it." He also told me that drugs were ubiquitous at the parties—the older men had a big-time affinity for cocaine.

When I first watched *Conspiracy of Silence*, and Boys Town was repeatedly mentioned, I wondered how the kids were able to just up and leave the campus for a weekend—I posed this question to Harris. "I specifically don't know how it was arranged, but it was taken care of—it wasn't difficult for me to get off campus. Plus, you were compensated very well to keep it hush-hush. I got a lot of perks at Boys Town for my participation with King. I'm sure my house parents don't know about King and me to this day." He also said that King issued very dire threats about talking: "You do not want to discuss this with anyone, and if you do there will be consequences out of our control."

Harris, like Carter, felt a loyalty to Boys Town, even though he felt King treated him as if he were "a piece of meat" and exploited him. "I don't want to tarnish Boys Town's name, but that hush-hush needs to stop. It's amazing that it happened period, and especially with such ease. It's also amazing to me that it's never come out throughout the years. It's not my place to judge, but there's a lot of kids who have been sexually exploited and may be experiencing adverse effects in their lives." Harris, though, denied that *he* had been adversely affected by the experience.

I interviewed Harris for about forty-five minutes. He said that I was the first person he ever talked to about his participation with Larry King. Harris provided me with a lot of details, and he expressed a heartfelt sincerity. I also hadn't paid him for the interview, and he didn't have any financial motive to be untruthful. After the interview, Harris went upstairs and retrieved Hill, and the three of us drove to a sports bar. I didn't have a drink, but Hill and Harris imbibed a number of drinks. Though I felt both were being honest with me, I have a tendency to believe that *in vino veritas* can be a useful tool for excavating the truth in some situations. As Hill and Harris became slightly intoxicated, they never diverged from their original statements to me, and I subtly doubled back on them quite a bit. They also repeatedly spoke of sexual conquests with women to the point of overkill, and I felt that their respective abuses had left both deeply scarred.

After dinner and drinks, we drove back to Harris' place. The three of us exchanged hugs on the street—Harris walked to his house as Hill and I headed back to Omaha. I continued to keep in touch with Hill, but Harris moved and I lost touch with him. I made repeated trips to Nebraska over the years, and in February of 2007 I took a jaunt to Kansas City to see Harris. Hill didn't accompany me, because he had been busted for selling crack—street level dealing—and was riding out his second stretch in prison.

I found Harris living in a rickety apartment building in the worst of Kansas City neighborhoods. Several of the buildings surrounding his apartment were gutted or boarded up, and the neighborhood had a Berlin-circa-1945 feel to it. His apartment was practically devoid of furniture, and the pictures of his children where nowhere to be found. Harris seemed as desolate as the abandoned buildings near his apartment—his body had become withered, his face sunken, and his skin was sallow. He looked like he had aged ten years since I first met him. It was obvious to me that he had fallen prey to either crack or crystal meth—his girlfriend was still supporting him. As I drove away from Kansas City that day, I concluded that though Harris had put up a good front three years earlier, his sexual exploitation had wreaked indelible damage that would require extensive help if he were ever to recover.

I gleaned the name of another former Boys Town student, Nikolai Cayman, from John DeCamp—Cayman said that he had been a victim of King's while a Boys Town student. However, the story DeCamp conveyed to me was so strange—even by the standards of the Franklin narrative—I initially had major difficulties taking it too seriously, and I put it on the back burner.

DeCamp recalled being contacted by Nevada law enforcement who were delving into the background of one Frederick Paine, a former Boys Town student, and Cayman's reported brother. Paine had shot a Las Vegas cabdriver in the head and was sitting on Nevada's death row. The law enforcement officials had apparently read *The Franklin Cover-Up,* or someone affiliated with them had read the book, and they told DeCamp they were looking for answers about Paine and Boys Town.

The law enforcement officials also said that Paine had a brother named Andre Paine, whom the feds had apprehended for possession of child pornography. DeCamp eventually managed to talk to Andre, and Andre related a peculiar tale indeed. Andre maintained that he arrived at Boys Town in the mid-1980s, and, shortly thereafter, he had started flying with Larry King. He also told DeCamp that Boys Town personnel, without rhyme or reason, suddenly placed him on an early morning flight to Georgia, where he was abruptly deposited in a psychiatric facility. Andre said his abrupt relocation occurred in late 1988; so I believe DeCamp surmised that if Andre's story was true, his quick exodus from Boys Town would have been brought about by the credit union's collapse and the subsequent attention focused on Larry King. And to cap off a very strange story, Andre Paine had changed his name to Nikolai Cayman.

After DeCamp relayed the story to me, I nodded and smiled. It was just too strange, and I didn't have a clue about where to start in search of corroboration. Paine/Cayman also wasn't on Caradori's Leads List; I didn't have the slightest paper trail connecting him to Boys Town.

But one day I found myself with a little time on my hands, and I wrote a letter to "Nikolai Cayman"—he was in a federal prison in Butner, North Carolina. In the letter, I wrote that I had garnered his name from John DeCamp and asked him about his Boys Town experiences. A month or so elapsed before I received a short letter from him. His handwriting was truly unique—almost like a medieval calligraphy. He didn't seem very happy about receiving my letter: "Since I met Mr. DeCamp, my name has been tossed carelessly to anyone who inquires about past abuse or situations concerning Boys Town and the like without my permission. I am not pleased.... Why on earth would you want to talk to me about my experiences at Boys Town? There are thousands of people who lived at Boys Town as a child. Why not them?"

In my second letter to him I was much more specific: I told him about the story I was working on, and I asked him whether or not he had been affiliated with Larry King. His second letter, considerably longer, with the same calligraphy-like handwriting, followed. He started out with "Dear Nick" instead of "Mr. Bryant," and I felt like my second letter had made a little progress. He thanked me for my candor, even though he didn't give me an answer about his involvement with Larry King; rather, he plied me with a number of questions and also remarked on an issue that is particularly germane: "When you write your story my name would be mentioned (which I don't mind) and anybody who would like to challenge what I say would be quick to point out my criminal history. Unless the rules changed, felons are not to be trusted—ever."

Most convicts I've talked to over the years, especially if they've experienced horrific childhoods, have had a tendency to blame their incarcerations on a variety of factors other than themselves—their upbringing, snitches, lawyers, prosecutors, judges, etc. But Cayman took full, unflinching responsibility for his current circumstances: "I've created a lot of problems in my adult life, and I cannot blame anybody but myself. When I was getting sentenced my lawyer wanted to bring up my childhood and the many factors that made it so impossible. He had access to documents that reported abuse by a lot of people.... His reason was that he felt that the judge would have mercy on me and give me a lesser sentence. However, I objected to this.... My firm belief is that, though you are not responsible for how you are raised and how you turned out, you are responsible for your actions. The law is the law...."

I wrote a third letter to Cayman and also sent him *The Road Less Traveled*. His second letter had been introspective, and I felt that the book might be beneficial to him. His third letter thanked me for *The Road Less Traveled*, and he wrote that he was "enjoying" it. Cayman initially discussed Boys Town: "Boys Town, as a whole to me, was a successful failure. I learned a lot about social skills and how to treat people. Yet, I did so at the price of losing my soul.... Still, as I stated before, I have had good times, bad times, and scary times at Boys Town. Through it all, it was the best I was going to get at the time."

His letter then shifted to Larry King: "You asked me about my interactions with him [King]. What can I say? Whatever I tell you I believe you already know. I can supply an answer, but before I do I ask this question of you: What do you know or have heard about him? I don't mean to frustrate you, but I don't want to tell you something you already heard or know. My interaction with Larry King was through child prostitution.

I suppose you want some detail, but refer to my question before you ask. Please."

After Cayman and I had a few correspondences, I opted to take my first incremental steps to corroborate his story. I knew where to find his purported brother—Nevada's death row—so I wrote him a letter, inquiring if he had a brother who had changed his name to Nikolai Cayman. I received a letter from him about a month later—he wrote that his brother had, in fact, changed his name to Nikolai Cayman and had also attended Boys Town. The information of a death row inmate is dubious at best, but he had absolutely no reason to lie—I decided to continue exploring Cayman's story.

In the interim, I had written a letter to Cayman, explaining the exact allegations that I was investigating. Though I wanted additional details about King, I requested that he provide me with a short biography—he acquiesced: "Coming to Boys Town was perhaps the best thing that could have happened to me. The year was 1985, and I had just turned eleven years old. At that time life wasn't so good. My father kicked me out of his house after only living with him two years of my entire life. I went through many foster homes but eventually ended up at a mental hospital. I wasn't crazy. I was depressed. Nobody wanted me because I was too old. Most people wanted a child eight years or younger. My caseworker put me in the hospital for storage until Boys Town would accept me. After five months I arrived there. My brothers were at Boys Town, and things seemed to be getting better. I did not live with them, but they were not far away.

"Boys Town was more than I expected. Father Peter became the new director, and MGM was making a movie called *Miracle of the Heart*. My Family-Teachers were OK, and my first month was OK. Yet serious problems began to arise. I was the youngest student in our house, and I was not well liked because of it. I was hit, kicked, slapped, and almost raped by some of the older boys. My Family-Teachers did their best to protect me by giving me a room by myself and kept me near them when we ate or went on family outings. Though my brothers were near, I hardly visited them. I became miserable and ran away to my mother's apartment often. I would stay for a day and then return back to Boys Town, who eventually barred me from seeing her...."

"My school grades were average, but my behavior was different. I had this, 'I don't give a damn,' attitude and usually did what I wanted within reason. I might curse a student out but certainly not the teacher. No. The most I would do is test their limits—pushing the envelope. This attracted my peer group, and thus popularity followed from within the school. At home, however, things weren't getting any better. Eventually I was moved to another home....

"At one point they were considered to be one of the best houses on campus. But, like most Family-Teachers, they seemed to be frustrated with the system Boys Town wanted them to follow. Soon their attitude went sour, and they began to play mind games. One moment they liked you and the next they didn't—for no reason. At one point, for example, they told me that they received permission for me to visit my mom, whom I haven't seen or heard from in a long time. I received weekend passes to see her, but I didn't. There was another agenda at hand, and in truth they never knew her address or phone number. But I would get these passes to leave campus under the assumption that I would visit my mother. Then one day out of the blue, they denied ever getting permission for me to visit her....

"Then one day early in the morning I was put on a plane to Georgia with no explanation other than saying I was terminated. Previously ... I was given a pass to see my mother (which I didn't) and when I returned, Boys Town said that I ran away.... When I arrived in Georgia, I was a mess. I hardly knew my name, date, month, and even my location. That was all that was needed for a commitment to the mental ward. For two and a half years I was in a mental hospital. I was in the hospital so long that nobody knew why any more. Eventually I returned back to Boys Town."

In the letter chronicling his Boys Town experiences, Cayman didn't mention Larry King. But I surmised that if he had flown with King, it would have been during the alleged bogus trips to visit his mother. He and I had a number of correspondences—he seemed sincere and provided sound details, so I encouraged him to phone me. After a workday of writing, I have great difficulties composing letters, and I also wanted a taped interview. He eventually phoned me, and we had the first of many phone conversations.

I was somewhat struck by Nikolai's voice—it was gentle and had the inflection of a naïve teenager. I thought he would have the sharp edges of a con who'd been through myriad institutions, and I was reminded of the way Alisha Owen had sounded when Gary Caradori initially interviewed her: She too had experienced horrific events, but came across on the videotapes as being frozen in adolescence.

Cayman, like Harris, said a fellow Boys Town student hooked him for King, but it was a different student: "I was introduced to King by another student who told me I could make a lot of money and meet a lot of different people—I could make something of myself. I was never told what I had to do to make the money, but that's how everything got started."

He recalled being taken to the Twin Towers on his first King-related outing, and photographed in the nude—he described the photographer as white, thin, and having blondish hair. Though his description was vague, it loosely fit Rusty Nelson. After the Twin Towers "photo shoot," he recounted subsequent outings to the Travel Lodge in Omaha for a pedophilic encounter and then to "some place out in the sticks" of Nebraska. He maintained that his first flight with King was a charter to Colorado. He couldn't remember exactly how many flights he was on, but he estimated approximately twenty.

"I was eleven years old when I started to fly with Larry King," said Cayman. "There were always other Boys Town kids on the flights, and there were always drugs involved. As I got older, I attended the parties more infrequently. When I was eleven, I was the man. My Family-Teachers said that I had a pass to my mother's. My mother is schizophrenic, and she didn't do too well—she was living in poverty. They would take me to places that I knew my mother could not afford, and one of King's people would pick me up. I never submitted the weekend passes—I never knew who submitted the passes."

Unlike Harris, Cayman told me he received cash only once—$50. "King always said 'I'll get you later, but you can have anything you want at Boys Town.'" Cayman claimed that his Family-Teachers provided him with clothes and toys that weren't afforded other Boys Town students. "As I'd get ready to go on a pass, my Family-Teachers would say ... 'let's go get you some new clothes.' If I said I wanted a keyboard, I would get a keyboard. Boys Town provided for clothes, but they wouldn't provide for the stuff that I received—watches, necklaces, and nice, fine clothes. King said he had an arrangement with Boys Town—'Whatever you need, all you got to do is say it and you'll get it.'"

Also, unlike Harris, Cayman divulged that he was subjected to extremely sadistic pedophiles—he related stories of pedophilic sadism similar to those conveyed by Alisha Owen, Troy Boner, Danny King, and Paul Bonacci. "A lot of the parties were outrageous—it was like one big orgy, but some of these parties weren't always nice. You'd get tortured, handcuffed, beaten, and videotaped. To this day, I have scars all over my body from flying with King. Doctors have asked me where I got all these scars."

I didn't broach the subject of Satanism, but Cayman, like Moore and Bonacci, said that some of the gatherings were satanic: "They would have these weird rituals, but I didn't realize what they were. At first I thought whatever, but, as I got older, I started to realize that these were satanic rituals. There was cutting, blood drinking, chants, and dancing."

Cayman said that he could no longer keep the abuse to himself after a weekend of extremely sadistic treatment in 1988, and he told his Family-Teachers about his outings with Larry King. "I came back, and it wasn't a good weekend. In fact, it was really bad. It was very sadistic, and I drank a lot of alcohol that weekend. I sat down with my Family-Teachers and attempted to tell them what was going on. I had never spoke about Larry King before. The next morning, early in the morning, they put me on a plane to Georgia and said I was terminated. The funny thing about it is that the caseworkers in Georgia were surprised too, because they said 'Listen we just got this call two hours ago, saying you were on the plane and you were coming to Georgia.' So they weren't really given a full reason as to why I was terminated either."

In the biographical letter Cayman wrote, he mentioned that he was at the psychiatric hospital for "two and a half years" before returning to Boys Town—a very strange story indeed. Though Cayman sounded very sincere and provided certain nuances that lent credibility to his account, I initially had no idea of how to corroborate his story: I felt Boys Town would never give me his records.

When I located a 1986 Boys Town yearbook, Cayman's picture was nowhere to be found—I didn't jump to conclusions one way or the other. Instead, I wrote a letter to his brother in Nevada, inquiring about the first year Cayman attended Boys Town. His brother wasn't exactly sure— he recalled that it was around 1987. If his recollection had been around 1986, it would have been an acceptable margin of error. It wouldn't have corroborated Cayman's story by any means, but I understand that recollections can get fuzzy over the years. But, given the fact that his brother said 1987, and that Cayman wasn't in the 1986 Boys Town yearbook, I couldn't help doubting his story, even though he seemed sincere.

I wrote him a letter about the discrepancies, and he phoned me. He stuck to his story—he arrived in 1985, he was sent to a Georgia psychiatric hospital in 1988, and then returned to Boys Town in 1990. He continued to stick to his story as I grilled him. I felt terrible about grilling him, because he had obviously been subjected to a brutal childhood and had suffered greatly—whether or not he had actually flown around with Larry King. He sent me a letter after I grilled him, and he continued to stick to his story: "I've asked nothing from you, and I did not contact you. I have told you what I remembered. I have not lied to you. There is no reason to. I understand the conflict and its implications on my character and my word."

As I more or less gave up on trying to corroborate Cayman's story, I encountered affiliates of federal law enforcement who offered to help me out—I could not help noting the irony. Like most Franklin-related encounters, it took a while for trust to be established. But after they deemed me trustworthy, they gave me the dates of Cayman's attendance at Boys Town: They said Cayman initially attended Boys Town in 1985, and that on March 30, 1988, he was abruptly flown to the Georgia Regional Hospital. He spent approximately twenty-two months being hospitalized in Georgia before returning to Boys Town.

So ultimately everything Cayman told me about his dates corresponded to the federal sources. The only discrepancy is that he spent approximately twenty-two months at Georgia hospitals instead of two and a half years. In his state, as he looked back on his life, I thought it was certainly understandable that twenty-two months in a psychiatric hospital when he was fourteen or fifteen years old felt more like thirty months.

Now I felt considerable remorse about grilling him, and I sent a letter apologizing. He phoned, and, though he seemed a bit miffed, he accepted my apology. He said that he wasn't so much angry with me, but at the fact that he didn't appear in the 1986 yearbook—it had been yet another example of his "invisibility" as a child. In response to my question of how he ended up back at Boys Town, he replied that he eventually wrote Boys Town a letter from the psychiatric hospital in Georgia requesting to return.

Perplexed, I asked him why he wanted to return to Boys Town. He said that though Boys Town had been a succession of painful ordeals, it was still better than the mental hospital. In fact, it was probably the best place he'd been sent to as a child.

Locating former Boys Town students on Caradori's Leads List has been practically a mission impossible. They seem to be nomadic and marginalized—none have permanent addresses. After considerable effort, I did manage to find two more, but one refused to talk to me, and the second, Jeff Hubbell, denied any affiliation with King.

Another former Boys Town student on the Leads List was Rue Fox. Though I knew how Caradori came up with Hill, Carter, and Harris, I had no idea how he garnered Fox's name. In my database searches for Fox, he initially came up in Nebraska, but then he appeared in Texas. In 2006, he started to reappear in Nebraska, and I collected various addresses for him and started knocking on doors in Omaha. I never quite managed to get a track on his current address—his nomadic, marginalized ways made it difficult to catch up with him. Omaha's White Pages were also loaded with that surname: Calling every Fox would have been far too time-consuming.

I finally hired an Omaha-based private detective in April of 2007 to find Rue Fox. The detective gave me the address of Fox's father, and told me that Fox was probably living with him. The private detective discharged a grave warning about Fox: He had a "rap sheet a mile long," a "history of violence," and had been incarcerated for armed robbery. I found Fox's father's house in a run-down neighborhood of South Omaha. He lived in a dilapidated two-story, yellow frame house. I knocked on the door without getting any response, so I left a note for Fox on the front door. I introduced myself, said I was a journalist, and left the number of my cell phone.

Fox phoned me later in the afternoon and immediately asked if I were a cop. I replied that I was a journalist—I said that I wanted to ask him a few questions about Boys Town and Larry King; he became quite emotional after I mentioned Larry King's name. He then repeatedly inquired if I were a cop, and I repeatedly responded that I was a journalist.

He agreed to meet me at 7:00 P.M., and he chose a bar in South Omaha. He said if I were a cop, he would "snap" my neck. I arrived at the bar about ten minutes early—its front room was filthy, and there were perhaps ten patrons bellied up to the counter. The bartender was a portly middle-aged woman, wearing a loose-fitting dark red housedress and dark-framed glasses. Her shoulder-length, black-grayish hair and overall appearance were unkempt, and her face had the premature grooves of acute alcoholism—she seemed somewhat dumbfounded when I ordered just a cranberry juice. A few patrons also gave me strange glances.

The patrons said little among themselves as they drank and watched television—they were there to drink, and to drink until they died, whether it was the next day or in ten years. I sat at a corner table that gave me a panorama of the front room and nursed my cranberry juice, which didn't taste quite right. As I sipped the cranberry juice, I thought I should probably pop an antibiotic after leaving the bar.

I also braced myself for Rue Fox—he sounded dangerous and paranoid on the phone; I suspected drug addiction. Fox eventually arrived with two friends; a few of the patrons greeted him by his first name. He was a stocky, barrel-chested 5'10", wearing a black T-shirt, blue jeans, and boots. He had obviously hit the weights pretty hard during his prison stretch for armed robbery or at some other point. His thick, brown hair had been cropped into a flattop; he had a square jaw and his face was scarred up—he looked like a pit bull that had taken on human form.

I stood up and piped, "Rue," extending my hand. He didn't take my hand, but nodded his head in the direction of the back room, blurting, "Back here!" The four of us walked into the darkened back room in silence, and we took a seat at the table farthest from the bar's entrance. We were the only patrons in the back room, and I quickly noted the location of the back door—just in case I needed to make a hasty departure.

Shortly after we sat down, Fox again asked me if I were a cop. Once more, I said I was a journalist. He told me to stand up—after I stood up, he frisked me. When he was sufficiently satisfied that I wasn't armed or wired, we sat down and he started firing questions at me about how I came by his name. I felt that only tangible evidence would abate his paranoia, so I pulled out Caradori's Leads List from my backpack and showed him his name on the list. In addition to stating that Fox was a former Boys Town student, the Leads List also mentioned a foster home where he had resided.

He snatched the Leads List from my hands and walked over to an adjacent pool table—he paged through it underneath the pool table lights. After he studied the Leads List for maybe five minutes, he walked back to the table and handed it to me, saying, "I believe you." Fox's acknowledgement certainly brought relief to me—his friends relaxed too, as if an electrical current nettling the three had suddenly been cut.

I bought a pitcher of beer to further ease the tension. After Fox and his friends promptly pounded down the pitcher, Fox asked me for a lift to whereabouts unknown—I quickly consented. I wanted to get him away from his friends—I thought it best not to broach the subject of sexual abuse around them.

After Fox and I left the bar, he wanted me to stop at a liquor store. He bought a pint of cheap vodka, and then he directed me to the proximity of a cop spot—as in copping drugs. He took long pulls off the vodka and repeatedly said, "You opened the wrong door. I had that door locked and bolted." He eventually directed me to pull over and park. Holding up the pint of vodka, he said, "This is the only thing that keeps the door closed."

In the bar, I had noticed the tracks on his arm, and after we parked I asked him what he was shooting—"Crystal meth," he replied. I then attempted to get him to talk about Larry King, but he kept saying, "You opened the wrong door." At one point, his ferocious façade briefly crumbled, and he actually started to cry. I then delicately pressed him on the subject of Larry King—he became increasingly hostile and belligerent, and I decided to back off. Before Fox departed into the dusk, he gave me the name and number of either his "half-sister" or "stepsister." He inexplicably told me I should call her.

I found Fox extremely frightening, and I felt that I might need a little help with him. So I phoned the "sister" the following day, and I related our conversation of the previous night—she agreed to have lunch with me the next day. I picked her up at either a therapeutic community or a long-term treatment center—she too had been hooked on drugs prior to cleaning up. As we ate lunch, we talked about Fox. She said that she and Fox had been very close as kids—she thought that Fox giving her number to me was a plea for help. I asked her if she was cognizant of Fox being sexually abused at Boys Town—she said that she suspected it, but he never overtly discussed the circumstances. She told me that Fox had attempted to clean up before, but she felt he just couldn't stay clean because of the unaddressed sexual abuse.

Following lunch, we drove over to Fox's father's house. Fox was in the driveway, and he was extremely hostile to me. "You opened the wrong door," was his first remark. His sister scolded him for his rudeness—I was surprised by her tone. After we reached a détente of sorts, I realized that the time just wasn't right, and I gave his sister a ride back to her facility.

I felt both ethical and practical quandaries over Fox. My ethical quandary was rooted in the fact that his reaction to the name of Larry King had been so intense and dysphoric that I felt surely something must have gone down, but I was unsure if he was psychologically equipped to "open the door." My practical quandary was that he was dangerous, and he might transfer that hostility to me and simply shoot me. At that point, I had been on my Franklin odyssey for over four years: I had thought that being taken out by men in black was always a possibility, but to be shot by an unhinged crystal meth addict was a little too anticlimactic for me.

I pondered these considerations for a few days before I decided to give Fox one final shot. As I drove to his father's house, I felt quite uneasy. I didn't have his sister along to buffer his fierce hostility, and I thought the situation had the potential to quickly spiral out of control. I arrived around noon and found Fox and two of his buddies working on a mini-van in the driveway. As I tentatively approached the three, my mouth parched and my fight-or-flight urges began to kick in. But Fox, surprisingly, gave me a very warm greeting—he had hit up crystal meth an hour or two earlier, and swilled maybe a pint of vodka too, and he was comfortably anesthetized, even though he didn't appear buzzed. Fox's meth addiction and alcoholism had progressed to the point where the fix and vodka merely made him "normal."

Fox gestured to the garage, and I followed him. When he felt we were out of earshot of his buddies, he said he had been thinking about giving me an interview. I was shocked by his sudden metamorphosis and decided to stick around. Fox even invited me into the house and introduced me to his father, who had spent several years in prison. He was laid out on the couch watching television. With longish, straight gray hair and a gaunt, blanched face, he didn't appear long for this world. As he watched television, he alternated between an oxygen mask and a cigarette. Fox had told him about me, and he didn't seem too happy to make my acquaintance.

Fox and his friends either had warrants out for their arrest or their driver's licenses were suspended, and my mobility made me a welcome addition to the group. Throughout the afternoon, Fox and his buddies used me as a go-fer—I drove them to various places, including an auto parts store and a McDonalds. After four or five hours, and a handful of stops, I gave his two friends rides home, and then Fox and I talked about Boys Town and Larry King.

Fox confided that he had consulted with his sister and father about giving me an interview—his sister said yea and his father said nay. He said his sister told him that he would never be able to overcome his drug addiction and alcoholism unless he started talking about his sexual abuse; I guess the father was taking his ex-con mentality of telling no secrets to his grave. Fox said that he usually listened to his father, but this time he felt that his sister was right.

Fox was born in Galveston, and his mother died when he was just an infant. Fox's father—with Fox and his older brother in tow—moved to Omaha in the late 1970s. After the move, his father was incarcerated, and Fox began his long odyssey from "foster home to foster home to foster home"—he ended up in Boys Town at the age of "twelve or thirteen." By the time he made it to Boys Town, he had already been molested by one of his previous caregivers.

Shortly after arriving at Boys Town, Fox maintains, he was shepherded into counseling for his prior sexual abuse. His counselor, Leslie Collins, had a master's in social work and a Ph.D. in sociology from Yale, and his specialty was counseling sexually-abused kids. Throughout the 1980s and into the mid-1990s, Collins counseled numerous Boys Town residents who were the victims of sexual abuse.

According to Fox, Dr. Collins introduced him to Larry King. It may sound unlikely that a sexual-abuse counselor would introduce a troubled adolescent who has already been sexually victimized to a notorious pedophile like King, but the counselor had a few secrets himself—he too was a pedophile. In 1996, Collins was charged with repeatedly molesting his two stepdaughters. Only after these allegations surfaced would Boys Town terminate its long-standing association with Collins. Nikolai Cayman asserts that Dr. Collins was also his counselor.

After his introduction to King, Fox told me, he initially liked the man: "I thought King was a cool dude." King took him to various places around Omaha, including Crossroads, a popular Omaha mall, and also to movie theaters. But Fox's honeymoon with Larry King was short-lived. "One night he started touching me inappropriately," stammered Fox, almost convulsing as he fought back tears. "He started rubbing my legs, saying that it was all right, that he wasn't doing anything bad. He asked me to unbutton my pants, and then he started playing with my penis. He molested me ten or eleven times."

Fox claimed their pedophilic encounters were always one-on-one and often in a park. In this respect, Fox's story is very different from the other alleged victims, because he said he never attended pedophilic orgies at the Twin Towers and was never flown around in chartered planes. Fox became quite frenetic when he discussed King's increasing aggression and viciousness: King started practicing anal intercourse, resulting in a laceration. "I had thirteen stitches put in me. My house parents took me to get the stitches, but they didn't know how it happened—it was my little secret. I was ashamed and scared—I didn't know how to deal with it at that time. King told me if I said anything, he would just deny it—they would believe him over me."

Fox told me he refused to have additional encounters with King, but the emotional turmoil of being tossed among various foster homes and repeatedly molested had taken a severe toll on him, and he started acting out at Boys Town. At first, Boys Town staff sent him to a "farm" for troubled students, and then they sent him to a psychiatric ward at Saint Joseph Hospital.

"Larry King took a lot of trust out of me," he said. "I put needles in my arm every day and drink every day just to hide from it. King took away my dignity; he hurt my self-esteem and pride. I'm thirty-six years old, and I have a lot of anger in me. I've been locked up in penitentiaries and mental institutions—all over this. I wasn't a bad child. I didn't ask for this to be done to me. If this didn't happen to me at Boys Town, I could have had a football scholarship. I could have graduated. I could have done anything I wanted. Larry King killed my motivation—I just gave up."

Hill, Carter, Harris, and Cayman all alleged abuse while at Boys Town, but they still felt that Boys Town had redemptive qualities that helped them. Fox, however, looks back at Boys Town with absolutely no fond memories. "Boys Town ain't nothing but a get-up. My world got crushed when my father was taken, and Boys Town crushed me even more."

As I interviewed Fox, he occasionally broke down in tears. The spite and rancor he wore like a protective suit of body armor dissolved. The ex-con with a "history of violence" that I was warned about morphed into a damaged boy before my very eyes. Actually, the damaged boy had been there the whole time—I just hadn't noticed him.

I left Nebraska three days after interviewing Fox—I gave him a calling card before I departed, and he phoned occasionally. When his father died, he called me. He was seriously broken up about his father. He was also on the threshold of being homeless. I suggested a rehab program that was affiliated with the shelter where Hill had crashed, and he eventually took me up on my suggestion.

We kept in touch as he started to clean up. I returned to Nebraska in November of 2007—I looked him up and took him to lunch. He had changed considerably since our first meeting: His anger had abated, and he seemed to be much more at peace with himself. I dropped him off at the facility and haven't heard from him since. I truly hope he hasn't reverted to his former ways.

After I met Fox, I started looking into the background of Dr. Leslie Collins—the counselor at Boys Town who Fox said introduced him to Larry

King. Collins was arraigned for molesting his two stepdaughters, starting at the ages of ten and thirteen. During the course of his trial, a depraved profile emerged: In addition to recurrently molesting his stepdaughters, sometimes on a daily basis, he also required that they videotape or photograph sexual encounters with their boyfriends.

He even held his elder stepdaughter at knifepoint for hours when she attempted to break off their "relationship." Collins also threatened to kill her boyfriend if she ended her "relationship" with Collins—she took his threats very seriously: he had previously disclosed to her that he carried out covert activities for the CIA.

Collins would ultimately be sentenced to thirty-to-fifty years for the sexual assaults on his stepdaughters. He appealed his hefty sentence, but the three appellate judges hearing his appeal wouldn't budge: "Collins' abuse of these girls is so bizarre that even those of us who think we have 'seen it all' are appalled," the judges wrote in their decision.

I found that Boys Town Press published two books that were co-authored by Collins: The first was written for the victims of sexual abuse, and the second was intended for therapists who worked with the victims. I managed to acquire Collins' first book published by Boys Town Press, and it was dedicated to the "American People whose love and concern for neglected and homeless children and generosity and support of Father Flanagan's Boys' Home have since 1917 made our famous motto a reality in the lives of thousands of children—"He ain't heavy, Father ... he's my brother."

I never managed to acquire Collin's second book, but I did find a synopsis. The book's introduction was written by Father Valentine Peter, Executive Director of Boys Town from 1985 until 2005.

Gary Caradori noted that Peter was "very uncooperative" with his investigation, and Father Peter wasn't receptive to talking to me either. I also found it very difficult to interview former employees of Boys Town. I've interviewed some who claimed they didn't have a clue about the sexual abuse of Boys Town students, and I have a tendency to believe them. I've also talked to former Boys Town employees who seemed to have knowledge of various improprieties, but they declined to meet with me. I arranged to meet with a former Boys Town police chief, who didn't show up. After he snubbed me, I phoned him—he never returned my calls. Moreover, the makers of *Conspiracy of Silence* found Boys Town administrators unwilling to talk to them regarding allegations that Larry King used the orphanage as a pedophilic reservoir.

Eulice Washington told her foster mother, Julie Walters, investigator Lowe, and the FBI that Larry King exploited Boys Town students, and she stands by her previous statements. In the testimony of Owen, Boner, and Bonacci, videotaped by Caradori, they said Boys Town students were involved in King's pedophile network. If they're telling the truth, and if Carter, Harris, Cayman and Fox are being truthful, then Larry King plundered Boys Town throughout the 1980s.

Bonnie Cosentino— 2007

Karen Ormiston — 2007

—Chapter Four—

A Carefully Crafted Hoax

O ne of Gary Caradori's ultimate objectives was to move the Committee's child-abuse investigation beyond the shady margins of provincial law enforcement and into a grand jury. As I've already mentioned, after the Committee submitted Caradori's videotaped statements of Alisha Owen, Troy Boner, and Danny King to Attorney General Spire in January of 1990, Spire requested that Douglas County's district judges convene and call for a grand jury to investigate Franklin-related child-abuse allegations. And on January 31, Douglas County's Presiding Judge, James Buckley, announced that the Douglas County judges had signed an order to impanel a grand jury. Spire didn't consult with Senator Schmit about the grand jury, but Schmit weighed in on the Committee's role in the grand jury's formation: "I think we contributed to the facts that led to the calling of a grand jury," said Schmit. "There would not have been a grand jury if there had not been a legislative committee."

Though Caradori initially welcomed the impaneling of a grand jury, he also realized the inherent flaws of the grand jury process, which makes the initial decision to indict—formally accuse—a criminal defendant to stand trial. Unlike a trial, a grand jury proceeding is private, and there is no cross-examination or presentation of the defense's case. The special prosecutor calls the witnesses, questions the witnesses, and selects the evidence that is shown to the grand jurors, who are ordinary citizens. Generally, only witnesses and evidence deemed relevant by special prosecutors are pursued by grand juries, and special prosecutors are in a unique position to twist grand jurors' judgments in a particular direction. A former Chief Appellate Judge of New York State once quipped that a special prosecutor could persuade a grand jury to "indict a ham sandwich."

The Douglas County judges originally wanted to name Douglas County Attorney Ronald Staskiewicz as the grand jury's special prosecutor. But Staskiewicz publicly rejected their offer, citing a possible "conflict of interest" because of innuendo that Douglas County law enforcement had abetted a cover-up of the child-abuse allegations. In early February 1990, the Douglas County judges tapped Samuel Van Pelt as the special prosecutor.

The tall, lean, fifty-three-year-old Van Pelt grew up in Lincoln, Nebraska and was a graduate of the University of Nebraska Law School. In 1972, Nebraska Governor J.J. Exon appointed him as a district judge in Lancaster County. Van Pelt had a judicial pedigree—his father had been an esteemed US District Court Judge—but he concluded that being a judge was an "unpleasant job" and resigned after eleven years on the bench. Van Pelt lived on a farm in rural Hickman, Nebraska, and he was twice divorced with two sons, one from each marriage.

Nebraska Attorney General Spire said that Van Pelt was an "absolutely outstanding" choice for special prosecutor, but outside the Attorney General's Office, Van Pelt received mixed reviews, ranging from bafflement to outrage. Some government insiders felt that Van Pelt's rubbing shoulders with Nebraska's high-flyers was integral to his appointment and questioned whether or not he possessed the wealth of experience required to tackle Franklin's complexities. "There's a good-old-boy aspect to Van Pelt," commented a former state senator. "He likes to get together with, and buddy up with, influential people.... Van Pelt's probably not the most experienced person for the job he has right now."

Though some Nebraskans gave Van Pelt a lukewarm appraisal, others viewed him with scalding contempt. Shortly after Van Pelt's appointment had been announced, forty-three Nebraskans sent a letter to the Speaker of the Legislature charging that Van Pelt was merely a "hired gun for the state." Their feelings about Van Pelt centered on an investigation he had directed five years earlier—they claimed he covered up the shooting death of a Nebraska farmer by an NSP SWAT team. The farmer was holed up in his house after the bank foreclosed on his farm, and NSP officials claimed that he charged into his front yard with a blazing M-16, where an awaiting SWAT team mowed him down.

The farmer's friends and family argued that he never fired his weapon—their allegations were reinforced by the fact that the NSP never performed gunpowder tests on the farmer's hands. The farmer's son commented on Van Pelt's 607-page report exonerating the NSP of any misconduct: "A lot of it was not true. There were little nooks and crannies that changed the outcome of the way the story read."

Van Pelt declined to comment on the citizens' letter that declared his appointment proved the fix was in, but a *World-Herald* editorial lauded Van Pelt and insisted he had simply "followed the evidence" in the farmer's shooting. The editorial maintained that the letter was a "cruel" denunciation promulgated by wayward citizens entwined in a "conspiracy theory," and didn't merit Van Pelt's response: "The accusation that he is a 'hired gun' for the government didn't deserve the dignity of his reply. But others need not be silent. The accusation deserves to be condemned."

Van Pelt granted an interview to the *World-Herald* in the first week of February. He confirmed that the grand jury would convene in March 1990, and he pledged to bring himself up to speed on the investigation in the interim. "I feel the integrity of the system is being challenged," he said. "I feel the system needs to work." To help ensure the system's integrity, Van Pelt stressed he would curtail his public comments on the upcoming grand jury, because he hoped to quell the "unsubstantiated and unfounded" rumors that had arisen thus far. It's telling that Van Pelt would already be focusing on unsubstantiated and unfounded "rumors" in early February, prior to commencing his investigation.

In a March *World-Herald* article, Van Pelt commented on his seeming obsession with Franklin: "It's the most fascinating thing I've ever encountered in my life," he said. "It's just a fascinating tale." The newspaper reported that because of his preoccupation with the case, he had narrowly avoided three car accidents in recent weeks: "I think about it when I'm driving—it's all consuming. I've been barraged with so much information."

As Van Pelt was reportedly having difficulties behind the wheel, a three-member panel was tasked with the duty of selecting sixteen grand jurors and three alternates. The panel included presiding Judge Buckley, a lawyer chosen by Judge Buckley, and Douglas County's Election Commissioner. The panel claimed to have interviewed forty individuals randomly chosen from a pool of eighty citizens who were at least nineteen years old and either registered to vote or licensed to drive. The panel released a statement that said they were striving to ensure that the nineteen grand jurors represented a wide cross-section of society regarding "age, gender, occupation, race, and station of life." The identities of the nineteen grand jurors were kept secret and the press was not even allowed to take their pictures. I eventually obtained the sealed transcripts of most of the grand jury's proceedings.

The grand jury formally convened in the landmark Douglas County Courthouse on March 19, 1990, in a courtroom that was normally used by the Douglas County Juvenile Court, and the proceedings had all the pomp and circumstance of a media spectacle. Nebraska's citizens and the media from far and wide eagerly anticipated the grand jury. All and sundry seemed to have countless questions and uncertainties about the "lurid" allegations, and, starving for answers, they expected Van Pelt and company to nourish them with the truth.

Before Van Pelt called his first witness, Judge Buckley gave a litany of instructions to the grand jurors, including their ultimate objective, or "charge." Buckley said he was placing "no limits on the grand jury's power and duty to investigate every aspect of this case." The grand jurors were "empowered to uncover any wrongdoing by all individuals, however prominent or obscure, who have been accused in the Legislative Committee's investigation, whether or not they have any relationship to the Franklin Credit Union."

After Buckley dispensed with the opening instructions and formalities, Van Pelt called the grand jury's first witness, Patricia Flocken, and introduced the first exhibit: Julie Walters' interviews of Eulice Washington. As noted, the grand jury's proceedings and testimony were blanketed in secrecy, but if Flocken had been able to tell the press about her grand jury experience, the hopes of everyone who wanted to see justice on behalf of children would have been dashed. "Van Pelt was a jerk," Flocken told me. "I don't think he was brought in to find the truth—I think he was brought in to expose the children as liars. I didn't think he was at all interested in the kids I represented."

Van Pelt and his assistant, Terry Dougherty, fired questions at Flocken for an hour or so. Their questions primarily pertained to the inferno that was the Webb household, and the unadulterated abuse the Webbs had doled out to the children living in their home. Van Pelt grilled Flocken on the sexual abuse allegations levied against Jarrett Webb by

Eulice Washington–Flocken discussed the NSP polygraph that Eulice had passed concerning Webb's repeated molestations and also the Washington County Attorney's refusal to press formal charges against Webb.

Flocken told the grand jury that she, an NSP Investigator, and two DSS caseworkers had a meeting in the office of Washington County Attorney Patrick Tripp. Everyone at the meeting, except Tripp, believed Washington's allegations about Jarrett Webb. Flocken testified that Tripp said the Webbs' attorney informed him the Webbs found a book Washington was reading that had "a story line" similar to the allegations she was making about Jarrett Webb, and Tripp felt "it was possible for her to pass a polygraph exam because she had somehow psyched herself into believing that it was all true."

Van Pelt eventually asked Flocken about Julie Walters' report, and she gave him the chronology of her receiving the report from Julie Walters and handing it off to Carol Stitt. Though Van Pelt inquired about the sequence of events leading to Stitt's acquiring the report, he didn't focus on the contents of the report.

When Van Pelt and Dougherty finished questioning Flocken, the grand jurors had an opportunity to question her too. The grand jurors followed the lead of Van Pelt and Dougherty, so they didn't concentrate on the Julie Walters' report either. Rather, they focused on the Webbs' physical and emotional abuse of the children. After the grand jurors' questions, Assisstant Special Prosecutor Dougherty asked Flocken if she believed Eulice Washington's allegations regarding Jarrett Webb and also the allegations about Larry King contained in Julie Walters' report. "I believe everything the child has said," Flocken replied. Dougherty then pressed Flocken on why she believed Washington was telling the truth about both series of events, and she replied that Washington's accounts of her abuse by Jarrett Webb to the NSP and to Julie Walters had "enough similarity and commonality" for her to believe that Eulice was telling the truth on both accounts, even though she hadn't told the NSP about her interstate flights with Larry King.

The grand jury didn't release its final report until July, but it filed an "Interim Report" in May that specifically dealt with the allegations regarding Jarrett Webb's molestations of Eulice Washington. The Interim Report found that Webb molested Washington "on or about" May 15, 1985, and also on June 1, 1985, after her sixteenth birthday. It urged Washington County authorities to pursue third-degree sexual assault charges against Webb. The Interim Report neglected to mention the allegation that Webb started molesting Washington as a child.

Van Pelt and company filed the Interim Report in May, because they ostensibly wanted the prosecution of Webb to fall within a 1989 Nebraska law that extended the statute of limitations on felony sexual assault from three years to five years. But the Interim Report noted that "certain legal questions may exist" about whether Webb could be prosecuted under the 1989 statute of limitations extension.

Bystanders who wanted to see justice on behalf of the children were reassured by the Interim Report—they felt that the first steps were being taken toward bringing child molesters to justice. But the Interim Report was little more than a sham.

Webb was charged with third-degree sexual assault, a misdemeanor, and misdemeanors in Nebraska carried a mere eighteen-month statute of limitations, so Jarrett Webb walked on the misdemeanor charges. One would expect Van Pelt, a former judge, to realize that Webb's misdemeanor charges had an eighteen-month statute of limitations and that the 1989 law extending the statute of limitations for felony sexual assault had no bearing on a misdemeanor.

Under Nebraska statutes, second-degree sexual assault, a mandatory felony, should have been charged if "serious personal injury" occurred during the assault. I realize that "serious personal injury" is open to interpretation, but Webb beat Washington with the railroad prop before molesting her, and he could easily have been charged with second-degree sexual assault.

The Douglas County grand jury admittedly spent the majority of its deliberations on "the videotaped statements" taken by Caradori, but it called several witnesses to address the "early allegations" prompted by the Foster Care Review Board's report. In addition to Flocken, witnesses called by Van Pelt to deal with the early allegations included Kirstin Hallberg, Dennis Carlson, Officer Irl Carmean, Kirk Naylor, and NSP Investigator Charles Phillips.

Hallberg was the second witness called by Van Pelt, and he questioned her about her relationship with Shawneta Moore. Hallberg testified that she first met Moore at the Uta Halee facility in June of 1986, and Moore told her that she had been enmeshed in a child-pornography and prostitution ring. Hallberg then testified that Moore started to call her periodically from her mother's home in June of 1988. She then recounted her conversations with Moore's school counselor, and the events that led to Moore's first hospitalization at Richard Young Hospital. The Board's Carol Stitt, Dennis Carlson and Burrell Williams followed Hallberg, and they testified about the early allegations and law enforcement's unwillingness to investigate them.

One of the standard procedures for Van Pelt seems to have been to hear the message and then kill the messenger: Following the testimony of Hallberg and the Foster Care Review Board's Executive Committee, a succession of witnesses deconstructed their accounts and questioned their credibility. NSP Investigator Phillips would be called to give testimony to the grand jury on at least eight different occasions, and he would invariably taint the testimony of previous witnesses or upcoming witnesses.

Phillips testified that NSP personnel jumped right into action when they received the Board's materials on December 16, 1988: He and the FBI questioned Moore on December 19. Dougherty then questioned Phillips about the three homicides that Moore discussed with him and the FBI agents. Phillips stated that Moore didn't provide any specifics concerning victims, perpetrators, and locations, and her statements to him were completely untrustworthy. It's certainly true that Moore's allegations are virtually incomprehensible, and the statements she made to Phillips and the FBI contradict the statements she made to Carmean, hospital staff, and Lowe, but the NSP and FBI had Moore committed under duress, and, according to Moore, they were extremely hostile—her accounts of their animosity are repeatedly corroborated by other FBI interviewees.

Though she wasn't specific with Phillips and the FBI, she named specific perpetrators and locations to Carmean and hospital personnel that perhaps law enforcement could have investigated. Phillips would say that he had read the OPD's reports on Moore, and those reports lacked specifics too, which isn't true. In Carmean's initial interview with Moore at Richard Young Hospital she was vague, but in her subsequent phone calls to him she provided a number of details.

Phillips also testified that Moore was recommitted because "everybody" had been told that there were "threats against Shawneta's life," and he implied that Hallberg was integral to fostering those fears. The truth of the matter was that the Douglas County Attorney's Office recommitted Moore for reasons that included a pair of falsehoods—that she was both living on the street and suicidal.

After Phillips demolished Moore's veracity, Dougherty and Van Pelt asked him questions about Hallberg. Phillips testified that he interviewed a Richard Young coworker of Hallberg's, who disclosed that Hallberg took it upon herself to shuttle Moore around from place to place after she had left the hospital in early December of 1988; in reality, several Richard Young Hospital personnel took it upon themselves to shuttle Moore around.

Van Pelt questioned Phillips about an interview he conducted with one of Hallberg's Uta Halee supervisors. It just happened to be the supervisor that Hallberg initially briefed concerning Moore's earliest allegations, and who had neglected to contact Moore's mother about the allegations. The very same supervisor had also suggested that Hallberg interrupt Uta Halee residents who confided in her to ask them, "Are you sure you can trust me with this information?" Phillips told the grand jury that Hallberg's former supervisor said Hallberg was guilty of rumor mongering while working at Uta Halee.

Van Pelt then queried Phillips about Hallberg's exchange with the Kansas City detective who had made statements about Larry King's exploitation of children to Hallberg. Phillips cited the FBI report that said the detective in question denied making those statements. Van Pelt had the Committee's information that the Kansas City detective made similar statements to Stitt and Carlson regarding Larry King, and Stitt had phone records proving a phone call, but either he hadn't read the Committee's materials or he opted not to discuss evidence that would have corroborated Hallberg.

Following Phillips' hatchet job on Hallberg's credibility, Van Pelt turned his attention to Eulice Washington's allegations of interstate flights. With Phillips still on the stand, Van Pelt focused on the FBI's interview of Kathleen Sorenson. Phillips testified that Sorenson told FBI agents that Eulice and Tracy Washington said Larry King flew them to Paris, New York, Chicago, Washington, DC, California, and Texas.

Phillips' account of Sorenson's FBI interview was vastly different from the notes that Sorenson provided to Lowe. Sorenson's notes make no mention of Tracy being on interstate flights, and she explicitly stated that Eulice was flown to Chicago and New York—Sorenson writes that Eulice may have been to DC, but she wasn't sure. The Julie Walters' report also makes no mention of Tracy being on interstate flights or of Eulice flying to Paris, California, or Texas, and Sorenson was present for those interviews.

Sorenson's FBI interview, as conveyed by Phillips, portrays Eulice and Tracy as given to flights of fancy or outright delusions, and they contradict Sorenson's notes, Walters' report, and also Eulice and Tracy's accounts. The FBI interviewed Sorenson in February of 1989, but by the time the Douglas County grand jury convened, anybody could have attributed anything to Sorenson, because she had been in a fatal car accident.

Though Franklin lore is rife with Sorenson's accident being a contract murder, she died as the result of an eighteen-year-old woman with an infant swerving into her lane. I've talked to a member of Sorenson's family about it, and he came to the conclusion that her death was merely an accident.

Phillips then discussed an interview with Boys Town teacher John Barksdale that he and the FBI conducted. Barksdale was apparently a workaholic—Boys Town and the Franklin Credit Union simultaneously employed him. Barksdale told Phillips and the FBI that he had traveled extensively with King, and freely admitted he accompanied King in chartered planes to several destinations, including San Francisco, New York, and Washington, DC. Barksdale maintained that he witnessed no inappropriate sexual activity during the trips, but he *eventually* came to believe that King was a homosexual through rumors at the credit union.

Earlier I mentioned that Julie Walters heard rumors that a Tojan sports car leased by King prowled the Boys Town campus, and three Boys Town teachers had been spotted driving the car—Barksdale was reportedly one of the teachers. But Barksdale, Phillips said, claimed that he knew nothing of a Tojan sports car on the Boys Town campus. Phillips also testified that Barksdale said he wasn't aware of Boys Town youth having sexual relations with King. In fact, he said, he had never seen King on the Boys Town campus or heard his name mentioned by Boys Town personnel. He recalled, though, noticing a Boys Town graduate at King's Café Carnivale.

It's interesting that Barksdale would mention seeing a former Boys Town student at Café Carnivale: In my interview with Monsignor Hupp, he said that he found out Barksdale was taking Boys Town kids off the campus and allegedly bringing them to Café Carnivale. One of the grand jurors asked Phillips if he and the FBI felt Barksdale was being honest during the interview, and, without missing a beat, he said, "Yes, we did."

Phillips testified that the FBI essentially conducted a national dragnet to find the Boys Town students who were purportedly linked to Larry King, and he discussed an FBI interview with a former Boys Town student named "Brant"—Eulice Washington had said that Brant left a party in Chicago with a nationally prominent politician. As it turned out, Washington hadn't conjured up a Boys Town student named Brant who had ties to King.

The Franklin Committee discovered that Brant graduated from Boys Town in 1983 and had actually moved into King's home upon his graduation. Brant's name also shows up in a document from the Youth Affairs Committee of the National Black Republican Council, authored by none other than Larry King. In his capacity as an "advisor" to the Youth Affairs Committee, King apparently wrote letters to various "Black college campuses" requesting that they contact Brant to establish a National Black Republican Council affiliate on their campus.

According to Phillips, the FBI interviewed Brant in rehab, where he was said to be recovering from a $2,500-a-day cocaine habit. Brant told FBI agents that King hired him to babysit King's son, and as a babysitter he accompanied King on numerous trips around the country. Brant said at no time did he see Eulice Washington on any of the flights, but, interestingly, he commented to the FBI that he recalled seeing her in New York with the Webbs. Both Washington and the Webbs maintained that Washington never traveled with the Webbs; so it's interesting that he would confess to seeing her in New York. Brant would tell FBI agents that Washington was mistaken about his presence in Chicago during September or October of 1984, because he was then in the Navy.

In Larry King's interview with the FBI—the very interview where he said he never lied—he acknowledged that Brant was one of three Boys Town students who moved into his house to babysit his son. King said that he didn't meet Brant via Boys Town, but at his church. He admitted that Brant frequently traveled with him, but asserted that he wasn't involved in any sexual improprieties.

I was most interested in talking to Brant, and I found him residing in Detroit. I attempted to contact him a number of times, but he never responded to my messages.

Jerry Lowe and Kirk Naylor appeared before Van Pelt and company to discuss the "early allegations," and their respective accounts vastly differed. Lowe stated that he didn't think criminal prosecutions could have been conducted with the information that the Franklin Committee had cultivated when he resigned, but he thought there were enough leads to warrant further investigation. He said that the public hearings the previous June, before the Committee ruptured, had spurred people to come forward with additional information, and their leads might have been fruitful.

As Van Pelt questioned Lowe, he took several opportunities to hammer Kirstin Hallberg. He maneuvered Lowe to discuss the OPD's opinion of her, and Lowe said that he talked to three OPD officers who found Hallberg "unreliable" and "flaky." Van Pelt then asked Lowe, "Did you receive a lot of information from her that you didn't think was important?" Surprisingly, Lowe didn't agree with Van Pelt's assessment: "I think she's a very credible person, a committed person," he said. Lowe then described what he thought was an OPD campaign to discredit her. Van Pelt then worked over both Hallberg's and Stitt's credibility by questioning Lowe about discrepancies between their claims and those of the Kansas City detective.

Midway through Lowe's testimony, Van Pelt dropped a surprise on him—he questioned him about Michael Casey, whose name hadn't surfaced in the proceedings thus far. Van Pelt referred to Casey as a "very colorful individual." Lowe disclosed that Casey claimed he had a videotape of King engaged in sexual acts with children. Van Pelt pounced on the lack of any evidence for the tape and quickly established Casey as not credible.

Whereas Lowe said the Committee had numerous leads that may have been fruitful, Naylor's testimony about the Committee painted it black—he told the grand jury that he sided with the FBI's conclusions concerning Larry King's non-exploitation of children. He felt that Shawneta Moore was lying, and Eulice Washington was a "victim" of "delusion." And taking a page from the FBI's debriefings of Owen, Boner, and Danny King, he stated that the allegations surrounding Larry King were the byproduct of "screwed-up kids" capitalizing on the "glamour and excitement" of the scandal. Van Pelt also had Naylor chime in on Hallberg—Naylor said he felt that Hallberg bore "a lot of the responsibility" for the "distortion."

With Naylor on the stand, Van Pelt editorialized on how an election year superimposed on a crazy public had created a synergy that triggered the unruly rumors. Van Pelt commented on the "unsubstantiated and unfounded rumors" shortly after he was named special prosecutor, and, given his remarks to Naylor on April 3, it's obvious that his thoughts on King's pedophile network hadn't changed. He nevertheless continued to call witnesses for nearly four more months.

Van Pelt initially called Gary Caradori to the stand on March 28—he had a little over three months to live. Before Caradori's videotaped interviews were shown to the grand jurors, Van Pelt ostensibly wanted him to provide the grand jurors with a brief synopsis of the investigation that led to the interviews. After extensively quizzing Caradori on his background as an NSP investigator and a private detective, Van Pelt inquired about the Franklin investigation. As Caradori attempted to explain the investigation, Van Pelt repeatedly cut him off. Caradori eventually talked about his earliest forays into Franklin, working the streets and bars, cultivating informants. At one point, Van Pelt interrupted Caradori and asked him if he was a "homosexual," to which he simply replied, "No."

Van Pelt assured Caradori that he would appear before the grand jury again, and he did on two subsequent occasions. Before Caradori's next grand jury appearance, however, the grand jurors watched his videotaped interviews of Alisha Owen, Troy Boner, and Danny King. Though the grand jurors could not know this at the time, much of the corroborating content of Caradori's Owen and Boner interviews was *edited out*. Before Caradori's second appearance the grand jurors also heard Boner and Danny King give the FBI's revised versions of their stories, recanting allegations of their abuse.

Though Caradori's March 28 appearance before the grand jury had been brief, he realized that the process was a *fait accompli*. A forlorn Caradori kissed his wife that night and told her, "It's all over."

The day after Caradori's initial appearance before the grand jury, Troy Boner made his first appearance—Boner made a second appearance in June. Of the initial three victims videotaped by Caradori, Boner was the logical choice to be the first to testify—Danny King lacked the gray matter and charisma of Boner, and he would have major difficulties juggling the lies that were required of him, whereas Boner's innate intelligence, drug addiction, and hustling had forged a gifted and well practiced liar. Amazingly, Alisha Owen was sticking to her story; so it was important to have both Boner and Danny King deconstruct her account before she took the stand.

Though Boner's testimony was littered with discrepancies and contradictions, he had been given the FBI's seal of approval by virtue of his passing the FBI polygraph with "excellent results." Van Pelt was quick to point out that Boner had the FBI's endorsement, and it was a point that was not lost on the grand jurors.

At the outset of Boner's testimony, Van Pelt took him through his initial meeting with Caradori and his videotaped statement. Boner maintained that Caradori and Ormiston brought him back to the offices of Caracorp, where, over the phone, he conversed with Owen for twenty minutes, and she brought him up to speed on the "plan." But, as I've noted before, according to Caracorp's phone records, the phone call that Boner pinned the entire "hoax" on never happened.

During Boner's two grand jury appearances, he spilled a morass of conflicting lies about the events that led to the phantom phone call and about the call itself, but his conflicting accounts didn't seem to bother Van Pelt.

Boner testified that Caradori sold him on the idea that the individuals he would be making statements against were very "bad" people, and

Boner would reap five to six million dollars by suing them—he said a book and movie deal were discussed too. But in response to a question by a grand juror, he denied that money motivated him; he replied that he was stirred by the moral calling of putting child abusers in jail—child abusers he'd never heard of. Boner also testified that he disclosed to Caradori "countless times" that his story was a scam, but then he denied that Caradori knew it was a scam.

As previously mentioned, the FBI apparently felt it was imperative that Boner and Danny King immediately disavow the flight to California, where Boner claimed that Larry King sold the two little boys. Boner told the grand jury that immediately upon arriving at the offices of Caracorp, Caradori described the flight to California with Larry King, Danny King, Owen, the two little boys, and himself. But later in his testimony, Boner couldn't recall how he had gleaned the details of the trip.

Boner's phone conversation with Owen at Caradori's office was the focal point of numerous contradictions. His FBI statement alleged that Caradori phoned Owen and handed the phone to him, but before the grand jury he testified that Owen phoned him at Caradori's office. When Boner appeared before the grand jury a second time, he couldn't recall if Owen called Caradori or Caradori called Owen. Boner then gave the grand jury two completely different accounts of where the conversation with Owen actually took place in the offices of Caracorp—"Jill's office" and then "Joe's office."

Boner told Van Pelt that during his twenty-minute conversation with Owen, she gave him 85% of the content that was contained in his seven-hour, videotaped statement to Caradori. He initially testified that he didn't take notes while he was talking to Owen—he jotted down dates, times, and places afterward. But during his second appearance before the grand jury, Boner maintained that he didn't take any notes and that Caradori didn't provide him with notes—he said Caradori would help him "over the hump" by giving him "hints." In complete contradiction to his FBI statement and earlier testimony, he also stated that he had a number of calls with Owen to craft the hoax. Boner initially testified that he briefed Danny King for five minutes on the hoax at Danny King's apartment, and then he said he briefed King for twenty minutes at King's apartment; but during his second appearance, he claimed King had several calls with Owen too.

During Boner's first appearance, a grand juror asked him if he was currently employed, and he let slip that he was too "busy" meeting with the FBI "every other day it seems like." His taskmasters at the FBI spent a considerable amount of time refining him for the grand jury, and their game plan was obviously for him to disavow everything regarding Larry King. In Boner's taped statement to Caradori, he elaborated on his first meeting with Larry King at The Max, but he flat out told Van Pelt that he had never been to The Max—he then later admitted to hanging out at The Max, and Van Pelt reminded him of his earlier statement. Boner gave a befuddled reply: "Oh, yeah, I have been. I thought maybe you meant, you know, now or something."

Boner's "lie or die" affidavit explicitly conceded that FBI intimidation forced him to disavow the vast majority of his abuse and the names of his abusers. But before the grand jury, he inculpated Baer as a john. Boner maintained he was Nebraska's age of consent—sixteen years old—when they started having their dalliances; so Baer wouldn't be charged with child molestation in Boner's case. However, since Danny King would have been under the age of consent when he started having dalliances with Baer, he simply told the grand jury that he had never even met Alan Baer.

Boner maintained that Baer was his one and only homosexual relationship, and he received money and drugs for services rendered. A grand juror inquired why he frequently hung out at The Max if he wasn't gay, and he responded, "I don't know." A grand juror then asked Boner about his last contact with Baer, and Boner responded that he was seventeen or eighteen years old. Though Boner told the grand jury that he hadn't had any contact with Baer in four or five years, he disclosed to FBI agents that he had phoned Baer in January of 1990.

Before the grand jury, Boner also named Eugene Mahoney as a homosexual. Mahoney was a former state senator and the Commissioner of Nebraska's Parks and Games—he was also a power behind the throne in Nebraska politics, with numerous friends among Nebraska's power elite, including Harold Andersen. Boner alleged that Mahoney requested oral sex from him at an adult bookstore. Alisha Owen and Paul Bonacci had also implicated Mahoney as a pedophile.

Though Boner denied ever attending parties at the Woodman Tower or the Twin Towers, he testified that he was present at a January 1985 party at the Brandeis Building. Then a minute or two later, he told Van Pelt that he was never at the party: two contradictory statements within just minutes of each other. But Van Pelt was undeterred and abruptly changed the subject. Boner also gave conflicting accounts about his FBI debriefings within a minute or two of each other: He originally said that he stuck to the story as he related it to Caradori during his first meeting with the FBI, but, shortly afterward, he told the grand jury that he immediately recanted that Owen and Danny King had any involvement with Larry King, Alan Baer, or Robert Wadman.

Boner would make contradictory statements about Wadman in rapid succession too. He initially testified that he had previously met Wadman, but then said he'd never met Wadman. At first he stated that everything he conveyed to Caradori about the relationship between Owen and Wadman was imparted by Owen during the phantom phone call, but he later maintained that Caradori said, "You can't forget Wednesdays when you would take Alisha to meet Bob Wadman at the Starlite Hotel."

Boner would have considerable problems keeping it together when testifying about his relationship with Owen. He initially said they met in the summer of 1988, then asserted it was absolutely the summer of 1987. Boner would tell the grand jury he knew Owen for three months, and then he recalled their relationship lasted six to eight weeks. He disclosed that they parted on very bad terms in the middle of 1988.

Boner testified that he had two subsequent communications with Owen after their breakup. The first was at the end of 1988 when she called him from a jail in Greeley, Colorado and asked him to bail her out—shortly afterwards he said Owen actually called him from Greeley in February or March of 1989. Though Boner couldn't remember the month of the call, he said the upshot of the conversation was that he refused to bail her out—their next contact was in Caradori's office, where they hatched the hoax. So, ultimately, Boner spun an extremely implausible yarn to the grand jury: He and Owen had a very short relationship, they parted on bad terms, he was unwilling to bail her out of jail, and yet he concocted an elaborate scheme with her even though he was engaged to another woman.

Danny King would be called to the stand only once—shortly after Boner's first appearance. Boner, admittedly, had been schooled by the FBI concerning his testimony, and he was considerably sharper than Danny King. If the FBI enrolled King in a memory retention seminar and pumped him full of ginkgo biloba, it would have all been for naught—he didn't have the cognitive chops of Boner, and years of repeated molestations and drug abuse had beaten him down. Though Van Pelt pretty much spoon-fed Boner, he would have to pull out an eyedropper for Danny King. Van Pelt usually allowed Boner to give short, three or four sentence responses to his questions, but he would have to lead Danny King, whose answers were often "That's correct," "Yeah," or "No."

Given Danny King's shortcomings as a witness, the strategy for him was to deny just about everything. But, even then, he still became bogged down and mired in uncertainty. Boner told the grand jury that he imparted the hoax to Danny King in the latter's apartment while Caradori waited outside. But Danny King testified that Caradori drove Boner and him to Lincoln's Residence Inn, where Boner gave him the low-down on the hoax in the bar over beers.

His story of becoming tuned into the hoax at a bar is just one of many inconsistencies—he repeatedly had problems with reality impeding on the FBI's version of events. The following Q & A is between an agitated Van Pelt and an acutely confused Danny King:

Q. And is that true, is that what went on and what went through your mind the night you were visiting with Troy in the bar at the motel?
A. Yeah.
Q. And is that why you decided to do this?
A. Yeah.
Q. And was any of this true at that time?
A. Any of what true?
Q. Any of the business about the basis for suing these people, the parties with all these people? Other than ... and the other people that you mentioned, anything about Alan Baer or any of those—Larry King, any of those people true at that time?
A. Yeah, so I wasn't really—
Q. I beg your pardon?

A. Yeah, I was—I wasn't really making nothing up about any of the persons.

Van Pelt was again forced to walk Danny King through his conversation with Boner at the bar, and help him snap back into line—but King still had considerable difficulties staying on track. Boner testified that Alan Baer had been his only homosexual relationship ever, but Danny King testified that he and Boner had previously engaged in homosexual acts together. Both Boner and Danny King told Caradori that Larry King forced them to sodomize each other during a party at the Woodman Tower. Danny King, once more, outright contradicted Boner and came perilously close to the story he had conveyed to Caradori.

Danny King initially testified that he met Alisha Owen in the summer of 1988. They hung out "four times and each time was, you know, a couple of hours." But in response to a grand juror's question, he discussed a trip to California that he took with Owen. Boner also mentioned Danny King and Owen's trip to California during his testimony. Moreover, Owen discussed a short jaunt to California with Danny King when interviewed by Caradori and the FBI.

By the time Danny King stepped down from the stand and was unshackled from his confusion, his role in generating the hoax, contradictions aside, would be distilled to talking to Boner at the Residence Inn bar for an hour, discussing the "case" with Caradori for an hour, and then giving a five-hour videotaped statement. Throughout his testimony, Danny King, like Boner, suffered repeated bouts of amnesia about his ability to provide such intricate details to Caradori over the course of his videotaped statement. A grand juror was even inspired to ask him about the elaborate minutiae he provided Caradori, and he responded, "I just played it by ear."

When Boner and Danny King appeared before the grand jury, they recurrently lost themselves in a labyrinth of lies and contradictions—I've mentioned a rather limited litany. Their testimony had a comedic aspect—a sort of *Abbott and Costello Meet the Grand Jury*—but the grave abuses they would later admit to covering up severely detract from the comical facets of their testimony, rendering their grand jury appearance a disfigurement of American justice and a true tragedy.

Danny King testified in front of the grand jury on April 5, and Alisha Owen was slated to appear on April 30, but her appearance would be pushed back to May 8. Prior to her grand jury testimony, she would be subjected to a merciless campaign of viciousness and betrayal that was to become an all-too-familiar occurrence in her life. Owen had been confined to segregation at York since January—she was isolated, and FBI agents essentially had her in a vise that they were screwing tighter and tighter. But, astonishingly, she wouldn't even bend ... let alone break.

On April 10, York's Visitor's Register shows that FBI agents paid a final visit to Owen. She said the FBI made her an attractive offer that day: If she recanted her story, she would be granted her freedom. She still refused to recant. The FBI would now be forced to put all of its cunning, resources, and power to bear upon a twenty-one-year-old. Needless to say, the FBI had a number of potent weapons in its arsenal to carry out its objective, including Pamela Vuchetich.

Owen had given Vuchetich, her trusted lawyer, a folder of letters, poems, and other personal papers that she didn't want the FBI to snatch, because she felt an FBI search was imminent. One of the documents in the folder was a list of Owen's former friends and relationships—Vuchetich had told Owen to write out the list. Though Owen and her mother initially objected to Owen's making such a list, Vuchetich convinced them that the list optimized Vuchetich's ability to defend Owen—it ensured Vuchetich wouldn't be sandbagged by people from Owen's past who held grudges and might be called as witnesses. In response to subpoenas, Vuchetich didn't invoke attorney-client privilege, but, rather, surrendered the folder—including the list—to the NSP and FBI! Witnesses who played pivotal roles in deconstructing Owen's credibility before the grand jury were on that list.

For example, two of the witnesses called by Van Pelt to impugn Owen's integrity came from that list. The first witness had sex with her when she had been a minor and he was an adult. He was also fond of smoking marijuana, even though he had a security clearance to work at Offutt Air Force Base. So, because of the possibility of jail time and at least the loss of his job, he would have been particularly vulnerable to threats from the FBI. Law enforcement also found other witnesses who were willing to testify against Owen. As a teenager and young adult, Owen certainly had bouts of being dissolute, and many of her friends and acquaintances were dissolute too; so their lifestyle made them particularly vulnerable to intimidation by law enforcement.

Vuchetich also left Owen high and dry just prior to her testimony before the grand jury. Though Danny King started to recant his video-taped statements to Caradori in early March, Vuchetich didn't skip a beat in her representation of Owen—in an apparent conflict of interest, she would continue to represent Owen for nearly two months after Danny King began to sing the FBI's tune. Fortunately, Donna Owen had sensed trouble with Vuchetich, and she contacted Omaha attorney Henry Rosenthal, who consented to represent her daughter. When Vuchetich deserted Owen shortly before her grand jury appearance, the sixty-year-old Rosenthal would sprint to Owen's rescue. "The poor girl was floundering," he told me about Owen. "Nobody wanted to represent her."

Rosenthal's first official act as Owen's attorney was to request that her grand jury testimony be postponed while he brought himself up to speed on her predicament. Van Pelt would have the benevolence to push back her grand jury appearance until May 8, but the damage Vuchetich had wreaked upon Owen by then was considerable and, perhaps, irreversible.

Before Owen took the stand to testify, Troy Boner, Danny King, NSP Investigator Phillips, and also a prominent Nebraskan had thoroughly tainted her character and testified she was a liar—several subsequent witnesses also leapt on the bash-Alisha Owen bandwagon. Chuck Phillips repeatedly took the stand and recounted NSP and FBI interviews that were extremely damaging to Owen—I'm aware of a friend of Owen's who refused to sign his FBI statement, due to the fact that it significantly differed from the actual disclosures he had made to the agents.

Over the course of two separate appearances, Phillips discussed FBI interviews with Jeff Hubbell—Owen named Hubbell as the Boys Town student who introduced her to Larry King et al. (Bonacci alleged Hubbell's involvement with the Franklin pandering network too.) Caradori had attempted to find Hubbell, and FBI agents informed him that Hubbell was living in California, but they wouldn't disclose his exact location.

Phillips testified that Hubbell was living in Arizona, and an Omaha FBI agent initially made "telephone contact" with him, and then he described Hubbell's having a face-to-face interview with FBI agents. According to Phillips, Hubbell told the FBI that he did indeed attend Boys Town and met Owen at a dance, but he didn't know Larry King—nor had he ever been enmeshed in a sex network. Hubbell reportedly said Owen was "demented" for insinuating such a story.

Alisha Owen spent two days in front of a hostile grand jury that had been primed to look upon her as a petulant, pathological liar. She was also painted as a wanton tramp who would sleep with just about anyone, anywhere, anytime. Owen attempted to explain that her teenage promiscuity was the result of her sexuality having been so deeply disfigured at an early age: "I had absolutely no concept of what sex ... was supposed to mean because my sexual experiences started in such a warped way." But her explanations apparently stirred little sympathy among the grand jury, as evinced by a grand juror ruminating aloud, "I can't imagine Alisha being around a man and not having gone to bed with him."

As Dougherty grilled Owen, she was unwavering about the truth of the videotaped statements she gave to Caradori. Dougherty's meticulously choreographed examination of Owen touched upon her psychiatric hospitalizations, suicide attempts, drug deals, bounced checks, flight from the law, etc. He also focused on her relationship with Michael Casey, and the brief period of time she had spent at the home of Casey's friend. Owen said that Casey made repeated efforts to contact her while she was incarcerated at York. Though she really didn't have a favorable opinion of him, she had written him one letter to be polite.

Dougherty also pressed Owen about her relationship with Robert Wadman. She claimed that Wadman was definitely the father of the child she had given birth to at sixteen, and stated she would be willing to take a blood test and also a polygraph. She provided details of their Wednesday afternoon encounters and also described the French Café's basement. Dougherty questioned her about social services documents that listed someone else as her daughter's father.

Owen replied that she and her mother went to social services to enroll her daughter in Medicaid, and social services personnel required her to provide a name for the father. She said she attempted to skirt around providing the father's name, but social services insisted; so she jotted down the name of an acquaintance—Owen's mother corroborated her account of this impasse when she appeared before the grand jury. As a sixteen-year-old, Owen told the grand jury, it would have been extremely unwise for her to name the OPD Chief as her daughter's father—her daughter's birth certificate didn't list a name for the father.

A grand juror inquired if she thought of having an abortion, and Owen discussed her difficult decision to have her baby. She claimed that while Larry King's enforcer was trying to threaten her into having an abortion, she attended her parents' pro-life church and a video on abortion had been shown to the congregation. "I looked at it," she told the grand jury, "and thought that's almost as bad as what happened to me. And I thought I can't do that—I can't—I can't do that." She concluded that having an abortion was a moral line she just wouldn't breach, even though she felt that her decision was potentially life threatening.

Dougherty asked Owen why she didn't reach out to her parents for help, and she replied with a pair of rhetorical questions: "What power do they have? Who are they going to go to?" She then said, "They can't call the police.... They can't go to the FBI." Owen further related her quandary of powerlessness to the grand jury: "There is [sic] two ways to do things. You either do it the easy way and you don't get hurt as much or it isn't as painful, or you do it the hard way. Either way you're going to do it. I would much rather have it be as pleasant as possible, and in that situation nothing was pleasant, but at least I wasn't bleeding and at least I wasn't dead."

Dougherty interrogated Owen regarding Danny King's participation at the Twin Tower parties in the fall of 1983, and she continued to stick to her original story. Dougherty then brought out the smoking gun that would prove beyond a reasonable doubt that Owen was lying: Danny King's school records. He held up Danny King's school records and handed them to Owen—the records were "proof positive" that Danny King attended school in Texas from September of 1983 to January of 1984. Owen didn't flinch, replying, "He was in the state, I saw him"—she said he stayed with Boner's family. Owen then looked at the records and showed Dougherty that Danny King had missed forty days of school over the four-month period: half of the school days.

Danny King's mother would then be hauled before the grand jury to testify that her son had never left the state when he attended school in Texas. During Boner's second grand jury appearance, however, a grand juror asked Boner if Danny King lived with him while King's mother was in Texas and Oklahoma, and Boner replied, "He was only gone for a couple weeks, and he came back and moved in with me ... he lived with me for about six months." The grand juror then started to make specific inquiries about King's stay with Boner—Boner quickly realized that he had told an inconvenient truth and started to backpedal. But he floundered and barked out a swift succession of contradictory stories about when King lived with his family. Finally, Van Pelt had to intervene and come to the rescue:

Q. Troy, are you saying was there ever a time that Danny was way down in Texas or Oklahoma with his family for four to five months?
A. Yeah, yeah.
Q. During that four to five month period, did he come back and visit you in the Omaha area?
A. He came back and moved in with me.
Q. After the four to five months?
A. Yeah.
Q. Okay. So what you're saying is that during that four- to five-month period he didn't live with you, he was down in Texas?
A. Yeah, he was in Texas with his family, and he called me a couple times.

As the grand jury trudged onward, the family of Al and Donna Owen would be subjected to a Kafkaesque assault. For months the Owens heard incessant racket on their phones, and they had no doubts that someone somewhere was listening to their conversations. Mysterious individuals in unmarked cars also routinely parked outside their home.

On the night of Friday May 25, the grand jury's looming specter rolled up to the Owens' front doorstep in the inhospitable form of the NSP's Chuck Phillips and a second NSP officer. They had an order, signed by a Douglas County Judge, "to effect whatever detention is necessary to obtain" a blood sample from Alisha Owen's five-year-old daughter. If Owen's daughter failed to "comply with the provisions" of the order, she would be "guilty of contempt of court and punished accordingly." The type of order Van Pelt had Phillips serve was usually reserved for the alleged perpetrators of a sexual assault, not for the alleged victims—let alone the five-year-old daughter of a victim.

Al and Donna Owen had seen their daughter subjected to truly shocking injustices by the end of May, and attorney Rosenthal had insisted that Robert Wadman, Alisha Owen, and Owen's daughter simultaneously submit to blood tests to ensure that the testing would at least have an air of integrity. Though Rosenthal and the Owens made a reasonable stipulation, Al and Donna Owen felt that Van Pelt and the NSP might pull something underhanded like snatching their granddaughter. As a result, the Owens took precautions guaranteeing their granddaughter was nowhere to be found the night Phillips showed up "to effect whatever detention is necessary."

Phillips served the order on a Friday night, and the blood test wasn't scheduled until Wednesday, and, given the order's wording and the prior conduct of the NSP, the Owens believed it was certainly within the realm of possibility that the NSP would "detain" their granddaughter for five days. After Phillips' visit, Donna Owen quickly contacted Senators Schmit and Chambers, who vociferously voiced their objections to the order.

Their criticisms even inspired Samuel Van Pelt to break his code of silence on the machinations of the grand jury and issue a public statement. "I just think this needs some explanation," he told the *World-Herald*. Van Pelt said he obtained the order only after the voluntary plan fell apart. In the article, Henry Rosenthal stated that his client was perfectly willing to take a blood test: "I have authority to tell you that my client and her daughter will submit to a blood test at either the pathology center at Creighton University or the University of Nebraska Medical Center, as long as the alleged father is there."

Donna Owen appeared before the grand jury on the Wednesday following Phillips' Friday night visit—she was still shell-shocked by the fact that a Douglas County Judge had issued an order of detention against her little granddaughter. She no longer had any illusions about the grand jury vying for justice—she felt it was rigged, and nothing she could possibly say would affect its outcome.

Dougherty initially quizzed Donna Owen about her and her daughter's background. She described Alisha's abnormal behavior, starting as a teenager—abnormal behavior that was both perplexing and inexplicable to her parents. Dougherty then questioned Donna Owen about Alisha's relationship with Troy Boner. She testified that Alisha announced her engagement to Boner in July 1988, and the Owens invited Boner to their house for dinner.

Alisha claimed to have recently met Boner, but Donna Owen said, "No one at the dinner table thought they had just met." She felt that they were just too familiar with each other—"It was almost like they had been married for four or five years." After the dinner, Donna Owen asked her other children if they were previously aware of Boner, and Alisha's younger sister said that a "Troy" had repeatedly phoned their home over the years.

Dougherty then inquired about the Owens' first contact with Gary Caradori. Donna Owen responded that Caradori phoned the Owen's home, looking for Alisha, and her husband told him that she was incarcerated at York. After Caradori's call, Al and Donna visited their daughter at York and informed her that someone had phoned their home, inquiring about her whereabouts. Donna Owen said that her daughter had a "panic attack" about Al Owen disclosing she was at York, and she made her parents promise they would never disclose her whereabouts again. Dougherty asked Donna Owen if Caradori promised "benefits" to Alisha for her cooperation, and Donna Owen said point blank, "That is a rumor started by the *World-Herald*. That is absolutely not true."

By the time Senator Schmit made his first appearance before the grand jury on May 15, Van Pelt had called witnesses who either portrayed the senator in an unfavorable light or severely ravaged his credibility. One witness in particular commented on Schmit's "paranoia," testifying that he wasn't "well physically or mentally." Van Pelt also seemed to be obsessed with illuminating Schmit's ties to John DeCamp and establishing DeCamp's undue influence over Schmit and the Committee.

Van Pelt interrogated Schmit about his relationship with DeCamp, and Schmit replied that they had met in the legislature twenty years earlier—they were close friends, and DeCamp represented him in a legal capacity. Van Pelt asked Schmit if DeCamp had seen the Committee's reports or records—Schmit flat-out denied that DeCamp ever had access to any of the Committee's files, reports, or tapes.

The grand jury had been primed about Schmit's "paranoia"; so when he talked about the fact that he thought his phones were tapped, it likely became easy for grand jurors to dismiss him. Schmit testified that his suspicions about his phones being tapped were confirmed when he provided Caradori with the name of a possible witness over the phone: Before Caradori contacted her, she received a visit from the FBI. He told the grand jury that he didn't want to sound "melodramatic," but he wouldn't discuss "anything over the telephone that I didn't want repeated over the television, I'll tell you that."

Schmit departed the grand jury feeling perturbed, because he felt that Van Pelt had neglected to address numerous pertinent issues. Van Pelt also hadn't left time for the grand jurors to ask him questions. He requested that he appear before the grand jury once more, and his request was granted. Between Schmit's first and second appearance before the grand jury, he heard murmurs that Alisha Owen would be indicted for perjury and Caradori for obstruction of justice.

During his second appearance, he read a prepared statement and gave an impassioned plea for the grand jury to carefully consider all the evidence. Schmit said that "based upon the evidence the Committee has heard, we are convinced that certain prominent citizens have abused children, are abusing children, and will abuse children in the future. It would be a great tragedy if nothing is done about it." He also discussed law enforcement's unwillingness to act and its hindrances: "Too many unanswered questions, ladies and gentlemen, too many leads not followed and too many roadblocks placed in the way of the investigation." Prior to Franklin, Schmit had been an almost dogmatic believer in "the system," and it clearly broke his heart when he realized that his pleas had fallen on deaf ears.

Caradori was called before the grand jury a second time at the end of April and would make a third appearance in the middle of May—in the wake of Boner and Danny King telling Van Pelt and company that they lied during their videotaped statements. Though Caradori had concluded that the grand jury was essentially a runaway train after his first appearance, he had an unyielding optimism and again hoped that just maybe his sincerity and honesty had a chance of saving the day.

Caradori was familiar with the grand jury format, and he knew that grand jurors had the prerogative to request the subpoenaing of witnesses; so his underlying strategy was to provide the names of prospective witnesses whenever Van Pelt gave him the latitude. He dropped the names of three pilots who had flown charters for Larry King and had said kids were on the flights. He also named the woman at the charter service who informed him that King and a gaggle of young men made almost weekly flights. The grand jury wouldn't subpoena any of them.

After Van Pelt went to great lengths to address the "relationship" between Caradori and Michael Casey, he focused on Casey's providing Caradori with Alisha Owen's name. Caradori stated that "Alisha Owen" was just one of countless names Casey and others had rattled off that he scribbled on his "scratchpad." Caradori maintained Casey told him that he had no idea where Owen lived, her connection to Franklin, or even if she was still alive. Caradori told the grand jury that he located Owen weeks after gleaning her name, and, even then, it took him an additional three weeks before he made his initial trek to York.

Following Van Pelt's examination, Caradori had to contend with Dougherty, who inquired about the phone call Owen made to Boner or vice-versa, depending on Boner's various accounts, in Caradori's office, which was the supposed linchpin of their cooking up the ruse. Caradori recalled that he took Boner directly to the Residence Inn. He said if, in fact, they stopped by his office, it would have been a brief pit stop for videotape, but he was certain that Boner was never "out of my sight." Boner's purported phone call to Owen ultimately came down to a "he said" versus a "he said and she said," meaning it was Boner's word against the word of Caradori and Ormiston.

Dougherty questioned Caradori about the day he and Boner drove to Omaha and met Danny King, and Caradori replied that Boner and Danny King were alone for "maybe a minute to a minute and a half." In response to a grand juror, Caradori said he brought Boner and King back to his office that night—he sent Boner to his apartment, and then he took King to the Residence Inn, where they both spent the night. A grand juror questioned Caradori about Boner and Danny King having beers in the lounge of the Residence Inn before Caradori videotaped King—Caradori replied that *the Residence Inn didn't have a lounge.*

After Caradori's stint in front of the grand jury in April, he found and videotaped Paul Bonacci, who corroborated the allegations by Owen, Boner, and Danny King on various perpetrators and numerous details. Caradori was called before the grand jury in May to discuss Bonacci. "The believability to me came when he kept talking about Troy, Danny, Alisha, and not a whole lot of people knew about Troy, Danny, and Alisha and some of the circumstances," Caradori said to Van Pelt of Bonacci. "He described people that I knew he was on target with."

Van Pelt questioned Caradori about Bonacci's previous statements to the OPD regarding Larry King et al., which he had recanted. Caradori testified that Bonacci was frightened to death of Larry King and Alan Baer, but he recanted only after an OPD officer threatened to charge him with additional crimes if he didn't. Caradori then elaborated on Bonacci's videotaped interview, where Bonacci mentioned a host of improbable occurrences, including his sexual liaisons with politicians in Washington, DC and the filming of a boy being murdered near Sacramento. Caradori said the following about Bonacci's Sacramento account: "I don't know if it happened, but one thing I do know is this kid described three people—Troy, Danny, and Alisha—in similar circumstances that matched their stories."

Caradori told the grand jury that he retrieved a number of Bonacci's notebooks and letters from his grandmother's apartment, where he was living at the time of his arrest. Caradori came across one of Bonacci's diaries that had a number of pages ripped out of it, and he asked Bonacci about the missing pages—Bonacci stated to him that the OPD was previously in possession of the diary, and someone with the police must have purloined the missing pages.

After Caradori testified to the grand jury about Bonacci, and before Bonacci testified, Van Pelt called an OPD detective to the stand who demolished Bonacci's credibility. This wasn't exceptionally difficult, considering Bonacci suffered from multiple personalities and was an incarcerated sex offender. The detective talked about Bonacci's "wild stories," and he said the OPD had polygraphed him, but the results were inconclusive because of his psychiatric disorder. The detective testified that Bonacci eventually recanted all of his tall tales; Van Pelt asked him if the OPD threatened Bonacci into recanting his prior statements. He replied with an unequivocal "No."

Before Bonacci recanted his "wild stories" to the OPD in March of 1990, he had told investigators about a sexual relationship between Alisha Owen and Robert Wadman. A grand juror inquired of the OPD investigator how Bonacci could have come by that information. The investigator unhesitatingly replied, "Out of a newspaper I would imagine." The grand juror mentioned that Owen's name had yet to appear in the paper. The detective then said that "word spreads like wildfire" through the jailhouse grapevine. The grand juror remarked that they were incarcerated at different prisons. The OPD investigator responded that the jailhouse grapevine more or less had telepathic powers: "It's a network that you couldn't imagine."

A subsequent grand juror questioned the detective about his thoughts on Caradori's interviewing Bonacci, and he was amusedly dismissive, as if Caradori had lost his mind: "I just heard he went and interviewed Bonacci, and I said, 'Oh, my God.'"

Bonacci was called before the grand jury at the end of June—about a month after the OPD officer impugned his credibility. Bonacci had been diagnosed with multiple personality disorder in April, and he was still in the midst of struggling to understand his condition. He told me that appearing before the grand jury was like being dragged in front of a hostile inquisition; he found the experience extremely stressful. To cope with the stress, he said, his psyche started to unconsciously shift into different personalities or "alters."

Throughout the majority of Bonacci's testimony, he was apparently in a color-blind alter, because Dougherty asked him about the color of an individual's eyes, and a grand juror asked him the color of an individual's hair—he replied in each case that he couldn't say for sure because he was color-blind. Dr. Mead's report on Bonacci stated that one of his alters was color-blind.

Bonacci reiterated much of the information he gave to Caradori about perpetrators, victims, places, and times. He testified that he recanted his statements to the OPD only after threats from a particular officer—it was the very same officer whom Van Pelt called to shred Bonacci's credibility. When Caradori interviewed Bonacci, he had named a renowned multi-millionaire as one of his abusers—Van Pelt questioned him about this, and Bonacci denied being molested by him.

The grand jury took a brief recess, and then Bonacci returned to the stand. Bonacci told Dougherty that he lied about the renowned multi-millionaire, because he was scared to death of him, but he had, in fact, been abused by him. Dougherty then questioned Bonacci about their liaisons—he was very specific about the locations and said Larry King arranged them.

After Dougherty interrogated Bonacci, the grand jury recessed for lunch. During the lunch break, Bonacci told me, someone affiliated with the grand jury threatened him and advised that he recant his morning's testimony. When the grand jury reconvened, Van Pelt immediately asked Bonacci if he wished to change any of his prior testimony—Bonacci said, "No."

As the grand jury was in its homestretch, Van Pelt paraded several witnesses before the grand jurors who testified about the moral turpitude and conniving of Michael Casey. Two of the witnesses testified that Casey took them for a ride financially, and Casey's termination from Boys Town was extensively discussed. NSP Investigator Phillips was called in to give a summary of Casey's criminal history.

The "Hollywood producer" whom Casey coaxed to Nebraska was called to the stand. The FBI tracked him down in Beverly Hills and served him with a federal subpoena, demanding that he appear before the federal grand jury looking into Franklin. The day he showed up to testify in front of the feds, he was handed a state subpoena that required him to appear before the Douglas County grand jury. The FBI had him jot down notes on his sojourn to Nebraska with Casey; Dougherty just happened to have a copy of the notes, and handed them to the producer to "refresh" his memory.

Both Van Pelt and Dougherty questioned the producer. Dougherty guided him into making a number of unsavory disclosures about Casey, including the fact that Casey had burned him for $3,225. But Dougherty was particularly interested in his meeting with Casey and Caradori at the Cornhusker Hotel in Lincoln. The producer testified that he introduced himself to Caradori after the latter came to the door of his suite—he said they had a brief discussion before Casey entered the room, corresponding to what Caradori told Franklin Committee counsel Berry shortly after he met the producer.

The producer testified that he spoke to Caradori about the possibility of Caradori assisting in a movie that included "immoral crimes and espionage and very powerful individuals." Dougherty then stated that he had read the producer's notes and it "appears to me that it was Mr. Caradori who came up with the idea that the emphasis would need to be on child sexual abuse." The producer initially responded that he received the same impression, but then he said that he may have "miswrote" Caradori's comments, because he quoted Caradori: "He said that, well, 'I can't say anything right now but it's big, real big. Heads are going to roll. This is an important issue.' And that was primarily, to answer your question, what he said."

In addition to Caradori's telling Berry about his "meeting" with the producer, he discussed their interaction in front of the Franklin Committee when it surfaced that the FBI was building a case against Casey and Caradori for scripting the child-abuse allegations. Caradori told the Committee that he talked to the producer for approximately ten or fifteen minutes before Casey slipped into the room. He said he and Casey had a fairly acrimonious exchange about Casey's not delivering on the promised pictures, and then he left.

Though the producer's grand jury testimony essentially recounted the same story Caradori related to the Committee, he said that Caradori and Casey also discussed Alisha Owen. The producer said that Casey wanted Caradori to compensate him for providing Owen's name, but Caradori wasn't willing to even entertain the idea. At that point, Van Pelt went on a tear, attempting to squeeze everything he could from the producer's comments on Casey and Caradori's exchange about Owen. However, the producer could provide little additional information.

Van Pelt asked the producer if Caradori wanted a "percentage" of the project, and he replied that "it's a sales technique" to offer someone a cut of a project. Van Pelt pressed the producer, asking if he and Caradori specifically discussed a cut of the movie. "I believe *I* would have said that," the producer replied. Van Pelt continued to press the producer—"to the best you can remember"—if Caradori specifically requested a cut of the movie. The producer responded, "At least the best that I can remember. Because why else would he show up?"

According to Caradori, the producer in question didn't discuss a movie deal or Michael Casey when they initially talked over the phone, and Caradori was under the impression that he wanted to make use of Caracorp's investigative or protective services. I think this account is to some extent corroborated by the fact that Casey didn't show his face for the first "ten or fifteen" minutes of their conversation, and that Caradori split shortly after Casey emerged from the other room. The producer also explicitly testified that Caradori told him, "I can't say anything right now" about the investigation; so it seems counterintuitive that Caradori would request, or a producer would offer, a cut of a story that Caradori wasn't even willing to discuss.

After Van Pelt evidently thought he'd established that Caradori was making clandestine Hollywood deals, he inquired if Caradori told the producer that he would have "to cut anybody else in on the deal like members of the Legislative Committee" or anyone else. The producer replied, "No, sir." Van Pelt then seemed to be given to flights of fancy for Caradori's upcoming Hollywood career, because he asked the producer if Caradori requested a specific movie star play him in the movie. "I don't think Caradori mentioned to me, sir, anything like that," said the producer.

Van Pelt forgot to ask the producer if Caradori followed through on his quest for Hollywood notoriety, but a grand juror asked the producer if Caradori contacted him after their initial meeting. The producer said that Caradori didn't contact him again, and they didn't have a second meeting, even though he phoned Caradori requesting one. So Caradori didn't contact the producer after their first meeting, and he obviously wasn't receptive to a second meeting, but Van Pelt nonetheless asked the producer if Caradori requested a particular star to play his role. Van Pelt seemed to be considerably more enthralled about Caradori's box-office potential than Caradori himself.

The producer was also questioned about whether or not he had heard that the victims were recruited to tell their tales of abuse—he said "third parties" had related that fact to him. A grand juror asked him to identify the third parties, and the only definitive third party he mentioned was the FBI. The producer also discussed an Omaha FBI agent flying to Southern California to take his statement, and, after reading that statement, he noticed several inaccuracies.

Though Michael Casey would become a focal point of the grand jury, and was subpoenaed, he was inexplicably nowhere to be found. In June 1990, NSP investigator Chuck Phillips was called to the stand and questioned about Casey's whereabouts. Phillips sounded as if Casey had become one of the FBI's Ten Most Wanted and a national dragnet was being conducted to find him. Phillips testified that the FBI received word that Casey had suffered a heart attack and was hospitalized in Las Vegas—he said the FBI quickly mobilized, but they arrived at the hospital too late. He told the grand jury that Casey managed to slip out of the hospital, and the FBI missed him by a mere "40 minutes." One of the grand jurors speculated that he had snuck "out the window." It is absolutely astonishing that despite the national manhunt for Casey, authorities just weren't able to collar him to testify before the Douglas County grand jury.

Though Senator Ernie Chambers had resigned from the Committee, he remained a very vocal critic of law enforcement's handling of Franklin-related child-abuse allegations and of the Douglas County grand jury. Chambers had a reputation among Nebraska's disenfranchised as their Saint Jude, the patron saint of lost causes, and he was trusted and revered by the downtrodden and oppressed. Now he was also becoming a champion for citizens who had lost faith in the willingness of Nebraska's judiciary to prosecute child abuse.

Chambers made it known, loud and clear, that the Douglas County grand jury was a kangaroo court, and he refused to testify before it. A local television station filmed him addressing a meeting of Concerned Parents: He unabashedly told the meeting's attendees that the grand jury was an unequivocal sham and that Van Pelt and Dougherty were merely putting the state of Nebraska's seal on a cover-up. Chambers told me that he talked to additional victims of the Franklin pandering network, but he advised them not to step forward because of the horrors that had befell the victims who spoke out.

As a consequence of Chambers' outspoken and scathing criticisms of Van Pelt, he became a lightning rod for grand jury witnesses who felt abused by law enforcement—two grand jury witnesses visited Chambers and leveled charges of improprieties directly against Van Pelt or Dougherty. Bonnie Cosentino of Concerned Parents approached Chambers after giving testimony to the grand jury, and said that Dougherty had harassed her shortly before she took the stand. Initially, Cosentino gratefully volunteered to appear before the grand jury, but then she heard about the NSP attempting to detain Alisha Owen's little girl and quickly realized that all was not well with the Douglas County grand jury.

According to her affidavit, the day before she took the stand, Cosentino phoned the number provided by the grand jury. She conveyed to the person fielding her call that she wished to cancel her grand jury appearance—the phone was summarily handed to Terry Dougherty. She stated that she expressed her misgivings about the grand jury proceedings to Dougherty—she claims he then single-handedly played "good cop, bad cop" with her: He told Cosentino that her testimony was important and preemptively offered a peculiar statement—he said they "weren't trying to drag this thing out just to make money." After Dougherty played good cop, she says, he threatened to subpoena her. So, under threat of subpoena, Cosentino showed up at the Douglas County Court House the next morning.

Cosentino was ushered into a small room while she waited to be called as a witness. In her affidavit, she stated that she was alone, reviewing her notes, when Dougherty walked into the room and introduced himself. Cosentino maintained that Dougherty dispensed with the cordial formalities that are customarily reserved for an initial encounter and launched into a hostile diatribe, portraying the Owen family as troublemakers. As Dougherty's diatribe became louder and louder, Cosentino wrote, she suggested that he talk to Senator Chambers, who was better informed on the issue—Dougherty barked, "'Oh, Ernie Chambers,' and waved his hand downward, then made a sound with his mouth as though he were spitting." Evidently, Dougherty didn't hold Chambers in very high esteem.

"I was aware that Mr. Dougherty," Cosentino continued in her affidavit, "a complete stranger to me, intended to let me know that he knew my private opinions, my knowledge of the situation, and also my friendship with the Owen family. He made me aware through his demeanor in angrily discussing this that I was not in an impartial and fair environment of truth, but rather that I was sort of in enemy territory."

Approximately two months after Cosentino gave her affidavit to Chambers, a twenty-year-old woman who had testified before the grand jury in the latter half of June turned up at his office with a very bizarre story. Alisha Owen had mentioned the young woman during one of her videotaped statements to Caradori: Owen thought she had seen the young woman with Larry King's enforcer, but Owen said she had never seen her at a sex party.

Caradori and Ormiston found her living in Lincoln, Nebraska, and they interviewed her. She confessed to being repeatedly molested by her father since the age of ten. She also said that her father brought her to a "trailer house" to be used for kiddy porn. She told Caradori that after high school she had drifted into prostitution and dabbled in Satanism. Though she said that she hadn't attended King's parties, nor could she recall meeting Owen, she was somewhat familiar with the names of certain individuals involved with King but lacked first-hand information.

FBI agents interviewed her too, and she gave the agents basically the same story. Despite the fact that she was in the dark concerning Larry King, she was subpoenaed to appear before the Douglas County grand jury: She would be a perfect candidate to discredit Owen, because Owen had tangentially mentioned her, and yet she knew nothing of Larry King. The FBI wouldn't even need to threaten her.

After she received the subpoena, she phoned the grand jury and requested that she be provided with transportation to Omaha—her lift to the grand jury came in the form of Samuel Van Pelt, who actually chauffeured her to Omaha! The young woman told Chambers that she initially didn't have a clue regarding Van Pelt's status with the grand jury until he disclosed that he was its special prosecutor. After Van Pelt informed the woman of his role, she said she would "plead the Fifth" unless he divulged how the grand jury had acquired her name. Van Pelt reportedly revealed to her that Alisha Owen mentioned her name on "some tapes." Van Pelt also reportedly told her that Owen had made accusations of sexual abuse against OPD Chief Wadman and that the grand jurors didn't believe her.

In the woman's statement to Chambers, she said that Van Pelt confessed to her that he was weary of the grand jury proceedings and coveted returning to his farm—Van Pelt hoped the grand jury would be "over soon" and complained that it had been drawn out too long. Van Pelt theoretically had ultimate control over the scope and span of the grand jury. If the woman's statements are truthful regarding Van Pelt's complaint about the grand jury's duration, one must wonder who was actually controlling the grand jury?

The woman also told Chambers that Van Pelt plied her with a number of questions concerning parties at the Twin Towers, and she replied that she had never been to a party there. "I didn't have or know about any of the information the grand jury was dealing with," she said. "So it seemed to me like he was going to use me just to discredit Alisha."

The woman said she felt threatened by Van Pelt too, because she thought that he might use her previous transgressions as legal leverage: "There were some things in my past that I was afraid he was going to charge me with." In addition to mentioning misconduct on the part of Van Pelt, she discussed an utter lack of decorum and concern on the part of the grand jurors. She said that the grand jurors talked among themselves and laughed while she testified: "Nobody from the jury actually seemed to care what was going on at all about the case."

After the woman testified to the grand jury, Van Pelt had the generosity to shuttle her back to Lincoln. During the ride back to Lincoln, she maintained, Van Pelt told her he had an "easy day" coming up because the witness being called before the grand jury on the following day would take the Fifth. "He told me that he was a homosexual and that he had sex with little boys," she said. "So he would plead the Fifth so he wouldn't get indicted."

The woman's statement to Chambers on this detail is very telling—Alan Baer was the witness called before the grand jury the following morning. He took refuge behind the Fifth and didn't even show up. The grand jury proceedings were blanketed in secrecy, which included the witnesses called to testify; so it would have been nearly impossible for the woman to be aware that a homosexual who had "sex with little boys" would be called by Van Pelt the next morning unless he had actually told her. Van Pelt was also seemingly admitting that he knew Alan Baer had sex with little boys.

Chambers sent the woman's statement and an accompanying letter to the media and also to Douglas County Attorney Ronald Staskiewicz. In the letter, Chambers stated that Van Pelt appeared to have been in violation of the grand jury's "secrecy requirement" and also guilty of "tampering with a witness." In response, Staskiewicz wrote that Douglas County Deputy Attorney Bob Sigler and an "investigator" interviewed the woman for more than two hours and concluded that Van Pelt hadn't committed a crime.

I tend to believe that the vast majority of the grand jurors were most likely good citizens, who were simply worn down and utterly confused by a four-month deluge of unremitting testimony that gushed truth, lies, irrelevancies, and outright absurdities. The last category was made absolutely evident when Van Pelt called a man to the stand who was clearly unhinged and knew nothing of Franklin. Van Pelt told the grand jurors that the man had written a letter to the grand jury requesting to appear as a witness, and after he personally talked to the man over the phone, he had decided to call him as a witness

Van Pelt didn't even ask this witness questions, but, rather, let him rant. He went off on various tangents concerning Communist plots and was particularly piqued about KGB infiltration of the Food and Drug Administration: "Now, so I believe that Communism is a simplex theory, which has no practical application in reality, and Communists are lacking in judgment, and also that both the CIA and the three FDA networks are manipulated by double agents of the KGB." The witness then discussed the "models and theories" he developed that would aid the treatment of cancer, high blood pressure, and muscular dystrophy; unfortunately medical researchers in Nebraska, whom he concluded were KGB agents, had undermined his revolutionary medical advances—he demanded that the Douglas County grand jury take action on his behalf! "Now, I do have a request for the grand jury, I mean, I came here with that specific purpose, and I'm asking for an indictment against the Nebraska Medical Center." None of the grand jurors felt compelled to question the witness.

During the third week of July, an exhilarating hum saturated Nebraska's airwaves: Television newscasters and radio talk show hosts tingled with excitement as they quoted "sources" in the know who whispered that the Douglas County grand jury was in the homestretch of its deliberations. Van Pelt had pledged to restore "integrity" to the system, and his grand jury had worked unremittingly to that end for month after month. Finally, all the confusion and uncertainty would be cleared up—criminals would be indicted and the innocent cleared.

On July 23, 1990, within two weeks of Gary Caradori's conveniently timed demise, the Douglas County grand jury released its whopping forty-page report, and it seemed as if Moses had descended from Mount Sinai with the Ten Commandments. The *World-Herald* bore a banner headline, flaunting a font size that probably hadn't been seen since Apollo 11 landed on the moon or, perhaps, the Kennedy assassination: "Grand Jury Says Abuse Stories Were a 'Carefully Crafted Hoax.'" A sub-headline stated: "Three Indicted; Many Rumors Debunked." Below the banner headline were three blown-up pictures—Alan Baer, Alisha Owen, and Senator Schmit. (The *World-Herald* had the tact to use a police mug shot for Owen.) The grand jury concluded that "Franklin" entailed absolutely no child abuse except within the confines of the Webb household: Alisha Owen was indicted on eight counts of perjury, Paul Bonacci was indicted on three counts of perjury, and Alan Baer received two indictments for *adult* pandering.

The *World-Herald* published the Douglas County grand jury report, and on the report's first page Van Pelt and company discussed the thoroughness of their deliberations—convening for "82 days," reviewing "395 exhibits," issuing "136 subpoenas," hearing from "76 witnesses," and watching "over 30 hours of videotapes." The first page of the report also included an introductory comment on Owen: "Two of the victims recanted their video statements and testified that a third victim, Alisha Owen, was perpetrating a hoax for personal gain."

There were some difficulties with the truth even on the report's first page—I have trouble with "reviewed 395 exhibits." On July 23, the very day that the grand jury foreman Michael Flanagan signed off on the report and it was released to the public, Van Pelt introduced eighty-seven exhibits into evidence. I find it inconceivable that the grand jurors could have adequately "reviewed" eighty-seven exhibits on the grand jury's final day of "deliberations," even if they had been enrolled in an Evelyn Wood speed-reading crash course and were provided with bottomless cups of espresso.

However, here's where it gets interesting: sixty-two of those exhibits were given the same number—exhibit "394." So it ultimately appears that Van Pelt only introduced twenty-six exhibits on that final day. And here's where it gets even a little more interesting: Among those eighty-seven exhibits introduced on July 23 was a "review" of Caracorp's phone records. NSP investigator Phillips picked up a copy of Caracorp's phone records on May 23, and they weren't introduced into evidence until July 23! Thus, Van Pelt had possessed evidence that the phantom phone call never existed, but never questioned Boner about his veracity concerning the call.

The grand jury's report was remarkably bizarre in its own right, even though it was intended for public consumption. The report declared that the child-abuse allegations concerning Larry King et al. were nothing more than the insidious work of "rumormongers," and it even quoted Shakespeare's *Henry IV*: "Rumor is a pipe, blown by surmises, jealousies, conjectures." The grand jury's foreman would later confess that Van Pelt had an integral role in writing the report; so perhaps its literary contrivances were a byproduct of Van Pelt's fertile imagination:

> Perhaps never in the history of Douglas County has the discordant multitude played so feverishly upon the rumor pipe as in the allegations of sexual misconduct surrounding Franklin. As Shakespeare observed, nearly four centuries ago, the local rumors have been blown by surmise, jealousy, and conjecture. Although many in the community both spread and received the gossip, three individuals are particularly illustrative.

The grand jury report named three primary rumormongers who couldn't get enough of playing so feverishly on that old rumor pipe:

Michael Casey, Kirstin Hallberg, and Bonnie Cosentino. The grand jury report gave a rundown of Casey's countless transgressions and extensive "criminal record." Casey was the fountainhead of all those nasty rumors—he labored incessantly, surely around the clock, to weave his web of innuendo that entangled the gullible masses, the Franklin Committee, Concerned Parents, Gary Caradori, etc. According to the report, the city and greater metropolitan area now had to recover from the blight of Michael Casey—an ethical eunuch who had masqueraded as a freelance writer: "Meanwhile, Omaha must go forward and try to leave behind the rumors, fear, accusations, and lies which Casey helped spread."

The report then gave an account of Casey admitting himself to Saint Joseph Hospital and befriending Alisha Owen—they "lived under the same roof" and even "corresponded" after Owen was incarcerated. "We believe that Caradori would not have found Owen if it were not for Casey. Owen then led Caradori to other potential victim/witnesses." The grand jury report clearly distorted reality when it discussed Casey and Owen's relationship: Owen wrote Casey one letter from York—they didn't have a continuing correspondence.

Casey's primary impetuses for being a rumormonger were "grudges" and "creating a sensational story," but the grand jury felt that Kirstin Hallberg concealed a different motive: "Hallberg believed that she was acting in the public's best interests. However, many of those testifying disagreed, viewing her as a troublemaker, gossip, and self-appointed conscience of the public."

The report made another departure from reality when it stated, "Hallberg's name surfaced in almost every stage of this investigation." Hallberg accompanied her friend, Kathleen Sorenson, when the latter brought Eulice Washington to meet Julie Walters—she certainly wasn't the prime mover in Walters' report. Moreover, Shawneta Moore merely told Hallberg that she had been in a prostitution and pornography ring while Hallberg worked at the Uta Halee facility and Moore was a resident—she was too frightened to name names. Moore told her school counselor about the specifics of the ring and named Larry King—the counselor then phoned Hallberg, requesting her assistance. Conversely, Hallberg played absolutely no role whatsoever in identifying Owen, Boner, Danny King, or Bonacci. So Hallberg's name "surfaced" in connection with two victims. Assigning her an almost ubiquitous role in the investigation was ridiculous.

The report fingered Bonnie Cosentino as a key rumormonger "who appeared to react from emotions rather than fact." Cosentino supposedly colluded with Casey in the spreading of "misinformation, rumor, and innuendo." The report flat out excoriated her as if she had emerged from some murky, reptilian netherworld: "If indeed there was a spawning ground in which Franklin rumors were born, nurtured, and grew, Cosentino would be found as an inhabitant."

The report ripped Cosentino for discussing Dougherty's diatribe with Senator Chambers: "We believe that Cosentino reported, in violation of her oath, to Senator Chambers, and eventually indirectly to the media, that the Grand Jury was not attentive, cohesive, or effective." The grand jury found Cosentino's "misrepresentation" to be "inappropriate, unfair, and untrue" and designed to "harass and demoralize the grand jury" and "its prosecutorial staff." It appears Van Pelt and company tell an outright lie in their statements concerning Cosentino contacting Chambers: The events described in Cosentino's affidavit occurred *before* she entered the grand jury, so she wasn't in "violation of her oath." Furthermore, the report asserted that Cosentino harassed Dougherty rather than vice versa. I've personally known Cosentino for over five years, and I find it difficult to believe that she would "harass and demoralize" anyone.

The grand jury smeared and castigated the rumormongers for three and a half pages before it tackled the early allegations, which consisted of the abuses recounted by Eulice Washington and Shawneta Moore. I never managed to acquire the grand jury testimony of Washington and Moore, but Washington has told me that she's never recanted her allegations, and the grand jury report implied that she stuck to her story. The report, however, mentioned that a number of witnesses who traveled extensively with King were interviewed by the grand jury, and it found no evidence that Lisa Webb (Eulice Washington) or any other children were ever transported on interstate flights for illegal purposes.

Examples of the grand jury's lack of due diligence are practically inexhaustible, but its unwillingness to track down passenger manifests or interview the pilots who flew Larry King's charters was particularly egregious. The grand jury had access to scores and scores of Larry King's flight receipts, as accumulated by both the Committee and the feds, and the overwhelming majority of them didn't have accompanying FAA-mandated passenger manifests.

The missing passenger manifests, in and of themselves, should have triggered red flags for the grand jury. Caradori's testimony and his Investigative Reports also provided the grand jury with the names of pilots and employees of the charters who could have corroborated that children were on Larry King's flights, but the pilots and employees named by Caradori were never subpoenaed. The grand jury ultimately demoted the missing passenger manifests to an almost inconsequential afterthought: "It is recommended that the FAA enforce requirements that all charter airline flights have a passenger manifest filed along with flight plans and logs similar to commercial airline flights. Since this investigation included allegations that certain persons were transported by charter flights for illegal purposes, passenger records would have facilitated the grand jury's work."

Shawneta Moore was seventeen years old when she appeared before the grand jury, and, given the phrasing of its report, it is difficult to discern whether or not she recanted portions of her story or the crafters of the report decided she recanted portions of her story: "Although the girl insisted that some of her events did occur, she admitted that it is difficult for her to now distinguish between reality and fantasy because of her heavy alcohol and drug use at the time." The report remarked that the "young woman" was under the treatment of a therapist, and "possible prosecution would be counterproductive to further rehabilitation and would not be in the girl's best interests." So the grand jury demonstrated its abounding compassion and opted not prosecute Washington and Moore for perjury. Van Pelt and company would indict two victims for perjury, but indicting four might create problems.

The grand jury felt that the Nebraska Attorney General's Office could have responded to the Foster Care Review Board "in a more timely manner" concerning the early allegations, but it "followed the proper policies and procedures." The report then blasted Carol Stitt and Patricia Flocken! The report stated that Stitt should have personally contacted the Uta Halee facility, Richard Young Hospital and Boys

Town instead of the Nebraska Attorney General "regarding Kirstin Hallberg's allegations."

Yet again, the grand jury made a departure from reality concerning Hallberg. Yes, it's true, Hallberg had a dialogue with Stitt about Uta Halee residents, a former Boys Town student hospitalized at Richard Young, and also about Shawneta Moore. But Stitt's initial concerns were sparked by a conversation she had with Flocken, and Flocken provided her with Julie Walters' report. Also, various Richard Young Hospital employees discussed Moore's allegations with either Stitt or Dennis Carlson once they realized that the OPD was unwilling to follow up with Moore.

The report noted that Flocken should have "pressed for the filing of charges" against the Webbs, even though Washington County Attorney Tripp refused to file charges. Two DSS employees, an NSP officer, and Flocken painstakingly attempted to persuade Tripp to file sexual abuse charges against Webb, but he had rebuffed all of them. If the County Attorney was unwilling to file charges after listening to four individuals who were intimately familiar with the case, Flocken in effect had no other options.

After the report reprimanded the rumormongers, consigned the early allegations to mere delusions, and took pot-shots at the various people who sided with the victims, it tackled the statements videotaped by Gary Caradori. Van Pelt and company admitted that they spent the majority of their comprehensive "fact finding and deliberative effort" on Caradori's videotapes and came to the following conclusion: "There is no doubt after reviewing all relevant evidence, that the story of sexual abuse, drugs, prostitution, and judicial bribery presented in the legislative videotapes is a carefully crafted hoax, scripted by a person or persons with considerable knowledge of the people and institutions of Omaha, including personal relationships and shortcomings."

But here's where a very strange report becomes even a little stranger: It never definitively named the careful crafters who "scripted" the hoax; rather, it simply listed several individuals with an accompanying paragraph or paragraphs. Alisha Owen was the first person mentioned. "We think that Owen might have been sexually abused during her early years, but not by the people and in the way she has alleged," the report stated. "Owen, being a promiscuous young woman, has had many experiences from which to draw the details of her allegations." The grand jury found that Owen's "motivation" for fabricating her statement to Caradori was "a reduced sentence" and to "collect money from her story or from civil litigation."

Paul Bonacci is the next person the report ravaged: "Bonacci was perhaps the most pathetic witness to appear during the entire proceedings." Bonacci was a young man struggling with a mental illness, and the grand jury report labeled him as "pathetic." Van Pelt and company seemed to have lost the abounding compassion that they exercised with Moore. I'm also unsure of the grand jury's groupthink connotation of "pathetic"—if, in fact, groupthink was involved in its characterization of Bonacci.

The report made yet another swerve from reality when it addressed Bonacci's inability to tell the truth: "He has been diagnosed as having multiple personalities, and his psychiatrist doubts that he can tell the truth." Bonacci's psychiatrist, Dr. Mead, testified before the Franklin Committee, because its members wanted to understand Bonacci's disorder, and he was questioned about the grand jury's report panning Bonacci's veracity. Mead told the Committee that he had appeared before the grand jury, but his appearance had been extremely brief, and he couldn't recall if Bonacci was even mentioned: "For the life of me," he said, "I can't even remember that we talked about Paul."

It's peculiar that the grand jury report discussed Mead, and Mead confirmed that he appeared before the grand jury, even though his name is nowhere to be found on the grand jury's "Witness Schedule." Whether or not this was an oversight or willful neglect is open to speculation, but Mead had explicitly told the Committee that he didn't doubt Bonacci's capacity for truthfulness: "I can't really believe that I said that he was not capable of telling the truth. I don't believe I would, because that's not what I believe now, and that's not what I believed then."

Mead's belief in Bonacci's veracity would have been an extremely inconvenient truth for the authors of the grand jury report, as Bonacci was a monkey wrench in the workings of the "carefully crafted hoax." The report implied that the hoax was imparted from Casey to Owen, who in turn conveyed it to Boner, who imparted it to Danny King. Bonacci's intricate knowledge of the perpetrators and the nuances of the network don't fit into the "script" with the greatest of ease, and it would have been imperative that the crafters of the grand jury report allotted him absolutely no credibility.

The grand jury report then discussed Troy Boner and Danny King, who possessed the good sense to see the light and had "cooperated with the grand jury." Boner and King were inspired to participate in the hoax for untold "monetary gain" through "litigation" and the "sale of movie and book rights." The report emphasized that they were never "threatened" into recanting their original statements to Caradori.

After the Douglas County grand jury concluded that the six victims who accused Larry King of child abuse and pandering children were lying, its acute discerning powers shifted to Larry King and separated the man from the myth. The report found that King shelled out cash and gifts for homosexual trysts, but his sexual activities were limited to consenting adults, and he certainly wasn't an interstate, pedophilic pimp: "Lawrence E. King, Jr. was mentioned by Owen as a regular participant in Twin Towers parties involving minors and out of town drug/prostitution activities. We have found no evidence that King was involved in these activities as stated by Owen."

The report reads as though Owen was the only one connecting Larry King to "out of town drug/prostitution activities." The report's authors seemed to have overlooked Eulice Washington, Troy Boner, Danny King, and also Paul Bonacci. All five link Larry King to the "out of town" pandering of children. It's true that Boner and Danny King recanted, but, even then, Eulice Washington and Paul Bonacci testified about King's cross-country child-pandering network. Maybe Van Pelt and company had too much on their minds to recall such trivial facts?

The grand jury "found probable cause" that Larry King "used money or items of value" to procure men in their late teens or early twenties, and, thus, "committed the crime of pandering"—adult pandering—but the majority of "these activities occurred in the early eighties." The grand jury prudently decided that since King was facing forty felony counts in federal court, it would defer his prosecution to the feds. "Should the matters pending against King in the federal system come to naught, we implore state authorities to act upon the overwhelming evidence against King relating to both pandering and theft offenses."

King would ultimately enter into a plea bargain with the feds for his financial crimes, but he was never charged with a single count of pandering by state or federal authorities—let alone child abuse. King was safely ensconced at the US Medical Facility in Rochester, Minnesota while the grand jury ostensibly deliberated his fate.

The report noted that the grand jury didn't subpoena King because he invariably would have taken refuge behind the Fifth Amendment. The report also commented on King's psychiatric malady: "Evidence and testimony heard regarding the issue of King's incompetence to stand trial for his crimes have shown much disagreement on the incompetency ruling." The grand jury apparently believed King to be a "very clever and manipulative person" who had most likely inveigled himself into the federal hospital. The report neglected to mention that King had been whisked off to the federal facility in Springfield, Missouri, where he was found incompetent without a motion from him or his attorneys.

King would be magically restored to sanity about five weeks after the Douglas County grand jury released its report. He returned to Omaha at the end of August.

After the report discussed King, it focused on Alan Baer: "We have found no direct connection between Alan Baer and [Larry] King or the Franklin Credit Union, other than limited social and business dealings." Even if Gary Caradori's videotaped testimony of Owen, Boner, Danny King, and Bonacci is to be discounted, the grand jury heard from an accountant whom the NCUA conscripted to ascertain how Franklin's $39 million evaporated—he testified about financial breadcrumbs that led directly from Baer to Larry King.

The accountant's inopportune disclosure didn't occur during his examination by Van Pelt or Dougherty, but was in response to a grand juror's question. He was asked if there was a "connection" between Baer and Larry King, and the accountant replied, "Well, there must be some connection, because Alan Baer wrote him a check for $12,000 in December of 1988 after the close." The grand juror apparently thought he was onto something, because he started to spout other names, seeking additional connections. But Van Pelt cut him off after only three names: "Excuse me, are you done?" The grand juror managed to squeeze in a fourth name.

If Baer and Larry King had only "limited social and business dealings," it seems highly unlikely that Baer would cut a $12,000 check for King after Franklin had been closed. Since King was facing meager employment opportunities in December, demonstrated by the fact that he ended up working for a florist, it's difficult to imagine that he and Baer would have had "business dealings" necessitating a $12,000 exchange.

Though the grand jury would conclude that Larry King and Baer "had no direct connection," it also found that "Baer enticed other persons to become prostitutes or commit acts of prostitution" and indicted him on two counts of *adult* pandering—so Baer wasn't charged with a single count of child abuse either. Each of Baer's indictments carried a maximum penalty of five years in prison: he was potentially looking at ten years in prison. An Omaha newscaster said of Baer after the grand jury's report was released: "He's in for the fight of his life!"

Baer evidently realized, or maybe he was even informed, that he would be the grand jury's fall guy, because he reached out to the Committee and inquired about the possibility of immunity, which, according to an affidavit from Senator Schmit, prompted a death threat from FBI agents. Baer did indeed snap back in line and keep his mouth shut. Despite his indictments, he would ultimately be handsomely rewarded for remaining mute and enduring a little public disgrace.

The grand jury report then commented on the various individuals who were written into the "script," but it persisted in never actually naming the scriptwriters. For example, Peter Citron had been "written into the script because of his known homosexual and pedophile behavior."

The report absolved Nebraska's political godfather Eugene Mahoney of any "sexual misconduct" and offered suspected reasons for writing him into the script: "Mahoney may have been included because of his personal friendship with Harold Andersen as well as his long-time political connections within the state of Nebraska." Boner testified to the grand jury that Mahoney requested that Boner perform oral sex on him in an adult bookstore, but apparently the grand jury didn't believe Boner's account of their interaction. The writers of the grand jury report thus believed Boner's testimony concerning Owen but evidently didn't believe his testimony concerning Mahoney. Though that would justify an indictment for perjury, Boner was never indicted.

The grand jury report ascribed striking incompetence and deception to Gary Caradori, who was dead and unable to defend himself when it was released. The report concluded that he "fed" information to the victims he interviewed: "He led the witnesses, and the videotapes were stopped and started at suspicious intervals with the substance of the witnesses' stories changing." The report also mentioned that Caradori was "duped into working with Casey."

The interviews conducted by Caradori were lengthy and tedious—the victims were periodically overwhelmed by emotion and broke down in tears; Caradori would take breaks and allow them to recuperate. I've watched Caradori's videotaped interviews, and it's just not true that the videotaping was "stopped and started at suspicious intervals" with the victims' stories thereafter undergoing substantial alteration. Moreover, Ormiston's polygraph results on the subject clearly indicated that the victims videotaped by Caradori weren't coached.

I've also talked to a handful of people who were acquainted with both Caradori and Casey, and I've asked them if Caradori could have possibly been "duped" by Casey—they found the idea preposterous and laughable.

The grand jury report unleashed scathing criticism on the Franklin Committee and Senators Schmit and Chambers. The report cited the Committee's "several hidden agendas" and declared that if Committee members had acted as "statesmen," instead of politicians, the "grand jury would not have been necessary." The report also remarked that the Committee lost focus on its original task—looking at Franklin's financial improprieties—once it ventured into investigating the child-abuse allegations. It is true that Schmit was only cognizant of financial improprieties when he originally drafted Resolution 5 during a special, year-ending session of the Unicameral in November of 1988; but after the Unicameral was in full session in January and monies were allocated to the Committee, the mandate of Resolution 5 included probing the child-abuse allegations.

The report ripped Schmit for a "lack of security during the Committee hearings and investigations," and more or less held him personally responsible for the leaks that ignited the widespread rumors. Van Pelt and company also pronounced that Schmit was politically irresponsible on several occasions, and they were deeply concerned about his unsubstantiated comments "to the media that there were people who wanted to see Caradori dead."

The report reserved its harshest rebukes for Senator Chambers, noting that his "recalcitrant attitude is counterproductive to the overall outcome that is desired by the community and its citizenry." The grand jury apparently felt that it labored slavishly to uncover the truth and that Chambers did everything in his power to undermine its quest: "In most circumstances, Chambers' information was far from the truth and was one-sided. However, because of the secrecy of the proceedings, we legally could not defend ourselves, as Chambers was fully aware. Nevertheless, he continued to taunt and harass the grand jury system. We found this practice to be unethical."

Chambers filed a lawsuit in Douglas County District Court to have all references to him expunged from the grand jury report. He contended that the grand jury overstepped its legal authority by commenting on individuals that it hadn't indicted, but a Douglas County Judge disagreed and let the report stand, warts and all. Chambers then appealed the judge's ruling to the Nebraska Supreme Court, and it handed down a unanimous ruling in his favor: "A grand jury has no right to file a report reflecting on the character or conduct of public officers or citizens unless it is accompanied or followed by an indictment charging such individuals with a specific offense against the state." The Nebraska Supreme Court not only expunged Chambers' name from the grand jury report: It expunged the entire report and ordered it sealed. But Nebraska's high court didn't make its ruling until December of 1993, and its decision was too little, too late. By then, the grand jury report had propagated irrevocable damage.

The grand jury's proceedings and report were macabre and surreal, and its indictments of Owen and Bonacci were also extremely unconventional. Perjury indictments generally specify exact statements where the indicted gave false accounts that were designed to mislead, but the report didn't pinpoint the definitive statements where Owen and Bonacci perjured themselves—it only offered excerpts from their testimony.

Each of Owen and Bonacci's perjury counts contained various exchanges with either Van Pelt or Dougherty that included several questions and answers—one of Bonacci's perjury indictments was spread out over three pages of rambling testimony on a number of subjects. So it's difficult to identify the precise statements of Owen or Bonacci that the grand jury concluded were false and misleading. With that in mind, I've distilled the sprawling exchanges that underlay each of their perjury indictments into a single sentence:

- Alisha Owen's first count of perjury included statements she made about meeting Robert Wadman and then-*Omaha-World* publisher Harold Andersen at Twin Towers parties in the fall of 1983.
- Owen's second perjury count consisted of her statements regarding her second party at the Twin Towers alleging that Larry King, Harold Andersen, and Robert Wadman were present.
- Owen's third count of perjury included a series of statements she made regarding accusations of Harold Andersen fondling an eleven- or twelve-year-old boy at the first Twin Towers party she attended.
- Owen's fourth perjury count consisted of statements concerning an alleged first sexual encounter with Robert Wadman at the Twin Towers.
- Owen's fifth count entailed a series of statements relating to a liaison with Robert Wadman at the French Café, subsequent liaisons on Wednesday afternoons, and also her allegation that Robert Wadman was the father of her child.
- Owen's sixth count was based upon a series of statements regarding Robert Wadman's inserting the barrel of a handgun into her vagina.
- Owen's seventh count included statements she made about "Larry the Kid" telling her that "Rob" was, in fact, Robert Wadman.
- Owen's eighth count of perjury consisted of her statements about performing oral sex on Douglas County District Court Judge Theodore Carlson as a fifteen-year-old.

- Paul Bonacci's first count of perjury included statements he made about witnessing Alisha Owen and Robert Wadman having sexual relations on two occasions.
- Bonacci's second count entailed accusations regarding Harold Andersen tying him up, burning his genitals with a cigarette, and cutting him with a knife.
- Bonacci's third count of perjury consisted of a statement about witnessing Robert Wadman snorting cocaine.

The individual perjury indictments leveled against Owen and Bonacci carried a penalty of one to twenty years of imprisonment: Owen was staring at up to one hundred-sixty years in prison, and Bonacci was looking at a maximum of a mere sixty years. I've talked to Bonacci about his perjury indictments, and he's still perplexed that the grand jury only indicted him on his statements regarding Wadman and Andersen—he also testified about alleged underage sexual encounters with Larry King, Alan Baer, Peter Citron, and a host of others. Though the grand jury report concluded that those statements were also false, Van Pelt and company inexplicably opted not to indict him on that content. It's also interesting that the *World-Herald* published the grand jury report, but it failed to publish the indictments of Owen and Bonacci.

After Samuel Van Pelt fulfilled his civic duty of restoring integrity to the system, he receded back to the obscurity of his farm in Hickman, Nebraska. Van Pelt for all intents and purposes handed the torch of integrity to the *World-Herald*. His carefully crafted grand jury report gave the newspaper free rein to use the Franklin Committee for batting practice, and it started swinging for the bleachers.

The *World-Herald* began with a series of editorials pounding Schmit and the Committee. The first editorial following the report minced no words: "The Franklin Committee a Disgrace to Nebraska." The two opening sentences of the editorial succinctly sum it up: "Members of the Nebraska Legislature should be embarrassed at the behavior of the Franklin Committee. The Committee has disgraced itself and the state." The editorial then proceeded to trash Senator Schmit, a deceased Gary Caradori, and also Alisha Owen and Paul Bonacci.

The editorial essentially commended Troy Boner for having the courage to stand tall and "recant" before the grand jury, and it commented on his superior veracity compared to the other videotaped victims: "Boner was the most believable of the three young people on the Caradori videotapes." In Boner's 1993 affidavit, he largely confessed to being the most accomplished liar of the three. The *World-Herald*, like the grand jury, didn't seem to hold Paul Bonacci in very high esteem: "Caradori later found a fourth person who claimed to be a victim of sexual abuse. This person, Paul Bonacci, told a story so patently ridiculous that none but the most naïve could swallow it."

The editorial also pounced on Caradori, whose "shortcomings as an investigator were plain"—he was "influenced by Michael Casey, a strange, shadowy man with a history of duping people...." The *World-Herald* then made a sly departure from reality and parroted the grand jury report: "It was Casey who put Caradori in touch with Boner, Miss Owen and James Daniel King, who has also recanted stories he told on the videotapes about sexual abuse by prominent men." In actuality, Casey simply provided Owen's *name* to Caradori; Casey never mentioned Boner or Danny King.

A second *World-Herald* editorial—"Schmit Panel Can't Duck its Responsibility in the Hoax"—gave Schmit a public flogging for criticizing the grand jury's report. A third editorial excoriated the Committee for leaking the first federal subpoena served on Caradori, and also Caradori's videotaped statements: "Reporters who were friendly to the Committee came into possession of the subpoena that was issued to the Committee's investigator and were among the first to get selected parts of the videotapes."

Mike McKnight was the first television reporter to come by the tapes, and he told Alisha Owen that the FBI sold him the tapes. Moreover, McKnight almost immediately recruited J. William Gallup to publicly view the tapes, and Gallup severely rebuked Caradori's interviewing techniques. McKnight appeared to be about as "friendly to the Committee" as Woodward and Bernstein were to the Nixon administration.

As the *World-Herald* raked the Committee with vicious editorials, it ran articles that buttressed the grand jury report. In one article, "Lawyer: Client Told Caradori of His Lies," Pamela Vuchetich discussed Danny King's chipping in on the hoax: "Mrs. Vuchetich said she agreed with a

Douglas County grand jury report that used the words 'carefully crafted hoax' to describe a series of sexual abuse allegations uttered by Danny King and two friends and encouraged by some older adults." Vuchetich said that Danny King told Caradori "five or six times" that his video-taped statement was fictitious, but Caradori just "wouldn't give up on him." She also commented on her gradual realization of the hoax: "It came slow for me."

The *World-Herald* also battered the Committee with an article on Troy Boner, "Witness: I Lied Seeking Riches," who confessed that "a promise of riches" was his primary motivation for cooking up the hoax. Boner said Caradori assured him that big, big money was to be made: "When we're done, Troy, you can sue for 10 or 15 million dollars. At the very least 5 million dollars guaranteed." In the article, Boner asserted that every statement he made to Caradori had been fabricated: "The only thing on the tape that is the actual truth is my name."

I've talked to conservatives and liberals alike who feel that "Pravda of the Plains" is an apt depiction of the *World-Herald*, even though no one denies its influential sway among Nebraska's populace. Despite the *World-Herald*'s incessant assaults on everyone who took a stand for the victims, Abraham Lincoln's adage about fooling all the people all the time still rings true: A *Lincoln Journal* poll found that 56% of Nebraskans felt illegalities had been covered up in the Franklin investigations; Omaha's KETV conducted a call-in poll in which the station's viewers disagreed with the grand jury report by a margin of ten to one; and an Omaha radio station found 72% of its listeners were disbelieving of the grand jury report.

The grand jury report declared that the Franklin Committee had "hidden agendas," but the majority of people I've interviewed felt that the *World-Herald* had an agenda of discrediting the victims and their supporters. The *World-Herald* also made a very minimal effort to pursue information that could have countered the grand jury report, even though Van Pelt's grand jury appeared to be a perversion of justice, and a preponderance of Nebraskans thought it facilitated a cover-up.

But the *World-Herald* wasn't the only media source to trumpet the Douglas County grand jury report: The *New York Times* essentially acted as a mouthpiece for the manufactured story. Shortly after the Douglas County grand jury's report was released, America's paper-of-record announced, "Omaha Grand Jury Sees Hoax in Lurid Tales." The article began, "Lurid reports of sexual abuse, drug trafficking, pornography and political intrigue that have held Omaha enthralled for nearly two years were a 'carefully crafted hoax,' a county grand jury in Nebraska has concluded."

The *New York Times* article noted that the grand jury didn't name the crafters of the hoax, and it also included a quote from Senator Schmit who called the report "a strange document." But the crux of the article was the findings of the grand jury. The article concluded with the perjury charges leveled against Alisha Owen and Paul Bonacci, and commented that they were currently incarcerated for "unrelated offenses." The *New York Times* article also discussed "a state investigator" being "duped" by a disgruntled former employee of Boys Town "identified as Michael Casey"—who "might have fueled the 'fire of rumor and innuendo' because of personal grudges."

As fate would have it, Casey testified before the federal grand jury on the very same day the Douglas County grand jury released its report. Inexplicably, the FBI had been able to collar Casey with a subpoena for the federal grand jury, even though its national dragnet failed to locate him for the Douglas County grand jury. If the Douglas County grand jurors had actually scrutinized Casey in the flesh, perhaps his portrayal as the personification of dishonesty would have been undermined?

Shortly after Casey testified in front of the federal grand jury and stepped out of the federal courthouse, synchronicity intervened in his life for a second time that day—he would be quickly arrested by the OPD on a South Dakota bench warrant. Casey was thrown in the Douglas County Jail and eventually extradited to South Dakota for committing the offense of bouncing a $1,430 check—a Douglas County Judge ordered him held on $100,000 bail.

Michael Casey granted the *World-Herald* an interview from the pokey. In the subsequent *World-Herald* article, "Casey Says He Shared Franklin Data with Caradori," published three days after the grand jury released its report, Casey acknowledged that he and Caradori swapped information, but he didn't think Caradori acted improperly: "He had information and I had information and I think we were both after each other's information. I don't think Caradori at all betrayed the confidence and responsibility of his job." The *World-Herald* article quoted Casey on the role he played connecting Caradori and Owen: "I told him about Alisha, where she was at, that she claimed she was abused and was very familiar with street life in Omaha." Caradori's Investigative Reports, his grand jury testimony, and Karen Ormiston refute Casey's latter statement—Owen refutes this statement too.

Casey was a bit perplexed about his newfound infamy—he told the *World-Herald* that he was puzzled that the Douglas County grand jury had anointed him as the supreme hoaxer without ever hearing his testimony. Also in the article, Casey said that Van Pelt had actually requested that Casey furnish the grand jury with background research on King and Franklin "within the first two weeks" of its formation.

Van Pelt and company's report asserted that they had "little knowledge" of Casey when commencing their deliberations in March, but as their investigation pressed forward "his name kept surfacing." Casey's account of Van Pelt conscripting his assistance shortly after the Douglas County grand jury was impaneled was in direct contradiction to the grand jury report—Van Pelt "could not be reached" for comment on Casey's contention.

The federal grand jury investigating the credit union was initially impaneled in September 1988, and it issued indictments against Larry King in May 1989 for his financial crimes. The federal grand jury would then shift its focus from Franklin-related financial improprieties to Franklin-related child abuse, and then be given a six-month extension in April 1990 to continue exploring the allegations; so it was ultimately impaneled for two years. The federal grand jury didn't have the sweeping "charge" of the state grand jury: It focused on whether or not federal statutes had been violated. The FBI served as the investigative entity for the federal grand jury.

Though I have never seen the witness schedule for the federal grand jury, I've been able to identify some of its witnesses through newspaper clippings and Douglas County grand jury testimony: The federal grand jury subpoenaed the Hollywood producer whom Casey had coaxed to

Nebraska, Casey's friend who put up Owen for a handful of nights, and the "shadowy" Michael Casey himself.

The federal grand jury's pursuit of hoaxer extraordinaire Michael Casey indicated that it chased the same red herring as Van Pelt and company. Casey's friend who briefly accommodated Owen broke his vow of secrecy and commented to the *World-Herald* about testifying before the federal grand jury—his remarks revealed that the feds were fixated on Michael Casey and had also depicted him as an ethical eunuch. "Most of the questions had to do with Mike," said Casey's friend. "One of the jurors asked me if I still consider Mike Casey to be a friend. I said, 'Yeah I still consider him a friend.' And the juror said, 'Then you're a better person than I am.'"

Alisha Owen alleged to me that one of the federal prosecutors pilloried her with threats at the federal courthouse before she took the federal grand jury's oath. She said that he was livid and discharging spittle as he shouted that she would suffer grave consequences if she didn't recant her prior statements to Caradori, but Owen still refused to recant. The feds, like Van Pelt and company, cast Troy Boner as their star witness to impeach Owen.

The day after Boner signed his federal immunity agreement, he was apparently frightened and confused, making a late-night phone call to Gary Caradori. He told Caradori that a high-ranking official in the US Attorney's Office, who frequented adult bookstores and had a sexual predilection for "young kids," had threatened Boner with perjury charges. According to Caradori's Investigative Report, the threat issued by that esteemed federal official seemed to have left Boner utterly demoralized. It was evidently the critical mass that crushed whatever will he might have mustered to stand by his videotaped statement.

I've never been able to corroborate Boner's allegations about the official in question, but that official played an instrumental role prosecuting the federal grand jury: He was the very same prosecutor who allegedly pilloried Owen with threats before she took the stand there.

In September 1990, the federal grand jury released a three-page report stating that it found absolutely no evidence of interstate transportation of children for illicit purposes, and also indicted Alisha Owen on eight counts of perjury. Both the *New York Times* and *Washington Post* reported on the federal grand jury's findings.

The grand juries and the merciless media onslaught were the final coffin nails for the Franklin Committee. One Committee member confessed to me that they had been brutally overmatched and outgunned by federal firepower and media manipulation—he likened the Committee's task to bear hunting with a BB gun.

In 1992, Senator Schmit lost his Unicameral seat of twenty-four years, and he discussed the personal and political fallout he had endured, because he refused to be warned off from pursuing the Franklin investigation.

"I had, I think, as distinguished a record as anyone could put together in twenty-four years—I was told that that would be curtailed, and it was," Schmit told Yorkshire Television. "I was told I would have financial problems, and I did. The message was not lost on most of the politicians in Nebraska—I think the message that was delivered was that if any legislative committee ever tries to conduct a thorough investigation again, the same thing will happen. It has shaken my faith in the institutions of government. I used to be a firm believer that the system would work."

Larry E. King's rented residence in Washington, DC — 2441 California St., NW

Larry King's party house and Craig Spence's party house were just blocks apart in Washington, DC's most affluent neighborhood, Sheridan-Kalorama. Nearby on W Street NW, only about a 7-8 minute car ride away, were the houses where the Finders kept their "kids." The Finders warehouse was located about 4 miles to the east in northeast DC.

Craig Spence's residence in Washington, DC
2445 Wyoming Ave., NW

—Chapter Five—

Washington, DC

Though the overkill of federal firepower focused on vaporizing Franklin initially seems bizarre and perplexing, events were concurrently unfolding in Washington, DC that shed light on the events in Nebraska. As I've previously noted, Gary Caradori was in contact with *Washington Times* reporter Paul Rodriguez, who was in the process of illuminating the skin trade in our nation's capital while Caradori was working for the Franklin Committee. Rodriguez appeared in *Conspiracy of Silence*, and, shortly after I made my initial Franklin-related trek to Nebraska, I phoned him, and we talked for twenty minutes or so. Our first conversation centered primarily on Gary Caradori—he was greatly impressed with Caradori's investigative talents. Rodriguez thought Caradori was neither corrupt nor delusional, and he too was of the opinion that Caradori and his son had been murdered.

Our subsequent conversations not only touched on Franklin but also on child exploitation in the United States—I found him to be deeply concerned about the organized sexual abuse of children. We talked on four or five occasions before I visited him at the *Washington Times*. By 2003, the *Washington Times* had promoted Rodriguez from a reporter to the managing editor of *Insight*, a magazine that accompanied its Sunday paper.

The *Washington Times* has a reputation for echoing the views of the conservative right; it is owned by the Reverend Sun Myung Moon. And driving down DC's New York Avenue to the newspaper's headquarters, I traversed a gauntlet of "Moonies" selling flowers. As I've attempted to sort out Franklin's facts from fictions, I've navigated metaphorical and literal streets that have never ceased to surprise me, and my jaunt down New York Avenue to the *Washington Times* encompassed both types.

Rodriguez's secretary ushered me into his cluttered office, and he gave me a firm, gracious handshake. He took a seat behind his desk and leaned backwards as we talked. Though Rodriguez projected the appearance of several Ivy League, New York publishing apparatchiks I've dealt with over the years, his outward demeanor belied his exceptionally seasoned street smarts. He was born in Haiti, and as a child he moved with his family to Venezuela. Revolution swept Venezuela in the 1950s, and his stepfather "disappeared," prompting the family to move to Texas. After a short time there, they relocated to the Washington, DC area.

As a teenager, Rodriguez combined flirting with hooliganism and being an altar boy. He eventually drifted to college for a year or two before a news service hired him. Rodriguez gradually worked his way up the news service's totem pole to become a senior White House correspondent. He then leapt to a second news service, where his beat was the US Congress—the *Washington Times* hired him as a reporter in February of 1989.

Shortly after Rodriguez joined the *Washington Times*, the US Secret Service and DC's Metropolitan Police Department busted a DC escort service being run out of a house located on a quiet cul-de-sac of two-story colonial homes at 34th Place Northwest. The raid garnered very little fanfare in the media, and it was downplayed by law enforcement, even though the Secret Service played an integral role in the bust. When Rodriguez started poking around for information about the escort service, he had no idea that he was dancing on the edge of a wormhole that would deliver him to a parallel universe.

Purveyors of the skin trade and their customers are loath to cough up information to journalists who might shine a light on their illicit activities, but Rodriguez was dogged as he pried into the workings of the escort service. He eventually managed to glean the escort service's mother lode: lists of hookers and clients and also the customers' credit card vouchers and canceled checks. Rodriguez followed the vast paper trails to a shocking and murky underworld that was fraught with perils: His house was broken into, his life was threatened, his children were threatened, and he was followed.

As Rodriguez delved deeper and deeper into DC's skin trade, he found that children were prized commodities among some of our nation's power-brokers. Rodriguez eventually met a "particularly unsavory" male hustler who claimed that he dealt in children. After Rodriguez cultivated a rapport with the hustler, he challenged him to back up his claims of dealing in children.

"He boasted that he snatched kids off the street and sexually abused them for days if not weeks at a time," Rodriguez told me. "He passed the kids around to various clients, and then dumped the traumatized kids on the street. He arranged for me to have an extended purchase of a minor for sex services, and he set up a meeting to effect that purchase. He called me to say that the 'package' had been procured, and I needed to cough up a substantial sum of money for the quote, unquote 'rental,' which of course I did not carry out, but, rather, I turned the information over to law enforcement."

Rodriguez also cultivated a rapport with a male prostitute who had a long rap sheet of felonies that included possession of obscene material, production of obscene material involving a juvenile, and distribution of cocaine. This hustler was the subject of a series of *Washington Times* articles written by Rodriguez. The articles were a window into the hustler's upper-echelon clientele, which included Massachusetts Congressman Barney Frank, who confessed to purchasing his wares. The hustler told Rodriguez that he had a protracted relationship with Frank and actually serviced clients at Frank's apartment, which Frank confirmed.

"In this business, the term 'sugar daddy' is popular for a person that supports you and sponsors you financially as well as otherwise," the hustler said. "In this case, I had a nickname for Barney—it was 'Sweet'N Low'—sweet guy, low on cash, that's what the moniker stood for.... And I told him that.... And he said, 'Hey, I'm only a congressman, I don't make a million dollars a year.'"

Frank admitted to Rodriguez that the hustler accompanied him to several political functions, and also assisted him in arranging a speaking engagement at a conference sponsored by the American Association of School Administrators. The hustler revealed to Rodriguez that he accompanied Frank to the White House in 1986 to witness President Reagan's signing of immigration and naturalization legislation.

The same hustler plied his trade with the principal of an elementary school who hid behind the guise of a happily married heterosexual. The principal gave the hustler around-the-clock access to an office at the elementary school, where he napped, phoned clients, and reportedly turned a trick. Rodriguez interviewed the principal about his arrangement with the hustler, and, after he brought up the hustler's prior conviction for the production of obscene material involving a minor, he asked the principal if the hustler had abused the elementary school's students. "Oh God, no," the principal replied. "He couldn't have. I don't think so."

Both Frank and the principal interceded on the hustler's behalf with Virginia parole officials after his conviction for producing obscene material with a minor. Frank wrote at least four letters to probation officials with his official letterhead: "Congress of the United States, House of Representatives, Washington, DC." The principal also had a meeting with the hustler and probation officials in Frank's apartment, though Frank stated to Rodriguez that he didn't attend the meeting.

In addition to servicing Frank and the principal, the hustler sold his wares to a DC lobbyist, who requested that the hustler provide him with children. The hustler told Rodriguez about the lobbyist's request, and Rodriguez coaxed him into helping law enforcement set up a sting to nail the lobbyist. The lobbyist offered the hustler at least $500 if he arranged "an evening with either a female or male child." Virginia's Alexandria Police Department had the hustler phone the lobbyist to discuss a transaction for a thirteen-year-old "blonde girl," and they recorded the conversation.

The police then wired the hustler, who stopped by the lobbyist's house to consummate the transaction. After fifteen minutes, the police had heard enough—they moved in and arrested the lobbyist. The lobbyist had the big bucks to hire a top-flight attorney, who sprung him on a technicality—the police's wiretap was ruled illegal. The lobbyist's attorney would later be appointed a federal magistrate.

Rodriguez had been burrowing into DC's seamy underside for months, enduring a succession of horrors, when he got wind of an actual auction of children. He was never able to corroborate the auction's existence, even though the mere mention of it shocked him. Both Paul Bonacci and Rusty Nelson told me about auctions they attended in Nebraska and Las Vegas, but the very idea of children being auctioned off in America was anathema to me, and I found it almost impossible to believe them. However, I eventually befriended a reputable and top-notch private detective in Nebraska named Dennis Whalen, who told me that he had actually attended such an auction in search of an abducted child.

The documentation that Rodriguez salvaged from the escort service on 34th Place was one strand of a vast, tightly woven rug shrouding an enormous pile of dirt. As Rodriguez doggedly tugged on the strand, more and more dirt piled up. After Rodriguez managed to unravel a corner of the rug, he started to uncover the shady exploits of a DC "powerbroker" named Craig Spence, who was in the habit of racking up a monthly $20,000 tab at the raided escort service. Spence had ties to the CIA, blackmail, and Larry King.

A 1982 *New York Times* profile of Craig Spence, "Have Names, Will Open Right Door," had described the then-forty-one-year-old Spence as "something of a mystery man." The svelte Spence was fond of dressing as an "Edwardian Dandy." At the time, Spence had an unblemished, boyish face that seemed to contradict his receding brown hair and moustache. The article talked about Spence's diverse business ventures: consultant, party host, registered foreign agent, and, last but not least, "research-journalist."

The *New York Times* article also commented on Spence's enigmatic personality. The reporter talked to a handful of Spence's business associates who found him to be "extremely conservative in his political views and secretive about his work, refusing to disclose the identity of his clients."

The *New York Times* made a point of discussing Spence's lofty social connections, and his "ability to master the social and political chemistry" of Washington. Spence had the uncanny guile and connections to assemble "policy makers, power brokers, and opinion shapers" at the parties he threw at his posh Victorian home on Wyoming Avenue in DC's upscale Kalorama neighborhood. According to the *New York Times,* Spence's parties and black-tie affairs sparkled with a veritable Who's Who of "congress, government, and journalism." The article read as if Spence had a direct line to Mount Olympus.

Indeed, throughout the 1980s, Spence collected the rich, powerful, and influential with the dexterity of a coin collector amassing rare coins. His parties and seminars boasted journalists Eric Sevareid, Ted Koppel, and William Safire. High-powered politicians—including Senators John Glenn of Ohio and Frank Murkowski of Alaska—attended. Former Ambassadors Robert Neumann, Elliott Richardson and James Lilly also came. John Mitchell, the disgraced former Attorney General under Richard Nixon, was a close friend of Spence and a frequent party fixture. Spence's soirees also attracted high-ranking military and intelligence officials. In fact, CIA Director William Casey seemed to be particularly fond of Spence and his high-flying get-togethers. Spence once threw a glitzy birthday bash for his friend and right-wing closet homosexual Roy Cohn, and his friend William Casey was one of the guests of honor. Larry King, as you will recall, discussed his friendship with William Casey in an article in Omaha's *Metropolitan*.

In addition to having an apparent direct line to Washington's elites, Spence had a penchant for capes, stretch limos, and brawny bodyguards. He also had an extremely inflated sense of self-importance that was evinced by his telephone etiquette: It wasn't uncommon for him to answer telephone calls by saying, "This is God—speak." After being arrested for driving under the influence, he listed his occupation as "millionaire."

To the outside world, journalists writing fluff, and even among his friends, Spence truly was "something of a mystery man"—a Jay Gatsby of sorts. Various friends of Spence attempted to delve into his childhood and background, but abruptly hit a firewall. Spence also had a habit of spinning various yarns about himself that were contradictory, and seemingly designed to obfuscate his origins. So putting together a brief chronicle of his life is somewhat like trying to reassemble an excavated mosaic that has missing pieces, and pieces from other mosaics haphazardly strewn in the mix.

Popular consensus suggests that Spence was born in upstate New York, even though it's been reported that he claimed to have sprung from New England Brahmins. Popular consensus also suggests that Spence attended Syracuse University before transferring to Boston College. A former Boston College classmate recalled him tooling around campus on a Vespa motor scooter, listening to folk music in coffeehouses, and covering his tuition with student loans. If her account about the student loans is accurate, I think Spence being a Boston blueblood can be ruled out. A second former classmate at Boston College said Spence was fond of faking an Australian accent and passing himself off as an exchange student. In 1963, Spence graduated from Boston College with a degree in Communications and Broadcasting.

After Spence's graduation, Massachusetts' governor hired him as a press assistant. Spence then became a press secretary for Massachusetts' State Speaker prior to landing a job as a correspondent for New York's WCBS. He then signed on as an ABC-TV Vietnam correspondent in

1969. Spence was always a conundrum among his fellow Vietnam correspondents. He would often disappear for weeks at a time, and one fellow correspondent remarked about Spence's inside track on seemingly clandestine information: "Craig always looked like he had learned something that no one else knew."

As a Vietnam correspondent, Spence also started to display the bombast that would characterize his later life. Vietnam correspondents sarcastically referred to the US Army's afternoon press briefings as the "Five O'clock Follies," and they would look on amazed while a grandstanding Spence asked Army personnel snide and provocative questions that were disruptive to the briefings.

Spence left both ABC and Vietnam in 1970 and moved to Tokyo, where he ostensibly made a living as a freelance radio correspondent throughout the early and mid-1970s. While in Tokyo, Spence forged a business relationship with Japanese politician Motoo Shiina, who was the president of the Policy Study Group (PSG), a Tokyo-based enterprise funded by monies from both Japanese government agencies and private industry. The primary objective of PSG was to encourage and advance Japanese business interests by teaming up Japanese businessmen with influential Americans and captains of industry. Shiina would be Spence's first documented victim of blackmail.

Spence and Shiina signed a formal agreement in July of 1979—Spence would serve as an "overseas representative" for PSG and receive a baseline salary of $10,000 a month. Under the contract, Spence was to receive additional compensation for conducting seminars, producing reports, and other ancillary services. Spence's agreement with PSG turned out to be lucrative, netting him well over $600,000 between 1979 and 1983. In 1979, Shiina also put cash on the barrel for Spence to buy his showpiece Kalorama home. In addition to serving as a residence for Spence, the home would be "Shiina's embassy" in DC and the American headquarters of PSG.

Motoo Shiina was in his late forties when he joined forces with Spence. Shiina wasn't just a run-of-the-mill Japanese politician—he descended from a noble family that had groomed him for political prominence. His father, Etsusaburo Shiina, was a wealthy businessman who had held several key Japanese cabinet positions. Japan's political pundits considered Shiina's father to be the behind-the-scenes kingmaker of Japanese politics. "Motoo's father, Etsusaburo, who was a great man, asked me to help his son, who he saw as playboy," said Spence of his relationship with Shiina.

The younger Shiina's political pedigree swept him into the Japanese Diet or parliament—he was a rising star in the country's ruling Liberal Democratic Party, and political insiders felt he was a shoo-in to become Japan's Prime Minister. "Liberal Democrat" was a misnomer for Shiina's politics: He was an arch-conservative and a hawk. The younger Shiina had the juice to convince the leaders of his party to break Japan's postwar one-percent cap on defense spending and also to cooperate with President Reagan's missile-defense initiatives.

Though Shiina amassed considerable power in his homeland, he never actualized the political stardom of his birthright, because bad press in Japan would plague him during the 1980s. Some of the bad press was engendered by his relationship with Craig Spence, but the first spate of truly damning press revolved around accusations of Shiina's passing US military secrets to the Soviets: Shiina's stance as a hawk had enabled him to become a leading authority on the Japanese military and a principal link between the Japanese Diet and the US government concerning matters of defense.

He was courted by various US defense contractors vying for contracts with the Japanese government, including General Dynamics Corporation, which manufactured the state-of-the-art F-16 fighter. A Japanese magazine implied that General Dynamics allowed Shiina to photograph specifications of the F-16 on microfilm, because he consented to promote the company's participation in a joint US and Japanese venture to produce a new cutting-edge jet fighter. Though the magazine didn't specifically mention Shiina's name, it reported that technical data about the F-16 had been leaked to the Soviets by "the son of an influential Japanese politician" and then gave a fairly definitive description of Shiina's father. In some Japanese political circles, it was thought that the CIA had hatched the story to discredit Shiina and nullify his rise to power.

A second wave of negative press entailed Shiina's relationship with Spence. The Washington Times reported that Shiina shelled out $345,000, via two bank transfers, so Spence could purchase his posh digs in DC. Shiina initially denied that the "loan" to Spence was made specifically for the house, but PSG documents describe the house as a "joint venture" between the two. By 1983, however, the partnership of Shiina and Spence had gone seriously south, and Shiina demanded that Spence vacate the premises. In court papers, Shiina stated the following about the home: "I was advised that staying at the house while Spence was there could be damaging to my reputation."

Spence's refusal to leave the house provoked Shiina to sue him, and Spence filed a countersuit. Spence readily admitted that he had signed two promissory notes for the $345,000, and he didn't deny that the money hadn't been repaid. But Spence apparently had an ace up his sleeve—he told friends that the $345,000 was "hot" and had been wired illegally. Spence's attorneys made repeated attempts to force Shiina's disclosures about his personal finances, but he invariably refused, citing his congested schedule in Japan. Finally, in June of 1984, Spence's attorneys succeeded in obtaining a subpoena that required Shiina to sit for a deposition and also required him to turn over financial documentation that pertained to the purchase of the house.

The *Washington Times* reported that Shiina and Spence came to an accord on the day of the scheduled deposition. "The money came into the country illegally from Hong Kong, and I knew it," Spence said of their settlement then. "That's why I could be so sarcastic in my deposition. I knew they wouldn't push it." The *Washington Times* also quoted a business associate of Spence's chiming in on the last-minute settlement: "He pretty much blackmailed the Japanese client." Shiina dropped his colossal damage claims against Spence, and Spence received a nice bonus. Spence agreed to pay Shiina $345,000 with 6% interest for the home—Spence sold the house in 1988 for $900,000. He pocketed over $500,000 from the sale and paid Shiina $376,000.

The *Washington Times* articles on Spence and Shiina sparked concern among some federal officials and members of Congress. A Republican congresswoman, citing the *Washington Times* and also articles from the Japanese media, voiced her concerns on the House floor about the links between Spence and Shiina. She surmised it might have been Spence, instead of General Dynamics, who furnished Shiina with the F-16 specs that were possibly turned over to the Soviets. "I bring this to the floor today, Mr. Speaker," she said, "because I am frankly puzzled that these stories are out—in print both in Japan and in

America—and there seems to be no official investigation into what to me are very grave charges."

In court papers, Shiina disclosed he was "advised" that lodging at Spence's house "could be damaging" to his "reputation," and a series of articles by the *Washington Times* on both Spence and his home confirm Shiina's concerns. Spence's house was bugged for blackmail, and his specialty was sexually compromising the powerful. The *Washington Times* claimed that he spent thousands a month on prostitutes to fuel his blackmail enterprise. Party-goers to Spence's home would be provided with whatever tickled their fancy—even children. Rodriguez heard from various sources that Spence and Larry King had a partnership of sorts when it came to pandering children and blackmail.

"I had been told by several prostitutes along with law enforcement that there were connections between Craig Spence and Larry King," Rodriguez told me. "The allegations were that Spence and King hosted parties and were involved in a variety of nefarious activities: The allegations included Spence and King hosting blackmail sex parties that included minors and illegal drug use."

In interviews I conducted separately, Rusty Nelson and Paul Bonacci also reported a pandering partnership between Spence and King. I interviewed Nelson first about the connections between Spence and King, and he disclosed to me that he met Spence on three occasions, twice in DC and once in Omaha. Bonacci said King repeatedly flew him to DC and that he met Spence on approximately ten occasions. I questioned both Nelson and Bonacci about the sexual blackmail parties and inquired if it was Spence or King who provided the children. Nelson and Bonacci gave me almost identical answers: They encountered children at the DC parties who hadn't been flown from Omaha to DC by King, and they believed that Spence had provided those children.

Rodriguez and his fellow reporters at the *Washington Times* expended considerable amounts of ink fleshing out Spence's blackmail enterprise: A *Washington Times* article from June of 1989, "Power Broker Served Drugs, Sex at Parties Bugged for Blackmail," revealed the strange goings-on at Spence's DC home: "Several former associates said his house on Wyoming Avenue was bugged and had a secret two-way mirror, and that he attempted to ensnare visitors into compromising sexual encounters that he could then use as leverage."

According to interviews conducted by *Washington Times* reporters, Spence had an eight-foot-long, two-way mirror overlooking his library that gave him a prime vantage point for "spying on guests." Bugs were also scattered throughout various nooks and crannies within his house. A Georgetown law professor and longtime friend of Spence's remembered being at Spence's home and having a conversation with a second friend of Spence's about their host's seeming physical deterioration, as Spence was HIV positive. "We were sitting in a corner, talking about our mutual concern about Craig's physical condition," said the law professor. "He came down later and said he had been listening to us and didn't appreciate it at all." The other friend, a veteran NBC and CBS correspondent, corroborated the law professor's story.

A business associate of Spence's told the reporters that Spence delivered him to one of his parties in a limousine; and when he arrived at the party, a number of young men made friendly overtures towards him. "I didn't bite; it's not my inclination," said the business associate. But he too remarked on Spence's predilection for blackmail: "He was blackmailing people. He was taping people and blackmailing them."

A former Reagan administration official who worked at the US Information Agency attended soirees at Spence's home, and he disclosed to *Washington Times* reporters that he personally observed a cornucopia of recording and taping equipment. "It was my clear impression that the house was bugged," he said. An Air Force sergeant whom Spence employed as a bodyguard corroborated accounts of blackmail: "The house was definitely bugged. I can't say what he was doing with the information. I don't know that. But he was recording what occurred there."

The same article also mentioned that some of Spence's parties were a snowstorm of cocaine. "I know he was a coke freak," said a business associate of Spence's. The article also quoted one of Spence's friends: "I heard he was selling drugs or smuggling drugs into the country from El Salvador." The *Washington Times* interviewed other party-goers who said the coke had less exotic origins—dealers in DC.

In a July 1989 article, *Washington Times* reporters interviewed a female prostitute whose services were occasionally procured by Spence—she too discussed blackmail. The prostitute said that Spence summoned her to his house on at least four occasions to have trysts with soldiers Spence employed as bodyguards—he boasted to her that he was blackmailing the soldiers. Spence once coerced the prostitute into taking a bath with two men and himself—she told the reporters that the bathtub foursome devolved into "an unhappy outing."

A couple of months after the bathtub foursome, the prostitute was contacted by one of the participating soldiers. The soldier said Spence had pictures of the "unhappy outing," and that he had blackmailed the soldier into "beating up a couple guys" in lieu of his wife being slipped the pictures. The soldier carried out Spence's directives, but Spence didn't live up to his word: He showed the wife the pictures nonetheless because the soldier refused to have sex with Spence. The soldier told the prostitute that the pictures had resulted in a separation from his wife.

The *Washington Times* amassed a number of sources—on and off the record—confirming Spence's blackmail enterprise, but the *Washington Post* was having none of it. A *Washington Post* article cited the *Washington Times* headline "Power Broker Served Drugs, Sex at Parties Bugged for Blackmail" and scoffed, stating that Spence's former Kalorama home was "attracting gawking news hounds." The *Washington Post* attempted to debunk the *Washington Times'* accounts of Spence's house being wired for blackmail with an unnamed source, whom it christened the "skeptical guest."

The skeptical guest said that he was at a party where a friend of Spence's challenged Spence's assertions that his home was bugged. The *Washington Post* reported that the friend got down on her knees and "found wires and cables all over the room at the floor level." The friend "also found metal fasteners that could have been listening devices." But the skeptical guest assured the *Washington Post* that "one of the so-called bugs was a button-release on a table."

The skeptical guest also claimed that he just happened to attend the party where the Georgetown law professor and veteran NBC and CBS correspondent were discussing Spence's ill health when Spence suddenly appeared and expressed his disapproval to them for talking behind his back. The skeptical guest declared that there "was never a bug hanging over their heads." A second unnamed source at the same party said it was "obvious" to all that the two were "gossiping about Spence."

The *Washington Post* concluded that "Spence may have been up to something with the electronic equipment," but his "clairvoyance, it seems, was strongest when his bodyguards were present and within earshot of the supposedly bugged conversations." It's interesting that the *Washington Post* at least admitted "Spence may have been up to something with the electronic equipment," even though it just couldn't bring itself to ponder the possibility of blackmail. The *Washington Post* shot down Spence's bugging by saying "it seems" his extrasensory powers were a byproduct of his bodyguards being "within earshot" of guests, but the newspaper didn't provide sources for "it seems," except for, perhaps, the "skeptical guest." I suppose it didn't strike the newspaper as strange that Spence had bodyguards in the first place.

The *Washington Post* also reported that Spence's parties were dull affairs. After dinner, Spence's guests would sit around "in a perimeter" and have rather drab conversations about "trade policy." The newspaper dusted off a quote from a 1980 article extolling the virtues of Spence's little get-togethers: "Not since Ethel Kennedy used to give her famous Hickory Farms seminars for great minds of our time during the days of Camelot has anyone staged seminars successfully on a continuing social basis in Washington."

Spence would divulge to *Washington Times* reporters that "friendly" intelligence agents bugged all the parties at his Kalorama home, and he repeatedly alluded to the fact that he was in the CIA. Rodriguez and his fellow reporters looked into Spence's claims of being CIA. "We had sources disclose that Spence wasn't a direct employee of the CIA, but they confirmed Spence was a CIA asset," Rodriguez told me.

The *Washington Times* also reported on Spence's frequent hints to friends and associates that he was affiliated with the CIA, and the *Washington Post* targeted that too. The newspaper quoted a friend of Spence's who was a former unofficial liaison to Communist China: "If he's CIA, we're in worse shape than I thought." Interestingly, the *Post* actually included remarks from an associate of Spence's who concurred with the *Washington Times'* reportage. "I really thought he was CIA," said the associate. "He always tended to be a bit mysterious."

Neither the *New York Times* nor the *Washington Post* disputed Spence's stratospheric connections among DC's power elite, but the

Washington Times ran a salacious June 29, 1989 story that highlighted Spence's astonishing ability to play the puppeteer and pull strings: "Homosexual Prostitution Inquiry Ensnares VIPs with Reagan, Bush." The article's subheadline read: "'Call Boys' Took Midnight Tour of White House." The article reported that Spence arranged a 1:00 A.M. tour of the White House that included a couple of male hookers!

The article also revealed that Spence stopped by DC's ABC studios shortly before the midnight tour and introduced a fifteen-year-old boy to his old friend Ted Koppel. The *Washington Post* quizzed Koppel about his friendship with Spence, but Koppel declined to speak "in-depth" about Spence, because Koppel said that he planned to write a story about him—two decades later I'm not aware of Koppel ever writing anything about Spence.

The *Washington Times* disclosed in subsequent articles that Spence arranged similar "midnight tours" of the White House on at least three additional occasions, and one of the late-night sightseers was a fifteen-year-old-boy. But the articles didn't report if it was the same fifteen-year-old boy that Spence introduced to Koppel. Paul Bonacci also claims that he went on late-night White House tours.

Though President George H.W. Bush's staff was initially mum on the midnight tours, a "White House source" parceled out a few words, insisting on anonymity. "Mr. Bush knows about the story. Yes he does. He's aware of the story." Presidential spokesman Marlin Fitzwater eventually discussed a Secret Service probe into the tours, but maintained the probe didn't raise concerns about the security of the first family. Responding to questions about hustlers roaming the White House in the middle of the night, First Lady Barbara Bush replied that she didn't feel threatened and said it was "good" that the *Washington Post* wasn't pursuing the story. It would later come out that a Secret Service officer purloined some of the White House's Truman china collection for Spence—Spence proudly displayed a plate of the china in his living room.

The Secret Service concluded that a uniformed White House officer who moonlighted as a Spence bodyguard had arranged the late-night White House tours. But Spence begged to differ—he implied that they were set up by Donald Gregg, who had been a national security adviser to Bush when he was Vice President, becoming President Bush's ambassador to South Korea. Gregg dismissed Spence's allegation as "absolute bull." Gregg later told the *Washington Times* that he had met Spence once—at a party Spence threw for a former Prime Minister of South Korea. Though Gregg said he only had one encounter with Spence, the latter must have made an extremely bad first impression. "It disturbs me that he can reach a slimy hand out of the sewer to grab me by the ankle like this," Gregg said of Spence.

As the Secret Service investigation into Spence's late-night White House tours started to heat up, he would reportedly be targeted with a federal subpoena. The subpoena-wary Spence surreptitiously slipped out of DC and was nowhere to be found—rumors had him surfacing in Florida, Boston, and even New Hampshire. In true Spence fashion, he emerged from the shadows in New York with a bang: The NYPD busted him for possession of a handgun, cocaine, and a crack pipe.

On July 31, 1989, New York police received a frantic phone call from Spence—he phoned the NYPD from his room at Manhattan's swanky Barbizon Hotel on the Upper East Side. The police intercepted Spence galloping out of his room: "This guy Craig Spence comes running out of the room screaming that the other guy has a gun." As it turned out, Spence just happened to have been smoking a little crack with a twenty-two-year-old male prostitute who attempted to rob him. "Spence claimed the kid had taken the gun and intimidated him and snatched $6,000 out of his hand," said a responding police officer.

Spence was charged with criminal possession of a pistol and possession of an illegal drug. He was thrown in "the Tombs," an immense jail in lower Manhattan that houses those awaiting arraignment or trial, and then released on his own recognizance three days later. Spence was looking at a maximum sentence of eight years. "They put me in the Tombs for three days without a phone call," Spence said of the experience. "I survived by offering to be the valet to the biggest thug there, a man appropriately named Heavy, and giving him half my bologna sandwich. I had to teach him not to pronounce it 'val-ay' like some parking attendant."

After Spence's arrest in New York, a pair of *Washington Times* reporters bustled off to the Big Apple, where they located Spence at a friend's ritzy East Side apartment. The journalists duly noted that the political bigwig looked the worse for wear: Spence had eschewed his trademark Edwardian-cut suit for a rumpled and soiled white knit shirt, crumpled khakis, and scuffed-up Reebok running shoes—he was unshaven. Spence eventually granted the reporters an eight-hour interview that was indeed bizarre.

Throughout the interview, Spence clutched a dispenser of double-edge razor blades, eventually dispensing one. He caressed his arm with the razor blade, smiled, and suddenly thrust the razor to the chest of the first reporter and then to the chest of the second reporter. "I am not a person to fool with," Spence declared after an uneasy pause. "You should know that by now."

After Spence threatened the reporters with the razor blade, he launched into a protracted diatribe of self-importance, asserting he had carried out assignments for the CIA on numerous occasions—assignments that were crucial to covert actions in Vietnam, Japan, Central America, and the Middle East. "How do you think a little faggot like me moved in the circles I did?" Spence asked. "It's because I had contacts at the highest levels of this government. They'll deny it, but how do they make me go away, when so many of them have been at my house, at my parties, and at my side?"

Spence also intimated to the reporters that his various comings and goings exposed by the *Washington Times* were merely the tip of a vast, clandestine iceberg. "All this stuff you've uncovered, to be honest with you, is insignificant compared to other things I've done. But I'm not going to tell you those things, and somehow the world will carry on." The two reporters went to dinner with Spence at an Italian restaurant, and then "he disappeared into the night, not to be seen again."

Spence lay low for the next couple of months, but in October of 1989 he threw a lavish birthday bash for himself in DC. "The rumors of my death are greatly exaggerated," he said to his friends at the party.

Shortly thereafter, he had a "video postcard" delivered to various friends and associates. In the video, Spence was seated on a leather chair in his dark green dining room as he waxed philosophic about the government, intelligence community, life's changing fortunes, and Winston, his Maltese dog, whom he said news reports had slandered as "a terrier." "The pressures on us over the past several years have been, let us say, significant," he said in the videotape. "Keeping a cheerful spirit in the midst of these pressures isn't easy, but Winston's holding up, and I'm working at it."

After Spence dished out criticism of the *Washington Times*, calling it "a local, cult-owned newspaper," he conveyed a parable about the intelligence community: "Some of you may know when it comes to the intelligence community, there is no such thing as coincidence. Now, I'm not sure I've seen the whole picture yet myself." Spence then ended the video on an upbeat, patriotic note, like Edward R. Morrow signing off: "I'll close by telling you I'm sure that in the end the truth will come out, and this too will pass. Now, I may be naïve about my optimism, but I'm an American, proud of my country and confident of the fairness of its people. So take heart, good friends, and share that pride and that confidence with me. Good night and God bless."

Spence was, in fact, signing off—approximately two weeks later he would be dead. His body was found on a bed in a room at Boston's Ritz-Carlton Hotel, attired in a black tuxedo, white shirt, bow tie, white suspenders, black socks, and shoes. Walkman headphones were straddled around his neck—he had been listening to Mozart's "A Little Night Music." The enigmatic Spence left an enigmatic suicide note on the room's mirror: "Chief, consider this my resignation, effective immediately. As you always said, you can't ask others to make a sacrifice if you are not ready to do the same. Life is duty. God bless America." The suicide note even had a thoughtful postscript: "To the Ritz, please forgive this inconvenience."

Citizen Kane was Spence's favorite movie, and he had signed into the hotel as C.F. Kane, its protagonist. His death would be ruled a suicide—an overdose on the antidepressant amitriptyline. Next to Spence's body on the bed was one final enigma: a newspaper clipping about then-CIA Director William Webster's attempts to protect CIA agents summoned to testify before government bodies—the *Washington Times* reported that Spence had indeed been subpoenaed by a grand jury investigating the 34th Place escort service.

Inexplicably, the US Attorney for Washington, DC took an unusual interest in Spence's death. The Boston Medical Examiner's Office customarily released the cause of an individual's death within days of his or her demise, but a high-ranking Boston city official said the US Attorney's Office in Washington requested that the information not be released. A second Boston official said "there has certainly been an interest" by the US Attorney's Office in police and autopsy reports in the case. A spokesman for the US Attorney declined to comment on the odd request: "The investigation is ongoing before the grand jury. I cannot make any comment about it."

The US Attorney's excessive interest in Spence's death and its request that his information not be released are the final enigmas in the life and death of Craig Spence, who emerged from a mysterious, shadowy netherworld to linger at the apex of power in our nation's capital for a decade or so before receding over death's threshold, leaving innumerable questions unanswered. But, perhaps, Spence had an insight into his final destination: "At 48," he told *Washington Times* reporters, "I'll still look good in hell."

The escort service on 34th Place that was busted by the Secret Service and DC police—the very same escort service Spence flooded with cash on a monthly basis—was owned by Henry Vinson. Like Japanese politician Motoo Shiina, Vinson woefully regrets the day he met Craig Spence.

Vinson's name popped up in a number of the *Washington Times'* articles on Spence, and I made my first phone call to Vinson shortly after I embarked on this investigation. I did a White Pages Internet search for all the Henry Vinsons in the US and started making calls. Both the *Washington Times* and the *Washington Post* mentioned that Vinson was a native of West Virginia, and I initially targeted the Henry Vinsons in the Southeast, a relatively short list. After just a handful of calls, I reached the Henry Vinson in question—he was living in his native West Virginia.

Vinson had transformed himself into a successful, legitimate businessman, and he wasn't too enthusiastic about talking to a journalist about his past. I apologized for imposing on him, and he consented to answer a few questions. At this point, I had yet to interview Rodriguez, Nelson, or Bonacci, and the only ties I had found linking Spence and King were rather vague allusions in DeCamp's *The Franklin Cover-Up* and also in *Conspiracy of Silence*, where Bonacci described a pedophilic pandering partnership between Spence and King. One "on the record" assertion connecting Spence and King, especially by an individual with the troubled history of Bonacci, and DeCamp's vague aspersions, certainly didn't provide the corroboration I felt such an allegation deserved. I knew that Bonacci's assertion, in and of itself, would never satisfy editors or publishers in New York.

I asked Vinson two questions: "Were Spence and King partners in pedophilic pandering?" and "Were Spence and King hooked up with the CIA?"

He responded with an unhesitant, nonchalant "Yes" to both questions. He then mentioned a former high-ranking official in the Department of Justice, whom he described as a "pervert"—he said that Spence and King provided him with "little boys." I was shocked by the name, but Vinson made such a preemptive, impromptu mention of the individual that it rang with authenticity. In fact, because I had completely surprised Vinson with these questions, and his answers about Spence and King were so unhesitating and prompt, those answers had a ring of authenticity too.

I certainly wasn't expecting to track down *the* Henry Vinson with such relative ease, and at that time I still harbored considerable skepticism concerning the purported partnership of Spence and King. So I really wasn't expecting the answers he gave me. Given that I was utterly unprepared to find Vinson, let alone talk to him, I didn't even tape the conversation. After our brief conversation, I asked Vinson if he would give me an "on record" interview. He didn't say yes, but then he didn't say no.

I would spend the next two years courting Vinson for an interview. I attempted to be tactful by occasionally phoning him and writing letters, but, like most individuals I've interviewed about Franklin, Vinson wasn't eager to go "on record." I attempted to be friendly yet persistent. Vinson, though, would prove to be unresponsive. Finally, I made a trek to rural West Virginia where he lived and worked—I left an after-hours voicemail on his office phone. In my message, I said I just happened to be in the neighborhood, and I would like to talk to him. I emphasized that my jaunt to West Virginia had been unsolicited, and he certainly wasn't obliged to meet with me. We talked the next day, and he acquiesced to a meeting.

Vinson wanted to size me up, and we talked for maybe half an hour in one of his business' vacant offices. He didn't grant me an interview at the time, nor did I request that he grant me one—I just wanted to introduce myself and start forging a rapport with him.

By the time I made my trip to see Vinson, a source in DC had told me that Vinson had confided in him about his relationship with Spence and King: I offered Vinson obscure details I knew, and he was impressed by the fact that I had done my "homework." At the conclusion of our conversation, Vinson assured me that he would seriously consider granting me an interview—he consented approximately six months later.

Vinson's route from his humble origins as a West Virginia coalminer's son to running the "largest homosexual prostitution ring" ever uncovered in Washington, DC is a winding one, and not without darkly humorous aspects. After Vinson graduated from high school in a remote corner of West Virginia, he attended and graduated from Cincinnati College of Mortuary Science. In 1982, Vinson was hired as a funeral director at a funeral home in Williamson, West Virginia. A couple of years later, Vinson opened a funeral parlor in West Virginia and was also appointed interim medical examiner for West Virginia's Mingo County. Vinson served as Mingo County coroner from 1985 to 1986 before resigning amidst controversy—one of the controversies centered on a widow who alleged that Vinson left her husband's body in his funeral home for several weeks because she didn't pay him. He, however, blamed his troubles on prejudice against gays.

Vinson left small-town West Virginia in 1986, seeking his mortuary fortunes in the big city of Washington, DC—he went to work as a mortician for a family-run chain of funeral homes in the DC area. A trio of brothers managed the funeral homes for their elderly parents. "Henry Vinson was a nice fellow when I hired him as a funeral director," said the eldest brother, who ran the business. "He was very good with grieving families."

Vinson, however, quickly grew disenchanted with the funeral biz and decided on vocational redirection. The plan he hatched to nearly monopolize the gay escort services in the capital was nothing short of brilliant. Escort services tend to be fly-by-night operations and they have relatively short half-lives—when their operators bolt to whereabouts unknown or they fold, their phone bills are almost always in arrears. So Vinson went through the DC Yellow Pages, phoning escort services. If the escort service's phone number was disconnected, he would simply call the phone company and agree to pay the defunct escort service's phone bill in exchange for the number. "I started buying all the phone numbers, and before long I was running the largest male escort service in Washington, DC," said Vinson. He assumed the phone numbers of such businesses as "Man to Man," "Jack's Jocks," "Dream Boys," etc.

Shortly after Vinson leapt into the escort business, his phone was ringing off the hook. He also hired a bevy of the gay clubs' version of Chippendales to moonlight as escorts, and he quickly had a thriving enterprise. The small-town kid from West Virginia had become a high-flying success in the big city, but Vinson would fly a little too high: Mysterious figures started drifting into his life that would mark the beginning of the end of his escort service and freedom. The first one was a muscle-laden man in his thirties, who identified himself as "Tony." "Tony just sort of showed up—he knew everything about everybody."

Vinson claims that Tony suggested he expand his business by developing the capability to process credit cards. Vinson had kept in touch with one of the brothers who helped to manage the funeral homes where he was employed, and the latter agreed to process credit cards. The brother opened a credit card merchant account under the auspices of selling funeral accessories. So frolicking with one of Vinson's escorts might be chocked up to an urn or two, burial markers, or, perhaps, for extended sessions, a mahogany casket.

All was well in the world of twenty-six-year-old Henry Vinson until the fateful day he received a call from Craig Spence. At first, Vinson welcomed the prolific business Spence solicited, thousands and thousands of dollars a month. Though Vinson was a "whiz kid" of sorts, he had yet to shake the vestiges of naïveté that were part and parcel of growing up in rural West Virginia. It would take him a while before he realized that doing business with Spence was equivalent to making a Faustian pact, and by then it was too late.

Vinson told me he became Spence's go-to guy for hookers and also his confidante, and Vinson maintains that Spence invited him to his Kalorama home on numerous occasions. "I was probably at Spence's house twenty to twenty-five times," Vinson told me. "Spence loved cocaine and little boys—he was addicted to sex and addicted to drugs. He was definitely a pedophile."

In addition to Spence's flaunting his depraved lifestyle, Vinson said Spence was also fond of flaunting his connections and blackmail equipment. "Spence showed me the hidden, secret recording devices that were scattered throughout his home," Vinson recalled. "Spence often alluded to the fact that he was connected to the CIA, and it was obvious to me that he was very well connected. There were people at his home who said they were CIA, and at least one or two Secret Service agents—I believe that it was some of the CIA operatives who installed Spence's blackmail equipment. Much of Spence's influence came from the House of Representatives and the Senate, and he told me he was blackmailing Congressmen. I believe that Spence was blackmailing for both the CIA and for his own personal purposes."

Dropping by Spence's house on one occasion, Vinson says, he was introduced to Spence's friend Larry King. Vinson remembers meeting King perhaps ten times. "King and Spence were in business together, and their business was pedophilic blackmail," said Vinson. "They were transporting children all over the country. They would arrange for children to be flown into Washington, DC and also arrange for influential people in DC to be flown out to the Midwest and meet these kids. I think that these kids were most likely marginalized—kids that no one cared about. King would talk about bringing in boys from Boys Town in Nebraska, and Craig Spence talked about that too."

Vinson found both Spence and King abusive, bullying, and manipulative. He remembers that Spence and King initially attempted to coax him into procuring children for them via a soft sell, but he said he refused to be a party to pedophilia or pedophilic pandering—"I made it clear to both that I didn't want to get involved with underage children." Vinson asserts that Spence and King then overtly pressured him and made threats in an attempt to have Vinson provide them with minors—he still refused. Despite Spence's significant infusions of cash into Vinson's business, he grew weary of Spence and King's threats and opted "to stop dealing" with them, "because they were such a pain in the ass."

When Vinson decided to disengage from Spence and King, he maintains, he discovered that his Faustian pact didn't have an exit clause. By this time, Spence had disclosed to Vinson that "Tony" was, in fact, the alias of a CIA operative who worked with Spence—"Tony never said he was in the CIA, but Spence said he was in the CIA." After Vinson severed his ties to Spence and King, Spence sent Tony and some of Tony's colleagues over to Vinson's home to have a little chat with him and help him reassess his decision.

"Tony and a few others actually came over to my house and broke out the windows and busted up the place!" Vinson's voice amplified considerably, as if the event happened just last week. "I was afraid he was going to kill me! He was very violent, and Spence used Tony and his group for a lot of his dirty work. They were very well trained, especially in covert operations." Tony's visit to Vinson forced him to reassess cutting off Spence and King, but he insists that he still refused to provide minors—I've talked to a former DC employee of Vinson's who supported that insistence.

As Vinson discussed the sordid exploits of Spence and King, I asked him a few questions specifically about King. He didn't hold King in very high esteem and described him as "cunning." Vinson then recalled a conversation he had with King that was "strange as hell," literally. "King said they had clients who actually liked having sex with kids as they tortured or killed the kid. I found that totally unbelievable. I thought it was the most far-fetched thing I had ever heard." Later in my interview, Vinson actually backtracked to King's grisly disclosure, inquiring if it were true.

In February 1989, Vinson claims, Spence wanted him to participate in a creative financing scheme involving government monies that Vinson felt was a tad too shady—he balked at Spence's idea. This time, however, Spence didn't send Tony over to Vinson's house: He summoned Vinson to his condominium on Massachusetts Avenue—he had sold his Kalorama home the previous year. An uneasy Vinson showed up at Spence's condo to find only Spence and an extremely high-ranking official in the Department of Justice—Spence had previously disclosed to Vinson that he provided this official with adolescent boys.

According to Vinson, the Justice Department official attempted to intimidate him into joining Spence's scheme, and Vinson continued to balk. Finally, the official dispensed an overt threat: "I can withstand a background check. Can you?" Those words apparently rang in Vinson's ears for a very long time, because shortly after their meeting, Vinson told me, he started to encounter considerable federal difficulties: "The Secret Service served a search and seizure on my house within seventy-two hours—I assumed the Secret Service was used because they also worked with Craig Spence."

Vinson's escort service was initially raided on February 28, 1989. The US Attorney for DC, Jay Stephens, impaneled a federal grand jury to investigate the escort service in June of 1989. Stephens said that "credit card" fraud would be the focus of the grand jury, and the *Washington Times* reported that the Secret Service was the primary investigative entity behind the investigation, but a Secret Service spokesmen declined to discuss the case with reporters—saying they were ordered to refer all inquiries to DC's Assistant US Attorney Alan Strasser, who was assigned to present evidence to the grand jury. Strasser wasn't very talkative either: "There is nothing I care to say to you about this at this time."

After the grand jury commenced, the *Washington Times'* Rodriguez questioned Vinson about the federal investigation. "Somebody set us up because they were scared about what we knew about high government officials," said Vinson. "I think it's because they wanted to get our files. We had some very big-name clients in all walks of life—on Capitol Hill, the military, and even the White House. You'd be surprised. Barney Frank isn't the only one in a high-powered job that uses such services." (Frank Gobie, the hooker who carried out services for Congressman Frank, had been employed by Vinson's escort service.) Vinson also dispensed a quote that suggested he was the man who knew too much, and the feds wouldn't dare come after him: "And anyways, if they do try to indict me, I'll have some good stories to tell."

In a July 1989 *Washington Times* article, Rodriguez reported that six plain clothes Secret Service agents kicked in the front door of a Vinson relative who lived in West Virginia. The relative said that the Secret Service agents didn't even bother to knock before smashing the door open, and they held a gun on her husband. After ransacking the house for well over two hours, the agents left with "small scraps of paper." The relative told Rodriguez that the agents warned her "not to tell anybody about the raid." The Secret Service also descended on the dwelling of Vinson's mother.

Meanwhile, back in DC, *Washington Times* reporters discovered that the federal grand jury prosecutors had been rather lackadaisical: "The *Times*, in contacting a number of principal witnesses and active participants in the case, discovered that few of them had been interviewed and only a handful asked to testify before the grand jury. Several key figures had not been contacted at all." The *Washington Times* would report that Vinson and his cohorts in the escort service hadn't been called before the grand jury—nor had Craig Spence, even though it had issued him a subpoena.

"I haven't heard one word from the US Attorney, the FBI, or anyone else," said a participant of a late-night White House tour interviewed by the *Washington Times*. "The Secret Service talked to me back in the summer, after the stories were out, but nothing since then."

Washington Times reporters talked to one midnight White House tour attendee who testified before the grand jury. The grand jury witness had been a "long-time acquaintance" of Spence's and "spent considerable time" in his home. He described a prolonged interview with prosecutor Strasser and Secret Service agents and then a brief Q & A in front of the federal grand jury. "They pulled out a picture book containing the White House china collection and asked me about the Truman china," said the witness. "They wanted to know if I had seen anything like that. They strongly intimated that more things were missing."

The witness disclosed that questioning by federal authorities became most detailed when it turned to the subject of the late-night tours. "They asked if we went in any offices, if I had seen any documents or if any documents had left the White House," he said. Though the witness spent numerous hours at Spence's home, *Washington Times* reporters noted that the grand jury didn't pose any questions to him about credit cards, about Spence's involvement with the homosexual call-boy ring, or about the ring itself. Moreover, federal prosecutors apparently didn't feel compelled to question him about Spence's blackmail equipment and blackmail activities, which, by that time, had been the subject of *Washington Times* articles. The feds seemed considerably more concerned about missing china than Spence's sexual compromise of public officials.

The federal grand jury would eventually indict Henry Vinson and three of his lieutenants on various felony charges, and Vinson was arraigned in July of 1990. Vinson's forty-three indictments included credit card fraud, racketeering, money laundering, and violation of the Mann Act—he was staring at 295 years in prison and fines exceeding $2 million. Shortly after Vinson's indictments were unsealed, he told me his mother received a phone call from someone claiming to be a reporter for the *Washington Post*, suggesting that her son hire DC attorney and future Fox News star Greta Van Susteren, whose services he promptly enlisted.

Interestingly, Van Susteren had grown up in Wisconsin, where her father was a judge and a political mover and shaker—her father had been a campaign manager for the infamous Wisconsin Senator Joseph McCarthy, and McCarthy had been the best man at the wedding of Van Susteren's parents. As I've previously mentioned, Roy Cohn was a good friend of Craig Spence, and Cohn more or less served as McCarthy's "best man" during the latter's notorious witch hunt for Communists in the 1950s.

"At first, Greta Van Susteren said we'll go to trial instead of entering a plea agreement," Vinson said, "because with all these high-ranking officials the government will not want to go to trial. She said that the government wouldn't want this type of embarrassment."

In fact, Rodriguez reported that Van Susteren filed an eleven-page motion to mandate the release of Vinson's clientele list. Van Susteren argued that the names of Vinson's patrons should not be protected, because, if the government's claim was accurate, and the "escort" service was actually a prostitution ring, the clients were criminals or aided a criminal enterprise.

But Assistant US Attorney Alan Strasser, who had overseen the grand jury and was prosecuting Vinson, refused to make "unedited" client lists public—his dubious excuse was that he feared "intimidation of government witnesses due to the embarrassing nature of the case." US District Judge Harold Greene sided with the prosecution and barred public disclosure of the client lists.

The feds then reached into their bag of tricks in an effort to silence Vinson: Assistant US Attorney Strasser filed a memorandum with the court that recommended Vinson be sentenced above the statutory guidelines for his crimes, even though he was already facing life in prison, since his escort service allegedly hadn't screened its escorts for HIV and, therefore, had spread the virus.

Vinson maintains that as the government was squeezing him to keep his mouth shut, Van Susteren started dancing to a different tune and suggested a plea bargain—he consented. He told me that she allowed the feds to debrief him for hours on end and wasn't even present at the debriefings. "Everything the government wanted to do is what happened," said Vinson. "Greta Van Susteren didn't make herself available for the debriefings, which I find incredible, thinking back on it. But I had never been through anything like that before; so I didn't know what to do or expect."

Vinson also claims that he disclosed all of Spence and King's nasty little secrets to the feds. "They spent about a week debriefing me, and I was very honest and cooperative with them—I told the feds that King and Spence were using children to blackmail politicians. I told them that Spence and King were affiliated with the CIA."

Vinson ultimately settled on a plea bargain of sixty-three months—"They explicitly told me not to talk to the media for that minimal sentence." By the time of Vinson's sentencing, the feds had emotionally pulverized him, and the person who showed up to be sentenced was vastly different from the person who boasted he had "some good stories to tell" if indicted. Before Judge Greene meted out five years, Vinson contritely told Greene, "My behavior has certainly not been very complementary. I'm sorry if I did hurt society." The judge then went on a bizarre rant about the lenient sentence Vinson was receiving, considering prosecutors had originally called for him to be sentenced above the guidelines, but the judge opted not to buck the prosecutors. So Vinson was sentenced, he kept his mouth shut, and the feds sealed all the evidentiary documentation in his case, effectively putting the US seal on a cover-up in Washington, DC that would reach all the way to Nebraska.

After Vinson pled guilty, the *Washington Post* reported that US Attorney Stephens declared that the federal investigation into Vinson's escort service found no evidence that its patronage had ties to anyone "with any political or military organization" except for the federal employees whose names had already been made public.

Though Vinson initially thought the truth would set him free, he eventually realized that he had the misfortune of being the locus of a sprawling government cover-up: "I think that my arrest was orchestrated from the highest levels of the government. I thought the truth would come out, but it just kept getting worse and worse and worse. Later it came out that there were no high-ranking officials involved with my escort service—everything about the government's investigation was a lie."

In addition to interviewing Vinson, I've talked to two of the three individuals who were arraigned and sentenced with Vinson for operating the escort service—the third refused to talk to me. In my conversations with Vinson and his associates, the names of eminent government officials who patronized the escort service have come up, including a US Congressman. The escort service's documentation salvaged by the *Washington Times* corroborates their contentions: "There were high-ranking US government officials, foreign government officials, law enforcement, clergy, and members of the press," said Rodriguez about the lists of Vinson's clientele retrieved by the *Washington Times*. "There were members of the United States Congress on those lists too," he added.

The *Washington Times* documentation corroborates Vinson's claim that the "government's investigation was a lie." The feds then sealed thousands of documents, ensuring the investigation was covered up, and they have been absolutely unwilling to unseal the documents. "I've been told that over 25,000 documents were sealed in perpetuity," said Rodriguez. "We've attempted to unseal those documents on two occasions but were rebuffed. We've been told 'It will be a cold day in hell' before those documents are ever unsealed."

Should we believe Vinson, the convicted felon, whose statements concerning his VIP clientele are corroborated, or the government, which covered up the names of Vinson's clientele and refuses to unseal the documents in his case? Absent any evidence to the contrary, it seems obvious that the government was protecting Vinson's customers and perhaps Spence and King's pedophile blackmail enterprise.

Shortly after Vinson and his accomplices were sent up the river, the *Washington Post* ran an article dismantling the *Washington Times* reportage on Spence, Vinson, blackmail, etc.: "The Bombshell that didn't explode; Behind the *Times'* Scoop and Press Coverage of the Call-Boy Ring." In the article, the *Washington Times* reportage was slandered as "yellow journalism" and having not "much substance." The article's author said she had talked to other reporters around DC: The reporters had been interested in pursuing the story until they "checked with the Secret Service," who said that the "raid was relatively routine." The article also discussed "a key law enforcement official" who had been gracious enough to have "lunch at the *Post*" and "assured the staff that the investigation was primarily on credit card fraud."

The *Washington Post*, the very same newspaper that broke the Watergate story, said it concluded that the *Washington Times* "Bombshell" had no substance because an unnamed government official said so. Government officials had also been adamant that the allegations swirling around Nixon during Watergate had no substance, so the *Post's* rationale for its hatchet job on the *Washington Times* seems a bit disingenuous.

The "Bombshell" article also quoted the *Los Angeles Times'* DC bureau chief: "To tell the truth, the reason editors in L.A. weren't interested in it was that the *New York Times* and the *Washington Post* hadn't been interested in it," he said. "If they had, our editors would have said, 'Where's the story?'"

So the major media concluded that there was no story, and kicked the *Washington Times* to the curb. The *Washington Post* dedicating so much ink to dismantling the *Washington Times* reporting could be written off as competition, or there may have been a more ominous reason. Vinson disclosed to me that a high-flyer at the *Post*, who paraded as a married heterosexual, frequently used his escort service. This individual doesn't show up in any of the *Washington Times* documentation, and I've never been able to corroborate Vinson's disclosure. But if it is true, the individual in question would likely have had the juice to seriously malign the *Washington Times* reportage to the *Post's* editorial staff, and might have had a hand in putting the kibosh on the *Post's* pursuit of the story.

The *Washington Post's* "Bombshell" article prompted a rebuttal article from the *Washington Times'* managing editor—"A little outrage for the children?" The managing editor commented on federal law enforcement's informing the *Post* that the story was a non-starter: "That's the energy and curiosity level of a lot of Washington reporters. They get a press flack's lie and that satisfies them." He also commented on the reach of his newspaper's reportage wrapping around various institutions, including a school. "This morning's accounts show the male prostitution ring to have reached into Congress, the White House and a public elementary school," he wrote. "*But unless this city, the Congress, the journalists who live here, and the US Attorney's Office have lost the last vestige of public and private decency*, we can expect a little outrage on behalf of our children" [my emphasis].

Rodriguez and his colleagues were sliced and diced for their reportage on Spence et al., but their investigative feats were remarkable, revealing a large mound of dirt that had been left intact for quite some time, and their series of articles were nominated for a 1990 Pulitzer Prize in Local Investigative Specialized Reporting.

The *Boston Globe*'s articles on the Boston transit system won the Pulitzer that year. The *Washington Times* series of exposés wouldn't even make it to the status of a Pulitzer finalist: Texas' Port Arthur *News* reporting on "shoddy waste disposal" and *Newsday*'s investigation into a "Long Island sewer scandal" would be nominated finalists.

I, too, found the mainstream media unreceptive to my reportage on King and Spence, even though I didn't wear the albatross of being affiliated with the Reverend Moon. Shoehorning Franklin into an article was very tough, but I managed to whittle the story down to the barest of facts. My efforts, however, were met with only incredulity and rejection—I think two or three mainstream magazines gave the story a hard look, but the rest dismissed it out of hand.

But as I shopped the article around, I found myself having an extraordinary encounter with serendipity. A friend phoned me and excitedly said he wanted to meet. Throughout my Franklin investigation, my home phone has at times clicked like someone is transmitting Morse code on the line—current technology enables phone taps to be silent; so either my phone line has had snags that the phone company couldn't find or the incessant clicking has been overt harassment. A number of my friends are aware of my problematic phone line, but most don't have paranoid inclinations, and we generally talk quite freely. My friends and I also live extremely mundane lives, devoid of illicit activity and deviance; so if, in fact, my line has been tapped, those listening in are privy to humdrum conversations. Consequently, for a friend of mine to insist that we discuss something face to face is very, very rare.

We met at a bar on 14th Street in Manhattan—he told me an interesting tale indeed: A close friend of his is a retired, highly-decorated NYPD detective, who had actually been at the Barbizon Hotel the night Spence was busted for possession of a handgun and cocaine. The detective had a confidential informant, a hustler, who parceled out information to him about illicit drug activity, and the retired cop said his informant was one of three hustlers with Spence at the Barbizon that night. As the acrimony was escalating between Spence and the hustler who was arrested with Spence, the informant phoned in an SOS to the detective. When the informant had scrapes with the law, the cop would intervene on his behalf, and the informant definitely felt that the Barbizon bedlam required him to call in a few markers.

So the detective arrived at the Barbizon to find his confidential informant, two other hustlers, Spence, and a high-ranking NYPD honcho. The high-ranking NYPD honcho was livid about the cop being at the Barbizon, because he had been in the midst of partaking of the hustlers' wares along with Spence, and the detective was out of his jurisdiction. A second high-ranking NYPD official had arrived on the scene a few moments earlier, and he told the cop and his informant to split.

The cop and the hustler took off and bid each other a good night. The cop didn't have a clue about Spence, and he thought the second high-ranking NYPD official was primarily there to run interference for the NYPD honcho, who had been caught with his hand in the honey jar—rumors about his homosexuality had floated around the NYPD for years.

But this was not the end of the story for the detective. The next morning he received a call from the second NYPD official at the Barbizon, and he had a little mission for the cop: He wanted him to drive Spence's car down to the Watergate Hotel in Washington, DC—of all places.

This mission struck the cop as extremely peculiar; so he phoned his informant, and they agreed to meet after the cop picked up Spence's car. After the phone call about Spence's car, the detective quickly came to the realization that the informant's call from the Barbizon had opened up a Pandora's box—he wanted to know the box's exact dimensions and its contents. The cop collected Spence's car, a navy blue Datsun 280Z, and then picked up the informant, and they had a long chat as they drove south on Interstate 95.

The informant divulged that he had been a "boy-toy" in a nationwide pedophile network, and that the pimps were Craig Spence and Larry King. He had been in the network since early adolescence, and had recruited other kids for the network. The cop was dumbstruck by the informant's disclosures.

Before the cop made it to the Watergate, he dropped off the informant a few blocks away. After he arrived at the Watergate, he was greeted by a handful of "suits"—he said they were "CIA, FBI, or Secret Service."

The suits had the cop proceed to the hotel's parking lot, and he was directed to a parking space that was right next to an identical navy blue 280Z! The suits then ushered the cop to the hotel's lobby, where he said he had the good fortune of meeting a seated Larry King. The cop distinctly remembers that King wore a tropical shirt and khakis and didn't bother to stand up when the cop introduced himself: He merely offered his left hand for a lackluster handshake. The cop was given an envelope that contained his "expenses," and instructed to drive the replica 280Z back to New York. He left the Watergate, picked up his informant, and they drove north.

I initially wondered about the rationale for switching cars while Spence was sleeping off his coke binge in the Tombs. Towards the end of his life, though, Spence had become an unrepentant coke and crack addict, and thus an extremely loose cannon. It would have been a major hazard to have him ricocheting around New York with compromising pictures stashed in his car—if he had any—and the switch while he was incarcerated makes sense from that perspective.

The cop's story is certainly a strange one, but when it comes to Franklin strange is the norm. The story becomes even a little stranger because of what happened just before my friend phoned me, requesting that face-to-face.

While I had been shopping my Franklin article around to New York-based magazines, the cop's informant received a call from someone claiming to be with a "magazine." The caller wouldn't disclose the name of the magazine and asked the cop's informant a number of questions relating to Franklin and my article. Here's the interesting part: The informant wasn't mentioned in any of the newspaper articles regarding Spence's bust at the Barbizon; the newspapers only named the hustler arrested with Spence. After the informant was contacted, he immediately phoned the cop and said they needed to talk.

I've surmised that the informant may have been contacted to determine if, since I live in New York, I had stumbled upon any of Spence's or King's New York shenanigans. But the truth of the matter is that I hadn't been digging in New York, even though victims told me they had been flown there, because the *Washington Times* articles offered me such a rich compost in DC to dig around in. If my surmise is correct, it is certainly ironic that I never would have discovered the cop and his informant had someone not learned of my investigation, and decided to make a phone call to the informant to find out what I might have discovered.

My friend had given the cop a thumbnail sketch of me and my Franklin investigation months earlier, but the cop's run-in with Spence had been approximately seventeen years earlier, and he didn't make the connection until the day his informant phoned him. Following the cop's talk with his informant, he gave my friend a call that elicited a rapid-onset interest in my work.

After my friend and I had our chat about the cop, the informant and the phone call, I requested that he introduce me to the cop. When the cop retired from the NYPD, he started working security for a variety of New York nightclubs. The cop finally agreed to meet me because my friend vouched that I was a stand-up guy. I met him at a nightclub where he worked security. The cop knew Spence and King were tied to something extremely heavy, and he wasn't too enthusiastic about imparting information to me. But I intermittently showed up at the nightclub and gradually earned his trust.

As I cultivated the cop's trust, he gave me more and more of the story, but I never pushed him. At a certain point, I asked him if I could use his information—he said he would have to give it some consideration. He was impressed that I kept my word about our conversations being off the record—I easily could have taken the information and run.

I turned up at the club a couple of weeks later, and he consented to be a source.

I then questioned him about the nuances of his misadventure, and he filled me in further on the story I've just related. The cop even attempted to coax his informant into meeting with me, but the informant was absolutely unwilling to emerge from the shadows.

The cop's account of King and Spence running a nationwide pedophile ring was my fifth confirmation on their partnership, and it provides further proof of Franklin's DC flipside. Though the Nebraskan heartland is a world removed from the capital's bustling hub of power, a number of parallels emerged. The first parallel was unbridled malfeasance by the federal government: The Department of Justice under US Attorney General Richard Thornburgh played an integral role in the cover-up in both Nebraska and DC.

According to both Alisha Owen and Troy Boner, at least one esteemed official in Nebraska's US Attorney's Office threatened them with perjury charges if they did not recant their tales of the Franklin pandering network. But even if one has difficulties embracing Owen's and Boner's words at face value, Nebraska's federal grand jury conclusion that Franklin didn't entail the transportation of children across state lines for immoral purposes was so contrary to the abundant evidence indicating otherwise that it's difficult to conclude that this grand jury wasn't also a cover-up.

On the DC flipside of Franklin, Washington's US Attorney's Office is reported to have exerted the same inexorable pressure on Vinson that the FBI exerted on Owen, Boner, and Danny King. A federal grand jury in DC, conducted by the US Attorney's Office, nailed Vinson with a forty-three-count indictment. It then directed that he be sentenced above the guidelines: Vinson was looking at untold years in prison. And he said that on the advice of his lawyer, Greta Van Susteren, he ultimately caved in—just as Boner and Danny King caved into the government's will.

Though the US Attorneys for Nebraska and DC had relatively comparable roles in their cover-up of Franklin, it appeared that the FBI primarily carried out the feds' dirty work in Nebraska, and the Secret Service served as the feds' principal heavy in DC. We've already seen FBI tactics of intimidation in Nebraska, and the *Washington Times* provided a couple of examples of the Secret Service's terrorizing of Vinson's relatives, which included kicking down a door and holding a Vinson in-law at gunpoint. So ultimately, the evidence points to several federal agencies being used to cover up Franklin: the US Attorney's Offices of Nebraska and DC and both the FBI and Secret Service.

As noted earlier, an *Omaha World-Herald* editorial gave the seal of approval to the state's grand jury report and severely trashed Paul Bonacci's credibility: "This person, Paul Bonacci, told a story so patently ridiculous that none but the most naïve could swallow it." However, when Gary Caradori first videotaped Bonacci in May 1990, the latter related King's "compromise" exploits in DC. Though Bonacci has made some outlandish statements as he's struggled through the acute throes of his mental illness, it would have been nearly impossible for him to know about the DC blackmail had he not been deeply involved with King—even Owen, Boner, and Danny King weren't privy to Larry King's DC deeds. In a later interview that wasn't videotaped, Karen Ormiston told me, Bonacci stated to her and Caradori that King's pedophilic pandering partner in DC was Craig Spence.

Bonacci also told Caradori that King's DC townhouse was fitted with a basement room that only locked from the outside, and kids who were acting up would be thrown in the room for an indefinite spell. Rodriguez was granted access to King's DC townhouse after he vacated the premises, and, in fact, found a basement room that only locked from the outside. Again, it would have been nearly impossible for Bonacci to be cognizant of the basement room had he not actually been to King's DC townhouse. So even some of the DC nuances of Bonacci's "patently ridiculous" story are corroborated.

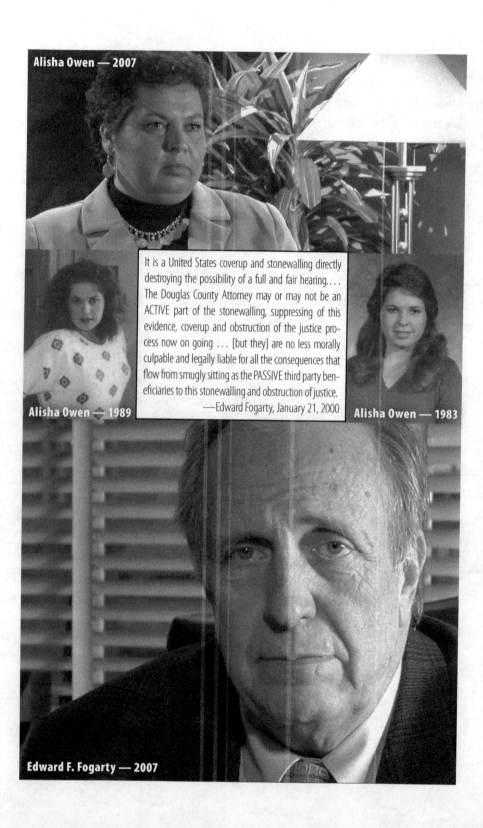

Alisha Owen — 2007

Alisha Owen — 1989

Alisha Owen — 1983

It is a United States coverup and stonewalling directly destroying the possibility of a full and fair hearing.... The Douglas County Attorney may or may not be an ACTIVE part of the stonewalling, suppressing of this evidence, coverup and obstruction of the justice process now on going ... [but they] are no less morally culpable and legally liable for all the consequences that flow from smugly sitting as the PASSIVE third party beneficiaries to this stonewalling and obstruction of justice.
—Edward Fogarty, January 21, 2000

Edward F. Fogarty — 2007

—Chapter Six—

State v. Owen

The US Department of Justice and the Secret Service, abetted by the media, executed a perfect cover-up of Larry King and Craig Spence's enterprise in DC. Moreover, federal and state authorities and the media also executed a near perfect cover-up of King's pandering in Nebraska. But the cover-up in Nebraska was confronted by a pair of wild cards: Alisha Owen and Paul Bonacci—they would have to be found guilty of perjury in a court of law in order for the "carefully crafted hoax" to become the official story. The Douglas County judiciary elected to prosecute Owen first.

I first attempted to talk to Alisha Owen on my maiden Franklin-related trip to Nebraska in January of 2003—I contacted her mother and left a message, but Owen didn't return my call. On my second trip to Nebraska, eight months later, Edward Fogarty, a lawyer who had represented Owen, contacted her on my behalf—Owen, Fogarty, and I subsequently met for half an hour or so at Fogarty's law office in downtown Omaha. At Fogarty's behest, I signed an agreement that stated our discussion would be completely off the record.

The media had skewered Owen, so I understood her apprehensions about talking to a journalist. Indeed, the last freelance writer Owen had contact with was Michael Casey, and, needless to say, that contact, albeit minimal, certainly had an adverse impact on her quality of life. So I didn't fault Owen's reluctance to talk to me. Despite all the hoopla Van Pelt made about Owen seeking attention, she had never granted an on-record interview to anyone in the media, and she had shunned all publicity over the years.

The afternoon I met Owen in Fogarty's law office I found her extremely guarded. I got the vibe from Owen that she really didn't want to meet with me, but she did so as a favor to Fogarty. Because of her reluctance, I didn't push for a second meeting. Over the years, I opted not to reach out to Owen again, even though I made a number of trips to Nebraska. However, I continued to cultivate a rapport with Fogarty as well as relationships with two other individuals who were on friendly terms with the Owens. Though I never contacted the Owens, they kept tabs on my various comings-and-goings from Nebraska. But truth be told, I completely relinquished any hopes of an on-record interview with Alisha Owen.

The state grand jury had signed off on their report on July 23, 1990, and Douglas County law enforcement spared little time booking Owen and Bonacci for perjury. On July 27, Douglas County Deputy Sheriffs picked up Owen at York, and Bonacci at the Lincoln Correctional Center, and hauled them to the Douglas County Sheriff's Office, where they were booked for perjury. Owen and Bonacci sat in the Douglas County Jail for nearly two weeks as they awaited their formal arraignment for perjury on August 8.

A *World-Herald* article on their respective arraignments showed unbecoming pictures of Owen and Bonacci—she wore county-issued light-blue Dickies, and he was in an orange jumpsuit. Owen, represented by Henry Rosenthal, and Bonacci, represented by a public defender, pleaded not guilty to the perjury charges. After their respective arraignments, Owen was eventually returned to York and Bonacci to the Lincoln County Correctional Center—Owen's trial was slated to start on December 10, 1991, but it was pushed back.

Owen lingered in solitary segregation at York throughout the fall as she prepared and girded herself for her upcoming trial—her family did the same. Al and Donna Owen had been given a crash course on government intimidation and malevolence—they had seen both state and federal legal "steamrollers" in action. Despite the threats and intimidation, their determination to stand by their daughter was unwavering. The Owens had profound spiritual beliefs that were the bedrock of their existence, and even the seismic cataclysms that they endured throughout their Franklin trials and tribulations didn't shake their faith.

In 1970, Al and Donna had a spiritual awakening that irrevocably altered their lives. They started attending Temple Baptist Church every Sunday, and church quickly became the focal point of their lives: They both taught Sunday school and became church leaders. Al and Donna also played an instrumental role in their church's creation of a private parochial school—Temple Christian Academy. Al labored long hours during the day taking care of the concerns of Owen Drywall and Construction, and he toiled into the wee hours making sure Temple Christian Academy was up to code.

From 1966 to 1973, Al and Donna had four children—Al Junior, Alisha, Andrea, and Aaron. Though Al's business had a series of ups and downs throughout the 1970s and 1980s, Donna never took a job outside the home, and they scrimped and saved so their four children could attend Temple Christian Academy.

Teenage children frequently present parents with a series of frustrations, but Al Junior and Andrea proved to be relatively low-maintenance teenagers. Al was a good-looking, popular kid, who played fullback for Central High School, and he was even nominated to be Central's Homecoming King. After graduating from high school, he joined the Marines and excelled as a sharpshooter. Alisha's younger sister, Andrea, was also into athletics—she gave her all to track and field. Andrea was a beautiful young woman, albeit somewhat shy, who was in constant demand as a prom date.

Alisha's younger brother, Aaron, became a handful for the Owens. Tall and lanky, Aaron vibrated like a human tuning fork—he was prone to attention deficits and extreme freethinking. As a child, Aaron jumped off a two-story roof using an umbrella as a makeshift parachute, which resulted in a trip to the emergency room. Donna also witnessed Aaron flirting with the hazards of gravity as a teenager when she peeked out the kitchen window into the backyard: Aaron had leaned two sheets of plywood against the swing set—his plan was to climb atop it and rollerblade down the sheets of plywood. Donna quickly pointed out to her son that the sheets of plywood weren't even fastened to the swing set, and his daredevil exploits would probably land him in the hospital—Aaron took his mother's advice and abandoned his emulation of Evil Knievel.

Aaron also had episodes of delinquency, but they were always ill-fated, because he invariably felt the pangs of conscience and quickly surrendered himself to law enforcement. Aaron and his friends once stole a car for a couple of weeks and took turns taking it on joy rides.

One night, when Aaron was on a solo joy ride, the values that his parents instilled in him suddenly kicked in—he phoned the OPD from a pay phone and waited around with the car until the police arrived. Though Aaron gave himself up, the police were vexed because he refused to name his accomplices.

Aaron's next act of delinquency occurred a few months later. He was hanging out with the same crew that stole the car, and they decided to break into a store that sold skateboards. A week or so later, Aaron spilled the beans about the break-in to his father. Al drove Aaron back to the store, where he returned a pilfered skateboard. Aaron once more turned himself into the OPD, but again he wouldn't name his accomplices.

Shortly after Alisha ended up at York, her younger brother had his third and final run-in with the law. In the fall of 1989, sixteen-year-old Aaron Owen visited his girlfriend at her parents' house—his girlfriend's uncle was also visiting. The uncle had a reputation for being a browbeating bully, and he didn't care too much for the sprite and spirited Aaron Owen. The two exchanged words and the uncle threatened Owen with bodily harm. Aaron Owen bolted from the house, and his girlfriend's uncle gave chase. After several blocks, Owen still hadn't managed to shake the surly uncle—he ran by a gas station, jumped into a vacant, idling car and took off.

The uncle immediately called the OPD to report the act, and shortly thereafter two or three squad cars showed up at the Owens' home. Donna Owen was on the porch talking to a couple of OPD officers when her son prowled by the house in the purloined car. Not only did she notice her son in the car, but the responding police officers noticed him too. The sight of the cops gave Aaron Owen a serious adrenal boost and, unfortunately, he didn't surrender—he hit the gas. "There he goes! We got a runner!" Donna Owen recalled a cop hollering. Aaron Owen suddenly found himself hotly pursued by a handful of squad cars. The chase ended in North Omaha, and Aaron Owen was arrested.

After Aaron's latest mishap, a reeling Al and Donna visited Alisha at York, and it was then that she told them about her abuse. When Al and Donna were driving away from York that night, Donna turned to Al and pierced a short silence: She said if their daughter's story was indeed true, then she'd been through a horrific nightmare.

It was initially painful for Al and Donna to reconcile the fact that their daughter had managed to pull off a double life while living under their very roof. However, as the Owens recounted various recollections, they finally had answers to their daughter's baffling and secretive behavior starting in early adolescence. They had been devastated when sixteen-year-old Alisha announced her pregnancy and was absolutely unwilling to name the father. Donna also remembered a sequence of incidents when Alisha exploded with undue paranoia concerning her daughter—she repeatedly phoned home and inquired about her daughter's welfare. Donna recalled working in the yard while Alisha's daughter was playing on the Owens' gated front porch—Alisha came home from school and screamed that she didn't ever want her daughter left unattended on the porch. She subsequently demanded that her daughter never be alone on the porch or in the yard.

The Owens were also constantly baffled by Alisha's difficulties following high school. They couldn't fathom the acute hopelessness that smothered their daughter prior to her first stint at St. Joseph's psychiatric ward, and they were utterly devastated by the suicide attempt that preceded her second stint there. They didn't understand the bounced checks and her clandestine flight from Nebraska, either. The Owens were also puzzled by law enforcement's ambivalent treatment of their daughter. Law enforcement initially put a "hold" on Alisha during her hospitalization at St. Joseph's, and then the hold was inexplicably withdrawn. Nebraska authorities then opted not to extradite Alisha when Donna informed them that her daughter was incarcerated in Colorado. Yet, after Alisha returned to Nebraska, a Sheriff's hold prevented the Owens from posting bail for her.

After Alisha Owen gave her first videotaped statement to Gary Caradori in early November of 1989, a constellation of events started to unfold around her as she languished in prison. Owen's nexus with Caradori gave his investigation considerable momentum, but it propelled her and her family on a collision course with the NSP and FBI. In previous chapters, we've looked at Alisha Owen through the lenses of Gary Caradori, the Franklin Committee, law enforcement, a grand jury, and the *Omaha World-Herald*. But the perspective of the then-twenty-one-year-old Owen has been more or less absent. It is now time to look at Owen's travails from her own perspective and that of her family.

Caradori contacted Al and Donna Owen shortly after Alisha made her first videotaped statement, and he suggested they rendezvous the following night at a restaurant near Interstate 80. When the Owens showed up at the restaurant, they spotted Caradori and Ormiston sitting at a corner table. The Owens were brimming with apprehensions and burning with questions. Caradori gave them a cursory history of his background in law enforcement, and then filled them in on his affiliation with the Franklin Committee. He immediately struck the Owens as honorable and truthful, so many of their initial apprehensions were quickly dispelled.

Caradori told the Owens he believed their daughter because the information she provided him was consistent with the information he had previously cultivated. He also said that her statement had too many details and intricate nuances for it to be fabricated. Caradori warned Al and Donna Owen that the NSP and FBI were actively engaged in a cover-up of Franklin, and he portended that their family would probably be subjected to threats and intimidation.

Though Caradori emanated integrity, the Owens were absolutely stunned by his disclosures. In addition to corroborating that Alisha had managed to pull off a double life as a teenager, Caradori's remarks about the NSP and FBI covering up child abuse were incomprehensible to the Owens. They were hard-working churchgoers and salt-of-the-earth Midwesterners who believed in the decency of law enforcement, especially the FBI. Al and Donna Owen found it inconceivable that the FBI would cover up crimes involving child abuse.

A month or so after Al and Donna Owen initially met Caradori, they brought their granddaughter to York to spend a long weekend with their daughter. York's exemplary inmates were granted extended visitations with their children, and Alisha had earned that privilege. On Friday, December 15, 1989, Owen was relishing her first extended visitation with her daughter—they spent the morning in York's "toy room," which was decked out with toys and games and also had a kitchen that enabled the inmates to bake cookies and cakes with their children.

Owen and her daughter played in the toy room throughout the morning, and then they made their way to the prison cafeteria for lunch. As they ate lunch, Owen noticed the conspicuous presence of two men also eating lunch there. The men wore suits, but it was obvious to the inmates that they were plainclothes law enforcement. Owen attempted to ignore the men, but she felt that they periodically shot menacing looks at her.

After lunch, Owen and her daughter were in the midst of finger painting when Owen was summoned to the warden's office—the NSP's Chuck Phillips and a colleague gave her a hostile reception. You will recall from an earlier discussion of this meeting that Owen told Caradori the NSP investigators said the Franklin Committee didn't exist, and Caradori was merely a private detective who had no affiliation with the Nebraska legislature.

Whereas the NSP's waylaying of Owen angered Caradori, it absolutely mortified Owen. Caradori's December 16 Investigative Report mentioned that the NSP investigators asked Owen intimidating questions about her daughter—Alisha Owen was still extremely frightened about her daughter's welfare, and their questions only served to intensify her fears. Caradori also noted that the NSP investigators threatened to transfer Owen from York at their whim. Owen found the NSP's threat of a prison transfer particularly upsetting—she worried that being transferred to a distant prison in western Nebraska would make weekly visits by her family very time-consuming and nearly impossible. Alisha also worried that a different prison might not permit her daughter to have extended visitations.

Al and Donna made the trip back to York over the weekend to retrieve their granddaughter, and they found that their daughter was still extremely shaken about being browbeaten by the NSP investigators—she specifically named Chuck Phillips to her parents. Though Caradori had forewarned Al and Donna about the NSP, the NSP's intimidating tactics nonetheless bewildered them. The Owens conceded that Caradori might be right regarding the NSP, but they just couldn't bring themselves to believe that the FBI would actively cover up crimes against children.

After the NSP sandbagged Owen in the warden's office, an innuendo that she was a snitch started to percolate among some of York's inmates. Before long she was viciously attacked by three inmates in the shower room—two of her three assailants were serving time for murder. Within days of being attacked, Owen was placed in solitary segregation for her own "protection." Owen found herself sitting alone in a cell for twenty-three hours a day—she was allowed to venture outside one hour a day if the weather permitted.

Owen wasn't used to social isolation, and she initially found the prospect of solitary confinement terrifying. She coped with the solitude by spending hours reading the Bible. Owen ultimately fell back on the faith that was the foundation of her upbringing—the very faith she had rebelled against as a teenager. Immersing herself in the faith of her childhood, she started to experience a profound metamorphosis. When Gary Caradori originally videotaped Owen, she came across as a helpless child who had been severely victimized and traumatized. But in months, Owen had transformed herself into a confident young woman who possessed the steely and unfaltering will to endure unbelievable acts of malice. As the harms and evils visited upon her escalated to an almost unfathomable scale, her faith took on the biblical proportions of Job's.

After his initial discussions with Alisha Owen, Gary Caradori had the acumen to see an impending legal maelstrom descending upon Owen, and he suggested she retain Pamela Vuchetich as an attorney. Owen trusted Caradori's judgment, and Vuchetich stated her willingness to represent her pro bono, so Owen consented to Vuchetich's representation. Throughout January 1990, Vuchetich attempted to coax Owen into talking to the NSP and FBI, but Owen's December 15 encounter with the NSP had been so caustic and disconcerting that she refused to enter into a dialogue with either branch of law enforcement.

Alisha Owen's refusal to have further talks with the NSP or FBI forced the FBI to take the initiative. On January 31, 1990, around 8:00 A.M., the Owens received a phone call from FBI Supervising Special Agent John Pankonin—he invited them to come to the Omaha FBI Field Office that day. Al and Donna were startled to receive an unexpected phone call from the FBI, and they told Pankonin that they wanted to discuss the proposed meeting with Vuchetich. When they managed to reach her after a few hours, Vuchetich instructed Donna and Al to meet with the FBI, and she agreed to attend the meeting as well.

Donna phoned Pankonin back, and the Owens consented to a meeting at the FBI's Omaha Field Office later in the day. Pankonin greeted them wearing a finely tailored suit that accentuated his tall, athletic frame. According to the Owens, Pankonin introduced himself as the FBI's agent-in-charge of Nebraska and Iowa.

Pankonin then escorted the Owens through a security door and into a cramped office. Three men and Pamela Vuchetich awaited them. Al and Donna had anticipated that Vuchetich would meet them in the reception area; they found it slightly odd to find her already seated in the crowded office. Pankonin introduced the Owens to Special Agents Mickey Mott and William Culver. Agent Mott was in his late thirties to early forties, favoring suits less expensive than Pankonin's. Culver was the youngest of the three, with a style more akin to Pankonin's than Mott's.

A fourth man was seated at the far end of the table—Pankonin introduced him as an NSP investigator. Donna immediately asked the NSP officer if he was Chuck Phillips, because her daughter had found Phillips so threatening. Pankonin quickly provided a different name for the NSP officer. The Owens would find out much later that the NSP investigator they met that day was, in fact, Chuck Phillips.

Pankonin had a commanding presence as he informed the Owens about his background in child-abuse investigations—Mott also chimed in and discussed his experience investigating child abuse. Culver and Phillips were silent as Pankonin and Mott put the Owens at ease. After an hour or so, the FBI dropped the hammer: The Owens were told that their daughter would be moved to a federal prison out of the state—for her own protection—if she didn't cooperate with the NSP and FBI.

The Owens made the two-hour trip to York on an almost weekly basis, and they didn't have the financial resources to routinely visit their daughter if the FBI relocated her outside of Nebraska. Vuchetich then assured the Owens that she was in the midst of working out an immunity agreement for Alisha with the US Attorney.

The Owens made a pilgrimage to York the following weekend, and they talked to their daughter about signing a federal immunity agreement and cooperating with the FBI so they could continue to see her on a regular basis. Alisha had revisited the Fifth Commandment—honor thy father and mother—and she ultimately consented to sign a federal immunity agreement and cooperate with the FBI.

On February 5, Pankonin and an NSP investigator made their first foray to York—Pankonin was thoughtful enough to exclude Phillips—and they met Owen and Vuchetich in the same conference room where Owen had initially met Caradori and Ormiston. Three days later, Pankonin, Vuchetich and the same NSP investigator made a second foray to York. Pankonin and Vuchetich discussed Owen's forthcoming immunity agreement, and they explained that she would be required to be entirely truthful. Though Owen had no qualms about being honest, she still didn't trust the NSP or FBI. She requested that Caradori attend her upcoming interviews, but the FBI unequivocally vetoed her request.

The following week, Vuchetich arrived at York with Special Agents Mott and Culver—Vuchetich presented Owen with her immunity agreement, which she signed. Owen was then subjected to eight protracted "interviews" with a hostile FBI during February, and Vuchetich exposed her to the FBI without a recitation of her Miranda rights.

Owen found the FBI agents to be derisive and condescending, and she quickly concluded that they weren't interested in the truth. She also started to feel that Vuchetich, her trusted lawyer, was developing a rather cozy relationship with the FBI agents. Owen desperately wanted to confer with Vuchetich either before or after the FBI interviews, but York's Visitor's Register shows that Vuchetich often signed in and out at the same time, or almost the same times, as the FBI agents.

Throughout February, Owen received the same hours-on-end FBI full-court press that collapsed Danny King and Troy Boner like two houses of cards, but she still refused to recant her videotaped statements to Caradori. Though Owen displayed a steely will with the FBI, their bullying tactics took an extreme toll on her. York's inmates in segregation were checked on every fifteen to thirty minutes, and the prison's records indicate that Owen had several sleepless nights in February, and she frequently declined meals. When Al and Donna visited her on weekends, they were stunned to see their daughter's rapid physical deterioration: She had lost considerable weight, her hair was falling out, and purplish bags bulged beneath her drowsy eyes.

By March, Owen's unwillingness to recant her account provoked FBI personnel to completely take their gloves off, and they raided her cell with a federal search warrant on March 8. Earlier I commented on Senator Schmit's perspective on the raid—he was utterly baffled by the search because the Franklin Committee had given the FBI numerous leads by then. But the FBI apparently wasn't interested in the Committee's leads—their primary concern was terrorizing Owen and impeaching her credibility.

The ever-congenial Chuck Phillips accompanied the FBI agents executing the search warrant, so Owen felt even greater intimidation and trepidation. Owen was in her pajamas when the FBI burst into her cell. The FBI agents tore apart all of her scant possessions—they even squeezed out her toothpaste!

Owen felt the FBI was after her red folder, where she kept the list of former lovers and friends that Vuchetich had requested she pen. But the red folder was nowhere to be found in the small cell—Owen had sensed that the FBI might pull something underhanded, and she had given the folder to Vuchetich. The day after the FBI tossed Owen's cell, Phillips served a subpoena on Vuchetich for the coveted folder, and Owen's trusted attorney failed to invoke attorney-client privilege—the folder would prove to be a precious little trinket for Van Pelt and company. In response to a federal subpoena, Vuchetich later surrendered the folder to the FBI as well.

The day after the raid, the FBI had Troy Boner phone Owen from FBI headquarters and recorded the call—Boner had flipped and become the FBI's boy, so it recruited him to inculpate Owen in the "hoax." At one point in the conversation, Boner said to Owen, "You concocted this whole thing Alisha." Owen responded, "You're full of shit."

A little later in the call, Boner told Owen, "I'm not gonna go to jail for you, and that's what's gonna happen." Owen then replied, "Why would you go to jail? Jail for telling the truth?" Owen repeatedly advised Boner to simply tell the truth: "So, all you can tell 'em is what you know, and if you don't know don't lie about it."

It's rather ironic that as Boner was attempting to make Owen look like a liar, he was telling her lies: He told Owen that he was alone, phoning her of his own volition, and had yet to be interviewed by the FBI. Boner would eventually start yelling at Owen—he had never yelled at her before, and she worried that he was being threatened and coerced.

On April 10, 1990, the FBI made one final foray to York: Pankonin and Mott made the jaunt with an NSP investigator. Vuchetich had previously ridden out to York with the FBI, but that day she arrived a couple of hours before the agents—she apparently wanted to confer with Owen. According to Owen, the final meeting consisted of the FBI agents unleashing a flurry of veiled threats. Owen, however, would not recant her story of abuse.

Al and Donna Owen had a hectic spring of 1990—they had two children who were bogged down in legal quagmires: Aaron had an upcoming trial for auto theft, and Alisha had an impending grand jury appearance. Al and Donna decided on a strategy of division—Al focused on Aaron's difficulties as Donna concentrated on Alisha's legal travails.

As Alisha was being subjected to the FBI's full-court press, Al and Donna Owen began to experience telephone glitches. Donna contacted the telephone company, and it sent out a repairman. Donna was in the midst of cleaning the house and listening to a faith-based radio station when the repairman arrived—she directed the repairman to the basement's telephone box. After fifteen minutes or so, the repairman emerged from the basement—he seemed a bit nervous as he asked Donna about her faith. When Donna confirmed her faith, he requested that she step outside—he whispered to her that the phones were tapped. The repairman's revelation didn't shock Donna—she suspected tapped phones because of the background racket that often accompanied her calls.

Shortly after the Owens had confirmation that their phones were tapped, Donna also started to have an uneasy feeling about Vuchetich—she voiced her concerns about Vuchetich to a member of Concerned Parents, who provided her with the names and numbers of a handful of attorneys. The first attorney Donna Owen contacted was too busy to grapple with her daughter's case, and Donna phoned the next attorney on the list—Henry Rosenthal. The *World-Herald* reported that Vuchetich lined up Rosenthal for Alisha Owen, but Rosenthal, Donna Owen, and Alisha Owen all told me that this was not true.

Rosenthal grew up in rural western Nebraska, and he had served as a Marine in the Korean War before receiving his law degree from Omaha's

Creighton University Law School in 1957. Rosenthal practiced law at a prestigious Omaha firm for fourteen years, becoming a senior partner, before signing on with Omaha-based Northern Natural Gas Company, which eventually evolved into Enron. Northern Natural Gas Company employed Rosenthal as a corporate attorney for seventeen years.

The sixty-year-old Rosenthal retired from Northern Natural Gas in 1989, and he had been in private practice for a year or so. Rosenthal practiced law at a firm that was housed in an upscale West Omaha office building. He wasn't an actual employee of the firm—he merely rented one of its offices. Rosenthal had made a good living as a corporate lawyer, and he retired with a comfortable pension; he was in the twilight of his career, and he could afford to be highly selective in the cases he chose to take.

Donna Owen made a solo trip to see Rosenthal on a Friday afternoon. A few minutes later, Rosenthal walked into the reception area and greeted her. Rosenthal stood a burly six feet tall and wore a gray Brooks Brothers suit with a crisp white shirt and blue tie. Introducing himself, he thrust out his fleshy right paw. Donna Owen shook his hand and then followed him into a conference room.

Rosenthal and Donna Owen were joined by one of the law firm's senior partners. The three sat at one end of the conference room's large oblong table as Donna Owen explained her daughter's predicament. Rosenthal and the firm's senior partner were following the Franklin fiasco as it unfolded in the *World-Herald*, and they had an almost glib curiosity about the man Alisha Owen alleged was the father of her child. Donna Owen unhesitatingly said, "Robert Wadman, the police chief." Rosenthal and his colleague erupted in incredulous laughter.

As Rosenthal struggled to take Donna Owen seriously, one of the firm's secretaries walked into the conference room—she handed Rosenthal a note and whispered in his ear. After the secretary's brief interruption, Rosenthal and his colleague were suddenly somber and attentive—as if they had just been zapped by a jolt of electricity. A startled Rosenthal looked Donna Owen in the eye and immediately inquired if she had told anybody about her appointment with him that afternoon—she replied that she hadn't uttered a word to anyone, including her husband.

Rosenthal held up the secretary's note and said that he had just received a call from the FBI—he was supposed to call Omaha's FBI Field

Office after their meeting. Donna Owen then told Rosenthal that her home phones were tapped, and the FBI probably gleaned the details of their meeting from the wiretap. Rosenthal's sidekick promptly excused himself as Rosenthal phoned the number on the note. Alisha's attorney, Pamela Vuchetich, answered the phone at the FBI Field Office! Donna Owen's account of the FBI tapping the Owen's phone would have seemed preposterous to the savvy Rosenthal had he not received a call from the FBI and then talked to Vuchetich.

After Rosenthal hung up the phone, he turned to Donna Owen and suggested they make a trip to York the next day—she smiled and gave him an affirmative nod. Donna talked to her daughter that night, and she told Alisha to expect an afternoon visit from her and Rosenthal. Donna Owen informed Alisha that Rosenthal charged $300 an hour, an especially hefty sum in 1990, and she expected her daughter to fully cooperate with him.

The following morning, Donna Owen rendezvoused with Rosenthal at the latter's office, and the two drove to York in Rosenthal's black Cadillac. As they drove along a desolate stretch of highway, the windshield suddenly cracked. Rosenthal cursed as he chalked up the cracked windshield to a ricocheting rock. Donna Owen surveyed the highway and commented that there wasn't a vehicle in sight. Rosenthal agreed, and both thought someone had probably taken a shot at them.

When Rosenthal and Donna Owen arrived at York, they were escorted into the same conference room where Alisha had initially met Caradori and then the FBI. Alisha was eventually shepherded into the conference room by a guard. She was noticeably tense and nervous as she seated herself next to her mother and across from Rosenthal.

Rosenthal visited Owen in the aftermath of a series of horrendous events: The FBI had besieged her in February, her cell was raided in March, and Boner's set-up phone call had left her thoroughly mortified. Though Owen had come to the painful realization that Pamela Vuchetich wasn't serving her best interests, she still felt ambivalent about the prospect of a new attorney. She apparently had defaulted to "The devil that you know is better than the devil you don't." In other words, she had become disillusioned with Vuchetich, but she thought that an unfamiliar and untested Rosenthal might put her in even worse circumstances.

Rosenthal was no-nonsense and brusque—he fired a fusillade of questions at Alisha that were designed to test her veracity. By April 1990, Alisha had become a whiz at Q & A, and her answers were quick and unflinching. After Rosenthal talked to Alisha for an hour or so, his prior doubts about her honesty were dispelled. He consented to represent her pro bono, but his representation had a caveat—their association would be summarily terminated if he ever caught her lying.

After Rosenthal and Donna Owen returned to Omaha, he parked his Cadillac next to Donna Owen's car—she drove home and he proceeded to his office. As Rosenthal worked into the early evening, catching up on paperwork, he had his first encounter with Franklin's reign of terror, receiving two death threats over the phone, but Rosenthal was undaunted. The two death threats only served to reinforce the Owens' story.

Two weeks after Rosenthal made his first visit to York, Alisha Owen was scheduled to appear before the Douglas County grand jury. Upon her arrival at the courthouse that day, April 30, 1990, she was given a terse letter from Pamela Vuchetich: "I find it necessary to withdraw as your lawyer due to a conflict of interest. I will do everything I can to effectuate a smooth transition."

If Donna Owen hadn't lined up Rosenthal to represent her daughter, she would have been left without an attorney when she appeared before a hostile grand jury. Rosenthal had Alisha Owen's grand jury appearance postponed. He sensed that the chips were being stacked against his young client, but he had no idea that Van Pelt and company intended to completely annihilate her until he witnessed their conduct firsthand. Rosenthal was absolutely appalled—he told me that he had never witnessed such flagrant abuses of justice, and he was further enraged by the subsequent grand jury report.

When Rosenthal opted to lock horns with the powers who wanted Alisha Owen silenced, he was at a crossroads in his life. He'd recently retired from Northern Natural Gas Company, and his marriage of thirty-three years had also recently ended in an amicable divorce—the marriage had yielded two sons who were now adults. Rosenthal found himself facing a void in his life; so he turned to his long-time mistress—the law—to fill the void. He had a fundamental and abiding belief in the legal system—he took on Owen's perjury case not only for the sake of Owen, but also as a crusade to rectify a grave miscarriage of justice that was anathema to his reverence for American jurisprudence.

As Alisha Owen made her stand before the Douglas County grand jury, Vuchetich sprung an additional surprise on her: Owen received an initial bill for Vuchetich's legal services, even though Vuchetich had pledged to represent her pro bono. Vuchetich maintained that the $5,407.77 bill was only for starters—"telephone expenses incurred at this point." Vuchetich wrote that Owen would receive forthcoming charges for "client conferences and conferences with witnesses, local mileage and mileage for trips to York or Omaha on behalf of the client, meetings with the Legislative Committee and legal research."

So Vuchetich opted not to invoke attorney-client privilege when the NSP and FBI came calling for Alisha Owen's coveted folder; she abandoned Owen on the threshold of her appearance before the grand jury; and in a glaring conflict of interest, she represented Danny King at the grand jury as he testified that Owen was lying. Now she was billing Owen for thousands of dollars, even though Owen was incarcerated and had no prospects of repaying her.

Vuchetich's subversion of Owen was certainly an about-face from her earliest interviews in the *World-Herald*, where she sounded dedicated to saving the children. Donna Owen had a hunch that Vuchetich was literally and figuratively in bed with the FBI, because Vuchetich talked about Special Agent Mott with a particular amour. The letters Rosenthal started to receive from Alisha Owen after the Douglas County grand jury proceedings also alluded to Vuchetich and Mott's dalliance.

One of Owen's first letters to Rosenthal elucidated Vuchetich's U-turn from catcher in the rye to duplicity: Owen described a relationship between Vuchetich and agent Mott that surpassed professional courtesy and seemingly entailed airborne pheromones. Her letters mentioned that the married Vuchetich and the married Mott "flirted outrageously." Vuchetich also reportedly referred to Mott as "cute," showed Mott a sexy picture of herself in dance garb, and told Owen that she had met with Mott "several times" and even had "dinner" with him.

In addition to Vuchetich's providing materials to law enforcement that sabotaged Owen, Owen wrote letters to Rosenthal that detailed Vuchetich's effort to poison her mind against the people who were attempting to help her. According to Owen's letters, Vuchetich made disparaging comments about some of the senators on the Franklin Committee: She said one of the senators had been having an affair with a friend of hers, a second senator was guilty of falsifying government documents, and a third senator stole parts for his helicopter and abused his daughters. The letters also noted that Vuchetich told Owen that Concerned Parents were a bunch of "loonies."

Vuchetich turns up on York's Visitor's Register for the last time on April 18, 1990, and a letter Owen wrote to Rosenthal discussed their final meeting. Vuchetich, Owen stated, said that the FBI had authorized an eleventh-hour "deal" requiring that she "lie" for her freedom: "I would have to say that Gary Caradori and Mike Casey conspired the entire Franklin abuse case.... They wanted me to say that Gary gave the three witnesses scripts and cash to make the tapes. I told her if I said that then I would be guilty of perjury. She still urged me to take the deal. I told her I couldn't do that to innocent people."

Owen's letters prompted Rosenthal to subpoena the phone records of Vuchetich, who was rather fond of dialing the FBI's Omaha Field Office. From January 23, 1990 through February 21, 1991, she made 177 phone calls to the FBI—155 of the calls were placed from her office and 22 of them were from her home phone. Over the thirteen months, Vuchetich racked up 2,185 minutes talking to the FBI, and she placed the calls day and night—between 7:40 A.M. and 10:00 P.M. One call was nearly three hours in duration. The day before Vuchetich dated the letter to Owen terminating her legal representation, she talked to someone at the FBI for a whopping 132 minutes.

Rosenthal was extremely interested in talking to Vuchetich after he subpoenaed her phone records, because they corroborated the belief of both Alisha and Donna Owen that Vuchetich and Mott were having an extramarital affair. Rosenthal attempted to depose Vuchetich, but she sent him a letter outlining a number of conditions that the Owens and Rosenthal had to meet in order for her to sit for a deposition.

Vuchetich's demands included that Al, Donna, and Alisha Owen provide her with affidavits "waiving all attorney-client privileges" and also releasing her from "any and all liability." She also wanted to know the names of "all individuals and the facts or information to be given by these individuals during the course of my deposition."

Vuchetich also demanded "two hours of time alone" with Alisha Owen, and she wanted prior payment for her time and attorney's fees to be placed in her "trust account." If the deposition was taken outside of Lincoln, Nebraska, Vuchetich required Rosenthal or the Owens to spring for her "travel expenses."

Vuchetich's letter angered Rosenthal, and he quickly acquired a subpoena that required her to sit for a deposition. But Rosenthal had second thoughts about the milieu of a formal deposition, which would include Vuchetich, a lawyer representing Vuchetich, a court reporter, Rosenthal, and Rosenthal's newfound paralegal—Donna Owen. Though Donna Owen had dropped out of high school in the tenth grade, she had a steel-trap memory, and she was an indefatigable spark plug.

Rosenthal ultimately decided to have Vuchetich stop by his office for an informal talk in lieu of sitting for a formal deposition. Before Vuchetich arrived that day, Rosenthal and his paralegal, Donna Owen, had a fiery argument about whether or not Rosenthal should broach the subject of Vuchetich's affair with Mott. Rosenthal thought that Vuchetich would never confess to the affair, because it would jeopardize her family and career. But Donna Owen lobbied hard for Rosenthal to at least bring it up.

After Vuchetich showed up at Rosenthal's office, Vuchetich, Rosenthal, and Donna Owen seated themselves at the conference room table. As Rosenthal talked to Vuchetich about her representation of Alisha Owen, Donna Owen started kicking him under the table, prompting him to pose the million-dollar question.

According to both Rosenthal and Donna Owen, Vuchetich bowed her head, became teary-eyed, and confessed to the affair—she repeatedly muttered that she was "sorry." They both claim that she pleaded with them not to tell her husband.

Vuchetich later denied that she confessed to an affair with Mott. In fact, she even disavowed setting foot in Rosenthal's office for the chat. However, her denials are in stark contradiction to a sworn affidavit of Rosenthal's that detailed both the meeting and her confession. Donna Owen was also polygraphed about the meeting and Vuchetich's confession, and her polygraph examiner found no indications of deception. Moreover, as the story of Alisha Owen's trial unfolds, along with Rosenthal's vigorous defense, it will become evident that it is highly unlikely he would have gone to the trouble of subpoenaing Vuchetich without following through with at least an interview.

The month before the Douglas County grand jury indicted Alisha Owen for perjury, her little brother, Aaron, had an extremely bizarre interaction with the Douglas County judiciary. Aaron Owen was sixteen years old when he stole the car to escape the wrath of his girlfriend's uncle, but Douglas County opted to try him as an adult, and threw the book at him. In addition to auto theft, he was charged with criminal mischief and operating a motor vehicle to avoid arrest.

Al and Donna Owen hired an attorney to represent their son, and the lawyer suggested to the Owens that they forgo a trial by jury and opt instead for a Douglas County District Court judge to single-handedly rule on Aaron's fate. The attorney assured the Owens that their son would most likely end up with probation and/or have to spend some time in a juvenile reformatory. But the Douglas County Judge hearing Aaron Owen's case disagreed with his lawyer's prognosis—he sentenced the now seventeen-year-old Aaron Owen to between four and seven years in prison. Though the judge sentenced Aaron Owen as an adult, he declared him to be a juvenile when it came to reimbursing the city for damages incurred during the chase, making Al and Donna Owen responsible for those costs too.

Around the time Aaron Owen was packed away to prison, Henry Rosenthal lodged a complaint against Pamela Vuchetich with the Nebraska Bar's Counsel for Discipline, which assesses the misconduct of Nebraska attorneys—he had a laundry list of her failings as a lawyer for Alisha Owen. Lodging a complaint with the Counsel for Discipline can be a protracted process, and Rosenthal's complaint against Vuchetich wended into the fall before there was an actual hearing in Lincoln.

In Vuchetich's written response to the Counsel for Discipline, she characterized Owen as having a "history of nymphomania, promiscuity, suicide attempts, and untreated mental illness." Vuchetich also wrote that "she worked very hard to prove" Owen's story, but she "found no evidence to support her statements." She then reflected on the traumatic decision that weighed so heavily on her conscience: "I took a hard and gut wrenching look at all the statements and documents before me and had to decide who was telling the truth."

Vuchetich's response to the Counsel for Discipline contradicted her statements in a *World-Herald* article that discussed her discarding Owen as a client. The article reported, "Ms. Vuchetich emphasized that she continues to believe the account of the 21-year-old woman...." The article then quoted Alisha's ex-lawyer: "There is a conflict of interest," said Vuchetich, "but I do believe she's been sexually abused."

As Rosenthal and Alisha Owen followed through on their Counsel for Discipline complaint against Vuchetich, Owen had a disturbing intuition about her little brother—she felt that Aaron's life was imperiled. Owen told me she voiced her suspicions to a guard at York—I contacted the former guard, and she corroborated Owen's account.

The week of Vuchetich's November 1990 hearing before the Counsel for Discipline, a guard awoke Alisha Owen in the early hours, and she was ushered to a prison caseworker's office—a somber caseworker handed Owen the telephone and instructed her to call her mother. Donna Owen's voice cracked as she told her daughter that Aaron Owen was dead—he had allegedly hanged himself. Alisha and Donna both erupted in tears—Alisha Owen continued to intermittently break down in tears throughout the upcoming weeks; she had dearly loved her little brother.

The official account of Aaron Owen's suicide was that his girlfriend visited him on the night of November 8, 1990 at the Lincoln Correctional Center and broke up with him. The lovesick seventeen-year-old Owen was then plunged into an abyss of despair and hanged himself in his cell—Owen's suicide note even mentioned his girlfriend, confirming the official account.

But the official account of Aaron Owen's death contained some salient anomalies. First, Aaron Owen had slash marks on both wrists, a bone-deep gash on his forehead, and a large bruise under his left eye. The official account essentially found that Owen succumbed to extreme masochism before he decided to hang himself, and it doesn't seem to have a problem with the bone-deep gash on his forehead. The official account contended that after Owen's body was found hanging in his cell, he was "cut down," and he plummeted to the floor of his cell, landing on his forehead. Aaron Owen's autopsy doesn't state whether or not the "abrasion" on his forehead and the bruise under his left eye occurred before or after his death.

The jailers who found Aaron Owen seemed to have little respect for him, which was evidenced by the fact that they simply cut the bed sheet that he ostensibly used to hang himself, and he fell to the floor. They nonetheless had him transported to Lincoln General Hospital, where "cardiopulmonary resuscitative efforts" were performed. The suicide note was problematic too: He signed the terse note "A.J."–he had never referred to himself as A.J. before. The Owens felt that Aaron Owen's writing "A.J." on the suicide note was a clear sign that he had been coerced; so they were extremely dubious of the official account of his death–they were also dubious when the Nebraska Bar's Counsel for Discipline concluded that Pamela Vuchetich had committed no ethical improprieties during her representation of Alisha Owen.

Approximately two and a half months after Aaron Owen's death, Troy Boner's younger brother, Shawn, shot himself in the head playing "Russian roulette." He was reportedly with three friends, and they were drinking and "toying" with a thirty-eight revolver in military housing north of Omaha near Offutt Air Force Base, which houses the US Strategic Command, a major nerve center of America's nuclear capability.

A *World-Herald* article quoted law enforcement on the shooting: "It still looks like it was accidental. We believe that at the time, Shawn felt it wasn't loaded." The *World-Herald* article featured a picture of Troy Boner, his mother, and her new husband–Troy Boner looked gaunt and horrified. The article quoted Boner's mother: "I know what Shawn's stand on guns was. I know what his thoughts about death and suicide were. He was very verbal about it. I want to see that this isn't swept under the rug." Troy Boner also interjected a comment into the article: "Shawn hated guns." The Boners seemed to be insinuating that foul play was involved in Shawn Boner's death, even though they didn't explicitly mention it in the *World-Herald* article.

According to their affidavits and comments made to friends, Troy Boner and his mother felt that Shawn Boner had been murdered. Troy was finding it difficult to remain mute about all the tall tales he had told the grand jury, telling several family members that threats had forced him to perjure himself there. The stories of Boner's perjured testimony had even leaked out of the Boner family and made their way to various people, including a retired Douglas County Deputy Sheriff, who had the fortitude to submit an affidavit stating that three of Troy Boner's relatives confessed to him that Troy had lied before the grand juries.

I've seen an outtake from *Conspiracy of Silence* that showed Troy and his mother standing in front of Shawn Boner's gravestone, voicing their belief that Shawn had been murdered as a tactic of intimidation. In Troy Boner's 1993 "lie or die" affidavit, he said that at one point he stood up to the FBI agents by telling them that he was the focal point of too much media scrutiny for them to hurt him. Boner maintained that an FBI agent responded that he was probably right, but the FBI still had the means of seeking retribution through a "family member." Boner's affidavit stated that his brother's "murder" was a "message" to him, because the FBI thought, "I might back down and tell the truth at the Alisha Owen trial.... After Shawn got killed, I had no doubt at all that they really were as dangerous as I had originally feared."

Boner's mother also submitted a 1993 affidavit that substantially corroborated her son's affidavit. She swore that Shawn Boner "never had anything to do with guns" and "never would have been playing Russian roulette." She further swore that she was "quite certain" her son "was executed as a message to Troy that he had better stick with his lies at the upcoming Alisha Owen trial or else." She too discussed her fear of the FBI: "When I told the FBI people that 'Nobody will ever convince me that Troy's original story was not the truth,' the FBI people became very angered and upset. Their actions and their questions after that convinced me that I was in danger."

After reading the affidavits of Troy Boner and his mother, I was extremely interested in finding at least one of the three individuals who reportedly played Russian roulette with Shawn Boner that January night in 1991. I eventually managed to track down one of the three—he was also the purported gun owner. I initially found him extremely resistant about talking to me, but I was unaccustomedly aggressive with him, because I truly wanted to tease out the reality of Shawn Boner's death. He told me it was an "unfortunate accident," and then he started to give either "No, sir" or "Yes, sir" answers to my questions. I finally persuaded him to open up, and we talked for approximately twenty minutes.

Law enforcement said that Shawn Boner believed that the gun wasn't loaded, but this individual first told me that he "thought" the gun was loaded—he then gave me two differing accounts as to whether or not the gun was loaded. The shooting had occurred fourteen years before I interviewed him, and it was certainly an event that he would want to delete from his memory. So I understood his vague and contradictory answers to my questions.

At one point in our conversation, though, I asked him if he was aware that Shawn Boner's brother, Troy, was a pivotal figure in the Franklin scandal, because he conveyed to me that he had known the Boner family for years. He responded that he wasn't aware of Troy Boner being enmeshed in Franklin. I found this latter statement very hard to believe: Troy Boner's scrambled visage and voice saturated the Omaha airwaves prior to his grand jury appearance, and he granted various interviews to television stations and the *World-Herald* after the grand jury—I think it would have been next to impossible for someone in Omaha, acquainted with the Boners, not to be aware of Troy Boner's involvement in the Franklin investigations. I ultimately came away from that interview questioning this individual's truthfulness—I'm just not certain about the *scope* of his lies.

Aaron Owen's death occurred four months after Gary Caradori's mysterious demise, and both deaths caused devastating emotional upheavals in Alisha Owen and her family. The Owen family had trusted Caradori, and they felt that his tenacity and guile would somehow, some way manage to save the day. Henry Rosenthal ultimately replaced Caradori as the Owens' knight in shining armor, and Rosenthal grew increasingly fond of Alisha Owen and her family—a friendship that lasted until his death in 2009.

State v. Owen was tried in the Douglas County Courthouse, the same site where Van Pelt restored "integrity" to the system, and Rosenthal was determined that it wouldn't be the scene of a second flagrant miscarriage of justice against Alisha Owen. He managed to have her trial postponed until May 1991, and he put in sixteen-hour days backtracking on Caradori's investigation and the Douglas County grand jury. He spent enormous out-of-pocket sums to finance his defense of Owen. As Rosenthal immersed himself in Owen's case and Caradori's investigation, he shared Caradori's astonishment over the perfidious power of state and federal law enforcement to twist truth into lies and vice versa.

Alisha Owen's perjury trial turned out to be one of the longest criminal trials in Nebraska history. The state of Nebraska pulled out all stops and spared no expense: Her trial represented much more than a simple case of perjury—her jurors would also be evaluating the grand jury findings. If Alisha Owen were found guilty of perjury, the Douglas County grand jury report would be validated. But if she were found innocent, its findings would be called into question.

The state of Nebraska and the United States of America had vital vested interests in the guilt of Alisha Owen, since both state and federal grand juries had disavowed the existence of Larry King's pandering network. FBI agents had been the field marshals behind the front lines of the Douglas County grand jury, directing the firebombing of Owen's credibility, but in *State v. Owen* they would be called to testify against Owen's integrity. Of course the *Omaha World-Herald* would play an integral role in underscoring the state's case, but, lo and behold, CBS—as in the Columbia Broadcasting System—would give the state a helping hand too. So Rosenthal and Alisha Owen found themselves squaring off against the state of Nebraska, the United States government, and the local and national media.

Just as Samuel Van Pelt had been plucked out of retirement to lead the Douglas County grand jury, retired jurist Raymond "Joe" Case would be dusted off to serve as the judge in the trial. Whereas tapping Van Pelt was ostensibly a collective decision of the Douglas County District Court judges, Case was chosen to oversee Alisha Owen's trial by the highest court in the state—the Nebraska Supreme Court.

The seventy-three-year-old Case was tall and lumbering: He had gray hair, a benign, creased face, and sagging jowls—he wore dark-framed glasses with thick lenses. Case was born in Iowa, but grew up in a small town in southeastern Nebraska. He received an undergraduate degree from the now defunct Tarkio College in Missouri, where he was a standout football player. Case graduated from college in 1941, and then he enrolled in Omaha's Creighton Law School. He was originally appointed a judge in Nebraska's rural Cass County in 1950. His tenure as a Cass County judge lasted forty years, and he retired in 1990. After Case retired from the bench, he went into private practice. Though Nebraska law prohibits practicing attorneys from serving as judges, Case was appointed Owen's trial judge nonetheless.

Douglas County Deputy Attorney Gerald Moran stepped into the ring to represent the state and its vast supporting cast. Moran was a youthful looking forty-three years old. He was fond of inexpensive suits, favoring navy blue and brown. A native son of Nebraska, Moran attended Omaha's Holy Name High School and graduated in the class of 1966. Holy Name was a small parochial school whose student body was primarily Catholic and from working-class backgrounds.

Moran had been a popular kid at Holy Name—he was Holy Name's Homecoming King as a senior and a center for the football team. After high school, he attended Creighton University as an undergraduate, and he was a 1973 graduate of Creighton University Law School. Moran then spent the lion's share of the next decade practicing criminal law for an esteemed Omaha firm before signing on with the Douglas County Attorney's Office in 1981. According to the grand jury testimony of Douglas County Attorney Ronald Staskiewicz, Moran had attended the January 1990 conclave of the top brass from the US Attorney's Office, Nebraska Attorney General's Office, FBI, NSP, OPD and the Douglas County Attorney's Office, where the FBI played their federal trump card by announcing that the Franklin interviews would be conducted on "FBI terms."

Alisha Owen's fate would be decided in a courtroom on the fourth floor of the Douglas County Courthouse—courtroom number twelve. Before the trial, Rosenthal filed a series of motions with Judge Case. One of Rosenthal's pretrial motions argued that Alisha Owen's statements to the NSP and FBI had been coerced and not voluntary, and were thus inadmissible at her perjury trial—Case granted Rosenthal a hearing to determine whether Owen's statements to the NSP and FBI had been voluntary or coerced. The three-day pretrial hearing was held on May 6, 13, and 15, and the jurors were not present.

In early May, prior to the pretrial hearing, Owen was transported from York to the Douglas County Jail, where she resided over the course of her trial. Throughout the pretrial hearing, Owen started a pre-dawn to dusk ritual that would become the hallmark of her life for the duration of her trial. She awoke around 4:00 or 4:30 A.M., showered, dressed, and, if lucky, she had a chance to eat a quick breakfast. She then bided her time in the jail's "transportation room" awaiting her armed escort to the Douglas County Courthouse. She arrived at the courthouse anywhere from 7:30 A.M. to 8:45 A.M., and she was then ushered to a holding cell on the sixth floor.

When Owen was summoned to the courtroom, she and her guards would take an elevator to the fourth floor, circle the courthouse's rotunda, and proceed to the courtroom. As Owen was escorted back and forth from the courtroom to the elevator, she was essentially "perp walked," and the Nebraska media had their prime opportunity to take pictures or film her. She never dispensed a quote to the media.

At the close of each day's proceedings, Owen would be transported back to the jail. By the time Owen made it back to the Douglas County pokey, she had already logged a sixteen-hour day. But her return to the jail usually didn't mark the end of her day's travails, because Rosenthal often visited her in the evening to discuss the upcoming day.

During the pretrial hearing, Al and Donna Owen also embarked on a ritual that would become integral to their lives for the next six or seven weeks. They awoke early in the morning—showered, ate breakfast, and dressed in their Sunday best. They then drove downtown, parked, and walked to the courthouse. Courtroom twelve was unlocked shortly before 9:00 A.M., and the Owens always arrived at the courtroom before its doors were unlocked so they could grab a seat in the first row of the spectators' seating, just behind the defense table. Initially, Donna Owen sat at the defense table with Rosenthal and her daughter, but Judge Case quickly put a stop to her helping Rosenthal—he ruled that she had to sit in the spectators' seating.

The pretrial hearing proved to be a microcosm of the trial, and it quickly became evident to Rosenthal that he wouldn't be trying Alisha Owen's case in a fair and impartial court of law. Just minutes into the hearing, Case cocked his head downward and peered at the "bunch of motions" that Rosenthal had submitted to him—Case barked out that April 29 was the deadline he had issued for submitting motions and the motions had been filed after that deadline. But the week that Case set the deadline, Rosenthal had been hospitalized for a heart condition; so he had phoned Case, explained his medical predicament, and requested two additional days to file his motions—Case agreed to Rosenthal's timetable, and instructed Rosenthal to notify Moran about the deadline being pushed back. In accordance with Case's decision, Rosenthal called Moran and explained his quandary.

Shortly after Case brought up Rosenthal's "bunch of motions," Rosenthal reminded him of their phone call, in which Case extended the deadline for his motions: "Your Honor, so the record is clear; when I got that order, I called you and I said, 'Judge I need a couple of extra days." And you said, 'Fine, but please don't take more than a couple of days, and notify Mr. Moran.'"

Case told Rosenthal that he remembered the phone call, but he couldn't recall that the crux of the conversation was an extension of his deadline to submit motions. Rosenthal then said if Case hadn't issued an extension for the motions, he would have filed them on time by hook or by crook—he also added, "Two days one way or another is not going to harm anybody here."

Moran quickly interjected that Rosenthal hadn't notified him of the extension until after Rosenthal submitted the motions. But Rosenthal disagreed and remarked, "That's absolutely a false statement to the Court—I notified that man and certainly, judge, I would not be in violation of your order." Judge Case all of a sudden had full recall of his conversation with Rosenthal, and he said that he explicitly stipulated that Moran had to be in agreement with the extension.

The discussion about whether or not the motions were belated was put off until later in the hearing when Case finally declared that Rosenthal had missed the deadline for the motions, and they wouldn't be taken into consideration. A perplexed Rosenthal pleaded with Case to stick to his word and rule that the motions were admissible. But Rosenthal's pleas angered Case, and the judge threatened him with a contempt of court charge. "I gave you permission if you got an agreement with the opposing counsel!" barked an angry Case. Rosenthal said, "That is not true. What you said to me, judge—" Case cut off Rosenthal with a razor-sharp rebuke: "Now, listen, if you call me a liar once more, you are going to try this case from jail!" Rosenthal was utterly stunned—he had practiced law for decades and previously experienced judicial ineptitude and inequity, but he had never witnessed an opposing counsel essentially rule on the motions he'd submitted to a judge.

One of the motions Rosenthal submitted to Case, which Moran essentially shot down, dealt with the wacky, rambling nature of Alisha Owen's eight perjury indictments. During the pretrial hearing, Rosenthal wanted Case to clarify what exactly the "prosecution has to prove." Rosenthal told Case that each one of the "voluminous indictments" contained several questions and answers—he asked the judge if the prosecution had to prove every statement that was contained within each of the individual counts of perjury for Owen to be found guilty on that respective count. *Moran* responded, "Nope, nope, nope," and he gave a nebulous answer about the "gist of the count." Moran then said that Rosenthal filed his motion "out of time," and his question was little more than "playing Franklin trivia."

"Your Honor, you are never too late to seek justice," Rosenthal replied. "We should have had that in the grand jury, and it flew by them." He inquired if Owen would be found guilty on an individual count of perjury if the prosecution proved just "one out of ten questions" and answers contained in each of the indictments—Case reacted to Rosenthal's inquiry by telling him his motion had been filed past the deadline. Rosenthal was a bit perplexed by Case's response, and he returned to his question—he simply wanted to know if the prosecution had to prove every statement contained in each of the individual perjury indictments. But Case wasn't too sure himself! After considerable wrangling, Case, in effect, declared that Rosenthal had to refute Owen's guilt regarding all the "allegations" that were "set out in each count." Rosenthal wouldn't be defending Owen on just eight statements—he would be defending her on numerous statements.

Nebraska law requires attorneys to question witnesses from their respective tables—they're allowed to approach the witness or the bench only after the judge has granted them permission. So during the pretrial hearing, Rosenthal waged a war from the defense table to prevent Owen's statements to law enforcement from being admissible at her trial, because he knew that the NSP and FBI would paint a very unbecoming portrait of her. In addition to contending that Owen wasn't coerced, Moran and the FBI agents maintained that the FBI and NSP treated Owen as the victim of a crime, instead of a suspect, throughout all their interviews, so they weren't required to dispense Miranda warnings to her. Though the FBI searched Owen's cell with a federal search warrant, and then seemingly had Boner phone York prison in an attempt to entrap her, Moran and the FBI declared that these were investigative techniques appropriate for victims.

During the pretrial hearing, Moran called the NSP's Chuck Phillips and FBI agents John Pankonin and Mickey Mott to the stand to testify that Alisha Owen hadn't been coerced into making statements and that she had been treated as a victim when they interviewed her. Phillips was the first witness Moran called to the stand, and Al and Donna Owen were shocked as Phillips seated himself and was sworn in. They initially laid eyes on Phillips at the FBI's Omaha Field Office on January 31 when he was introduced as an NSP investigator: Donna Owen remembered explicitly asking John Pankonin if the NSP investigator in question was Chuck Phillips, and Pankonin's introducing him by a different name.

Rosenthal noticed that Phillips was extremely nervous when he testified, whereas the FBI agents testifying at the pretrial hearing were calm, cool, and collected. Moran's examination of Phillips was short and sweet: Phillips testified that he had talked with Alisha Owen at York on December 15—he said he never threatened or coerced her and that she was treated as a victim. As Rosenthal attempted to cross-examine Phillips, Moran's voice bellowed as he began belting out objections. Moran objected nearly two hundred times during the pretrial hearing—Case sustained the vast majority of his objections, keeping Rosenthal on a short leash.

Against Moran's torrent of objections, Rosenthal questioned Phillips about Miranda rights and inquired if Phillips had ever issued a Miranda warning to Owen—Rosenthal was then absolutely staggered by a comment made by Case after a Moran objection: Case announced there was no need for Phillips to give Owen a Miranda warning because the NSP was merely in an "investigative stage" when Phillips interviewed her.

"Your Honor, please, I object to that statement," protested a baffled Rosenthal. "It shows prejudice—prejudice on your part, your Honor, because that is the very thing you have to decide. And if you've already decided it, there is no use to us being here." Case then gave a response that was antithetical to his previous statement: "Well, I haven't decided it..." Alisha Owen and her parents looked on in disbelief as Case backpedaled.

After Case tipped his hand, Rosenthal attempted to question Phillips about Alisha Owen's reactions and emotional state during the December 15 interview—he wanted to illustrate that the NSP's coercive tactics and badgering had made her "upset." Moran apparently didn't want it to come out that Phillips had upset Owen, and, just possibly, treated her as a suspect instead of a victim; so he countered with a chorus of seventeen objections as Rosenthal touched on the issue from different angles. Though Case finally overruled one of Moran's objections, Moran continued to object. But Rosenthal at long last made Phillips concede that he had been informed that Owen was "upset" after the interview.

The next witness called by Moran was FBI Special Agent John Pankonin, who had supervised the FBI's "investigation" of Franklin. After Pankonin had been sworn in, Judge Case disclosed to Moran and Rosenthal that Pankonin's mother was a stepsister of his—Case said that he had seen Pankonin probably only once in the last twenty to twenty-five years. Rosenthal offered no objection—he had a number of questions he was dying to ask the G-man.

Moran questioned Pankonin about his four forays to York to interview Owen. Like Phillips, Pankonin said that Owen was never coerced and that her statements were given freely and voluntarily. Pankonin also mentioned that Owen's trusted attorney, Pamela Vuchetich, was always at her side during the interviews. Moran quizzed Pankonin about promises he may have made to Owen—Pankonin replied that Owen requested that he "get her out of prison," but he said that the "most he could do for her" was to write a letter to her attorney acknowledging her cooperation.

Moran's examination of Pankonin had been brief—Rosenthal commenced his cross-examination of Pankonin by telling him to "sit back and relax, because I am going to talk to you for a little while." Against a gale of Moran's objections, Rosenthal attempted to establish Alisha Owen's reluctance to talk to the FBI. Pankonin eventually slipped in a bald-faced lie—he said that Alisha Owen wanted to talk to the FBI, but Vuchetich insisted that she be given an immunity agreement.

Rosenthal brought up the FBI's meeting with the Owens on January 31 to show that FBI agents had coerced Alisha Owen by telling her parents she would be transferred to a remote federal prison if she didn't talk. Rosenthal asked Pankonin about the call he placed to the Owens that day—Pankonin denied phoning the Owens! Rosenthal pressed Pankonin about the call, and Moran objected. Pankonin then asserted that Vuchetich had set up the meeting, to the "best of my recollection."

As Rosenthal questioned Pankonin about the meeting, Pankonin said that Vuchetich had accompanied the Owens to Omaha's FBI Field Office. Rosenthal pointed out that Vuchetich was already at FBI headquarters when the Owens arrived—Pankonin agreed, replying that Vuchetich was at the FBI "waiting for them to come." Pankonin gave contradictory accounts of Vuchetich's accompanying the Owens and not accompanying the Owens in a matter of seconds. Rosenthal inquired which account was true: Pankonin couldn't "recall," and Moran objected.

Rosenthal asked Pankonin about the "gist" of the meeting, and Pankonin responded that the FBI agents' primary concern was to assure the Owens of their extensive background "working sexual exploitation cases." Rosenthal queried Pankonin as to whether or not the Owens would be wrong if they testified that the FBI agents wanted them to talk to their daughter about granting the agents interviews—Pankonin was again struck by amnesia and just couldn't remember.

Rosenthal started plying Pankonin with questions about Vuchetich riding out to York with the FBI, and Moran began firing objections. Rosenthal inquired if Vuchetich ever met with Owen one-on-one before any of the FBI interviews he conducted. "To the best of my recollection," said Pankonin, "I believe that Ms. Vuchetich talked to her client prior to every interview." Rosenthal called Pankonin's attention to his reports on the FBI interviews of Owen, and only one report noted that Vuchetich talked to Owen prior to the FBI interviewing her. Pankonin's response to Rosenthal impeaching his "recollection" yet again was to put forth that it wasn't "important" for Vuchetich to meet with Owen prior to Owen's FBI interviews, because the FBI hadn't declared Owen to be a "defendant."

Pankonin then testified that Alisha Owen only became a suspect after her final interview with FBI agents on April 10; so FBI agents weren't legally obligated to dispense Miranda warnings to her throughout their interviews. Rosenthal had Pankonin read from his April 10 report: "It was explained to her that in view of the fact that she had signed an immunity agreement with the federal government, failure to testify would constitute a contempt citation and expose her to further incarceration."

Rosenthal asked Pankonin if he informed Owen that "under certain circumstances" she could have exercised her Fifth Amendment rights without the prospect of incarceration. Pankonin replied that her attorney was present—Rosenthal said that he wanted a simple yes or no. Moran objected on the grounds that Pankonin wasn't a lawyer, and also pointed out that Owen's trusted lawyer, Vuchetich, was present to inform Owen of her rights—Moran said about Vuchetich's presence: "I mean I don't know how much better it can get than that."

Rosenthal had already heard some whopping lies at the hearing, but he was absolutely astonished by Moran's comment: "That is as false a statement as has been made this afternoon, your Honor!" Rosenthal then launched into a short speech, stating that Owen "didn't have effective counsel." He also told Case that one of his rejected motions dealt specifically with Vuchetich leading Owen down a primrose path that ultimately left her susceptible to FBI coercion. But Case snapped that Vuchetich had "nothing to do" with the issues that were to be decided at the pretrial hearing.

Rosenthal realized that the tandem of Moran and Case wouldn't allow him to fully explore the FBI's terrorizing of Owen with additional prison time, and he shifted to the federal search warrant executed on Owen's cell in March. Rosenthal asked Pankonin if the FBI usually served "search warrants on people who are not suspects." Pankonin replied that it all depended on the evidence the investigators were looking for—Rosenthal inquired what specific evidence the FBI was after when it searched Owen's cell. Pankonin said that he wasn't quite sure—he had nothing to do with procuring the search warrant. A now incredulous Rosenthal attempted to pin down Pankonin on exactly when Owen's status changed from victim to suspect, but Moran began objecting, and Case sustained his objections.

At the conclusion of the pretrial's first day, Alisha Owen kissed her mother and father good-bye—she was then handcuffed and shackled and taken back to the Douglas County Jail by deputy sheriffs.

When the pretrial hearing resumed the following week, Rosenthal continued his cross-examination of Pankonin. Rosenthal questioned Pankonin about who was the prime mover in setting up the FBI's meetings at York with Owen—Pankonin couldn't recall. Rosenthal inquired who informed the NSP of the meetings—Pankonin couldn't recall.

Pankonin testified that his interviews of Owen didn't chronicle a year or a year and a half of her past—Rosenthal inquired what time frame was missed. Pankonin again defaulted to the best of his "recollection," and answered that it was late 1988 and 1989—Rosenthal pointed out that in actuality it had been 1983 and 1984. Rosenthal was a bit baffled that Pankonin didn't touch on those years with Owen, because the FBI was theoretically investigating child abuse and those were the years when Owen was allegedly subjected to the majority of her abuse. Rosenthal said that Owen's videotaped statement to Gary Caradori focused on her abuse in 1983 and 1984, and he asked Pankonin if he had watched Caradori's videotape of Owen—Pankonin replied, "Yes I did, but I tried to ignore the tapes."

The third witness called to the stand by Moran was FBI Special Agent Michael Mott. Again, Moran's examination of Mott was quite brief—Mott testified that Owen hadn't been coerced or threatened; nor had the FBI made any promises to her.

Rosenthal quizzed Mott about the FBI interviews of Owen lacking detailed information concerning 1983 and 1984—Moran objected because he said it was irrelevant. Rosenthal countered Moran's objection by saying that the FBI was supposedly treating Owen as a victim of child abuse, and it was rather "odd" the interviewing agents seemed to focus on Owen's life "five or six years" after her abuse. Moran then objected on the grounds that Rosenthal's contention was "paranoid." Rosenthal explained to Case that he simply wanted to know if the FBI interviews touched on the years when Owen was a victim of child abuse. Moran objected once more, and Case caught Rosenthal completely off guard—he overruled a Moran objection. As Mott identified excerpts from an FBI report where agents actually talked to Owen about the years she was alleging abuse, Moran belted out two objections.

Rosenthal then shifted gears to the federal search warrant that the FBI executed on Owen's cell. To obtain a federal search warrant, FBI agents generally provide an affidavit to a federal judge or magistrate stating the grounds for the search warrant. Rosenthal felt Mott's affidavit was suspect because it wasn't signed or notarized, and he started to question Mott about it—Moran began yelping out objections. Rosenthal told Case that Mott's affidavit wasn't signed or notarized, and he simply wanted to find out if Mott had submitted a "complete" affidavit. Moran responded, "I feel I should object, but I'm not sure—" Case cut off Moran, "sustaining" the objection, even though no objection had actually been made, nor any grounds for one offered.

Rosenthal had asked Pankonin exactly when Owen became a suspect, and he posed the same question to Mott. Moran objected on the grounds of irrelevancy—Moran then maintained that Owen became a suspect only after she committed perjury before the grand jury in May. Rosenthal asked Mott again when Owen became a suspect—Moran objected, and Case sustained his objection. Rosenthal told Case that the question had paramount relevance—he said if FBI agents ever had an inkling that Owen was a "suspect" throughout their interviews of her, they violated Owen's Constitutional rights by never dispensing a Miranda warning to her. Case was unmoved, and yet again sustained Moran's objection.

Rosenthal returned to questioning Mott about the search warrant, attempting to establish that the FBI viewed Owen as a suspect long before she was indicted by either grand jury for perjury. Mott's "affidavit" stated that a rationale for acquiring the search warrant was the fact that Danny King had told FBI agents that "Owen was fabricating allegations." Mott also asserted in the affidavit that "records" supported Danny King's statements. Rosenthal asked Mott to tell him about the specific comments made by Danny King that contradicted Owen. Mott replied that Danny King said everything he told Caradori was a "total fabrication."

Rosenthal inquired whether Mott believed Danny King's recantation—Mott responded that it wasn't his "position" to believe him. Rosenthal pointed out that Mott must have believed Danny King, because he decided to "run and get a search warrant" after Danny King contradicted Owen. Moran, evidently, didn't want Mott to state that he believed Danny King's FBI-version of events, because that would potentially paint Owen as a suspect: He objected to Rosenthal's inquiry as "irrelevant," and, after a brief discussion, Case sustained the objection.

Though Moran and Case had effectively shut down Rosenthal's quest to demonstrate that the FBI's obtaining the search warrant was proof positive that Owen was the hunted, his resolve was unabated. In the face of objection after objection, Rosenthal attempted to ask Mott what exactly the FBI was looking for when it raided Owen's cell. When Moran and Case blocked that avenue of inquiry, Rosenthal tried to question Mott about the federal subpoena served on Vuchetich to acquire Owen's coveted red folder—he wanted to show that Mott had gleaned information about the folder directly from Vuchetich. The state couldn't afford to have it surface that Vuchetich had seemingly abetted the FBI's mutilation of Owen's rights and had made her vulnerable to coercion—Rosenthal's questions on that topic were met with a flurry of sustained objections.

Rosenthal turned to a second FBI tactic that he felt showed FBI coercion and the fact that the FBI viewed Owen as a suspect: the call Boner placed to Owen at York in which he tried to inculpate Owen in the "hoax." Mott admitted that the call had been placed from Omaha's FBI Field Office and that it had been made at Mott's request. Rosenthal inquired why Mott had Boner call Owen, and Mott replied that it was to "lock" Boner into his story and to find out if Boner had the ability to pick up the phone and call Owen.

As Rosenthal pressed Mott on Boner's phone call to Owen, Mott was stricken with a bad case of amnesia. Rosenthal inquired if Boner had, in fact, told York personnel that he was Gary Caradori—Mott replied: "I can't remember unless you have a record." Rosenthal questioned Mott about what Boner asked Owen during the call—Mott couldn't remember. Rosenthal finally asked, "You remember nothing of the conversation?" Mott responded, "No, I don't."

Rosenthal asked Mott if Owen sounded "upset" during the phone call. The state just didn't like the word "upset" to be used in conjunction with Owen and the FBI's tactics—Moran objected on the grounds of irrelevancy, and Case sustained the objection.

Rosenthal lobbed a few softballs at Mott concerning his interviews with Owen, prompting a relative lull in the storm of objections, but a tempest followed shortly thereafter: He started to inquire about the relationship of Mott and Vuchetich: "Weren't you and Alisha Owen's attorney, Pamela Vuchetich, playing toesies?" Mott snapped out an unequivocal "No," and Moran exploded: "For crying out loud! Judge, I am going to ask that you order him to terminate this!" Case didn't skip a beat: He said that the issue was the subject matter of a "civil case."

Rosenthal was flabbergasted as he characterized Alisha Owen's allegations: "She looks down, and she sees this woman having her shoe off and rubbing up and down this gentleman's leg, and she says, 'Would you like me to leave for a while until you complete what you want.'" Moran retorted, "And that's being told to him by a three-time convicted felon!" Moran had previously slandered Owen, and Rosenthal had objected—now he jumped up and shouted, "Your Honor, he is not going to say this much more before I—I'll take some action!" Moran barked out once more, "She is a three-time convicted felon!"

Case shot a stern look at Rosenthal and rebuked him: "It is certainly out of order for you to be asking those questions! I've ruled on them!" Rosenthal gazed up at Case and exclaimed: "You haven't even heard the question before! Now how could you say that, Judge, unless you are prejudiced?" Rosenthal and Case had a few acrimonious exchanges before Case asked Rosenthal about the "relevancy" of the dalliance between Mott and Vuchetich. Rosenthal said that it "has to be obvious to everyone what happened"—Vuchetich led Owen "down the primrose path" that left her almost defenseless against FBI coercion and intimidation.

To Rosenthal's disbelief, Case continued to insist that the affair between Mott and Vuchetich was the subject matter for a civil case. Moran interjected again that "a three-time convicted felon" was scandalizing a vaunted G-man and beseeched Case to return to the "issues" of the hearing. Case later called Rosenthal into the judge's chambers and once more threatened him with contempt of court and jail if he brought up the Mott and Vuchetich dalliance again. Case wielded "contempt of court" over Rosenthal's head a number of times throughout the trial, and Rosenthal once remarked to Owen that both of them might eventually end up in the Douglas County Jail.

After Moran called Phillips, Pankonin, and Mott to testify that Alisha Owen hadn't been coerced, threatened, or promised anything, it was Rosenthal's turn to call witnesses supporting his contention that Owen had been subjected to FBI intimidation and coercion. The first witness he called was Donna Owen, and the first issue he addressed was Pankonin's phone call to the Owens on January 31—he also introduced Donna Owen's calendar into evidence, which had Pankonin's name and number written on it.

Moran objected on the grounds of relevancy—Rosenthal replied, "It shows that Pankonin lied when he said that he never called the Owens and set up the meeting." Moran again objected on the grounds of relevancy—Rosenthal explained to Case the relevancy of Pankonin's phone call to the Owens: "It goes to show, your Honor, that they could not talk to the girl because she wouldn't talk to them; so what they did is they got the parents to come down. And if we can just get the testimony in, they tried to persuade them through threats and coercion to get the daughter to talk." Rosenthal then introduced the Owen's phone bill from January 31, establishing that the Owens phoned Vuchetich that morning.

Rosenthal had Donna Owen recount her and Al's visit to the FBI's Omaha Field Office—she discussed Pankonin introducing himself as the agent-in-charge of Nebraska and Iowa, Pankonin telling the Owens that Chuck Phillips wasn't Chuck Phillips, and Vuchetich awaiting their arrival in Pankonin's FBI office, sipping coffee.

Rosenthal then focused on Donna Owen's discovery during the pre-trial hearing that Chuck Phillips was, indeed, Chuck Phillips. Moran started objecting, and Case asked Rosenthal to defend his line of inquiry. Rosenthal said he intended to demonstrate that the FBI had been duplicitous with Al and Donna Owen from the outset, and that the agents had told the Owens they would "shove" their daughter into a remote federal facility if she didn't talk to the FBI, thereby coercing Alisha Owen via her parents. But Case's response signified that he didn't grasp Rosenthal's logic: "This defendant has to be responsible for her own acts." Rosenthal spouted an incredulous, "What?"

After a few exchanges, Rosenthal explained his intentions: He said that Pankonin invited the Owens to the FBI Field Office under the pretext of a "blatant lie"—Pankonin told the Owens that the agents wanted to explain their protocols and experience in the investigation of child abuse. "We're going to show that they threatened these people," Rosenthal asserted. Moran cut in and interjected that Rosenthal wasn't following the correct "format" for the "impeachment" of Pankonin's testimony. Case then said he couldn't "perceive the relevancy" of Donna Owen's testimony concerning her and Al's visit to the FBI's Field Office.

Case and Rosenthal haggled over the relevancy of Donna Owen's testimony before Rosenthal finally spelled it out in the simplest of terms: "Threats, coercion, voluntariness—I thought that's what this hearing was about. That's what we're showing." Case remarked that he wanted Rosenthal to concentrate exclusively on threats to Alisha Owen. Rosenthal responded, "I can threaten your son by threatening to harm you—it's very simple." Case ultimately sustained Moran's objection.

Rosenthal told Case that he was being "deprived" of presenting "any evidence" on behalf of Owen to demonstrate her "statements were not voluntary," adding, "I am kind of dumbfounded."

Rosenthal then circled back and again simplistically explained to Case that he could show that the FBI coaxed Al and Donna Owen to the FBI Field Office on a false pretense and issued a threat to Alisha Owen via her parents. Moran objected to this as irrelevant, but, lo and behold, Case overruled Moran. Rosenthal walked Donna Owen through her and Al's meeting with the FBI, he then started to review the FBI's threat of relocating their daughter to a distant federal prison.

Now Moran took a different tack and objected on the grounds that Donna Owen's testimony was "hearsay"—Case sustained his objection. Though Moran had effectively blocked Donna Owen from testifying about the FBI's threats and intimidation, he couldn't leave well enough alone—he said Rosenthal wasn't conducting his "impeachment" of an FBI agent in "the way that a trial lawyer properly does." Rosenthal cut him off and whispered under his breath, "Oh, you and your 'trial lawyer'—you're so full of shit." Moran hollered, "Judge, did you hear what he said?" Rosenthal continued with his examination of Donna Owen, but Moran looked at Case and hollered once more, "Did you hear what he just said to me?" An oblivious Case replied, "No, I didn't." Moran yelped, "He said I was full of shit!"

Case brandished another contempt of court threat at Rosenthal, who attempted to defend himself by saying that Moran had repeatedly slandered his client, and yet Case had never admonished him for that conduct. "It seems to be a one-way street," he said. Indeed, Rosenthal's efforts to prevent a second miscarriage of justice against Alisha Owen, and Moran's incessant objections and jibes, were turning the courtroom into a pressure cooker.

Rosenthal carried on with his examination of Donna Owen about her afternoon at FBI headquarters—he inquired if there was a discussion regarding her daughter not wanting to talk to the agents, and she replied, "Yes, there was." Moran, right on cue, objected to the question as "leading." Rosenthal gazed at Case and inquired, "How could that be leading your Honor?" Case responded by stating that the question could have been answered with a "yes or no." An infuriated Rosenthal kept his cool and posed basically the identical question—Donna Owen responded with a "Yes." Rosenthal then asked her which FBI agent brought up the subject of her daughter's not wanting to talk to the FBI—she answered "Mr. Pankonin." Rosenthal asked her what Pankonin said to her—Moran objected as "hearsay," and Case again sustained this objection.

Undeterred, Rosenthal approached the same line of inquiry from different angles. After a little wrangling, he asked Donna Owen if Pankonin ever discussed the ramifications facing her daughter for not talking to the FBI—Moran objected, Case overruled, and Donna Owen said, "Yes." Rosenthal requested that Donna Owen embellish her answer, but Moran objected twice, and Case sustained the second objection. Rosenthal peered up at Judge Case and said that he had just overruled a Moran objection on essentially the same question—Case snapped at Rosenthal: "I sustained the objection, and I will!"

Rosenthal posed a few questions to Donna Owen on a different subject, and he returned to her meeting at the FBI Field Office—he inquired about her frame of mind during the meeting. Moran objected, but Case was benevolent enough to overrule his objection. Donna Owen replied that she was frightened, because she and her husband wouldn't be able to afford to visit their daughter regularly if the feds moved her to a different state. In response to Rosenthal's next question, Donna Owen said that she conveyed the FBI's warning to her daughter.

Rosenthal had finally managed to breach Moran and Case's seemingly impenetrable barricade concerning the FBI's threats to Al and Donna Owen; so he moved on and started to explore Alisha Owen's reaction to the FBI interviews from the perspective of her mother. He questioned Donna Owen about her daughter's emotional state after the first FBI interview, and she said her daughter "was very upset." The word "upset" when applied to Alisha Owen being interviewed by law enforcement just might imply coercion, and the fact that she wasn't treated as a victim; Moran had previously demonstrated his distaste for the word when used in conjunction with Alisha Owen and the NSP, and he cut off Donna Owen after she voiced the word "upset," with an objection that was sustained by Case. Rosenthal assailed the issue from different angles, but all his efforts were blocked by sustained objections.

Rosenthal eventually started to tackle the reign of terror that was wrought upon the Owens—he asked Donna Owen if she had reasons to believe that the FBI tapped the Owens' phone. She imparted a rather interesting account that confirmed the FBI was listening to the Owens' phone calls. Donna Owen said that she had one of her friends phone the Owen household so she could tell the friend that her daughter would take the Fifth in front of the Douglas County grand jury. Shortly afterwards, she was approached by a television reporter, who informed her that the FBI had told him Alisha would invoke her Fifth Amendment rights before the grand jury. Rosenthal attempted to raise another example of the FBI's tapping the Owens' phone, but he was met with a flurry of sustained objections.

Moran's cross-examination was extremely short—he inquired if Donna Owen and Rosenthal had "scripted" her testimony, and she responded that Rosenthal had merely provided her with a number of written questions.

After Moran's cross-examination of Donna Owen, Rosenthal called her daughter to the stand—Rosenthal had Alisha Owen describe her life in "protective custody." She said that she was locked up alone and not allowed to mingle with other prisoners—if the weather permitted, she could venture outside one hour a day.

Rosenthal questioned Alisha Owen about her December 15 encounter with Chuck Phillips. She testified that she was playing with her daughter when she was ordered to proceed to the warden's office, where Chuck Phillips and a second NSP officer gave her an icy, hostile reception—she said that she risked punishment for disobeying a direct order from prison personnel, and she felt forced to meet with Phillips. After Phillips told her that there was no Franklin Committee and Gary Caradori was a "nut," Owen asserted that she requested to be excused from the warden's office so she could phone Caradori, but Phillips wouldn't let her leave, and she felt "really frightened." She disclosed that though there was a phone in the warden's office, she didn't want to have a conversation with Caradori in front of Phillips.

Rosenthal asked Alisha Owen if Phillips made any promises to her—she said Phillips promised her that her statements to him would be confidential and kept within law enforcement. She said she didn't believe Phillips, though, because she sensed he was lying about Caradori—her suspicions were confirmed the next morning at 7:30 A.M., when she was listening to the radio and heard that the NSP had interviewed an alleged victim, providing details about Owen without naming her.

Rosenthal then questioned Owen about her aversion to being interviewed by the FBI—she gave three reasons. The first was her treatment by the NSP. Second, she was cognizant that Chief Wadman was working joint investigations with the FBI. Third, she felt that the FBI was covering up the child abuse, because it had supposedly investigated the charges for a year prior to Caradori's videotapings but hadn't uncovered anything.

Rosenthal asked Owen about her first meeting with the FBI, and she described extremely coercive circumstances. On the day of her initial FBI interview, she testified, she wasn't even aware that the FBI had made the trek to York until Pamela Vuchetich sprung it on her that morning. Alisha Owen then testified that Vuchetich informed her that the FBI would prosecute her for the drug offenses she discussed on Caradori's tapes if she didn't meet with Pankonin. A York guard also gave Owen a "direct order" to meet with Pankonin. Defiance of a direct order had the potential to land an inmate in solitary. But Owen was already in solitary segregation when the FBI came calling; so she believed her defiance of prison personnel would have resulted in unfavorable letters to the parole board.

Rosenthal started to explore Owen's mental and physical deterioration over the course of her FBI interviews. Owen said she found the FBI interviews very grueling—she couldn't sleep and lost twenty-five pounds. She often cried and spent hours pacing in her tiny cell.

Rosenthal then introduced York's twenty-four hour segregation logs into evidence that corroborated Owen's account of her extreme sleep deprivation and loss of appetite—and the logs showed that Owen ate very little, declined meals, and suffered from acute insomnia throughout the FBI's interviews in February. At one point, Moran interjected that the FBI or the NSP wasn't "keeping the defendant up at night"—it had been "her decision" not to sleep.

Owen stressed that the genesis of her turmoil and agitation was the FBI's hostility and threats towards her. She said that the FBI agents derided her too, and she didn't think they were acting in good faith. To emphasize the FBI's terrorizing of Owen, Rosenthal had her discuss the federal search warrant executed on her cell—she talked about the FBI agents and Chuck Phillips ripping apart all of her possessions.

Owen initially thought the FBI agents and Phillips were looking for drugs, but then she came to the realization that they executed the search warrant to harass her and confiscate her red folder. She told the agents and Phillips that the red folder fell under the safeguard of attorney-client privilege, and she phoned Vuchetich, who confirmed that her red folder was protected by attorney-client privilege—the very folder that Vuchetich surrendered the following day. Rosenthal also had her speak to the fact that her mail postmarked after the March 8 search warrant mysteriously ended up in the hands of law enforcement and the Douglas County grand jury.

Moran's cross-examination of Alisha Owen began with an *ad hominem* attack: "Miss Owen, have you ever been convicted of a felony?" Rosenthal objected on the grounds of relevancy—he asserted that the hearing was about whether or not her statements to law enforcement were voluntary and her criminal record was of no import. Case overruled his objection.

Taking a cue from Van Pelt, Moran started questioning Owen about Vuchetich's representing her on a "contingency" basis so she could launch civil suits against Larry King, Baer, Wadman, etc. Rosenthal again objected on the grounds of relevancy, saying that the question had nothing to do with voluntariness. He also pointed out that Case had limited *him* to issues pertaining to Alisha Owen's interviews and interactions with law enforcement—Case overruled Rosenthal.

Once Case gave Moran carte blanche to grill Owen, he brought up "movie rights or book rights." Owen responded that she never wanted her private life dragged into public scrutiny, which was evinced by the fact that she hadn't granted interviews to reporters. Moran then made inquiries about her relationship with Michael Casey. Moran also questioned Owen about her other supposed motivation for concocting the allegations: She wanted a get-out-of-jail-free card. He said that at "virtually each and every interview" with law enforcement she requested that either the NSP or FBI liberate her from incarceration—Owen replied with a resounding, "No." Moran's badgering of Owen ultimately became so frenzied and blatant that even Case agreed with Rosenthal that he was badgering the witness.

Moran returned to the idea that Owen had been treated as a victim, and he belted out the party line: "And, in fact, isn't it true that during the eleven interviews with Pankonin and Mott and Phillips you were treated as a victim and a potential witness?" Owen looked Moran in the eye and replied, "Absolutely not. I was called names. I had to put up with snide remarks. Absolutely not. I don't believe they ever treated me like a victim."

At the conclusion of the pretrial hearing, Judge Case ruled that Owen wasn't threatened or coerced and had been treated as a victim throughout her interviews with the NSP and FBI. Thus all her statements to the NSP and FBI were admissible at her trial. For all intents and purposes, Case had announced that he had made up his mind within ten minutes of the hearing's commencement, when Phillips was testifying, so his ruling didn't take Rosenthal or the Owens by surprise. But they were nonetheless troubled by Case's lack of impartiality—it was painfully obvious to Rosenthal and the Owens that they faced two foes in the courtroom.

Rosenthal wasn't too worried though. He would be contesting the trial in front of a jury, and he felt he had more than enough evidence to establish reasonable doubt.

On May 17, at 9:40 A.M., a Thursday, the Honorable Raymond "Joe" Case declared that the court was convened in the matter of the *State of Nebraska versus Alisha J. Owen*. In a criminal trial, the state gives its opening statement, and afterwards the defense presents its opening statement: summations of the case from the perspectives of the state and of the defendant. The state initially calls its witnesses, then the defense calls witnesses to refute the state's witnesses or testify to the innocence of the defendant. The state's case precedes the defendant's case because the "burden of proof" is on the state. After the state rests its case, if the judge believes a sufficient case has not been presented, he may grant a defendant's request that the charges be dismissed.

Ultimately, Moran's job was to sell the "carefully crafted hoax" to a jury of twelve, and his opening statement rambled on and on. First, he went over the indictments, and then he discussed the publicity generated by the fall of the Franklin Credit Union and Larry King. He touched on the formation of the Franklin Committee, Ernie Chambers' shepherding the child-abuse allegations into public consciousness, Gary Caradori, and the Douglas County grand jury.

He said that in reality *State v. Owen* actually began in the fall of 1988 when Alisha Owen met Michael Casey at St. Joseph's—Moran then went off on a tangent, thrashing out Casey's history of lies and deception. After Casey and Owen were discharged from St. Joseph's, Moran maintained, Casey "showed" Owen his notes on the "tabloid" version of the closing of the Franklin Credit Union, and the two continued corresponding even after Owen was sent off to York. Moran claimed that Owen gleaned all her information about Larry King from the media and Casey's notes.

Owen's meeting Troy Boner in the summer of 1988 was the next event Moran discussed in his opening statement. He depicted Boner as a "hustler," and he defined hustler: "someone who trades sex for money with men." He said that Owen was "infatuated" with Boner and even contemplated marrying him, but Boner didn't share her affections. He told the jury that Boner sold his sexual wares to Alan Baer, and Owen had garnered her intricate knowledge of Baer through Boner—she was introduced to a "street hustler and opportunist" named Danny King through Boner too.

Moran subsequently leapt to Gary Caradori's first encounter with Owen at York, and he gave a terse description of the meeting: "Gary Caradori says there are also two other people that I know you are involved with, and I want you to verify it for me." Moran said at that point Caradori preemptively dropped the names of Robert Wadman and Harold Andersen to Owen.

Moran now focused on Owen's relationship with Wadman—he detailed Owen's account of their initial meetings at the Twin Towers. Moran described an imaginary tale of Owen going to Brandeis at Wadman's behest, picking out a black dress, and their "lunch" at the French Café. Moran stressed that Owen testified to the grand jury that she had sex with Wadman between twenty and twenty-five times, but she told Chuck Phillips that they had sex on approximately one hundred occasions.

He then announced to the jury that his next point was "very, very, very, very important"—he said that Owen didn't mention that Wadman had surgical scars when she described his anatomy to the Douglas County grand jury. Moran then flashed back to 1973 and depicted Wadman as a valiant federal agent in Yuma, Arizona—Wadman was shot by a heroin dealer during a bust: The bullet hit him in the left forearm and took out "two inches of bone." Moran then discussed the extensive surgeries Wadman underwent after the shooting. Moran said Wadman had bone taken from his leg and grafted into his forearm—he also had a rod temporarily inserted in his forearm.

Moran explained to the jury that the surgeries had left Wadman's arm "withered," and he had a colossal scar. The resultant injury made it extremely difficult for Wadman to rotate his hand upwards. In addition to Owen's testifying that she didn't notice a scar on Wadman's forearm, she testified that he had muscular arms. Moran also called attention to the fact that Owen testified Wadman inserted a gun inside her vagina. But surely she was lying about that too, because Wadman never carried a gun as the Police Chief of Omaha.

Moran also addressed the fanciful tales Owen fabricated about Douglas County Judge Theodore Carlson to Caradori and before the grand jury. Owen testified that her first encounter with Carlson was during a Saturday afternoon reception at the French Café—Larry the Kid forced her to meet with Carlson in the basement of the French Café and perform oral sex on him. Moran said that Owen never even mentioned the French Café incident to FBI agent Mickey Mott, which was significant proof that it didn't happen. Moran commented on Owen's second alleged encounter with Carlson—Larry the Kid delivered her to the Starlite Motel, and she was again required to perform oral sex on Carlson.

No variation on the theme of a "carefully crafted hoax" would be complete without a bumbling, gullible, corrupt, and now dead-and-unable-to-defend-himself Gary Caradori. Moran conveyed to the jurors that Boner would tell them he initially thought Caradori was talking absolute gibberish and had no idea about Larry King. But after Caradori so belabored the matter, Boner had a revelation: "Perhaps another target of opportunity is presenting itself to me." Moran added that Caradori told Boner that "within six months" of making a videotaped statement he'd "pocket" no less than a million dollars via civil lawsuits, and, naturally, book and movie deals. Taking a page directly from the grand jury report, Moran described how Caradori prepped Boner for his videotaped statement and stopped and started the interview if Boner forgot something pertinent.

Moran's opening statement ran approximately two hours, but his discussion of the phantom phone call, where Boner talked to Owen from an office at Caracorp on the day of Boner's videotaped statement, was exceptionally brief. Though the phantom phone call was the linchpin of the hoax, Moran spent only about a minute elucidating it.

Moran finally proclaimed that all of Owen's stories were nothing more than "lies," and that he would parade witness after witness before the jurors who would attest to her lies. He provided three motives for Owen's lies that were essentially on loan from Van Pelt and company. First and foremost, she wanted "to get out of prison." Moran told the jurors that three beacons of truth—Chuck Phillips, Mickey Mott, and John Pankonin—would testify that Owen's lies were part of an elaborate scheme to be granted her freedom. And, of course, Owen savored the mere thought of cashing in on her "fantastic" tales—she planned to make between five and ten million dollars from civil lawsuits, and book and movie deals.

Moran also offered a third, "very clear" motive: Owen was a nobody who wanted to be "somebody." She constantly mentioned "champagne" and "lavish lifestyle," because she yearned for wealth, creature comforts, and the limelight. She craved the "public spotlight," and she "relished" all the attention that had been "lavished on her" since she made the tapes.

After lunch, Rosenthal commenced his opening statement. He started out by saying that he represented a "young girl now twenty-two years old" who came from an upstanding "Christian family." In 1983, though, she went astray and ended up over her head. He said that Owen, in fact, had a relationship with Robert Wadman that resulted in a pregnancy—Rosenthal voiced the various alleged threats Wadman dispensed to Owen, and to her family by way of Owen, if she didn't consent to an abortion. Owen nonetheless opted to have the child, and she never told a soul about the identity of the child's father—nor did she attempt to collect a penny from Wadman: "She was scared because she had been threatened, and went about her business."

Rosenthal then discussed Owen and Boner transporting drugs for Alan Baer: He noted that she lived "high, wide, and handsome" on a part-time job—she had a car, motorcycle, and lived in a beautiful home. He informed the jury that a person didn't have to be an "Einstein" to figure out her income wasn't on the up-and-up. After Rosenthal talked about Owen's illicit revenue, he jumped to the summer of 1988, when he said the "word is out"—Owen had to disappear: "You've got to leave Omaha, something is going to break; we can't afford to have you around." Rosenthal maintained that Owen had no idea that the Franklin story was on the verge of busting open, and she decided not to hightail it out of town. Alan Baer consequently pulled the plug on Owen's finances, her checks started to bounce, and her world quickly imploded.

He spoke about her two hospitalizations at St. Joseph's and her ill-fated flight from Nebraska with the young man she had met at St. Joseph's. Rosenthal brought up the fact that Owen eventually turned herself into Nebraska authorities, and she was sentenced to prison—he mentioned she had been in segregated custody "four hundred and some days."

Rosenthal made the point that Owen wanted to quietly serve out her sentence and then get on with her life. But one day Gary Caradori showed up at York: His visit completely shocked her, because she hadn't confessed her abuse to a soul—it was like he just "dropped out of the sky." He said that Owen was "petrified," and she told Caradori she would have to think long and hard about giving him a formal statement. Rosenthal stressed that Owen didn't tell the *World-Herald* or "blab" it around to "ruin" Wadman's reputation, but, rather, she talked to the prison psychiatrist, who referred her to the warden.

He summarized Owen's confessions to the warden and disclosed that the warden initially didn't believe her. He conceded that the warden kept a close eye on Owen and mulled over her conduct before he came to the conclusion that she was telling the truth. So approximately five weeks after Caradori first videotaped Owen, York's warden phoned Nebraska's Attorney General and told him that he thought Owen had been the victim of Franklin-related child abuse. Rosenthal explained to the jury that the Attorney General contacted the governor, which resulted in Owen's being visited by Phillips and a second NSP investigator on December 15.

Throughout Rosenthal's opening statement, he emphasized that Owen was extremely fearful for her life and certainly didn't seek publicity—she consented to be videotaped by Caradori only after he assured her that her statements wouldn't be made public or wind up with the media. Rosenthal said that the NSP investigators made the same promise to Owen, but it was, almost immediately, a broken promise.

Rosenthal then touched on Al and Donna Owen's being summoned to FBI headquarters and being threatened, as well as the threats and taunts Alisha Owen endured during her FBI interviews in February. He talked about the FBI's executing a federal search warrant on Owen's cell, Vuchetich violating her attorney-client obligations and surrendering Owen's red folder to the FBI, and the FBI's intercepting Owen's mail.

Rosenthal stressed that the FBI agents' treatment of Owen certainly wasn't appropriate for someone whom they perceived to be a "victim." He also said that if the FBI agents were sincerely investigating child abuse, they would have more reports that documented Owen's sexual abuse allegations—he pointed out that a number of the FBI reports generated from the Owen interviews never broached the subject.

After Rosenthal discussed the FBI's treatment of Owen, he shifted to the Douglas County grand jury. He talked about Van Pelt and Dougherty "scurrilously" interrogating Alisha Owen for three days, and how she never refused to answer their questions and never took refuge behind the Fifth Amendment. Rosenthal told the jurors that the grand jury's conclusion regarding Owen's motivation for making her statements to Caradori—riches via movie and book deals—was an utter absurdity.

He then focused on the state's star witness: Troy Boner. Rosenthal said that a second absurdity was that Boner's nearly seven-hour statement to Caradori was supposedly gleaned from a twenty-minute phone call. He repeated that Boner's videotaped statement was a "solid six hours"—he specified "times, places, names," etc. Rosenthal stated that even if Boner had mastered shorthand to the tune of "5,000 words a minute" he couldn't have jotted down everything that he articulated on his videotaped statement. He told the jurors to carefully scrutinize the videotaped statement of Boner and decide for themselves if Caradori acted deceitfully, and he remarked on the phantom phone call: "Because if you don't believe the phone call, and if you don't believe the phone call was made, then the cookie crumbles."

After Rosenthal's discussion of the phantom phone call, he noted Boner's appearance before the grand jury and some of his blatant lies. Boner had testified that he worked at Kelly's Furniture while he was living in San Diego, California; Rosenthal said he had easily discovered that there was no Kelly's Furniture in San Diego. Boner testified to Van Pelt and company that he had recently joined the Navy—Rosenthal stated that this was an absolute lie. Boner testified before the grand jury that he was employed by various temporary services—Rosenthal said he subpoenaed the various temp agencies and found they had never employed Boner. Rosenthal told Owen's jurors that the Douglas County grand jury had access to the almost limitless resources of the NSP and FBI; yet it never checked out whether or not Boner was truthful on relatively straightforward matters.

Rosenthal then discussed Boner's repudiation of his recantation in the aftermath of Caradori's death. He pledged to the jury that he would call three credible witnesses, including two former state senators, who would testify that Boner recanted his recantation. "I submit to you at the time Boner's conscience was burning up inside him," said Rosenthal, "and he was torn between telling the truth and the threats of the investigating officers." He also mentioned to the jury that the FBI descended upon Caracorp after Caradori's death, when his body wasn't "even cold," to subpoena all of his records, even though most didn't "have a damn thing to do with this case about child abuse."

Moran had harped on the inconsistencies in the videotaped statements of Owen, Boner, and Danny King, but Rosenthal maintained that they were merely "human frailties." He acknowledged that people's accounts of events can become a little fuzzy over time regardless of their circumstances, but "the theme is abuse and that's what it is—all throughout these tapes."

Rosenthal also talked about the vast sums of money the state and federal governments had spent—"hundreds of thousands of dollars"—to charge a young woman with perjury: "Not murder, not arson, not insurrection, not treason—perjury." He again voiced the theme that a number of witnesses had perjured themselves before the grand jury, and their stories were never investigated despite the grand jury's vast resources.

Rosenthal concluded his opening statement by concentrating on the primary impetus behind Owen's perjury indictments—she had accused distinguished men of child abuse: "Alisha Owen is charged here today and they're not going to give up until you bring in your verdict because she accuses prominent people. If she had accused Henry Rosenthal or Joe Blow, it would have been all over and done."

For months on end, Van Pelt had flung shovel after shovel of mud on the victims, and everyone who sided with the victims, and gradually worn down the grand jurors until they simply capitulated to the "carefully crafted hoax"—Moran and the state would deploy the same modus operandi, but they only had to focus their mudslinging on Owen. The state would parade witness after witness—week after week—who testified about Owen's moral turpitude and create a mudslide that was designed to completely engulf her and obscure the slightest vestige of her humanity.

Whereas Van Pelt and company had to discredit legions of people who believed the child-abuse allegations, Moran merely had to discredit a twenty-two-year-old girl who had a history of drug use, psychiatric hospitalizations, and, of course, was also a convicted felon. The grand jury, though, had the luxury of free rein without an adversary—Moran and the state had an adversary in the form of Henry Rosenthal, and a trial jury to convince.

One of the state's first witnesses was a DSS caseworker for the state of Nebraska, and Moran called her to testify that Alisha Owen had named someone other than Robert Wadman as the father of her child when applying for her daughter's medical assistance. The Nebraska statutes on "Paupers and Public Assistance" explicitly stated that such information was confidential and not to be used outside the confines of social services, and the caseworker initially cited the statute's "strict rulings" on confidentiality and voiced her reluctance to furnish such information in a public forum like a trial—she said that she had discussed the matter with a state attorney. Moran requested that Judge Case give her "permission" to disclose the confidential information, and Case graciously obliged.

Alisha Owen told the Douglas County grand jury that the caseworker had pressured her to provide a name, any name, for the father of her child, because she was unwilling to name the OPD chief. Rosenthal objected to the caseworker's discussing Alisha Owen's disclosures on the grounds that a specific statute was very straightforward regarding her confidentiality on the matter, but Case would have none of it. In response to a Moran question, the caseworker testified that Alisha Owen provided a name other than Wadman's when she applied for her daughter's medical assistance, even though the caseworker hadn't required her to provide the father's name. The caseworker also said that social service applicants weren't required to provide the father's name when requesting assistance.

Also on the first day of the trial, Moran called the foreman of the Douglas County grand jury, Michael Flanagan, who was an "administrator" at the Union Pacific Railroad. Rosenthal had deposed Flanagan the previous month, and Flanagan had arrived at the deposition accompanied by Moran. Though Rosenthal had numerous questions for Flanagan during the deposition, he and Moran weren't very receptive to many. Rosenthal had inquired which judge appointed Flanagan to be the grand jury foreman, and, at Moran's insistence, Flanagan wouldn't answer his question. Rosenthal asked Flanagan who wrote the grand jury report, and the latter declined to comment. After Flanagan said he was married and had a twenty-one-year-old daughter, Rosenthal delved into previous conduct that might make him susceptible to being blackmailed or leveraged—he questioned Flanagan about sexual advances he had purportedly made towards a young man who was formerly employed by Union Pacific. Moran snapped, "That's the end of the deposition!" He and Flanagan then stormed out of the room.

As Flanagan took the stand, Rosenthal recalled Flanagan and Moran scurrying from the deposition. Rosenthal felt that Moran most likely knew of Flanagan's purported advances with respect to the young man, because Moran had fired an objection at the deposition after Rosenthal simply brought up the young man's name, and *before* he mentioned Flanagan's alleged sexual advances.

After Flanagan was sworn in, Moran asked him a few general questions about Alisha Owen's appearance in front of the Douglas County grand jury. Flanagan testified that the grand jury "tried to corroborate" Owen's testimony by "calling other witnesses" and by "reviewing the tapes" and the other information that had been submitted to the grand jury.

Moran's examination of Flanagan was quite brief, and then he yielded to Rosenthal's cross-examination. Rosenthal quickly piggybacked on Moran's inquiries regarding Alisha Owen's indictments: "You said you indicted her based on her testimony?" Moran objected, citing the "secrecy oath" of the grand jurors. Rosenthal told Case that Moran had just asked Flanagan about Owen's testimony and subsequent indictments—Case agreed with Rosenthal, and ruled that Moran had already opened the door to that line of inquiry with Flanagan. Rosenthal repeated the question, and Moran objected once more. Rosenthal suggested to Case that Flanagan's previous testimony be read back by the court reporter and Case agreed. Rosenthal again requested that Flanagan answer the question—Moran objected.

"Your Honor," replied Rosenthal, "I think it is very clear now to everybody that he said, based upon her testimony on the tapes, she was indicted." Moran responded with a salvo of "No, no, no!" Moran and Rosenthal then had a few protracted exchanges before Rosenthal said, "I am going to ask him what Mr. Moran opened up." Moran objected, and Case finally came to the rescue and sustained his objection. A perplexed Rosenthal reminded Case that he was merely asking Flanagan questions about the grand jury in the same context as Moran. Case told Rosenthal to go ahead with the question, which Rosenthal repeated. Moran barked out another objection—Case sustained the objection! As Moran quibbled with Rosenthal, Case suggested that the court take a fifteen-minute recess. After the recess, Rosenthal had the court reporter reread the question that had caused Moran so much consternation: "You said you indicted her based on her testimony?"—Rosenthal asked Case if he could proceed with the question. Case said, "You may."

"Now, Mr. Flanagan," inquired Rosenthal, "based on her testimony, then, and your failure to corroborate her testimony, she was indicted?" True to form, Moran objected, but Case overruled his objection. "I don't feel that we failed to corroborate the testimony," Flanagan responded. "We looked at every witness that we felt was available and formed our indictments upon the evidence presented to us."

Rosenthal tossed a few soft questions at Flanagan about the grand jury report, and then he touched on the "over fifty-five exhibits" that were introduced into evidence on the grand jury's last day of deliberation, because he wanted to show that the grand jurors couldn't possibly have given that much evidence careful consideration in one day. Moran objected—Case sustained the objection. Rosenthal attempted to haggle with Case, but the judge was inflexible. So Rosenthal skipped to his next question.

"Isn't it a fact, Mr. Flanagan, that long before July 23, 1990, the attorneys were preparing the indictment against Alisha Owen?" Moran objected on the grounds that Flanagan would be breaking his secrecy oath if he answered the question. When Case sustained this objection, Rosenthal said he had no further questions.

When the court reconvened after lunch, before the jury was called in, Moran brought up a rather bizarre incident to Case—he said that he was walking out of the courtroom and a "fella" asked him if he was "sleeping" with grand jury foreman Flanagan. Moran insinuated that Rosenthal was somehow in cahoots with the man, and Case questioned Rosenthal about the matter—Rosenthal was taken aback: "Your Honor, you know it bothers me when you say that. I don't even know who the hell he is talking about."

In a second bizarre twist shortly thereafter, Moran called a man to the stand who he previously said had committed suicide the week before.

The man's name was Alfie Allen—Alisha Owen told Caradori that Alfie Allen resided at one of the Twin Towers apartments rented by King. The thirty-three-year-old Allen was a flamboyant African-American homosexual, and he sashayed to the stand. Moran inquired if Allen ever lived in the Twin Towers—Allen denied ever residing at the Twin Towers, and also denied ever meeting Alisha Owen. Allen told Moran he had resided in a house near downtown Omaha for the last decade; so surely he hadn't lived at the Twin Towers, but he did acknowledge formerly working at the French Café.

During Rosenthal's cross-examination of Allen, he inquired how many times Allen had been to the Twin Towers—Allen responded, only "once." The FBI had interviewed Allen on his living arrangements throughout the 1980s, and Rosenthal asked Case if could approach the witness to show him the FBI report that was garnered from the interview. Case said, "You may," and Rosenthal walked up to Allen and handed him the FBI report. Rosenthal asked Allen if FBI agent Mott and NSP investigator Phillips had interviewed him. "Yes, that's true," replied Allen.

Rosenthal then read aloud from the FBI report that stated Allen was living in New York City in August of 1983—when Alisha Owen said she attended her first party at the Twin Towers. Rosenthal asked Allen whether or not he told the FBI and NSP that he had lived in New York in August of 1983, contradicting his prior testimony of being stationary in Omaha for a decade. Allen said that he didn't "mean to say" he was living in New York in 1983: He was just visiting—a protracted visit. Rosenthal pressed Allen on the report's wording, and Moran objected—Case sustained the objection.

In response to a Rosenthal question, Allen maintained that he did not know Alisha Owen—Rosenthal mentioned Moran's opening statement where Moran put forth that Owen had previously met Allen in a gentrified, hip section of downtown Omaha known as the "Old Market"—the French Café was located in the Old Market. "Alfie Allen will tell you that he has lived at 29th and Jackson for the last ten years, and he has never had an apartment or hung around in or stayed at the Twin Towers," said Moran in his opening statement. "He at one time—Troy Boner will tell you about this: He did meet this defendant, and he did meet Troy Boner, because he was kind of an Old Market character."

After Allen denied meeting Owen, Rosenthal mentioned Moran's opening statement that suggested Allen and Owen had at least been introduced to each other. Moran objected—he argued that Boner said Allen and Owen had previously met. Rosenthal had the court reporter read the excerpt from Moran's opening statement that touched on the meeting. Moran objected once more on the same grounds.

Case sided with Moran: "That's what that statement says—that Troy Boner was saying that." Rosenthal looked up at Case and huffed, "You are interjecting yourself in this trial." Rosenthal and Case had a number of exchanges on the subject before an exasperated Rosenthal said, "Please, your Honor, I just really object. I just really do, judge. I think you are interjecting yourself so much into this trial that I've got two lawyers I have to fight." Case finally let Rosenthal ask Allen if he agreed with Moran's statement that Allen had met Owen—Allen replied, "No, it is not true."

Rosenthal also questioned Allen about his "dealings" with Larry King—Allen replied that he "had no dealings with Larry King" other than a "casual hello."

On my second Franklin-related trip to Nebraska, I managed to locate Alfie Allen, and he appeared to be free-falling in an abyss of drug abuse—he said he would only talk if I gave him some cash. I opted not to give Allen any cash, and he opted not to open up. Though Allen refused to say much, he did nonetheless clearly imply that his relationship with Larry King went far beyond a "casual hello."

When Rosenthal was presenting the defense's case, he called a witness who was a "service merchandizing" representative for a company that supplied convenience stores with food, toiletry articles, pet supplies, film, etc. The witness testified that a convenience store across the street from the Twin Towers was on his route, and he serviced the store on a weekly basis from late 1983 to early 1984, and then again from late 1984 to April of 1989. He said that Alfie Allen frequently came into the store and bought snack foods, and the two periodically chatted. He also mentioned that he watched Allen "coming and going" from the Twin Towers on numerous occasions.

In Moran's cross-examination of that witness, he focused on the witness' affiliation with Concerned Parents. The witness admitted that he was affiliated with Concerned Parents, but that affiliation didn't change the fact that he had witnessed Allen coming and going from the Twin Towers. Case allowed Moran to explore various tangents regarding the beliefs of Concerned Parents, which Rosenthal objected to as irrelevant. Moran asked the witness, "And you wouldn't come down here and falsify some testimony to try to bolster a sinking ship, would you?" The witness replied, "No, sir, I would not, even if it was a sinking ship." Moran quipped, "It is."

Moran also called a Twin Towers security guard to the stand. He was an elderly white man whose vocal inflection was deep and slow like a locomotive running out of steam. The security guard testified that he had been employed by the Twin Towers for thirteen years and had never set eyes on Alfie Allen. He also told Moran that King only had two parties at the Twin Towers, and the attendees were primarily seniors—people whose ages ranged from sixty to seventy years old—"No young people, no white people was ever at that party."

The security guard's testimony was in stark contrast to an interview he had granted a Caracorp employee a year and a half earlier. According to the Investigative Report, droves of young men who were possibly "teenagers" came and went from the Twin Towers. The Caracorp employee inquired if the security guard ever confronted the young men—he replied that he would occasionally stop them, and they said they were employees of Larry King. The security guard also mentioned that the "young men" never had to sign in.

To further attest to the jury that Alisha Owen hadn't been to sex parties at the Twin Towers, Moran called the Twin Towers' owner to the witness stand—she was a stylish woman in her late forties to early fifties. She testified that she and her husband bought the Twin Towers in 1984—she said that Alan Baer was already renting an apartment at the Twin Towers in 1983, and Larry King started renting a penthouse in August of 1987—he also rented a one-bedroom apartment on the third floor starting in February of 1988. She told Moran that she had never laid eyes on Alfie Allen prior to Moran's introducing him to her that morning.

The owner maintained that elderly and "retired individuals" rented the majority of the Twin Towers apartments when she and her husband purchased the buildings. She also discussed the Twin Towers' "high security" that was manned by security guards around the clock, and she said the entryway doors to the buildings were locked sometime between 6:00 and 7:00 P.M. every night. A second feature of the Twin Towers' unbreachable security system was that each floor had a foyer, and no one would be able to pass beyond the foyer unless they had a key or one of the floor's occupants granted them entry—Moran even provided the jury with a videotape of the Twin Towers' virtually impenetrable security. Moran inquired if it would be possible for anyone who rented an apartment in the Twin Towers to have teenage "sex and drug parties" without the owner's being aware of them, and she said, "With our high security and tenant mixture, no, I would say."

After Moran established that the Twin Towers had a security system ostensibly rivaling that of Fort Knox, Rosenthal began his cross-examination: Rosenthal informed the owner that he had wandered through the Twin Towers the previous night at around 7:00 P.M.—the doors weren't locked and "nobody bothered" him—and he even took Polaroid pictures of his little field trip. He asked her if people were "usually allowed" to wander about the Twin Towers and take pictures at their leisure. She said, "No." Rosenthal then had her leaf through his pictures—she identified the lobbies and the other locations he had photographed.

Rosenthal put forth to the owner that if Alisha Owen wanted to visit a Twin Towers apartment, she merely had to walk through the lobby and into an elevator and press the desired floor, and, after she exited the elevator, she simply had to pick up the phone in the foyer and a Twin Towers occupant could grant her entry—the owner agreed.

When Alisha Owen testified before Van Pelt and company, she said that Larry King's Twin Towers penthouse faced downtown. The owner acknowledged that the penthouse rented by King faced downtown—Rosenthal asked her if King had the penthouse "off and on for a period of time." She replied, "That's correct." Earlier, she had testified that King rented the penthouse for less than a year, starting in August of 1987.

Moran attempted to thrust a final dagger in Alisha Owen's Twin Towers story by calling former Boys Town student Jeff Hubbell to the stand. Owen hadn't seen the twenty-five-year-old Hubbell in seven years, and she was struck by his physical transformation. As a Boys Town student, Hubbell had been cute, svelte, and athletic, but when he took the stand, his hair was receding, his face was pockmarked, and he had a hefty paunch.

On direct examination by Moran, Hubbell confirmed that he had met Owen at a dance, and they had "fondled, kissed, stuff like that." Hubbell testified that he never talked to her again—nor had he ever attended a party at the Twin Towers.

Rosenthal highlighted Hubbell's statement to the FBI where he said he was "drunk" when he met Owen. Rosenthal thought it was rather strange that Hubbell had only met Owen once, and in an intoxicated state years earlier, yet he remembered that night with such clarity, even though he couldn't recall the exact year they met—Hubbell eventually came up with the summer of 1983.

Though Hubbell testified that he and Owen had only one encounter in 1983, Owen had told Gary Caradori that Hubbell was sent to an Omaha drug rehab in 1984—she specified that it had been "Eppley Methodist Midtown Treatment Center." Hubbell confessed to the FBI that he had done a 1984 stint at Omaha's Midtown Methodist Hospital rehab. Rosenthal attempted to shed light on the fact that Owen knew where Hubbell went to rehab in 1984. But when he started to discuss Hubbell's treatment for alcoholism, Moran objected on the grounds of irrelevancy and added that Rosenthal was striving to "embarrass and humiliate" the state's witnesses—Case sustained Moran's objection.

When Rosenthal presented the defense's case, Donna Owen recalled receiving a number of calls from Hubbell. Rosenthal inquired how it was possible for Donna Owen to remember Hubbell's calls, and she said that Hubbell was one of the few young men calling for her daughter over those years who actually left his full name. Donna Owen also remembered driving her daughter to a Kmart so she could buy a bracelet that was engraved with the name "Jeff." She specifically recalled that incident because it went against the grain of her feelings about girls giving boys presents, and she was slightly peeved.

FBI agents Mott and Pankonin were the spearhead in the state's case against Alisha Owen. When prosecutor Moran called Supervising Special Agent Pankonin to the stand, he inquired how Pankonin "became involved with that person, this Alisha Owen." Pankonin told the jury that he reviewed Caradori's videotaped statement of Owen in early January of 1990—he then talked to Owen's attorney, Pamela Vuchetich, who then made all the arrangements for his initial foray to York.

Pankonin summarized his first meeting with Owen, testifying that he gave Owen a general overview of "how a federal investigation was conducted." Moran asked him what else was talked about at the meeting. According to Pankonin, a primary concern of Owen's was Pankonin's clout "to get her out of jail." Pankonin revisited the theme of Owen yearning for a get-out-of-jail-free card throughout his testimony.

Following Moran's lead, Pankonin brought up a letter Owen wrote to her sentencing judge prior to being sentenced on her bad check conviction. At the behest of Owen's public defender, she wrote the letter in an attempt to solicit leniency from the judge. The letter contained a lot of blarney for two reasons: First, Owen was trying to explain the downward trajectory of her life without mentioning Wadman, Baer, or Larry King. Second, Owen wanted a lenient sentence from the judge, so she had written a tale of woe that integrated various falsehoods.

In the letter, Owen wrote that her pregnancy was the result of a "date rape." She also discussed meeting Troy Boner in 1988, and how Boner had coerced her into writing bad checks. She said in the letter that Boner was a cocaine addict, and because she came from a "religious background," she didn't have "firsthand knowledge of drugs" or their "use" or "symptoms."

The letter had been like chum in the water for the grand jury, and it incited a feeding frenzy that devoured large chunks of Owen's credibility. In front of the Douglas County grand jury, Owen had attempted to explain the letter by saying that she hadn't initially met Boner in 1988, but she *did* come from a religious background and hadn't been cognizant of drug addiction until after meeting him. Just like Van Pelt, Moran emphasized the letter, and he had Pankonin explain the various falsehoods it contained.

Pankonin discussed Owen's relationship with Michael Casey too—he discussed Casey's having a large quantity of cocaine and how Owen said she helped him sell it. Agent Mott also elaborated on the fact that Owen had sold cocaine for Casey. Owen actually admitted to this particular drug dealing enterprise in her testimony before the Douglas County grand jury, saying that she had aided and abetted Casey in dealing cocaine when she briefly resided with his friend, because she had a number of contacts that he didn't.

Upon cross-examination, Rosenthal had a number of questions he was eager to pose to the supervising special agent who had overseen the FBI's Franklin investigation. One of his first questions pertained to the FBI's selling Caradori's videotapes to the media—Pankonin denied that the FBI had sold the tapes.

During the pretrial hearing, Rosenthal had asked Pankonin if he phoned Al and Donna Owen on the morning of January 31, requesting that they meet with Pankonin at the Omaha Field Office later in the day, and Pankonin disavowed making the call. Rosenthal now plied him with the same question, and Pankonin said, "I do not recall calling them." Rosenthal also explored Pankonin's telling the Owens that Chuck Phillips wasn't Chuck Phillips, but again Pankonin couldn't "remember" if an NSP investigator was even present at the meeting—then he seemed to "recall" an NSP investigator attending the meeting; he just couldn't recall the name of the NSP investigator in question.

Rosenthal pressed Pankonin about the presence of an NSP investigator upsetting the Owens—Pankonin said that it couldn't have created too much "commotion," because he just didn't recall the Owens voicing their displeasure. Responding to Rosenthal's questions, Pankonin denied that Alisha Owen didn't want to talk to the FBI and that he had threatened to move her to a federal prison out of the state.

In Alisha Owen's videotaped statement to Caradori, she confessed to transporting drugs from California to Nebraska for Alan Baer and Larry King, and she told Rosenthal that Pankonin questioned her about those activities at their first meeting before she even signed her immunity agreement. Owen also alleged to Rosenthal that Pankonin threatened to prosecute her for those offenses if she didn't sign her immunity agreement and grant interviews to the FBI.

Rosenthal questioned Pankonin about his first meeting with Owen at York, and Pankonin denied talking to Owen about her transporting drugs. Rosenthal called Pankonin's attention to his report on their first meeting, which discussed Owen's transportation of cocaine. Rosenthal hoped he could refresh Pankonin's memory by showing him the report, but Pankonin still denied discussing the subject with Owen, replying, "It was mentioned that we would talk to her after she got her immunity."

Rosenthal, in due course, brought up Owen's federal immunity agreement—it stated that "upon request" Owen had to submit to a polygraph. Pankonin agreed that the feds had the authority to mandate Owen take a polygraph, even though he admitted they never requested that she take one. Rosenthal said he felt it was rather odd that the FBI held that Owen wasn't telling the truth, but had never requested she take a polygraph.

Owen's federal immunity agreement also stated that if the government thought Owen wasn't telling the truth, she "will be so informed." Rosenthal asked Pankonin when the FBI informed Owen that she wasn't being truthful. Pankonin said he related his "concerns" to her at their last meeting on April 10. Rosenthal inquired if Pankonin wrote about his concerns in his report on their April 10 meeting—Pankonin replied, "Yes." In actuality, Rosenthal noted, Pankonin made no mention of his "concerns" in his April 10 report.

Rosenthal eventually delved into the set-up call Boner made to Owen from the Omaha's FBI Field Office. Pankonin asserted that the set-up call was merely a test to see if Boner could talk to Owen "directly at the institution." Pankonin offered a second reason too—he said the FBI wanted to probe the "reasons for the inconsistencies between the two."

Rosenthal described Boner's disposition when he phoned Owen: "It is very threatening isn't it?" Pankonin said, "I don't recall that," and Moran objected. Rosenthal asked Pankonin if FBI agents coached or instructed Boner on what to say before he made the call, and, again, Pankonin had amnesia: "I don't recall." Though FBI agents had Boner phone York in an effort to incriminate her, Pankonin insisted that Owen was still a "victim" in the view of the FBI.

After Rosenthal questioned Pankonin about the phone call, he explored the FBI's treatment of victims and suspects in its Franklin investigation. Rosenthal inquired if Pankonin ever interviewed the perpetrators Owen named throughout her videotaped statement to Caradori, and Pankonin said, "I didn't interview any of them." Rosenthal asked Pankonin if any FBI agents had interviewed the men Owen named as perpetrators—Pankonin replied, "They might have, but I'm not sure."

Rosenthal eventually started to ply Pankonin with questions about Alisha Owen's supposed phone call to Boner from Caradori's office shortly before Boner gave his videotaped statement to Caradori. Rosenthal squeezed Pankonin about whether or not the FBI checked out if Owen phoned Caradori's office that day. Moran apparently didn't like that line of questioning—he started firing objections, and Case sustained them.

Rosenthal tried to explain to Case that this particular issue was "deadly important," and he was attempting to establish if the Douglas County grand jury requested that the FBI investigate the phone call—Moran shouted out, "We don't care what you are trying to establish!"

I'm uncertain what Moran meant by "we"—we the state or we as in Judge Case and Moran—but, either way, Case sustained Moran's five objections concerning Rosenthal's inquiries about the phantom phone call.

Special Agent Mott followed Pankonin—Mott didn't have the refinement, fashion sense, or commanding presence of Pankonin, but he made up for his relative shortcomings by spinning quite a yarn about Alisha Owen. He painted such a sordid, pathological portrait of Owen that it was nearly impossible to distinguish her from one of Charlie Manson's harem. While Mott's depiction of Owen became increasingly over-the-top, Rosenthal was prevented from broaching the fact that Special Agent Mott had been Vuchetich's "special agent" too, because Rosenthal would have been thrown in jail for contempt of court.

Mott told the trial jury a rather fanciful tale about Owen's experiences dealing and taking LSD that made her seem a peer of Timothy Leary. He discussed Owen's clandestine visit to an "acid lab," and said Owen took LSD for thirty days straight. He gave the lowdown on an acid deal Owen attempted to put together with the Sons of Silence motorcycle gang: Mott testified that Owen "planned to purchase one hundred sheets of acid" from the gang—each sheet contained "one hundred hits" of acid. Mott then brought his expertise to bear and informed the jury that a "hit was one dosage unit."

Mott's testimony about Owen at her trial corresponded to Chuck Phillips' testimony about Eulice and Tracy Washington before the Douglas County grand jury: Owen and the Washington sisters supposedly made disclosures to the FBI that they made nowhere else—disclosures that made them appear to be delusional liars. Phillips told Van Pelt and company that deceased foster mother Kathleen Sorenson told FBI agents that Eulice and Tracy Washington said Larry King flew them to Paris, New York, Chicago, Washington, DC, California, and Texas. Phillips' account of Sorenson's FBI interview was vastly different from the notes that Sorenson provided to Jerry Lowe.

In addition to exploring Owen's fictitious drug trafficking, Moran delved into the FBI's version of Owen's relationship with Michael Casey. Mott testified that Owen told the FBI that she first met Michael Casey at a political function—Mott then testified that Owen said her second meeting with Casey was at St. Joseph's, and that Casey checked himself into the hospital just to pick her brain about the Franklin affair.

Mott went on to say that after Owen was discharged from St. Joseph's, she informed the FBI, Casey offered to hire her as an "assistant" and teach her the ropes of "investigative reporting"—she was "highly impressed" with Casey's investigative work and accepted his offer. Casey's offer also included room and board at his friend's house. Mott said Owen lived with Casey for three weeks, and it was during this period that Casey really started to pick Owen's brain.

Mott's testimony about the relationship between Owen and Casey, as Owen purportedly related it to the FBI, was vastly different from the version of events she gave to the Douglas County grand jury. There she testified that she first met Michael Casey at St. Joseph's. Mott's version also doesn't make a lot of sense: Owen and Casey were hospitalized at St. Joseph's before the feds even raided the Franklin Credit Union; so it's unlikely that Casey had the slightest inkling of "Franklin" before the closing of the credit union.

After Mott had been testifying ad nauseam about Owen's interactions with the Sons of Silence, drug deals, Michael Casey, etc., Rosenthal interrupted the proceedings and asked Judge Case if the witness could be directed to discuss the years 1983 and 1984, when Owen said she had been a victim of sexual abuse.

"Our argument," Moran responded, "is that she is telling the FBI agents what she thinks they want to hear so that they will, in turn, help her get out of prison because she is a valuable witness." Rosenthal replied, "Well, she was obviously a failure, Judge, because she is still in there." Judge Case allowed Moran's line of questioning to proceed.

Mott spent approximately three hours on the stand answering Moran's questions and imparting the tall tales that he alleged were spun by Owen. At the very end of Moran's examination of Mott, Moran asked him if he attempted to "verify" the information that the FBI had harvested throughout Owen's interviews. Mott said the FBI obtained Danny King's school records from the fall of 1983, and they confirmed he was in Texas when Alisha Owen told Caradori he had attended parties at the Twin Towers. The second piece of verifying information Mott mentioned were Troy Boner's records from a juvenile facility in Iowa—the records showed that Boner had resided at the facility from June 1984 through November 1984. Owen had, in fact, told law enforcement that Boner had spent time in a juvenile facility.

Rosenthal was looking forward to his cross-examination of Mott—he was practically salivating at the prospect of grilling the FBI special agent. But before Rosenthal started his cross-examination of Mott, Moran called Judge Case's attention to a "federal case" that limited cross-examination "to forty-five minutes per witness." He also discussed a Nebraska case that limited cross-examination to the judge's "discretion." Moran's plea was so ridiculous that even Case wouldn't rule on it, and Rosenthal quipped, "We are not going to be done anywhere near forty-five minutes, so I don't need to look at those cases."

Rosenthal continued to explore if the FBI agents ever relayed to Owen that they didn't believe her—Mott was vague and evasive. Rosenthal eventually explained his question in the simplest possible terms—he asked Mott if the FBI agents ever told Owen they couldn't corroborate her story. Mott just wasn't in sync with Rosenthal as he replied, "There were things we attempted to corroborate, and, offhand, I cannot recall any at this minute." Rosenthal restated his question so Mott would give him a yes or no: "Did you ever come back to Alisha Owen and say, 'Miss Owen, we've tried to establish these facts and we can't, we think you are lying to us'?" Mott muttered, "Well, I would say that—" Rosenthal interrupted him and said the question required a "yes or no." Mott finally replied, "Yes ... we did go back at least once." Rosenthal asked Mott when FBI agents informed Owen that they didn't believe her, and Mott again replied, "I can't recall."

Rosenthal amended his question by requesting that Mott answer it to the best of his "recollection," and Mott finally accommodated him: "Unequivocally on the 10th of April." Pankonin had testified during the pretrial hearing that Owen became a suspect only *after* April 10, and Moran maintained that Owen was a suspect only after her grand jury testimony—Mott had just unleashed an inconvenient truth.

Rosenthal had nailed down Mott on April 10, and now he commenced with his second pincer: "Isn't it a fact that the April 10th, 1990, interview has nothing whatsoever to do with 1983 and 1984?" Mott attempted to backpedal, but Rosenthal handed him the FBI's report from its April 10 interview of Owen, and Mott confessed that the dates 1983 and 1984 "do not appear in the report." Mott, essentially, had just told the courtroom that the FBI agents didn't discuss the years Owen said she was abused when they "unequivocally" conveyed to her that they felt she was a lair.

Rosenthal then embarked on a little exploration of the FBI's tampering with evidence—he handed Danny King's federal immunity agreement to Mott and had him look it over. Rosenthal directed Mott's attention to the third page, where it discussed Danny King's sworn statements videotaped by Caradori. The sentence Rosenthal cited read as follows: "You hereby acknowledge that such tapes were made freely and voluntarily and without any promises whatsoever." After Mott read the sentence, Rosenthal handed him Danny King's federal immunity agreement, which was introduced as evidence to the Douglas County grand jury—he pointed out to Mott that the sentence regarding "freely and voluntarily" was deleted from the federal immunity agreement as submitted to the grand jury.

"And without it," remarked Rosenthal, "without that sentence in there, isn't it true, then, that the jury was led to believe that Mr. King's tapes were not made voluntarily and freely?" Mott conceded Rosenthal's point, but denied that the FBI had tampered with evidence. Rosenthal then showed Mott that the same sentence had been deleted from Boner's federal immunity agreement, which also had been introduced as evidence to the Douglas County grand jury—Mott had no idea who might have tampered with Boner's federal immunity agreement either.

After Rosenthal focused on evidence tampering, he skipped to the set-up phone call Boner made to Alisha Owen at the behest of his FBI masters—Mott said Boner claimed he could phone York and talk directly to Owen, and testified that the purpose of the call was to see whether or not Boner had been "leading us astray or giving us the truth" about placing a phone call directly to Owen.

If the FBI simply wanted to determine if Boner could phone Owen at York, Rosenthal asked Mott, why didn't they terminate the call once Owen answered? Mott had suffered a bad case of amnesia when Rosenthal asked him about the call at the pretrial hearing, but his memory of the call was markedly improved now: He said the FBI wanted to "elicit a response" from Owen relative to her counseling Boner on the "stories"—Rosenthal eventually got Mott to confess that the FBI was using Boner to set up Owen.

Rosenthal's next line of questioning with Mott also dealt with phone calls—he introduced Vuchetich's phone records into evidence, even though he realized that he would be flirting with contempt of court. Rosenthal had Mott look over the phone records that showed Vuchetich's 177 calls to the FBI Field Office, noting that one of the calls lasted 132 minutes and that several were approximately 30 minutes in duration. He asked Mott if Vuchetich's calls had been made to him: "I would assume so." Rosenthal attempted to have Mott elucidate the subject matter of the phone calls, but Mott was again stricken by amnesia. Rosenthal pressed Mott on the content of the conversations, and Mott eventually countered, "I have no idea."

But Mott's memory became fully restored when Rosenthal asked him if he ever threatened or coerced Boner to change his original statement to Gary Caradori. Mott gave him a very definitive answer: "No coercion whatsoever." Rosenthal inquired if Boner had ever visited Omaha's FBI Field Office and told the agents he wanted to recant his recantation—Mott maintained that Boner never made such a visit.

Rosenthal brought up the subpoena that the FBI served on Caracorp shortly after Caradori's death, and also Mott's exchange with Sandi Caradori, when Mott allegedly confessed that Boner had visited the FBI Field Office and Mott had said something to the effect that the FBI couldn't waste its time with Boner because he had lost all credibility. Rosenthal asked Mott if he did in fact make that confession to Sandi Caradori in front of Karen Ormiston—once more Mott was stricken with amnesia: "I can't recall."

Mott's amnesia on a number of subjects wasn't an auspicious development for the state, and Moran again raised the issue of a "time limit" on Rosenthal's cross-examination—Moran asked Case if the judge had had an opportunity to read the ruling he'd submitted that put a limit on the duration of cross-examinations. "I can't rule on that, I don't think," replied a befuddled Case. Rosenthal added, "I think we're more interested in justice than in time." Rosenthal responded that since Moran took an entire afternoon with Mott on direct examination, he could certainly spend an entire morning cross-examining him. "So we are even," said Moran. Rosenthal begged to differ—he had long realized that the cards he was being dealt were from a stacked deck: "We are not ever, ever even," Rosenthal replied.

The *World-Herald* had reporters cover Owen's trial every day, and it even provided a daily synopsis of the trial. The *World-Herald*'s reportage on Owen's trial had the same bias that had marked the newspaper's previous coverage of Franklin, and G-man Mott would prove to be the perfect foil for a protracted article: "Agent Michael Mott said he never had encountered anyone who claimed to have as many drug dealings as Miss Owen did during eight interviews with him during February 1990," related the article's second paragraph. The article then went on to trash Owen's credibility from the perspective of different witnesses, including agent Mott's. Under the rubric of "other claims," the article bulleted the drug dealing ventures Owen had supposedly confessed to agent Mott:

• "She once arranged a drug deal on the set of a pornographic movie while in Los Angeles with Boner."
• "She set up a drug deal that involved the Sons of Silence motorcycle gang."
• "She became involved with the Hell's Angels gang."
• "In 1987 and 1988 she made at least three trips to the Los Angeles area to transport cocaine to Omaha."
• "One drug deal involved two Sicilians who spoke French and said they smuggled cocaine into this country in fabric shipments."

- "She and two other people shared a $4,000 profit on one deal."
- "Among the drugs she was dealing were LSD 25, Window Pane and Orange Barrel—forms of the hallucinogen LSD."

The state, of course, called Troy Boner and Danny King to the stand in its campaign against Alisha Owen. The state made the logical choice of calling Boner before Danny King—as had Van Pelt. Boner wore a maroon shirt and blue slacks, and he had put on some weight since he had initially talked to Gary Caradori.

By the time Boner testified in *State v. Owen*, his story had been considerably hemmed and hedged. For example, in front of the Douglas County grand jury Boner gave three conflicting accounts of imparting the hoax to Danny King: Boner testified he conveyed the hoax to King the night before he and Caradori went to King's apartment, he then testified that the hoax was transmitted while he and Danny King were alone in King's apartment for twenty minutes, and finally he testified that he imparted the hoax to King while Caradori filled his gas tank. Danny King told Van Pelt and company that Boner imparted the hoax to him over beers at the Residence Inn. Evidently, the state preferred Danny King's version of events, because Boner's testimony now incorporated King's version.

When Boner testified at Alisha Owen's trial, he definitively said that he gave Danny King a "five minute" overview of the hoax at Danny King's apartment, but he laid out the meat and potatoes of the hoax after Gary Caradori drove them to the Residence Inn, and before Danny King made his videotaped statement to Caradori: He testified that he detailed the hoax to Danny King at the Residence Inn's whirlpool and at the bar over the course of three hours. After the state rested its case, Rosenthal called a "general manager" of the Residence Inn in Omaha to the stand who testified that Lincoln, Nebraska's Residence Inn didn't have a bar.

From the stand, Boner lapsed into a false bravado—Owen had seen Boner display the same bravado when he was stressed out or frightened. He testified that he first met with Caradori because the latter threatened to subpoena him, but Caradori's promises of vast riches ultimately compelled him to make his videotaped statement. Boner portrayed Caradori as naïve, bumbling, and corrupt—Moran had Boner discuss the phantom phone call, and also Caradori's feeding him information before and during his videotaped statement. Boner also testified that the FBI never threatened or coerced him into changing his statement. In fact, they were a swell bunch of guys.

Moran took on the role of dog trainer and Boner acted like a toy poodle—Moran held up a succession of hoops for Boner, and an obedient Boner unhesitatingly jumped through each one. At one point, Moran had Boner cozy up to the microphone, so he could convey an anecdote that Moran described as a "classic." Boner discussed Karen Ormiston's boyfriend making runs to the store for Boner and Danny King—Boner said that Ormiston's boyfriend was initially averse to providing Boner and King with "beer and cigarettes," but Boner threatened to discontinue his cooperation with Caradori and the Committee; so the boyfriend reluctantly made deliveries that included beer, cigarettes, and cat litter.

After Boner had renounced just about everything that was in his videotaped statement to Caradori, and depicted Alisha Owen as a pathological liar, Rosenthal commenced his cross-examination. Boner had spewed numerous lies to the Douglas County grand jury with impunity—now he would have to face a grilling.

Almost immediately Rosenthal started pouncing on the lies Boner had mass-produced for Van Pelt and company. Boner told the Douglas County grand jury that he had turned his wayward life around—he had become a "confident heterosexual," he was attending community college, and he enlisted in the Navy. Rosenthal said he talked to the community college in question and had been informed that Boner was never even enrolled—Boner exclaimed: "That's a lie!"

Rosenthal then started to explore Boner's whereabouts over the years. Though Boner attempted to be cagey, Rosenthal was able to eventually nail Boner on his claim of living in California from March of 1987 to April of 1988—Rosenthal reminded Boner that he had been a patient at Saint Joseph Hospital in August of 1987, and Boner grudgingly agreed: "Then I guess I was there."

Boner then came to the realization that he had ventured to California in 1988 and returned in February of 1989. Rosenthal refreshed Boner's memory from earlier in the day when he had told Moran that he originally met Alisha Owen in the summer of 1988. Moran apparently didn't like the looks of Rosenthal shredding Boner, and he complained to Judge Case that Rosenthal was "arguing with the witness." Moran then said,

"We have beaten this California thing to death." Boner suddenly recalled returning from California in February of 1988 and meeting Alisha Owen shortly thereafter: "March or May, April, May, something."

Rosenthal reminded Boner that he told the FBI he originally met Alisha Owen in July of 1988—he asked Boner how long their relationship lasted, and Boner said, "Just a couple of months." Rosenthal jogged Boner's memory by mentioning that his FBI debriefings noted he had seen Owen on a regular basis through November. Boner ultimately confessed that he had lied to the FBI—a federal felony.

Rosenthal asked Boner if he had ever lived with Owen, and Boner denied that too, prompting Rosenthal to bring up a law enforcement interview with Owen's former landlord that had been submitted to the Douglas County grand jury—the landlord said that Owen and Boner lived together. Boner continued to deny that he had ever lived with Owen.

Rosenthal then began delving into the phantom phone call—Boner said that eighty-percent of the information on Caradori's tapes had come from Owen via the phantom phone call. Boner revealed to Rosenthal that he took notes during the call—Rosenthal directed his attention to his grand jury testimony, where he had said he didn't take notes. Rosenthal asked Boner which account was true—Boner responded that he took notes.

Rosenthal inquired who placed the phantom phone call—Boner testified Caradori made the call. Rosenthal again directed Boner's attention to his testimony before the Douglas County grand jury—Boner initially told Van Pelt and company that Caradori made the call, but he then explicitly amended his answer and said Owen phoned Caracorp. Once more, Rosenthal asked Boner which account was true—Boner couldn't recall.

Rosenthal disclosed to Boner that he had the phone records for Caracorp the day of the phantom phone call, and the phone records showed that no calls were placed to or from York on that particular day—Boner said that the phone records were "incorrect." "If there was no phone call," Rosenthal inquired, "then you didn't learn all of this from Alisha Owen, did you?" Boner fired back: "But you see, there was a phone call, and I did learn this from Alisha Owen!"

Boner said that his first meeting with the FBI was on March 12—Rosenthal held up his federal immunity agreement, which was signed on March

8, and Boner suddenly remembered that his first meeting with the FBI was March 8–he recalled his second meeting with the FBI was on March 12. In a comeback to Rosenthal's questions, Boner declared that he had stuck to his guns about his statements to Caradori throughout his first and second FBI interviews.

Rosenthal told Boner that he made the set-up call to Owen on March 9, sparking Boner to have an epiphany that he had recanted his story by then. Boner eventually admitted to Rosenthal that the FBI wanted Boner to "entrap" Owen, which contradicted the prior testimony of both Pankonin and Mott. Rosenthal pointed out to Boner that Owen simply told him to tell the truth seven times during the March 9 phone call. Boner also admitted to Rosenthal that he told a number of lies to Owen during the phone call, including that he had yet to talk to the FBI.

Referencing Boner's Douglas County grand jury testimony, Rosenthal nailed Boner in lie after lie. Boner testified to the grand jury that he was employed by a temporary agency–Rosenthal subpoenaed the agency's records, which showed it never employed Boner. Though Boner testified to the grand jury that he last had sex with Alan Baer in 1986, at Alisha Owen's trial he said his last dalliance with Baer was in 1984. Boner told the Douglas County grand jury that he watched part of his videotaped statement to Caradori; however, he denied watching any portion of his videotapes at Alisha Owen's trial.

Rosenthal asked Boner if Alisha Owen ever mentioned suing the perpetrators or other third parties–Boner replied, "I don't remember if she did or not." Rosenthal then called Boner's attention to his Douglas County grand jury testimony where he said, "Oh, she was going to sue everybody."

Rosenthal brought up the fact that Alisha Owen discussed Alan Baer quite a bit when she gave her videotaped statements to Caradori, and Boner contended he gave her the lowdown on Alan Baer, because Owen had never met Baer. Rosenthal reminded Boner that he told the grand jury he never furnished Owen with information about Alan Baer–Boner stated that he had made a "mistake."

Rosenthal touched on the phone calls Boner placed to Sandi Caradori after the death of her husband and youngest son. Rosenthal made an effort to rekindle Boner's memory about his conversation with Sandi

Caradori, when he said her husband hadn't acted with duplicity, and he confessed to being coerced into changing his story. Boner responded to Rosenthal's question just like a seasoned FBI agent: "I don't remember saying that."

As Rosenthal attempted to jog Boner's memory about the call, Boner became extremely agitated and started talking about the "pressure." Rosenthal asked Boner who was pressuring him. Boner replied "nobody"—"It's just a sense of pressure, you know, a sense of pressure." Rosenthal again asked Boner who was pressuring him. Moran objected, and Boner called Rosenthal a "jerk." Judge Case didn't even admonish Boner for his outburst, but Rosenthal was undaunted.

Rosenthal posed the same question from a slightly different perspective: He asked Boner if Sandi Caradori would be lying if she testified that Boner told her he had been threatened and coerced into recanting the videotaped statement he gave to her husband. Boner suddenly had total recall of the conversation: "If she testifies and says that I said that, she is lying."

Rosenthal next inquired about Boner's phone call to Sandi Caradori on the day after he stopped by Omaha's FBI Field Office to recant his recantation—the phone call where he told Sandi Caradori that the FBI agents he confronted laughed in his face. Boner adamantly denied both visiting the FBI and telling Sandi Caradori that he had.

Rosenthal also touched on Boner's visit to Senator Schmit's office the day before Caradori's funeral. Boner recanted his recantation in Senator's Schmit's office to at least eight people. Rosenthal pressed Boner on his visit to Schmit's office and asked him if he recanted his recantation, and Boner replied, "I don't remember if I did or not." Rosenthal was eventually able to make Boner concede that he visited Schmit's office, even though Boner had told the *World-Herald* that he never set foot in Schmit's office. Rosenthal also made Boner concede that he had lied to the *World-Herald*.

When the state rested its case, Rosenthal had Sandi Caradori testify about Boner's recanting his recantation to her over the phone shortly after her husband's death. Rosenthal also called the Caracorp employee, Robert Nebe, who gave Boner a ride to Schmit's office—he testified that Boner recanted his recantation. Rosenthal then called three people who were at Schmit's office that day, including Schmit himself, and all three testified that Boner recanted his recantation.

At one point during Rosenthal's cross-examination of Boner, Rosenthal referred to Moran as Boner's lawyer—Moran was deeply offended. "No wait a minute!" he barked. "Number one I am not his lawyer." Moran then made a rather impassioned plea to the judge that bordered on a soliloquy: "He is making it sound like I am somehow bringing these witnesses here and fashioning the testimony—I am not. I work for the people of the state of Nebraska, and not Troy Boner or Danny King or anyone else." An obtuse Case didn't grasp Rosenthal's jibe, and he actually sided with Rosenthal on the subject. "I don't think that's really a misrepresentation when he calls you his lawyer," said Case, "because you are the one who called him as a witness originally." But Moran was having none of it: "I am an attorney for the state of Nebraska—I am not Troy Boner's attorney!"

In addition to Moran's taking offense at the intimation that he was Boner's lawyer, he seemed to be flustered by Rosenthal's cross-examination of the state's witnesses. After Rosenthal spent the afternoon skewering Boner, and Case recessed court for the day, Rosenthal still had more than a little unfinished business with the witness. But the following morning, Case called Rosenthal into the judge's chambers: Both he and Moran were waiting there, but Case did all the talking. Case showed Rosenthal three cases where a time limit on cross-examination was upheld, and he instructed Rosenthal that he could only cross-examine Boner until the morning break at 10:30 A.M. Rosenthal argued that Boner was a "very important witness," and he didn't feel that time limitations should be imposed on him when he was cross-examining important witnesses. But Case wasn't receptive to Rosenthal's pleas.

Though Rosenthal had become accustomed to Judge Case siding with Moran, he nonetheless decided to discuss a ruling Case had made the previous day that he thought was patently unjust. Rosenthal had attempted to bring up the issue that Boner had a long history of drug addiction. Moran had objected on the basis of relevancy, and Case sustained the objection. Rosenthal now told Case that the issue was extremely germane: Boner was taking methadone and several courts had ruled that drug addicts are notoriously "unreliable" witnesses, because their perceptions are distorted by the drugs themselves, and they're also more susceptible to coercion. Case was unmoved, ruling Boner's drug addiction to be "irrelevant."

By the time Boner stepped down from the stand, Rosenthal had snared him in numerous lies—I've mentioned a rather limited litany. The next witness called by the state was Danny King, who was noticeably frightened and tentative as he took the stand. He wore a plaid shirt and blue jeans to court. Boner was a brain trust compared to Danny King, so Moran's direct examination was short. Pamela Vuchetich continued to represent King as he testified that Owen's statements regarding Larry King, Wadman, Baer, etc. were nothing but lies.

Rosenthal's cross-examination of Boner had been like shooting fish in a barrel, and he also impeached Danny King's testimony with relative ease. Boner told Moran and the jury that he imparted the hoax to Danny King over the course of three hours at the Residence Inn, but Danny King testified it only took two hours for Boner to impart the hoax. Rosenthal asked Danny King if it took two hours or three hours, and King replied, "I'm not sure." Rosenthal handed Danny King a copy of his Douglas County grand jury testimony and then called his attention to where he said that Boner imparted the hoax to him in an hour. Rosenthal inquired if it took one hour, two hours, or three hours for Boner to convey the hoax. "If I had to make an estimate," said King, "I would say an hour and a half to two hours."

As Rosenthal pored over Danny King's grand jury testimony with him, King started to experience amnesia, a common affliction among the state's witnesses. Moran eventually accused Rosenthal of conniving to "humiliate" the state's witnesses—he added that Rosenthal's line of questioning had "absolutely nothing to do" with the case of Alisha Owen. Rosenthal replied that he was merely questioning Danny King about his grand jury testimony—he said if the grand jury deemed the subject matter relevant, he should be permitted to delve into it. Case ruled that he didn't "see the relevancy" of Rosenthal's line of questioning.

Rosenthal returned to the day Danny King initially met Caradori—he had King reiterate that he and Boner had hit the Jacuzzi at the Residence Inn before King made his videotaped statement. Rosenthal inquired if

King brought a pair of swim trunks to the Residence Inn—King said Caradori just happened to have a pair of swim trunks at the hotel, and Caradori had lent King the trunks. Rosenthal asked King if the swim trunks fit him, and King replied that they were a "little big."

Rosenthal questioned King about whether or not Boner relayed to him that Boner had talked to Alisha Owen prior to their statements to Caradori—King couldn't remember. Rosenthal again called King's attention to his grand jury testimony where he related that Boner didn't tell him he had spoken to Owen. Rosenthal then asked King if Boner told him they would acquire bountiful riches via lawsuits—King said, "Yeah." Rosenthal inquired whom Boner said they would sue, and King gave him a succinct, unflinching answer: "Alan Baer and Larry King." Rosenthal reminded King that in his testimony to the grand jury King said Boner never informed him who would be the target of their lawsuits.

Rosenthal eventually switched gears and explored Danny King's interviews with the FBI—he asked King if FBI agents emphasized to him that he didn't have to tell them the same story he conveyed to Caradori. King replied that the FBI just stressed that he tell the "truth." After King had decided to come clean with the FBI about the hoax and become "totally honest," he purportedly told Special Agents Mott and Culver that Boner made a surreptitious, nocturnal jaunt from Lincoln to Omaha to clue him in on the hoax. Though King just couldn't remember making that statement to the FBI, Rosenthal showed Danny King the FBI report, and he suddenly recalled both making the statement and Boner's nocturnal jaunt.

Rosenthal also questioned Danny King about his friendship with Alisha Owen—King maintained that he only met her on three occasions and their interactions only lasted for a couple of hours. Rosenthal refreshed King's memory with his Douglas County grand jury testimony—King testified to the grand jury that he and Alisha Owen had taken a trip to California. Rosenthal got King to admit that a trip to California takes more than a couple of hours. "And, at most," queried Rosenthal, "didn't you tell the grand jury you knew her one week?" Danny King responded with a "Yeah." Rosenthal asked, "That wasn't true was it Danny?" King replied, "I'm not sure."

Rosenthal asked King if Boner ever informed him that he and Owen had decided to marry, and King replied, "No, never." Rosenthal called

King's attention to his grand jury testimony—King testified that Boner told him that he and Owen were tying the knot. Rosenthal questioned King about the veracity of that particular statement—King said it wasn't true. Rosenthal inquired why Danny King would not tell the truth to the grand jury on such a relatively straightforward issue, and a befuddled King said, "I must have got mixed up on that question."

As Rosenthal shredded King's credibility, Moran decided to play the improper impeachment card once more. Moran acknowledged that King had answered Rosenthal's questions "inconsistently" with his prior statements, but Rosenthal wasn't giving him "an opportunity to explain what he meant by his answer." Case jumped on Moran's bandwagon, and ordered Rosenthal to read King's prior statements and ask him if he had made such a statement.

Over the years, I've looked high and low for Danny King, but he had become so marginalized, I found it impossible to unearth a viable paper trail on him. I finally hired a private investigator who managed to collar him. King and I talked on the phone, and two hours later I found myself at his fiancée's Omaha apartment.

King gave me a genial, yet guarded, reception at the apartment's front door—he was now thirty-seven years old, but at first glance he looked strangely similar to the twenty-year-old that Caradori had videotaped in 1989. He still had shoulder-length hair, and a blanched, boyish face, even though he had put on probably twenty or so pounds—he still spoke with a guttural rasp. Though King's face retained a certain boyishness, as I took a closer look, and we made eye contact, I could see the grooves that years of addiction had prematurely carved on it.

After King checked me out, he invited me into his fiancée's apartment— she was a portly, blonde woman from Eastern Europe who struggled with major mental health issues. Danny King was unemployed, and they lived on the dole. Their apartment had odd smatterings of threadbare furniture, and it was absolutely filthy. As I stood between the kitchen and the living room, King's fiancée opened up the refrigerator door—I caught a whiff of the open refrigerator and thought it was in my best interests to decline a soda or even a glass of water.

By the time I found myself sitting next to Danny King on a dirty aqua-blue couch, I had made contact with numerous people who were reportedly enmeshed in the underlying events or the cover-up of Franklin, and they generally gave me one of three responses: They told me they were involved and provided details; they said they weren't involved in Franklin and/or hadn't lied for law enforcement; or they simply refused to talk to me.

As it turned out, Danny King more or less fell into his own category: He told me that he had attended sex parties at the Twin Towers, alleged that the FBI threatened him with perjury charges if he didn't recant his allegations about being sexually abused, admitted that he lied at Alisha Owen's trial, and stated that Paul Bonacci was a permanent fixture at the Twin Towers pedophilic parties. He corroborated Owen, Boner, and Bonacci down the line except, oddly, when it came to Larry King: He fingered Alan Baer as a pedophile, but he refused to accuse Larry King. In fact, he maintained that he had never met Larry King.

Danny King had made a number of definitive statements about Larry King to Gary Caradori, and I had trouble squaring up his current denials with his admissions on just about everything else. I reminded him of the fact that he had told Caradori that he passed out while drinking with Alan Baer and Larry King, and woke up handcuffed to a chair with Larry King hitting him in the face with his penis. King replied that he had been handcuffed to a chair in Baer's Twin Towers apartment, but it was Baer and someone else who handcuffed him to the chair when he passed out. I attempted to probe whether or not he was telling the truth about Larry King, but he was adamant that Larry King wasn't involved.

As we talked, it appeared to me that untold molestations and years of drug and alcohol abuse had left Danny King little more than a shell of a human being. Unbelievably, he didn't even remember testifying before Van Pelt's grand jury. He remembered testifying at Owen's trial, but his only memories were of Rosenthal's cross-examination.

In the aftermath of the Douglas County grand jury, and before Owen's trial, Pamela Vuchetich had told the *World-Herald* that she planned to pursue a $200,000 molestation civil law suit on behalf of Danny King against the lone pedophile named by the grand jury. But King said that he never saw Vuchetich, or the FBI agents for that matter, after he testified at Alisha Owen's trial. Danny King had served his purpose, and it seems he was discarded like gum that had lost its flavor.

As I drove away from Danny King's apartment, I was perplexed that he had come clean about everything except his involvement with Larry King. The following day, I was slated to meet one of Larry King's reported "henchmen," who told me, over the phone, he had "nothing to hide," and he was willing to meet with me. I had previously reached out to two of King's reported henchmen, but they weren't at all interested in talking to me; I was most interested in finally talking to one. When I phoned him the next day, he related various details of my conversation with Danny King the previous day, and then he refused to meet me. The notion that Danny King knew one of Larry King's minions, without knowing the man himself, was difficult for me to swallow.

The grand jury had called two witnesses from Owen's past—Darlene Hohndorff and Steve Solberg—who knew nothing of her teenage detour into darkness. Hohndorff and Solberg had made very disparaging statements about Owen to the Douglas County grand jury that severely impugned her credibility, and Moran yet again took a page from Van Pelt's playbook and also called Hohndorff and Solberg to testify against Owen. Solberg was on the list of former friends and lovers that Vuchetich had Owen compose, the list she later released to the NSP and FBI.

Alisha Owen and Darlene Hohndorff had been friends as children—their parents attended the same church, and Owen and Hohndorff also attended Temple Christian Academy together throughout grade school. Owen and Hohndorff drifted away from each other in junior high school as Owen surrendered to her shadow life.

Owen became reacquainted with Hohndorff when they had a chance meeting on a bus in 1986 and exchanged numbers. Both Owen and Hohndorff graduated from high school that year, and they hung out a handful of times that summer. They would see each other intermittently before Owen fled Nebraska in 1988 and eventually ended up in Colorado. After Owen returned from her ill-fated flight to Colorado, she moved in with Hohndorff for a month or so in May and June of 1988. Owen opted to move in with Hohndorff because Hohndorff wasn't aware of her past, and, with the exception of Troy Boner, her past wasn't aware of Hohndorff.

Hohndorff testified to the Douglas County grand jury from the perspective of someone who had known Owen since "preschool"—she said

Owen was a liar and an all around bad egg. Moran quickly piggybacked on Hohndorff's grand jury testimony and used Hohndorff to make Owen appear as a tart. He plied Hohndorff with questions about how many "boys" Owen slept with in the summer of 1986, but Hohndorff couldn't remember. Moran then called Hohndorff's attention to her Douglas County grand jury testimony: She told Van Pelt "based upon the things" that Owen said to her, Owen had sex with "around ten to fifteen people" in the summer of 1986. After Hohndorff's memory was refreshed, she suddenly became crystal clear on the fact that Owen had sex with ten to fifteen guys that summer.

When Moran asked Hohndorff if Owen ever mentioned the names of Larry King, Robert Wadman, Troy Boner et al. during the summer of 1986, Hohndorff replied with a "No" to each of the names except for Boner. She acknowledged meeting Boner in the summer of 1986. But when Moran questioned her about Boner again, she replied, "No, that was probably later on."

Rosenthal found it relatively easy to make mincemeat of Hohndorff's testimony. Before the grand jury, she claimed to have had a friendship with Owen during high school, but she now testified that Owen graduated from Benson High School when, in fact, she graduated from Central High School.

Then, in an about-face, Hohndorff testified that she and Owen didn't renew their friendship and pal around until after both had graduated from high school in 1986. Rosenthal pointed out to Hohndorff that her statement to the grand jury regarding Owen telling Hohndorff the name of her child's father in high school had been false, because their friendship wasn't renewed until after they graduated from high school. Moran objected on the grounds that Rosenthal was characterizing the statement as false.

Rosenthal recycled the question by asking Hohndorff which of her two statements was true: She and Owen didn't pal around in high school or Owen disclosed the name of her child's father to Hohndorff in high school? Moran objected on the grounds of improper impeachment— Judge Case sided with Moran. Rosenthal attempted to outflank Moran and Case by breaking the question down into its two separate components. He asked Hohndorff if her testimony to the grand jury about

Owen's divulging the name of her child's father was true—Hohndorff answered, "Yes." Now he asked Hohndorff about her previous statement regarding her and Owen reacquainting themselves with each other only after they graduated from high school. "I don't remember," she replied. "I thought we were still in high school."

After Hohndorff's last bout of amnesia, Moran made a few guttural sounds before firing up an objection: "Huh-uh, huh-uh, I am going to object to this as arguing with the witness, and now he is misstating the evidence on direct examination." Rosenthal complied with Moran's wishes and withdrew the question, but Moran was still piqued: "I don't care if he withdraws it!" barked Moran. "I want him to be ordered to stop doing this to the witness!" Case backed up Moran and rebuked Rosenthal: "Well, in order to maintain order here, you are going to have to limit those kinds of questions."

"That are damaging, you say," Rosenthal sarcastically rejoined.

The grand jury had been hard pressed to come up with an explanation of how Alisha Owen knew so much about Alan Baer until Hohndorff testified. Hohndorff testified to the grand jury that Alan Baer and Alisha Owen attended the same church. Hohndorff mentioned that she had personally seen Baer at Owen's church on various occasions and seemed to imply that Baer assisted Owen in landing a job. Hohndorff's testimony concerning Baer was outlandish, given that Baer was Jewish and had never set foot in Owen's church.

As Rosenthal questioned Hohndorff about Baer, Moran fired off eight objections. Apparently, Hohndorff had been filled in about Baer's being Jewish, because she backpedaled and said that she had met a second Alan Baer at Owen's church. In one of the trial's noteworthy moments, Rosenthal played "What's My Line"—he gazed into the audience and requested that the real Alan Baer stand up, and, in fact, he stood up. Hohndorff then confessed to seeing a different "Alan Baer" at Owen's church. Considering that the FBI had purportedly threatened to murder Baer if he cooperated with the Franklin Committee, it was quite remarkable that he showed up at Alisha Owen's trial and actually helped her out. Rosenthal hoped that Baer's gesture wouldn't be lost on the jury.

One of the many apparent falsehoods Hohndorff had told the grand jury was that Alisha Owen called Hohndorff "from outside the state of

Nebraska" to tell her she was traveling with "Michael Casey"—Hohndorff testified to the grand jury that Owen "was working for him on some sort of newspaper or something like that." She reiterated basically the same story to Moran. Hohndorff pinpointed the call to early 1989—Owen had been incarcerated for at least four months when Hohndorff claimed she was junketing with Casey.

The next witness the state resurrected from the Douglas County grand jury was twenty-six-year-old Steve Solberg—he had dated Owen some years earlier. The two had started dating when Solberg was nineteen years old and Owen was fifteen. He now wore a pricey dress shirt, tie, and crisp slacks.

With Moran's guidance, Solberg too would spin quite a yarn about the wicked Alisha Owen. Almost immediately, Moran had Solberg imparting anecdotes of Owen's depravity. Solberg said that the first night he met Owen was at a high school football game in the fall of 1983—though he couldn't remember the high school. He told Moran and the jury that he attended the game with his girlfriend, and Owen was with a couple of friends who were acquainted with his girlfriend. After the game, a group that included Solberg and Owen went to a pizza parlor.

Moran asked Solberg if "anything of an unusual nature occurred" at the restaurant. Solberg testified that Owen was sitting across the table from a young man, and she took her shoe off and began "fondling" his "testicles" underneath the table with her foot.

Moran moved Solberg to his second "encounter" with Owen: Solberg testified that he was in a mall arcade, playing a video game, when Owen crept up behind him, reached between his legs, and "grabbed ahold" of his testicles. He also said that a friend, Rick Southwick, had accompanied him to the arcade—Owen had her cousin in tow, and the foursome decided to see a movie. All four bought tickets for the movie, but they collectively decided to bypass it and proceed to the home of Southwick's parents.

Solberg informed Moran and the jury that he and Owen paired off and had "sexual intercourse" in Southwick's bedroom while Southwick and Owen's cousin made their way to Southwick's parents' bedroom. Solberg told Moran that after he and Owen had sex, Owen insisted that they jump into bed with Southwick and Owen's cousin. Solberg maintained that he and Owen watched a little television and had sex again. Afterwards, Solberg and Southwick gave Owen and her cousin a ride to Owen's parents' house.

Solberg related to Moran that he dated Owen "three or four times a week" from January of 1984 through May of 1984, even though he alleged to the grand jury that he saw Owen "practically every day." Moran then had Solberg convey anecdote after anecdote about his and Owen's sex life. Solberg said that he ultimately decided to end their relationship due to Owen's extreme freakiness. Moran also recited a list of Franklin's cast of characters and Solberg replied that Owen hadn't mentioned a single one. Moran asked Solberg if Owen could have attended parties at the Twin Towers while they were dating—Solberg contended that they often spent weekends together, and she couldn't have possibly been able to sneak off to parties at the Twin Towers.

Rosenthal wasted little time pouncing on the discrepancies between Solberg's testimony to the Douglas County grand jury and at Alisha Owen's trial. In response to a Rosenthal question, Solberg said that after his first tryst with Owen at the home of Southwick's parents, he and Southwick gave Owen and her cousin a ride to Owen's house around midnight. Rosenthal reminded Solberg that he explicitly told the grand jury that he had dropped Owen and her cousin off at a supermarket about a half-mile from the Owen household.

Solberg testified to the Douglas County grand jury that he picked up Owen from high school "always on Wednesday" between 1:00 and 1:30 P.M.—Owen told Gary Caradori that she and Wadman frequently rendez-voused on Wednesday afternoons. Before the grand jury, Dougherty implied that Owen's regular Wednesday afternoon assignations were partly based in reality, but they involved Solberg and not Wadman; Moran would make the same intimation.

Rosenthal spent considerable time deconstructing Solberg's accounts of his Wednesday afternoons with Owen. He asked Solberg if he ever actually entered Central High School when he picked up Owen on Wednesdays, and Solberg replied that he entered Central High on one occasion. Solberg testified to Van Pelt and company that after he wandered into Central High to meet Owen, she introduced him to her drama teacher.

Solberg also testified to the grand jury that Owen's drama teacher was a man and that Owen claimed to be having sex with him—Rosenthal told Solberg that Owen's drama teacher was, in fact, a woman. Moran objected on the grounds that Rosenthal was questioning Solberg on a "collateral matter"—an objection Moran was becoming fond of making.

Undeterred, Rosenthal started to make inquiries about Solberg's meeting Owen's drama teacher—Solberg was stricken with amnesia. As Solberg's amnesia became more acute, Moran began rattling off objections—Case also failed to see the relevancy of Rosenthal's questioning Solberg about the drama teacher. Rosenthal peered up at Judge Case and commented that Moran interviewed the witnesses "ad nauseam" about Owen's sexual mores, but "the minute I try to see whether they are really truthful, I get stopped."

Rosenthal argued that his questions were designed to gauge Solberg's "credibility"—Case's response was either one of astonishing obliviousness or mendacity: He said "it seems" Solberg had made the "same" statements to both the grand jury and during his current testimony. A bewildered Rosenthal replied that Solberg conveyed one thing about Owen's drama teacher to the grand jury and now "he doesn't remember"—Case sustained Moran's objection.

As Rosenthal continued to question Solberg about his Wednesday afternoon liaisons with Owen, Solberg testified that he and Owen had sex on all of their Wednesday get-togethers. Rosenthal introduced an FBI interview of Solberg into evidence wherein Solberg told FBI agents that he and Owen didn't have sex every Wednesday afternoon—Solberg denied making that statement to the FBI.

Solberg said that he occasionally dropped off Owen at her church after their Wednesday afternoon trysts, because she had to attend a church activity. Rosenthal asked Solberg to provide a time frame when he delivered Owen to church on Wednesdays—Solberg replied between 3:30 P.M. and 4:00 P.M. Rosenthal responded that Owen had choir rehearsal on Wednesdays, but her rehearsals didn't start until 6:00 P.M.

On direct examination, Solberg testified that he often gave Owen a ride back to her house on Wednesday afternoons, where they would have sex in Owen's room or her parents' room—he specifically noted that her parents had cable TV at the time. Rosenthal asked Solberg additional questions about the Owens' home and its furnishings, and he mentioned they "may have" had a computer in the family room.

When Rosenthal called Donna Owen to the stand, she testified that Wednesday afternoons were the busiest day of the week for her, and she seldom ventured outside the house on Wednesdays, nor had she ever met Solberg—she also testified that the Owens didn't have cable TV or a computer until May of 1984. She provided an invoice from July of 1984, when the Owens initially had cable installed, and also a receipt from January of 1986, when they purchased their first computer. Both were entered as evidence, refuting Solberg's testimony.

Rosenthal now delved into the exact nature of Solberg and Owen's relationship: In addition to portraying Owen as a floozy, Solberg told Moran that their primary bond was simply sex. But Rosenthal called Solberg's attention to the various "mementos" he kept from his 1984 relationship with Owen: a robe, bracelet, and love letters. Solberg confessed to Rosenthal that he had held onto the mementos even after he married. After Rosenthal discussed the mementos Solberg had retained from his relationship with Owen, he suggested to Solberg that his relationship with Owen had been much more than sexual and that he had "feelings and emotions" for her—Solberg agreed.

Solberg had implied that he broke up with Owen because she was kinky, but Rosenthal contended that their relationship ended because Solberg had "stepped out" on Owen—Solberg denied Rosenthal's contention. Rosenthal then mentioned the name of a girlfriend of Owen's, and Solberg confessed that he had sex with her on two occasions. Though Solberg testified that he never laid eyes on Owen after 1987, Rosenthal produced the receipt from a hotel where Solberg and Owen had spent a night in 1988.

I've talked to both Hohndorff and Solberg and asked them if they were coerced into testifying before the grand jury, and also at Owen's trial—both had unpublished numbers, and they didn't seem particularly enthusiastic about talking to me. I found Hohndorff to be fairly amicable—she told me about FBI intimidation, but fell short of saying she was coerced. Conversely, Solberg was quite hostile while denying FBI coercion. Solberg started dating Owen when he was nineteen years old and she was a fifteen-year-old; he also had a second skeleton in his closet that possibly made him susceptible to coercion. When I brought up these two indiscretions, he became exceedingly hostile, denied he had been coerced, and hung up the phone.

After Rosenthal finished his cross-examination of Solberg, Case recessed court for the day. Rosenthal then asked Moran whom he would be calling to the witness stand the following morning and Moran said, "I don't know." The last utterance the court reporter recorded was Rosenthal saying to Moran, "You know who you are calling."

Rosenthal assumed that Moran would be calling Rick Southwick, Solberg's friend, as the first witness; but the next morning Moran threw a curveball at him—he called a different witness. Though Rosenthal had carried out extensive research on this witness, he had left that particular file at his office, which was ten minutes from the courthouse. Moran claimed that he told Rosenthal to call him at 8:00 A.M.—Rosenthal replied that he was en route to the courthouse at 8:00 A.M. Rosenthal implored Case to let him hop in a cab and grab the file, but Moran wouldn't think of it, and Judge Case backed Moran.

Rosenthal realized Moran's game plan at about 8:50 A.M., and he appealed to Case—a discussion among Case, Rosenthal, and Moran on the issue was eventually held in the judge's chambers. "Your Honor," pled Rosenthal, "it is now 9:15. If I had been allowed to leave the courthouse at 9:00, I would probably be back to the courthouse by now." Rosenthal called Case's ruling an "injustice" and "highly prejudicial to the defendant." Rosenthal made one final appeal to Moran's sense of justice: "You owe something to the defendant—whether your office believes it or not." But Moran just wasn't fazed, "I owe nothing—let's go."

After this, the hostility between the two attorneys escalated to a scalding boil—Moran demanded that Rosenthal not talk to him directly. At one point in the trial, Rosenthal requested to approach Judge Case, and he turned to Moran and asked him if he also wanted to approach the judge about the matter at hand. "He is talking to me again, Judge!" snarled Moran. "I don't want him doing that!" Rosenthal replied, "I'll write to him." The humor appeared to have been lost on Moran.

Rosenthal had a great veneration for law, but he felt that the tandem of Moran and Judge Case was making a mockery of the judicial process he so revered. Donna Owen remembers that Rosenthal once turned towards her with tears welling up in his eyes and whispered, "This isn't the law that I love."

The state would ultimately call three of the alleged perpetrators who were singled out in Owen's perjury indictments: Douglas County Judge Theodore Carlson, Robert Wadman, and Harold Andersen. The first to be called was Carlson—Owen alleged to Gary Caradori and the Douglas County grand jury that Judge Carlson had molested her during a Saturday afternoon reception at the French Café. She said that Larry the Kid coerced her into meeting Carlson in the basement of the French Café, where she performed oral sex on him. Owen recalled that the incident occurred shortly after her fifteenth birthday, and she concluded it most likely happened on the first or second Saturday in October of 1983. She also discussed a second encounter with Carlson at the Starlite Motel.

Caradori showed Owen small, stock portraits of the Douglas County judges, but Owen didn't recognize Judge Carlson from the pictures. She told both Caradori and the Douglas County grand jury that Judge Carlson's name was never disclosed to her, but she learned it through a chance encounter a few years after their last rendezvous at the Starlite Motel: She maintained that she was in the basement of the Douglas County Courthouse, waiting in line to pay a speeding ticket, when she saw Judge Carlson emerge from an elevator—he was wearing a suit and carrying a briefcase.

She said that his sudden appearance startled her, and she couldn't prevent herself from staring at him, with her "mouth hanging open," as he walked by her. Owen testified to the grand jury that the person ahead of her in the line moved forward, but she felt like she was in a state of suspended animation while she gazed at Carlson. Finally, a woman behind her suggested that she move up in the line, and Owen gestured toward Carlson and asked the woman if she knew his name—the woman replied that the man in question was Judge Theodore Carlson.

Van Pelt and Moran contended that Owen had gleaned the various details and intricate nuances regarding the men she named as perpetrators or pedophiles from various sources. The state would have been hard pressed to explain how Judge Carlson ended up in the "script" had it not been for Owen's informing Caradori that a fellow prisoner at York had purportedly bribed Carlson.

Owen told Caradori that she knew an inmate at York who had committed vehicular homicide while intoxicated, and Carlson had been her sentencing judge. The inmate divulged to Owen that she had befriended a drug dealer who had the clout to float Carlson a bribe via a lawyer he knew. The inmate claimed that the drug dealer talked to the lawyer, and then the drug dealer relayed to the inmate that it would cost her $2,500 if she wanted her case fixed. The drug dealer put up the $2,500 and the inmate, a pharmacist, allegedly ripped off a cache of narcotics from the pharmacy where she was employed to compensate the drug dealer. Carlson nonetheless sentenced her to a year in prison—she spent four months at York.

The Douglas County grand jury called the inmate to testify, and she essentially related the same story she had told to Owen. The grand jury then subpoenaed the drug dealer, the lawyer, and, of course, Carlson, and all three disavowed the inmate's story, even though the lawyer confessed to having the drug dealer as a client. Van Pelt gave the inmate immunity for ripping off the cache of narcotics from the pharmacy. Both the grand jury report and Moran declared that Owen fingered Carlson to exact vengeance for the inmate.

When Owen appeared in front of the Douglas County grand jury, she had difficulty gauging Judge Carlson's height, but she finally settled on "closer to five-ten." She testified that Carlson was in his forties, with dark hair, and about fifty pounds overweight; she also mentioned that he had a "roll" of a paunch and "bird legs." She pointed out that she could tell he wore glasses, but he never wore them during their encounters. Owen also testified to the grand jury that Carlson said she had a "nice mouth," but she wasn't his "type." Owen felt Carlson had homosexual tendencies, because he allegedly didn't fondle her breasts, had anal sex with her, and he called out a boy's name when they were having sex.

When Carlson made his appearance before the Douglas County grand jury, he didn't have any problems accounting for his whereabouts on the first or second Saturday afternoons in October when Owen alleged his abuse. His Saturdays were completely consumed by Nebraska football—he lived and breathed Nebraska Cornhusker football, or "Big Red" as Nebraskans affectionately call the team. "Well, like everybody else, I think, in Nebraska," Carlson told Van Pelt, "I'm kind of a nut, Big Red fan, and I go down and yell and holler and scream and wear my red sweater at Nebraska football games."

On the first weekend of October, Carlson told the grand jury, he and his wife were at the University of Nebraska's stadium in Lincoln, watching "Big Red" demolish Syracuse University. Though the game was a blowout, Carlson said he didn't mind "lopsided" games—he and his wife stuck around to the very end. On the second weekend of October in 1983, he "distinctly" remembered Big Red playing Oklahoma State University in Oklahoma: He listened to the game on the radio as he and his wife drove out to a "barbecue" sponsored by Senator Loran Schmit—every year Senator Schmit sponsored a bash for the state's senators, judges, mayors, county commissioners, etc.

Prior to calling Carlson, Moran had called two other judges to the stand who attended Schmit's 1983 bash on the second Saturday in October. The state evidently felt that Carlson being corroborated by two judges would give him an ironclad alibi—both judges acknowledged seeing Carlson at Schmit's.

On the stand at Owen's trial Carlson vehemently denied taking bribes and molesting Alisha Owen. Moran told Carlson that Owen claimed that one of their encounters occurred in the first or second week of October at the French Café between 1:30 P.M. and 4:00 P.M.—Carlson reiterated that he was in Lincoln, watching Big Red wallop Syracuse on the first Saturday in October. On the second Saturday afternoon in October, Carlson testified, he and his wife drove to Schmit's barbecue, and he listened to the Big Red game on the radio—Carlson gave Moran the score of the game and even recapped a few of the highlights.

On cross-examination, Rosenthal eventually inquired why Owen would possibly implicate him as one of her abusers. Carlson replied that he had pondered that very question, and he cited the explanation promulgated by the grand jury report and also the media—she wanted to get out of jail and garner money from the writing of a book. Rosenthal asked Carlson how Alisha Owen had come up with a fairly apt description of him. Moran objected to the question as calling for speculation, and Judge Case sustained the objection.

Rosenthal asked Carlson if he received special treatment from Van Pelt and the grand jury, and Carlson replied, "No, I didn't." Carlson then confessed to a probing Rosenthal that he had a conversation with Van Pelt prior to his grand jury appearance, and Van Pelt had advised him to retain a lawyer. "Your attorney advised you," pressed Rosenthal, "did he not, that you were to check your calendars for October of 1983 and April of 1984?" Carlson's initial response was "No," but then he said that he and his lawyer accounted for "certain areas and times" after his attorney had talked to Van Pelt.

Rosenthal then read a question Van Pelt put to Carlson before the grand jury: "Prior to your coming in here today did your attorney advise you that I asked him for you to check your calendar for October of '83 and April of '84?" And Carlson responded to Van Pelt, "Yes that was my understanding from my lawyer." So Rosenthal plied Carlson with the same question about double-checking October of 1983 and April of 1984, and Carlson answered, "That apparently is correct."

Now, Rosenthal embarked on a line of questioning about Big Red football, and weekends in October of 1983. Rosenthal asked Carlson if he simply went down to the *World-Herald* and looked up articles on the 1983 Husker games when his lawyer informed him that Van Pelt would question him about Saturday afternoons in October of 1983—Carlson denied Rosenthal's contention.

After Carlson rejected Rosenthal's allegation, Rosenthal questioned him about the Huskers game on the fourth Saturday in October of 1983, when Big Red played Colorado—Carlson clearly remembered that the Huskers scored forty-eight points in the third quarter. Rosenthal backtracked on Moran, and quizzed Carlson about the Huskers game on the first weekend in October of 1983—Carlson replied that it had been "a blowout" against Syracuse. Rosenthal then decided to play Husker trivia with Carlson, who presented himself as an expert witness on Nebraska football: He asked Carlson where the October 7, 1984 game against Oklahoma State was played—Carlson wasn't sure. Rosenthal inquired about the score—Carlson couldn't provide it.

Rosenthal requested that Case allow him to question Carlson further about Husker football, but Moran was absolutely opposed—he said, "Oh, no, you can't, because it is improper cross-examination!" Rosenthal started to say that he was merely testing Carlson's credibility, but he was cut off by Moran: "No, no, no! It is a card trick!" Rosenthal argued that Carlson should have an easier time remembering facts about more recent games.

Both Case and Moran began bombarding Rosenthal with rebuttals about playing Husker trivia with Carlson. Rosenthal again said that he simply wanted to test Carlson's credibility, because, after all, Carlson was a self-proclaimed "football nut" and "he knows everything about the Big Red." Moran interjected the "collateral matter" objection once more, and Judge Case ultimately ruled that Rosenthal could only ask Carlson questions about Big Red's 1983 season.

Rosenthal felt that he had made his point, and he moved on to question Carlson about his outing at Senator Schmit's on the second weekend of October in 1983. Carlson testified that he left Omaha around 11:30 or 11:45 A.M. and arrived at Schmit's between 1:00 and 1:15 P.M. Rosenthal told Carlson that one of the judges Moran called had testified to pulling up at Schmit's "shortly after 4:00 P.M.," and listening to the "last four or five minutes" of the game—he also testified that Carlson pulled up to Schmit's at approximately the same time. The second judge testified that he arrived at Schmit's around 4:00 P.M. or shortly thereafter, about fifteen or twenty minutes after the game was over. He further testified that he thought Carlson arrived fifteen to thirty minutes after him—he recalled talking to Carlson about how close "the game had been." When Rosenthal called Schmit to the stand as a witness for the defense, Schmit testified that nobody arrived at his place before 4:00 P.M.

After Rosenthal edified Carlson about one of his fellow judges testifying that Carlson didn't arrive at Schmit's until after 4:00 P.M., Carlson evidently realized he had to change his tune a bit—he testified that he left Omaha "around 12:30, 1:00, 12:30, something like that."

Carlson testified to the Douglas County grand jury that he arrived at Schmit's in the midst of the game and that he had been peeved because Schmit hadn't provided a radio for the Big Red fans to listen to the game, noting that he and another judge periodically strolled over to their cars to grab updates on the game. He had attempted to tell the same story at Alisha Owen's trial, but he now provided a variation on the theme—people were standing around their cars with the car doors open to catch the game.

If Carlson arrived at Schmit's after 4:00 P.M., when the game was in its waning minutes or was over, he had perjured himself to the Douglas County grand jury, and did so again at Alisha Owen's trial. He stuck to a story that Senator Schmit and two of his fellow judges had attested was a fabrication—it takes approximately two hours to drive from Omaha to Schmit's Bellwood home; so Carlson had not accounted for his time on the afternoon when Alisha Owen accused him of molesting her.

The two judges who essentially testified that Carlson was spinning a fabrication were witnesses for the state and called by Moran, who must have realized that Carlson's account wasn't jibing with their accounts. When attorneys present testimony they know to be false, they are guilty of the crime of suborning perjury. Regarding the testimony of Troy Boner and Danny King at Alisha Owen's trial, Rosenthal suspected Moran of suborning perjury, because their testimony was riddled with so many lies—even without their later recantations. But in the case of Judge Carlson, Rosenthal definitely felt that Moran had suborned perjury.

Robert Wadman was the second of Owen's alleged abusers that Moran called to the stand—Wadman had left the OPD in October of 1989, signing on as the Police Chief of Aurora, Illinois that same month. Naturally, Wadman said that he had never molested Owen, and he denied ever meeting her in 1983 and 1984.

Moran had Wadman illuminate a 1973 shooting incident when Wadman took a bullet in his left arm, working undercover for the feds in New Mexico. Wadman went on at length about the many operations on his left arm—he also mentioned that his left arm was severely handicapped, and the subsequent surgeries had left extensive scarring. Moran previously had a physician testify that Wadman suffered from a fifty-percent disability of his left arm, and introduced pictures of Wadman's left forearm and hand into evidence.

Wadman had told Van Pelt and company that his left arm and hand were so disabled from the shooting that he had to button his shirtsleeves with both hands and then slip his arm through the sleeves. When Owen described Wadman's anatomy to Caradori and the Douglas County grand jury, she hadn't mentioned that Wadman's left arm was scarred or handicapped—Owen's whiffing on Wadman's arm was the primary rationale that the grand jury report cited to demonstrate that she had never met Wadman, and for indicting her on the statements she made pertaining to him.

Rosenthal began his cross-examination of Wadman by discussing the photographs of Wadman's left arm and hand that the state had introduced into evidence—he told Wadman he was "having a terrible time seeing any scar in those photographs." After Rosenthal commented on the pictures of Wadman's arm and hand, he directed Wadman's attention to the application he filled out when he applied to become the OPD Chief. The application asked Wadman if he had any serious injuries, and he wrote—"Shot left arm 1973, okay now." Rosenthal inquired if Wadman was being truthful when he wrote his arm was "okay now" on the application—Wadman said, "Yes, sir."

Rosenthal also pointed out that the physician who examined Wadman before his appointment as OPD Chief noted that Wadman had only a "10% loss of rotation of upper forearm," and wrote that Wadman was in "general good health" too. So Rosenthal quickly dispelled the notion that Wadman's left arm was severely disfigured and handicapped.

Owen told the Douglas County grand jury that Wadman regularly had a "dark" handgun when she would meet with him, and alleged he had actually inserted the gun into her vagina on one occasion. Testifying before the grand jury, Wadman said that he hadn't "carried a gun" since his days as a federal agent. Rosenthal knew better though, because he'd acquired a 1980 deposition where an attorney deposing Wadman commented on a pistol Wadman was wearing in his "waistband."

Rosenthal asked Wadman if he had, in fact, packed a gun after being a federal agent, and Wadman replied: "Well, I've periodically carried a gun since then, yes." Rosenthal reminded Wadman of his grand jury testimony, and he had Wadman read his grand jury statement to the courtroom: "I don't carry a gun. I've never carried a gun from the time I was a federal agent." Wadman attempted to mince words, but Rosenthal pressured Wadman on whether or not he made that statement to the grand jury— Wadman finally coughed up a "Yes." Wadman even confessed to owning a blue-steel, thirty-eight revolver while residing in Omaha.

Owen had told the Douglas County grand jury that Wadman brought a gym bag to their encounters, and that he played racquetball, but Wadman testified to Van Pelt and company that he never carried around a gym bag or played racquetball. Again, Rosenthal knew better, and he asked Wadman if he played racquetball, and Wadman replied, "No sir, I don't." Rosenthal piped, "Never have?" Wadman then confessed to playing racquetball a "couple of times," but it wasn't something he did "regularly"—he then quickly amended his answer: "I probably played three times in my life."

Rosenthal inquired when Wadman played racquetball, but Wadman couldn't recall. Rosenthal jogged Wadman's memory a bit, and Wadman conceded that he had played racquetball when he had been the OPD Chief. Rosenthal mentioned to Wadman that racquetball is a two-handed game—Wadman said, "I don't know." Rosenthal made a point illustrating how one hand held the racquet while the other hand dropped the ball; Wadman finally responded with a "Yeah." Rosenthal also commented on Wadman's coaching his sons in baseball, football, and basketball—Wadman acknowledged that he used both hands when coaching his sons.

When Moran was questioning Wadman on direct examination, Wadman testified that he had submitted blood for DNA testing in conjunction with Alisha Owen and her daughter, and the DNA test confirmed that he wasn't the father of Owen's child. A DNA test was certainly incontrovertible evidence that Wadman hadn't fathered Owen's child, and it should have been game, set, and match for the state; but for some inexplicable reason the state didn't introduce the DNA test into evidence. If the state had introduced the test into evidence, it would have been in the public record and accessible to the scrutiny of anyone.

The *World-Herald*'s former publisher, Harold Andersen, was the last of the alleged perpetrators named in the indictments against Owen whom Moran called to the stand. Though Andersen had stepped down as the publisher of the *World-Herald* in 1989, he still sat on the newspaper's board. During direct examination by Moran, Andersen absolutely repudiated Alisha Owen's allegations about his affinity for boys.

Rosenthal brought up Andersen's long-standing relationship with Larry King and his role on Franklin's advisory board. Andersen said he had been affiliated with the credit union since the early 1980s. Rosenthal cited Andersen's grand jury testimony, in which Andersen stated that he only became aware of King's homosexuality through an *Omaha World-Herald* article in 1989. An incredulous Rosenthal asked, "You had never been aware of it before that?" Andersen responded with a resounding "No."

On Friday June 7, after three weeks, thirty-five witnesses, and scores of exhibits, Moran and the state rested their case. The following Monday morning at 9:00 A.M., Rosenthal met with Moran and Case in the judge's chambers. Rosenthal had a long list of reasons for Judge Case to dismiss perjury charges against Owen or, at the very least, declare a mistrial.

As Rosenthal conversed with Moran and Case in the judge's chambers, he was very tired because he hadn't slept well the night before. But he was keyed up nonetheless—he felt he had found the smoking gun that proved out-and-out that the Douglas County grand jury had been a travesty of justice and that his client should be exonerated. But before Rosenthal unfurled his newfound revelation to Moran and Case, he offered the following reasons for Judge Case to declare a mistrial:

• The state's use of confidential material plundered from Owen's Social Services records.
• The state's use of confidential material plumbed from Owen's Presentence Probation Report.
• The Court's refusal to accept the motions Rosenthal submitted to Case on May 1.
• The vague wording of Owen's grand jury indictments.
• Misconduct on the part of Van Pelt and company that "destroyed the impartial administration of justice."
• Misconduct by Owen's previous attorney, Pamela Vuchetich, who provided state and federal law enforcement with various communications—both written and verbal—that were unlawful for the state to use against Owen, because Owen had at no time waived her attorney-client privilege.
• The state's use of information obtained by the NSP and FBI that was involuntary, coerced, and obtained without a competent counsel, violating Owen's right against self-incrimination.

Judge Case didn't seem to be particularly moved by the reasons Rosenthal cited for declaring a mistrial, so Rosenthal revealed his new discovery: He told Moran and Case that the Caradori videotapes shown to the grand jurors had been "doctored"—much of the content in Troy Boner's videotaped statement that corroborated Alisha Owen's statement had been deleted.

Case had allowed Rosenthal to take the videotapes submitted by the grand jury home over the weekend, and Rosenthal had watched them until "way early in the morning this morning." Rosenthal said he had a copy of Caradori's original, undoctored videotaped statements, and he suggested that "we"—he, Moran and Case—watch both sets of tapes so he could point out where the videotapes had been altered. In addition to having Caradori's original, unedited tapes, Rosenthal had a synopsis of the tapes written by FBI Special Agent Culver the previous January, shortly after the Franklin Committee surrendered the tapes to state and federal law enforcement, and Culver's synopsis of the videotapes included details that weren't on the tapes shown to the Douglas County grand jury.

Rosenthal insisted that the indictments against Owen should be dismissed after he demonstrated to Moran and Judge Case that the videotapes watched by the Douglas County grand jurors had been doctored. But Moran wasn't receptive to Rosenthal's proposal, and said, "What he is saying is a lie. No one has doctored up any tapes unless he has done it himself." Moran's response didn't take Rosenthal by surprise—Rosenthal replied that he wasn't "casting stones" at Moran or law enforcement, but he was certain the tapes that went to the grand jury had been altered.

Judge Case didn't grasp exactly what Rosenthal was putting forth and its implications, so Rosenthal explained it to him a second time. Case responded that maybe Franklin "Committee members" could have doctored the tapes. Rosenthal said that he didn't know who altered the tapes, but they had surely been altered, and again he suggested that he, Moran and Case watch Caradori's original videotapes and the tapes that had been provided by the grand jury. Case balked at Rosenthal's suggestion, but Rosenthal was undeterred, saying he would show the jury both sets of videotapes. Rosenthal's latter comment seemed to spark the ire of Moran: "Oh, no, you are not!" Case backed up Moran.

Rosenthal asked Judge Case why he couldn't play both sets of tapes for the jury, but, before the judge responded, Moran interjected, "Because the *State versus Packett* says that if someone gets up and recants a prior recorded statement, then it is not relevant, and I've got the case—it's a Nebraska case."

Rosenthal argued that the grand jury used "illegal evidence to bring about the indictment"—"Everything that corroborates Alisha Owen has been cut out of the grand jury tapes, and that's the only thing I want to show," said Rosenthal. Rosenthal's latter statement led to Rosenthal and Moran bickering back and forth as Case silently looked on. Moran—and not Case—seemed to rule on the matter: "*State versus Packett* says you can't, so."

Judge Case suddenly jumped in and told Rosenthal that his concerns were "pretrial stuff"—Rosenthal asserted that he had a "right to rely" on the grand jury not tampering with evidence. Case asked Rosenthal where he acquired original copies of Caradori's tapes, and Rosenthal replied that they had come from Sandi Caradori. Case then insinuated that Sandi Caradori was up to no good! "What's her part in this?" Case subsequently raked Rosenthal with questions about Sandi Caradori—a befuddled Rosenthal replied, "I don't know what you are trying to ask me?" A dubious Judge Case inquired how Sandi Caradori suddenly came up with original copies of her late husband's tapes. Rosenthal responded that she had kept material left over from her husband's investigation.

After Case implied that Sandi Caradori somehow, some way played a deceptive role in the emergence of her late husband's original video-tapes, he again made the point that Rosenthal should have realized that the tapes had been doctored earlier in the trial—Rosenthal, once more, countered with the assertion that he had a "right to rely on" the grand jury or law enforcement not to tamper with evidence.

Rosenthal fought to hold his ground against Moran and Case, and he pleaded for justice: "It goes to show that the indictment, your Honor, is just wrong, and should be dismissed." Moran then accused someone in Rosenthal's office of accidentally erasing the tapes! Rosenthal replied that he certainly wouldn't erase the parts of the tapes that corroborated his client.

Moran eventually declared that Rosenthal's contention was merely "wishful thinking"—Moran described the thoroughness of the Douglas County grand jury and commented that Rosenthal was "not looking at reality to consider or suggest" that someone had "doctored the tapes." Both Case and Moran suggested that Rosenthal could bring up the issue on appeal, but Rosenthal wasn't buying it: "We are entitled to a fair trial, Judge," he said. "That's what we are entitled to without bothering about appeals."

After further bickering, Moran recycled his accusation that the tapes were recently erased: "This couldn't have happened last night, could it? Could somebody have accidentally hit the erase button?" Rosenthal still attempted to present a professional decorum as he responded to Moran's accusation: "I've been trying to be very charitable with you, counselor." Moran shouted at Rosenthal, "Don't be!" Rosenthal reiterated that he wouldn't erase the statements from the videotapes that corroborated his client.

After an hour or so, Moran went on a diatribe in which he spewed that "everybody connected with this case is paranoid" and "everyone connected with this case believes that the truth means absolutely nothing—it is the cause that's important and they will lie. They will phony up evidence." Did Moran have any idea of just how much truth was encapsulated in his *ad hominem* appeal to Case?

Rosenthal and Moran eventually argued to a stalemate on the admissibility of the grand jury's doctored videotapes being admitted into evidence at Owen's trial, and Case didn't make a definitive ruling about their admissibility. But the battle plan for both sides had been drawn up—Rosenthal would attempt to introduce the doctored tapes, and Moran would counter with *State v. Packett*.

Rosenthal had talked about the state tampering with evidence earlier in the trial when he demonstrated that the immunity agreements of Danny King and Troy Boner were altered before they were presented to the Douglas County grand jury. The doctored videotapes weren't an exception to the rule—they were yet one more example of what appeared to be widespread taint and corruption.

Ironically, the loophole that Moran planned as a barricade against Rosenthal showing the doctored videotapes to Owen's jury was a decision of the Nebraska Supreme Court that upheld a conviction against a perpetrator: Larry Packett, in *State v. Packett*, abducted a woman at gunpoint and before he had an opportunity to sexually assault her or, perhaps, even murder her, she leapt out of his moving truck and notified the police about the kidnapping.

Packett claimed he had an alibi when the woman alleged he abducted her—he was at a service station purchasing gas and having his tractor batteries charged. The service station owner gave a recorded interview to law enforcement stating that Packett was at his gas station while the abduction occurred. The service station owner also told authorities that he was called on by a salesman after servicing Packett, but the state showed that the salesman had visited the service station at least an hour before the owner said Packett had left the service station. On the stand, the service station owner couldn't recall exactly when Packet left the service station.

Packett appealed his guilty verdict on the grounds that the service station owner had given law enforcement a recorded statement that Packett's trial judge had ruled was inadmissible. But the Nebraska Supreme Court found that Packett's judge hadn't erred when he ruled that the tape was inadmissible, because the recanting witness had an opportunity to "explain or deny" his prior statements and Packett's attorney had the "opportunity to interrogate the witness" making the recantation. Moran's invocation of this precedent to justify barring evidence that the Caradori videotapes shown to the grand jury had been doctored is nothing short of voodoo jurisprudence.

As Rosenthal presented Owen's defense, he called a number of witnesses to the stand whom I've already mentioned: Sandi Caradori, Senator Schmit, Donna Owen, and Caracorp employee Robert Nebe. Rosenthal also threw a curveball of his own by subpoenaing Chuck Phillips to testify. Rosenthal had a little more business with Phillips—a few questions regarding the doctored videotapes.

Rosenthal asked Phillips if he had ever watched Caradori's videotaped statements of Owen, Boner, and Danny King—Phillips said that he had watched the videotapes in January 1990 at the NSP's headquarters in Omaha. Rosenthal then handed Phillips a synopsis of the videotapes prepared by FBI Special Agent Culver, which included an unedited account of Boner's original statement to Caradori—Phillips acknowledged reading the synopsis. A little later in his testimony, he said he had not read it!

Rosenthal started pointing out details in Culver's synopsis that weren't in the videotapes provided by the grand jury, but he had yet to mention the videotapes—Moran cut him off and made a beeline straight for Case without first seeking Case's permission. Standing in front of the bench, Moran told Case that Rosenthal shouldn't be raising the issue of the videotapes in front of the jurors, and Case reprimanded Rosenthal for "bringing that out in front of the jury," even though Case had yet to make a definitive ruling on the matter.

Rosenthal sidestepped the predicament by saying he was merely asking Phillips about Culver's synopsis of the tapes. Rosenthal next asked Phillips if he had delivered Caradori's videotapes to the Douglas County grand jury—Moran objected. Judge Case sustained Moran's objection: "This is exactly what you went over this morning, and I haven't ruled on it yet." Rosenthal responded that he was just asking Phillips who delivered Caradori's videotapes to the grand jury—Phillips confessed to transporting Caradori's videotapes from the NSP office in Omaha to the grand jury.

After Phillips confessed to being the custodian of the videotapes, the jury was dismissed for the day and Rosenthal and Moran squared off— Rosenthal told Case he wanted to enter the grand jury's edited videotapes into evidence. Moran objected: "They are irrelevant, and I would like to remind the court of the State v. Packett, which I presented to you." Judge Case cocked his head downward, read from the State v. Packett decision, and ruled that the doctored videotapes were inadmissible.

Case signing off on this move demonstrates that the trial of Alisha Owen wasn't concerned about whether or not child abuse had occurred—it was only concerned with putting Owen in prison for perjury. Rosenthal wandered out of the Douglas County Courthouse that night exhausted and heavy hearted—Alisha Owen was handcuffed and taken back to the Douglas County Jail, where she cried late into the night.

The defense took a huge, demoralizing hit when Moran and Case shot down Rosenthal's attempt to show Owen's jury that the grand jury's videotapes had been doctored. But Rosenthal knew he still had an ace up his sleeve concerning the phantom phone call: Caracorp's phone records and York's phone log. He had attempted to introduce Caracorp's phone

records into evidence earlier in the trial—Moran, however, had strenu-
ously objected, usually on the grounds of relevance, and Case invariably
sustained Moran's objections on the matter. Rosenthal finally called an
employee of Lincoln Telephone Company as a witness to enter Caracorp's phone records into evidence without an objection from Moran—
Lincoln Telephone was Caracorp's local and long-distance provider.

Prosecutor Moran was evidently aware that he couldn't stave off
Rosenthal from introducing Caracorp's phone records into evidence for-
ever, so he cooked up a theory: The cunning Gary Caradori had used an
MCI or maybe an AT&T credit card that was obtained under a fictitious
name, and the bill was delivered to an unknown address or post office
box. Though Moran had absolutely no evidence to bolster his theory,
he extensively questioned the Lincoln Telephone employee about it.
Caradori just couldn't catch a break: The state originally portrayed him
as bumbling and incompetent, but to account for the phantom phone
call, he was now sly and crafty enough to set up a fictitious credit card
account that had even eluded the FBI.

As Rosenthal cross-examined the state's witnesses, Moran's game plan
had been to barrage him with objections—Rosenthal was consequently
kept on a very short leash concerning the questions he could ask the
witnesses called by Moran. Conversely, Case gave Moran considerable
latitude when he cross-examined Rosenthal's witnesses. In addition to
brutalizing Rosenthal's witnesses with verbal brass knuckles, Moran questioned them about matters that were far afield of Owen's case.

Robert Nebe was the Caracorp employee who gave Troy Boner a lift
to Senator Schmit's office five days after Caradori's death. After Rosenthal called Nebe to the stand, he testified about Boner's recanting his
recantation while they were en route to Schmit's office.

Moran then had a chance to work him over, and inquired if Nebe assisted Caradori, "in the investigation of the so-called Franklin child-abuse
allegations?" Once Nebe responded with a succinct "Yes," Moran started
firing questions at him that were designed to flesh out his theory about
Caradori's acquiring credit cards under a pseudonym. He asked Nebe
if Caradori had "false IDs"—Rosenthal piped, "Just a minute." Moran
retorted, "No, not just a minute"—Judge Case also chastised Rosenthal,
"Don't talk to him about just a minute!" Nebe replied that he wasn't

"aware" of Caradori using false IDs. Moran then questioned Nebe about "dummy corporations" that Caradori had possibly set up.

Moran eventually broached the subject of Michael Casey, and Casey's relationship with Caradori. Nebe acknowledged that Caradori had contact with Casey, but he wasn't sure about the extent of their contact. Moran asked Nebe if he knew the Hollywood producer Casey had coaxed to Nebraska—Nebe replied that his name had come up in the course of Caradori's investigation. Moran questioned Nebe about the "meeting" Caradori had with Casey and the Hollywood producer at the Cornhusker Hotel in Lincoln—Nebe said he hadn't discussed the meeting with Caradori.

Moran then insinuated that Caradori kept "two sets" of investigative reports—one set of reports included "everything that a witness said" and a second set that would "leave out or omit" anything that didn't jibe with Caradori's "theory" of child abuse—Moran contended that Caradori submitted the latter set of reports to the Franklin Committee. Again, Nebe replied that he wasn't aware of Caradori's having a second set of investigative reports.

After Moran implied that Caradori falsified his investigative reports, he questioned Nebe about Caracorp double-billing the Committee. Finally, Rosenthal had heard enough—he objected on the grounds that Moran's cross-examination was "way beyond the scope" of Nebe's testimony about giving Boner a ride to Schmit's office. Moran's response to Rosenthal was unflinching: "When he puts a witness on the stand, he does so at his peril!" Judge Case backed up Moran on the matter, and Moran battered Nebe with the "double billing" question once more—"No, not to my knowledge," Nebe told Moran.

Case gave Moran carte blanche to flail away at Nebe, and Moran's questions concerning Caradori were so far-fetched that Nebe found it difficult to provide reasonable answers, allowing Moran to assault Caradori's character with impunity.

The following day, Rosenthal called Senator Schmit to the stand, and Schmit testified that Boner had recanted his recantation in Schmit's office, and he also testified that Judge Theodore Carlson arrived at his annual barbecue well after Carlson claimed. Moran then had an opportunity to target Schmit with the same vitriol that had been hurled at Nebe.

Moran initially cross-examined Schmit on his prior testimony to Rosenthal, but then began firing question after question about Schmit's financial interests in "video slots." Rosenthal objected as "clearly immaterial," and again Moran barked: "When he puts a witness on the stand, he does so at his peril!" Judge Case was consistent too—he overruled Rosenthal's objection. Moran also embarked on a bizarre Q&A in which he attempted to link Schmit to a far-right fringe group—Rosenthal objected to this as "irrelevant," and Case overruled that objection. Rosenthal eventually voiced an "ongoing objection" to Moran's tactics with Schmit.

The next morning, Rosenthal met with Case and Moran in the judge's chambers. Rosenthal was a bit miffed, and he made a motion for a mistrial, because in the wake of an ongoing objection Case had allowed Moran to interrogate Senator Schmit regarding his interests in "video slots," "his association with various organizations," and other matters that were "clearly irrelevant" to Owen's perjury trial, even though they were "highly prejudicial" to her. Case ruled that Moran's cross-examination was a litmus test for Schmit's "credibility" and overruled Rosenthal's motion.

Alisha Owen was the last witness called by Rosenthal—she wore a pink suit, a white blouse, and a pastel chiffon bow in her hair as she stepped up to the witness stand. After a handful of questions on Owen's background, Rosenthal questioned her about meeting Jeff Hubbell at a dance in late August of 1983. Owen testified that her parents had given her and a girlfriend a ride to the dance, and she had planned to spend the next two nights at her girlfriend's. She said she met Hubbell at the dance, and Hubbell asked her if she wanted to "go out with him that weekend"—she gave Hubbell the number at her girlfriend's house, and he phoned her the following afternoon. She agreed to go out with Hubbell that night; he and Larry the Kid dropped by her girlfriend's place, picked her up, and they eventually made their way to the Twin Towers.

When Owen made her first videotaped statement to Gary Caradori, she recalled Hubbell and Boner picking her up at her parents' house. Prior to the night Caradori initially videotaped Owen, she hadn't detailed her adolescent shadow life to anyone, and she certainly didn't think Caradori's interview would be so thorough and in-depth. So she had some difficulties cutting through the haze of her drug-addled adolescence and remembering the precise details of specific nights seven or eight years earlier. However, Owen's months in seclusion at York had given her an opportunity to really mull over her early adolescence—she alleged to the grand jury that Hubbell and Larry the Kid gave her a lift to the Twin Towers that first night, and she stuck by this at her trial, though conceding she had been wrong about the detail of where they picked her up.

Upon further questioning by Rosenthal, Owen mentioned that Larry the Kid had a key to the foyer door after they exited the elevator. The descriptions she provided to Rosenthal of the party, and the people who attended the party, were consistent with the descriptions she gave Caradori and also the grand jury. She said she drank, smoked pot, and played the "501 game" at the first party, but she didn't engage in any overt sexual acts. Owen said that Hubbell and Larry the Kid gave her a ride back to her girlfriend's around 1:00 A.M.

Owen called Larry King's henchman "Larry the Kid"—Bonacci called him "Larry the Enforcer" and Danny King talked about him too. Before Caradori died, he had come to believe that Larry the Kid was most likely an African-American male named Larry Walker who was a DJ at The Max. Rosenthal found out that Larry King had rented an apartment for Larry Walker, and I've interviewed someone who was acquainted with Larry Walker—he alleged to me that Walker was a drug dealer and pedophile.

Owen testified that the next party she attended at the Twin Towers was either the following Friday or Saturday night. She originally told Caradori she thought Troy Boner gave her a ride to that party, but now she remembered Hubbell and Larry the Kid again giving her a lift—she also discussed losing her virginity to Boner that night. She was consistent about losing her virginity to Boner when she attended her second Twin Towers party in her testimony to Caradori, the grand jury, and at her trial. Owen told Rosenthal that her third party at the Twin Towers in September of 1983 marked her initial sexual encounter with Chief Wadman. Owen told Caradori that she performed oral sex on Wadman at the third party, but, when testifying before the grand jury and at her trial, she said that Wadman disrobed and fondled her at the third party. She testified that she performed oral sex on Wadman at the Twin Towers, but that it was during a later encounter.

Rosenthal then questioned Owen about her alleged Wednesday afternoon encounter with Wadman at the French Café, and she essentially recounted the same events she had related to Caradori and the grand jury: Larry the Kid phoned her and said that Wadman felt "bad" about how he had treated Owen the previous weekend: He wanted her to pick out a dress at Brandeis & Sons and meet him at the French Café at 2:00 P.M. the following Wednesday.

Rosenthal had Owen discuss her lunch, and then she described the basement of the French Café. Her description of the French Café's basement corresponded to the description she had given Caradori and the Douglas County grand jury. She recalled the basement as having ornate trim and a wood pillar—she also said it was dank and dirty and had a cement floor. After Owen gave a description of the French Café's basement, Rosenthal introduced pictures of the basement into evidence—the pictures corroborated Owen's description.

Owen told Caradori and the Douglas County grand jury that a woman named Sheila let her into the French Café that afternoon. Owen wasn't sure about Sheila's affiliation with the French Café, but thought she was most likely an employee. Moran had previously called the manager of the French Café to the stand—she testified that a Sheila had never worked at the French Café. The manager neglected to mention that Sheila Calder had an apartment above the French Café—a Franklin employee testifying in front of the Douglas County grand jury said that Calder told him Larry King had "unusual parties" at the French Café. Jerry Lowe, Caradori's predecessor, was told that Sheila Calder had an affiliation with Larry King: Lowe phoned Calder, who moved to the West Coast after the fall of Franklin, but she denied any connections to Larry King.

After Owen testified about her "lunch" with Wadman at the French Café, Rosenthal asked her questions regarding her various assignations with him. She said that her "relationship" with Wadman lasted from September of 1983 to September of 1984. She maintained that they often rendezvoused on Wednesday afternoons and that Larry the Kid delivered her to various motels for Wadman—she stated that Wadman personally picked her up after school on only three occasions.

Before the Douglas County grand jury, Owen gave a fairly definitive description of Wadman's physique, and Rosenthal had her restate the description. In both accounts, she said that Wadman had a "bunion" or a "knotty knuckle" on one of his little toes. The state never provided Owen's jurors with a picture of Wadman's toes, despite its eagerness to provide them with a picture of his arm.

Owen testified that Wadman always took a shower after their encounters, and once she had an opportunity to look through his wallet, which had his initials—"RCW"—in gold leaf. Owen told the grand jury and also her trial jury about two pictures that were in his wallet: The first picture was of a girl and "two or three boys" wearing sweaters, and the second was a black-and-white photo of a woman with a necklace and a 1960s beehive hairdo. Owen also claimed that Wadman often "berated" one of his sons as "irresponsible" and "a troublemaker"—Wadman even mentioned to her that the son in question had broken a "china" or a "crystal" family heirloom of his wife's, and his wife was extremely upset about it.

In Owen's testimony before the grand jury, she was convinced that Wadman was the father of her child, and she expressed the same certainty at her trial. She testified that her daughter had eczema and asthma, two "hereditary diseases" that weren't in her family, but two diseases that afflicted Wadman.

Rosenthal questioned Owen on the chain of events that led to her making her first videotaped statement to Gary Caradori—Owen said that Caradori's first visit to York had utterly astounded her and left her in a state of "shock." She then discussed seeking out York's psychiatrist and warden to mull over the ramifications of her making a formal statement to Caradori. In a rather bizarre twist, Moran had called York's warden as one of the state's witnesses, and the warden testified that he thought Owen was telling the truth about her abusers.

Rosenthal walked Owen through her first "interview" with NSP investigator Phillips on December 15, and her subsequent interviews with the FBI: She stressed that she was never informed that she had a right not to grant the NSP and FBI interviews, nor that her statements could be used against her in a court of law. FBI agents had previously avowed that Owen had set the agenda for every interview, but Owen testified that was absolutely false. Owen also said she quickly realized that the FBI agents interviewing her weren't interested in the truth, but, rather, their primary concern was dismantling her credibility. So she brought a tape recorder to her third FBI interview—Mott and Culver, she said, wouldn't allow her to use it.

Rosenthal inquired about the physical and emotional toll the FBI interviews took on his client. "I couldn't sleep," she replied. "I didn't like it at all. I couldn't eat. I think I lost twenty pounds during that." Owen also discussed the terror she experienced when Phillips and the FBI raided her cell, and the distress she felt during and after Boner's "set-up" call to York because Boner sounded like "his life was in danger."

Rosenthal spent a considerable amount of time dispelling the state's account of the phantom phone call: Owen testified that prior to making her first videotaped statement to Caradori in early November of 1989, she hadn't talked to Boner since that June. Rosenthal then had Owen discuss York's telephone policy to hammer home the point: She testified that inmates were only allowed one personal phone call a day, and they had to sign up for it, and a York guard was required to initial the sign-up sheet when an inmate placed the call. Rosenthal then introduced York's November and December telephone sign-up sheets into evidence, and they confirmed that Owen hadn't made a call on the day of the phantom phone call. She then stated that York inmates couldn't have credit cards and, "under no circumstances," were inmates allowed to bill calls to a third party or a credit card. Owen acknowledged that York inmates were occasionally granted "special permission" to use the phones of prison personnel, but permission had to be explicitly granted by York's hierarchy, and a guard invariably monitored the inmates when they placed those calls.

Rosenthal had Owen address Moran's belief that her primary impetus for granting Caradori an interview was release from prison—Owen responded that his contention was "totally ludicrous." Owen also brought up the fact that she hadn't granted on-record interviews to anyone, including CBS, even though several reporters had requested them. Throughout Owen's trial, Rosenthal had repeatedly made the point that Owen had shunned all publicity and only talked to the Franklin Committee and state and federal law enforcement about her abuse.

At the conclusion of Owen's direct examination, Rosenthal asked her, "And regardless of what happens to you, are you going to change your testimony?" Owen's response was unwavering: "I will never, never change my story—the truth is the truth." Rosenthal's direct examination of Owen lasted all of Friday, June 14, and Case recessed the court shortly after 4:00 P.M.

Owen had the weekend to gird herself for Monday morning's showdown with prosecutor Moran—she felt that Moran's prior taunts to Rosenthal about putting a witness on the stand at his own "peril" were directed exclusively at her. She thought Moran would be nasty and cruel and would unabashedly attempt to humiliate her. She also thought that Rosenthal's objections to Moran's conduct would be overruled by Case, and she was walking into the lion's den all by herself. The night before, she prayed for God to guide her, and she also meditated on the 23rd Psalm: "Though I walk through the valley of the shadow of death, I will fear no evil: For thou art with me; thy rod and thy staff they comfort me."

Judge Case reconvened the "matter generally entitled the State of Nebraska versus Alisha J. Owen" at 9:00 A.M. on Monday. Owen stepped up to the stand and once more she was sworn in—Moran spared absolutely no time assaulting her character with his first question: "Miss Owen, have you ever been convicted of a felony in the past three years?" Owen confessed to being convicted of three felonies.

When Owen testified on Friday, she frequently made eye contact with her jurors. As Moran interrogated Owen, he pounced on her for looking directly at her jurors: He called it "a little bridge-building technique." Owen replied, "Those are the people that are deciding this trial—those are the people that need to know the truth."

One of the first issues raised by Moran was the phantom phone call, and he discussed Boner's phoning Owen at York from the FBI's Omaha Field Office. Owen responded that a guard invariably monitored her calls, and they were always logged. Moran then discussed Boner's imparting the hoax to Danny King, and he insinuated that Caradori let Boner and Danny King hop in a whirlpool on the same day Caradori and Boner made contact with Danny King, even though Caradori told the grand jury that he let Boner and Danny King take a whirlpool at the Residence Inn only after Danny completed his videotaped statement; Caradori was adamant that they had been kept apart until then.

Moran twisted Caradori's grand jury testimony and came up with the following scenario: "So after Danny's taping, though, he went to the apartment—so the only time they could have gone to the hot tub was the first night?" Owen replied, "I think Residence Inn has a late check out, and Gary Caradori clearly states that they went to the hot tub. But that's Gary's testimony. I wasn't there—I can't tell you what happened."

Moran shifted gears, firing a question at Owen that she thought was designed to make her capitulate and hoist the white flag: "Miss Owen, given the physical injuries that he [Wadman] has got, you really want to keep on with this story about Chief Wadman?" Owen simply said, "It is the truth." Moran, of course, neglected to remind the jury that Wadman had written—"Shot left arm 1973, okay now"—on his application to become OPD Chief, and that an examining physician had found a mere ten-percent disability.

Moran also blasted Owen with the fact that the "blood tests" Wadman, Owen, and her child submitted "confirmed one hundred percent that Robert Wadman was not the father" of her child—Owen replied, "I've never seen the results of the blood tests." Throughout Owen's trial, Moran never gave a rationale for the state's inexplicably opting not to enter the "blood tests" into evidence, even though they would have been absolute proof that Owen had committed perjury before the grand jury when she testified that Wadman was the father of her child.

Rosenthal's evidence that Wadman's arm wasn't nearly as disabled as the state claimed sowed doubt in the minds of various jurors concerning Moran's argument that it would have been next to impossible for Owen not to notice Wadman's "atrophied" arm, and the state not introducing the "blood tests" into evidence sowed further doubt. Moran, however, ultimately brought up a point about Owen and Wadman that carried significant weight with Owen's jurors: Wadman would have risked "everything," including his "family" and "career," to "fool around." Owen countered Moran's contention: "I think men have done more or risked more." This may have seemed feeble in 1991, but had she thrown the same counterpunch after the dalliance of Bill Clinton and Monica Lewinsky, it would have landed with a much heavier impact.

Moran spent considerable time grilling Owen on the Twin Towers—her testimony focused on the events that she had personally observed, and she was reluctant to speculate. Moran eventually fired another smoke-screen question at Owen: "And is the reason you chose the Twin Towers as the setting for your stories because of what Troy Boner had told you about he and Alan Baer getting it on in that second floor apartment?" Owen didn't back down, but rather offered a compelling rebuttal that cited Boner's grand jury testimony, where he stated that he hadn't edified Owen about Alan Baer.

Moran deployed the same tactic as Van Pelt to try to show that Owen couldn't possibly have met Danny King in the late summer or fall of 1983—he said King's school records proved he had been in Texas. Owen explained to Moran that King had been enrolled in the Texas middle school for "sixteen weeks," but he outright skipped "eight weeks." She also reminded Moran of Thanksgiving and Christmas holidays and teachers conferences—she concluded that Danny King, in actuality, "probably" attended the school for maybe "six weeks."

Owen's explanation of Danny King's missing ten weeks of school, when he was only enrolled at the Texas middle school for sixteen weeks, seemingly neutralized Moran's contention that it just wasn't "possible" for Owen to have met King in 1983. So Moran came roaring back with Jeff Hubbell's testimony—Moran pointed out that Hubbell confessed to meeting Owen at a dance, but he testified that was the only time he ever talked to her.

Owen responded that when Caradori initially videotaped her, she knew the rehab where Hubbell had been sent in 1984—before anyone "could even quote, unquote, as you say, feed me information." Owen then thrust a jab at Moran: "That's the part you can't get around—you go back on my tapes, and I just know too much." Moran may have been slightly taken aback by Owen's retort—he initially said "Okay" prior to shooting his next fireball: "Did you use Jeff's name because you thought that nobody would be able to find him and check your story?" Owen responded, "No—I used his name because he was there."

Moran interrogated Owen about the inconsistencies between her videotaped statement and the videotaped statements of Boner and Danny King. Owen wasn't willing to speculate too much on the videotaped statements of Boner and King, but, again, she conceded that Caradori had completely shocked her with the thoroughness of his initial videotaped interview; she had been forced to recall events from years earlier that she had never discussed with anyone. She also mentioned that

Caradori didn't provide her with a calendar for 1983 during their initial interview, and it had been very difficult for her to pinpoint, or even approximate, certain events from that year.

Moran frequently brought up the testimony of the FBI agents and NSP investigator Phillips to scorch Owen's credibility—Owen flat-out denied making many of the statements the FBI and Phillips attributed to her. Owen was "a three-time convicted felon," and it was essentially her word against the word of the FBI and Phillips, but some of the jurors had become dubious about the veracity of the FBI agents and Phillips. So Moran's repeated references to the testimony and reports of the FBI agents and Phillips, and Owen's refutations of their statements, weren't nearly as devastating to her credibility as the state might have envisioned.

Rosenthal's direct examination of Owen lasted an entire day, but Moran's cross-examination was short in comparison—just two and a half hours. Owen took the stand at her "peril," and Moran repeatedly blasted her—Owen, however, wasn't reduced to smoldering ruins. In fact, the jurors were able to see that she actually possessed human qualities, and she wasn't the personification of evil. At the conclusion of Owen's testimony, the defense rested its case.

The state now had an opportunity to call "rebuttal" witnesses to refute the defense's case, and Moran's two rebuttal witnesses were conspicuously bizarre. Moran's first rebuttal witness, Kathy Croson, and Owen were Central High classmates. Owen initially didn't recognize Croson when she took the stand, because she had undergone such a profound physical metamorphosis since high school, five years earlier. As a teenager, Croson was a waif with short, feathered brown hair, freckled alabaster skin, and a turned-up, button nose—she was fond of skin tight jeans and T-shirts with the logos of rock-and-roll bands. When Croson appeared at Owen's trial, she was obese and had curly, shoulder length hair—she wore a blue smock dress.

At the onset of Croson's direct examination, Moran had her announce to the courtroom that she was a diabetic and that her diabetes had the potential to suddenly debilitate her. "When I am under stress," she said, "my sugar level can fluctuate very high or very low, and I need to take a break and take a natural sugar."

Croson testified that she and Owen "frequently" went to Friday night football games together and also hung out on Saturday nights as Central High sophomores—she said they attended the same drama class as sophomores too. Croson told Moran that she was "ninety-nine percent sure" that she and Owen had attended all of Central High's football games in 1984. Moran then tossed out a flurry of names—Larry King, Robert Wadman, Alan Baer, etc.—and Croson replied that Owen hadn't mentioned any of those people.

Croson testified that when she and Owen were juniors, she suggested that Owen see her doctor after Owen became pregnant—Croson had given birth earlier in their junior year. Croson estimated she had "taken" Owen to her doctor's office "two or three times." Croson also said that her drama teacher assigned her to keep a diary in her junior and senior years—Moran cited specific dates and requested that Croson read little snippets from the diary. The little snippets started out with an innocuous "Dear Diary," but invariably depicted Owen as dishonesty incarnate.

Rosenthal had grown accustomed to Moran's throwing curveballs at him, but Croson was a screwball that he hit out of the park without too much trouble: The entries from Dear Diary that Croson read aloud to the courtroom were from January 21 and February 12 of 1985. On cross-examination, Rosenthal asked Croson if she was aware that Owen had severe complications with her pregnancy, and she had been bedridden during the time of those journal entries. After Croson confessed to Rosenthal that she hadn't even visited Owen when she was bedridden, Croson put the back of her hand to her forehead and crumbled—her gesture reminded the Owens and Rosenthal of the melodramatic faint of a silent-film actress. "We need to take a break here, judge!" Moran quickly interjected.

When Croson collapsed and was helped off the stand, Rosenthal had an opportunity to talk to Alisha and Donna Owen about the particulars of Owen's pregnancy. Alisha Owen told Rosenthal that she had one appointment at the clinic mentioned by Croson, but Croson hadn't accompanied her. After that first appointment, confirming her pregnancy, Owen started seeing an obstetrician at the Nebraska Medical Center, and her mother, not Croson, always accompanied her—Donna Owen backed up her daughter's account.

So, when Croson returned to the stand, Rosenthal started to question Croson about her prior statements relative to Alisha and Donna Owen's account, and Croson, again, seemed to be on the verge of slipping into a diabetic coma: "I'm sorry—I'm just feeling very nauseated." She was helped off the stand once more.

After Croson's second diabetic episode, Moran approached the bench—he complained to Judge Case that Rosenthal shouldn't be allowed to "torture" Croson. Moran also criticized Rosenthal for "pawing" through Croson's Dear Diary, and he implored Case to instruct Rosenthal not to damage it. Case warned Rosenthal about making an alteration to Dear Diary, and Rosenthal voiced his umbrage that Case would accuse him of altering evidence in front of the jury—Case denied making the accusation. Moran said that he wanted Croson's Dear Diary back intact—Rosenthal responded that he would return Dear Dairy when he finished leafing through it. Moran then told Rosenthal not to talk to him in front of the jury.

When Croson was resuscitated a second time, she was put back on the stand. Rosenthal told her that he'd had an opportunity to look over her Dear Diary, and he didn't notice any entries on the weekends—he thought that was somewhat peculiar. Croson replied that she never went out on the weekends during her junior and senior years in high school. "That's all I have," said Rosenthal.

Terry Clements was Moran's second rebuttal witness—he had attended the Owens' church. Clements was gay, and had come out of the closet shortly after high school. His sexual preference created a rift between him and his family, and the Owens frequently invited him over to their house for Thanksgiving and other holiday festivities.

Al and Donna Owen had been very generous to Clements, and they were shocked to see him milling around their daughter's trial with an investigator for the Douglas County Attorney's Office. But the Owens were in for an even greater shock: When Clements took the stand as the state's second rebuttal witness, Pamela Vuchetich represented him! Clement's name had been on Owen's list of friends and lovers contained in the red folder that Vuchetich surrendered to law enforcement.

Clements conceded that the Owen family had been very kind and generous to him, but he severely trashed Alisha Owen nonetheless—he testified that she was a wanton tramp and a pathological liar. Owen thought she and Clements were friends, and she was flabbergasted when he started to spew such scathing contempt for her. In the midst of a Clements' diatribe, he remarked that Owen told the FBI he could corroborate her story, and, indeed, one of the FBI's reports on Owen's interviews said, "She further stated Clements was one of the only people she told about being sexually abused and that he now lives in Lincoln." Owen denied ever telling the FBI that Clements had been a confidante, and she never brought up his name to Gary Caradori or the Douglas County grand jury as someone who was privy to her abuse.

Clements also testified that Owen took his virginity, and Moran specifically asked him if he knew of other virgins whom Owen had deflowered, prompting Clements to wax poetic: "She told me that I was like the eighth or ninth virgin that she had ever slept with and that she especially liked virgin penises, because there was like a soft, silky, satiny sheen on them, which eventually rubbed off with wear and tear—although it might be the aging process in general. But she especially liked to lay virgin penises." With Clements' testimony the state underscored two realities: It had no shame, and Clements had devoted a great deal of thought to penises.

Rosenthal's cross-examination of Clements was relatively short, but, even so, Moran blasted him with sixteen objections, so he had minimal latitude. Rosenthal inquired whether or not the Owens treated Clements "like one of the family." Clements promptly replied, "Yes, they did," before Moran objected to Rosenthal's question as "irrelevant."

Clements testified that he lost his virginity to Owen on December 16, 1984, and Rosenthal asked him if he was aware that Owen had been pregnant for months when she purportedly took his virginity. Clements responded with an unflinching "Yes" and even tossed in a little humor—he said that proved he wasn't the father of Owen's child. On the subject of paternity, Clements said that Owen showed him a picture of her child's father in her Central High yearbook—he named the same individual whose name Owen had provided to Social Services. Rosenthal pointed out to Clements that the individual in question had never even attended Central High.

As Rosenthal questioned Clements, his answers grew increasingly strange. Clements seemed to imply that he originally made contact with the Douglas County Attorney's Office or law enforcement, because he sought a "restraining order" against Alisha Owen. Rosenthal reminded Clements that Owen had been in "protective custody" for months and months, and a restraining order against her didn't make too much sense. Clements' response was a wacky non sequitur: He was afraid to "break off" his "relationship" with Owen—he worried that when he became "famous or prominent" she would write a tell-all book about him.

Though the state's rebuttal witnesses provided the exhausted jury with a bit of comedic relief, their testimony was just too bizarre to have a major impact on the jurors. Vuchetich's representation of Clements also left the jurors perplexed. And the mere fact that the state had resorted to such tactics just to sling additional mud on Owen demonstrated its seeming desperation.

The closing arguments of Moran and Rosenthal followed the state's rebuttal witnesses. Moran reiterated Owen's motives: a get-out-of-jail free card, vast riches, and to be "somebody." And he also recapped his parade of witnesses who had shown that all of Owen's accusations were nothing but lies. Moran said Owen's statements about Danny King were "just beyond belief"—she "obviously" didn't know he was living in Texas when she concocted "her story."

Moran in due course elaborated on Judge Theodore Carlson's testimony—he maintained that Carlson couldn't possibly have molested Owen at the French Café on the second Saturday afternoon of October, because he was at Loran Schmit's barbecue, and two judges had supported his alibi. Moran also brought up the fact that the FBI's wellspring of truth, Special Agent Mott, had testified that Owen never even mentioned to him that she had been molested by Carlson at the French Café.

Moran ultimately put all of Owen's "ideas for her stories" into a nicely wrapped box with a bow, and handed it to the jury. Gary Caradori, either "wittingly or unwittingly," fed her information on Robert Wadman and Harold Andersen, and Michael Casey and the media turned her onto the idea that Larry King was an alleged interstate pedophilic pimp. Troy Boner provided her with the lowdown on Alan Baer, and a former York inmate gave her the goods on Judge Carlson.

Though a number of witnesses testified that Boner recanted his recantation after Caradori's death, Moran focused his vitriol on Loran

Schmit and attempted to puncture holes in his credibility: He said that Schmit was the chairman of "that nutty Committee," and he seized upon Schmit's interest in "that video slot thing" and his purported affiliation with right-wing lunatics.

When Moran was in the homestretch of his closing argument, he commented on the heroics of Kathy Croson, who risked lapsing into a "diabetic coma" to dispel Owen's lies. He also contended that Judge Carlson, Robert Wadman, and Harold Andersen had been the real victims, and he flung a final gratuitous insult at Owen: "Given the small size of this courtroom, I'm glad she is not heavier."

Rosenthal commenced his closing argument by saying that he didn't take Moran's repeated assaults on his character personally, "but when somebody stands here and calls my client a pathological liar and a fat bitch that does bother me." Rosenthal likened Moran's vicious smear campaign against Owen to McCarthyism, and he paraphrased the Army attorney, Joseph Welsh, who confronted McCarthy at the US Senate Army-McCarthy hearings: "Is there no decency to you at all." Rosenthal said that though Alisha Owen was charged with perjury, the state has tried a "promiscuity case."

Rosenthal quickly assailed the contradictions between Wadman's testimony to the grand jury and his trial testimony, stressing Wadman's claim to be fifty-percent handicapped and also his claim that he hadn't carried a gun since his days as a federal agent. Rosenthal also requested that the jurors scrutinize the pictures of Wadman's arm to see if they discerned a "deep scar" or any scar "that's going to jump out at you." Rosenthal directed the jurors' attention to Moran's opening statement, where he said Wadman had a "Frankenstein-type scar" on his hip that was six to seven inches in length—Rosenthal said that if Wadman had such a scar surely the state would have presented pictures of it.

Rosenthal then went after Judge Carlson's testimony—he asked the jury why, if Judge Carlson had nothing to hide, he put himself at Schmit's barbecue at 1:30, even though two judges and Schmit said he arrived after 4:00 P.M. Rosenthal also called the jurors' attention to the fact that Carlson proclaimed himself an unrepentant Big Red "nut"—he had the team's 1983 scores memorized, but he couldn't seem to recall more recent scores.

After Rosenthal discussed Carlson, he attacked the phantom phone call: He pointed out that Caracorp's phone records and York's phone logs proved that the call never occurred. Rosenthal told the jury that the grand jury had subpoenaed Caracorp's phone records, and yet they didn't question Boner regarding the phone records: "Because if they told Mr. Boner there was no phone call, he would have admitted it, and it would make the [Caradori video-] tapes legitimate."

Rosenthal also declared that, even if the jurors believed in the reality of the phone call, it would have been impossible for Boner to give a six-hour statement to Caradori with such intricate details after talking to Owen for only twenty minutes. Rosenthal then attacked Boner and King's conflicting accounts of how the hoax was imparted, and reminded the jurors that the Residence Inn didn't have a bar, which is where Boner and King said they had colluded. Moran had described Owen's statements about Danny King's attending Twin Towers parties as "beyond belief," because King's school records demonstrated unequivocally that he was in Texas. But Rosenthal cited Boner's grand jury testimony in which Boner stated that King lived with Boner's family in 1983.

Rosenthal touched on Jeff Hubbell too—he said it was miraculous that Hubbell only met Owen once, when he was drunk, and they never talked again, but seven years later he recalled her with precise clarity. Rosenthal brought up Alisha Owen's telling Caradori about Hubbell's 1984 stint in rehab, Donna Owen's receiving phone calls from Hubbell, and the bracelet Alisha Owen bought for Hubbell, which Donna Owen corroborated.

Rosenthal's final surge was directed at the FBI and Pamela Vuchetich: He argued that the crux of Owen's FBI interviews wasn't to garner information about child abuse, but, rather, to collect dirt on Alisha Owen that would force her recantation. Rosenthal stressed that the FBI's focusing its interviews on the years after Owen alleged her abuse had occurred made its strategy all too transparent.

Rosenthal's concluding crescendo was reserved for Vuchetich. He discussed Vuchetich's driving out to York with the FBI and not affording Owen the opportunity to talk to her before or after Owen's FBI interviews. Rosenthal then risked contempt of court by bringing up Vuchetich's repeated phone calls to the FBI. He didn't come right out and say that Vuchetich and Mott were having an affair, but he highlighted the inordinate number, length, and times of Vuchetich's phone calls to Omaha's FBI Field Office.

At the very end of Rosenthal's closing argument, he tackled the motives that Moran said compelled Owen to hatch the hoax. Rosenthal commented on the fact that Owen had never granted an on-record interview to the media or initiated a civil lawsuit. He then told the jurors that Owen wouldn't change her testimony regardless of their decision, and he thanked them for sitting through the "long, long" trial. It had now lasted 22 days spread over five weeks.

Earlier in the day, prior to closing arguments, Moran and Rosenthal met with Case in the judge's chambers, and they attempted to hammer out the judge's final instructions to the jury—Rosenthal appealed to Judge Case to revise his prior decision wherein he ruled that if Owen's jurors concluded that just one of the statements in each of her multi-statement perjury counts was a willful giving of false testimony, Owen would be found guilty of perjury on that particular count. Rosenthal pointed out that Case's ruling was "highly prejudicial" to Owen and "shifted the burden to the defendant to prove that they are false." He told Case "if they prove one, they can fail on ten and I lose." But, again, Judge Case was a paragon of consistency, and he stuck by his previous ruling.

After Moran and Rosenthal wrapped up their closing arguments on the afternoon of Tuesday, June 18, Case informed the jurors that they would begin their deliberations the following day. It had certainly been a "long, long" trial for Rosenthal, and he felt severely handicapped by the duo of Moran and Case—Rosenthal had essentially played a game of chess without his queen. Moreover, Case's instructions to the jury concerning Owen's perjury counts were an additional handicap—perhaps even a backbreaker. Surprisingly, the jury was in deliberation for the entire day on Wednesday. Indeed, in their initial ballot the vote was split seven to five.

Owen's fate still hung in the balance as her jurors left the Douglas County Courthouse on Wednesday night after deliberating all day. The day before, Judge Case had sprung a "surprise" on the jury: a program, "named *48 Hours*," was to be telecast on Wednesday night at 9:00 P.M. Case mentioned that the program "may have some elements of this case," and he instructed the jurors not to watch it. But, according to one juror, "almost all if not all" of Owen's jurors opted not to heed Case, and they tuned into *48 Hours* that night.

Dan Rather hosted *48 Hours*—Rather's CBS predecessor, Walter Cronkite, had been thought of as "the most trusted man in America," and Rather, at least hypothetically, took over that mantle from Cronkite after his retirement. The *48 Hours* episode on that particular night just happened to be entitled, "Accusing Prominent People of Sex Crimes." And the fourth segment of the show just happened to start out with a shot of Troy Boner, who was making his network debut: "My name is Troy Boner—I was involved in a big scandal in Omaha, Nebraska. I said that I was abused by a prominent Omaha man and that I witnessed them abusing other children and young female girls."

After Boner confessed that he had falsely accused prominent men of abuse, the *48 Hours* reporter, Phil Jones, cut in and discussed Gary Caradori: "According to Boner, Caradori, who later died in a plane crash, encouraged him to videotape his allegations of sexual abuse." A dead-and-buried Caradori had been battered and bruised by the *World-Herald,* but now the big boys at CBS were also kicking him around.

The next stop for *48 Hours* reporter Phil Jones was the home of Robert Wadman—his wife sat next to him on their living room couch. Wadman fought back tears as he described the ordeals of a prominent man accused of child abuse: "It just is the most damaging, God-awful experience that you could wish on anybody." Then there was an abrupt cut to reporter Jones interviewing Boner, who confessed to saying "a lot of damaging things." Reporter Jones asked Boner, "Were they lies?" A contrite Boner replied, "They were all lies." Reporter Jones then commented on the deliberations of Van Pelt and company: "A grand jury found the allegations to be a hoax, but the damage was already done."

After reporter Jones and Wadman readdressed the "God-awful" allegations, footage of Alisha Owen was beamed coast to coast, and it was followed by Jones' commentary: "This woman testified before a grand jury that Wadman sexually abused her when she was a teenager and fathered her child—she is now on trial for perjury." Reporter Jones then carried on his interview with "former police chief" Wadman, who continued to express his hurt, outrage, and indignation.

Reporter Jones circled back to Troy Boner in his quest to unearth the truth about the genesis of those "God-awful" allegations. Boner fingered Caradori as the true culprit behind the sordid stories: "Gary had convinced me that, you know, these people really are abusing, and I thought, 'Hey, they really are abusing people.'" Boner told the national audience that Caradori said he would pocket "millions," and "greed" ultimately motivated him to concoct the allegations. Reporter Jones had Wadman chime in on Caradori: "The grand jury's report very clearly says that their investigator, Caradori, led witnesses, fed information to witnesses and acted irresponsibly." Wadman then discussed the impact of the allegations on his professional life, but he was too choked up to discuss their impact on his family life.

Reporter Jones had James Martin Davis, the former attorney of then-incarcerated, inveterate pedophile Peter Citron, sprinkle in quotes throughout the episode. Attorney Davis led with a quote he recycled from a *World-Herald* interview: "Omaha was going to be the first city in history to gossip itself to death." Davis also discussed the irrevocable harm that had been visited upon Wadman, "Bob Wadman has been scarred for the rest of his life. It has completely destroyed a reputation he has taken twenty-some years to build up." As the segment faded, Davis provided a quote that was the show's *pièce de résistance*: "The danger is that it can happen anywhere, because the allegations of child abuse are so volatile and so deadly that, like nitroglycerin, unless they're handled properly, they can explode and destroy individuals, families, communities."

The *48 Hours* reporter just happened to mention that Owen was "now on trial for perjury" after Wadman had professed his innocence. Boner had confirmed Wadman's innocence, and Peter Citron's former attorney, Davis, had condemned the "allegations." Of course it could have been a mere fluke that CBS broadcast the program during the jury deliberations at Owen's trial, even though the footage had been shot months earlier. Or were some extremely powerful people attempting to sway the perjury trial of a twenty-two-year-old in Omaha, Nebraska?

When Owen's jurors arrived at the Douglas County Courthouse on Thursday morning to continue deliberating Owen's fate, the *48 Hours* segment was a hot topic of discussion—a few of the jurors confessed to being profoundly influenced by the program. After all, the show's host was the heir apparent to the most trusted man in America. A subsequent juror affidavit stated the following: "I believe I would have never even known about the program or watched it except for the attention given it by the Court during the trial. I believe this may well be the case of the other jurors also ..."

In addition to protracted discussions about *48 Hours,* Owen's jurors later reported other strange goings-on in the jury room: Jurors have the right to examine exhibits that have been introduced into evidence during a trial, but Owen's jurors said they were denied the right to review certain exhibits, including Danny King's Texas school records and the 1980 deposition of Wadman where the attorney deposing him commented on the pistol Wadman wore in his "waistband."

The strange goings-on in the jury room didn't stop there—an "exhibit" that wasn't introduced during the trial "mysteriously" found its way into the jury room. The "exhibit" in question was a letter purportedly written to Owen on a yellow legal pad, and signed by none other than "Michael Casey."

The "Casey letter" was nowhere to be found among the exhibits after Owen's trial—yet it was passed around the jury room and read by "all or most" of Owen's jurors: One of the jurors ultimately concluded that the letter had been planted. In American justice, the jury room has the sanctity equivalent to the Catholic confessional, and breaching that sanctity is a serious crime.

I've been told that a shady investigator for the Douglas County Attorney's Office, Damien Turner, had the capabilities and the wherewithal to puncture the sanctity of the jury room and plant the Casey letter, and his subsequent deeds would bear that out. Turner was employed by the Douglas County Attorney's Office as an investigator from 1986 to 1993, and worked in close conjunction with the office's prosecutors. He flitted in and out of Alisha Owen's trial like a shadow, and he periodically sat next to Moran at the state's table—he also accompanied Terry Clements into the courtroom before Clements waxed poetic about Owen's affinity for "silky satiny" virgin penises.

Turner was arrested in 1992 for possession of an unregistered firearm: He pled "no contest" to the charge and was fined a whopping $10—the Douglas County Attorney opted not to fire him. In 1993, Turner committed his next recorded crime as an employee of the Douglas County Attorney—he was busted for illicitly selling criminal histories culled from the National Crime Information Center. Turner's rummage sale of criminal histories was a potential felony, but the Douglas County Attorney inexplicably didn't prosecute him, even though he was finally fired—he, then, amazingly, was accepted to law school and became an attorney! Turner saved his sociopathic *tour de force* for 2003 when he murdered his wife and, after a high-speed chase with police, committed suicide.

Despite weeks of unabated character assassination, the *48 Hours* episode, and the Casey letter, Owen's jurors were still unable to reach a consensus. So Judge Case took it upon himself to lend a helping hand. On one occasion, a juror asked Case the meaning of "reasonable doubt." The judge told the juror that he could not discuss the case outside the presence of both counsels, and it was up to each juror to decide his or her definition of reasonable doubt.

Case's instruction drove some jurors to use a dictionary to define reasonable doubt, and dictionary definitions of "reasonable" and "doubt" without "beyond" as a precursor are antithetical to the standard legal connotation of *beyond a reasonable doubt*—proof of such a convincing character that you would be willing to rely and act upon it without hesitation in the most important of your own affairs. Merriam-Webster defines "reasonable" as "being in accordance with reason" and "doubt" is defined as "be in doubt about" or "to lack confidence in: distrust." So the jurors who resorted to Merriam-Webster for "reasonable doubt" most likely came up with the following: A person acting in accordance with reason would have doubt about, or distrust, Owen's contentions.

Even after this, the jurors were deadlocked after casting several ballots. The domineering jury foreman was quite vociferous concerning Owen's guilt, and heated exchanges started to boil over in the jury room. One of the jurors later said that he felt there was "zero chance of a unanimous decision." The jurors conveyed their deadlocked quandary to the bailiff, and the bailiff consulted Case, who informed the bailiff to tell the jury to "keep deliberating."

In criminal law, instructions given by judges to ensure that deadlocked juries "keep deliberating" are called "Allen charges," or "dynamite charges," because they often strong-arm the holdouts into capitulating, and some states have barred such admonitions as coercive. An Allen charge suggests to the holdouts that they may be mucking up the jury deliberations and preventing their fellow jurors from rejoining their lives—children, spouses, livelihoods, etc.

In fact, the Allen charge that Case dropped on the jury was against Nebraska law, which mandates that such instructions are to be delivered "in the presence of or after notice to" both counsels—in this case Rosenthal and Moran. If Rosenthal had been informed about the deadlocked jury, he certainly would have moved for a mistrial.

Despite the *48 Hours* episode, the planted Casey letter, jurors deciphering reasonable doubt with a dictionary, and the Allen charge, Owen's jury was still deadlocked when they went home after deliberating all of Thursday—they were even deadlocked well into Friday morning. Around 10:30 A.M., the jury foreman handed a note to the bailiff indicating that the jury had reached a verdict.

Shortly thereafter, Douglas County Deputy Sheriffs escorted a terrified Alisha Owen into the courtroom—past Al and Donna Owen who were already seated. But when Owen made eye contact with her parents, she had a flashing sense that everything would be all right, regardless of the jury's verdict. She was led to the defense counsel's desk, where Rosenthal gave her a hug. The jury then entered the courtroom single-file. Owen immediately noticed an acute pathos in the eyes of two or three of the jurors who seemed to be the most attentive towards her.

After the Douglas County District Court Clerk said "guilty" on the first count, Owen heard a gasp from the audience, and she felt as though she had just been kicked in the stomach—with each successive "guilty," she felt that kick in the stomach again. She was guilty on all eight counts. Before the trial's observers had a chance to leave the courtroom, Owen was surrounded by deputy sheriffs and quickly ushered out. When the courtroom's door opened, Owen was barraged by camera flashes and swarmed by media—tears welled in her eyes, but she didn't utter a word.

On Friday afternoon, the *World-Herald* trumpeted Owen's guilt with a banner headline—"Alisha Owen Convicted On All 8 Perjury Counts." The size of the headline even eclipsed the newspaper's name on the front-page. The article quoted Douglas County Deputy Attorney Gerald Moran, who ripped the Franklin Committee and lauded Nebraska's judiciary: "How did our institutions of government fail us so badly that this case got to this point? Maybe the institutions of government failed us, but the criminal justice system worked every time. We've now had two grand juries, and a petit jury, say it was all a lie." Now everyone in Nebraska could sleep soundly, because the fire-breathing dragon—the nasty rumors of child abuse and its cover-up—had finally been slain.

The following day, a *World-Herald* editorial, "Prosecution Crushed Lies With Avalanche of Truth," showered accolades on Moran just as previous editorials had praised Samuel Van Pelt: "Moran showed Miss Owen's story to the jury as a concoction of lies brewed in the twisted minds of people who were seeking power, money, or political gain." The *World-Herald* couldn't get enough of chastising Gary Caradori, and the editorial confirmed the state's cockeyed speculation: "Caradori, who worked for state Sen. Loran Schmit's Franklin committee, suggested to Miss Owen that she could have her bad-check sentence shortened and receive large sums of money if she told a story about sexual abuse of minors by prominent men. He even mentioned a movie contract."

Judge Case set August 8 as the date for sentencing, and Owen was detained in the Douglas County Jail. The trial had left her absolutely spent, and after being found guilty, she found it extremely difficult to get out of bed for the next day or so.

Prior to Owen's trial, she had been confined to solitary for over four hundred days. Now, at least, she had a cellmate at the jail—a cellmate was a welcome novelty in her life. Her cellmate had been pinched on a federal drug conspiracy—she had never been to prison and was also staring at a decades-long sentence. Owen and her Douglas County cellmate had protracted talks about their daughters and families, and Owen also explained the ropes of doing time.

Around noon on August 8, Owen was transported from the Douglas County Jail to the courthouse. Douglas County Deputy Sheriffs escorted her into the courtroom shortly before 1:30, and she seated herself at the defense table alongside Rosenthal. Moran was conspicuously absent for the sentencing hearing—his boss, Douglas County Attorney Jim Jansen, represented the state.

The United States government, the state of Nebraska, and Douglas County had spent hundreds of thousands of dollars and innumerable man-hours finding Owen guilty of perjury, and she felt Case would throw the book at her. An FBI agent had also told her she wouldn't see the light of day until she was "an old lady" if she didn't recant—she expected the worst as she faced a possible sentence of 160 years.

Though Owen fully expected Judge Case to wallop her with many years in prison, she didn't feel the same sense of foreboding as when she entered the courtroom to hear the jury's verdict. Rosenthal had told her she would have an opportunity to address the court before being sentenced, and her thoughts were transfixed on finally saying her piece. Case called her in front of the bench and asked her if she had anything to say before sentencing—Owen responded with an eloquence that belied all the nasty innuendo that the state had used to paint her portrait:

"There have been many accusations as to why I gave my testimony. I believe that my reasons are so basic they are easy to see. But Mr. Moran, the *World-Herald*, Mr. Andersen, and Mr. Wadman have all tried to cloud the issues with stories of money, attention, and obtaining an early release from prison. The undisputable fact remains that I have never given an interview, nor have I ever sued anyone. Not one of the principals involved can say that.

"The fires of gossip, lies and innuendos have been fueled not by me but by the news media, the *World-Herald*, Mr. Andersen, and Mr. Wadman. Mr. Wadman says he had suffered, and yet he is the one that continually makes the statements to the press, TV, and the radio, and he is the one who has filed lawsuits. Various people, including the news media, the grand jury prosecutors and the prosecutor in this case have all made accusations concerning me about making movie deals, writing books, or trying to obtain an early release from prison. We now know all of these accusations are incorrect. When the FBI came to me on April 10th, 1990, they told me what they wanted me to say. In exchange for lying for them, I would receive my freedom, the chance to be a mother to my daughter, and all of this would simply, quietly go away. I told them—no—I wouldn't lie for them no matter what the penalty for the truth was.

"I left that meeting, and as I walked back to my cell, I began to think of all the things I was giving up, and I wondered what was it inside of me that made lying not an option. I entered my cell and something caught my eye in the mirror—I looked in the mirror, and that's when it hit me: I could look in the mirror and know that I did the right thing. No one ever said that doing the right thing was easy. But, your Honor, if a person cannot look into the mirror with a clean conscience and know that they did the right thing, you are truly in a prison in which no man has the key. I believe that children ask for mercy while adults plead for justice. Your Honor, I stand before you today and ask for justice."

After Owen said her piece, Case called for responses from Rosenthal and the Douglas County Attorney. Rosenthal pled for leniency—Jansen, however, contended that Alisha Owen had not only "victimized" Wadman and Andersen, but also "our community" and "our system of criminal justice." Though Jansen wasn't quite sure how to quantify Owen's "substantial" damage to the community and "the system," he requested that Case take that into consideration.

Indeed, Judge Case took that into consideration and also Owen's prior stints at St. Joseph's and York. As Case recounted all of Owen's "bad checks" and "forgeries," his voice became thunderous. "There is [sic] two grand juries who said you weren't telling the truth!" Case hollered down at Owen. "One petit jury who came to the conclusion that you weren't telling the truth! And now you are telling me that you did the right thing! That you simply want justice!" Case then categorized Owen as a serial offender: "With your history, what am I to believe? With your history, there is going to—a good chance that you are, again, going to engage in other criminal activity! I truly believe that!"

Judge Case concluded one of the longest trials in Nebraska history by sentencing Owen to between nine and fifteen years for her eight counts of perjury. She was eventually remanded back to York and, once more, thrown into solitary—Owen took a slight amount of solace in the fact that she had expected a longer sentence.

The Douglas County judiciary now had to deal with Alan Baer and Paul Bonacci, who had also been indicted by Van Pelt and company. Baer was potentially facing ten years in prison for his two counts of felony "pandering"—an Omaha newscaster had remarked that he was in for the "fight of his life" when the grand jury's report was released. Incredibly, Baer's "fight of his life" turned into a rather benign skirmish—he was charged with a misdemeanor and fined $500. Baer had kept his mouth shut, even though it took a reported death threat from the FBI, and, evidently, he was handsomely rewarded.

Then there was that little matter of Paul Bonacci's three perjury indictments: Shortly after Owen was found guilty, the Douglas County Attorney dismissed the perjury indictments against Bonacci. According to a *World-Herald* article, Moran offered three reasons for dismissing Bonacci's perjury charges: "The first reason," said Moran, "is that the truth is out—it is evident that the allegations of sexual misconduct were a lie from start to finish." Moran's second rationale was that Bonacci "has a multiple personality disorder," even though he made the point that Bonacci wasn't "incompetent" to stand trial. The third reason cited by Moran was that Bonacci's testimony wasn't material to the grand jury's investigation.

Not material to the grand jury's investigation? The Douglas County grand jurors "charge" was "to uncover any wrongdoing by all individuals, however prominent or obscure, who have been accused in the Legislative Committee's investigation, whether or not they have any relationship to the Franklin Credit Union." Bonacci's grand jury testimony certainly fell under the aegis of the grand jury's charge, and two of his perjury indictments, in essence, mirrored the indictments against Owen. Bonacci's testimony was unquestionably material to the grand jury's investigation.

Moran offered three rationales for dismissing Bonacci's perjury indictments. So I'll offer three of my own: First, the Douglas County judiciary convicted Owen only by the hair of its chinny, chin, chin, even though Judge Case was basically a puppet and various tricks had been deployed, including the planting of fabricated evidence. If Bonacci were to be found innocent, then Owen's convictions would have been jeopardized and, perhaps, even overturned.

Second, Bonacci was essentially a full-time employee of the Franklin pandering network and made no bones about it, while Owen had been part-time and managed to hide a secret life. Bonacci knew numerous potential witnesses who could vouch for his participation in King's sex network, and Bonacci was cognizant of King's DC involvement, whereas Owen had no idea about that activity.

Third, John DeCamp had signed on to represent Bonacci. DeCamp had been a prominent Nebraska statesman, he was a gifted orator, and also a loose cannon. The Douglas County judiciary was unsure of the various moves DeCamp might make. DeCamp also loved to grandstand, and Bonacci's trial would grant him innumerable opportunities. If DeCamp learned that the Caradori videotapes shown to the Douglas County grand jurors had been doctored, he would have screamed that inconvenient truth from Omaha's highest rooftops and, most likely, called a well-attended press conference.

The federal grand jury investigating Franklin had also indicted Alisha Owen on eight counts of perjury. The feds surely would have been hot on her heels if the state had failed in its campaign to convict Owen. But the state triumphed, albeit narrowly, and the feds were benevolent enough to dismiss Owen's federal perjury indictments. The feds, however, weren't derelict in their duties when it came to dispensing justice to Larry King for his financial crimes, even though state and federal law enforcement concluded that he never took part in the abuse of a single child. King was sentenced to fifteen years in a federal prison for plundering the Franklin Community Federal Credit Union.

After Owen's conviction and King's plea bargain, the national media still hadn't finished kicking around Gary Caradori, Alisha Owen, and the Franklin Committee. *GQ* sent a journalist to investigate Larry King's activities, and its December 1991 issue featured an article entitled "Other People's Money." The magazine article was essentially a thumbnail encapsulation of the grand jury report, but it failed to report on even those fabricated facts accurately, and it was fraught with falsehood after falsehood. For example, the article didn't even report the accurate amount Larry King plundered from Franklin, reporting that he had stolen $20 million, even though the *World-Herald* and the grand jury report conceded that the figure was roughly $40 million.

The *GQ* article acknowledged that Larry King had extravagant homosexual appetites, but it absolutely denied that King was an interstate pedophilic pimp, "so far as is known." The article also discussed the "hoax" generated among Owen, Casey, and Caradori as a sanctified truth: "a transaction between a liar, a con artist, and a delusional investigator was the foundation upon which a staggering conspiracy theory came to be built." The *GQ* article ripped Senator Schmit as gullible and "mistrusting of city life," but the article was particularly vicious toward Alisha Owen: "Owen's gaudy fabric of lies was being torn to tatters in a protracted perjury trial. The conspiracy theory, which had grown in the twilight of rumor and misinformation, was now being exposed to the merciless light of the trial process." *GQ* repeatedly hammered away on the "conspiracy theory" until even the remnants of the truth it presented became merely dust swept away by gusts of deceit.

But *GQ*'s account of Larry King's extravaganza at the 1988 Republican Convention *may* contain an ominous detail, considering the role of the *48 Hours* broadcast on the outcome of Alisha Owen's trial. Among the influential in attendance, only one is identified: "And they remember seeing Dan Rather there, and King wrapping him in a big embrace. Larry King, a black man from Omaha, had bought his way into the club."

Thus, local and national media as well as local, state, and federal law enforcement had effectively branded Franklin as a "conspiracy theory." Though the media played an instrumental role in dispelling the reality of Franklin, state and federal law enforcement did most of the heavy lifting, and the officers of the court who participated in the prosecution of Alisha Owen experienced fairly expeditious upward mobility on the judicial totem pole. Douglas County Deputy Attorney Gerald Moran was appointed a Douglas County District Court Judge in October of 1993. Generally, District Court judges work on their judicial chops in a lower court, Omaha Municipal Court, before being appointed to the District Court. But Moran leapfrogged over all the Omaha Municipal Court judges to become a Douglas County District Court Judge.

Federal Magistrate Richard Kopf and First Assistant US Attorney for the District of Nebraska Thomas Thalken experienced upward mobility in the wake of Owen's conviction too. Federal Magistrate Kopf signed off on the federal search warrant that enabled the FBI to raid Owen's cell at York, and he also made the preemptive decision to send Larry King to the federal Springfield, Missouri facility when George H.W. Bush visited

Nebraska on a fundraiser—he also sealed King's Springfield psychiatric report. Approximately a year after Owen's conviction, Kopf was bumped up from federal magistrate to US District Court Judge, which carries a lifetime appointment.

Thomas Thalken, Nebraska's First Assistant US Attorney, was the lead prosecutor of the federal grand jury that found Franklin didn't entail the interstate transportation of children for immoral purposes and indicted Alisha Owen on eight counts of perjury. The federal grand jury that Thalken directed not only validated Van Pelt and company, but also provided a back-up plan if Moran and the state had failed to validate Van Pelt's grand jury with Owen's conviction. In 1993, Thalken was appointed a US magistrate.

In February of 2007, I was poking around Nebraska on my eleventh Franklin-related visit when one of the Owens' friends, with whom I'd cultivated a rapport, contacted me and said Alisha Owen was willing to meet with me. She gave me Owen's number—I was both amazed and delighted. When I phoned Owen, I was surprised to find her voice brimming with élan, because she had been so hesitant when we first talked at Fogarty's office. I've since met with Alisha and her parents on numerous occasions over the last couple of years.

Owen was reluctant to give me an on-record interview, but, at that point, I'd been enmeshed in Franklin for over four years, and TrineDay had agreed to publish this book—I told her I would proceed with or without her input, but I would greatly appreciate an interview. She talked it over with her husband and her family, and eventually agreed to be interviewed.

"One of the hardest hurdles for me to get over in my decision to be interviewed was that I supposedly made up these stories for a book or a movie," said Owen. "If I stayed silent for the rest of my life because they said I did it for book and movie deals, then they really did win. I've also tried every appropriate venue to get the truth out through the Nebraska judiciary, but the court in Nebraska is broken. So the only way anybody is ever going to know what really happened to me in Nebraska is for me to tell them."

I was also interested in her motives for granting Gary Caradori that first interview: "I knew these guys were still doing what they were doing.

There was still a Peter Citron and a Gene Mahoney out there. I was no longer a kid, and I knew if I kept my mouth shut and didn't say something, then nothing would separate them from me. If I kept my mouth shut, then I'm a criminal too. I initially told my folks, and it was really hard. My folks understood that this had to be a family decision, and we decided that we had to do it."

In November of 2007, I was driving to Alisha Owen's South Omaha home. Though she gave me straightforward directions, I was lost yet again. My mental GPS had malfunctioned somewhere along the line: I was guilty of zigging when I should have zagged, or vice versa. I phoned Owen and provided her with my whereabouts, and she gave me a new set of directions. When she initially imparted the directions, I had confessed to her that I was geographically challenged, and it wasn't uncommon for me to get lost in Omaha. So my call from God-knows-where and subsequent admission of being off-course didn't take her by surprise. In fact, she seemed to be mildly amused at my self-professed ability to end up lost despite seemingly clear-cut directions.

I eventually found Alisha Owen's house on a quiet, oak-lined street. I parked on the street and walked to the front door—her home was a ranch style house with green siding. Owen had seen me walking up the driveway from the living room's picture window, and she met me at the front door—she had light brown hair, stood 5'4", and wore a matching salmon-colored top and pants. Her hazel eyes were keen, and the initial indicator of her sharp mind. Owen was gracious and articulate.

She directed me to an easy chair that was in front of the picture window, and sat on the loveseat next to the easy chair. As I sat down, I scanned the living room. An oak wall unit with a television and several vinyl albums was in front of the loveseat. The living room's distant wall, to the right, had a "lawyer's shelf" containing about a thousand CDs, and a curio cabinet of Swarovski crystals. The wall just to my left had a grandfather clock and a color print of Frank Zappa sitting on an earthmover. Owen's husband is a big-time Zappa fan, and she bought the limited-edition print for him as a birthday present.

A box of newspaper clippings rested in front of the loveseat. Owen had been leafing through the articles before I arrived, and she continued to leaf through the box's contents after we sat down—her mannerisms were delicate and introspective as she gave each a careful look. She hadn't looked through the box's contents in many years, and each newspaper snippet evoked various memories. She recalled her memories in a verbalized free association, but the events described in the newspaper clippings were a distant memory—almost like artifacts from a long-lost civilization. "That was a really, really bad day," Owen spoke softly, gazing at the *World-Herald* article that showed her being taken out of the Douglas County Courthouse after she was found guilty of perjury.

I had thought it was patently unfair and cowardly of the Nebraska judiciary to prosecute Owen to the hilt and opt not to prosecute Paul Bonacci, because two of Bonacci's perjury indictments were quite similar to Owen's. Owen, however, had a different take on Bonacci's perjury charges being dropped. "Nobody ever said life was fair, and I was happy for Paul. There is no way that a reasonable person or a decent person would wish upon someone else what I went through. Plus, if Paul was found innocent, and I was found guilty on the same matters, then that opened up a whole can of worms for them."

Local, state, and federal law enforcement repeatedly voiced the belief that Franklin did not involve the interstate transportation of children for illicit purposes. So, theoretically, the FBI shouldn't have played such an integral role in the prosecution of Alisha Owen, especially after state and federal grand juries concluded that such interstate violations never occurred. I asked Owen about her thoughts on why the feds were so heavy handed.

"I believe the FBI was brought in because I don't think that local law enforcement was capable of covering up Franklin by themselves, following it all the way through to its completion. There were so many witnesses and so much corroboration. The FBI was one of the few law enforcement entities that had the power, resources, and wherewithal to execute such a massive cover-up."

After Owen's trial, Henry Rosenthal would have continued to represent her, but his heart condition and declining health made it practically impossible for him to continue waging war on her behalf. "I didn't have a lot of pro bono attorneys beating down my door to represent me, and

John DeCamp stepped in as my appellate lawyer," said Owen. DeCamp originally represented Owen pro bono, but he later charged her $5,000.

As DeCamp immersed himself in the record of Owen's trial, he was absolutely stunned by the innumerable examples of malfeasance. Moreover, one of Owen's alternate jurors contacted Donna Owen in the aftermath of her daughter's conviction. Steadfastly believing that Alisha Owen was innocent, the alternate juror had some rather interesting tales to tell. She volunteered to contact her fellow jurors, and juror affidavits illustrating a tainted deliberative process followed thereupon.

Two of the affidavits discussed the *48 Hours* episode that was watched by most, "if not all, of the jurors," and how it "impacted the decision of any juror who in fact did watch it." One of the affidavits cited jurors using a dictionary for "reasonable doubt." An affidavit also mentioned the mysterious Michael Casey letter. The juror who submitted the affidavit on the planted letter said that it had been "the piece of evidence that ultimately tipped me to vote conviction"—he also stated that the letter "was read and handled by all or most of the jurors." The juror, just to make sure, even went through the trial's exhibits after the trial, and the Casey letter was nowhere to be found.

DeCamp had plenty of fodder to start churning out appeals. Indeed, Lady Justice had been raped so many times throughout Owen's trial that DeCamp had difficulty choosing the most egregious miscarriages of justice to target first. In 1992, DeCamp appealed Owen's conviction, citing the following actions or inactions of Judge Case:

- Judge Case erred in refusing to dismiss the charges against Owen based upon the misconduct of the Douglas County grand jury.
- Judge Case erred in refusing to declare a mistrial of Owen's case based on prosecutorial misconduct during the course of the trial.
- Judge Case erred in committing judicial misconduct during the course of Owen's trial.
- Judge Case erred in refusing to grant Owen a new trial based upon the misconduct that occurred during the jury's deliberations.
- Judge Case erred in admitting into evidence, over Rosenthal's objection, contents of a presentence investigation.

• Judge Case erred in admitting into evidence, over Rosenthal's objection, testimony from an employee of Social Services.

• Judge Case erred in allowing the prosecution to introduce irrelevant, immaterial, and prejudicial evidence regarding Owen's character.

• Judge Case erred in allowing the prosecution to admit into evidence statements of Owen's made while she was in custody without having been notified of her Miranda rights.

• Judge Case allowed Wadman to testify about the results of "genetic blood testing" by means of "hearsay" and without establishing a proper "foundation and custody" that demonstrated the blood tested was, in fact, from Wadman, Owen, and Owen's daughter.

• Judge Case had improper contact with the jury—the appeal cited Case's verbal directions to the jury concerning "reasonable doubt" and also the Allen charge.

• Judge Case erred in overruling Rosenthal's pretrial motions.

• Judge Case's quashing of subpoenas deprived Owen of a fair trial.

• Judge Case improperly limited Rosenthal's cross-examination of witnesses.

• Judge Case repeatedly allowed "hearsay evidence" to be used against Owen.

• Judge Case repeatedly allowed "prejudicial and irrelevant" evidence to be used against Owen.

As DeCamp started launching Owen's appeals like salvos of Trident missiles at the Nebraska Court of Appeals, Owen was eventually returned to the prison's general population. With her "good time" credits, she was slated to wrap up her bad-check sentence on February 13, 1992. Because Owen's perjury conviction was under appeal, she was theoretically eligible for an appeal bond that would release her from prison until her various appeals had been adjudicated.

Judge Case was the ultimate arbitrator of whether or not Owen would be granted an appeal bond. DeCamp thought it would take a miracle for Case to grant Owen an appeal bond, because Case's parting shots at Owen had been extremely harsh, and his nine-to-fifteen year sentence wasn't particularly benign either. Owen, however, still hadn't lost faith in miracles, even though Lady Luck hadn't smiled on her recently.

One night, as Owen sat in her cell, she recalled the Old Testament story of Gideon "putting out a fleece." In the Book of Judges, God directed Gideon to assemble the Israelite troops and defeat the Midianite invaders. But Gideon was wracked by doubts, and he wanted to make sure it was actually the voice of God he heard—he requested that God provide him with a sign to prove that this command was truly God's will. So Gideon put out a fleece of wool, and asked God to moisten it while keeping the surrounding earth dry: The following morning, the earth was dry but the fleece was drenched enough to produce a bowl of water after being wrung out.

Owen would put out her own fleece, which took the form of applications for scholarships to college. A scholarship would be her proxy for a wet fleece: if granted a scholarship, she would again request an appeal bond, even though Judge Case had thwarted her two previous efforts. "At one point I was really down about spending all those years in prison," she said. "I just knew that I wasn't supposed to spend the majority of my life in prison. I got down on my knees, on the cement floor, and asked God to cut me some slack—I did the right thing and told the truth, and I couldn't seem to catch a break. I started applying to colleges, and if I was given a full-ride scholarship, I felt that would be a sign, and I'd do whatever it takes to go to college—I knew that I was supposed to fight. I also started researching the criteria for a bail bond. Nebraska law reads that you're allowed an appeal bond unless you're convicted of a capital offense or you're going to be an extreme flight risk or danger to the public. Obviously I wasn't going to run away, because I ultimately turned myself in; so that nixed that, and perjury isn't a capital offense. I also wasn't a danger to the public."

Lo and behold, Omaha's Metropolitan Community College gave Owen a full-ride scholarship. Though her fleece had been soaked, she still had the problem of a recalcitrant Judge Case. "I called John DeCamp and I said, 'John you go to the judge and tell him I want an appeal bond—tell him to give me a number.' I told John that under Nebraska law Case has to give me a bond—it's just wrong that he's denying me a bond. So John tells Case that Alisha said give her a number, and Case set the bond at $500,000. I didn't have any money, but I just knew I was destined to go to college. My mom and dad thought that I was cracked, and the prison personnel said, 'Alisha you are doing a nine-to-fifteen-year sentence—you are not going to college next semester.'"

Case required Owen to shell out $500,000 cash—he wouldn't allow her to post the customary ten percent; so her parents' house wouldn't even come close to the required collateral. Owen had to somehow come up with $500,000. A Nebraska entrepreneur had followed Owen's case very closely, and he too perceived a flagrant miscarriage of justice—he contacted a bail bondsman in Grand Island, Nebraska, and they worked out a $500,000 surety bond to liberate Owen from prison.

On Thursday, February 12, 1992, Owen was transported from York to the Douglas County Jail, and the next morning Al and Donna Owen showed up at the jail. Al said to his daughter, "I've come to take you home."

Al and Donna Owen threw a huge party for their daughter on her first night home—Henry Rosenthal was an honored guest. Owen hadn't slept in her own bed in nearly three years, and she slept soundly that first night—she started attending classes at Metropolitan the following month. Owen met her husband-to-be at the junior college—they were married in June of 1994.

"I immediately started taking paralegal classes so I could do these appeals. They certainly weren't happy to see me out and about, and they really weren't happy when they started to see my legal work come in, because I had one goal and one goal only, and that was to get this case overturned and get vindicated. I worked day and night for that. I made really good grades, and the prosecution knew that if they could get me back in prison, I wouldn't have access to the Douglas County law library and the Creighton College law library; so they were constantly trying to revoke my bond to get me back in prison. The entire law library in York is very small, and the books are outdated—you also have to sign the books out; so sometimes you only get them for a half hour or an hour a week."

Legal appeals are generally protracted, and, as the Nebraska Court of Appeals started shooting down Owen's appeals, DeCamp and Owen submitted additional ones citing other errors. Owen felt that she was in a Catch-22—her appeals cited considerable malfeasance by the Nebraska judiciary, and she felt her only chance of winning an appeal was to move it to a federal appellate court.

While Owen slogged through the appellate process, Gerald Moran would be robed as a judge, and Douglas County Deputy Attorney Robert Sigler replaced him as Owen's principal prosecutor. The forty-six-year-old Sigler and Moran were old buddies—Sigler graduated from Creighton University Law School in 1974, a year after Moran, and he went to work for the same law firm as Moran. Sigler, though, opted to leave private practice and become a Douglas County Deputy Attorney a few years before Moran took his leap into the Douglas County Attorney's Office.

Sigler had accompanied Moran to the January 1990 conclave where the FBI played their federal trump card by announcing that Franklin interviews would be conducted on "FBI terms," but his name had surfaced in connection with Franklin well before then.

Besides overseeing Owen's prosecution for "bad checks," you will recall that Sigler's name surfaced in the highly suspicious 1986 "suicide" of body builder and Max bouncer Charlie Rogers: Two weeks prior to Rogers' death he stopped by his sister and brother-in-law's home and told them that he was in the midst of attempting to extricate himself from an ominous endeavor that was linked to Larry King. Rogers revealed that he had taken several trips with King to Washington, DC—he also said that he felt he was in over his head and feared for his life.

Rogers explicitly told his sister and brother-in-law that if something should happen to him they should contact Douglas County Deputy Attorney Bob Sigler—he said that Sigler would be mindful of his situation. After Rogers' death, however, his father phoned Sigler, and the latter contended that he had no idea why Rogers insisted that he be contacted if Rogers turned up dead or went missing.

Omaha World-Herald reporter James Allen Flanery was also puzzled about Sigler's connection to Rogers after he talked to Rogers' family. Flanery started poking around into Rogers' death and visited the Douglas County Sheriff's Office, requesting Rogers' autopsy report, but the Sheriff's Office phoned Sigler, who refused to provide the report. A perplexed Flanery wandered over to Sigler's office.

But Sigler wasn't receptive to Flanery's inquiries and detonated: "There's no interview here!" shouted Sigler. "I don't affirm, I don't deny! I don't have any comment!" Sigler also made a remark that Flanery found very odd: He asked Flanery if then-*Omaha World-Herald* publisher Harold Andersen was aware that Flanery was poking around into Rogers' death.

Sigler was also the Douglas County Attorney's point man in the prosecution of Peter Citron. In addition to being charged with molesting two children, Citron was arrested with a vast cache of child pornography; but, strangely enough, the Douglas County Attorney's Office didn't charge him with a single count for possessing child pornography: Citron was given a mere three- to eight-year sentence for molesting the two boys, and he skated on kiddy-porn charges. Though both Owen and Bonacci named Citron as a child molester, Sigler said that Citron's case was never linked to Franklin "in the beginning, middle, or end."

Sigler's name surfaced yet again in our tale when he "investigated" whether or not Samuel Van Pelt had committed any improprieties when he picked up the twenty-year-old woman in Lincoln and drove her to the Douglas County grand jury. According to the young woman, Van Pelt had quite a talk with her on their treks back and forth from Lincoln to Omaha that day: Van Pelt had plied her with threatening questions, mentioning Alisha Owen's name and her predicament, and told her he had an "easy day" coming up because the witness he intended to call "was a homosexual and ... had sex with little boys."

After the woman provided Senator Chambers with her account, he sent the details and an accompanying letter to the Douglas County Attorney, who had his trusted subordinate, Sigler, look into the matter. Sigler and Damien Turner interviewed the woman for over two hours, concluding that Van Pelt wasn't guilty of any improprieties.

So even before Sigler stepped up to the mound as a relief pitcher for his old buddy, Gerald Moran, and became Owen's principal prosecutor, he had played quite a significant role in Franklin-related events. Owen also experienced another judicial changing of the guard: Judge Joe Case receded exclusively into private practice, and Judge Everett Inbody replaced him as Owen's presiding judge. Inbody, like Case, had been recruited from the hinterlands of Nebraska.

In October of 1993, Owen's appellate efforts to vindicate herself were given a booming boost: Troy Boner came forward and provided John

DeCamp with his "lie or die" affidavit. Boner's affidavit is fourteen pages long, but the first page offers a succinct rundown of both his motives for the affidavit and his sins against Owen: "I, and my mother and my family, are exhausted from living in fear of death or injury as a result of my personal involvement in the Franklin matters which ended up in my testifying at the Grand Jury hearings as well as at the Alisha Owen trial. I lied at the Grand Jury hearings, and I lied at the Alisha Owen trial. I lied when I 'recanted' my original statement to Gary Caradori. I lied because I truly believed and still do believe that it was a situation where I must either 'lie or die,' and at the insistence primarily of the Federal Bureau of Investigation officials who were dealing with me at that time..."

Boner's affidavit further stated, "From the age of 14 to 17, I was seriously involved in sexual and drug related activities with a wide range of individuals, but primarily and specifically with Alan Baer, Larry King, Robert Wadman, Peter Citron, Eugene Mahoney and others of prominence and wealth whom I will identify for any legitimate investigative officials who seriously wish to correct the problems and stop the conduct these individuals are and were engaged in rather than cover up that conduct."

Boner's affidavit explicitly mentioned the relationship between Alisha Owen and Wadman, parties at the Twin Towers, Paul Bonacci's participation in the pedophilic parties, and the ensuing cover-up: "It has been repeatedly publicly stated that my story and the stories told by Alisha Owen, Paul Bonacci, and a large number of other young people not previously identified who were simply intimidated from talking or who were ridiculed, were a 'Carefully Crafted Hoax.' The stories were not a hoax. The only carefully crafted thing that occurred was in fact the cover-up of the facts and the subsequent conviction of Alisha Owen and the original Grand Jury Investigation."

Boner's affidavit exonerated Caradori of any wrongdoing, witness tampering, and involvement in the phantom phone call: "Gary Caradori did not intimidate, threaten, coach, make things up, or in any way improperly or falsely portray the information I provided him." Boner maintained that the videotaped statement he gave to Caradori was "substantially the truth and substantially accurate." He said "substantially" because he "exaggerated" on some points and couldn't exactly recall "the date or place or time of this or that event or particular person or persons involved."

Is Troy Boner to be believed? The state's grand jury report and Moran maintained that Boner met Owen in 1988, and they then dated for a brief period. It seems highly unlikely that a hustler and a drug addict who had only briefly dated Owen would come to her defense after she was convicted. Boner surely would have just walked away from the "matters" if he had not been involved. But, once again, his conscience was burning—just as it had shortly after Gary Caradori's death.

Boner's affidavit even provided a caveat for the naysayers who would simply write him off as a hustler and drug addict who shouldn't be believed, and he specifically predicted that response from the FBI: "'You can't believe these kids and you can't believe Troy Boner. If he lied once, he will lie again. He's a drug addict. He's a sex pervert. Who are you going to believe, these kids with their wild stories or the respectable people like Alan Baer or the FBI…. Besides, these kids were as guilty or more guilty than anybody else. They were using drugs, and they were selling their bodies and they were getting paid well for it, and they did it all voluntarily.' I have heard that before. But, let me give you the other side of that story.

"Yes, we kids, from an early age, sold our bodies. We became drug addicts. We got lots and lots of money from these people. But today we are ruined because of that. And we were turned into sex perverts and drug addicts by these people. In my particular case, just like a lot of other young boys, I was turned into a true drug addict by Alan Baer. He was the one who first taught me to mainline and who first injected heroin directly into my veins—same as he did to a lot of other boys."

When Owen and I discussed Boner's zigzagging, I was a bit surprised that she harbored no animosity toward him. "I know that the grand jury and my trial were very hard on Troy, and I was pleased that he finally started to stand up for himself," she said. "But I was more pleased for him than for me. I know that Troy was really bothered by what he did to me, and I thought that this was maybe his first step in making things right with himself. I thought that Troy could now become a real person."

Around the time Boner submitted his affidavit to DeCamp, Yorkshire Television was filming *Conspiracy of Silence*, and Boner was interviewed by the Brits. Again, he confessed to lying before the grand jury and at Alisha Owen's trial. He also provided graphic allegations of the extreme pedophilic perversity of Larry King and Alan Baer.

John DeCamp thought Boner's affidavit and subsequent testimony assured Owen of a new trial, and he submitted it to Judge Inbody—Owen was granted a hearing in November 1993. At the hearing, Boner was expected to testify that he lied at Owen's trial and thus assure Owen of a new trial. But Boner was a no-show. Interestingly, Yorkshire Television turned up at the hearing, and the producer of *Conspiracy of Silence* was prompted to ask Sigler if MIA Boner had been subpoenaed by Douglas County, because Boner's changing his testimony at Owen's hearing potentially made him liable to perjury charges.

"Oh, no comment," replied a smiling Sigler.

DeCamp wasn't deterred by Boner's no-show—he coaxed Boner to come in from the cold once more, reassured him of a legal haven, and lined up a second hearing in December 1994 at the Douglas County Courthouse. Boner was provided with a "safe house" so he would be tucked away from the FBI and NSP, and also state or federal subpoenas. That December morning was cold and foggy—Alisha Owen, her husband, Troy Boner, his girlfriend, and DeCamp all made it unscathed to the courthouse. DeCamp was particularly excited about the prospect of securing a new trial for Owen.

As the group walked towards the courtroom, they saw prosecutor Sigler, and then they noticed a handful of men conspicuously milling around Sigler—the men were either Douglas County Deputy Sheriffs or NSP. The men approached Boner, snatched him, and dragged him into a vacant room—their abduction had the swift, well-rehearsed choreography of a SWAT-team takedown. After the men, Sigler, and Boner disappeared into the vacant room, and its door was locked, pandemonium quickly broke out: DeCamp started hollering, but no one was about to let him into the room. Shouts could also be heard emanating from the room.

A terrified Boner eventually emerged, and he pointblank told DeCamp that he would invoke his Fifth Amendment right against self-incrimination when called to testify at the hearing; Boner said if he didn't take the Fifth he'd end up in prison just like Owen. When DeCamp called Boner to the stand, he repeatedly took the Fifth: Judge Inbody ultimately ruled that Owen wouldn't be granted a new trial. Though it had required tactics reminiscent of the Gestapo, the state had again triumphed over Alisha Owen.

By this time, Owen had become a veteran at witnessing the wanton perversion of justice. "After everything I'd been through at that point, I can't say I was surprised by what they did to Troy. I was happy that he was finally able to stand up for himself; so I felt really bad that he got crushed again. On the other hand, only an individual can make the decision that he or she is not going to break. I had to do it, and I ultimately had to pay a really high price. But if you can't live with yourself, then what type of life do you have? I was hoping that Troy would be able to get a real life that was happy."

The strong-arming of Boner at the Douglas County Courthouse essentially marked the end of his efforts to help Owen. Needless to say, I was quite interested in talking to him when I made my first Franklin-related trip to Nebraska. At that point my background information on him was next to nil—I didn't even know that his mother had remarried and taken a new name. I made a few half-baked attempts to find him, but I had no luck by the time I left. As fate would have it, within two weeks Troy Boner turned up—unfortunately he turned up dead in Abilene, Texas.

Boner apparently spent his final days in a psychiatric facility in Abilene. My information on Boner's death is from a second-hand source, and the psychiatric hospital where he reportedly died has refused to provide any confirmation. With that caveat, I will tell you what I have been told: On or around February 11 of 2003, thirty-six-year-old Troy Boner sought medical treatment at Abilene Medical Regional Center's emergency room. He wore blue jeans, a casual shirt, and a jacket. A birth certificate was his only form of identification.

He told emergency room personnel that Blue Cross in Nebraska insured him, and a friend had promised to deliver his insurance card and additional belongings later in the day. He reportedly complained of chest pains. At the time, Boner was evidently living with his mother, who had relocated to Texas.

The Abilene Medical Regional Center transferred Boner to the psychiatric facility by early evening. When Boner arrived at the psychiatric facility, he reportedly seemed "shaky" and "dazed," and he also mentioned to facility personnel that he had missed his methadone that day.

Boner's first night at the facility was unremarkable—he was friendly when introducing himself to the staff and his fellow patients, but he was heard to ramble on about Franklin-related matters. The next afternoon, Boner was seen wandering the halls of the psychiatric facility. That night, however, the facility's personnel reportedly found him unconscious, sitting up in bed, with blood coming from his mouth. Facility personnel attempted to apply CPR, which caused additional blood to surge from his mouth.

An autopsy was performed on Boner the following morning by Tarrant County's Chief Medical Examiner, who concluded that Boner died of "acute respiratory failure"—he also dismissed "evidence of foul play." The Chief Medical Examiner noted that Boner had a "perimortem scalp injury"—perimortem trauma is sustained at or about the time of death—but he concluded that the scalp injury had no effect whatsoever on Boner's death.

So, just as I was leaping into Franklin with both feet, Boner was exiting feet first. I received word of Boner's demise about a month or so after he died. Shortly after I received the news, I talked to someone who had been affiliated with the Franklin Committee. This individual had seen a number of eerie "coincidences" occur, and he was convinced that the synchronicity of my initial visit to Nebraska and Boner's death was not coincidental.

Alisha Owen certainly didn't have a dearth of injustices in her trial, and they would eventually become the fodder for appeals. But by the end of 1994, both the Nebraska Court of Appeals and Nebraska Supreme Court had denied several of them.

One of the appeals shot down by the Nebraska Court of Appeals dealt with the planted "Casey letter." The juror who submitted the affidavit about the Casey letter said that he had combed through all of Owen's exhibits after her trial and couldn't find the letter in question. But the Nebraska Court of Appeals stated the letter was part and parcel of "Exhibit 55," which was a hodgepodge of letters and documents that the FBI seized during the March 1990 search of Owen's cell. The letter certainly would have been a smoking gun for the state, but Moran never singled it out during the trial. Rosenthal and Owen also scrutinized all the state's exhibits during the trial, and they didn't see the letter among the contents of "Exhibit 55" either. But here's the kicker on the Casey letter: The FBI supposedly seized the letter on its March 8 search of Owen's cell, *but the letter is dated March 15*—a week after the search and supposed seizure of the letter! Unfortunately, the implication of this was lost on the Nebraska Court of Appeals.

Owen's newfound ability to write her own appeals and her deftness at dodging the state's repeated onslaughts to toss her back in prison were evidently having an unpleasant effect on Douglas County Deputy Attorney Sigler, because he seemed rather gung-ho about getting her back behind bars. At a February 1995 hearing, Sigler commented on Owen's perpetual sequence of appeals: "The time has come to stop this. Enough is enough." At the hearing, Sigler even gave Owen quite a compliment at the expense of John DeCamp. "She's a smarter lawyer than he is," said Sigler, pointing to DeCamp. DeCamp said, "If there is a God above and a conscience somewhere," Owen should be spared a second stretch in prison. The judge sided with Owen, and she remained free on bond.

Shortly after the hearing where Boner was shanghaied, Judge Inbody was elevated to the Nebraska Court of Appeals, and Owen was given a new judge, also imported from outside of Douglas County, whose judges continued to disqualify themselves from Owen's legal travails. Owen's new judge was named Mark Fuhrman. The exploits of former LAPD Detective Mark Fuhrman were all over the news in 1995 in conjunction with the O.J. Simpson case—Owen felt having a judge by the same name didn't bode well for her. In August of 1995, Fuhrman ordered Owen back to prison, even though her appeals hadn't been adjudicated. A DeCamp motion pointed out to the judge that Owen was out on appeal and that her appeals weren't exhausted, and Owen once more sidestepped being sent back to York.

At that point, Owen was appealing her case on the grounds that Judge Case had been a practicing attorney: Nebraska law prohibits judges from practicing law. However, in November of 1995 the Nebraska Court of Appeals didn't seem to mind that fact, because it found that Owen's case hadn't been prejudiced by practicing lawyer Case.

Owen assumed that DeCamp would appeal the Court of Appeals ruling on Judge Case to the Nebraska Supreme Court. By February of 1996, though, Owen's appeal wasn't yet before the Supreme Court, and the Nebraska judiciary acted swiftly and mercilessly. On February 23, Judge Fuhrman ordered Owen to surrender herself on March 4 and begin serving her nine-to-fifteen-year perjury sentence. "I knew my position was precarious," said Owen. "I saw how hard they were fighting to get me back into jail. But I was going to fight, and I wasn't going down easy."

On March 7, three days after Owen surrendered, DeCamp filed a petition for habeas corpus, objecting to Owen's incarceration on the grounds that her conviction should be overturned because her trial judge "was a practicing attorney in violation of the Nebraska State Constitution." De-Camp's habeas corpus petition was dismissed, and Owen found herself back at York, staring at years in prison.

"After I was sent back to York, I decided I wouldn't hold myself to the normal standard of inmate behavior—I aspired to exceed even the standard of an ordinary citizen. I didn't want my time to be wasted— I wanted to make a difference. I went to work on York's road crew, and it was a lot of hard work. We toiled in the winter when it was three degrees and in the summer when it was ninety degrees, filling in potholes with asphalt and removing dead deer from the highway. Prior to working on the road crew, my idea of the great outdoors was a detached garage."

Owen was on York's road crew for approximately a year, and during that time she demonstrated that she wasn't a flight risk. She was eventually granted work release in Lincoln. The facility in Lincoln required her to be employed, and she had to adhere scrupulously to its draconian rules, or she would quickly find herself back at York. Owen also felt that she was under additional scrutiny because her character had been so publicly tainted. "It was no secret that the *Omaha World-Herald* had publicly called me a liar, so if I said anything it had to be the God's honest truth."

She was eventually granted work release in Omaha, and her job was to drive a prison van, delivering her fellow prisoners to various sites. Shortly after Owen started work release in Omaha, the College of St. Mary's in Omaha gave her a scholarship.

Nebraska's Department of Corrections was reluctant to let Owen attend college; so she phoned her long-time advocate, Senator Ernie Chambers, and he went to bat for her. Chambers' advocacy enabled Owen to enroll at the College of St. Mary's on an education release. Owen's meticulous conduct allowed her to make enormous strides at St. Mary's, but she never lost sight of her primary goal: to return to her husband, daughter, and family, and to have her conviction overturned.

In June of 1997, the Nebraska Supreme Court made a ruling that significantly impacted Owen's case. In *State v. Anderson*, a second-degree murder conviction, Anderson's appellate attorneys argued that jury misconduct had been prejudicial to their defendant. When *State v. Anderson* had been appealed before the Nebraska Court of Appeals, the court ruled that Anderson didn't present "clear and convincing" evidence demonstrating that the jury had been prejudiced, and Anderson's appeal was shot down. But the Nebraska Supreme Court decreed that the Nebraska Court of Appeals had erred in applying "clear and convincing" as an evidentiary standard to Anderson's claim of jury misconduct. The Nebraska Supreme Court ruled that Anderson's appeal should have been judged by a "preponderance of the evidence," which is a lower standard of proof.

The Nebraska Court of Appeals had applied the "clear and convincing" standard of proof when dismissing Owen's appeals on jury misconduct. So, in theory, the Nebraska Supreme Court had decided that the decisions against Owen were "overruled" too. "The Nebraska Court of Appeals essentially declared that it could use a heightened evidentiary standard against me so it could use it against Anderson," said Owen. "When *State v. Anderson* came out, I wrote a letter to the court, and said you overruled my case, why am I still incarcerated? It took them a while to find an attorney to try my case."

Her new attorney was Edward Fogarty, whose office later served as the site of my initial meeting with Alisha Owen. As Fogarty took the baton to see justice served on Owen's behalf, she continued to live in the Omaha facility and attend the College of St. Mary's. Fogarty was a seasoned attorney and well respected in Omaha's legal community—he had graduated from Creighton University Law School in 1965, and was a senior partner at his law firm.

Fogarty too had great reverence for the law, and when he delved into Owen's case, he was absolutely stunned by the injustices that had been inflicted on her. Given the numerous injustices suffered by Owen, and her exemplary behavior as a prisoner, he initially thought that a pardon or, at the very least, a commutation of her excessive sentence would be in order. But the Douglas County Attorney's Office wasn't willing to give an inch where Owen was concerned, and Fogarty let it be known that he planned to slug it out for her in the courts.

Shortly after Fogarty decided to take on Owen as a client, he had a chance encounter with Robert Sigler. Sigler referred to Owen as "Miss Piggy."

State v. Anderson had provided Owen with one more crack at the Nebraska judiciary, but Fogarty decided to go beyond *State v. Anderson* and seek "post-conviction relief" on the grounds that several injustices had been perpetrated against Owen. The legal parameters for granting post-conviction relief in Nebraska are very narrow: The only previously-raised appellate issues that can be revisited for post-conviction relief are issues of "plain error," which are errors so egregious that they undermine the fabric of either the state or federal constitutions, and thus scream out for redress.

Though the post-conviction relief process is like threading a needle, Fogarty still felt he could secure post-conviction relief for Alisha Owen due to the fact that her constitutional rights had been so dreadfully trampled upon. As Fogarty stepped into the ring to duke it out for Owen against the state and its vast supporting cast, her carousel of judges continued: Judge Fuhrman, who had sent Owen back to prison, receded out of sight, and Judge James Livingston replaced him. Livingston was Owen's fourth judge from Nebraska's hinterlands.

Fogarty perceived Owen's case to be laden with plain errors. Moreover, as a member of the bar for over thirty years, he had never encountered a more devastating case of attorney-client betrayal than Pamela Vuchetich's representation of Owen. One of Fogarty's motions for Owen's post-conviction relief summed up his thoughts on the issue: "Pamela Vuchetich, contrary to her obligation to defendant and other Franklin youth she represented, entered into an unprofessional, personal, romantic relationship with FBI Agent Mickey Mott that allowed Mott to corrupt Vuchetich and cause her to betray the defendant and develop a mass of evidence against the defendant.... The actions of Pamela Vuchetich are substantively so shocking and in violation of the defendant's rights under the Fourth, Fifth, Sixth, and Fourteenth Amendments of the US Constitution and comparable State provisions as to require setting aside the judgment of the conviction and sentence."

Fogarty was quite interested in deposing Vuchetich and Mott, as well as FBI agents Pankonin and Culver, and he subpoenaed the quartet. After Fogarty had Mott served with a subpoena, he wrote a letter to him: "I have no doubt Pam Vuchetich said what she said. Given Pam Vuchetich's history, I'm working on two premises: (1) her confession was true, or (2) it was the product of love-struck wishful thinking. Either way, it helps to explain Ms. Vuchetich's incompetent performance as a defense lawyer." In the letter, Fogarty also requested that Mott take a polygraph. If Mott was, in fact, culpable, Fogarty promised "to keep this mess as dignified and low profile as possible" by having the judge seal Mott's polygraph results, or possible confession, for presentation only before a judge.

Fogarty quickly found out that the FBI didn't want to bare any of its dirty secrets: The US Attorney for the District of Nebraska requested that Fogarty's subpoenas of FBI agents Mott, Pankonin, and Culver be quashed: Judge Livingston agreed. The US Attorney for Nebraska offered a number of rationales for quashing the subpoenas, but Fogarty found one to be particularly vexing: Disclosures by the agents "would reveal investigative techniques and procedures, the effectiveness would be impaired." If the FBI was worried that Mott's disclosures would compromise investigative techniques, Fogarty quipped to me, the FBI must be a dream job for every healthy, heterosexual young man.

Fogarty, like Rosenthal and DeCamp before him, had profound respect for his profession and believed that it was incumbent upon attorneys to show deference to each other. But after he began having a bird's-eye view of Owen's case and its toxic effect on the judicial process, he became incensed: He wrote a letter to the US Attorney for the District of Nebraska and CC'd the Douglas County Attorney. For starters, he characterized the US Attorney's actions as a "US cover-up and stonewalling directly destroying the possibility of full and fair hearing of these issues." The letter also stated that while the Douglas County Attorney's Office "may or may not" be an active participant in the "stonewalling, suppressing of evidence, cover up, and obstruction of justice," it was still "morally culpable and legally liable" for sitting by "smugly" as the feds obstructed justice.

Fogarty's subpoena of Pamela Vuchetich hadn't been quashed. And in June 2000 he made a jaunt to Topeka, Kansas, where she was living—she was divorced and had surrendered her license to practice law in Nebraska. Douglas County provided a new Deputy Attorney to oversee Vuchetich's deposition, because Sigler was no longer involved in Owen's case: He had experienced his very own upward mobility—the feds had moved him up to Assistant US Attorney for the District of Nebraska.

Fogarty found Vuchetich hostile and recalcitrant, and the Douglas County Deputy Attorney sitting in on the deposition rattled off objections to Fogarty's questions of Vuchetich as had Moran at Owen's trial. Vuchetich absolutely denied confessing to Rosenthal and Donna Owen that she had an affair with FBI agent Mott. And Vuchetich, like Mott at Owen's trial, had a bad case of amnesia when it came to recalling the content of all those protracted telephone calls to the FBI office that she had placed from her business and home phones.

Fogarty also found Vuchetich woefully lacking in candor, but, nonetheless, she made a number of interesting, yet bizarre, disclosures. About midway through the deposition, Vuchetich went on a rant concerning Owen's shortcomings: "She's a liar ... there was not one person that could corroborate anything she said ... her parents would give me information that directly disputed anything she told me ... she slept around with a large number of men, young men ... she's had sex in her parents' house in the bathroom ... she'd sneak out the window and run around at night ... she ran around with gay guys ... she wrote a lot of bad checks...."

Vuchetich had told the *World-Herald* that she believed Owen, but withdrew as Owen's counsel when Owen was on the verge of facing the grand jury because of a conflict of interest. Vuchetich, however, gave Fogarty a different explanation: She withdrew from Owen's case due to the fact that Owen explicitly confided to Vuchetich that she would "knowingly and willingly" commit perjury before the Douglas County grand jury.

Fogarty was also curious about Vuchetich's subversion of Owen with the FBI, but Vuchetich didn't feel that she had committed any transgressions against Owen: "I know that I never did anything to hurt Alisha in my conversations with the FBI or with anyone else." Vuchetich repeatedly said that Nebraska's Counsel for Discipline had cleared her of any improprieties, and indeed it had.

Fogarty brought up a number of examples of Vuchetich's subversion of Owen: He mentioned a *World-Herald* article published after the Douglas County grand jury and before Owen's trial, wherein Vuchetich publicly stated she agreed that the child-abuse allegations were a carefully crafted hoax—he thought it was a prime example of Vuchetich's hindering Owen's prospect of a fair and impartial trial. Fogarty actually broached that *World-Herald* article twice: The first time he raised the issue, the Douglas County Deputy Attorney objected, and the second time Vuchetich denied making such an admission, even though it was there in black and white.

Then there was that little matter of Vuchetich representing Terry Clements at Owen's trial. Clements—at Moran's behest you will recall—discussed Owen's affinity for "virgin penises." Vuchetich replied that she didn't represent him in terms of the "content" of his testimony, but, rather, to ensure he wasn't "harassed" by Moran or Rosenthal. Fogarty asked Vuchetich how she ended up with Clements as a client—after all, Clements seemingly had his pick of all the lawyers in the Yellow Pages. Vuchetich said, "I believe he called me."

Vuchetich also provided Fogarty with a rather outlandish non sequitur regarding Owen's sticking to her "story." She claimed that Owen did so "to get out of prison," even though the facts and logic dictate just the opposite. Alisha Owen has taken exception to Vuchetich's explanation of why she stuck to her story: "For Pam to say that the reason I stuck to my story was to get out of prison defies all reason and is absolutely insane," said Owen. "The only way I could have gotten out early was to go along with the FBI and prosecution—that was my only option for getting out of prison."

In February 2000, Fogarty and Owen had their day in court—Fogarty was in for a succession of shocks before, during, and after the hearing, whereas Owen was a weathered veteran of injustice. Shortly before the hearing, the Douglas County Deputy Attorney told Fogarty that if Owen repeated any of the statements that were part and parcel of her perjury conviction on the stand, she would be charged with perjury again.

After Fogarty had called Donna Owen and Henry Rosenthal to the stand, Judge Livingston ruled that he wouldn't hear any more testimony about Pamela Vuchetich, because it was irrelevant to Owen's receiving a fair and impartial trial. Livingston declared that there was a "firewall" between Vuchetich's resigning as Owen's attorney and Rosenthal's taking over for Owen at the state and federal grand juries and at her trial. In other words, Vuchetich would bear no responsibility whatsoever for Owen's judicial travails, because she hadn't represented her during the grand juries or at trial.

Fogarty argued that even if Livingston let Vuchetich off the hook for enabling the FBI to deconstruct Owen's credibility without announcing her Miranda rights, she still represented Danny King during the grand jury and at Owen's trial, and she had also acquired a new client, Terry Clements, who further damaged Owen at her trial. These arguments were lost on Livingston, and he decided that Owen shouldn't be granted any post-conviction relief. In addition to finding Fogarty's arguments regarding plain errors to be spurious, Livingston ruled that even after applying the *State v. Anderson* "preponderance of evidence" standard to Owen's case, he didn't find that she had been prejudiced.

Fogarty was "absolutely furious" at Livingston's antics, and he appealed for post-conviction relief to the Nebraska Supreme Court, citing many examples of plain error. The Nebraska Attorney General's Office moved to dismiss Fogarty's petition and the Nebraska Supreme Court acquiesced, concluding that Fogarty's petition was "so unsubstantiated as not to require argument." Fogarty had bypassed the Nebraska Court of Appeals for the obvious reason that Judge Theodore Carlson had been elevated from Douglas County District Judge to the Court of Appeals in 1998.

Owen greatly appreciated Fogarty's efforts, but she had come to the realization that the Nebraska judiciary would never cut her one inch of slack. In September 2000, Owen was given her first shot at parole—she had served approximately four and a half years on her perjury conviction. But she faced a major hurdle in her quest for parole—she wasn't about to show the slightest signs of contrition, because she considered herself to be fully innocent.

"Throughout my time in prison, I exceeded every standard and my GPA in school was just about straight A's—I had been an exemplary prisoner," Owen told me. "When you go before the parole board, they want to hear you say that you're contrite. When prison officials confronted me about what I would say before the parole board, I said that I would do the exact same thing all over again. I did not lie, and I'm not going to say I'm a liar just so I can get out of prison—I made that very, very clear. I let the parole board know that I'm innocent and if it means that I have to do every single day of this sentence then that's exactly what I'll do."

Remarkably, the Nebraska Parole Board voted unanimously—a five to zero margin—to give Owen parole. A Parole Board member said that he had never seen an inmate with a more impressive record of accomplishments. Senator Ernie Chambers wrote a letter on Owen's behalf: He discussed her many accomplishments as well as her mentoring fellow prisoners for their GEDs, along with mentoring nontraditional students at the College of St. Mary's.

"The parole board does not like to be embarrassed by people breaking parole, and I was a high-profile case. Very few people ever get their first parole on a long sentence, but the parole board gave me a unanimous vote for parole," Alisha said. "These people had scrutinized me twenty-four hours a day, and if you watch someone for twenty-four hours a day—if she's a liar you'll know it. I told the Board that they had watched me since 1988, and it was now 2000, so for 12 years they had watched me—I said let me have parole, and I'll make you proud. So they gave me parole, and that was a good day. The parole board was kind to me."

Thirty friends and family members awaited Owen with hugs and kisses as she left the parole hearing. As Owen walked away from her state-sponsored nightmare, holding her husband's hand, she still refused to make any comments to reporters. Since Owen's release from prison, she has been happily married and also a productive member of society—she is self-employed.

"I think most Nebraskans knew something was wrong; they just don't know the extent of it. I decided I can't change the past, but I'm going to outlive them all, and I'm going to live a wonderful life. I live every single day and enjoy it—I have a wonderful husband and daughter. I have to admit, though, that there's some unfinished business: I hope that one day I'll be pardoned, but in the state of Nebraska you have to say you're guilty and admit remorse. I believe wholeheartedly that an innocent person has the right to say they're innocent, and the judicial system did something wrong to them. And I'm going to keep fighting."

I've spent many hours talking to Alisha Owen, and I've even spent a Thanksgiving and an Easter with her family. She is extremely close to her family, and she has many close friends. She is well-read and has traveled extensively. The horrific events of her youth and early adulthood notwithstanding, she's managed to build a successful, productive and happy life. Before Judge Case sentenced her to between nine and fifteen years, he said she was a serial offender, and he predicted that she would continue to be a serial offender. He was wrong.

As she sits in her living room, holding a cup of coffee, a universe removed from the horrors that have been visited upon her, she appears to have transcended her bygone inferno, but looks can be deceiving: "I've made peace with most of the things that have happened to me in the past, but I still have nightmares—my nightmares are usually of nondescript people who come to my home and take me back to prison. There's no way you can be in solitary confinement for almost two years and not have it affect you."

The Washington Times

THURSDAY, JUNE 29, 1989 •   WASHINGTON, D.C.   PHONE (202) 636-3000 SUBSCRIBER SERVICE (202) 636-3333   25 cents

Homosexual prostitution inquiry ensnares VIPs with Reagan, Bush

'Call boys' took midnight tour of White House

By Paul M. Rodriguez
and George Archibald

A homosexual prostitution ring is under investigation by federal and District authorities and includes among its clients key officials of the Reagan and Bush administrations, military officers, congressional aides and U.S. and foreign businessmen with close social ties to Washington's political elite, documents obtained by The Washington Times reveal.

One of the ring's high-profile clients was so well-connected, in fact, that he could arrange a middle-of-the-night tour of the White House for his friends on Sunday, July 3, of last year. Among the six persons on the extraordinary 1 a.m. tour were two male prostitutes.

Federal authorities, including the Secret Service, are investigating

criminal aspects of the ring and have told male prostitutes and their homosexual clients that a grand jury will deliberate over the evidence throughout the summer, the Times learned.

Reporters for this newspaper examined hundreds of credit-card vouchers, drawn on both corporate and personal cards and made payable to the escort service operated by the homosexual ring. Many of the vouchers were run through a so-called "sub-merchant" account of the Chambers Funeral Home by a son of the owner, without the company's knowledge.

Among the clients, names contained in the vouchers — and identified by prostitutes and escort operators — are government officials, locally based U.S. military officers,

businessmen, lawyers, bankers, congressional aides and other professionals.

Editors of The Times said the newspaper would print only the

names of those found to be in sensitive government posts or positions of influence. "There is no intention of publishing names or facts about the operation merely for titillation."

said Wesley Pruden, managing editor of The Times.

The office of U.S. Attorney Jay B. Stephens, former deputy White House counsel to President Reagan, is coordinating federal aspects of the inquiry but refused to discuss the investigation or the grand jury action.

Several former White House colleagues of Mr. Stephens are listed among clients of the homosexual prostitution ring, according to the credit-card records, and those persons have confirmed that the charges were theirs.

Mr. Stephens' office, after first saying it would cooperate with The Times' inquiry, withdrew the offer late yesterday and also declined to say whether Mr. Stephens would recuse himself from the case be-

cause of possible conflict of interest.

At least one highly placed Bush administration official and a wealthy businessman who procured homosexual prostitutes from the escort services operated by the ring are cooperating with the investigation, several sources said.

Among clients who charged homosexual prostitute services on major credit cards over the past 18 months are Charles K. Dutcher, former associate director of presidential personnel in the Reagan administration, and Paul R. Balach, Labor Secretary Elizabeth Dole's political personnel liaison to the White House.

In the 1970s, Mr. Dutcher was a congressional aide to former Mrs. Robert Bauman, Maryland Republican, who resigned from the House after he admitted having engaged in sexual liaisons with teen-age male.

see PROBE, page A7

Omaha World-Herald

JULY 25, 1990   EDITION 5
OUR 125TH YEAR
NO. 205   56 PAGES
25c
Nebraska Edition

Grand Jury Says Abuse Stories Were a 'Carefully Crafted Hoax'

Three Indicted; Many Rumors Are Debunked

By Robert Dorr
and Gabriella Stern
World-Herald Staff Writers

A Douglas County grand jury Tuesday called the Franklin Community Federal Credit Union child-abuse allegations a "carefully crafted hoax."

The grand jury's report said the hoax was "scripted by a person or persons with considerable knowledge of the people and institutions of Omaha ..."

While not specifically saying who authored the hoax, the report was critical of some state officials and others who made or supported the child sexual abuse accusations.

The grand jury said blame must fall on three young people who accused prominent Omahans of sexual misconduct. Two have recanted their original stories, and the third was indicted Tuesday on charges of lying to the grand jury.

The grand jury said "rumormongers" spread much gossip and misinformation.

It said "many in the community both spread and received the gossip," and

Baer ... Brandeis stores heir.

Full text of grand jury report begins on Page 14.

Miss Owen ... York inmate.

working with Casey."

It said the Legislature's Franklin committee had "hidden agendas" in pursuing the sexual-abuse allegations. Committee chairman Loran Schmit has been "politically irresponsible" in some of his statements, the grand jury said.

Former State Sen. John DeCamp's memorandum naming five people who, he said, were central figures in the investigation amounted to a "smear campaign" and further spread the ru-

part-time Omahan and fired Boys Town employee Michael Casey and Kirsten Hallberg and Bonnie Cosentino, who were active in the Concerned Parents group.

The grand jury criticized Gary Caradori, the Franklin legislative committee investigator killed in a plane crash

Schmit Rejects Report, Defends His Committee

By Henry J. Cordes
WORLD-HERALD BUREAU

Lincoln — State Sen. Loran Schmit of Bellwood said Tuesday that he did not accept a Douglas County grand jury's conclusions that alleged child sexual-abuse victims who had made videotaped statements to a legislative committee were a key part of a "carefully crafted hoax" scripted by someone with considerable knowledge of Omaha.

Two of the four people who gave the taped statements — Alisha Owen and Paul Bonacci — were determined to have committed perjury.

Two others interviewed by the legislative committee — Troy Boner and James Daniel King — were reported to have recanted their statements of child sexual abuse. They were not indicted.

Schmit, chairman of the Legislature's Franklin Committee, said Tuesday after the grand jury issued its report that he considered it unfortunate that the grand jury indicted Miss Owen and Bonacci.

"Their conclusions ... frankly do not coincide with the conclusions I have

Schmit ... called indictments "tragic."

He called the indictments "tragic." Once Miss Owen and Bonacci have a chance to tell their stories in court, Schmit said, different conclusions may result.

Schmit also said he resented the grand jury's criticism of the committee he heads.

If it had not been for the committee's investigation, he said, charges never

—Epilogue—

What is the Reality?

So what can be concluded from this sordid sequence of incidents, interviews, indictments, convictions, confessions, denouncements, and deaths? On one hand, a Douglas County grand jury found that Larry King never molested a child and certainly wasn't an interstate pedophilic pimp, but that grand jury is trumped by countless contradicting documents and the statements of Eulice Washington, Shawneta Moore, Alisha Owen, Troy Boner, Paul Bonacci, Rusty Nelson, Tony Harris, Fred Carter, Nikolai Cayman, Rue Fox, Paul Rodriguez, Henry Vinson, and a highly decorated NYPD detective. I concede that some of these sources are tenuous; but if just one of them is truthful, then the grand jury report was largely a fiction.

The grand jury also declared that Boys Town students weren't illicitly involved with Larry King and the "non-existent" pedophile network. It's surely hard to cast off the traditional saintly image of Boys Town. However, the statements of Eulice Washington, Alisha Owen, Troy Boner, Paul Bonacci, Rusty Nelson, Tony Harris, Fred Carter, Nikolai Cayman, Rue Fox, and Henry Vinson counter-balance the government's official account—I've included Vinson because he told me that both Larry King and Craig Spence disclosed to him that Boys Town kids were involved in their network. Again, if just one of them is truthful, then the Douglas County grand jury was a travesty.

When I refer to sources as tenuous, I touch on Franklin's built-in mechanism that has greatly facilitated its concealment. The victims were molested and turned on to drugs as children, and, after they outgrew their youthful marketability, they were discarded and quickly became drug addicts and/or felons, thereby compromising themselves and demolishing their credibility. Boner characterized their state as "ruined," and readily confessed, "we were turned into sex perverts and drug addicts by these people." In the case of Alisha Owen, a former victim who wouldn't recant, the feds and state garishly and unabashedly used her prior behavior to deconstruct her credibility. Nebraska's media and the national media have also depicted her as a pathological liar.

In addition to the names I've listed, two individuals who claimed to be victims of the Franklin pedophile network have approached me. I didn't have a paper trail on either one to King or to Boys Town, so I opted not to include their names, even though I have a tendency to strongly believe one of them. Senator Ernie Chambers has also told me that further victims approached him as Franklin unfolded—he didn't want to see them destroyed by the wrath of law enforcement and advised them to button up and hunker down. Sandi Caradori, too, has received a number of phone calls over the years from purported victims who have conveyed to her that they appreciated the crusade of her late husband. Finally, Gary Caradori's documentation lists several victims I never managed to contact. I probably could have used his documentation to locate additional victims, but I ultimately concluded that I had a critical mass of victim corroboration without seeking out other victims. Perhaps some will come forward as a result of this book.

The powerful sating their appetites for forbidden fruit via pedophilia and pedophilic sadism are evils that date back millennia: The Roman emperor Tiberius reportedly indulged in pedophilia and then murdered his victims. Moreover, since I started work on this story, pedophile rings linked to the powerful have been exposed in Portugal, Belgium, Chile, and Mexico. The Portuguese ring procured victims from Portugal's version of Boys Town, and the Belgian pedophile ring reportedly utilized blackmail and had satanic practitioners. The Belgian ring also mirrored Franklin in the respect that many Belgians, including law enforcement officers, concluded it entailed a massive cover-up. The situation prompted thousands of Belgians to take to the streets in protest. So powerbroker pedophile networks like Franklin aren't unprecedented around the globe.

Indeed, extraordinary and breathtaking power was deployed to orchestrate the cover-up and vaporization of the Franklin story, which generated deeply disturbing aberrations in the US legal system. When I made my first face-to-face pitch of Franklin to a news organization, I told the individual meeting with me that it was likely that state and federal grand juries in Nebraska had been co-opted, and I felt a federal grand jury in

DC was probably co-opted too: The sort of puppeteering I alluded to implied that the puppeteers were sitting at the apex of power. The individual I met with couldn't make the paradigm shift required to entertain the prospect that two, and possibly three, grand juries had been hijacked to protect child molesters, and he looked at me with unbridled skepticism, which became an all too familiar pattern. He is a former recipient of the Pulitzer Prize in investigative journalism.

In my Franklin investigation, the names of lofty politicians and powerbrokers who have pedophilic appetites have repeatedly surfaced. The names have been absolutely mind-boggling. Senator Schmit was anonymously implored not to pursue the Franklin Committee investigation because it would lead to the "highest levels of the Republican party." And shortly after Gary Caradori realized that he was in the feds' crosshairs and "being 'set up' for an arrest," he wrote a letter to a renowned lawyer noting that the pedophile network he uncovered extended "to the highest levels of the United States." Given the names that have surfaced in my investigation, I believe that without an immaculate cover-up of Franklin the administration of George H.W. Bush may have been jeopardized.

But to name names would serve no useful purpose, thanks to Franklin's built-in concealment mechanism: the victims' previous transgressions and the politicians' eminence. Eulice Washington continues to insist that she saw a nationally prominent politician at a pedophilic party she attended in Chicago. Washington has amazingly turned her life around, and has been gainfully employed as a youth worker, but she fell in with the wrong crowd after her liberation from the Webb household and has had four children out of wedlock; she lost control of one of her sons, who became enmeshed in gang activity and was later placed in Boys Town, of all places. Though Washington is an extraordinary example of someone overcoming a hellish childhood, her word against that of an eminent politician would be a first-round TKO.

Ultimately, an extremely uncomfortable question needs to be considered: Were the feds saving a specific administration or an extremely corrupt, institutionalized political system where blackmail is commonplace—or, perhaps, both? In other words, is it possible that the feds were the prime movers in Franklin's underlying events? Is it conceivable that Franklin may have been the blackest of black ops?

Rumors that Franklin Credit Union funds ended up in the Reagan administration's illegal Contra war chest even made it into the *Lincoln Journal*, and Larry King fondly name-dropped his friendship with CIA Director William Casey, but rumors and name dropping do not a CIA operation make. However, Paul Rodriguez and his colleagues had sources state that Craig Spence was a CIA asset; Spence himself claimed he was a CIA asset and confessed that his home was bugged by "friendly" intelligence agents. Henry Vinson also told me that Spence confessed to him he was a CIA asset and that his blackmail enterprise was CIA-affiliated.

Vinson claims to have informed federal officials that the pedophilic blackmail enterprise of King and Spence had connections to the CIA. The CIA has denied its affiliation to Spence, and Vinson is a convicted felon, but thousands of documents were sealed in Vinson's case. The documentation salvaged by the *Washington Times* is at odds with the statements issued by the US Attorney concerning Vinson's clientele, but it corresponds to Vinson's allegations.

Should we believe Vinson, the convicted felon, whose statements concerning his VIP clientele are corroborated, or the government that covered up the names of Vinson's clientele and refuses to unseal the documents in his case? The unsealing of Vinson's case files may elucidate the alleged connections of King and Spence's pedophilic pandering to the CIA. If Vinson's documentation is unsealed, and shows that he revealed to the feds that King and Spence were pedophilic pimps connected to the CIA, then it would be incumbent on the Department of Justice to tell America whether or not those allegations were investigated or simply ignored and covered up. If the Department of Justice has a sincere interest in the welfare of children, it should unseal those documents and provide the American public with answers.

Documentation from the CIA's mind-control program demonstrates that the agency carried out extremely ominous experimentation on children that included electroshock, drugs, hypnosis and "psychological tricks," and the documents discussed the experimenters' inducing disassociation and multiple personality disorder. The CIA apparently came to the rescue of the Finders, who were seemingly engaged in sinister activities with children, and a CIA official offered only "Hogwash" as a rebuttal when *US News & World Report* questioned him about the CIA's possible connections to the Finders.

Moreover, the CIA's Operation Midnight Climax in the 1950s and 1960s consisted of CIA-run safe houses in San Francisco and New York—prostitutes on the CIA payroll lured clients back to the safe houses, where they were surreptitiously slipped mickeys of various drugs, including LSD, and monitored behind one-way mirrors; sexual blackmail was reportedly used to secure the confidences of the unsuspecting victims who were surreptitiously drugged. The CIA has a track record of child abuse and blackmail, even though the leaked documentation about these particular endeavors has been scant. So is it possible that American politicians have been targeted by the CIA's spycraft?

The inordinate lust for power is often accompanied by the inordinate power of lust, which has the potential to cause the smartest of individuals to make foolish decisions: Bill Clinton is a stunning example of someone who craved power from a young age, but nearly forfeited his coveted seat at the pinnacle of power because of compulsive sexual behavior. In addition to lust making smart people foolish, arrogance and greed also make fools of very smart people, and many of our politicians have the trifecta of full-tilt libido, arrogance, and greed.

In recent years, America has witnessed the sexual downfall of New Jersey Governor James McGeevey, New York Governor Eliot Spitzer, US Senator Larry Craig, and US Congressman Mark Foley. Both Craig and Foley sat at the zenith of power in the US Congress: Craig attempted to solicit sex in an airport restroom and Foley sent instant messages with explicit sexual content to an underage Congressional page.

After Craig and Foley were outed, long-standing accounts of their brazen homosexuality began to surface—both were extremely susceptible to sexual blackmail: One sexually compromising picture leaked to the media or the public certainly would have marked the end of their political careers as well as public disgrace. If such pictures existed, whoever possessed them would have held these politicians in thrall. But homosexuality and pedophilia are by no means the only fodder for the blackmail of a politician—revelations of extramarital affairs and bribes have sunk many.

In 2008, the Congressional approval rating plummeted to an almost unfathomable low of 12%. If 88% of Americans feel that the Congress is not serving their will, whose will is it conceivably serving? One might say "special interests," but the story I have told suggests that Congress may be serving the will of covert masters. Perhaps there is a checks and balances system that is obscured from the American public—a checks and balances system of blackmail. Is it possible that our politicians' various improprieties are catalogued and then wielded over their heads, like some sword of Damocles? I consider the federal overkill involved in covering up Franklin, and, again, I ask were the feds protecting an administration, a corruption-laden political system, or both? The upward mobility of certain officers of the court who played a role in covering up the facts of Franklin, even after the administration of George H.W. Bush left office, may be an indication that "the system" is corrupt and compromised.

The government's abetting child abuse is extremely disturbing, but the media, or the fourth estate, played a role as well. The feds were aided and abetted by the press through either commission or omission: The "conservative" *Omaha World-Herald* and the "liberal" *Washington Post* loudly echoed the feds' official line. The *World-Herald* proactively dismantled the Franklin Committee's investigation and promoted the version of Franklin cooked up by the FBI and the Douglas County grand jury, just as the *Washington Post* proactively dismantled the *Washington Times'* investigation and promoted the malfeasance of the DC US Attorney's Office and the Secret Service. The *New York Times*, CBS' *48 Hours*, and *GQ* also participated by trumpeting what seems to be government propaganda.

The *Omaha World-Herald* published a retrospective 1998 article on "Franklin" echoing a familiar refrain: "The passage of time, Van Pelt said, has vindicated what the Douglas County Franklin grand jury did. Nothing has emerged in the intervening years that disproves the grand jury's conclusions, he said." In addition to owning a newspaper that is an arbiter of truth, the World-Herald Company co-owns Election Software & Systems, which has counted approximately fifty percent of the ballots in the last four major US elections.

I've written mostly about the *Omaha-World Herald* and its twisting and turning of facts, but the *Washington Post* steamrolled over the *Washington Times* reportage on Craig Spence, his purported CIA affiliation, and his blackmail enterprise. The *Washington Post* branded the *Washington Times* reporting as "yellow journalism" and having "not much substance." The *Post* also offered a disingenuous explanation for discounting the *Washington Times* stories on Spence—"a key law enforcement official" had "lunch at the *Post*" and "assured the staff that the investigation was primarily on credit card fraud." Again, it's rather interesting that the *Post* didn't listen to key law enforcement officials during Watergate, but it was all ears concerning the government's account of Spence.

Interestingly, Henry Vinson named a high-flyer at the *Washington Post*, who professes to be a married heterosexual, as one of his more gung-ho clients. I don't consider Vinson's word infallible, but his account does offer a plausible explanation for the newspaper's siding with the government concerning Spence et al.

The *New York Times* coverage of Franklin was quite interesting—America's newspaper of record jumped on the story almost immediately, reporting on the Unicameral's Executive Board meeting in December of 1988, when the first allegations of child abuse publicly surfaced. A week later, the *Times* had a follow-up article that further explored the child-abuse allegations, and it even included an interview with Julie Walters, who said that she felt Eulice Washington's contentions were credible. The newspaper also reported on the findings of the Douglas County grand jury. The final *New York Times* article on Franklin reported on the findings of the federal grand jury—both articles discussed Alisha Owen's perjury indictments.

The timing of CBS' *48 Hours* was uncanny: The episode even commented on the fact that Owen "is now on trial for perjury." The producers of that segment must have kept tabs on Owen's trial, and the *48 Hours* aired on the same day that Owen's jurors started deliberating her fate. Though the *48 Hours* episode had a profound impact on Owen's jury, I realize that to directly attribute malfeasance to the show would be mere speculation. But the feds spared no expense to cover up Franklin; is it possible that some very powerful people in government called in markers with a major network to facilitate the cover-up?

I think it would be difficult to interpret the *GQ* article, "Other People's Money," as anything other than a hatchet job on the Franklin Committee, Gary Caradori, Owen, etc. In addition to a derisive slant, the article had numerous inaccuracies—even in its pronouncement of the government's cover story on Franklin. For example, the article described Eulice Washington as a "9-year-old boy." Major magazines require articles to be scrutinized by "fact checkers," but *GQ*'s fact checkers were obviously asleep at the wheel that month.

I've heard of other media personalities who are possibly compromised, but it's also conceivable that many in the media found the story of Franklin too implausible, and opted to take their cue from the government instead of putting much legwork into excavating the truth. If, in fact, Franklin reportage was so skewed because the media has been heavily compromised and corrupted, it does not bode well for our society.

A third powerful entity in our society that has been implicated in Franklin is Boys Town, and, by extension, the Church. I have considerable corroboration that King plundered Boys Town for underage victims. Boys Town's administration initially seemed to be interested in investigating the allegations—Father Val Peter gave Julie Walters the thumbs-up to look into Eulice Washington's early allegations. But, later on, Caradori noted that Father Peter was "uncooperative" with his investigation. A paper trail, albeit scant, also links Larry King and his credit union to Boys Town.

Boys Town has had a positive impact on numerous children, but it is an organization with a shadow. This was illustrated once again by its character assassination of former students who stepped forward and attempted to litigate molestation lawsuits against the orphanage. A "report" commissioned by Boys Town to "investigate" the abuse allegations employed retired G-man John Pankonin as its chief investigator, and it was essentially déjà vu all over again: The report included the psychological and psychiatric records of the alleged victims, trashed their credibility, refuted their allegations, and exonerated the alleged abusers. The attorney representing the litigants as well as social services agencies were dumbfounded by Boys Town's "malicious" response to the lawsuits.

All the litigants had succumbed to drug addiction and/or antisocial behavior that made their credibility tenuous and easy to deconstruct except for one: Todd Rivers. So the Boys Town report published an absolute falsehood concerning him. The report said that Rivers had claimed recovered memories of his molestations by Boys Town's Father James

Kelly in March of 2002, and he gave an interview to the *World-Herald* about his molestations before February 23, 2002; therefore he wasn't being truthful. But Todd Rivers actually commented on his abuse in a *World-Herald* article from February 23, *2003*—almost a year after he recovered memories of being molested. The fact that Boys Town published an outright falsehood to deconstruct Rivers' credibility is very disturbing. It's also disturbing that the Boys Town report cleared Father James Kelly of molesting Boys Town youth, because I've talked to four former students who claim Kelly was their abuser, and his history suggests that of a serial predator.

After David Hill, Rue Fox, and Nikolai Cayman were allegedly molested at Boys Town, all three told me they were put in psychiatric facilities. Molestation will invariably have adverse effects on children, compelling them to act out, and to attribute sinister motives to Boys Town for depositing them in psychiatric facilities as a premeditated means to destroy their credibility, like the former Soviet Union discredited dissenters, would be problematic. But according to Cayman, after he told Boys Town staff about his alleged flights with Larry King, he was flown to Georgia and deposited in a psychiatric institution. His account of being summarily flown from Nebraska to Georgia and hospitalized is corroborated by affiliates of federal law enforcement. If Boys Town was actually concerned about Cayman's mental health, and he was in the midst of a severe mental health crisis requiring hospitalization, I would think that Boys Town would have hospitalized him in an Omaha facility.

Ironically, it was an exploration of Satanism which propelled me into the parallel universe of Franklin, and it's one of the facets of the story where I've accrued the least amount of corroboration: I have Shawneta Moore's accounts, and I also have the statements of Paul Bonacci, Nikolai Cayman, and Rusty Nelson.

The US Customs report on the Finders seemingly implicates that group in occult activities, but over the years I've heard several conflicting accounts about the cult's actual beliefs and its affiliation to the CIA. Nonetheless, the CIA shutting down an investigation into the Finders reminds me of the OPD and FBI's earliest efforts to slam the door on the early allegations against Larry King. The CIA apparently had no problem lowering an iron curtain on any investigation into the Finders—even when US Representatives pushed for an inquiry. If the US Representatives had possessed the same fortitude as members of the Franklin Committee, and not backed down, their hearing might have yielded some rather remarkable revelations that the CIA obviously didn't want publicized.

Though I only have four corroborations on the Franklin narrative's satanic component, the theme of Larry King confessing to or playing a role in the murder or sale of children has come from Troy Boner, Alisha Owen, Paul Bonacci, Rusty Nelson, and Henry Vinson. Though the selling or killing of children isn't necessarily satanic, it *is* unconditionally evil.

Satanism has numerous different sects with varying beliefs, but many of its adherents hold values that are an inversion of *idealized* Christian values, which put a premium on the preservation of a child's innocence—Satanists of this ilk look upon the defilement of innocence as one of their highest sacraments. They would be the perfect individuals to conscript in the creation of a pedophile network, or to carry out inhumane activities or "psychological tricks" on children in the perpetuation of sadistic mind-control experiments.

I recall the "satanic panic" that emerged in the 1980s, but I didn't give it too much credence because it was so off-the-wall. The FBI, though, responded to the escalating brouhaha with a 1992 report authored by a supervisory special agent at Quantico, Virginia's venerated Behavioral Science Unit. The report essentially debunked all that wacky innuendo about ritual abuse and reassured the American public that is was virtually non-existent and they could sleep soundly at night. Though the FBI report yielded scant evidence concerning ritual abuse, several studies and articles on the subject have been published in academic, peer-reviewed journals. The strength of their findings lies in the fact that the victims who claim to have been ritually abused are from disparate geographic locations and socioeconomic strata; yet they describe the same improbable, horrific events.

A 1995 study published in *The Journal of Psychohistory* surveyed five organizations throughout the United States offering a hotline for children, including Childhelp USA, a bellwether in the advocacy and assistance for abused children: The study found that in 1992 roughly

23,000 calls reporting the ritual abuse of children had been logged by the five hotlines.

Additionally, a 1991 study conducted by the National Center for the Treatment of Dissociative Disorders in Denver, Colorado, published in *The Journal of Child Abuse & Neglect*, surveyed thirty-seven adults who had reported ritual abuse as children and were diagnosed with either multiple personality disorder or dissociative disorder. All the subjects said they had been sexually abused, physically abused and/or tortured, had witnessed animal mutilations, been forced to take drugs, and received death threats—83% said they had witnessed at least one adult or child sacrifice.

The studies of ritual abuse survivors have contained relatively limited numbers of subjects, but in 2007 a team of researchers from the United States and Germany conducted the Adult Survivors of Extreme Abuse Survey (EAS), the largest study of ritual-abuse survivors to date. The team provided an online website for survivor advocates and survivors. The website featured a survey of 238 questions, ranging from demographics to categories of abuse. Of the 1,471 participants responding to the questionnaire, 987 completed the "Categories of Abuse" component: 191 participants claimed to have experienced only ritual abuse, 69 said that they had undergone only mind control, and 513 reported that they experienced both ritual abuse and mind control.

Of the 704 EAS respondents reporting ritual abuse, 543 respondents specifically reported satanic ritual abuse. When the EAS investigators crunched the numbers concerning the participants who claimed ritual abuse, they were amazed at how closely the types of ritual abuse reported by the EAS respondents matched the types of ritual abuse found in the 1991 study conducted by the National Center for the Treatment of Dissociative Disorders. The latter study found that 100% of the subjects had been sexually abused, physically abused and/or tortured, had witnessed animal mutilations, and received death threats: The respective percentages of the EAS respondents reporting abuse in those categories were 95%, 96%, 86%, and 93%. The National Center for the Treatment of Dissociative Disorders found that 83% of the subjects in its study had witnessed a human sacrifice, and 82% of EAS respondents had witnessed murder carried out by their abusers.

When I started to explore ritual abuse, I thought it was merely the stuff of nightmares, and, I have to confess, I was initially dubious of the therapists I contacted who worked with ritual abuse survivors and mind-control victims. But over the years, as I've cultivated a rapport with these therapists, I've concluded that they haven't lost their minds, nor are they religious zealots. In fact, a 1995 study published in the *Journal of Professional Psychology: Research and Practice* looked at the question of whether or not therapists who work with ritual abuse victims had a tendency to be religious. The study looked at 497 Christian therapists and 100 members of the American Psychological Association, and their respective diagnoses of dissociative disorder, sexual abuse and ritual abuse. The study concluded that Christian therapists and APA members diagnosed dissociative disorder and sexual abuse with the same frequency, and Christian therapists' diagnosis of ritual abuse was only slightly higher than that of the APA members questioned. A second study, published in *The Journal of Child Sexual Abuse*, concluded that religious beliefs had no relationship to a therapist's identification of ritual abuse.

To the average American, the Franklin story, even in its abbreviated version—a pedophile network that pandered children to the power elite, its cover-up by the federal government, and its possible affiliation with the CIA and blackmail—is wholly divorced from conventional reality, and to superimpose Satanism onto it makes it over-the-top incomprehensible, even approaching the absurd. It easily surpasses the darkest surrealism of a David Lynch movie. But there's a facet of Franklin that even eclipses Satanism in terms of the fantastic: mind control. Paul Bonacci, in fact, claims to be a victim of a government mind-control program.

Though Van Pelt and company concluded that Bonacci was a liar, Alisha Owen, Troy Boner, Danny King, and Rusty Nelson corroborate his participation in the pedophilic parties at the Twin Towers.

After some false starts, I've spent numerous hours with Bonacci, his wife, and their children. Today, Bonacci doesn't smoke, drink, or take drugs, and he's quite pious—he's also struggled through the acute throes of his multiple personality disorder. Before Bonacci became "integrated," sorting out his multiple personalities into a unified self, he related some fantastic tales. Unfortunately, as he was in the midst of unifying his various personalities, he was exploited by various parties on the fringe and perhaps also by major television networks, including ABC and FOX.

Bonacci has been relatively consistent, but he now admits that some of the statements he's made, especially in the earlier stages of his integration, were incorrect. So, that being said, I'll discuss Paul Bonacci and the accounts he's conveyed to me, and also the corroboration I've collected in his case.

When Gary Caradori initially videotaped Bonacci, Bonacci claimed that Larry King was engaged in the sexual compromise of politicians in Washington, DC. Karen Ormiston said that she remembers a later interview where Bonacci brought up Craig Spence's name as King's partner in pedophilic pandering and blackmail. Bonacci discussed King's DC townhouse with both Caradori and Yorkshire Television. As previously noted, he said that the basement had a room that only locked from the outside, and reporter Paul Rodriguez found that statement truthful. It would be next to impossible for Bonacci to relate such a detail unless he had actually been in King's DC townhouse.

Bonacci also told Yorkshire Television that he took midnight tours of the White House as an underage prostitute, and the tours were arranged by Craig Spence. Bonacci's claims sound extremely implausible, but *Washington Times* reporters were aware of at least four tours arranged by Spence, and one of the tours included an underage male. Though the *Washington Times* doesn't outright corroborate Bonacci on the midnight tours he's alleged to have taken, its reportage indicates Bonacci's seemingly far-fetched story was within the realm of possibility.

Bonacci maintains that his MPD was the result of a government mind-control program. According to Dr. Mead, Bonacci wasn't cognizant of his MPD until Mead diagnosed him in 1990. Bonacci told me he wasn't aware of the mind-control origin of his MPD until even later, when he started to integrate his alternate personalities. I've talked to accredited, licensed therapists who say they've counseled mind-control victims, and they've said that the majority of these patients initially aren't mindful of their MPD or its government origins.

The CIA documentation that I've collected discusses inducing MPD in children and the experimenters' use of electric shock, drugs, hypnosis, and "psychological tricks." Bonacci related to me that his mind was deconstructed through electroshock, drugs, hypnosis, sexual abuse, and ritual abuse. He also told me that he was initially molested in kindergarten by a serviceman at Offutt Air Force Base, where the mind-control program was conducted.

MPD is the result of dissociation, and dissociation is caused by traumatic events that compel the mind to distance itself from those events because an individual is unable or unwilling to process them at the time. It's impossible to infer the exact nature of the "psychological tricks" mentioned in the CIA documents I've acquired, and to specifically ascribe satanic ritual abuse and sexual abuse to the mind-control experiments is problematic; but the scant CIA mind-control documentation that has been recovered demonstrates that the agency was willing to use a variety of sadistic methodologies to further its research, including torture, concussions, large doses of psychotropic drugs, and frequent high-powered electroshock.

When I embarked on this investigation, I knew next to nothing about the CIA's mind-control programs, so I initially talked to therapists who counsel mind-control victims. The therapists included psychiatrists and psychologists, and I was eventually directed to individuals the therapists had diagnosed as mind-control victims and who themselves contended they were mind-control victims. Every self-proclaimed mind-control victim I've interviewed has said that satanic ritual abuse and sexual abuse were integral facets of the experimenters' methodologies.

I freely concede that these individuals strike me as psychologically damaged. If I hadn't been directed to them by therapists whom I found to be credible, I never would have believed their accounts, because they were so divorced from mundane reality. In fact, even today, I have difficulties discerning whether some of them were psychologically damaged simply by their dysfunctional childhoods or by the CIA's mind-control experimentation.

The CIA allegedly discontinued mind-control programs in the 1960s, but Paul Bonacci and the other alleged mind-control victims I've interviewed discuss being manipulated by mind control throughout the 1970s and into the 1980s. So we are faced with a dilemma quite familiar to our tale: Are we to believe the government? Or shall we believe these psychologically damaged individuals who insist that they underwent CIA mind-control efforts well after the CIA's declared termination date for these programs?

The CIA destroyed the overwhelming majority of its mind-control documentation in 1973, which could have been its way of hiding the efficacy of the programs and/or their sheer, sadistic brutality. The particular CIA document I've acquired concerning the creation of MPD wasn't released during the US Senate hearing on mind control in 1977—it was acquired through a Freedom of Information Act request years later. The majority of the documentation floating around the Internet regarding the CIA and mind control came out of a 1977 Senate hearing, and I'm not aware of the document I possess even being on the Net, though it very well may be.

Bonacci also told me about a high-ranking military officer who was in cahoots with King and Spence's pedophilic blackmail enterprise—he said that the military officer in question was a Satanist and a pedophile. The military officer Bonacci alluded to is an admitted Satanist, and he was implicated in the molestation of several children. I have the search warrant that police executed on his home during a molestation investigation—a child who was purportedly molested gave an apt description of the officer's house, which was detailed in the search warrant. After local police executed the search warrant, they found corroboration of the child's account, but the feds usurped the case and dropped the charges against the officer—a familiar theme.

Bonacci claims to have been in the officer's home, and he gave me an accurate description of the home; so either Bonacci came by the search warrant, a description of the home by someone else, or he was actually in the home—the officer's home is on the West Coast.

Shortly after Caradori found Bonacci, Bonacci confessed to participating in the kidnapping of twelve-year-old Johnny Gosch, who was abducted on the morning of September 6, 1982 while delivering papers in West Des Moines, Iowa. This is one of the more infamous abductions in American history—Johnny Gosch's photo and that of a second kidnapped child were the first to appear on milk cartons. Word of Bonacci's confession eventually drifted to Noreen Gosch, Johnny's mother, and, searching for answers, she met with Bonacci at the Lincoln Correctional Center in 1991. Bonacci provided Noreen Gosch with details about her son's abduction, and with details regarding certain physical characteristics that had never been released to the press. Noreen Gosch believed Bonacci, and her husband believed him as well.

The FOX network's *America's Most Wanted* picked up on the story, airing five segments on Johnny Gosch's abduction. *America's Most Wanted* interviewed and even polygraphed Bonacci, and his interview was integral to the show's coverage. *America's Most Wanted* also videotaped Bonacci's first meeting with Noreen Gosch at the Lincoln Correctional Center—he broke down crying and apologized profusely.

Bonacci told *America's Most Wanted* that the man who coordinated the Johnny Gosch abduction was named "Emilio," and he provided a very detailed description of him—he also provided a detailed description of Emilio's henchman, whose name was "Tony." Bonacci told me that Emilio shoved a gun in his mouth and threatened to kill him if he didn't accompany Emilio to abduct Johnny Gosch.

Bonacci imparted a highly improbable tale to *America's Most Wanted* about a sinister network of pedophiles, and he disclosed to the show's producers that Johnny had been held on a ranch in rural Colorado that was near an elephant-shaped rock. Bonacci said that Johnny attempted to run away from the ranch and, as a punishment, he was branded like livestock, which the producers thought was extremely far-fetched. After Bonacci's interview aired on *America's Most Wanted*, a runaway named Jimmy contacted Noreen Gosch, and *America's Most Wanted* eventually interviewed him.

Jimmy claimed to have been on the Colorado ranch after Bonacci had left, and he gave a description of the ranch and the elephant-shaped rock that coincided with Bonacci's description. He then dumbfounded the producers of *America's Most Wanted*: Jimmy showed them a brand on his leg—the precise type of brand that Bonacci had described! Bonacci and Jimmy also told the producers about a cavity beneath the Colorado house where the children were stashed. *America's Most Wanted*, Bonacci, and Jimmy took a field trip to rural Colorado, and they indeed found the elephant-shaped rock and the ranch. Bonacci walked up to the vacant house and burst out in tears. Bonacci and Jimmy then led the producers to the cavity under the house.

America's Most Wanted also interviewed a friend of the Gosch family, who said he had been to a Colorado restaurant where he saw "Johnny

Gosch was here" written on the men's room wall. This is a remarkable coincidence, and Jimmy's account certainly corroborated Bonacci's earlier account, but none of this is irrefutable proof that Johnny Gosch was in Colorado.

However, when Bonacci was incarcerated at the Lincoln Correction Center after the fall of Franklin, he received various letters from around the country. The letters were from Kansas City, Missouri; Sacramento, California; and Brockton, Massachusetts, and were written by kids who, Bonacci said, were enmeshed in the vast underground pedophile network that abducted Johnny Gosch. I've acquired some of the letters, and they discuss Emilio, and also "Johnny" and "JG." For example, "The Col is gone to Mexico and took JG with him. JG is back to blond and had face surgery." So either Bonacci had these letters sent to him from around the country to provide bogus validation for his participation in Johnny Gosch's abduction, or these kids were actually enmeshed in the network, have "broken away," and are aware of Emilio and Johnny or JG.

Bonacci offered details of Johnny Gosch's abduction that had never been released to the press; Jimmy corroborated Bonacci; a family friend of the Gosch's provided possible corroboration that Johnny Gosch may have been in Colorado; and Bonacci's letters supplied the names of kids who claimed to have been acquainted with Johnny Gosch after his abduction. But Iowa law enforcement never followed up on Bonacci's leads.

America's Most Wanted interviewed a law-enforcement official in Iowa who said that Iowa law enforcement hadn't interviewed Bonacci regarding Johnny Gosch because the Omaha FBI declared he was not credible. The FBI even pressured *America's Most Wanted* not to air its segments on Johnny Gosch, but its host, John Walsh, refused to knuckle under to the FBI's pressure.

I've provided a mere thumbnail account of the Johnny Gosch abduction and its related complexities, which would be a book unto itself. Early on, I simultaneously pursued both the Franklin and the Johnny Gosch stories, but I came to a fork in the road where time and money would permit my pursuit of only one—I ultimately opted for Franklin, because I concluded that its immense paper trial and potential for corroboration made it much more likely to yield real results.

The Johnny Gosch story is also overflowing on the Internet, and it occasionally pierces the mainstream media. In addition to *America's Most Wanted*, ABC spent a great deal of time and resources on the story, but its inquiry was eventually shelved. In 2006, Noreen Gosch received a color photo of three boys bound and gagged on a bed, and also a black-and-white photo of a single boy bound and gagged—she maintains that the black-and-white photo was definitely her son.

She posted the photos on JohnnyGosch.com, and the pictures quickly ricocheted around the world, creating a surge of interest—they were even broadcast on the ABC and FOX networks. Shortly after the pictures started to circulate, a former Florida investigator denied that the pictures were of Johnny Gosch—he said the pictures were from a 1978 or 1979 investigation, where law enforcement found no "coercion or touching." The retired investigator asserted that the pictures from the investigation were filed away, but he was never able to produce them.

Paul Bonacci's allegations have been out-and-out rejected by state and federal law enforcement as the ravings of someone who is mentally ill, but he has received a modicum of vindication from the civil suit he litigated against Larry King in a US District Court. As discussed, John De-Camp, acting as Bonacci's attorney, filed sixteen civil lawsuits in federal court on behalf of Bonacci. The lawsuits were directed at people Bonacci accused of molesting him or of covering up his abuse, and the lawsuits contended that these individuals had deprived Bonacci of his civil rights.

US District Court Judge Warren Urbom dismissed fifteen of the lawsuits. Larry King was incarcerated when Bonacci's lawsuits were filed, and he opted not to contest the allegations. "A lot of people conduct lawsuits from prison," said Judge Urbom. "There is no indication he wanted to dispute this.... The defendant King's default has made those allegations true against him." Urbom entered a "default judgment" against King in 1998, and DeCamp moved for a separate trial on the issue of compensation.

During the 1999 trial, DeCamp called Noreen Gosch, Rusty Nelson, Paul Bonacci, and Denise Bonacci, Paul's wife, to testify. Noreen Gosch made a stunning disclosure when she testified: She stated that her son, Johnny, had visited her a few years earlier and had corroborated Bonacci's account of his abduction—she said that she hadn't publicly divulged her late-night rendezvous with Johnny, and she was disclosing it only because she was under oath. She testified that her son feared for his life, and he had said that the pedophile network that abducted him was connected to the rich and powerful as well as the government.

Urbom's one-million-dollar judgment against King discusses Bonacci's "repeated sexual assaults, false imprisonments, infliction of extreme emotional distress, organized and directed satanic rituals," etc. The judgment also addressed Bonacci's suffering because of King: "He has suffered burns, broken fingers, beating of the head and face and other indignities by the wrongful actions of the defendant King. In addition to the misery of going through the experiences just related over a period of eight years, the plaintiff has suffered the lingering results to the present time."

I wrote that Bonacci received a "modicum of vindication" from the judgment, and DeCamp felt Judge Urbom finally believed Bonacci. But the real vindication ultimately came in the form of King's appealing the judgment, and then withdrawing his appeal after DeCamp began making "motions for depositions." King was released from federal prison in April 2001, after serving nearly ten years for his financial crimes, and he relocated to the Washington, DC area. Not a single dollar from the judgment has as yet been collected.

I've spent years corroborating the reality of these events, and I acknowledge that there are facets of Bonacci's story that sound implausible and are impossible to substantiate—he's also confessed to making untrue statements as he's struggled through the acute throes of his MPD. On the other hand, Bonacci has never wavered about his participation in Johnny Gosch's abduction, and he's provided numerous specifics concerning the abduction that were, in part, confirmed by *America's Most Wanted*. If the Omaha FBI hadn't been engaged in a proactive cover-up of the Franklin story and the discrediting of Bonacci, which was further evinced by the FBI's pressuring *America's Most Wanted* not to run the Johnny Gosch story, Bonacci might have provided law enforcement with valuable leads that could have solved the riddle of that boy's disappearance.

I've worked assiduously to prove that "Franklin" is a reality, but it's also important for me to debunk various Franklin derivatives that have floated around the Internet and been the subject of wild speculation and conjecture. The story of Johnny Gosch has become an integral facet of Franklin lore because of Paul Bonacci's purported participation in the abduction. In 2005, the Internet was abuzz with innuendo that Jeff Gannon, gay escort by night and White House reporter by day, was none other than Johnny Gosch. The Internet innuendo about Johnny Gosch emerging as Jeff Gannon became so fertile that it even pierced the mainstream media—MSNBC's short-lived show, *Dietl and Daniels*, aired segments tackling the Web speculation. I looked into the innuendo and quickly concluded that Jeff Gannon definitely wasn't Johnny Gosch.

A second Franklin-related fallacy that is all over the Internet involves Hunter Thompson's alleged participation in snuff films. When Gary Caradori initially interviewed Bonacci, the latter related that Larry King chartered a plane to Sacramento, where a boy named "Jeremy," who had been kidnapped, was filmed being shot in the head. Bonacci later said that the film's "producer" introduced himself as "Hunter Thompson." Bonacci didn't say that the producer was, in fact, the gonzo writer Hunter Thompson, but merely that he introduced himself by that name. To this day, Bonacci doesn't even know what the late Hunter Thompson looked like. And surely common sense would dictate that someone making a snuff film wouldn't provide his true name, especially if he was famous.

Though Bonacci never said that the actual Hunter Thompson participated in the production of a snuff film, Rusty Nelson gave an interview where he fingered Hunter Thompson as a snuff-film aficionado. I've previously discussed Nelson's living a very marginalized life after his incarceration, and then falling in love with a woman in rural Nebraska who footed the bill for him to start a photography studio. And shortly after the studio was opened, it was raided by law enforcement—Nelson was incarcerated for not registering as a sex offender, and his camera equipment was impounded. Those events ultimately led to the dissolution of Nelson's photography studio and his relationship.

Prior to the raid, Nelson had been consistent with me and generally snubbed Internet irregulars who requested interviews. After the raid, however, Nelson gushed interviews to all comers, and he gushed information that was contradictory to the accounts he related to me—he also made statements that I concluded were outright lies. In some of those interviews he implicated Hunter Thompson in the making of snuff films. I had spent hours with Nelson before his photography studio was raided, and he had never discussed Hunter Thompson's affiliation with King or snuff films. After those interviews, I confronted Nelson and showed him five pictures—one of the pictures was of Thompson and Nelson couldn't identify him.

Though Rusty Nelson has a propensity to tell tall tales, OPD documentation, Alisha Owen, and Paul Bonacci connect Nelson to King—I've also collected off-the-record corroboration linking Nelson to King. He's provided me with many nuances that have panned out regarding Franklin, so I believe that Nelson was part-and-parcel of Franklin's dark machinations. Though Nelson's moral barometer may be deeply flawed and he has told tall tales, I have a tendency to believe that he was able to smuggle some pictures out from under King's watchful eyes, and that he gave those pictures to Gary Caradori in Chicago. I also feel that he no longer has pictures. He maintains that he has as a life insurance policy.

In addition to spending numerous hours with Rusty Nelson, I've spent countless hours with Eulice Washington, Alisha Owen, Paul Bonacci, and members of their respective families. I initially cultivated relationships with them in order to determine their veracity, but, over time, I've developed friendships with each of them. Unlike Nelson, they've been consistent right down the line—their respective family members also believe and/or back up their accounts.

I've never snagged Eulice Washington in a lie, and I've corroborated various statements she's made to me via Kirstin Hallberg, Patricia Flocken, her sisters, and through the many social service documents I've collected—I also have multiple corroborations about her allegation that Larry King flew Boys Town students around the country to be used as underage prostitutes.

I've also never caught Alisha Owen lying to me, and I've corroborated numerous aspects of her story through Paul Bonacci, Rusty Nelson, Danny King, Troy Boner's affidavit, Karen Ormiston, Henry Rosenthal, her family members, a York guard, and through the other documentation I've collected. I've contacted various witnesses who testified against

Owen at her trial, and Danny King is the only one who has confessed to perjuring himself. However, Troy Boner's "lie or die" affidavit states that he also perjured himself at her trial because of FBI coercion.

Paul Bonacci's story is extremely bizarre, but he's also been consistent with me, and I've been able to corroborate bits and pieces of his story—I must admit though, I've encountered one contradictory statement: Bonacci told me that he related his sexual abuse to a high school counselor. I eventually found the former counselor, and he said that he remembered Bonacci's prolific truancy, but he couldn't recall him conveying accounts of sexual abuse.

I readily admit that there are aspects of Bonacci's story that are next to impossible to corroborate, but Alisha Owen, Danny King, Rusty Nelson, Troy Boner's affidavit, Paul Rodriguez, and a former producer of *America's Most Wanted* have confirmed nuances of Bonacci's very strange stories. Both of Johnny Gosch's parents have also stated that they believe Bonacci took part in the abduction of their son, because of the detailed information he provided them.

I was initially perplexed by Bonacci's ability to cut loose from his family for protracted periods at such a young age: He told me that his family life was completely dysfunctional, and his mother and his subsequent stepfathers never kept tabs on him—his account of non-existent parenting has been corroborated by a family member. Moreover, from the interviews I've conducted with Alisha Owen and Danny King, it's obvious to me that they clearly know Bonacci, even though Van Pelt and company denied that fact. It's also evident to me that Rusty Nelson and Paul Bonacci know each other.

Given the unbelievable amount of abuse that Alisha Owen and Paul Bonacci have endured from perpetrators and also law enforcement, I find it truly astounding that they've been able to forge lives for themselves. Both Owen and Bonacci have been happily married for years, and both are gainfully self-employed.

I feel that time has vindicated Owen and Bonacci and granted them a well deserved poetic justice: They refused to recant their abuse, and they've managed, against all odds, to put together productive lives for themselves. Troy Boner and Danny King recanted their allegations of abuse—Boner died a drug addict, and Danny King is well on his way to that destination. Moreover, the other victims I've talked to who never came forward publicly are mired in drug addiction and are living on the periphery of society or are incarcerated. The fact that Owen and Bonacci have been able to persevere and even flourish in various aspects of their lives is the only silver lining to Franklin's very dark cloud.

Contrary to the legions of government and media personnel who have labeled Franklin as a mere "conspiracy theory," overwhelming corroboration and documentation confirm both the existence of an interstate pedophile network and a government cover-up thereof. This is not a conspiracy theory—it is an account of a conspiracy. Unlike other government conspiracies that *have* been acknowledged—Watergate, Iran-Contra, Cointelpro, etc.—Franklin hasn't been exposed in the "authoritative" media as a bona fide conspiracy. In fact, mainstream media seems to have colluded in the cover-up, and thus it has been relegated to the dustbin of "conspiracy theories." Indeed, if I hadn't come across the US Customs report on the Finders, I never would have pursued this story, because of its absolute implausibility. But "implausible" does not mean "contrary to fact."

The Franklin story is a cautionary warning for America—not only does it provide a glimpse at a stratum of government corruption that is opaque and unfathomable to the majority of Americans, it also demonstrates that the government, together with the media, have the potential to spin fictions into facts and facts into fictions. Since the collapse of the Franklin Credit Union, the Patriot Act has eased restrictions on law enforcement, and the media has undergone considerable consolidation due to government deregulation. The titanic media conglomerates of today are beholden to the federal government because its policies allow for their existence. So early 21st century America may be even more susceptible to the cover-up of a scandal as horrific as Franklin than it was two decades ago.

Publisher's Afterword

This book has been "on my desk" for far too long; that it is *even on my desk* is in itself a story, and also a very, very sad commentary on the vacuous times in which we live.

I first heard about Nick Bryant long before I met him. The word came to me from folks in Nebraska: there was a reporter out there asking questions and saying he was writing a story about the Franklin scandal for a major magazine. Having pitched this very topic and other "suppressed" material to many magazines for years, I thought, "Yeah, sure, sounds like a 'vacuum-cleaner' operation to me. (That's spook parlance for sending someone out into the field to see what they can dig up, who's where and who's talking, and about what.) It will never be printed."

A short while later someone gave me Nick's phone number; I called and we spoke. He definitely knew the subject, and seemed undaunted by the challenges of reporting this tragedy. I had asked several other writers to look at the situation and pen a book; all came back and said they had kids and were frightened—all turned me down. So, Nick's courage impressed me, and then there was his advocacy, concern and heart-felt empathy for children, especially the disadvantaged and challenged.

I told Nick TrineDay wanted to publish an in-depth look at the Franklin scandal. He said he was looking to do the same, but he was hoping to get it placed at a major publishing house. Nick was a successful free-lance journalist living in Manhattan, with many friends in the news and print fields, and he was actively shopping a magazine article and a book project around the city. He was with America's top literary agency—surely they could do something.

"New York won't print it, but we will, or at the very least, they may publish it because they know TrineDay will," I bluntly said at the time.

For the next couple of years we stayed in touch. Nick would let me know of his progress, or lack of it, with NY magazine and book publishers, and I would send him TrineDay's latest outputs.

Later, after his agency dropped him, apparently, over this very story and his magazine article was turned down by everybody, TrineDay brought Nick out to Oregon; we met, sized each other up, and soon agreed to work together.

Now, years later, finally, a book. One that answers many questions, while spawning more. A big one being, "Now, what?"

What can we the people do when our institutions are so debased that terrible child abuse is covered up using some of our most vaunted governmental agencies, and our "free press" actively misleads us, participating in a venal bamboozlement of our body politic? How and for whom does this system operate when the "watchdogs of the press" turn into the lap dogs of the corrupt?

Inveterate champion of the "Franklin" cause, lawyer John DeCamp, tells the story of a judge, who, when asked in chambers about why this scandal keeps getting covered up, even though everyone knows it's for real, said, "You won't like it, but this will help you understand—read *Billy Budd*." To make a long story short, the judge was implying that sometimes one must allow evil to happen for the system to survive, that the tragedies of a few don't measure up to the security of all.

To that self-serving delusion I say, "Hogwash!"

There is no system so sacrosanct that it can condone sadistic child abuse. The terms "honey-trap" and "national security" do not absolve dirty deeds done at the expense of us all; those are simply terms used to deter investigations and consequences. In my opinion, any "security" bought by such a debasement brings us nothing but a deep stain. I believe an honest look at the facts reveals private agendas, systemic corruption, and very real, horrific abuse ... not legitimate "statecraft." Therefore, I hope and pray that this book will help us, "We the People," take notice of this gross crime and take some long overdue action.

What kind of action? Stand up, speak out and tell your friends. Get outraged, write your elected representatives, call your local news—ask them to cover this story. Get involved locally with your feet, speech and heart. Get involved globally on the Internet. For in this computer age, we the people do have tools to bring about true change. Do we have the courage, the will? We shall see, for time has certainly brought us a way.

Peace,
Kris Millegan
Publisher
TrineDay
June 15, 2009

Franklin Scandal Timeline

1965

Peter Citron arrested for sexual child abuse in Scarsdale, New York, but abuse charges were dropped.

Larry King began four-year hitch in Air Force, spending a year in Thailand, handling top-secret information.

1969

Craig Spence employed by ABC as a Vietnam correspondent.

1970

Larry King became manager of the two-year-old Franklin Community Federal Credit Union.

1978

Eulice, Tracy, and Tasha Washington placed in the Webb household.

1978

According to Paul Bonacci, he started attending orgies at Alan Baer's apartment.

1979

Craig Spence relocated from Tokyo, Japan to Washington, DC.

1982

Shawneta Moore alleged she was recruited for pedophilic parties at the Omaha Girls Club and within six months started attending satanic rituals—she was nine years old.

Robert Wadman hired as OPD Chief.

1983

Alisha Owen said she attended first Twin Towers party.

1984

Larry King held lavish party at "Southfork" ranch during the GOP convention—Paul Bonacci said that he and other children were served to pedophiles at the convention.

Autumn: Eulice Washington said that Larry King flew her and other underage children to Chicago.

1985

Spring: Eulice Washington alleged that Larry King flew her and other underage children to New York.

December: Eulice and Tracy Washington removed from Webb household.

1986

January: Eulice Washington passed NSP polygraph regarding repeated molestations by Jarrett Webb—no charges were filed against Webb.

March: Eulice and Tracy Washington, accompanied by foster mother Kathleen Sorenson, met with Boys Town youth worker Julie Walters on three occasions—Walters wrote a report on their allegations.

November: Charlie Rogers, a lover of Larry King's, "committed suicide"—having told family members he feared for his life and if anything happened to him they should contact Douglas County Deputy Attorney Robert Sigler.

November: Omaha Mayor Mike Boyle fired OPD Chief Wadman for insubordination.

1987

March: After Mayor Boyle's recall, a Douglas County Judge reinstated Wadman as OPD Chief.

1988

Larry King formed Council of Minority Americans—Jack Kemp, Alexander Haig, and former President Gerald Ford were on the "host committee."

May: OPD's Robbery and Sexual Assault Unit commenced "possible child pornography investigation" that implicated Rusty Nelson and Larry King.

June: OPD Robbery and Sexual Assault investigator Carmean interviewed Shawneta Moore at Richard Young Hospital, and she implicated Larry King in child exploitation and "devil worship."

July: Carol Stitt, Director of Nebraska's Foster Care Review Board, sent a letter to Nebraska Attorney General Robert Spire, notifying him of a "child exploitation ring" linked to "Larry King of Omaha."

August: Larry King and the Council of Minority Americans held a $100,000 gala at the Republican National Convention—a video featuring Larry King and Jack Kemp, urging blacks to vote for George H.W. Bush, was shown at the gala.

November: The National Credit Union Association and FBI closed the Franklin Credit Union—regulators quickly determined that millions had been embezzled and the credit union had a second set of books.

November: Senator Loren Schmit introduced Legislative Resolution 5 (L.R. 5) on the floor of the Unicameral, and it was unanimously approved—L.R. 5 called for the formation of a subcommittee to investigate the failure of the Franklin Credit Union.

December: The Foster Care Review Board's executive committee testified before the Unicameral and expressed their collective outrage about law enforcement's inactivity regarding the child-abuse allegations.

December: In response to the Foster Care Review Board's outrage, Nebraska Attorney General Robert Spire and OPD chief Wadman said that both agencies had conducted thorough investigations of the child-abuse allegations.

1989

January: L.R. 5 was given a sweeping mandate to investigate the Franklin Credit Union's financial collapse and also accusations that law enforcement hadn't properly investigated the child-abuse allegations—Senator Loren Schmit was appointed Chairman of the Franklin Committee and Senator Ernie Chambers was appointed Vice-Chair.

February: The Franklin Committee named Kirk Naylor as its special counsel.

February: FBI's Special Agent in Charge of Nebraska and Iowa, Nicholas O'Hara, and OPD Chief Wadman asserted that their agencies had found no evidence supporting child-abuse allegations.

May: Larry King was charged with 40 counts of embezzlement, fraud, and tax evasion.

June: The Franklin Committee held public hearings.

June: The *Washington Times* started publishing a series of articles on Craig Spence and Henry Vinson.

July: Senator Chambers, Kirk Naylor, and Jerry Lowe resigned from the Franklin Committee.

July: Concerned Parents formed because of law enforcement's unwillingness to investigate the child-abuse allegations.

August: Craig Spence was arrested in New York City for possession of a handgun and cocaine.

August: Gary Caradori replaced Jerry Lowe as the Franklin Committee's investigator.

September: Alisha Owen sentenced to between three and four years for writing "bad checks."

November: Craig Spence committed suicide in Boston, Massachusetts.

November: Gary Caradori took videotaped statements of Alisha Owen and Troy Boner.

December: Gary Caradori took videotaped statement of Danny King.

December: The Franklin Committee showed the videotaped statements to ranking officials from Nebraska law enforcement, and then submitted the videotapes to the Nebraska Attorney General and US Attorney for the District of Nebraska.

1990

January: Nebraska Attorney General Robert Spire called for a grand jury to be impaneled.

February: The Douglas County District Court judges signed an order for a Douglas County grand jury to be impaneled, and appointed retired Lancaster County Judge Samuel Van Pelt as its special prosecutor.

February: Federal Magistrate Kopf preemptively ordered that US marshals transport Larry King to the US Medical Center for Federal Prisoners in Springfield, Missouri for a "mental health evaluation."

February: Peter Citron arrested for felonious sexual assault on two children.

March: The Douglas County grand jury formally convened at the Douglas County Courthouse.

March: Larry King declared incompetent to stand trial and was sent to the US Medical Facility in Rochester, MN.

March: The FBI pressured Danny King and Troy Boner to recant their videotaped statements to Caradori.

March: The *Lincoln Journal* and *Omaha World-Herald* reported that two of the victims videotaped by Caradori had flunked FBI polygraphs.

April: The FBI interviewed Alisha Owen for the last time at York—she refused to recant her videotaped statements to Caradori.

May: Caradori videotaped Paul Bonacci at the Lincoln County Correctional Center, and he corroborated Owen, Boner, and Danny King on multiple accounts.

June: Caradori wrote a letter to renowned attorney, Gerry Spence, requesting legal representation because he was being "set up" to take a fall for fabricating the child-abuse allegations.

July: Caradori's airplane mysteriously broke up over Lee County, Illinois, killing Caradori and his eight-year-old son.

July: The Douglas County grand jury declared the child-abuse allegations were a "carefully crafted hoax"—Alisha Owen and Paul Bonacci were indicted on perjury charges.

July: A federal grand jury indicted Henry Vinson on 43 counts, which included racketeering, credit card fraud, interstate transportation for purposes of prostitution, and money-laundering.

September: A federal grand jury exonerated Larry King of being an interstate, pedophilic pimp and indicted Alisha Owen on eight counts of perjury.

November: After state and federal grand juries exonerated Larry King of child abuse, he was declared competent to stand trial.

November: Alisha Owen's brother was found dead in his cell—his death was ruled a suicide.

1991

January: The Franklin Committee was disbanded.

January: Troy Boner's brother shot himself in the head playing "Russian roulette."

January: Vinson pled guilty to conspiracy and credit card fraud.

February: Larry King pled guilty to his financial crimes and was sentenced to fifteen years in a federal prison.

February: John DeCamp filed civil rights lawsuits on behalf of Paul Bonacci against the Catholic Archbishop of Omaha, Larry King, Peter Citron, Alan Baer, Harold Andersen, Robert Wadman, and others.

May: The State of Nebraska v. Alisha Owen began with a pretrial hearing.

June: Alisha Owen found guilty on eight counts of perjury.

June: Vinson sentenced to sixty-three months in prison.

August: Judge Case sentenced Alisha Owen to between nine and fifteen years for perjury.

1992

February: Alisha Owen served her sentence for her "bad check" conviction, and was released on a $500,000 surety bond as John DeCamp appealed her perjury conviction.

1993

October: Troy Boner submitted his "lie or die" affidavit to John DeCamp, confessing that threats from the FBI forced him to lie at the Douglas County grand jury and also at Alisha Owen's trial.

1994

December: Troy Boner was strong-armed at the Douglas County Courthouse shortly before a hearing for Alisha Owen—his testimony would have reiterated the contents of his October 1993 affidavit.

1996

March: Alisha Owen was sent back to prison.

1999

February: Federal District Court Judge Warren Urbom granted Paul Bonacci a $1 million default judgement against Larry King.

2000

September: Alisha Owen was paroled after serving four and a half years.

2001

April: Larry King was paroled after nine years and ten months.

2003

February: Troy Boner died in a Texas psychiatric hospital.

Documentation

Document Index

OFFICIAL USE ONLY

DEPARTMENT OF THE TREASURY
UNITED STATES CUSTOMS SERVICE

REPORT OF INVESTIGATION

C-3

1 PAGE 1 OF 3

"FINDERS"

STATUS					
	Interim Report	Disp. Pending	[X] Closed Case	Index & Fwd	Closing Report

| DATE 87 | DATE ASSIGNED 021287 | CLASS II | PROGRAM CODE 700 | REPORT NO one |

DISTRICT FILE NUMBERS

DISTRICT LEADS TO
None

[checkbox section with "assistance to local LE" checked]

This office was contacted by the Tallahassee Police Department on
February 5, 1987, who requested assistance in attempting to identify
two adult males and six minor children, all taken into custody the
previous day. The men, arrested and charged with multiple counts of
child abuse, were being very evasive with police in the questions
being asked of them pursuant the children and their condition.

This agent contacted SS/A, Bob Harrold, RAC/Reston, Virginia, and
requested telephone numbers and names of police persons in area
police departments in an attempt to follow-up on two leads which
were a Virginia license number and that the children had commented
about living in a Washington, D.C., commune.

Subsequently, this office received a telephone call from the Washington,
D.C. Metropolitan Police Department inquiring about the men and children.
This office put the MPD and the TPD in contact with each other.

DISTRIBUTION		SIGNATURE	
RAC/JX; SAC/TA; RAC/DC		Walter F. Kreidlow II Special Agent	
SE		Fredric D. Haiduk Resident Agent in Charge	
E:SD:G:P	SE		
CPPU copy	Original	ORIGIN OFFICE Office of Enforcement 727 N. Franough St. Rm 6045	TELEPHONE NUMBER 965-7608

400 A

DEPAR°   T OF THE TREASURY
UNITED . ~TES CUSTOMS SERVICE

REPORT OF INVESTIGATION
CONTINUATION

4700-01 (37), P&PM (Special Agents Handbook)

DETAILS OF INVESTIGATION:

n Thursday, February 5, 1987, this office was contacted via telephone, by sergeant, JoAnn VanMETER of the Tallahassee Police Department, ʲuvenile Division. Sgt. VanMETER requested assistance in identifying wo adult males and six minor children ages 7 years to 2 years.

ᵀhe adult males were tentatively identified by TPD as Michael HOULIHAN ᵑnd Douglas AMMERMAN, both of Washington, D.C., who were arrested the previous day on charges of child abuse.

ᵗhe police had received an anonymous telephone call relative two well-ᵈressed white men wearing suits and ties in Myers Park, (Tallahassee), apparently watching six dirty and unkempt children in the playground ᵃrea. HOULIHAN and AMMERMAN were near a 1980 Blue Dodge van bearing ⱽirginia license number XHW-557, the inside of which was later described as foul-smelling filled with maps, books, letters, with a mattress ᵗituated to the rear of the van which appeared as if it were used as a ᵇed, and the overall appearance of the van gave the impression that all eight persons were living in it.

ᵗhe children were covered with insect bites, were very dirty, most of ᵗe children were not wearing underwear and all the children had not ᵇeen bathed in many days.

ᵀhe men were arrested and charged with multiple counts of child abuse and lodges in the Leon County Jail. Once in custody the men were somewhat ᵉvasive in their answers to the police regarding the children and ᵗtated only that they both were the children's teachers and that all were enroute to Mexico to establish a school for brilliant children.

ᵀhe children tentatively were identified as Mary HOULIHAN, white female, age 7; Max LIVINGSTON, white male, age 6; Benjamin FRANKLIN, white male, age 4; HoneyBee EVANS, white female, age 3; B.B., white male, age 2; and John Paul HOULIHAN, white male, age 2. The children initially indicated that they lived in tents in a commune in the Washington, D.C., area and were going to Mexico to go to a school for smart kids.

This office contacted the Office of the RAC/DC and spoke with SS/A, Bob Harrold. This agent requested telephone numbers and names of police persons in area departments that might be aware of said activities described by the children and to follow-up on the leads which were the Virginia license number and a check on the men's names with local law enforcement.

DEPART   T OF THE TREASURY
UNITED   TES CUSTOMS SERVICE

**REPORT OF INVESTIGATION
CONTINUATION**

4200-01 (371, PA7M (Special Agent Handbook)

1. PAGE		PAGES
3	OF	3

2. CASE NUMBER

3. REPORT NUMBER
one

A short time later this office was contacted by Detective, Jim Bradley of the Washington, D.C., Metropolitan Police Department. Bradley indicated that the case here in Tallahassee appeared to be strongly related to a case he was currently working in the Washington, D.C. area.

He stated that the actions of the two men in custody in Tallahassee relative the children just might give his case enough probable cause for search warrants to search premises occupied by a cult group called the FINDERS.

This agent directed Bradley to telephone TPD and discuss with police directly any activities forthcoming relative the instant case.

At this time it was determined that there was no Customs violations found to exist and therefore, this case is being closed pending receipt of additional information.

ACTION TO BE TAKEN BY LESD/TECS: Create a permanent DRR/TECS record.

IDENTIFYING DATA/TECS-FIN QUERIES:

AMMERMAN, Douglas Edward   SUBSTANTIATED   NCIC: Negative
 (F-23B attached)   TECS: "
                                                         CMIR: "
                                                         CTR :
                                                         FBA : Negative
                                                         PAIRS: Negative

HOWELL, James Michael   SUBSTANTIATED   NCIC: Negative
(CF-23B attached)   TECS: "
                                                         CMIR: "
                                                         CTR : Negative
                                                         FBA :   "
                                                         PAIRS: Negative

"FINDERS"   ALLEGED   NCIC: NEGATIVE
(CF-23B attached)   TECS: NEGATIVE
                                                         CMIR: "
                                                         CTR :   "
                                                         FBA :   "
                                                         PAIRS: "

The Finders' warehouse in northeast Washington, DC.

The Finders' house on W St., Washington, DC.

MEMO TO FILE

To   : Resident Agent in Charge   Date: 02/07/87

From   : Special Agent

Subject: Customs cooperation/interest in
          Tallahassee/Washington MPD child abuse investigation.

On Thursday, 2/5/87, the duty agent, SS/A Bob Harrold, received
a call from SS/A Walter Krietlow, USCS, Tallahassee, Florida.
SS/A Krietlow was seeking assitance in contacting an
appropriate local police agency to coordinate a child abuse
investigation in with the Tallahassee Police Department. SS/A
Krietlow further requested assistance in checking some names,
addresses and a vehicle through the Customs Child Pornography
Unit data base, and stated there was some suspicion of the
subjects being involved in supplying children for the
production of child pornography. Further, he was informed by
the Tallahassee Police Department that the children may have
been enroute to Mexico from the Washington, D.C. area. The
possibility of Customs interest in the investigation due to
possible violations of the Child Protection Act of 1984, and
the alleged nexus with the U.S./Mexican Border were discussed
and agreed upon. SS/A Krietlow related the following
background information. SS/A Krietlow was contacted by the
Tallahassee Police Department for assistance in identifying six
children and two adults taken into custody in the Tallahassee
area. U.S. Customs was contacted because the police officers
involved suspected the adults of being involved in child
pornography and knew the Customs Service to have a network of
child pornography investigators, and of the existance of the
Child Pornography and Protection Unit. SS/A Krietlow stated
the two aduls were well dressed white males. They had custody
of six white children (boys and girls), ages three to six
years. The children were observed to be poorly dressed,
bruised, dirty, and behaving like animals in a public park in
Tallahassee. The police were notified by a concerned citizen
and all eight persons were taken into custody. The subjects
were living out of a white 1979 Dodge van, Virginia license no.
XHW 557. Upon being taken into custody, the adult white males
refused to cooperate, one of whom produced a 'business' card
with a name on one side and a statement on the other. The
statement indicated that the bearer knew his constitutional
rights to remain silent and that he intended to do so. Upon
interviewing the children, the police officers found that they
could not adequately identify themselves or their custodians.
Further, they stated they were enroute to Mexico to attend a
school for 'smart kids.' SS/A Krietlow was further advised the
children were unaware of the function and purpose of
telephones, televisions and toilets, and that the children had
stated they were not allowed to live indoors and were only
given food as a reward.

After receiving the request from Tallahassee, SS/A Harrold
contacted me while I was on official business at Customs
Headquarters. He requested that I conduct computer checks on
the Customs Child Pornography Unit data base. The checks were
to be conducted on the names, addresses, and a vehicle provided
by SS/A Krietlow. After conducting the computer checks, I made
direct contact with SS/A Krietlow to inform him that all the
checks were negative. At that time I was informed by SS/A
Krietlow that the Tallahassee police had discovered large
quantities of records, to include computer discs and a U.S.
passport in the van. From some of these records the police had
obtained tentative identification of the two adults, and
partial identification of the children. Furthemore, the two
Washington, D.C. addresses had been discovered through these
documents, one of which was verified through the vehicle
registration. I advised SS/A Krietlow I was leaving
Headquarters and he would be receiving a response to the
remainder of his request from SS/A Harrold. I then left as
stated and proceeded to conduct other business in the District.

A short time later, at approximately 11:30 a.m., SS/A Harrold
contacted me by radio, and advised me that a Detective Jim
Bradley of the Washington, D.C. Metropolitan Police Department
(MPD) was interested in the information provided by SS/A
Krietlow, was in contact with Tallahassee, and would very
probably be conducting search warrants in the area later in the
day. He also informed me that U.S. Customs was invited to
participate due to the continuing possibility of violations of
law enforced by the Customs Service. As I was already in
Washington, I terminated my other business and proceeded to
make contact with Detective Bradley, Intelligence Division, MPD.

Upon contacting Detective Bradley, I learned that he had
initiated an investigation on the two addresses provided by the
Tallahassee Police Dept. during December of 1986. An informant
had given him information regarding a cult, known as the
'Finders' operating various businesses out of a warehouse
located at 1307 4th St., N.E., and were supposed to be housing
children at 3918/3920 W St., N.W. The information was specific
in describing 'blood rituals' and sexual orgies involving
children, and an as yet unsolved murder in which the Finders
may be involved. With the information provided by the
informant, Detective Bradley was able to match some of the
children in Tallahassee with names of children known alleged to
be in the custody of the Finders. Furthermore, Bradley was
able to match the tentative ID of the adults with known members
of the Finders. I stood by while Bradley consulted with AUSA
Harry Benner and obtained search warrants for the two
premises. I advised acting RAC SS/A Tim Holloran of my
intention to accompany MPD on the execution of the warrants,
received his permission, and was joined by SS/A Harrold. SS/A
Harrold accompanied the team which went to 1307 4th St, and I
went to 3918/20 W St.

During the execution of the warrant at 3918/20 W St., I was

able to observe and access the entire building. I saw large
quantities of children's clothing and toys. The clothing
consisting of diapers and clothes in the toddler to pre-school
range. No children were found on the premises. There were
several subjects on the premises. Only one was deemed to be
connected with the Finders. The rest were renting living space
from this individual. He was identified as Stuart Miles
SILVERSTONE, DOB/061941, U.S. Passport No. 010958991.
SILVERSTONE was located in a room equipped with several
computers, printers, and numerous documents. Cursory
examination of the documents revealed detailed instructions for
obtaining children for unspecified purposes. The instructions
included the impregnation of female members of the community
known as Finders, purchasing children, trading, and
kidnapping. There were telex messages using MCI account
numbers between a computer terminal believed to be located in
the same room, and others located across the country and in
foreign locations. One such telex specifically ordered the
purchase of two children in Hong Kong to be arranged through a
contact in the Chinese Embassy there. Another telex expressed
an interest in "bank secrecy" situations. Other documents
identified interests in high-tech transfers to the United
Kingdom, numerous properties under the control of the Finders,
a keen interest in terrorism, explosives, and the evasion of
law enforcement. Also found in the "computer room" was a
detailed summary of the events surrounding the arrest and
taking into custody of the two adults and six children in
Tallahassee, Florida on the previous night. There were also a
set of instructions which appeared to be broadcast via a
computer network which advised participants to move "the
children" and keep them moving through different jurisdictions,
and instructions on how to avoid police attention.

One of the residents was identified as a Chinese National. Due
to the telex discovered referencing the Chinese Embassy in Hong
Kong, he was fully identified for future reference:
WANG/Gengxin, DOB/092747, POB/Tianjin, People's Republic of
China Passport No. 324999, entered the U.S. on January 22,
1987, admitted until December 31, 1987. He is in the U.S. as a
graduate student in the Anatomy Department of Georgetown
University. His Visa was issued on November 10, 1986, in
London, England, number 00143.

During the course of the evening, I contacted Sector 4 to
initiate a TECS check on SILVERSTONE, and initiate an archives
check on him for the last four years. I also contacted SS/A
Holloran to keep him advised of the proceedings and asked for
and received permission to contact SS/A John Sullivan of the
CPPU to query some names through the CPPU data base. SS/A
Holloran told me he would call Southeast Region Headquarters to
keep them posted on the proceedings as well. I later contacted
SS/A Sullivan for the stated purpose, and in the discussion
that followed, I gave him some background on the purpose of the
request. I advised him that the information was not for
dissemination at Headquarters, that Region was being notified,

and that Region would probably contact Headquarters later if Jeemed necessary. SS/A Sullivan assured me that the information would go no further until official notification was made by Region. No positive matches were obtained from the CPPU data base. I was later joined at the W Street address by SS/A Harrold. SS/A Harrold advised me that there were extremely large quantities of documents and computer equipment at the warehouse, and that MPD was posting officers inside the building there and sealing the building until morning, in which a second warrant for that premises would be obtained and executed. SS/A Harrold also advised me that the news media had been notified and had been waiting for the execution of the warrant at the 4th Street address.. Detective Bradley later stated that the MPD Public Information Officer had been contacted by a Tallahassee reporter. When it became apparent the PIO had no information on the search warrants, the reporter contacted local media representatives and a check of public records containing the affidavits for the search warrants disclosed the locations and purpose of the warrants. Detective Bradley surmised that someone on the Tallahassee Police Department was the original source of information for the press. I advised SS/A Holloran of the involvement of the press, and he stated that he would, in turn, relay the information to Region. SS/A Harrold and I assisted in the transport of the evidence seized pursuant to the warrant and cleared MPD after the press left the area.

On Friday, 2/6/87, I met Detective Bradley at the warehouse on 4th Street, N.E. I duly advised my acting group supervisor, SS/A Don Bludworth. I was again granted unlimited access to the premises. I was able to observe numerous documents which described explicit sexual conduct between the members of the community known as finders. I also saw a large collection of photographs of unidentified persons. Some of the photographs were nudes, believed to be of members of Finders. There were numerous photos of children, some nude, at least one of which was a photo of a child "on display" and appearing to accent the child's genitals. I was only able to examine a very small amount of the photos at this time. However, one of the officers presented me with a photo album for my review.- The album contained a series of photos of adults and children dressed in white sheets participating in a "blood ritual." The ritual centered around the execution of at least two goats. The photos portrayed the execution, disembowelment, skinning and dismemberment of the goats at the hands of the children. this included the removal of the testes of a male goat, the discovery of a female goat's "womb" and the "baby goats" inside the womb, and the presentation of a goats head to one of the children.

Further inspection of the premises disclosed numerous files relating to activities of the organization in different parts of the world. Locations I observed are as follows: London, Germany, the Bahamas, Japan, Hong Kong, Malaysia, Africa, Costa Rica, and "Europe." There was also a file identified as

"Palestinian." Other files were identified by member name or "project" name. The projects appearing to be operated for commercial purposes under front names for the Finders. There was one file entitled "Pentagon Break-In," and others which referred to members operating in foreign countries. Not observed by me but related by an MPD officer, were intelligence files on private families not related to the Finders. The process undertaken appears to have been a systmatic response to local newspaper advertisements for babysitters, tutors, etc. A member of the Finders would respond and gather as much information as possible about the habits, identity, occupation, etc., of the family. The use to which this information was to be put is still unknown. There was also a large amount of data collected on various child care organizations.

The warehouse contained a large library, two kitchens, a sauna, hot-tub, and a "video room." The video room seemed to be set up as an indoctrination center. It also appeared that the organization had the capability to produce its own videos. There were what appeared to be training areas for children and what appeared to be an altar set up in a residential area of the warehouse. Many jars of urine and feces were located in this area.

I should also mention that both premises were equipped with satellite dish antennas.'

I discussed the course of action to be taken by MPD with Detective Bradley. He stated he was only interested in making the child abuse case(s). I was assured that all of the evidence would be available to U.S. Customs in furtherance of any investigative/criminal action pursued. MPD personnel were to begin around the clock review and sorting of the evidence until completed. Customs will have access after this is accomplished. This will include several U.S. passports discovered during the search.

Upon leaving the 4th Street premises, I encountered a news media representative and was asked the reason behind U.S. Customs involvement in the investigation. I advised the reporter that I could not discuss anything and referred her to the RAC/DC. I left immediately thereafter.

There is no further information available at this time. It should take three to five days for all the information to be sorted, reviewed, logged by the MPD. I will maintain contact with Detective Bradley until the evidence is again accessible.

Respectfully submitted,

Ramon J. Martinez
Special Agent, USCS

OFFICIAL USE ONLY

DEPARTMENT OF THE TREASURY
UNITED STATES CUSTOMS SERVICE

REPORT OF INVESTIGATION.

*200-01 (271, F&PM (Special Agent Handbook)

1. TECS ACCESS CODE		C-3
2. PAGE	PAGES	1 OF 2
3. CASE NUMBER		

4. TITLE

FINDERS

5. CASE STATUS						
☐ Initial Report	☐ Interim Report	☐ Disc/Pending	☐ Open & Close	☒ Incur & File	☐ Case Reopen

6. REPORT DATE	7. DATE ASSIGNED	8. CLASS	9. PROGRAM CODE	10. REPORT NO
04/13/87	02/05/87	I	700	1

11. RELATED CASE FILE NUMBERS

12. UNDEVELOPED LEADS TO

None

13. TYPE OF REPORT			
☐ Test	☐ Search Warrant Executions	☐ Penalty Case Report	☐ Memorandum of Interview	☐ Initial Source Documentation	☐ Source Debrief
☒ Investigative Finding	☐ Subpoena Service	☐ Surveillance Report	☐ Background	☐ Request for Collateral	☐ Other

14. NARRATIVE

On Thursday, February 5, 1987, Senior Special Agent Harrold and I assisted the Washington, D.C. Metropolitan Police Department (MPD) with two search warrants involving the possible sexual exploitation of children. During the course of the search warrants, numerous documents were discovered which appeared to be concerned with international trafficking in children, high tech transfer to the United Kingdom, and international transfer of currency.

15. DISTRIBUTION		16. SIGNATURE (Type Name & Title)
SAC/RAC SAC/VA Beach RAC/Tallahassee		Ramon J. Martinez, Special Agent
CA/SCR	SE	17. APPROVED (Type Name & Title)
HQ DIV EO:SD:G	SE	LINWOOD ROUNTREE, Resident Agent in Charge
HQ INT T-S	FILE RAC/DC	18. ORIGIN OFFICE 22	19. TELEPHONE NUMBER

DEPARTMENT OF THE TREASURY
UNITED STATES CUSTOMS SERVICE

REPORT OF INVESTIGATION
CONTINUATION

4200-01 (37), F&PM (Special Agent Handbook)

DETAILS OF INVESTIGATION:

On March 31, 1987, I contacted Detective James Bradley of the
Washington, D.C. Metropolitan Police Department (MPD). I was to
meet with Detective Bradley to review the documents seized
pursuant to two search warrants executed in February 1987. The
meeting was to take place on April 2 or 3, 1987.

On April 2, 1987, I arrived at MPD at approximately 9:00 a.m.
Detective Bradley was not available. I spoke to a third party who
was willing to discuss the case with me on a strictly "off the
record" basis.

I was advised that all the passport data had been turned over to
the State Department for their investigation. The State
Department in turn, advised MPD that all travel and use of the
passports by the holders of the passports was within the law and
no action would be taken. This included travel to Moscow, North
Korea, and North Vietnam from the late 1950's to mid 1970's.

The individual further advised me of circumstances which
indicated that the investigation into the activity of the FINDERS
had become a CIA internal matter. The MPD report has been
classified secret and was not available for review. I was
advised that the FBI had withdrawn from the investigation several
weeks prior and that the FBI Foreign Counter Intelligence
Division had directed MPD not to advise the FBI Washington Field
Office of anything that had transpired.

No further information will be available. No further action will
be taken.

ACTION TO BE TAKEN BY LESD/TECS:

No action to be taken on the basis of this report.

Lawrence E. King

Larry E. King at Southfork Ranch during 1984 GOP National Convention.

Larry and Maureen Reagan

Larry and Lyn Nofziger

Larry in custody.

ORIGINAL

OMAHA POLICE DIVISION

Page No. 1
of 3 Pages

☐ CONTINUATION — CHECK ONE — SUPPLEMENTARY ☒			R.B. No.: 50001-A		

Offense: SUPPLEMENTAL REPORT TO AN INFORMATION REPORT	☐ Victim Suspect ☐ SUBJECT: KING, Larry (NMI)	Address: 13232 North River Road
Day/Date/Time: Original Report: Thursday, 05 May. 88/1940 hours	Day/Date/Time: This Report: Wednesday, 25 May. 88/0800 hours	

SYNOPSIS:

This report will cover an interview with a KAREN BEVERIDGE, Property Manager of The MASON APARTMENTS (25th and Mason Streets) and also of The ORPHEUM TOWER, concerning information she possibly has of a LARRY KING, who had previously rented an apartment in The ORPHEUM TOWER between January of 1987 and January of 1988.

PERSONS AND PLACES MENTIONED IN THIS REPORT:

PARTY:

KING, Lawrence E.

DOB:
DATA NO:
ADDRESS:

Black Male.
07 Sep. 44.
1850547.
13232 North River Road,
Omaha, Nebraska.

Also Has Property At The
TWIN TOWERS, 2900 Farnam
Street.

PARTY:

BEVERIDGE, Karen.

Property Manager of
The MASON APARTMENTS,
345-8992.

Property Manager of
The ORPHEUM TOWER,
341-2974.

PARTY:

ADDRESS:

WALKER, Larry.

Unknown.

"D.J." at MAX'S BAR,
1500 Jackson Street.

REPORTING OFFICER:

HOCH, Michael, #525.

Robbery/Sex Assault Unit.

Report Typed By: LOUISE MARKLE,	Date: 25 May. 88/1100 hours	Time:	Signature Reporting Officer/Serial No.:
Approved By: (Commanding Officer/Serial No.)			Signature Reporting Officer/Serial No.: Officer MICHAEL HOCH, #525

PO 200A (84) OMAHA, NEBRASKA

ORIGINAL

OMAHA POLICE DIVISION

☐ CONTINUATION → CHECK ONE → SUPPLEMENTARY XX

R.B. No.: 50001-A

Offense: SUPPLEMENTAL REPORT TO AN INFORMATION REPORT	☐ Victim Suspect ☐ SUBJECT: KING, Larry (NMI)	Address: 13232 North River Road
Day/Date/Time: Original Report: Thursday, 05 May. 88/1940 hours	Day/Date/Time: This Report: Wednesday, 25 May. 88/0800 hours	

DETAILS OF THIS INVESTIGATION:

Reporting Officer, on Tuesday, 24 May. 88, went to The ORPHEUM TOWER, 405 South 16th Street, and interviewed a KAREN BEVERIDGE, Property Manager at that location. The property is managed by The KNUDSON (phonetic spelling) INVESTMENT COMPANY, who also manages The MASON APARTMENTS, 2500 Mason Street.

Reporting Officer stated to KAREN BEVERIDGE that his purpose for the interview was to obtain any information concerning LARRY KING, as it was believed that LARRY KING had previously or is presently renting an apartment at the ORPHEUM TOWER, and Reporting Officer wished to obtain any information concerning this matter.

KAREN BEVERIDGE stated that LARRY KING, in January of 1987, rented Apt. #1604, which rents for $550.00-a-month, and that he rented the apartment from January of 1987 until January of 1988. When KING rented the apartment, he paid the entire year's lease in advance.

KING had used the excuse that he had a catering business, and that he did business in the Downtown area on occasions. And then after working, because of his residence being quite a-ways north of Omaha, he would spend the night at the location in Downtown Omaha. KING would not always stay at the apartment and would only be seen in the building occasionally.

In September of 1987, KING sub-let his apartment (until the lease was up) to a LARRY WALKER, who is a "D.J." at MAX'S BAR, 15th and Jackson Streets. LARRY WALKER is described as a black male, 30 years of age.

KAREN BEVERIDGE stated that LARRY WALKER had resided at UNION OUTFITTING Apartment Buildings, 16th and Jackson Streets, prior to moving into The ORPHEUM TOWER. BEVERIDGE also stated that an individual by the name of MARY, at The UNION OUTFITTING Building, possibly could supply Reporting Officer with more information concerning LARRY WALKER.

KAREN BEVERIDGE was then asked if she knew any particulars or had heard any type of information about LARRY KING, as it seemed very strange that he would rent an apartment in The ORPHEUM TOWER and is presently renting an apartment at The TWIN TOWERS. BEVERIDGE indicated that she did not know any specifics about LARRY KING; however, she stated that she has heard rumors that he is a very heavy drug dealer, and that she has heard this from more than one individual. She could not relate from whom she heard the rumors, as she just passed them off as small talk.

Report Typed By: LOUISE MARKLE, 25 May. 88/1100 hours	Date:	Time:	Signature Reporting Officer/Serial No.:
Approved By: (Commanding Officer/Serial No.)			Signature Reporting Officer/Serial No.: Officer MICHAEL HOCH, #525

PO 200A (84) OMAHA, NEBRASKA

ORIGINAL

OMAHA POLICE DIVISION

CONTINUATION ☞ CHECK ONE ⟶ SUPPLEMENTARY	XX	R.B. No.:
		50001-A

Offense: SUPPLEMENTAL REPORT TO AN INFORMATION REPORT	☐ Victim Suspect ☐ SUBJECT: KING, Larry (NMI)	Address: 13232 North River Road
Day/Date/Time: Original Report: Thursday, 05 May. 88/1940 hours	Day/Date/Time: This Report: Wednesday, 25 May. 88/0800 hours	

KAREN BEVERIDGE stated that she has also heard that LARRY KING is a homosexual and has a preference of young men or boys.

BEVERIDGE was asked if she had any knowledge if LARRY KING had any investments in The MASON APARTMENTS, which she also manages. BEVERIDGE stated that she did not know who the main investors were, but did know that COMMERCIAL FEDERAL was handling most of the loans on the business, and that they would possibly have further information as to who some of the main investors were.

END OF THIS REPORT.

Report Typed By: LOUISE MARKLE, 25 May. 88/1100 hours	Date:	Time:	Signature Reporting Officer/Serial No.:
Approved By: (Commanding Officer/Serial No.)			Signature Reporting Officer/Serial No.: Officer MICHAEL HOCH, #525

200A (84) OMAHA, NEBRASKA

513

ORIGINAL

OMAHA POLICE DIVISION

Page No. 1
of 2 Page

☐ CONTINUATION → CHECK ONE → SUPPLEMENTARY ☒ X

R.B. No.:
50001-A

| Offense: INFORMATION REPORT | ☒ Victim Suspect ☐ | Address: |

CONCERNING POSSIBLE CHILD PORNOGRAPHY

| Day/Date/Time: Original Report: | Day/Date/Time: This Report: |
| THURSDAY / 05 MAY 1988 / 1930 | FRIDAY / 06 MAY 1988 / 1430 |

SYNOPSIS:

This report is relative to further information regarding this information submitted on this report.

PERSONS MENTIONED:

PANTOJA, Connie
1316 South 24th Street
Omaha, Nebraska
345-1375
Party supplying the information.

NELSON, Rusty
White male
Age 25 to 26 years
5'10", 145 lbs.
Blond hair, blue eyes
3000 Farnam Street #3B
Omaha, Nebraska

Rusty Nelson —2000

DETAILS:

This afternoon, I received a telephone call from PANTOJA, inquiring about the circumstances of the information she had supplied to this Division on Thursday. The report could not be located, however, I advised secretary, Louise MARKLE, that I would talk to the lady.

While I was talking to her, Louise MARKLE was able to locate the report, which is above captioned.

In talking to Mrs. PANTOJA, she related that her daughter was contacted at Shopko, by a male individual, who identifies himself as Rusty NELSON. He stated that he was looking for models, who have red hair and that he was extremely interested in photographing Mrs. PANTOJA's 17 year old daughter. He gave the girl a card with a telephone number only, and Mrs. PANTOJA has recently discovered that the telephone number is listed to an answering service only.

Report Typed By:	Date:	Time:	Signature Reporting Officer/Serial No.:
K.A. Nelson	06 May 1988	1858	
Approved By: (Commanding Officer/Serial No.)			Signature Reporting Officer/Serial No.:
			Marilou Lawson #314

PO 200A (84) OMAHA, NEBRASKA

ORIGINAL

OMAHA POLICE DIVISION

Page No. 2
of 2 Page

	CONTINUATION — CHECK ONE → SUPPLEMENTARY	X		R.B. No.: 50001-A

Offense: INFORMATION REPORT CONCERNING POSSIBLE CHILD PORNOGRAPHY	☒ Victim Suspect ☐	Address:
Day/Date/Time: Original Report: THURSDAY / 05 MAY 1988 / 1930	Day/Date/Time: This Report: FRIDAY / 06 MAY 1988 / 1430	

Mrs. PANTOJA said that when her daughter told her about this information, she and her daughter went to the apartment on Wednesday, 04 May 1988. She said the two of them spent approximately five hours in the apartment of Rusty NELSON. He claims to be self-employed, and then in later statements to Mrs. PANTOJA, stated that his company supplies the lavish apartment and furnishings where he resides.

She said that while she was looking through several photographs, she saw nude photos and she told the party, Rusty NELSON, that her daughter could not pose for that type of photo. He also wanted her daughter to pose for lingerie, which her daughter stated she did not wish to do.

Apparently NELSON did take some photos of the girl, Melinda, and on one of them, a portion of her breast was showing, apparently the girl and her mother, as well, were disturbed about this.

Mrs. PANTOJA states that she has called the various companies that this individual states he works for and no one has heard of him and she said that several people have told her that this is not a legitimate situation. She states that her daughter, Melinda HARRIS, is scheduled for another photo session on Sunday, 08 May 1988, at 1200 hours, and at that time she is suppose to come alone and not to bring her mother. Mrs. PANTOJA was requesting information on how they should proceed.

At this time I advised Mrs. PANTOJA, that it would appear unlikely that this is a legitimate photography situation, however, I indicated that it might be helpful to this investigation to "play the matter out". I advised Mrs. PANTOJA, that we would not want her daughter to go to that photo session by herself, but it is possible that we could set up some kind of an arrangment for the girl to be accompanied by either a young female police officer or other arrangements could be made. I advised Mrs. PAN-TOJA to have her daughter contact Rusty NELSON and to tell him that she can't make it to the photo session on Sunday, 08 May 1988, as scheduled, since other plans had been made and something had come up and she could not make it. I also advised Mrs. PANTOJA, that Officer Mike HOCH, does handle the pornographic investigations and would be in the office on Monday. She said she would either call Officer HOCH or I advised her I would have him call her, to attempt to perhaps make some kind of a stakeout on this photo lab, to determine the legitimacy of the operation.

There is no further information at this time.   END OF REPORT.

Report Typed By: K. A. Nelson	Date: 06 May 1988	Time: 1858	Signature Reporting Officer/Serial No.:
Approved By: (Commanding Officer/Serial No.)			Signature Reporting Officer/Serial No.: Marilou Lawson #314

PO 200A (84) OMAHA, NEBRASKA

Boys Town
Father Robert P. Hupp, Director

July 21, 1980

Mr. Lawrence E. King, Jr.
Treasurer/Manager
Franklin Community Federal Credit Union
Consumer Service Organization
33rd and Decatur Streets
Omaha, NE 68111

Dear Larry:

Thank you for your proposal dated July 14, 1980, to provide counseling services for our land acquisition program associated with the building of the Boys Town/Dominican alternative high school.

The proposal is, in my opinion, quite thorough and completed in a highly professional manner.

I would, however, suggest the following prior to my approaching Father Hupp, Executive Director, for acceptance:

1. If Father Flanagan's Boys' Home acquires or rents a home in or close to the site, would your agency staff the facility during reasonable hours to be available for counseling owners or renters who cannot otherwise, without inconvenience, travel to your central or branch office?

2. As a protective covenant in the event Father Flanagan's Boys' Home elects to cease its land acquisition activities, I would like to add the following clause:

"Should Father Flanagan's Boys' Home elect to cease activities within 30 days following acceptance of this agreement, its total obligation to Consumer Service Organization shall be a reasonable fee for services rendered, in any event, not to exceed $6,000.00.

Should Father Flanagan's Boys' Home elect to cease activities within 60 days following acceptance of this agreement, its total obligation to Consumer Service Organization shall be a reasonable fee for services rendered, in any event, not to exceed $10,000.00.

Robert M. Bigley, Director of Administration and Finance
Boys Town, Nebraska 68010, (402) 498-1017

516

Mr. Lawrence King
July 21, 1980
Page 2

> Should Father Flanagan's Boys' Home elect to cease activities
> within 90 days following acceptance of this agreement, its total
> obligation to Consumer Service Organization shall be a reasonable
> fee for services rendered, in any event, not to exceed $13,000.00."

A meeting of the Boys Town Urban Advisory Committee has been scheduled
for Monday, July 28, at 4:30 p.m., at the North Omaha Boys Club, 2200
North 20th Street. I would appreciate consideration of the above no
later than this date, as I would like to report on the status of our
efforts to contract for counseling services. In addition, if a decision
is made to employ your agency, I would request a representative be available to explain your services to the Committee.

I, therefore, request your consideration of the above at the earliest
possible time.

Sincerely,

Robert M. Bigley
Director of Finance and Administration

RMB/b

Larry E. King opening 1984 GOP National Convention.

517

EXHIBIT
13

DEPOSIT UPDATE
APRIL 21, 1981

V. J. SKUTT - MUTUAL OF OMAHA $25,000
LEO DALY -   25,000
PHILLIPS KILTNER, FIRST NAT'L BANK   50,000
PETER KIEWIT   100,000
INTERNORTH

ANTICIPATED

  BOYSTOWN, FR. HUPP   1,000,000
JOHN C. KENEFICK, U. P.
SYNOD OF LAKES + PRAIROS
PETE MARRDWICH / JACK McCOLLISTER - NWB
SALEM BAPTIST CHURCH $20 - $100,000
Mt. EASTERDAY @ WOODMEN TOWER
  EUGENE CONLEY

Interior view of Franklin Credit Union

518

ORIGINAL
OMAHA POLICE DIVISION
SUPPLEMENTARY REPORT

1168F

RB 11543E
PAGE 7
OF 19 PAGES

OFFENSE:	VICTIM:	ADDRESS:
SEXUAL ASSAULT	BAGLEY, PHILLIP	5721 Mayberry

ORIGINAL REPORT:	THIS REPORT:
Monday / 19 February 1990 / 2145	Monday / 26 February 1990 / 1040

5. Magazine - Team Mate, #2.

6. Magazine - Team Scene, #1.

7. Magazine - Team Scene, #2.

8. Magazine - Boys Who Seduce Other Boys.

9. Magazine - Check Mate, #1.

10. Magazine - Kids, #1.

11. Magazine - Play Time Pals, #2.

12. Magazine - Sennels Album, #3.

13. Magazine - Sennels, #69.

14. Magazine - Young Boys & Step Review.

15. Magazine - Young Boys & Masturbation.

16. Magazine - Nudest Studio Reviews.

17. Magazine - Boys, #3.

18. Magazine - Aquarius 106, #19.

19. Magazine - Puppy Dog Tails, Vol. 1, #1.

20. Magazine - Chicken Little, #2

21. Magazine - Sun Children, Vol. 1, #2.

22. Magazine - Beautiful Boys, Vol. 1, #1.

TYPED BY:	REPORTING OFFICER:
P.J. HOUSE 26 February 1990 2252	Michael HOCE, 525

OPD catalogue of Citron's kiddy porn collection.

ORIGINAL

OMAHA POLICE DIVISION
SUPPLEMENTARY REPORT

1168F

RB 11543E
PAGE 8
OF 19 PAGES

OFFENSE: SEXUAL ASSAULT	VICTIM: BAGLEY, PHILLIP	ADDRESS: 5721 Mayberry
ORIGINAL REPORT: Monday / 19 February 1990 / 2145	THIS REPORT: Monday / 26 February 1990 / 1040	

23. Magazine - American Boys, Vol. 1, #1.

24. Magazine - Boys Studies, Vol. 1, #1.

25. Magazine - Naked Boyhood, Vol. 1, #2.

26. Magazine - Naked Boyhood, Vol. 1, #3.

27. Magazine - Sun Children, Vol. 1, #1.

28. Magazine - Nek Kids, Vol. 1, #1.

29. Magazine - Kampy Kids, #4.

30. Magazine - Boys & Masturbation

31. Magazine - Chicken, Vol. 1, #1.

32. Magazine - Youngsters, #1.

33. Magazine - Boyland, #6.

34. Magazine - Phallic Development in the Pre-Adolescent.

35. Magazine - Hard To Beat, Vol. 1.

36. Magazine - Tales Before Midnight.

37. Magazine - Big D, Vol. 1. (Vol. 2)

38. Magazine - Kissy Boys, #2.

39. Magazine - Teenage Masturbation.

40. One roll of 35mm film, partial.

TYPED BY:
P.J. HOUSE   26 February 1990   2252

REPORTING OFFICER:
Michael HOCH, 529

Boner, right, in office with Delman ... "I would have never went and done any of it had I known it was going to get this big."

Enticed by Prospect of Lawsuit

Witness: I Lied, Seeking Riches

By Robert Dorr and Gabriella Stern
World-Herald Staff Writers

Franklin Inside

On Page 11: Troy Boner says he helped inmate Alisha Owen make up the story that she was assaulted by three fellow inmates at the Nebraska Center for Women in York.

On Page 12: Michael Casey says he shared information with the late Gary Caradori, the Legislature's Franklin committee investigator.

Troy Boner said Wednesday that a promise of future riches, the coaxing of a young woman friend and the urgings of a legislative committee investigator prompted him to lie in a videotaped statement before telling what he now says is the truth to a Douglas County grand jury.

"The only thing on the tape that is the actual truth is my name," said Boner, 23.

In the videotapes, Boner said that when he was in his late teens, two

the right thing because his testimony.

---

2 lawyers: We saw Boner with Schmit

Witness, lawyer deny Boner visited Schmit

By Bill Kreifel and Kathleen Rutledge
Journal Statehouse Bureau

Franklin videotape witness Troy Boner and his attorney, Marc Delman of Omaha, both say Boner did not go to the Statehouse to speak with Sen. Loran Schmit of Bellwood and did not say he wanted to recant his earlier recantation of what he said on the videotapes.

Delman said Wednesday that Schmit's assertion that Boner had done so was "unequivocal bull—."

However, Schmit stood by his statement Thursday, and two attorneys confirmed that they were present when Boner visited the Statehouse.

Schmit said Tuesday that Boner came to his Statehouse office on July 16 and 17 and told Schmit and Sen. Bernice Labedz of Omaha that he had told the truth to committee investigator Gary Caradori. Caradori was killed July 11 when his private plane crashed in Illinois and his funeral was July 17.

A Douglas County grand jury said in a Tuesday report that Boner and James Daniel King had recanted their "fabrications" on the videotapes before the committee.

Boner, 23, said on the tapes that he had been sexually abused as a minor, that he had run drugs for a prominent Omaha businessman and that he had witnessed sexual abuse of Alisha Owen, another Franklin witness who was indicted for perjury by the grand jury.

In a Wednesday interview with Jim Fagin of WOWT television, Boner stood by his testimony to the grand jury that the videotaped testimony was false.

Boner: All a lie

"Every bit of it was a lie, the whole tape, the only part of that videotape that was truth was when I stated my name," Boner said.

Delman said Boner told him he never wanted to recant his recantation. Delman said Boner claimed instead that Schmit and others, including R.J. Nebe and Karen Ormiston of Caradori's private detective firm, tried to get him to do that when Boner came to Lincoln for

jury the truth — that this whole thing was a hoax and that it was made up,'" Delman said. "I know what game Loran is playing. He is the captain of a sinking ship. The ship's going down and he's going to grab on to anything he can."

Two other attorneys said they were present at the Statehouse when Boner spoke with Schmit and Labedz. Jody Gittins, counsel to the Legislature's Natural Resources Committee and member of Schmit's staff, said she was present on both days Boner was at the Statehouse.

Schmit Says Boner Came To His Office

By Henry J. Cordes
WORLD-HERALD BUREAU

Lincoln — State Sens. Loran Schmit of Bellwood and Bernice Labedz of Omaha said Troy Boner told blatant lies when he said he did not come to Schmit's office last week and when he said he didn't recant what he told a Douglas County grand jury.

Boner, 23, who last November told the late legislative committee investigator Gary Caradori that he was a sexual abuse victim, appeared before the Douglas County grand jury and recanted his statement to Caradori. The statement was recorded on seven hours of videotape.

Schmit said at least eight people were in his office last week when Boner, in essence, recanted his recantation and said that what he had originally told Caradori was the truth.

Six of the eight appeared at a press conference Thursday, including four — Schmit, Sen. Labedz, Caradori associate R.J. Nebe and Jody Gittins, an attorney who works in Schmit's office — who said they heard Boner's comments directly.

Responding, Boner's attorney, Marc Delman, said in Omaha Thursday night that Boner had told him that he didn't go to Schmit's office and that he didn't take back the account he had given the grand jury.

Schmit said Boner first indicated he wanted to change the story he told the

---

Witness Says He Made False Accusations 'for the Money'

● Continued from Page 1

counts of pandering involving adult men, to which he pleaded not guilty Wednesday. Those alleged incidents had nothing to do with Franklin, the grand jury said.

'For the Money'

Boner, 6-foot-2½ and 220 pounds, said he tried to stop the hoax before it began, telling Caradori last fall when the investigator first contacted him that he knew of no sexual abuse.

But, he said, Caradori apparently thought Boner was afraid to name his abusers and encouraged him to tell all.

Although there was nothing to tell, Boner said, he followed the lead of a friend — Alisha Owen — and came up with a story of sexual abuse in his late teens, which was then captured on videotape by Caradori and his assistant, Karen Ormiston.

The grand jury indicted Miss Owen this week on eight counts of perjury.

Boner (pronounced "Bonner") said the did it mainly because he was told he would make money through civil lawsuits and movie and book rights. He also became convinced that men he was falsely accusing might have gotten away with abusing children in the past, even though he didn't have personal knowledge of that.

"I did it for the money and because I thought I was doing the right thing," he said.

Boner said he was told that for a time in late 1989 and early 1990 the Franklin legislative committee paid for his room and board.

'I Don't Know Any'

Boner gave this account of his role in the case:

Around last Thanksgiving 1989, Caradori contacted his mother, told her that her son had been sexually abused, and asked her to find him.

Contacted by his mother, Boner tele-

restaurant in Bellevue a few hours later, Boner said.

'It Didn't Happen, Gary'

Boner said Caradori told him he knew all about drug runs and sex abuse and said "he really felt bad for me."

Boner said he told the investigator: "It didn't happen, Gary."

Boner said Caradori then told him that the men "need to be put away. When we're done, Troy, you can sue for 10 or 15 million dollars. At the very least 5 million dollars, guaranteed," he said Caradori told him.

Boner said he continued to tell Caradori he did not know the people the investigator wanted him to identify.

Boner, who didn't have a steady job and came from a modest economic background, said he was tempted by the prospect of becoming rich.

Caradori told him he had interviewed a friend of Boner, Miss Owen. He said she had told him that she and some friends had been sexually abused by prominent Omaha men, Boner said.

Caradori brought Boner to Lincoln to be interviewed, Boner said. But before the interview, he put Boner in touch by phone with Miss Owen, who is an inmate at the Nebraska Center for Women in York.

Boner said that when he began talking to Miss Owen, she said: "Oh, you decided to go along with it, Troy, just trust him. I'm going to get out of prison. We'll be so rich."

During a 20-minute phone call, he said, Miss Owen told him to "remember" certain gasts of chuse then he

Jim Burnett/World-Herald

Boner said what started as a small lie mushroomed ... "I would have never went and done any of it had I known it was going to get this big."

Boner said he would cover only the "essentials" and no longer pay for such items as cigarettes, beer and food for Boner's car, Troy.

He said King said to him, "Sure I'll do it. What do I say?"

Boner said he prepared King for the taped interview with Caradori during a three-hour session in a Lincoln hotel jacuzzi.

Boner said Caradori told him and King that, after accusing prominent people of crimes, it was dangerous for them to return to Omaha. Caradori put them up in an apartment near downtown Lincoln and paid their room and board for the next month or two, he

'We'll Be So Rich'

Boner said he and Miss Owen met in 1987 and were acquainted for about three months. Boner and she apparently became "infatuated" with him, sending him flowers and gifts. He said that they were never romantically involved and that he had not seen or spoken to her in more than a year.

Boner said that when he decided to go along to Miss Owen, she said: "Oh, you decided to go along with it, Troy, just trust him. I'm going to get out of prison. We'll be so rich."

At their first meeting, Boner started telling Delman the story he had told Caradori. Midway through the conversation, he said, he paused and then told Delman: "It didn't happen. I just want to get out."

Although Boner told Delman he had been lying, he still wasn't ready to tell the absolute truth, both Delman and Boner said. The two said Boner did a "dance" for a week until the entire truth came out.

Shortly after, Boner told law enforcement officers that he had been lying and was ready to tell the truth. He came clean as an FBI agent was about to administer a lie detector test, he said.

He was hooked up to the machine and the test was about to begin, he said, when he asked the FBI agent to halt the process because he wanted to tell the truth.

The lie detector test was never administered, contrary to an earlier Lincoln Journal story based on the newspaper's information from a source who said he and King took the tests and failed them, he said.

Boner obtained immunity from prosecution for any past crimes from state and federal authorities, and in March testified before the grand jury.

Grand Jurors

The grand jurors had just seen a copy of the videotaped interview with Caradori and seemed shocked when Boner appeared before them and said he'd been lying, said Delman, who accompanied his client to the grand jury session.

Boner and Delman said the grand jurors seemed to be serious about their mandate, taking notes and asking tough questions. They said critics of the grand jury are wrong when they say the jurors were manipulated by special prosecutor Samuel Van Pelt.

"The only people who ever did their

Delman: "The Troy that sits before you today is not the Troy that came to see me in early March."

Boner said he is sorry about the lie he told because they hurt innocent people and cost taxpayers money, disturbed his and his finacee's families, and might make it difficult for actual victims of child sexual abuse to tell their stories.

He said he realizes that some people have the impression he changed his story after being bribed by those who accused Boner and Delman said flatly than there was no truth to that rumor.

The fact is, Boner said, what started out as a relatively harmless lie blew out of proportion and became impossible to live with.

"I would have never went and done any of it had I known it was going to get this big," he said.

At Funeral

Contrary to Miss Owen's charge, former Omaha Police Chief Robert Wadman is not the father of her 5-year old daughter, Boner said. Boner said he met a man who, Miss Owen told him at the time, is the real father, and that man is not Wadman. The grand jury cleared Wadman of all allegations.

Boner said the elaborate stories Miss Owen told Caradori involving both him and Danny King are also untrue.

Boner said he suspects Miss Owen lied and because she hoped it would result in her release from prison and financial reward.

He said as Caradori's funeral last week that Schmit and others apparently got the impression that Boner was going back to the story he originally told Caradori, he said.

While at the funeral, Boner said, he was approached by Schmit, Sen. Bernice Labedz of Omaha, Mae Ormiston and another investigator, R.J. Nebe.

"I took R.J. aside and told him that what I told the grand jury was the

FD-498 (.ev. 6-24,87)

POLYGRAPH REPORT

DATE OF REPORT 4/19/90	DATE OF EXAMINATION 3/20-21/90	BUREAU FILE NUMBER	FIELD FILE NUMBER 31C-OM-35967

FIELD OFFICE OR AGENCY REQUESTING EXAMINATION
FBI, Omaha

AUTHORIZING OFFICIAL
SAC, Omaha

DATE AUTHORIZED
3/16/90

EXAMINEE NAME (LAST, FIRST, MIDDLE)
Boner, Troy Donivan

CASE TITLE

LAWRENCE E. KING, JR.;
ET AL;
WSTA/SEOC;
DRUGS AND CORRUPTION
OO: OMAHA

00426510

ERENCES

CASE SYNOPSIS/EXAMINER CONCLUSION

The Omaha Division of the FBI has conducted an extensive investigation into the failure of the Franklin Credit Union, Omaha, Nebraska. Lawrence E. King, former President of the credit union, is a principal subject of that investigation.

Allegations have subsequently surfaced suggesting that KING and numerous other prominent individuals in Omaha have been involved in a child prostitution ring and in the transportation and sale of drugs. Funds from the defunct credit union were also allegedly used for financing those illegal operations.

A special Nebraska State Legislative Committee was formed to pursue this matter. This committee hired a private investigator, Gary Caradori, to investigate the allegations. Caradori has conducted videotaped interviews of three individuals identified as Troy Boner, James King, and Alisha Owen, who claimed to have knowledge of these alleged illegal activities. In those videotaped interviews, these individuals claim to have had sexual relations with prominent individuals in the Omaha business community, and they also provided details relating to the alleged transportation of male juveniles to California, Washington, and Iowa for purposes of prostitution, and to the purchase and transportation of illegal drugs.

Troy Boner has been interviewed by the FBI on several occasions regarding his videotaped interview and has retracted portions of his statement that do not deal with transporting male juveniles to other states for prostitution and illegal drug operations.

EXAMINER NAME:
SA Donald A. Gunnarson

FBI/DOJ

522

Pursuant to an agreement with the U. S. Attorney, Omaha, Boner agreed to submit to polygraph testing in an effort to determine the truthfulness of his statement.

On March 20 and 21, 1990, Boner voluntarily appeared at the Omaha FBI Office for a scheduled polygraph examination, accompanied by his attorney. He was furnished forms FD-395 and FD-328, which he read, stated he understood, and signed.

During a pre-test interview, Boner provided a detailed signed statement, a copy of which is attached, in which he retracted the statements made by him in a videotaped interview. He stated he has never met Lawrence King and never did travel with him. He said the information he provided during the videotaped interview was a fabrication. He said he was told by Gary Caradori that providing the statement could help get a friend, Alisha Owen, out of jail, and that he could sue King and others for millions of dollars.

A polygraph examination was thereafter administered wherein following relevant questions were asked:

A. Did you ever personally meet Larry King? (Answer: No)
B. Did you ever travel anywhere with Larry King? (Answer: No)

It is the opinion of the examiner that the recorded responses are not indicative of deception.

During Series II of this polygraph examination, the following relevant questions were asked?

A. Did you know Alisha before 1988? (Answer: No)
B. Did you take Alisha to any parties before 1988? (Answer: No)

It is the opinion of the examiner that the recorded responses t these questions are inconclusive.

In Series III of this polygraph examination, the following relevant question was asked:

A. Did you know Alisha before 1988? (Answer: No)

It is the opinion of the examiner that the recorded responses are not indicative of deception.

AFFIDAVIT   AFFIDAVIT   AFFIDAVIT   AFFIDAVIT   AFFIDAVIT AFFIDAVIT

Troy Boner, being first duly sworn, does depose and say of his own knowledge and experience as follows:

EXHIBIT

_A_

REASONS FOR THIS AFFIDAVIT:

I am making this affidavit freely and voluntarily and for the protection of myself and my family now and in the future; second, because it is right to do; and finally, because I want to undo some of the damage and injury I have caused and to help force legitimate and honest investigtions of such matters as my brother's death, Gary Caradori's death and ALL CIRCUMSTANCES SURROUNDING MY ALLEGATIONS HEREIN, PARTICULARLY THE ALLEGATIONS THAT I LIED TO THE GRAND JURY AND AT THE ALISHA OWEN TRIAL BUT THAT SUCH LIES WERE CAUSED BY OTHERS INCLUDING PARTICULARLY THE F.B.I. I, and my mother and family, are exhausted from living in fear of death or injury as a result of my personal involvement in the Franklin matters which ended up in my testifying at the Grand Jury hearings as well as at the Alisha Owen Trial. I lied at the Grand Jury hearings and I lied at the Alisha Owen trial. I lied when I "recanted" my original testimony to Gary Caradori. I lied because I truly believed and still do believe that it was a situation where I must either "...lie or die," and at the insistence primarily of the Federal Bureau of Investigation officials who were dealing with me at that time, specifically Mr. Mott and Mr. Culver.

The purpose of this affidavit, very simply, is to provide John De Camp the information he requires to file an action seeking protection for me and for my family from various individuals and the F.B.I. so that my true story can be told without fear of death or injury to myself or my family and so that others in a similar situation to myself can also come forward safely and tell their

(a)

stories which I believe will prove very clearly that what I am saying in this affidavit is true. I am also certain now that only by telling the truth as openly and publicly as I can will I ever stand a chance of providing protection for myself and my family for the future. I have asked John De Camp to do whatever is necessary to seek Witness Protection, including Federal Witness Protection if possible, for myself and my mother and my pregnant fiancee and child-to-be. Yes, I know full well the very great risk I run by taking this action but I and my mother and family can not go on the way we are and I can not live with myself unless I take this action.

I will be as brief as possible in this affidavit but I will also try to answer the questions that have to be answered in the situation I am in.

WHY JOHN DE CAMP IS MY ATTORNEY FOR THIS UNDERTAKING:

I know some of the people I am accusing in this affidavit, and the legal action accompanying it, will immediately claim that John De Camp somehow contacted me and convinced me to take this action for his purposes. So he has told me.

The exact opposite is true. Never have I spoken with John De Camp prior to this and he has never contacted me directly or indirectly. I had a friend of mine contact John De Camp several weeks ago and bring him to a meeting with me and my family at a secret location. At the time, John De Camp did not even know he was coming to meet me or my family. He thought he was being brought to meet a girl who needed representation on some matter. I searched him before our meeting began. We both agreed--with my entire family present--that anything said at the meeting could not and would not be recorded or ever used against me or to hurt me by John De Camp if I did not want to go ahead with this action. He agreed. I proceeded, along with my mother, to detail for John De Camp the fact that I had lied; why I had no choice but to lie; and many other facts. I then asked John De Camp whether he would represent me in helping to correct matters. I told him I went to him not because I liked him or knew him but because I felt he was the only honest one in this entire mess who could and would do something about my situation and who would not back down when the going got tough and who would "stick by me thru thick and thin if I (Troy) was telling the truth absolutely." He promised to do this so long as I told the truth and would agree to comply with any lie detector or other truth test he OR ANY LEGITIMATE INVESTIGATIVE OFFICIALS might ask for no matter what and so long as I and my family were doing this action not for money damages but for our safety and to get the truth told and myself and my mother and other kids protected. John DeCamp also told me that he could not and would not represent me and my family in this effort if he, De Camp, believed that I was lying or if he believed he had any conflict of interest between myself and any other clients of his, specifically Alisha Owen and Paul Bonacci. After researching and investigating what I, Troy Boner, had told him, De Camp said he would represent me and my family on a Pro Bono basis seeking only such compensation for representation as a Court might provide him. He also agreed to assist in any way he could personally in helping procure a secure and safe environment for me and my fiancee and child-to-be and to procure such other assistance for us as was possible thru social agencies or other groups or government agencies able to assist me and my family. He specifically refused in advance to provide any personal financial assistance in any way saying that he felt that would raise questions as to the correctness of his work on this case. I have included this information in this affidavit at his, De Camp's, request, to answer in advance questions he said others would ask.

MY ORIGINAL STORY TO GARY CARADORI:

What I told Gary Caradori in the original taped interviews Gary had with me was the truth. It is still the truth. From about age 14 to 17 I was seriously

4

involved in sexual and drug and related activities with a wide range of
individuals but primarily and specifically Alan Baer, Larry King, Robert Wadman,
Peter Citron, Eugene Mahoney, and others of prominence and wealth whom I will
identify for any legitimate investigative officials who seriously wish to
correct the problems and stop the conduct these individuals are and were engaged
in rather than cover up that conduct.

It has been repeatedly publicly stated that my story and the stories told by
Alisha Owen, Paul Bonacci, AND A LARGE NUMBER OF OTHER YOUNG PEOPLE NOT PREVIOUSLY
IDENTIFIED WHO WERE SIMPLY INTIMIDATED FROM TALKING OR WHO WERE RIDICULED, were
a "Carefully Crafted Hoax." The stories were not a hoax. The only carefully
crafted thing that occurred was in fact the cover-up of the facts and the
subsequent conviction of Alisha Owen and the original Grand Jury Investigation.
In short, there was a carefully crafted cover-up by the very people who were
supposed to be exposing the conduct of these people rather than covering it up.
And, YES, I WAS A VERY, VERY CRITICAL ELEMENT IN THAT COVER-UP BUT THAT
PARTICIPATION BY ME WAS DONE BECAUSE OF THREAT AND PROMISE MADE TO ME PRIMARILY
FROM THE F.B.I., AND MR. MARK DELMAN, THE ATTORNEY ARRANGED FOR ME BY OTHERS.

I repeat. The original story I told on taped interview to Gary Caradori was in
fact substantially the truth and substantially accurate. I say substantially
because I am sure on some points I exaggerated and on some points I did not
remember exactly the date or place or time of this or that event or particular
person or persons involved. But, specifically, the material and substantive
facts about the (1) Parties that took place at Twin Towers; (2) the use of
myself and other children as DRUG COURIERS FOR ALAN BAER AND LARRY KING; (3)
the involvement of Alisha Owen at the parties and as a drug courier also and
her involvement with former Omaha Police Chief Robert Wadman; (4) my relationship
with Alan Baer sexually and otherwise as well as the involvement of a number of

5

other children with him; (5) Wadman's presence and participation at these
parties in question ; (6) my delivering Alisha Owen personally to Bob Wadman on
several occasions; (7) my involvement sexually as a boy with Eugene Mahoney,
the former Game and Parks man; (8) Peter Citron's presence and involvement in
the parties and related sexual activities and filmings, WERE ALL TRUE, CORRECT
AND ACCURATE ON THE MATERIAL FACTS. And, contrary to what the F.B.I. and others
tried to get me to say and what I did say and in saying did lie about under
pressure and threat and promise from the F.B.I. and others, GARY CARADORI DID
NOT INTIMIDATE, THREATEN, COACH, MAKE UP THINGS OR IN ANY WAY IMPROPERLY OR
FALSELY PORTRAY THE INFORMATION I PROVIDED HIM. HE SIMPLY ASKED ME TO TELL THE
TRUTH, NO MATTER WHAT IT WAS, AND THAT IS ESSENTIALLY WHAT I DID WITH HIM. He
told me that was the law; that I had to report these things about Child Abuse
under the state laws. But that was the only pressure of any kind he applied.
And I know now it is the state law and all I want to do is comply with that law
without fear of me or my family being hurt or killed for having complied with
that law.

MY CONTACT WITH THE F.B.I. AND WHY I LIED AFTER THAT CONTACT:

After telling my story to Gary Caradori, I was assured that it was most important
that EVERYTHING I KNEW BE KEPT ABSOLUTELY SECRET. That I should talk to no-one
or reveal what I had provided Caradori or the Legislative Committee. Everybody,
including Caradori and the Committee and the Feds told me this. I KNOW NOW
THAT THIS WAS THE STUPIDEST THING I COULD DO AND THAT MY FOLLOWING THEIR VERY
INSTRUCTIONS TO CONCEAL THINGS IN FACT MADE ME AND MY FAMILY SUBJECT TO AND
VICTI S OF LATER THREATS AND INTIMIDATION. That is one of the main reasons
that I have definitely determined that I will now conceal nothing from any
legitimate investigative source--including the press. I am certain that had
the press really known what was happening and all the facts that they would
have done a far better investigation than others and would not have allowed the

cover-up to occur. I will explain later why I now believe this to be the case.

In my first contact with the F.B.I. the F.B.I. officials, particularly Mickey

Mott and Mr. Culver, made it clear to me that (1) They were ONLY interested in

DISPROVING everything I had told them; that (2) they were taking the position

that "...we know you are lying and we are only trying to figure out why and who

is your leader who is having you lie; and that (3) "if you will tell us you are

lying then we will let you off the hook but if you insist on sticking with the

story you told Caradori then WE will stick you in prison for a long, long time.

What you told on your tapes to Caradori can land you in prison for twenty years

each on a lot of different charges of perjury. If you insist on sticking with

your story, YOU WILL GO DOWN."

When the F.B.I. dealt with me, they made it clear that they had the power to

put me in prison--whether my story to Caradori was true or not--and the power

to put Caradori and others in prison including Alisha for providing the

information we did to Caradori. And they made it clear that was what they

intended to do unless I "recanted" my original story to Caradori and the

Legislative Committee.

The F.B.I. in conjunction with my new attorney, Marc Delman, who was arranged

for me by others including particularly Frank Brown of the Television Station

in Omaha, made it crystal clear to me that my only hope of staying out of prison

was in "recanting" my original story to Gary Caradori even though my story to

Caradori was and is the truth.

To make a long story short, I was put into the following situation by the F.B.I.

and my attorney, Marc Delman, and I am confident in my own mind that they knew

exactly what they were doing although I still do not understand all the reasons

why they wanted me to lie or who they were doing this for: I HAD TO LIE TO

STAY OUT OF PRISON AND I HAD TO SAY THAT THE TRUTH WAS A LIE AND THAT THE LIES

THEY WANTED ME TO TELL WERE THE TRUTH. So, when I went before the Grand Jury,

/

at the insistence and instruction of Marc Delman and the F.B.I., I told the Grand Jury what the F.B.I. and Delman wanted me to tell the Grand Jury which is that the story to Gary Caradori was a "hoax." But, as stated, the exact opposite is true.

Some time after my testimony to the Grand Jury, Gary Caradori was killed. I have no proof but I do believe he was deliberately killed. But, someone else will have to determine this because I acknowledge I have no information to prove or disprove this. Immediately after Gary Caradori was killed, and BECAUSE I DID BELIEVE HE HAD BEEN KILLED AS PART OF A COVER-UP AND AS A RESULT OF MY LIES TO THE GRAND JURY, I immediately called his home (from the Red Lion Hotel) at which time I spoke to his wife Sandy and told her I had in fact lied to the Grand Jury and that I was going to help straighten it out now. She suggested I go to Senator Schmit and provide him that information. This I immediately did and told Senator Schmit personally in his office that I had lied to the Grand Jury and that what I told Gary Caradori was the truth and that I only lied out of fear that the F.B.I. and others, particularly my attorney Marc Delman, would hurt me or my family and particularly because they promised me they would put me in jail if I did not say what the FBI and Delman wanted me to say which I, and I am sure they also knew WAS A LIE.

I also met Senator Berniece Labedz at the Caradori funeral and agreed I would meet her and Senator Schmit for lunch immediately following the funeral at which time we would go over my alleged "recantation" and I would provide her and the Committee all the facts. At the funeral, however, the F.B.I. agents, particularly Mickey Mott made it clear to me thru their actions that they knew what I was up to and gave me the clear impression that I was in "great danger" if I went ahead and met with the Legislative Committee and tried to tell them the truth. So, immediately following the funeral, I told my mother, who was with me, that we were not going to the meeting with the Senators and I was

going to stick with my lies to the Grand Jury because of what I feared the
F.B.I. or others associated with them or whom they were protecting would do to
me or the members of my family.

Later, Senator Labedz called me and asked why I did not show up at the meeting.
At first I pretended like I did not know what she was talking about because by
this time I was really scared especially because of Caradori's death. Then she
said she knew I was scared. So I was honest and I remember I flat told her I
was "scared" and could not do anything now. She said she felt sorry for me and
that she understood.

Then, Marc Delman and Mickey Mott saw Senator Schmit say on T.V. that I had
been in his, Schmit's office, and that my "recantation" had been false. They
both called me. Even though Marc Delman knew I had been at Schmit's office and
that what Schmit was saying was the truth, he, Delman, asked me whether the
conversation had been taped or whether there was any other record of my having
been in Schmit's office to talk to Schmit. I told Delman there was no tape or
any other record I had been with Schmit & that I had not signed anything. So,
acting on Delman's instructions I publicly lied and denied any meeting or
discussion with Senator Schmit and Delman publicly did the same and suggested
Senator Schmit was lying. Delman then instructed me to deny that I was in
Schmit's office and to simply imply that Schmit was lying about all these
things. Delman's exact words to me were, "It's your word against his...as long
as there are no tapes." Mickey Mott the F.B.I. man also met again with me and
again made it clear that if I told the truth--in other words, if I recanted my
recantation--that I was in big trouble and would go to prison and for the first
time Mickey Mott said something I interpreted then and now to have been a direct
and personal threat that later came to pass.

When I told Mickey Mott and Culver the F.B.I. people one time when I was feeling

9

a bit cocky about their threats to me that Alan Baer and others "could not afford" to do anything to hurt me now because too much publicity was focused on me and that they could not afford the risk of doing anything to me, Mott right away told me that they probably would not do anything directly to me, that instead "they will do something to a family member." And, of course that is what happened shortly thereafter after I had met with Schmit and talked to Sandy Caradori and when the F.B.I. and Delman and Baer and others thought I might break away from them, the F.B.I. and Delman, and tell the truth and confirm that I had lied when I testified to the Grand Jury.

I am completely certain in my own mind, which I believe a decent and honest investigation will show, that my brother Shawn was killed as a message to me to stick with my lies and not to back down because they were afraid I might back down and tell the truth at the Alisha Owen trial. After Shawn got killed, I had no doubt at all that they really were as dangerous as I had originally feared; that they would do anything and kill anybody to keep the truth contained and to keep me lying for them; and I complied with every request they wanted me to do or say with respect to the whole so called Franklin thing.

Before the Alisha Owen trial I was carefully rehearsed by the F.B.I. as to what I would say and what questions would be asked and then after rehearsing everything with the F.B.I. I was taken over to Mr. Moran the prosecutor to go thru the Rehearsal again. I do not know whether Mr. Moran knew I was lying but for sure the F.B.I. had to know because they were the ones who forced me to "recant" in the first place and threatened me with prison if I did not. Additionally, the F.B.I. themselves had actual pictures of me and other prominent individuals in their possession including particularly Alan Baer (1983 picture of he and me in very pornographic sexual acts) as well as checks from Alan Baer to me. So, they had to absolutely know I had a relationship with him and that they were forcing me to lie when I denied such relationships. Additionally, the F.B.I. had seized photos and tapes involving among others myself and a Mr. ANDREASEN and LARRY KING. These were video tapes of a party. And I know from having seen tapes at Peter Citron's house that the F.B.I. had access to tapes which clearly documented much of the conduct and the personalities I and other kids had identified as having occurred but which later I lied about before the Grand Jury and again at the Alisha Owen trial when I claimed--again to satisfy the F.B.I.--that the events never occurred. I do not know what the F.B.I. ever did with these pictures of me and Baer, for example, BUT I KNOW THEY HAD THEM BECAUSE I SAW THEM. So, they, the F.B.I. had to know the real truth all along and had to know what they were doing when they forced me to LIE. I am also sure that there are other pictures which would prove the things we kids told Caradori. Why do I say this? Because, the one thing I remember above all else is that these people like Baer, Mahoney, Citron, Andreasen, King, always loved to have pictures of themselves and others, particularly the kids, in weird sexual poses.

MY CREDIBILITY AND THE CREDIBILITY OF THE OTHER KIDS:

I know the first thing that the F.B.I. and Marc Delman and others involved in these Franklin and related matters will say when I submit my affidavit is something like: "You can't believe these kids and you can't believe Troy Boner now. If he lied once, he will lie again. He's a drug addict. He's a sex pervert. Who you going to believe, these kids with their wild stories or respectable people like Alan Baer or the F.B.I. or Attorney Marc Delman. Besides, these kids were as guilty or more guilty than anybody else. They were using the drugs and they were selling their bodies and they were getting paid well for it and they did it all voluntarily." Or something like this is what they will say. I have heard it before. But, let me give the other side of that story.

16

Yes, we kids, from early age, sold our bodies. We became drug addicts. We got lots and lots of money from these people. But today we are ruined because of that. And we were turned into sex perverts and drug addicts by these people. In my particular case, just like a lot of other young boys, I was directly turned into a true drug addict by Alan Baer. He was the one who first taught me to mainline and who first directly injected heroin directly into my veins-- same as he did to a lot of other boys. He was the one who made me a prisoner of drug addiction to where he could completely control me and use me to deliver drugs or deliver sex or anything else. Sure, he paid me well, but he also destroyed me in the process. It was Alan Baer who first injected me with a "speed ball", for example. A speed ball is a heroin/cocaine mix that zips you up immediately but brings you down mellow. And it was Marc Delman, my attorney arranged for me by others who claimed I owed him more than $500,000.00 for work he did protecting me, when what he really was doing was having me lie to protect others.

But to those who really want the truth it really is all there for you to find out if you will only check on the things that are available. And the truth is the truth whether it is told by us street kids whom you may not want to believe or the richest and most powerful people in Omaha who you think you have to believe. Same with a lie.

So, here are some things that any honest investigator can check out to see who is lying and who is telling the truth.

I. Marc Delman wrote my script for the program 48 hours wherein I claimed that the entire story of myself and the other kids was a "hoax." He promised me ten or fifteen thousand for this. I got virtually nothing. 48 hours told me that they had "paid my attorney." There should be records on this. I think Marc

– 12 –

got about $10,500.00 for doing that. And as everyone knows, the 48 hours program was played on television just before the Alisha Owen jury began their deliberations. Marc Delman also claimed that I had not met with Senator Schmit to tell the truth and I followed his instructions in denying it also. This sure can be checked out. There were people who saw me with Schmit. Same with my contact with Senator Labedz.

II. I saw the picture the F.B.I. had of me and Alan Baer. Some official sure ought to be able to get this picture to prove who is lying--me or the FBI.

III. Lots of kids, other than myself and Alisha and the ones who tried to come forward and tell the truth, know about Alan Baer, Larry King and the major drug dealing activity they and other prominent people were involved in. But, as long as they are scared for their lives because of what happened to Alisha and me, they are not going to say anything. If an honest prosecutor would step in and offer immunity and protection to these kids, many of them young men and women now, I am sure the entire network of drug dealing, use of kids for sex, and related things could be proven and corroborated to everybody's satisfaction.

IV. But, maybe the most important thing that any honest investigator should do is to ask me, Troy Boner, or any of the other kids such as Alisha or Paul Bonacci, to take polygraph, lie detector, tests SIDE BY SIDE ON THE SAME QUESTIONS WITH THE PEOPLE WE ARE ACCUSING OF THESE THINGS. Example, ask Alan Baer if he shot mainline drugs into me and if he is a major drug dealer and if he had sex with me. Ask Eugene Mahoney if he met me at the book store in Council Bluffs and used to regularly pay me to have sex with him as a boy? Ask ~~_____~~ to take a polygraph test on whether he is a big-time drug dealer. Ask the F.B.I. guys to take a polygraph test on whether they threatened

535

I 5

me with jail if I did not say the things they wanted me to say which things were a lie. Ask Marc Delman about the 48 hours thing and the Schmit meeting.

Obviously, either us kids are lying or the rich prominent people are lying. And just because they are rich and prominent does not mean they are telling the truth or because we are thought of as scum and kids who were supposedly all willingly involved in the drug trafficking and sexual activity does not mean we are lying. And like it or not, if we are not worth protecting then other young kids now and in the future will not be worth protecting either; and the prominent and respectable citizens who took us as children and made us a part of this drug dealing and sex abuse activity will continue without fear to do the same. Maybe to your children next time.

I promised my mother and myself after my lying at Alisha Owen's trial caused her to get convicted that if I ever got the chance to straighten things out I would come forward and do it and set the record straight. I owe it to my brother Shawn.

A couple months ago I met investigators from a British Television Broadcasting Company. They convinced me that they honestly wanted to tell the true story no matter what that story was.

I believed after talking with them that my and my family's safety lies in telling everything particularly to press sources outside Nebraska and not controlled by Nebraskans. I have done this in many hours of tapes with them. They have checked on many of the matters I told them about--not dealt with in this affidavit--and have satisfied themselves that I am telling the truth about my lying to the Grand Jury and to convict Alisha Owen and the reasons why I had to lie, just as I have explained in this affidavit. The reason I mention this is simply to establish that eliminating me or any member of my family will do

14

nothing to suppress the information or keep me from reporting it because I have already done so in many hours of tapes which have been taken outside this country but which will be made available to Federal Authorities and legitimate investigators here and in Washington, D.C.

But right now, I need protection for myself and my family so that I can tell the truth totally and without fear of being punished or jailed for doing it. That is the purpose of this affidavit. To help Mr. De Camp in filing the proper papers to seek that protection. Mr. De Camp has discussed with me the fact that someone may attempt to file perjury charges against me for taking this action at this time. I understand that. I want to repeat one final thing: I told the truth to Gary Caradori. I tried to tell the truth to the F.B.I. and Marc Delman but they did not want to hear the truth and the only thing they wanted was to have me say the truth was in fact a hoax; and they scared me with threats of jail and other things into lying to the Grand Jury and then later into lying for them at the Alisha Owen Trial. I want to tell the truth without fear and to help other kids who are and were in the same situation as I am and was. That is the reason I am doing this.

STATE OF NEBRASKA

COUNTY OF DOUGLAS

BEFORE ME A NOTARY PUBLIC ON THIS 27 day of October, 1993, PERSONALLY APPEARED TROY BONER, TO ME PERSONALLY KNOWN, WHO EXECUTED THE ABOVE AFFIDAVIT, AFFIRMED THE TRUTHFULNESS OF THE STATEMENTS MADE THEREIN, AFFIRMED THAT HE WAS VOLUNTARILY AND WILLINGLY SIGNING THE AFFIDAVIT AND DOING IT FOR THE PURPOSES STATED THEREIN.

DATED AND SIGNED THIS 27 DAY OF OCTOBER 1993 by NOTARY PUBLIC

GENERAL NOTARY-State of Nebraska
MARY ANN VERSAW
My Comm Exp July 16 1995

AFFIDAVIT   AFFIDAVIT   AFFIDAVIT   AFFIDAVIT   AFFIDAVIT   AFFIDAVIT

Lani Hicks, being first duly sworn, and based on her own knowledge and actual
experience does depose and say as follows and for the purposes stated:

I.   I am the mother of Troy Boner, whose affidavit I have read.

II.   Troy is telling the absolute truth about these matters as I know them and
I believe I have enough knowledge and experience in this entire matter to know
what the truth is and is not with respect to Troy Boner and his testimony before
the Grand Jury and in the Alisha Owen trial. Further, Troy is reporting exactly
what occurred with respect to our, his and my, arranging to meet with John De
Camp, the lawyer.

III.   When Troy first provided Gary Caradori information which he did I knew
that Troy was essentially telling the truth. Later, when Troy was reported to
have "recanted", I knew he was lying and I confronted him, Troy, about that
fact. At that time, Troy admitted to me that yes he had told Gary Caradori the
truth and yes, he, Troy, was lying when he recanted, but that he was scared for
himself and he had changed his story to satisfy the F.B.I. and an attorney
called Mark Delman. And he told me that for my and his own safety that if I
attempted to tell the truth and expose Troy as lying that he, Troy, would claim
that I, his mother, was in fact lying. This was just before Troy testified to
the Grand Jury.

IV.   Later, two F.B.I. individuals named Mott and Culver came to see me alone
at my house and ask my reaction to Troy's "recanting." When I told the F.B.I.
people that "Nobody will ever convince me that Troy's original story was not
the truth," the F.B.I. people became very angered and upset. Their actions and
their questions after that convinced me that I was in danger
and I remember saying to myself, "I've got to get out of here." I then made
some excuse to get away from them and I have never seen them since. I remember
feeling that they would actually attack me at that time. That's how strong my
feeling was at this time at this meeting with them.

V.   With respect to Attorney Mark Delman, he mainly tried to prevent me from
attending the Alisha Owen trial, but I attended much of it anyway. For whatever
reason, neither Mark Delman nor the F.B.I. wanted me to know anything. I know

('2 |

how scared Troy was of them because I know how much they frightened me.

VI. With respect to Alan Baer, I remember when Troy was a young boy and out with him at one of his parties and I told Troy that I was going to call Alan Baer and straighten him out, Troy warned me not to call him and stopped me from calling him and said, "This man can have you killed. He can cost you your job, Mom." I knew then that Troy was really scared of him way back then and was involved deeply with him in improper ways but I could do nothing about it. This was in 1983 as I recall.

VII. The information Troy provided in his affidavit about the meeting Troy and I were going to have to meet with the Senators, (Labedz, Schmit, the committee, I think) is exactly accurate. Troy had promised me right after Gary Caradori was killed that he was going to quit lying for the F.B.I. and for Delman and was going to go directly to Senator Schmit and the committee and tell them the truth. He did go and see Senator Schmit. He later refused to go to the meeting with Senator Labedz after the Caradori funeral because he was scared. I remember asking him after the funeral what was going on since we were supposed to meet with the Senators and he simply told me that he had cancelled it and we were going directly back home because he was scared because of Mickey Mott and the other F.B.I. man and how they acted towards him at the Caradori funeral.

VIII. Sometime after that, my son, Troy's brother, Shawn was killed. Supposedly in an accident playing Russian Roulette. Shawn never had anything to do with guns; would never have been playing Russian Roulette; and I am quite certain was executed as a message to Troy that he had better stick with his lies at the upcoming Alisha Owen trial or else.

After Shawn's death--and my attempts to get any information on what really happened since the death happened on Air Base Housing--I knew just how scared Troy was and why he was scared--because I was then in the same condition. So, I supported Troy in having to lie to save our family and himself.

IX. Troy and I agreed that if ever there was an opportunity for him to come forward and straighten things out after the Alisha Owen trial was over and if he could find someone he could trust, he would do it. That is what this is all about. Our family needs protection so that Troy can get out from under the lies he has been forced to tell and so that our family does not have to live in

(3)

fear waiting for whoever to eliminate Troy to keep the truth contained. Troy with my support and the family's support has told in detail his information to the British Television People so hurting or destroying Troy or his family at this point serves no point except vengeance. And, finally, I want a legitimate investigation of Shawn, my son's, death. I have an 11-year-old daughter to raise and I do not want her or me or Troy or Troy's fiancee to constantly have to live in fear and hang our heads in shame because of what Troy was forced to do, lie, to save himself and the family.

Further affiant sayeth not.

Dated and Executed this 27th day of October, 1993, at Omaha, Douglas County, Nebraska by: _Lani Hicks_

        LANI HICKS, mother of Troy Boner

State of Nebraska

County of Douglas

Before me a notary public on this 27th day of October 1993 personally appeared Lani Hicks, to me personally known, who executed the above affidavit, affirmed its truthfulness and executed it voluntarily and for purposes stated.

Marsha Jensen

NOTARY PUBLIC

GENERAL NOTARY-State of Nebraska
MARSHA A. JENSEN
My Comm. Exp. May 9, 1997

Troy Boner — 1993

Investigative Notes

The following is a written account of the happenings on July 11, 1990, and July 12, 1990, regarding telephone calls and conversations with Troy Boner.

I need to preface this writing by explaining that in the course of the Franklin Credit Union investigation, many calls were received at our home from Troy Boner. I was familiar with the individual's voice and can be 100% assured that I did, in fact, receive the telephone calls from him.

In the early evening of Wednesday, July 11, 1990, several telephone calls were received at our home by an individuals identifying himself as "Troy." Difference individuals answered the telephone and took the message from him. I was either talking to other visitors at our home or in no shape to come to the telephone. In any event, if necessary I can supply names of the parties who can attest to the fact that a "Troy" called for me during that evening.

Later in the evening, Troy again called and I was able to go to the telephone. It should be noted that I did not initiate the call, nor did I know what, if anything, he wanted to speak to me about.

The following is a synopsis of the conversation:

SC: Sandi Caradori

TB: Troy Boner

SC: This is Sandi Caradori... Troy, what do you want to say?

TB: First, you have to be careful.

SC: Troy, that is the least of my worries. How are you?

TB: I am so sorry. I am so sorry. He shouldn't have died.

SC: What are you saying Troy? What are you trying to tell me.

TB: Gary wasn't lying. He didn't tell me what to say. What I told him was the truth. (He spoke very rapidly as if fighting back tears.) They made me take it back. The threatened me.

SC: Troy, you should tell someone... Do you want me to call Senator Schmit? You need to come out with the truth once and for all. Troy, what has happened?

TB: You don't understand, they threatened me. They made me take it back. I was so scared.

(At this point I felt I needed someone else to hear this so I asked Troy to tell what he had just told me to our son, Sean.)

SC: Troy, I want you to talk to Sean, Gary's 16-year old son. Please tell him, alright?

TB: Yeah, sure.

Sean: Yeah, man what do you want?

I, along with the ten to 15 other people in our kitchen/family room heard Sean's portion of the conversation as follows:

Sean: Okay buddy, you need to do it for my Dad, man. Okay... Okay...

(I got back on the telephone and told him I would try to contact Senator Schmit or Karen. He said he'd be at 341-3031 but only for a short time. He said he was going to be "on the move" or something to that effect. He further stated,

"I'll go to anyone who'll listen. I'll go without my lawyer. I'm gonna come clean."

He then asked if I would talk with his mother. She wanted to talk. I said, "Of course."

Troy's mother's voice was familiar. She had called our house several times for Gary. One time she wanted to know if she could get reimbursed for collect telephone calls from Troy. She even said that Gary told her he'd pay for it, etc. Gary was home but didn't want to speak with her so I took the call and listened to what she had to say. She said that the telephone company was going to disconnect her telephone. Later, Gary said it was just a ploy and he was disturbed that she said that Gary had told her that he would take care of the telephone bill. Troy's mother related the following:

Mrs. Boner: Mrs. Caradori, I am so sorry. I'm so sorry. This is such a tragedy. I knew something happened to Troy. He got so scared just before he changed his story. They were threatening him. I knew he shouldn't have backed away from the truth (or some similiar expression).

Troy then got back on the telephone and I repeatedly asked that he would promise me that he would come through for me, for Gary, and for A.J. He said, "I promise... Tomorrow... To anyone who will listen... the FBI, the news - anyone."

I was unable to reach Senator Schmit and it was almost 11:30 PM. I thought that I should let Troy do this on his own in the morning.

The next day I did not hear anything on the television or the radio and I really felt that Troy had probably backed away. That evening he called me again. He said, "Sandi, I tried, I tried. I went to Mickey Mott and _____ (FBI agents). They laughed at me. They said they spent too much time and money on this case now for me to change my story. I also went to Frank Brown but he said he didn't want to take a statement because of my Grand Jury testimony." Troy sounded very down and disappointed, as was I. I related that I would let Karen know as well as Senator Schmit and that maybe they could help. Troy agreed.

The next day we planned a short meeting at the office to confirm our standing in the businss for our Lincoln staff. I arrived at the office at approximately 9:30 AM and found out that the FBI was in Karen's office serving Caracorp, Inc. with a subpoena. I was extremely upset because the timing certainly left much to be desired. I opened the closed door and noted two FBI agents, Karen Ormiston, and our security director, Joe Hebenstreit. They were all seated in the office. I said, "I don't think I need to introduce myself. What are you doing here? I can't believe this."

The smaller individual stammered a bit and looked at Karen and said, "Who... who is this?" "She's Gary's widow." He then halfway stood up and extended his hand as if to shake mine and expressed his/their sympathy. The whole ordeal was extremely unprofessional. He then looked over his shoulder at the other agent, gave him a smirk, and shook his head. He identified himself as Micky Mott. I again voiced my outrage and they indicated that Gary had been expecting this subpoena. The said that they were trying to deliver the subpoena when they received the news about the airplane crash on the radio. I sincerely question this.

544

I then asked them directly whether Troy Boner had tried to speak with them on the previous day.   Mr. Mott said, "We can't confirm or deny that."   I indicated that I did deserve an answer.   Mr. Mott then said,"Yeah, he came to the office but we can't waste our time with him. He has lost all credibility." I said, "Gentlemen, he is still a US citizen and he deserves to be heard."

End of notes.

Call Followed Investigator's Death

Mrs. Caradori Says Boner Felt Pressured

By Leslie Boellstorff and Robert Dorr

World-Herald Staff Writers

Sandra Caradori, widow of legislative investigator Gary Caradori, testified Wednesday that a young Omaha man told her during an emotional call on the day her husband died that he was sorry he had changed his story about sexual abuse of minors by prominent Omaha men.

Mrs. Caradori, testifying in the Alisha Owen perjury trial, said Troy Boner called her about 11 p.m. on July 11, 1990.

Caradori and the couple's son Andrew had been killed in the pre-dawn hours that day when the plane piloted by Caradori crashed into an Illinois cornfield.

According to Mrs. Caradori, Boner said: "Gary was telling the truth. I've been pressured to change (my story). I shouldn't have changed."

Boner, a former friend of Miss Owen, had told Caradori in late 1989 that he witnessed and experienced sexual abuse when he was a minor. Later, in interviews with the FBI and before a Douglas County grand jury, Boner said his original story to Caradori was a lie.

Miss Owen, 22, stuck to the original story she told Caradori. She told the grand jury, among other things, that she had a sexual relationship with former Omaha Police Chief Robert Wadman when she was a minor and that he fathered her child. She is being tried in Douglas County District Court on eight charges of lying under oath to the grand jury last year.

Caradori's death and Boner's call to Mrs. Caradori occurred after Boner had appeared before the grand jury and recanted his story.

In his earlier testimony at the perjury trial, Boner, now 24, had a different recollection of his call to Mrs. Caradori. He said he told Mrs. Caradori how sad he was about Caradori's death. He said Mrs. Caradori then told him that now was the time "to come forward with the truth."

Boner added: "How do you tell somebody (who has just lost a husband and son) it's all a lie?"

Mrs. Caradori testified Wednesday

Please turn to Page 10, Col. 1

Inside Today

U.S. Helps Soviets Buy Grain

The Soviet Union will be able to buy $1.5 billion in U.S. grain this year with loans guaranteed by the U.S. government. **Page 20.**

RELIGION, SCOUTING: An 8-year-old asks a federal judge to force the Cub Scouts to let him join even though he doesn't believe in God. **People, Page 3.**

ETHICS PROBE: The Senate Ethics Committee has received a complaint from a conservative group over Sen. Edward Kennedy's actions related to an alleged rape on Kennedy property. **Page 16.**

BASEBALL SALE: The Union Pacific Railroad, which bought part of a baseball team last week, is poised to sell Denver land for a new major league baseball stadium. **Business News, Page 24.**

Investigative Report

Case Name: Franklin Credit Union/Investigation

Report Date: July 11, 1990

Report By: Karen J. Ormiston

I received a telephone call from Gary A. Caradori's wife, Sandi, who informed me that I was to come to their residence immediately. When I arrived at their residence, I was informed that Gary and his son, Andrew, had been killed in a plane crash earlier this morning in Lee County, Illinois. Please note that Mrs. Caradori had to make numerous telephone calls in an attempt to determine what had actually occurred.

Due to Gary's work with the Franklin investigation, it is this writer's opinion that his airplane had been tampered with. According to reports to-date, the airplane "broke up" in the air and Gary and his son were killed on impact.

This writer received a telephone call from Trish Lanthier who expressed her sympathy, and who indicated that she thought Gary's airplane may have been tampered with also.

This writer received a telephone call from Donna Owen on the above date who informed me that Alisha Owen was extremely upset over Gary's death and that York prison officials had removed Alisha to a "safe" area of the prison. She went on to state that she had received information that Jim Parson had remitted information to Gary the week previous to his death that related to the Franklin investigation and stated that Gary was in possession of a firearm, possibly given to him by Mr. Parson, that he was going to have ballistic tests run on in the Chicago area by someone who he trusted in law enforcement there. She stated that it was her opinion that Gary's airplane had been sabotaged, and that this may have been the reason.

On the evening of the above date, this writer received a telephone call from Sandi Caradori indicating that Troy Boner had telephoned her residence several times, indicating that he was sorry for recanting his statement to Gary and that he wanted to come forward to state that he had lied when he stated that his statement to Gary were untrue and/or fabricated. This writer will attempt to contact Troy Boner at a later date.

End of report.

July 13, 1990

This writer requested that RJ Nebe transport Troy Boner to the offices of Caracorp, Inc. on the above date due to the fact that Troy had made several telephone calls to Sandi Caradori at her residence, and several telephone calls to my residence on Friday evening and Saturday evening. I informed RJ Nebe to call Troy on Sunday evening to make arrangements to meet with myself, RJ, and the legislative committee on Monday after Troy discussed certain issued with these investigators. R.J. Nebe called me at my office at approximately 11:00 indicating that he and Troy were out their way.

Investigative Report

Case Name: Franklin Credit Union/Investigation

Report Date: July 13, 1990

Report By: Karen J. Ormiston
                          Private Investigator

On the above date, FBI agents, one of whom was Nick Nott, served a subpoena on Caracorp, Inc., which requested numerous records relating to the Franklin investigation. I had been informed by Sandi Caradori previously that Troy Boner had gone to the offices of the Federal Bureau of Investigation earlier this week, however, they would not listen to him. I then asked Mr. Nott if Troy had attempted to set the record straight reference Troy's recanting of his statement to Gary Caradori. Mr. Nott would not comment. A copy of the subpoena will be remitted to the Franklin Legislative Committee.

Also on the above date, this writer received word that Investigator Nebe had proceeded to the capitol building to meet with the Legislative Committee. This writer then received a telephone call from Senator Labedz who indicated that the Committee would like me to come to the meeting also.

Upon arriving at the capitol building, I proceeded directly to the Hearing Room. Present were Senators Lynch, Labedz, Schmit, Baack, and Warner. Also present was attorney Craig Wittstruck.

I was questioned about records that I am in possession of. I stated that they were in possession of all of the information that I was in possession of. Please note that five volumes of material were remitted in April to the Legislative Committee, Samual Van Pelt, John Stevens Berry, and FBI agent, Nick Nott. I stated that the most recent reports, which were dictated by Gary Caradori, had also been remitted to Senator Schmit. I indicated that Gary Caradori had not dictated any notes or reports since the date of the last report Senator Schmit had received.

I was also questioned about the Franklin material was stored. I indicated that I had hard copy material and backup computer disks. Please note, however, that some information was not stored on computer disks due to the fact that so many hard copies of this material had been made for the above-stated entities.

They questioned me about Gary's trip to Chicago and whether I was aware of any work that he may have been conducting reference this case in the Chicago area. I indicated that I did not know what he was working on, but that he had attempted to meet with me several times over the previous weekend and I had been unable to meet with him in person. Please note that it is probable Gary had information that he wanted to share with me in person due to the fact that our telephone lines are being monitored.

I was questioned about Jim Parson, who had indicating on Omaha radio station, KKAR, that he had been a "volunteer investigator" for Caracorp, Inc. I stated that although Mr. Parson had telephoned our office several times over the course of this investigation, that he was not an employee of Caracorp, Inc., nor was

July 13, 1990
Page Two

I was questioned about my thoughts on whether Gary's airplane had been sabotaged. I stated that it was my feeling that his airplane had been tampered with. I stated that Gary was an excellent pilot who meticulously maintained his airplane. I also indicated that Gary would have taken no risks with his son, Andrew, in the airplane.

I stated that Troy Boner had contacted Sandi Caradori and wanted to "come forward." I stated that it was crucial to get Troy's statement again and have him testify in front of the Legislative Committee. I did attempt to telephone his mother's residence in Council Bluffs, Iowa, however, that telephone number had been disconnected. It was my intent to record the telephone conversation. I will attempt to contact Troy over the weekend. If I am able to contact him, arrangements were made by the Committee to meet with Troy at a location in Omaha in the area of 72nd and Pacific Streets.

The Committee stated that they would like Caracorp, Inc. to continue with the investigation. I stated that we would do so.

The Committee requested that I store my files and information at the capitol. I stated that I would get these items to them as soon as I was able, and an inventory of the information would be taken at that time.

Please note that Senator Labedz also read information which I will follow up on reference Anita Adams and Rue Fox.

End of report.

Supplemental Report

Case Name: Franklin Credit Union/Investigation

Report Date: July 13, 1990

Report By: Karen J. Ormiston
                          Private Investigator

This writer received word on the above date that a pickup which is frequently driven by me had been tampered with. Handfuls of nails had been placed behind three of the tires of this pickup which had been parked for two days in the west parking lot of Caracorp, Inc. located at 3426 O Street.

Upon returning from the meeting with the Legislative Committee, I telephoned the Lincoln Police Department. Officer Dennis Scott then came to the offices of Caracorp, Inc. and proceeded to the west parking lot in which the vehicle was parked. Please note that the LPD case number for this incident is 90-062923 and that a report of this incident is on file.

End of report.

Investigative Report

Case Name: Franklin Credit Union/Investigation

Report Date: July 16, 1990

Report By: R. J. Nebe

After several phone calls on Sunday evening, it was agreed upon that I would pick up victim-witness, Troy Boner, and bring him to Lincoln on Monday morning.

Monday morning I arrived at Troy Boner's mother's house in Council Bluffs, Iowa. Troy's brother came out to my car to inform me that Troy had just gone to the store and would be back in a few minutes. Troy arrived within a few minutes and entered the vehicle to proceed to Lincoln with this investigator.

INVESTIGATOR'S NOTE: I noticed that Troy's mother had a new car sitting in the driveway.

Before proceeding to Lincoln, Troy asked that I take him to the Equilibria Medical Center in downtown Omaha. Equilibria Medical Center is a methadone clinic for narcotic addictions. Troy informed me that he has been on the methadone program for slightly over a month and that he is almost finished going through the treatment.

INVESTIGATOR'S NOTE: I noticed that Troy is extremely paranoid and each time when he would get in and out of the car, he would look in all directions as if to see if anyone had seen him with me.

Throughout the entire trip to Lincoln, Troy talked openly concerning his connections with the Franklin Credit Union case.

Troy also stated that he recently had a baby boy by the name of Zachary last June with his girlfriend, Yvonne. Troy informed me that he recently enlisted in the Navy and was expected to begin basic training next January. His plans in the Navy are to begin working as a printer and receive training in printing.

INVESTIGATOR'S NOTE: At first glance, it would appear as if Troy was trying to clean up his life by going through the methadone clinic to cure his addiction to narcotics and his enlisting in the Navy. He also stated that he was planning to be married sometime in August.

In regards to Troy's testimony to both grand jury's, the federal as well as Douglas County, that after he recanted his story, the FBI began to treat him in his words "like a king." He said the FBI told him he had failed the lie detector test and at this time, he better change his story to the truth. Troy told me what he basically told them what they wanted to hear and they were happy that it was all that everything he had stated to Gary Caradori was made up.

It appeared to this writer that from Troy's statements that his new attorney, Dehlman, must have a great deal of contact with sources in the grand jury as well as the FBI. Troy stated that Delman told him Friday after Gary's death, the grand jury was planning to indict Gary in the near future. Troy did not state where Delman received this information. Troy also stated that Mark Delman had recently contacted him stating that a publishing company was offering to pay $20,000 for Troy's story. I questioned Troy to how Delman was being paid and he stated, at this time, he wasn't paying Delman anything but he was supposed to pay him in the future. Troy also stated that Delman would take 33 1/3 percent of any money that Troy would receive from any publishing companies.

Troy stated that both the FBI and U.S. Attorney, Tom Thalken, had threatened Troy in the past that if he did not recant his story, they would bring him up on perjury charges and send him to jail. This is a great concern of Troy's at this time.

Troy stated that he wanted to come down to Lincoln in order to set the records straight. It appears Troy feels some guilt towards recanting his story after Gary's death.

Upon arriving at the Caracorp office, Karen Ormiston and myself explained to Troy that we wanted to re-interview him on tape so that he could state he originally told Investigator Caradori the truth and later recanted his story due to threats from the FBI and the U.S. Attorney's office. As soon as we explained to Troy that we wanted to video tape his again, he became extremely upset and stated that he didn't want to go on video tape because of the fact that the U.S. Attorney would bring him up on perjury charges.

At this point, Troy asked me to step outside with him. Out on the porch of the Caracorp offices, Troy tried to tell me that it was all lies and he made up the story. He stated that I was the only one that would believe him. He stated he was with Alan Baer and Larry King a couple of times, but it was when I was 17 years old.

At this time, I told Troy that anything we would discuss we would discuss back in the office with Karen. At this point, we went back into the office.

INVESTIGATOR'S NOTE: The statements that Troy made to this investigator out on the porch appeared to have been what he has been coached to say, due to the fact, he was positive he was 17 years old when he was with Alan Baer and Larry King. I feel he was coached on this because by saying he was 17 at the time, he was passed the legal age of consent.

Once Troy was back in the office with Karen Ormiston and myself, he agreed he may be willing to testify again, but only if we could provide him with an attorney because of his fears of being arrested for perjury charges. At this time, Ms. Ormiston began attempting to contact Senator Schmit in order to line up an attorney for Troy.

At approximately 1:30 PM, Ms. Ormiston and myself took Troy Boner to the Capitol to Senator Schmit's office. While in Senator Schmit's office, we discussed the possibility of lining Troy up with several different attorneys, but it was also explained to Troy that he would have to make the call to get the attorney for himself and at the same time, he would have to contact his attorney, Mark Delman, to discontinue services.

Committee attorney, Robert Creager, also came to Senator Schmit's office in order to discuss where we stood as far as defending Troy against any perjury charges if he would state that he did tell Gary Caradori the truth in the original video tape.

It was determined that we would be unable to retain an attorney for Troy until the next morning; therefore, our meeting was discontinued.

End of report.

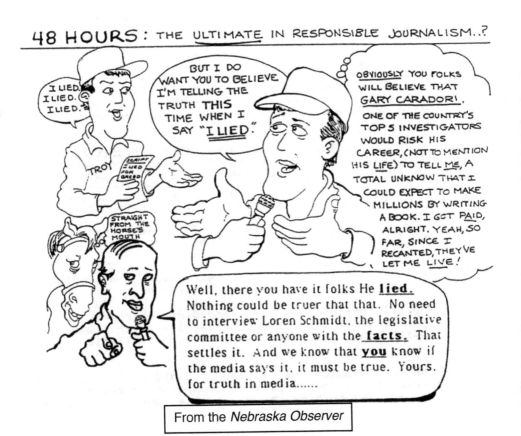

From the *Nebraska Observer*

EXHIBIT

Affidavit   Affidavit   Affidavit   Affidavit   Affidavit

My name is Donna Owen. I am the mother of Alisha Owen. I live at 3140 North 58th Street in Omaha, Nebraska. On or about the 13th of February 1992 my daughter Alisha Owen was released from prison and returned to live at my home at 3140 North 58th Street in Omaha along with my husband,' Alvin Owen, and our granddaughter (Alisha's daughter) Amanda Owen, age 6 at that time.

On March, 1992, I received a phone call at our residence, phone no. 402 551 5457, and the person calling asked for my daughter Alisha. I immediately recognized the voice as that of Troy Boner, because I was very familiar with Troy's very distinctive voice because of previous conversations I have had over the years with Troy both on the phone and in person. I immediately asked the caller to identify themselves as I always do for anybody who calls for Alisha.

The caller immediately identified himself as Troy Boner.

Troy then asked again to speak to Alisha. I advised Troy that I was sorry but that I could not allow him to speak with or to Alisha.

He, Troy, told me it was very important for him to talk to Alisha because he, Troy, wanted to help Alisha. I told him again that I would not be able to do that for reasons that should be obvious to him.

He continued to request to speak with Alisha, insisting the information was to help Alisha, but I declined. At about this point in the call, a call came thru on Call Waiting, and I asked Troy to hold a minute while I took the other call and checked who it was. I put Troy on hold. I went then and got my tape recorder and hooked it up to the phone.

I then made sure that in the ensuing conversation with him I ientified him as Troy several times for later reference and identification.

I then asked Troy how he wanted to help Alisha and simply let Troy talk himself from that point forward.

I have the original of this tape recording, which was operating on Voice Activated on the machine which I was not familiar with, and I wish to make this tape available to this court.

During the conversation that I tape recorded from Troy, Troy acknowledged without any urging or prompting or requests on my part in any way that he, Troy, had lied during the trial.

He explained that it was impossible for me, Donna Owen, to understand the fear and pressure that he, Troy, was under from the time he had gone to Senator Schmit's office and tried to recant and tell the truth up to and during the trial.

I interrupted one of the times he kept describing his fear and told him that people were prepared to keep him safe after he, Troy, had gone and visited Senator's Schmit's office when he first attempted to correct his alleged recantation. Troy immediately told me that was not true. He told me that in fact we, the Owen family, had not been able to keep our own son safe. Troy was referring to our son, Aaron, who allegedly committed suicide several months before the trial of Alisha. Troy also said that nobody was able to protect his own brother who was supposed to have accidentally shot himself in the face and killed himself. Troy emphasized that nobody could keep him safe and kept repeating, "You don't know the fear and the pressure."

Troy repeated that he had lied during the trial and now that Alisha was out of prison that together, they might be able to tell the truth and help free Alisha.

I told Troy that he could not talk to Alisha. That he had told us once before that he was going to tell the truth and had backed down and I told him that if he really wanted to help Alisha that he, Troy, should call Alisha's attorney, John De Camp. He, Troy, then said that he was afraid to do that because, as Troy explained, he was afraid that the same thing would happen as happened when he went to see Senator Schmit and tried to tell the truth and the next thing he knew it was in all the papers and on the news.

Troy repeated that he had lied in the trial for his own safety. That he had to look out for himself because nobody else would. And that he was all alone.

Further affiant sayeth not.

Dated and executed this 13th day of May 1992 at Omaha, Nebraska by:

Donna Owen _____
DONNA OWEN

STATE OF NEBRASKA

DOUGLAS COUNTY

BEFORE ME A NOTARY PERSONALLY APPEARED DONNA OWEN TO ME KNOWN WHO EXECUTED THE ABOVE AFFIDAVIT, ACKNOWLEDGED THE TRUTH OF ITS CONTENTS AND THAT IT WAS VOLUNTARILY GIVEN.

Jan C. Jewell _____   May 13, 1992
NOTARY

AFFIDAVIT   AFFIDAVIT   AFFIDAVIT   AFFIDAVIT   AFFIDAVIT
AFFIDAVIT

My name is Robert Janecek, Junior. I live at 4706 South 90th
Street in Omaha, Douglas County, Nebraska 68127.

During the period 1955 thru 1983 I was a member of the Douglas
County Sheriff's Department and from apprx. 1981 held the position
of Reserve Captain in charge of fifty-five Reserve officers of the
Douglas County Sheriff's Department.

I spent apprx. 12 years in the Criminal Investigation Division as
a Sergeant and had broad experience in the investigation of crime
in and around Douglas County, Nebraska. My educational background
in crime investigation includes the F.B.I. academy in Quantico,
Va., from which I graduated as well as the Institute of Applied
Science in Chicago, Ill., where I studied criminal investigation
and became a certified polygraph operator. In that position, I
performed polygraph examinations on behalf of the Douglas County
Sheriff's Department. Since apprx. 1983 I retired from the Douglas
County Sheriff's Department, but have kept active in law enforcement
and criminal investigation by being a licensed private detective
and operating Central States Intelligence Bureau, an investigative
service, located at 4911 South 25th Street in Omaha, Nebraska
68107.

I am today providing this affidavit and this information to assist
in efforts to obtain a new trial for Alisha Owen--whom I do not
know, have never met, have never talked to--but whom I believe was
convicted on the basis of perjured testimony from one Troy Boner.

In my private and business life I have known the "Boner" family
for approximately thirty or more years. On occasions, during that
period of time, various members of the Boner family have been
employed by me on a part time basis.

Subsequent to the Alisha Owen trial--which I had not particularly
followed or paid attention to but which I was aware of from
Newspaper reports--an incident occurred which gravely concerned me
and which I felt compelled me to investigate further.

The incident was as follows:
    1. Dave Boner was in my office and working for me at the
time and began discussing a newspaper article which involved the
Alisha Owen trial and a witness identified by the newspaper as
Troy Boner. At that time he shocked me by identifying the Troy
Boner in the newspaper article as his nephew. I had never made
any connection between the two--despite my longtime familiarity
with the Boner family--because the media pronunciation of Troy
Boner's name had always sounded to me like BONNER, RATHER THAN
BONER. As the discussion progressed between myself and David
Boner, David Boner stated to me, that another Boner who also worked
for me part time by the name of Ed Boner was in fact the Step-

554

father of Troy Boner, the individual identified in the news article. David Boner then pointed out to me--without my soliciting the information--that the Grand Jury and the Trial were a "big JOKE in the Boner Family,"...because Troy had stated to David's daughter, that he, Troy, had lied to the Grand Jury and also had lied to the Court in the Trial and also stated that he had received $12,000.00 for doing same. The money, according to David Boner, was provided to Troy under the disguise of being "rights for a book."

David Boner also stated that I should talk to Ed Boner for further information if I was interested.

At this time I asked Ed Boner to come in and talk to me. Ed Boner agreed to do so. Upon arrival at my office, also with Ed Boner, was Ron Boner. Ron Boner is the cousin of Ed Boner and a brother of David Boner.

At that time I told them that I would like to tape-record the conversation with their permission. They gave me their permission.

The essence of this tape, which I will provide to the Court, was this: that Troy had acknowledged and explained to relatives that he had no choice but to lie or he would never make it to trial. In other words, that he, Troy Boner, had perjured himself, had do so out of fear and also because of a promise of reward financially if he would lie at trial.

I felt after obtaining this information that I had no choice but to make such information available to appropriate individuals who could bring this matter to the attention of the Court for corrective action.

Other discussions I had over the following weeks with the members of the Boner family confirmed this story repeatedly. I believe I may have some of those other tapes available also. I would make them available to the court if requested. I am satisfied in my own mind based on the information I have obtained that Troy Boner did in fact perjure himself at the Alisha Owen trial and before the Grand Jury.

Dated and executed this 29th day of July 1992 at Lincoln, Lancaster County, Nebraska by

Robert Janecek, Affiant

State of Nebraska

County of Lancaster

Before me a notary public personally appeared Robert Janecek, Junior, to me personally known who executed the above affidavit and acknowledged it was his voluntary act and deed and done for the purposes stated.

A GENERAL NOTARY-State of Nebraska
JAN C. JEWELL

Jan C. Jewell

555

AFFIDAVIT AFFIDAVIT AFFIDAVIT AFFIDAVIT AFFIDAVIT AFFIDAVIT

My name is John De Camp. I live at 2215 South 70th Street in Lincoln, Lancaster County, Nebraska and am a practicing attorney at 414 South 11th Street in Lincoln, Ne. 68506 and am affiliated with DE CAMP LEGAL SERVICES, P.C.

We are providing legal assistance to Alisha Owen.

I have been contacted by at least five individuals who are either intimate with or who have or did have extremely close and confidential relationships with an individual named Troy Boner who testified at the original Alisha Owen trial.

Each of these individuals has provided me statements--independent of each other--which are essentially as follows:

1. That following the Alisha Owen trial their very close and direct relationship with Troy Boner provided them and Troy repeated opportunities to discuss the testimony and actions of Troy Boner with respect to the Boner testimony before the Court in the Alisha Owen trial.

2. That on repeated occasions Troy had voluntarily told them that he, Troy Boner, had lied and perjured himself in his testimony before the Court in the Alisha Owen case.

3. That he, Troy Boner, had felt compelled to do this out of fear for his own personal safety and that of other members of his family, because of pressure put on him, Troy Boner, by certain other individuals.

I, John De Camp, will be most happy and anxious to provide the names of these individuals to the Court for further examination, verification, and investigation by the court independently. The individuals have for their own protection or because, in some cases, it might constitute a violation of Confidentiality laws of the State of Nebraska, indicated they did not want at this time to have their names disclosed.

Further Affiant says not.

Dated and executed this 8th day of August 1992 by John W. De Camp.

JOHN W. DE CAMP

STATE OF NEBRASKA

COUNTY OF LANCASTER

Before me a notary public personally appeared John W. De Camp, to me personally known, who executed the above affidavit voluntarily.

Jan C. Jewell   8 August 1992

GENERAL NOTARY-State of Nebraska
JAN C. JEWELL
My Commission Exp. June 8 1996

556

Office of Chief Medical Examiner
Tarrant County Medical Examiner's District
Tarrant County, Texas
200 Felix Gwozdz Place, Fort Worth, Texas 76104-4919
(817) 920-5700 FAX (817) 920-5713

AUTOPSY REPORT

Name: Troy Bonner
Approximate Age: 36 years
Height: 77 inches

CASE NO: 03001536
Sex: Male
Weight: 227.3 pounds

I hereby certify that on the thirteenth day of February 2003, beginning at 0940 hours, I, Nizam Peerwani, M.D., pursuant to Statute 49.25 of Texas Criminal Code, performed a complete autopsy on the body of TROY BONNER at the Tarrant County Medical Examiner's District Morgue in Fort Worth, Texas on the request of Justice Bryan Smith of Taylor County, Texas and upon investigation of the essential facts concerning the circumstances of the death and history of the case as known to me, I am of the opinion that the findings, cause and manner of death are as follows:

FINDINGS:

I. Sudden death with:
    A. Acute respiratory failure with:
        1. Pulmonary vascular congestion and edema, bilateral, severe
        2. Hyper inflated lungs with aspiration of gastric contents
        3. Generalized visceral congestion, severe
        4. Postmortem toxicology.......pending
    B. Hypertensive atherosclerosis cardiovascular disease
        1. Cardiomegaly (weight = 464/1 gms)
        2. Left ventricular hypertrophy
        3. Multi-focal mild occlusive coronary atherosclerosis with 10-20% stenosis
        4. Generalized atherosclerosis, mild

II. Hepatomegaly (weight = 2976.2 gms) with moderate generalized fatty metamorphosis

III. Chronic cholecystitis with lithiases

IV. Perimortem scalp injury with:
    A. Left temporal subgaleal hemorrhage
    B. Absence of cranial or cerebral trauma

V. No evidence of foul play

Page 2 of 6

0301536
Troy Bonner

CAUSE OF DEATH: SUDDEN DEATH PENDING TOXICOLOGY

MANNER OF DEATH: PENDING

_____
Signature

Nizam Peerwani, M.D.
Chief Medical Examiner

The Associated Press

Crash wreckage . . . is examined in a farm field southwest of Ashton.

Caradori's Airplane 'Broke Up in Flight'

By Robert Dorr and Gabriella Stern
World-Herald Staff Writers

The small plane that carried Lincoln private detective Gary Caradori and his 8-year-old son to their deaths in Illinois early Wednesday apparently broke up in flight, two investigators said Wednesday.

"It was a scattered wreckage pattern," said Bill Bruce, an investigator with the National Transportation Safety Board. "It certainly demonstrates that it did break up in flight. The exact mechanism of the breakup is unknown."

Sheriff Tim Bivins of Lee County, Ill., who spent 12 hours at the crash site, said he didn't think an explosion occurred while the plane was in the air. He said he thought the plane "came apart in the air" and exploded on impact. Bivins said plane debris was scattered over an area three-quarters of a mile long.

Caradori was the private investigator looking into allegations of child sexual abuse for the Legislature's Franklin Credit Union committee. The commit-

Gary Caradori . . . He and his son were on way home to Lincoln from Chicago.

attending the Tuesday night All-Star

'I Hurt Real Bad,' Mother Says

By Gabriella Stern 7-13-90
World-Herald Staff Writer

Mary Caradori of Ralston was grieving Thursday for her son and grandson, Gary and Andrew Caradori, who were killed Wednesday in the crash of their private plane in Illinois.

Gary, 41, and Andrew, 8, were heading home to Lincoln after attending the All-Star baseball game in Chicago.

"I hurt real bad," Mrs. Caradori said in her home in Ralston. "I miss him. I love him. I'll miss him and my dearest Andrew.

"What can I tell you about Andrew? He was a New York Mets fan, and I was so proud of that because I'm from Brooklyn, New York. He loved tall buildings, and he was anxious to go to New York some day because of all the tall buildings.

"Gary, what can I tell you about

Gary Caradori   Andrew Caradori

Gary? He was a fine, fine pilot. You had to know Gary and you'd fall in love with the guy.

"My Andrew, my Andrew. He was like a Teddy bear, and you can't help but love him. I miss him and I miss the fact that I won't see him. It's bad enough that they're both gone, but I won't be able to see them. I understand their bodies were burned beyond recognition.

"It's bad enough that they're gone

but that part hurts terribly. I just can't get my mind to stop thinking: 'Did they suffer when they crashed? Were they still alive and in pain? What was the last thing he said to Andrew? He loved to call him 'my son.' I wonder, did he grab Andrew and say, 'Son, don't worry'? I'm thinking, what were his last words? What were Andrew's last words?

"I hate to think anyone would think otherwise of Gary. He was so dedicated. He never tried to hurt anybody. He never did."

Mrs. Caradori said that immediately after she learned of the plane crash she believed it was sabotage.

She told the Lincoln Journal: "I feel my son was murdered and my grandson was murdered."

After more than a day's reflection, however, she said, "I think I'm going to wait and see what the report from the FAA (Federal Aviation Administration) says. I think I'd better wait a little longer."

Initial Probe Finds No Sign of Sabotage

By Robert Dorr 7-13-90
World-Herald Staff Writer

Ashton, Ill. — A federal investigator said Thursday he hadn't seen anything pointing to foul play in the plane crash that killed Lincoln private detective Gary Caradori 41 and a son Andrew 8

Bruce said the plane — a single-engine, six-passenger Piper Saratoga — broke up in flight.

He said that he didn't know what part of the plane broke apart first and that he had seen no evidence of a fire before the crash.

Lee County Coroner Richard Schil-

and the corn shielded the wreckage.

The plane was spotted about daybreak by a medical helicopter.

Rain, Fog

Earlier, a National Weather Service forecaster in Rockford, Ill., about 40 miles away, said he thought there was

John DeCamp — 2000

559

National Transportation Safety Board
Washington, D.C. 20594

Brief of Accident

File No. - 2083   7/11/90   ASHTON, IL   A/C Reg. No. N43515   Time (Lcl) - 0221 CDT

----Basic Information----

Type Operating Certificate-NONE (GENERAL AVIATION)   Aircraft Damage

				Fatal	Serious	Minor	None
Type of Operation	-PERSONAL		DESTROYED				
			Fire	Crew	1	0	0	0
Flight Conducted Under	-14 CFR 91		ON GROUND	Pass	1	0	0	0
Accident Occurred During	-DESCENT						

----Aircraft Information----

Make/Model	- PIPER PA-32R-301T	Eng Make/Model - LYCOMING TIO-540-S1AD	ELT Installed/Activated - YES/YES
Landing Gear	- TRICYCLE-RETRACTABLE	Number Engines - 1	Stall Warning System - YES
Max Gross Wt	- 3600	Engine Type - RECIP-FUEL INJECTED	
No. of Seats	-. 6	Rated Power - 300 HP	

----Environment/Operations Information----

Weather Data

Wx Briefing	- FSS	Itinerary	Airport Proximity
Method	- TELEPHONE	Last Departure Point	OFF AIRPORT/STRIP
Completeness	- PARTIAL, LMTD BY FCSTR	CHICAGO, IL	
Basic Weather	- UNK/NR	Destination	Airport Data
Wind Dir/Speed-	UNK/NR	LINCOLN, NE	
Visibility	- UNK/NR		Runway Ident - N/A
Lowest Sky/Clouds -	UNK/NR	ATC/Airspace	Runway Lth/Wid - N/A
Lowest Ceiling	- UNK/NR	Type of Flight Plan - IFR	Runway Surface - N/A
Obstructions to Vision-	UNK/NR	Type of Clearance - IFR	Runway Status - N/A
Precipitation	- RAIN	Type Apch/Lndg - NONE	
Condition of Light	- NIGHT (DARK)		

----Personnel Information----

Pilot-In-Command   Age - 41   Medical Certificate - VALID MEDICAL-NO WAIVERS/LIMIT
Certificate(s)/Rating(s)   Biennial Flight Review   Flight Time (Hours)
    PRIVATE   Current   - YES   Total   - 1208   Last 24 Hrs - UNK/NR
    SE LAND   Months Since - 11   Make/Model- UNK/NR Last 30 Days- UNK/NR
                                       Aircraft Type - UNK/NR Instrument- UNK/NR Last 90 Days- UNK/NR
                                                            Multi-Eng - UNK/NR Rotorcraft - UNK/NR

Instrument Rating(s) - AIRPLANE

----Narrative----

THE FLT ORIGINATED AT 0151 CDT AFTER THE PLT & PSGR HAD SPENT A DAY SIGHTSEEING & ATTENDED A NGT BASEBALL GAME. BEFORE
DEPG, THE PLT RCVD A WX BRIEFING & FILED AN IFR FLT PLAN. OVC SKIES WITH CUMULIFORM CLOUDS & RAIN SHOWERS PREVAILED
ALONG THE ROUTE. THOUGH THE PLT WAS NOT BRIEFED ABOUT TSTMS, ONLY WIDELY SCATTERED TSTMS WITH MODERATE RAINSHOWERS
WERE FORECAST. WHILE EN ROUTE, THE PLT MADE A TRANSMISSION THAT HIS COMPASS WAS "SWINGING" & THEN CONTACT WITH THE
ACFT WAS LOST. SUBSEQUENTLY, AN INFLT BREAKUP OF THE ACFT OCCURRED & WRECKAGE WAS SCATTERED OVER A WIDE AREA. RADAR
DATA SHOWED THAT THE AIRPLANE MADE RAPID CHANGES IN ALTITUDE BEFORE BREAKING UP. AN EXAM OF THE WRECKAGE SHOWED THAT
BOTH WINGS FAILED IN POSITIVE OVERLOAD. THE STABILATOR FAILED DOWN & WAS BENT AFT BEFORE SEPARATING FROM THE ACFT. THE
REST OF THE AIRCRAFT WAS EXTENSIVELY DAMAGED BY IMPACT & FIRE.

Brief of Accident (Continued)

File No. - 2083   7/11/90   ASHTON, IL   A/C Reg. No. N43515   Time (Lcl) - 0221 CDT

Occurrence #1   LOSS OF CONTROL - IN FLIGHT
Phase of Operation   CRUISE

Finding(s)
    1. REASON FOR OCCURRENCE UNDETERMINED
    2. LIGHT CONDITION - DARK NIGHT
    3. WEATHER CONDITION - CLOUDS
    4. WEATHER CONDITION - RAIN
    5. FLIGHT/NAV INSTRUMENTS - UNDETERMINED

Occurrence #2   AIRFRAME/COMPONENT/SYSTEM FAILURE/MALFUNCTION
Phase of Operation   DESCENT - UNCONTROLLED

Finding(s)
    6. DESIGN STRESS LIMITS OF AIRCRAFT - EXCEEDED - PILOT IN COMMAND
    7.   FATIGUE - PILOT IN COMMAND
    8.   SPATIAL DISORIENTATION - PILOT IN COMMAND

Occurrence #3   IN FLIGHT COLLISION WITH TERRAIN/WATER
Phase of Operation   DESCENT - UNCONTROLLED

----Probable Cause----

The National Transportation Safety Board determines that the Probable Cause(s) of this accident was:
A LOSS OF AIRCRAFT CONTROL FOR AN UNKNOWN REASON, WHILE EN ROUTE IN INSTRUMENT METEOROLOGICAL CONDITIONS (IMC) ON
A DARK NIGHT, AND THE PILOT EXCEEDING THE DESIGN STRESS LIMITS OF THE AIRCRAFT WHILE ATTEMPTING TO RECOVER FROM
UNCONTROLLED FLIGHT. FACTORS RELATED TO THE ACCIDENT WERE: PILOT FATIGUE AND PROBABLE SPATIAL DISORIENTATION OF THE
PILOT AND/OR AN INSTRUMENT MALFUNCTION.

DOCUMENTS

Nebraska State Legislature

SENATOR LORAN SCHMIT

District No. 23
State Capitol
Lincoln. Nebraska 68509
(402) 471-2719

Box 109
Bellwood. Nebraska 68624

COMMITTEES

Chairman. Natural Resources
Banking. Commerce and Insurance
Executive Board
Reference
Legislative Council

Ninety-First Legislature
December 12, 1990

Mr. Bill Bruce, Aviation Inspector
National Transportation Safety Board
Chicago Field Office
DuPage Airport
31 West 775 North Avenue
West Chicago, Illinois 60185

Dear Mr. Bruce:

I have visited recently with the family of Gary
Caradori, the young man who, along with his son, was
killed in a Piper Saratoga aircraft approximately 100
miles west of Chicago, Illinois, on July 11th.

The brothers of Mr. Caradori would like to know
how long it will be before the wreckage of the aircraft
will be released. They have shown me photographs of the
wreckage, and I would like to know if it is standard procedure
not to try to reconstruct an aircraft which was destroyed in
this kind of crash.

I want to assure you that I am still concerned about the
cause of the crash. Mr. Caradori was an excellent and experienced pilot. I have never known him to incur any unnecessary
risk while flying an aircraft, and I also know that he would
be particularly careful while carrying his eight year old son
as a passenger. Mr. Caradori and I on numerous occasions
prior to July 11 discussed the possibility that his aircraft
or one of his vehicles might be sabotaged, although he did not
dwell upon the issue. He emphasized, and I agreed, that such
a possibility did exist. I must confess that I did not think
he would ever die in the crash of an aircraft because he was a
fine pilot and because the unexplained crash of his aircraft
would be suspicious at best.

If you have discovered the cause of the crash, it
would be extremely helpful to the Franklin Legislative
Committee if we could have that information prior to
December 31st as we are preparing a report to the
Legislature.

Thank you very much.

Sincerely,

Loran Schmit, Chairman
Franklin Legislative Committee

561

The Franklin Legislative Committee
Atten: Senator Loran Schmit, Chairman
State Capitol
Lincoln, Ne

January 5, 1990

Dear Senators:

I have watched the events surrounding the Franklin Investigation unfold with great interest, both before Gary's and AJ's deaths but more importantly-after their deaths. To say this investigation has impacted all of our lives is an understatement. The publicity and media coverage has been, as I see it, unprecedented. The stress on you, your families and your careers must have been and is staggering.

I know the feeling to get on with other work and leave this mess behind would be very tempting. For me, my heart wants me to forget what I instinctively know is right, and get on with our lives, meet new challenges and create new dreams. That is what my heart-shattered as it is-wishes for me. To mend, to heal, to live.

My gut, however, tells me that this THING is not finished. This monster of a thing can not be boxed up in archives. People, real people, fellow Nebraskans, have come forward-willingly asking for assistance. Gary and his staff and Investigator Lowe furnished the Committee with much information and evidence of some very distinct problems. This work cannot be ignored or overshadowed because certain entities have elected to call this thing a hoax.

It is frightening to think that in America, suppression of news has taken hold so firmly in the Midwest. A case in point: I had released pertinent information and results regarding a polygraph examination that Karen Ormiston had taken several months ago. The examiner was an out of state expert and president of the National Association of Polygraph Examiners. The specific issue that I wanted addressed was the fact that neither Gary nor Karen ever coerced witnesses, threatened victim witnesses, or scripted any testimony. She, of course, was cleared of any of those accusations. We were interviewed by radio and television and stories did run regarding this matter. The print media in Omaha however, elected to run a story about the interviews but never mentioned the polygraph examination nor the results. I feel utterly helpless and, at times, hopeless regarding the clearing of Gary's name.

What is more important, as I see it, is not to abandon innocent people who have "gone to bat" for the sake of justice. If a new approach, a different angle into the investigation could be created, I see no reason why the Committee should not rally against dissolution of the Committee. I have read the Mr. Colby has been retained. A more respected professional could not have been found. Now would definitely not be the time to pull away.

I write to you today with a simple request, please do not forget. Gary had nothing to gain by manufacturing a "hoax." He, in fact, had everything on the line from day one and he was very aware of that. He respected you and your responsibility and did not take his responsibility lightly. Please do not forget what has happened to so many. Whatever you decide in the near future, please do not take the easy road.

Respectfully,

Sandra L. Caradori

Sandra L. Caradori

Nebraska State Legislature

SENATOR LORAN SCHMIT

District No. 23
State Capitol
Lincoln, Nebraska 68509
(402) 471-2719

Box 109
Bellwood, Nebraska 68624

COMMITTEES

Vice Chairman, Banking, Commerce
and Insurance
Natural Resources

Ninety-Second Legislature

March 6, 1991

Mr. Bill Bruce
Aviation Inspector, Nat'l Transportation Safety Board
31 West 775 North Avenue
West Chicago, Illinois 60185

Dear Mr. Bruce:

I visited briefly with Mr. William Colby and he indicated that he thought you might soon be writing a report on the crash which killed Gary Caradori and his son, Andrew. I have visited with Mrs. Caradori and she was adamant about the fact that none of the seats were ever removed from the aircraft and she informs me that as of now the two rear seats of the six have never been found.

It seems to me that those two seats could not simply have disappeared. Certainly by now they should have shown up somewhere unless something unusual would account for their disappearance. I do not know anything about sabotage, but I have been told that a phosphorous type bomb would, in fact, vaporize metal and any other material with which it came in contact and that unless someone knew what they were looking for, it would be difficult, if not impossible, to detect.

I am sure there will be those who will scoff at such a suggestion, but there have been entirely too many violent deaths associated with this investigation for me to accept the conclusion that Caradori's aircraft simply came apart in the sky. If you have found those two seats, I would be most appreciative if you would confirm that fact for me.

Sincerely,

Loran Schmit, Chairman
Franklin Legislative Committee

LS:LR
cc: Committee Members
    Mr. Steve Berry

AFFIDAVIT AFFIDAVIT AFFIDAVIT AFFIDAVIT AFFIDAVIT

My name is ████████████████████████ ████████████████████████ I was a regular juror in the
Alisha Owen trial which occurred in Omaha on May 16 thru
June 22nd of 1991.

I am giving this affidavit voluntarily and without promise
or pressure of anything from anyone and strictly because I
believe a grave injustice has occurred and, to the degree
that it is possible, I have an obligation to try to help
correct it.

I have been asked whether the Judge, Judge Case, had any
contact or communication with the jury during the
deliberations of the jury.

On Wednesday, the first day of jury deliberations, Judge
Case gave the jury their admonishment to not watch the news
reports about the trial and not to read newspaper articles
about the trial and not to discuss the trial with anyone
other than other jurors. This discussion did not occur
during the regular trial but occurred instead in the jury
room after the trial was over and after the jury had been in
the jury room all day deliberating and before the jury was
dismissed for the day. At this point, one of the jurors,
Tim Yambur, asked the judge if he, the judge, could give us
a definition of "reasonable doubt." To the best of my
knowledge the judge said that he could not and that it was
up to each individual juror to come to his own conclusion as
to what "reasonable doubt" was.

Each day during the trial there were newspapers in the jury
room, particularly the World Herald, which I thought very
odd. The issue as to whether these newspapers should be in
the jury room, was raised by the news media after Harold
Andersen testified, and from that point forward the
newspapers were kept out of the jury room. But, prior to
that time, the newspapers in their entirety with articles
about the trial and proceedings and other articles about
Franklin and Alisha Owen were available to the jurors in the
jury room.

Other events occurred during the jury deliberations in the
handling of the evidence which was supposed to be available
to us which, upon reflection, convince me that there were
deliberate improprieties in the handling of the evidence and
providing the evidence to the jury members. Specifically,
evidence which the jurors knew and believed had been
introduced in the trial was denied the jurors review and
evidence which had never apparently been introduced was
mysteriously provided to jurors. I would be more than
willing to provide much more information on this point to
the court at the proper time if requested.

Further affiant sayeth not.

Dated and executed this 13th day of May 1992 at Omaha,
Nebraska by:

████████████████████████████████

State of Nebraska
County of Douglas

Before me a notary public personally appeared ████████
██████ to me personally known, who executed the above
affidavit and acknowledged it was her own voluntary act and
deed and done for the purposes stated.

Jan C. Jewell   May 13 1992
Notary Public   Date

AFFIDAVIT AFFIDAVIT AFFIDAVIT AFFIDAVIT AFFIDAVIT

My name is ▓▓▓▓▓▓▓▓▓▓▓▓▓▓▓▓▓▓▓▓▓▓.
▓▓▓▓▓▓▓▓▓▓▓▓ I was a regular juror in the Alisha Owen
trial in May and June of 1991.

I have thought long and hard before deciding to give this
affidavit. I have not been forced or pressured or coerced
in any way to give this affidavit and am doing it simply
because I believe as a responsible individual and citizen I
have a duty to right a wrong if it can possibly be done.

Three matters have bothered me considerably that I am
convinced affected the outcome of the trial and my decision
and the decision I am sure of the other jurors also.

The first of these has to do with the program 48 hours which
jurors had been asked not to watch by the Judge.

I did in fact watch the program. I believe I would have
never even known about the program or watched it except for
the attention given it by the Court during the trial. I
believe this may well be the case of the other jurors also,
all of most of whom watched the program also.

The day after the program 48 hours aired and I had watched
it and went into the jury room along with the other jurors
to await the start of the trial, the clear topic of
conversation was the 48 hours program. It was clear to me
that almost all, if not all, of the other jurors had done
exactly the same thing as I had and in fact watched the 48
hours program.

I am satisfied that this program—particularly along with
some of the other things I will identify in this
affidavit—did definitely affect the outcome of this trial.

The second matter that has bothered me has to do with the
fact that during the jury deliberations trying to reach a
verdict, I and other jurors specifically sought, and other
jurors specifically requested, that certain evidence which
had been introduced into evidence during the trial be
provided to us jurors to review in our deliberations. The
specific things I (we) sought were (1) Danny King's school
transcripts from Texas; (2) The transcripts of Chief
Wadman's shooting incident in Utah. These pieces of
evidence were not provided to us when we had our
deliberations although I am convinced that they were

admitted into evidence and were kept from us for some reason or other and by some means which I do not know.

A third matter that concerns me has to do with the pivotal piece of evidence on which I ultimately made my decision for conviction. This evidence was a hand-written letter signed by Michael Casey on yellow legal paper which was handled by me in the Jury Room deliberations and was handed around and read by myself and the other jurors.

I am one hundred percent satisfied that this critical piece of evidence was in the Jury room; was read and handled by me; was the piece of evidence that ultimately tipped me to vote conviction; and was read and handled by all or most of the other jurors.

I have been challenged since the trial was over to identify this piece of evidence since the claim has been made that no such letter exists or was ever introduced into evidence and could not therefore have been in the Jury room.

I have subsequent to the trial and these challenges been allowed to sort thru all evidence and exhibits in this trial and have been unable to locate this letter. It is no where to be found in the legal exhibits and evidence. Something improper had to have occurred to cause this critical piece of evidence to be available in the Jury room to the jurors and not to exist later when the official evidence was reviewed after the trial.

Dated and executed this 13th day of May 1992 at Omaha, Douglas County, Nebraska by:

State of Nebraska
County of Douglas

Before me a notary public personally appeared ▮▮▮▮▮ to me personally known, who executed the above affidavit and acknowledged that it was his own voluntary act and deed and done for the purposes stated.

Jan C. Jewell   _may 13, 1992_
Notary public   Date

GENERAL NOTARY-State of Nebraska
JAN C. JEWELL
My Comm. Exp. June 9, 1992

EXHIBIT (

Affidavit   Affidavit   Affidavit   Affidavit   Affidavit

My name is ███████████████████████████ Juror
in the Alisha Owen trial and was present and participated in
the proceedings.

As a part of the proceedings I was required to be present
during the trial and I associated and talked with ████
████ jurors during the trial and proceedings.

As a part of that trial the jury was instructed by Judge
Case not to watch a particular program being aired on
television just prior to the completion of the Alisha Owen
trial itself and just prior to the jury going into their
jury deliberations. The program was titled 48 hours and we
were informed that it could have an impact on our decision
and we were therefore instructed not to watch it.

The morning after the program, which I watched, I attended
the trial proceedings and immediately upon entering the jury
room to meet with the other regular jurors it became
apparent that almost all, if not all, of the jurors had in
fact also watched the 48 hours program and that it was
profoundly affecting their thoughts on the Alisha Owen case.

The program was pretty much the main topic of discussion as
the jurors waited for the proceedings to begin and
particular attention was centered on Chief Wadman's
discussions on the 48 hours program as well as the
statements and testimony on 48 hours of Troy Boner.

It was clear to me then and even clearer to me now that this
program had to have impacted the decision of any juror who
in fact did watch it.

I am providing this information now because I believe a
terrible injustice has been done to Miss Alisha Owen and the
48 hour program clearly played a major part in causing this
injustice.

Dated and executed this 13th day of May 1992 at Omaha,
Nebraska by:

_____ Juror Alisha Owen trial

State of Nebraska

County of Douglas

Before me a notary public appeared ████████████ to me
personally known who executed the above affidavit,
acknowledged it was her own voluntary act and deed, and was
true and accurate and for the purposes stated.

_____   May 13, 1992
Notary Public   Date

A GENERAL NOTARY-State of Nebraska
JIM C. JEWELL

567

AO 93 (Rev. 5/85) Search Warrant

SEALED

United States District Court

FOR THE   DISTRICT OF   NEBRASKA

FILED
DISTRICT NEBRASKA
APR 3 ... M

SEALED

Norbert H. Ebel, Clerk

By _____ Deputy

In the Matter of the Search of

(Name, address or brief description of person or property to be searched)

Room/cell of Alisha J. Owen at the
Nebraska Correctional Facility for
Women, York, Nebraska or any storage
facility maintained on her behalf
at said facility

SEARCH WARRANT

CASE NUMBER: 90-0052M

SW 026

TO: MICHAEL F. MOTT, Special Agent, FBI ___ and any Authorized Officer of the United States

Affidavit(s) having been made before me by Michael F. Mott _____ who has reason to
                                                              Affiant

believe that ☐ on the person of or ☒ on the premises known as (name, description and/or location)

Room/cell of Alisha J. Owen at the Nebraska Correctional Facility for Women, York, Nebraska
or any storage facility maintained on her behalf at said facility

in the_____ District of __Nebraska_____ there is now
concealed a certain person or property, namely (describe the person or property)

handwritten notes, letters, calendars, newspaper articles, diaries, telephone books, documents,
address books but excluding any correspondence or communication to or from her attorney
involving any attorney client privilege

I am satisfied that the affidavit(s) and any recorded testimony establish probable cause to believe that the person
or property so described is now concealed on the person or premises above-described and establish grounds for
the issuance of this warrant.

YOU ARE HEREBY COMMANDED to search on or before __March 18, 1990__
                                                                          Date

(not to exceed 10 days) the person or place named above for the person or property specified, serving this warrant
and making the search (in the daytime — 6:00 A.M. to 10:00 P.M.) (at any time in the day or night as I find reasonable cause has been established) and if the person or property be found there to seize same, leaving a copy
of this warrant and receipt for the person or property taken, and prepare a written inventory of the person or prop-
erty seized and promptly return this warrant to _Richard G. Kopf, United States Magistrate_
as required by law.   U.S. Judge or Magistrate

March __ 1990 at 5:40pm.   at   Omaha, Nebraska
Date and Time Issued   City and State

RICHARD G. KOPF, United States Magistrate   Signature of Judicial Officer
Name and Title of Judicial Officer

SEALED

FD-597 (Rev. 3-29-84)

UNITED STATES DEPARTMENT OF JUSTICE
FEDERAL BUREAU OF INVESTIGATION
Receipt for Property Received/Returned/Released/Seized

Page ___ of ___

On (date) _3/8/90_

item(s) listed below were:
☐ Received From
☐ Returned To
☐ Released To
☑ Seized

(Name) ALISHA J. OWEN

(Street Address) NEBR. CORRECTIONAL FACILITY FOR WOMEN

(City) YORK, NEBRASKA.

Description of
Item(s):

#1 FOUR NEWSPAPER ARTICLES
#2 MISC. GREETING CARDS AND POST CARDS (7)
#3 28 LETTER ENVELOPES OF VARIOUS
    SIZES
#4 ONE DATA COM LEGAL PAD
#5 NINETEEN PROGRESS REPORTS FROM
    NEBR. CORRECTIONAL FACILITY FOR WOMEN
#6 79 SEPERATE LETTERS ON VARIOUS
    PIECES OF STATIONARY
#7 5 LETTERS CONTAINED IN 5
    SEPERATE ENVELOPES

Received by: _Michael F. Mott_
(Signature)

Received from: _Alisha J. Owen_
(Signature)

569

AO 106 (Rev. 5/85) Affidavit for Search Warrant

United States District Court

FOR THE DISTRICT OF NEBRASKA

FILED
AT _____ M

APR 30 ____

Norbert H. Ebel, Clerk
BY: _____ Deputy

In the Matter of the Search of

(Name, address or brief description of person or property to be searched)

Room/cell of Alisha J. Owen at the
Nebraska Correctional Facility for
Women, York, Nebraska or any storage
facility maintained on her behalf
at said facility

**APPLICATION AND AFFIDAVIT
FOR SEARCH WARRANT**

CASE NUMBER: 90-0052M

SW 026

I Michael F. Mott _____ being duly sworn depose and say:

I am a(n) Special Agent of the Federal Bureau of Investigation _____ and have reason to believe
                    Official Title

that ☐ on the person of or ☒ on the premises known as (name, description and/or location)

Room/cell of Alisha J. Owen at the Nebraska Correctional Facility for Women, York, Nebraska
or any storage facility maintained on her behalf at said facility

in the _____ District of __Nebraska_____

there is now concealed a certain person or property, namely (describe the person or property)
handwritten notes, letters, calendars, newspaper articles, diaries, telephone books, documents,
address books

which is (give alleged grounds for search and seizure under Rule 41(b) of the Federal Rules of Criminal Procedure)
evidence of violations relating to sexual exploitation of children, obstruction of justice
and providing false statements to an agency of the United States

in violation of Title ____18____ United States Code, Section(s) 1001, 1510, 1511, 2251 and 2423
The facts to support the issuance of a Search Warrant are as follows:

See attached affidavit

Continued on the attached sheet and made a part hereof. ☒ Yes ☐ No

Michael F. Mott
Signature of Affiant MICHAEL F. MOTT, Special Agent
Federal Bureau of Investigation

Sworn to before me, and subscribed in my presence

March 8, 1990 _____ at Omaha, Nebraska
Date   City and State

RICHARD G. KOPF, United States Magistrate _____
Name and Title of Judicial Officer   Signature of Judicial Officer

SEALED SEALED SEALED SEALED SEALED

570

AFFIDAVIT FOR SEARCH WARRANT

I, Michael F. Mott, being duly sworn, depose and say:

1. I have been a Special Agent of the Federal Bureau of Investigation (FBI) for over fourteen years and am presently assigned to the Omaha Division. One of my investigative responsibilities is to investigation violations of statutes relating to Sexual Exploitation of Children, Obstruction of Justice, False Statements in violation of Title 18, Sections 1001, 1510, 1511, 2251 and 2423 of the United States Code.

2. Alisha J. Owen is presently incarcerated in the Nebraska Correctional Facility for Women, York, Nebraska and is assigned to a room/cell in said facility and is identified at said facility by Inmate Number 2947.

3. Between February 12, 1990 and February 26, 1990 the affiant was present during eight interviews by law enforcement officers of Alisha J. Owen at the Nebraska Correctional Facility for Women in York regarding various allegations relating to sexual exploitation of minors, controlled substance trafficking and public corruption. These interviews took place in a conference room at the said facility.

4. During the aforementioned interviews Owen was observed utilizing various notes, calendars, and other documents as a means of recollecting certain events allegedly occurring in August 1983 through May 1989 relating to her involvement and knowledge of offenses set forth in paragraph 1 above. These notes, documents, calendars and other such items would contain her handwritten notes. These documents include but are not limited to correspondence to and from other individuals together

with newspaper articles and other such items. During the interviews Owen based her recollection on the review of such documents and from time to time would change her recollection after her review of these documents.

5. The affiant has participated in an interview with another witness, Danny King, regarding the incidents inquired of through Owen and that witness has contradicted Owen with regards to various allegations and further stated that Owen was fabricating allegations of criminal conduct by others presently under investigation by the Federal Bureau of Investigation and other law enforcement agencies. Review of records supplied to the FBI regarding specific dates involved in the investigation support the statement of the witness contradicting Owen.

6. At the conclusion of each interview described above Owen would retrieve her documents and take them with her.

7. The affiant believes that said documents are taken back to Owen's room/cell and maintained in that area during her incarceration or provided to personnel in the Nebraska Correctional Facility for Women for safekeeping. These notes, documents, letters, calendars, newspaper articles, diaries, telephone books, address books and other such materials are evidence of the offenses of sexual exploitation of children, obstruction of justice and providing false statements to an agency of the United States.

The affiant does not seek any correspondence or communications from or to her attorney involving any attorney-client privilege.

michael Casey c/o Mueller   march 15, 1990
1002 PARK AV.   342-6150   OMAHA —
Omaha, Ne. 68105

Dear Alisha,

I hope this note finds you
with a smile on your face and in
your heart!

I know how trying these times
must be for you. Keep a strong
will and heart and things will
work well for you and the baby.

I've just returned to Omaha,
after spending the last few month in
L.A. working on the later development
of the Franklin Project script, and
likewise working together with a
playwrite putting together a 1 or 2
act Play for production (possibly) at
the Firehouse within the next couple
of month for a limited run. I'll
send you a copy of the 1st. draft
soon as it's available, all and any
of your ideas are welcome.
                              National
I've been contacted by many pub's to

Michael Casey's "lost and found letter" that was impounded by the FBI on
March, 8,1990—a week before it was written.

do features. "People" mag. called today
and I should have confirmation of
an assignment for them soon.

The most important part of this letter
is to let you know that a lot of
people here in the community believe
you should be released without delay, not
only for your protection but that you
have suffered enough. Your assistance
to the committee has allowed (aided
in a major way) them to accomplish
one of their major goals - with out your
help - I doubt a grand jury would of
ever have become a reality. You have
more than paid your debt to society.

I also know and feel that promises
were made - before I ever gave Story
your name and location - he assured
me that if your info checked out
you would receive favorable consideration
and protection outside of a prison
environment. I feel not responsible
if promises were made to you and
not kept! If negative action will hurt
by other prisoners or other reps of
our legal system, then, it's my fault
for not getting better assurances before

revealing your info and identity.

Enclosed you'll find a copy of a telegram I sent the Attorney General on your behalf. I am considering a petition drive to the Gov. Our (providing I have your permission) for your release. She has the power to pardon you — I think you deserve it. I've talked to several community leaders (today) and other reporters and they seem willing to support such a move.

There are some other matters I like to discuss with you — perhaps we can set up a phone call or visit?

I'm moving around alot these days so you might not be able to find me — Dick M. will always accept a call from you / he will be able to locate me or pass a message.
Hm: No. 342-6150   my cal. No. is 762-6592 88
Theatre   346-6009.
For now stay well and know you are not alone. A lot of people love and are pulling for you out here.
Love;
Michael

AFFIDAIT AFFIDAVIT AFFIDAVIT AFFIDAVIT AFFIDAVIT AFFIDAVIT

I, Loran C. Schmit of Bellwood, Nebraska, being first duly sworn on this
28th day of May 1994, do depose and say as follows:

On the morning that I was to meet Gary Caradori which morning was the same
day that Gary Caradori was in fact killed in an airplane crash, two attorneys
representing Alan Baer of Omaha--including one by the name of Selin--met
with me in my offices at the Capitol in Lincoln, Nebraska to discuss matters
relating to Franklin Credit Union INvestigation and particularly to discuss
matters relating to Alan Baer whom they represented.

Present at this meeting were MR. CREAGER, LINCOLN, ATTORNEY WORKING FOR THE
COMMITTEE AND JODY GITTINS, AN EMPLOYEE of my office who is also an attorney,
myself, Loran Schmit and the two attorneys for Mr. Alan Baer.

These two attorneys advised us with everybody present that the F.B.I.
officials dealing with them and with Alan Baer had instructed Mr. Alan Baer
to "Keep your (his) head down, or you'll (He) will get it blown off, your
(his) mouth shut and to talk to no one."
These were the instructions Alan Baer's attorneys advised us that the FBI
gave to Alan Baer in conjunction with the Franklin Investigation which we,
the LEGISLATURE--and others--were conducting.
Further affiant sayeth not.

Dated and executed this 28th day of May 1994 at Lincoln, Lancaster County,
Nebraska by

Loran Schmit

LORAN C. SCHMIT, AFFIANT

STATE OF NEBRASKA

COUNTY OF LANCASTER

BEFORE ME A NOTARY PUBLIC PERSONALLY APPEARED LORAN C. SCHMIT, TO ME PERSONALLY
KNOWN, WHO EXECUTED THE ABOVE AFFIDAVIT AND ACKNOWLEDGED IT WAS ACCURATE AND
WAS HIS OWN VOLUNTARY ACT AND DEED.

Jan C. Jewell 5-28-94

Notary Public

> GENERAL NOTARY-State of Nebraska
> JAN C. JEWELL
> My Comm. Exp. June 9, 1996

Fr: Michael J. Casey
    1002 Park Av.
    Omaha, Neb. 68105
    (402) 342-6150

Michael Casey

To: Senator Loran Schmit, Chairman
    Franklin Legislative Committee
    State Capital Building
    Linclon, Nebraska 68508

Sept. 4, 1990

Dear Sentor Schmit and Committee Members,

After reviewing the Franklin Committees response
issued on 7-28-90 to the report issued 7/23/90 by the
Douglas County Grand Jury I have found your response
most accurate and powerfully provocative while add-
vessing the tragic existence and state of current
affairs surrounding the franklin Committee's on going
probe/investigation into the matters of Child Abuse
accuring in the State of Nebraska.

I have devoted nearly two years reserching and
investigating the Franklin Community Federal Credit
Union as a journalist/reporter... I wish to thank
and commend you and the committee members, Senator
Jerome Warner, Senator Bernice Labedz and Senator
Dennis Boack, for having the courge and

577

confidence to denounce the deceptive allegations the Douglas County Grand Jury chose to make part of their misleading report. The over-all effect of their report has been to discredit well intentioned citizens wishing to assist the Grand Jury in their fact findin mission towards truth and justice. Instead, the Grand Jury has gone down a path of indicting abused victims formely along with those that have supported abused children informally. Many of our young people in this and other communities have viewed the Grand Jury report and resulting actions by our legal system as confirmation and cause not to trust in our system of laws. You the men and women of the Franklin Committee along with your support staff and investigator Gary Caradia have stood tall in face of presure and condemation unjustly bestowed upon you by the now defunck Douglas County Grand Jury.

Speaking for myself as one who was the target of the Grand Jurys tales and misleading alligations the worst and most painful being that I duped Mr. Caradori; I did not. The Grand Juries report further charged that I was motivated by personal grudges and for want of personal gain such as movie and book projects.

Let me tell you that most writers I know would love to complete a successful book or movie and live happy ever after. It dosen't often happen.

My motives however, never had anything to do with a movie or book deal, though, during my work on the Franklin various persons approached me about different types of journalistic and media projects, of which I chose not to be part of. With the exception of doing continued research for Steve Bowman of Bowman Marketing, Inc., (Omaha) regarding a book project Mr. Bowman is developing about Franklin.

So that you might have some additional background and insight I wish your committee to know that during the past two years that my work has continued, I have been supported in my research and investigative assignments by: I.E. The New York Times, The New York Village Voice, Omaha's KKAB Radio, and Bowman Marketing.

In addition, other support has come forth from people in this community who have loaned and given both financial support and/or in kind services such as Lodging, Food, Phone, office space and materials to keep my investigative effort afloat. My four wonderful and beautiful children have gone without and never complained so that I might persue the truth behind the Franklin Child Abuse Alligations.

I've come before you the members of the Nebraska

state Legislative Franklin Committee to share my thoughts because of the many media articales you may have read or viewed containing the misleading and false statements the Douglas County Grand Jury entered into their report of 7-28-90. Soon I hope to compel (via The Courts) the Franklin prosecutor and jury members to account for their actions and to prove or retract the information placed in the Douglas County Grand Juries report of 7-28-90.

Again, thank you for your time and consideration. Should you desire my assistance or an in person report on my activities during the past two years while investigating the Franklin feel free to call on me. There are area's and persons surrounding the Franklin I believe could have escaped the Committees attention.

Most Respectfully Yours,

Michael J. Casey

Michael J. Casey

CC / Bruce Mason, ATTORNEY AT LAW
8420 W. Dodge Rd.
Omaha, Nebraska 68114
Ph: 402-391-5400

Nebraska State Legislature

SENATOR LORAN SCHMIT

District No. 23
State Capitol
Lincoln, Nebraska 68509
(402) 471-2719

Box 109
Bellwood, Nebraska 68624

COMMITTEES

Chairman, Natural Resources
Banking, Commerce and Insurance
Executive Board
Reference
Legislative Council

Ninety-First Legislature

July 23, 1990

Mr. William Colby
Donovan Leisure Newton & Irvine
Counselors at Law
1850 K Street, N.W.
Washington, D.C. 20006

Dear Mr. Colby:

I have asked my daughter, Lorin, to deliver certain material to you, along with this letter. I will be providing additional material by Federal Express within several days. I would suggest that you contact the National Transportation Safety Board in Chicago--Telephone No. (708) 377-8177, and ask for the following information:

No. 1 - Transcripts of all audiotapes of conversation between Mr. Caradori's aircraft and Ground Control at Midway Airport, and also transcripts of all conversations between the Caradori aircraft and, I believe, Rockport Communication Center. This would include routine conversations from the time that Mr. Caradori switched from Ground Control to Rockport Communication Center until the aircraft went off radar at approximately 2:38 A.M., Wednesday, July 11. It should also include the "garbled" transmission which may or may not have come from the Caradori aircraft.

No. 2 - You should ask for any records of conversation between Mr. Caradori and the Fixed Base Operator at the National Safety Board may have acquired as a result of their investigation.

No. 3 - You should ask for a complete inventory of all personal items recovered from the crash site--particularly Mr. Caradori's briefcase and/or notes, papers, or photographs, which might be related to Franklin.

No. 4 - Was any attempt made to determine if Mr. Caradori might have suffered from carbon monoxide poisoning or if there was any indiciation that sabotage could have made carbon monoxide poisoning a possibility?

Mr. William Colby
July 23, 1990
Page two

No. 5 - Was there any indication that a phosphorus bomb might have been involved and did they, specifically, look for evidence of such a device?

I would also suggest that you ask the following questions of NCUA:

No. 1 - A list of all depositors of the Franklin Federal Credit Union for the past twelve years.

No. 2 - I would also ask for a breakdown of those depositors so that we would know the dates and times of the deposits, when some of the deposits might have been redeemed, was interest collected or rolled over, was there separate depositor's list for the account of record of approximately two million dollars and the secret account of approximately thirty-nine million dollars.

No. 3 - A list of all the claims paid by the NCUA and to whom and for what amount.

No. 4 - A list of those claims not paid and the amount.

This will give you something to start on. You might also call the Department of Justice and ask for the name of the FBI Agent in charge of the investigation here in Nebraska. Ask also if Mr. John Pankonin is still involved with the investigation. He was the Agency who first viewed the tapes with us on December 27, 1989. He also interviewed Aleshia Owen early in the investigation. I have just heard that he had Mr. Alan Baer almost ready to talk when he was taken off the case. This may or may not true. I will be in touch with you regularly by Fax.

Sincerely,

Loran Schmit, Chairman
Franklin Committee

LS:lr

Colby calls Franklin case 'fascinating'

By James Joyce 1-21-89
of The Lincoln Star

Former CIA Director William Colby said Friday that the $38.5 million reportedly missing from the Franklin Federal Community Credit Union makes the case fascinating.

Although he knows little about the case except what he has read in the newspapers, he said, the "paper trail" presumably left by the missing money is enough to capture his interest.

"It's a fascinating case. You start down one of these trails and it frequently goes into a lot of astounding areas," Colby said.

Colby, who was director of the Central Intelligence Agency from 1973-74, was in Lin-

coln to interview for the job of legal counsel for the special committee running the Legislature's investigation of the failed Omaha financial institution.

The committee met with Colby for nearly two hours behind closed doors where, among other things, his legal fees, association with Washington political figures and CIA connections were reportedly discussed.

The question of Colby's $250-an-hour legal fee has raised eyebrows among a number of senators because it could quickly exhaust the $100,000 that the Legislature has allocated for the investigation.

After the interview, however, Colby, who works in the Washington office of the New York law firm of Donovan, Leisure, Newton and Irving, said that the cost of his services is open to negotiation.

The $250 figure, he said, was simply what his firm normally charges and was included in his letter of application to provide the committee with some figure

rather than nothing at all.

Neither Colby nor Sen. Loran Schmit of Bellwood, chairman of the committee, would estimate what figure might be appropriate.

However, Schmit suggested, cost should not be a factor in whether Colby or anyone else is hired or be a limitation on any other aspect of the committee's investigation.

"The state of Nebraska can afford whatever is necessary. What it can't afford is a half-hearted effort," Schmit said.

Colby is one of six persons who have formally submitted applications for the position and the only one interviewed so far.

The others are former state Sen. Vard Johnson of Omaha, Bernard Glaser of Lincoln, counsel to the

Turn to: Colby, Page 12

Colby

582

Nebraska State Legislature

SENATOR LORAN SCHMIT

District No. 23
State Capitol
Lincoln, Nebraska 68509
(402) 471-2719

Box 109
Bellwood, Nebraska 68624

COMMITTEES

Chairman, Natural Resources
Banking, Commerce and Insurance
Executive Board
Reference
Legislative Council

Ninety-First Legislature

August 8, 1990

Mr. William E. Colby
Law Offices of
Donovan Leisure, Rogovin, Huge & Schiller
1250 Twenty-fourth Street, N.W.
Washington, D.C. 20037-1124

Dear Bill:

I want to express my appreciation to you for making yourself available to the committee this past week. I am sure that those of us who were able to meet with you gained a new understanding as to how we might proceed with the investigation from this point.

The committee members did not yet reach a decision as to the employment of your firm. Several of our members are out-of-state this week and I hope that I can get them together next week so that we can discuss it further.

They did agree prior to your traveling to Nebraska that it would be alright for you to question the National Credit Union Association and the National Transportation Safety Board, and I am sure that you could be of considerable help on anything which took place in the Washington area or the New York City area. We know that Mr. King spent considerable time in both cities.

The committee members take their responsibility very seriously and none of us want to make a decision hurriedly. I appreciated very much your suggestion that you would use your associates, paralegals, and Mr. Michael Curto in order to make the best use of committee resources. I will be out of the hospital tomorrow and will try to speak to you yet this week.

Sincerely,

Loran Schmit, Chairman
Franklin Committee

LS:lr
cc: Committee Members
    Mr. Steve Berry, Special Counsel

Dictated but not read.

583

Nebraska State Legislature

SENATOR LORAN SCHMIT

District No. 23
State Capitol
Lincoln, Nebraska 68509
(402) 471-2719

Box 109
Bellwood, Nebraska 68624

COMMITTEES

Chairman, Natural Resources
Banking, Commerce and Insurance
Executive Board
Reference
Legislative Council

Ninety-First Legislature

August 30, 1990

Mr. William Colby
Attorney-at-Law
1250 - 24th St. N.W. Suite 700
Washington, D.C. 20037

Dear Bill:

I am sorry that I did not mention this to you earler. We are agreeable to the terms you mentioned relative to your working for the Franklin Legislative Committee.

We need a letter from you to me as Chairman of the Franklin Committee stating the terms which we had agreed upon. Basically, that the committee would pay you a $7,500.00 retainer and that you would notify the committee when you have reached that point on your services so that we could then decide if we wanted to continue your employment with us.

I tried to call you today, but you were out, so I will Fax it to you.

Sincerely,

Loran Schmit, Chairman
Franklin Legislative Committee

Loran
Schmit
1993

584

Law Offices of

Donovan Leisure, Rogovin, Huge & Schiller

1250 Twenty-fourth Street, N.W.

Washington, D.C. 20037-1124

DONOVAN LEISURE NEWTON & IRVINE
30 ROCKEFELLER PLAZA
NEW YORK, N.Y. 10112
TELEPHONE: 212 632 3000
FAX: 212 632 3321

DONOVAN LEISURE NEWTON & IRVINE
SOUTH GRAND AVENUE
LOS ANGELES, CALIFORNIA 90071
TELEPHONE: 213 253 4000
FAX 213 617 2366

TELEPHONE: 202-467-8300
FAX. 202-467-8484

DONOVAN LEISURE NEWTON & IRVINE
130 RUE DU FAUBOURG SAINT-HONORÉ
75008 PARIS
TELEPHONE: 1-42-25-47-10
FAX: 1-42-56-08-06

DIRECT DIAL NUMBER
202-467-8333

August 31, 1990

Senator Loran Schmit
Chairman
Franklin Committee
The Legislature of the State of Nebraska
State Capitol
Lincoln, Nebraska 68509

Dear Mr. Chairman:

In response to your letter of August 30, 1990, we of this firm are delighted to be able to assist the Franklin Committee in its important work under the Resolutions which empowered it.

This firm would not displace the able counsel the Committee now has, but would contribute what it could to the Committee's work from the special access we have in Washington. We have already made contact with agencies of the United States Government which might have information of value to the Committee. We will maintain close personal contact with you so that you can consider the implications of any contacts we may suggest.

We will bill the Committee for our services at our usual hourly rates here in Washington, and will use our associates, paralegals, etc. to the extent possible to keep our charges down. We request that you provide us with a retainer of $7,500.00 in advance, for which we will fully account. We will not exceed that sum without your prior approval.

We look forward to working with you on this important matter, and hope that we can be of real assistance to the Committee.

Sincerely,

William E. Colby

William Colby 1993

585

Law Offices of

Donovan Leisure, Rogovin, Huge & Schiller

1250 Twenty-fourth Street, N.W.

Washington, D.C. 20037-1124

DONOVAN LEISURE NEWTON & IRVINE
30 ROCKEFELLER PLAZA
NEW YORK, N.Y. 10112
TELEPHONE: 212-632-3000
FAX: 212-632-3321

DONOVAN LEISURE NEWTON & IRVINE
333 SOUTH GRAND AVENUE
LOS ANGELES, CALIFORNIA 90071
TELEPHONE: 213-253-4000
FAX: 213-617-2368

TELEPHONE: 202-467-8300
FACSIMILE: 202-467-8464

DONOVAN LEISURE NEWTON & IRVINE
130 RUE DU FAUBOURG SAINT-HONORÉ
75008 PARIS
TELEPHONE: 1-42-25-47-10
FAX: 1-42-56-08-06

DIRECT DIAL NUMBER
202-467-8333

March 13, 1991

Senator Loran Schmit
Legislature of Nebraska
Lincoln NE 68509

Dear Senator Schmit:

Since I understand that the Franklin Committee of the Legislature has been terminated, I do appreciate your invitation to submit my billing for the time I have devoted to this matter. I only regret that we were not able to penetrate more effectively the clouds of confusion and contradiction which seems to have surrounded this whole case.

While I have not yet received the final report of the Transportation Safety Board, it seems clear from my telephone discussion with Mr. William Bruce, the examiner of Mr. Gary Caradori's aircraft crash, that the Board will conclude that there is no indication of sabotage as the cause. I will of course review the final report when it comes to ensure that it does not leave any substantial loose ends uncovered, but it seems unlikely that any leads will come of this crash which could affect the larger case on which you are concerned.

With respect to the National Credit Union Administration, the analysis prepared by its staff certainly shows that sufficient attention was not paid to the Franklin Community Federal Credit Union, the dollar figures appear roughly accurate and do not seem to raise substantial questions beyond the kind of high living Mr. Lawrence E. King Jr was known to have engaged in. Thus that area of investigation does not seem to warrant further effort.

With respect to the problems of sexual and child abuse which have arisen in the background of this matter, these are in the hands of some of your local authorities (for better or worse) and there seems little I could do about them from here. I regret that the journalist I suggested has apparently not found the necessary interest in the subject from a publisher. She does have your name as a possible contact, however, and I did supply her with several of the background documents on the case I had here. If she shows interest, of course, I will put her in touch with you.

Ms. Karen Ormiston, who worked closely with Mr. Caradori for several years, did write me the attached letter offering to be of assistance. I responded with the letter I have also attached, and will certainly be in contact with her when I next am in Lincoln (as I expect to be in connection with a separate matter). Since I am sure she was interviewed by your own Counsel, I doubt that there is much I could learn from her that you do not already know.

The attached invoice outlines my firm's time and expenses on this matter. If you have any questions about it, please let me know and I would be glad to respond.

While I close with the regret I stated above that we have not been able to clarify the many questions which this case raised, I do want to say how much I appreciate having met and worked with you on it. Your integrity, your sense of public duty and your straight forward personality were a great pleasure to have been associated with. May I wish you the best of good fortune in the future.

Sincerely,

William E. Colby

The "elephant" rock.

Noreen Gosch

Johnny Gosch

The ranch.

Paul Bonacci

James Daniel "Danny" King

Creighton University Medical Center *School of Medicine*
University of Nebraska Medical Center *College of Medicine*

CREIGHTON-NEBRASKA DEPARTMENT OF PSYCHIATRY
2205 South 10th Street
Omaha, NE 68108
(402) 449-4184

Frank J. Menolascino, M.D.
Chairman

REPORT OF PSYCHIATRIC CLINICAL INTERVIEWS
WITH PAUL BONACCI

As of April 9, 1990, I have conducted six interviews with Mr. Bonacci on November 22, 1989, January 10, January 24, March 7, March 16 and April 5, 1990. Mr. Bonacci is a 22 year old man (DOB 8/3/67), very light-build, dark hair, clean-shaven, always polite and well-mannered. He has pled no contest to a charge of sexually fondling a nine year old boy. He understands that I am to report as to whether or not I consider him to be a Mentally Disordered Sex Offender. He has been more than cooperative because the interviews have revealed that he is suffering from multiple personalities, an unusual form of psychiatric disorder. Mr. Bonacci presents a typical case. He has numerous alternate personalities, each one having an individual identity, a different name and certain individual characteristics. Many of the alternate personalities are aware of each other and are usually aware of what the original personality, Paul, is doing, but Paul is not aware of who the personalities are and what they are doing.

Because of the interviews, and some discussion of his problem, Paul does now have some awareness that he has multiple personalities although, typically, he is still mystified by the situation and finds it difficult to accept. He does know, however, that there have been reports from friends and relatives of his assuming different personalities, behaving in uncharacteristic fashion, and later not being able to recall some of the things reported that he had done.

This condition presents with bizarre symptomatology, but it is not a psychosis. It is classified as a dissociative disorder in which a person separates or "dissociates" himself from his usual pattern of thinking and awareness. A more common example of a dissociative disorder is amnesia.

It is typical that multiple personality disorder is associated with a very disorganized childhood during which they suffered severe, and often repeated abuse. According to the history that Mr. Bonacci presents, this is quite true in his case. He related a very detailed, complicated history of which the following seems to be most significant.

He was born and brought up in the Omaha area, the fifth of six children of Mr. John Bonacci. His parents were divorced before his younger brother was born. His father lives in Lake Manawa, Iowa, and he has no contact with his father until recently. "Father never claimed me, but he does now." His mother soon remarried a Mr. Robert Boukl who was very abusive to the children, particularly to Paul. He remembers this man as using any excuse to beat the children, and he remembers him doing such things as chopping toys in two with an axe. He doesn't remember how long this marriage lasted (perhaps no more than two or three years), but they broke up following an episode in which he beat Paul's mother quite severely.

Mother then soon remarried a Mr. Jack McCoy. He was a much better stepfather because he did not beat the children, but "he ignored me because I was different". Mr. McCoy died of a heart attack in July of 1983.

Mr. Bonacci said that much abuse also came repeatedly from his older brothers. The oldest child in the family was Tim and the next two were identical twins, John and Clifford. These brothers "beat me up all the time". "If others fought me, they would help them." He described himself as the one in the family who was always picked on. "They used to call me a girl - a fag." These boys had their share of delinquent problems, particularly Clifford who used a lot of drugs and had trouble with the law.

Mr. Bonacci said his worst experiences began when he was about six years old when he was repeatedly molested by a 14 year old male babysitter named Jason. He said that he told his mother what was going on, but his mother would not believe him. Jason was a pal of his older brothers and what would happen most of the time was that mother would leave him to be looked after by his older brothers, but his brothers wanted to go someplace to do something so they would leave him with Jason, and Jason would molest him again. The brothers would also set him up to get other people to pick on him, and when I questioned Mr. Bonacci as to why his mother or stepfather did not become aware of this and intervene, he said that mother just "didn't listen and Jack McCoy was not talkative and did not get involved".

As he remembers his school experience, it went fairly well until he was in the third grade and moved to Carter Lake. He then began to get bad grades simply because he did not care and he realized that others thought he was weird. He had some black friends, and some of the white boys would pick on him because of that and make fun of him. It was also about this time that he first began to notice blank periods of time in which he could not remember later what he had done. Evidently, these were the first experiences of having an alternate personality take over.

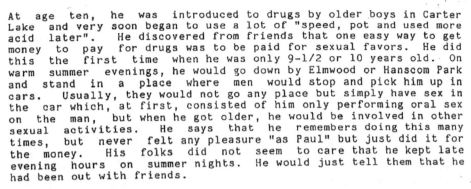

At age ten, he was introduced to drugs by older boys in Carter Lake and very soon began to use a lot of "speed, pot and used more acid later". He discovered from friends that one easy way to get money to pay for drugs was to be paid for sexual favors. He did this the first time when he was only 9-1/2 or 10 years old. On warm summer evenings, he would go down by Elmwood or Hanscom Park and stand in a place where men would stop and pick him up in cars. Usually, they would not go any place but simply have sex in the car which, at first, consisted of him only performing oral sex on the man, but when he got older, he would be involved in other sexual activities. He says that he remembers doing this many times, but never felt any pleasure "as Paul" but just did it for the money. His folks did not seem to care that he kept late evening hours on summer nights. He would just tell them that he had been out with friends.

Mr. Bonacci says that he also got "messed up with Satanism" beginning about age 12. It involved such strange rituals as drinking cat's blood and urine. He did not look back on this as anything that he enjoyed, but felt at the time that he had to do it to be accepted by some other boys who called themselves "Knights of Darkness". "I was trying to reach out for something."

He said that he got away from the Satanism after suffering some disappointments. An Aunt Mary who had been nice to him died and about the same time his stepfather died unexpectedly of a heart attack. Soon after that, a young friend his age committed suicide. He began going to church in January, 1984, and has had some intermittent interest in religion ever since. Despite this, however, he admits that he continued using a lot of drugs and going to a lot of parties where he served as a young male prostitute. Eventually, he was admitted to the Nebraska Psychiatric Institute in April of 1986 where the multiple personalities were not discovered but, because of strange symptoms interpreted as hallucinations, he was considered at that time to be suffering from schizophrenia. One important benefit of this hospitalization, however, was that he stopped using drugs on a regular basis although he admits that he has used them just occasionally since, and the last time was some LSD in August of 1989.

With all these activities, and several family moves, his education was repeatedly disrupted but, in one way or another, he continued and finally in 1988, at age 20 years and 10 months, he did get a high school diploma from the Individualized Study Center at 30th and Fort.

He described an interesting job experience in the summer of 1989 when he worked for three weeks at some recreation place named River Crest where his first duties were to help keep the place clean, mow lawns, clean the pool and sometimes act as lifeguard. During the second week, they advanced him to help out in the kitchen, but the entire third week he was working there, he has no recollection whatsoever, but he does know that at the end of that week, they fired him and he never knew what he did or didn't do that was the cause of his dismissal.

Regarding the incident with the nine year old boy, he remembers the occasion when they were lying down next to each other to go to sleep, but he has no recollection (as Paul) of deliberately touching the boy.

CONCLUSIONS: Mr. Paul Bonacci is suffering from a multiple personality disorder. I do not consider him to be a Mentally Disordered Sex Offender in the usual meaning of that term. The principle personality Paul has no wish to molest children, is quite religious and is not inclined to have homosexual interests.

I do, however, believe that Mr. Bonacci is very much in need of extensive psychiatric help such as may be available at the Lincoln Regional Center to help him create a personality structure, or structures, less inclined to dissociate. Currently, a majority of his alternative personalities are heterosexually oriented, but there are some with a homosexual orientation and some that actually identify themselves as female rather than male personalities. Having an alternate personality of a different gender may seem unbelievable, but it is actually typical of complex, multiple personality cases.

Without treatment, it is conceivable (and this is probably what happened in the contact with the little boy) that if placed in an unusual circumstance, an alternative personality might temporarily take over and commit such an act of fondling, although it is also true that such behavior will be stopped, or at least quickly checked, by another alternate personality which would disapprove of such behavior. It all gets quite complicated.

Beverley T. Mead, M.D.
Professor of Psychiatry

BTM/mlm

- 3 -

when subjects are divided into response types, these types
will tend to score at different levels in ESP tests. Of
course it is not assumed that adopting a particular pattern
can in any way effect scores (except in experiments where
the model involved in comparing guess and target sequences
is the matching distribution rather than the binomial
distribution, in which case the variance may be increased,
though the expectation is not effected). It is assumed
that the guessing pattern and the ESP score are both
related to a third factor.

The work with individual subjects who give
promise of extraordinary abilities will introduce a number
of experimental techniques which have been ignored or
barely hinted at in the past. A variety of models of the
manner in which information is transferred will be tested
by simple variation of the tasks imposed on the subject.
Preliminary learning studies, in which feedback of results
and other kinds of reinforcement are utilised, will be
introduced at the same time. If a subject is found who can
score reliably, an attempt will be made to increase the
quantity of transmitted information without increasing
the average probability of success, by making use of
straightforward techniques borrowed from the mathematical
theory of communication.

In working with individual subjects, special
attention will be given to disassociative states, which
tend to accompany spontaneous ESP experiences. Such states
can be induced and controlled to some extent with hypnosis
and drugs. Some of this work will make use of qualitative
stimuli, such as drawings and ideas with special
associations.

II. Methods

Group Experiments

Numerous mathematical models and experimental
designs enable the simultaneous assessment of two or more
independent predictors. Chief among these are multiple
regression analysis and factorial experimental designs,
which are closely related logically and mathematically.
The essential idea of the regression model is that each
individual's scores on the n independent variables and
the ESP criterion may be located at a point in an n + 1
dimensional space. The relation between the criterion
and the predictors is given by a multiple regression
equation which takes the form:

$$\tilde{Y} = A + \beta_{y1.23...N} X_1 + \beta_{y2.134...n} X_2 + ... + \beta_{yn.123...n-1} X_n$$

/where

- 4 -

where A is an intercept and the coefficients of the X's are
partial regression coefficients and indicate the weighting
allotted to each predictor.

The regression equation and each of the, independent,
predictors may be tested for significance. If the null
hypothesis is rejected, the accuracy of prediction is of
interest. This is best considered in the language of
estimation statistics, where one may speak of confidence
intervals. That is, for a subject characterised by a
certain pattern of scores on the independent variables,
one may predict with .95 confidence that the subject's
ESP score will fall somewhere between A and B percent
success. The clearest meaning of 'repeatability' is
expressed in statements of this kind, whereby the results
of a series of experiments, not the probabilities attached
to them, may be compared to see if they fit the same
pattern. The width of the predicted interval and the
confidence coefficient of course vary inversely and the
definition of 'repeatability' depends on assigning an
a priori ESP probability.

The variables to be considered can be classed
in several ways. They will be intrinsic psychological
and physiological factors and experimentally manipulable
factors. Intrinsic factors may be temporary and
characteristic of the experimental situation, such as
annoyance, or general personality characteristics, such
as intelligence. Experimentally manipulable factors
include induced attitudes, such as motivation produced
by positive reinforcement, and purely formal factors,
such as the number of ESP trials yielding the most accurate
predictions. The selection of variables will depend on a
detailed analysis of the results of past research, incidental
observations in experiments with single subjects, apparent
common factors in 'spontaneous' ESP, and intelligent
guessing. In the selection of variables, special attention
will be paid to technical problems in scaling and to the
reliability and validity of existing scales. In some cases
ad hoc procedures, such as the Q sort, will be used.

Response Patterns. Human beings are notoriously
inefficient randomisers, so would not be inappropriate to
treat response patterns as having two components, ESP and
guessing habits. Guessing habits represent subjects'
subjective evaluation of the sequential uncertainty
situation in the experiment and depend on such factors
as ability to judge probabilities and imitate randomness,
compulsions with respect to symmetry &c. Such habits will
necessarily interfere with exercise of ESP, because every
time a choice is made habit and psi-information are in

/competition

594

competition unless they should agree fortuitously. It
might be, for example, that the well known decline effect
phenomena are due to the gradual build up of habits and
their dominance over ESP.

It is, however, not only desirable to correct
for the destructive effects of guessing habits. It may
be that such habits could be used to predict ESP test
scores. When one decides to cross the street, his decision
about when to cross depends on his estimate of the chance
that he will be run over. Behaviour is largely determined
by concepts of probability, and systematic bias in
assessments of uncertainty situations are known to be
related to personality types. It is quite possible that
some of these types, whether or not they are similar to
the ones derived by psychometric techniques or ordinary
common sense, may be related to ESP ability. It might
in fact be possible to derive an ESP-typology from the
non-ESP component of the ESP guessing pattern.

The techniques which will be used to analyse
response sequences are too complicated to enter into here,
but will include the informational estimation of redundancy,
as used in the study of languages and the construction of
pseudo-languages, autocorrelation, and ad hoc methods to
reduce and classify the number of possible patterns. The
actual analysis will be carried out by an electronic
computer. It should be made clear that the quantity of
ESP in the results of even the best subjects is too small
to interfere with the elucidation of guessing habits. The
data used in this study will be obtained from group ESP
experiments which have yielded significant results, high
scoring subjects (including control series and records
taken after they lost their ability), from special groups
such as psychotics, children and mediums, and from
psychological and educational tests in which answers are
of the multiple choice type. The ESP data have been
promised by ▓▓▓▓▓▓▓▓▓▓▓▓▓▓▓▓▓▓▓▓▓▓▓▓▓▓▓▓▓▓▓▓▓▓▓

B
C

Individual Subjects. The amount of information
transmitted on the average per trial in ESP experiments
is: $\log_2 5 + (r/25)\log_2(r/25) + 4[(25-r)/100] \log_2 [(25-r)/100]$
in binits, where r is the number of correct guesses. (This
appears to be the correct model, since there is evidence
that subjects produce the same deviation from chance when
aiming below it as when they aim above, in spite of the
fact that $p \neq 1/2$). Good subjects will tend to have
somewhere between .2 and .6 bits of information generally

/available

595

available to them. This is one of the reasons why ESP
experiments are so difficult. But it may still be possible
to learn a good deal about the phenomenon, even if learning
studies should fail. For it is possible to vary the
experimental paradigm to discriminate between various
models for the operation of the phenomenon, such as:
ESP occurs sporadically but gives perfect information;
ESP always occurs and multiplies chances of success by
a constant factor; ESP tells the subject one of the
things the target is not; ESP, when it occurs, answers
a question of the form— is the target an X?. In addition
to psi-models, it will also be necessary to introduce
models which provide more sensitive estimates of ESP. For
example, target material will be introduced whereby guesses
instead of being of the 'all or nothing' type can be more or
less right. Again, a number of different p values will be
introduced and intermixed to imitate real life situations.

Learning studies will be instituted in which the
subject will be rewarded or punished for his overall
performance and reinforced in various ways — by being
told whether he was right, by being told what the target
was, with electric shock etc. In addition, an attempt
will be made to increase the transmitted information in
cases where the average probability of success remained
constant. Thus if N_{ia} = the number of trials in which
the ith distinguishable target is guessed to be the ath,
t_i = the frequency of i as a target, g_a = the frequency
of guesses of A, and N^1 = the number of trials, $(N_{ia})N/g_a(t_i)$,
which states the ratio of the frequency with which i is
guessed A to the expected frequency if there were no guessing
preference, may be used to determine which guess was the
best estimate of the target, and the resultant estimate,
which will depend on the number of trials and the quantity
of information available to the subject, will approach
certainty asymptotically.

But the main consideration will be the attitude
and general disposition of the subject. Wherever possible,
every attempt will be made to tailor the tasks required to
his preferences and his estimate of good working conditions.
In one case the experimental procedure will be designed to
achieve favorable motivation by such devices as instructing
him that he is participating in a study of subception. In
other cases drugs and psychological tricks will be used to
modify his attitudes. The experimenters will be particularly
interested in disassociative states, from the abaissement de
niveau mental to multiple personality in so-called mediums,
and an attempt will be made to induce a number of states of
this kind, using hypnosis. Hypnosis is seen not as a

/variable

Appendix

The Strange Case of Omaha FBI Agent Donald Rochon

The interviews I've conducted and the documentation I've collected demonstrate the mind-boggling lengths the Omaha FBI Field Office undertook to ensure Franklin's conspiracy of silence: Victims and potential witnesses were harassed and even terrorized, evidence was falsified, and Gary Caradori's investigation was ultimately sabotaged. This recurring malfeasance was to cover up the sexual abuse of children—the most depraved and evil of crimes. Various philosophers and social thinkers have argued that the willful, conscious cover-up of evil is almost equivalent to the hands on participation of evil, because evil can't exist without the lies it uses to conceal itself. For example, if Hitler or Stalin were candid about their respective genocides, they would have found scant support from their respective populaces.

I realize that accusing the Omaha FBI of not just evil but of a particularly odious strain of evil is a grave condemnation, but corroboration of a malignancy festering within the Omaha FBI exists outside the realm of Franklin and can be found in the legal documentation of Donald Rochon, an FBI special agent stationed in Omaha—he and his wife sued the FBI for "racial discrimination and harassment." The documentation from the Rochons' lawsuit provides an insight into an FBI Field Office that is depraved and dangerous.

Rochon was a distinguished African-American investigator for the terrorism division of the Los Angeles Police Department before he became an FBI special agent in 1981. Rochon would be assigned to the FBI's Omaha Field Office from January of 1983 to June of 1984, a period when King's pedophile network was purportedly in full swing, and he would quickly learn the strange ways of the Omaha FBI. Rochon started to receive harassing phone calls at his home and bogus messages at his office. When he returned the calls placed to his office, he would be connected to the recorded sermons of black preachers or recordings of gospel singers.

In addition to threats and harassment via the phone, Rochon said he began to find alarming photos and notes in his office mail slot, which was only accessible to FBI employees. The photos included the picture of a badly beaten black man, an African in native dress, and invitations to office functions with "don't come" scrawled on them. Rochon also found that the family photograph that he kept on his desk had been disfigured—a picture of a "monkey or ape" had been taped over the faces of his children.

When Rochon took up scuba diving, he said he noticed a picture of two black scuba divers swimming in a dump posted on the Omaha FBI Field Office's bulletin board—a picture of Rochon's face, illegally taken from his personnel file, was pasted over one of the diver's faces. Shortly thereafter, a battery-operated, toy scuba diver in a bowl of water was left on Rochon's desk—a felt-tipped marker had been used to blacken the diver's face, hands, and feet. When Rochon returned to his desk, the toy was switched on—Rochon "looked around in disbelief" as "many" FBI agents and employees looked on, laughed, and commented about blacks' inability to swim.

Rochon's lawsuit documentation is not only abounding with unfathomable racist conduct by special agents at the FBI's Omaha Field Office, but it cites acts of "sexual deviance" by the special agents too. Rochon stated that an Omaha special agent routinely kept pornography at his desk and that Rochon had personally witnessed this agent "exposing himself" to both male and female employees at the Omaha Field Office. Rochon heard that the same special agent plucked the "deodorant block" from a "men's urinal" and put it "in his mouth" and also allowed a fellow special agent to "urinate into his mouth."

The FBI conducted an investigation into Rochon's claims of sexual deviance by Omaha's special agents and found Rochon's observations were "taken out of context." The investigation unearthed a "mooning incident" at an office Christmas party, but found no "corroboration" of genital exposure. The investigation also concluded that the special agent in question wasn't guilty of inserting a urinal deodorant into his mouth or of permitting a fellow special agent to urinate in his mouth. However, the latter denial is in direct contradiction to an FBI agent who attended that party—his sworn statement to the FBI's Deputy Assistant Director explicitly stated that he actually witnessed an Omaha special agent urinating into the mouth of a second special agent at the party.

In 1985, Rochon maintained, he received an unsigned, typewritten letter in the mail, threatening him with mutilation and death and threatening his wife with sexual assault—attached to the letter was the picture of a black man whose body had been mutilated. In a subsequent letter Rochon wrote to the FBI's Equal Employment Opportunity Office, he mentioned that the "Omaha/Chicago clique has a long and established reputation for retaliation against persons crossing their path unfavorably." In the letter, he noted that special safeguards had been undertaken to protect him and his family from his fellow FBI agents after the FBI relocated him to Chicago. Rochon wrote that he essentially lived as a "protective federal witness," and to ensure his safety and the safety of his family only a handful of supervisors and agents had been privy to his new Chicago telephone number and address until it was leaked in a "memo." The letter further discussed that the "fear and intimidation" enveloping him was "becoming emotionally overwhelming for me and my family, especially since our address has been discovered."

The FBI denied nearly all of Rochon's allegations, and it didn't concede any misconduct, but the Bureau nonetheless decided to settle the Rochons' lawsuit for a considerable sum. Under terms of the settlement, the FBI forked over a full pension to Rochon, estimated at $1 million, and Rochon consented to leave the Bureau. The FBI also paid his legal team $500,000, and Rochon's wife received $150,000. Rochon said the FBI agreed to the settlement because a trial would have revealed that his fellow FBI agents had made death threats against him and his family, and that their supervisors covered up their egregious conduct.

It's almost inconceivable that a former highly decorated LAPD detective and seasoned FBI special agent would be so terrified of his fellow agents in the Omaha and Chicago FBI Field Offices that he feared for his life and for all intents and purposes lived as a protected witness. If Rochon was a member of the Gambino crime family, his fears would be well founded, but, unbelievably, he was in the FBI! Rochon essentially said that his case was a window into what happened to individuals who crossed the "Omaha/Chicago" FBI clique of the 1980s "unfavorably"— a clique that apparently viewed itself as above the law. The substantial corroboration I've collected confirms that Gary Caradori crossed the Omaha FBI unfavorably.

U.S. Departm' Justice

Federal Bureau of Investigation

In Reply, Please Refer to
File No.

219 South Dearborn Street
Chicago, Illinois 60604
June 3, 1985   **FILED**

Barbara Dean
Black Affairs Program Manager
Equal Employment Opportunity Office
FBI Headquarters

JUL 23 1990

CLERK, U.S. DISTRICT COURT
DISTRICT OF COLUMBIA

CONFIDENTIAL

Dear Ms. Dean:

Reference our telephone conversation on May 30, 1985, I have enclosed three EEO memorandums dated May 3, 1985, May 9, 1985, and May 21, 1985, concerning racially motivated death threats and harassment received by me. These latest events are the most serious problems I have incurred in a series of harassment.

The reason the harassment has occurred in the Chicago Division is the result of a complex and unique set of circumstances I will give you a brief overview to put matters into perspective.

Over two years ago while assigned to the Omaha Division, I had a racial conflict with a small clique of Agent's there. The principal person in this clique was THOMAS J. DILLON, currently assigned to the Chicago Division. DILLON caused his racial ideology to come to my attention while in Omaha by speaking boastfully about how he grew up in a racially segregated neighborhood in Chicago. He spoke about problems his neighborhood had with blacks moving in and how he lost some permanent teeth due to physical altercations with them. DILLON displayed a subtle contempt for blacks and other minorities.

This was reflected in his loud and overbearing discussions in which he made disparaging remarks about past and current black civil rights leaders, as well as contemporary black and white politicians in favor of civil rights. DILLON was openly supportive of J. EDGAR HOOVER'S reported campaign to discredit MARTIN LUTHER KING, JR. Even Judge WILLIAM WEBSTER was routinely and openly criticized because of his views on minority hiring and his general lack of HOOVER'S ideology.

EXHIBIT B

DEPOSITION
EXHIBIT
Sharp 23
6-19-90

603

I was not ashamed to make my views on civil rights and injustice known to this clique. What totally surprised me was their lack of tolerance to an opposing view. What I experienced as a result of this in Omaha was a series of pranks and harassment in which DILLON and his clique were implicated due to physical evidence, eye witness observations and confessions. Some of the pranks had insulting racial overtones. This clique was verbally advised to discontinue their activities during a special meeting with two Omaha supervisors in June, 1983, after I made a verbal complaint. Two other members of that clique, Charles Kemp and Larry Mc Gee, are from the Chicago Division. They were assigned there for many years prior to Omaha. KEMP now plans to return to the Chicago Division sometime this year. This clique was part of another clique in the Chicago Division where they had been assigned.

This clique was mad that I brought their activities to the attention of management. They had been spoiled by Omaha SAC, Herbert Hawkins' reputation for calling the only other black Agent, Charles Wiley, in the office a "nigger" to his face. This incident was not formally reported and that's the way this clique felt business should be conducted. This clique spread the rumor to make Hawkins appear as a macho SAC unintimidated by a black EEO counselor.

Wiley personally explained the incident in which Hawkins made the racial slur to him. He described Hawkins' behavior in this incident as causing hard feelings between the two of them. Wiley had to verbally admonish Hawkins for using this racial slur. He saw no reason to formally report it since Hawkins had been admonished by him.

What further complicated matters was my transfer orders to Chicago in March, 1984. This resulted in a current EEO complaint for racial discrimination in transfer orders caused by Hawkins' influence on the Transfer Unit, which he openly claimed to have.

The controversy with regards to my transfer orders dealt with the fact that while I was assigned to Omaha, every white Agent in Omaha, without exception, was transferred to a top 12 office in a geographical area where they wanted to be. There were 12 transfer orders during that period to white Agents in which 10 of them received the exact top 12 office expressly requested without any Office of Preference rights. I was the only black person transferred to a top 12 office. I received totally opposite treatment because of Hawkins. This claim is supported by Bureau documentation concerning transfer requests of all employees in Omaha during that period.

-2-

Dillon, now assigned to Chicago Division, and other Agents who benefited from Hawkins preferential treatment, became upset about my allegation made in Omaha concerning preferential treatment of whites. They felt I was hurting a white SAC who went out of his way to help white Agents obtain their desired offices. They made their views known to fellow white Agents and supervisors. They could not change the facts of my allegation, so they attempted to discredit me by making me the issue.

When I reported to the Chicago Division, June 11, 1984, I learned a controversy had been started in the office and on my squad specifically because of my past complaint against Dillon (Omaha/Chicago clique) and my allegation of discrimination in transfer orders to Chicago. I also learned because of this controversy, my assigned supervisor in Chicago had attempted to transfer me off his squad to a squad of a black supervisor prior to even meeting me. The internal transfer never came off. This sent signals to the Agents on my squad how management felt about blacks making racial complaints.

This controversy started some minor harassing pranks against me. Samples of which are a bag of chicken bones neatly placed on my desk and the posting of a derogatory editorial on Jesse Jackson on my desk.

Things were even further complicated later on that summer when Dillon learned that he (and a few members of his clique) was the subject of an administrative inquiry by the Office of Professional Responsibility for sexual misconduct. Myself and others personally observed Dillon violate criminal law by intentionally exposing his penis in the center of the Omaha Office to employees during normal business hours. Two black female employees, Gurthie Armstrong and Syn Parker, expressly complained to a white supervisor, Connie Wickman. This was also observed by a white Agent supervisor who did nothing. These ladies were told to keep quiet because it was a minor incident. They and others were upset that this violation was being covered up. I made it my responsibility to see that it was not.

Dillon was also investigated for a separate and unrelated incident of "french kissing" another male Agent, Terry Boley (recently assigned to Chicago), while they were intoxicated at a private social event. This was personally observed by myself and others who corroborated this event. It was a clear embarrassment to the Bureau. There were also other incidents of bizarre sexual type of misconduct this clique was investigated for.

-3-

605

Upon learning of this inquiry, Dillon and his clique immediately started an open propaganda campaign against me. He brought his administrative inquiry to the attention of other employees who had no idea of his behavior beforehand. This clique exploited racism to get back at me. Dillon and his clique were given letter of censures for their activities.

This agitation by the Omaha/Chicago clique resulted in further racially motivated harassment against me. This agitation has lead up to the present circumstances of receiving threats and harassment.

This has been a very emotion issue for the management in Chicago to handle. Because of my complaint against a few white Agents and my discrimination complaint against a white SAC, Hawkins, I believe I have not received much sympathy and help from management in Chicago. When I complained to ASAC Milt Ahlerich in writing about ongoing annoying calls to my temporary quarters, he did absolutely nothing to help me. I had to deal with the police and telephone company as a private citizen. On another occasion when I complained to management about someone intentionally flattening my tire on my assigned Bureau car, I was not assigned another Bureau car for a couple of months apparently to protect the fleet. When it was established that I was receiving obscene and annoying phone calls at my office extension, I was transferred from a popular organized crime squad to an unpopular applicant squad. This was because Dillon was on a squad next to mine. The SAC felt that if I was out of Dillon's sight, the agitation and harassment would stop in the office. This was not the case.

Since I moved into my permanent residence in September, 1984, I have been living as a "protective Federal witness." Only the Chicago SAC, a couple of supervisors and a few Agents have my telephone number and address. This Omaha/Chicago clique has a long and established reputation for retaliation against persons crossing their path unfavorably. By law, this is an unfair employment practice to cause an employee to work in fear of retaliation due to his race, when the situation could be easily amended by changing work environment.

Living with fear and intimidation is becoming emotional: overwhelming for me and my family, especially since our address has been discovered (memo dated May 3, 1985). The person responsible for these acts appears dangerous and mentally disturbed. This person is bent on violating my civil rights.

The Chicago Office has opened an administrative inquiry in order to identify this person. This person has apparently made an effort not to implicate the Chicago Office

-4-

TION,

For Summary Judgements As to Sept 13, 1989
Plaintiffs' "Chicago CLAIMS"

In responding to and investigating these complaints (the
"Chicago/Rochon Complaints"), the FBI compiled an administrative
record of more than 1,500 pages.[3] The entirety of the record is
submitted herewith.[4] Because of the record's length, a detailed
summary of the investigations pertinent to this motion is
presented below.

II.   The Sexual Deviance Complaint and Investigation

      (June - October 1984).

On June 4, 1984, seven days before he reported for duty in
Chicago, SA Rochon telephoned John D. Stapleton, a Supervisory
Special Agent ("SSA") in the FBI's Office of Professional
Responsibility ("OPR"), to make a confidential complaint about

---

[2](...continued)
SSA Jon W. Housley, interviewed the four members of the United
States Attorney's Office with direct personal knowledge of the
incident. Id. (AG 1523-33).

Based on the information that the investigation of the
prisoner-release incident produced, SSA Crocker concluded that SA
Rochon had not intended to secure the release of the inmate
"without the prior approval of the SAC as is required" and that,
accordingly, no action was required beyond the severe oral
reprimand that SA Rochon had already received. Id. (AG 1522).

The second was a complaint lodged by SA Kenneth Veach
regarding a confrontation between Veach and Rochon on January 9,
1986. This complaint is described in detail in Part VII, N, The
Rochon-Veach Confrontation, infra.

[3] References to the record are to specific FBI files, and to
specific page numbers within those files. Copies of the
foregoing files are submitted herewith. File numbers beginning
with the letters "HQ" refer to files maintained at FBIHQ; file
numbers beginning with the letters "CG" refer to files maintained
in the Chicago Field Office. The page numbers (e.g., "AG 1019")
have been added by the Attorney General's undersigned counsel for
ease of reference.

[4] As to the authenticity of the materials submitted
herewith, see declaration of Eric M. Dohogne, ¶ 2.

- 5 -

"homosexual activities" and other acts of sexual deviance on the part of SA Thomas J. Dillon, a former member of the Omaha Field Office who recently had been reassigned to Chicago.[5] HQ 62-120862 (AG 1019). Responding to these accusations, OPR opened an immediate investigation into the behavior of SA Dillon.[6] Id. (AG 1021). In the course of the investigation, OPR, operating out of FBIHQ, collected a series of signed, sworn statements from 18 witnesses to, or participants in, the alleged acts of perversion.

In response to his telephonic complaint, a signed sworn statement was taken from Rochon on July 3, 1984. In his statement, Rochon described a series of acts or events which he alleged were evidence of sexual deviance by SA Dillon and other SAs assigned to the Omaha Office. Specifically, Rochon alleged that he had "personally observed" Dillon "'French Kissing'" SA Terry J. Bohle, a male, at a going-away party for SA Bohle, and the he likewise had "personally witnessed" Dillon "exposing himself in the Omaha office during a regular work day to numerous

---

[5] OPR is the component of the Bureau, located at FBIHQ, responsible for supervising the investigation of all allegations of criminality or serious misconduct on the part of FBI employees. Manual of Investigative Operations & Guidelines, vol. II, pt. 1, § 263, at 966.407 (1988).

[6] The substance of these allegations do not pertain to racial harassment against SA Rochon. Nonetheless, as a result of SAs Dillon and Rochon's assignment in Omaha, this investigation is but one piece of the sequence of events in which they are both involved or implicated. Thus, both the timing and content of Rochon's allegations are relevant to the subsequent series of events that transpired in Chicago. Moreover, the extent of this investigation demonstrates that SA Rochon's complaint regarding SA Dillon was not ignored or covered-up by the FBI; instead it was made the basis of an extensive and careful investigation.

- 6 -

Omaha employees, both male and female." Id. In addition, Rochon said that he had heard reports that Dillon had allowed Bohle to urinate into his mouth and to "urinate in a beer bottle, [from] which he subsequently drank;" and that Dillon had been observed "picking out the deodorant block in men's urinal and placing this block in his mouth." Id. (AG 1020). Rochon further alleged that Dillon appeared preoccupied with homosexual sex, kept homosexual pornography at his desk, and had frequently spoken in the office of homosexual acts (AG 1074).

In concluding his statement, Rochon said that he had chosen to contact OPR on June 4, 1984 -- months after the events in question -- because he "did not want any more harassment from Dillon" after reporting for duty in Chicago on June 11, 1984, and because, after leaving Omaha, he thought he would be safe from harassment by that office's Special Agent in Charge ("SAC") and Assistant Special Agent in Charge ("ASAC"). Id. (AG 1080). And, he said, "I also had a feeling of retaliation against Dillon for the pranks and harassment which I felt he had performed against me and my family." Id.

Responding to the foregoing, OPR promptly took signed sworn statements from several witnesses, including the alleged participants in the activities as well as the sources of information to whom SA Rochon had referred in his statement. These statements provided conflicting accounts of the incidents described by SA Rochon. In all, eighteen statements were taken of SAs and support employees in the Omaha Office who were

- 7 -

witnesses to or had information regarding the incidents described by Rochon.[7] The statements of Dillon's superiors were also taken. Some of the statements confirm that certain events described by SA Rochon had in fact occurred, although not in the manner alleged. Specifically, a "mooning" incident involving two SAs at a going-away party and one involving SA Dillon at an office Christmas party in 1983 were confirmed. However, contrary to Rochon's assertions, none of the witnesses observed SA Dillon or any other SA expose his genitals during these incidents. SA Dillon also confirmed several of these incidents in his own statement, but denied certain details as well as the context in which SA Rochon described them. None of the statements supported the serious allegation that Dillon was involved in homosexuality or deviant sexual practices.[8]

More specifically, in a signed sworn statement executed on July 27, 1984, SA Dillon denied ever taking a bite from or placing a urinal mint in this mouth (AG 1242). Dillon also denied the allegation that he had given a "French kiss" or touched tongues with SA Bohle during a going-away party which was

---

[7] Statements were not taken from all persons attending the events when the incidents were alleged to have occurred. Specifically, statements were not taken from SA Dillon's wife or the other office members' spouses, nor was one taken from the mother of the host of one of the parties who was present.

[8] Instead what the investigation showed was that SA Dillon, as part of his official duties in the office's investigation of the kidnap, mutilation and murder of two young boys, had to interview homosexuals and young male prostitutes for any information they might have, as well as review homosexual publications periodically for leads. Id. (AG 1249, 1250).

- 8 -

attended by the spouses of office members. SA Dillon advised that he had hugged SA Bohle as well as several other people who were leaving the division, and had kissed them on the cheek and been kissed on his cheek in return. Id. SA Dillon advised, however, that this had been intended as a joke. Dillon also denied that he had ever drunk urine as alleged by SA Rochon, that he had intentionally permitted another SA to urinate on him or that he had taken any urine into his mouth, although he did admit that another SA had accidentally urinated on him during a private party at a cabin on a lake. The other SA, SA Bohle, also confirmed this incident.

SA Dillon did admit that he had exposed his buttocks during an office Christmas party in 1983, but denied that he exposed his genitals. SA Dillon explained that he had been encouraged by others to try to raise the morale and spirit of the people present at the party because office personnel had been under much stress and were very depressed over the office's then ongoing investigation into the kidnap, murder and mutilation of two young boys. To his later embarrassment, SA Dillon admitted that he "mooned" the people present at the party in an attempt to raise their spirits. However, Dillon advised that the incident consisted of the exposure of only a portion of his buttocks, not his full buttocks, that he had not exposed the front of this body or genitals, and that the incident was over in a matter of seconds. (AG 1248).

- 9 -

On August 3, 1984, SSA Stapleton forwarded to the
Administrative Summary Unit[9] ("ASU"), for "review and action
deemed appropriate," the results of OPR's investigation into the
acts of perversion allegedly committed by SA Dillon. In doing
so, Stapleton said that the investigation had "substantiated and
corroborated" certain of the allegations that Rochon had made
against Dillon, but that "SA Dillon's conduct, as alleged by SA
Rochon, was taken out of context and did not, for the most part,
occur as stated by SA Rochon."[10] Id. (AG 1000). For instance,
"no one present for the 'mooning incident' at the 1983 Omaha
office Christmas party" had corroborated Rochon's allegation that
Dillon had exposed his genitals. Id. On the contrary, all of
the witnesses had stated that Dillon had "exposed only his bare
buttocks" and that "the entire incident" had ended "in a matter
of seconds." Id. In addition, "[n]one of the witnesses [had]
corroborate[d] any genital or frontal exposure whatsoever." Id.

On October 11, 1984, SSA W. Lane Crocker of ASU responded to
the Dillon investigation. After summarizing in detail each of SA

---

[9] ASU is the component within the FBI's Administrative
Services Division responsible for reviewing the investigations of
agent misconduct conducted by OPR and making recommendations to
the Assistant Director, Administrative Services Division, with
respect to the taking of disciplinary action in response thereto.
Manual of Administrative Operations & Procedures, pt. 1, 13-2, at
153 (1987).

[10] The attribution of the above remarks to Stapleton is based
on the appearance of his typed initials at the foot of the
document from which the remarks are taken (the document is a
memorandum dated August 3, 1984, from John D. Glover to Mr.
Groover). The practice of attributing the authorship of
documents to those whose typed initials appears at their foot is
followed throughout this brief.

Rochon's allegations and the evidence obtained by OPR in response thereto, Crocker said that the available evidence had "failed to reveal any grounds to conclude that SAs Dillon, Bohle, or Kempf [had] engaged in sexually deviant behavior or that they ha[d] homosexual tendencies." Id. (AG 1009). At the same time, Crocker said that Dillon and Bohle had "used poor judgment" when they "mooned" the office Christmas party. Id. Acknowledging that the "mooning" had taken place "in a lighthearted vein [and] with no intention of offending anyone," Crocker described "such crude conduct in FBI office space" as "clearly inappropriate and unprofessional." Id. Accordingly, he recommended that Dillon and Bohle be censured. Id.

In addition, Crocker said that the failure of SSA Murphy SA Dillon's supervisor who was present at the Christmas party, to report the "mooning" incident to SAC Hawkins or ASAC Evans required that he, too, be disciplined. Id. (AG 1010). Characterizing Murphy as "a member of the Omaha supervisory staff," Crocker said that he had "had an obligation to report this misconduct to his superiors" and that his failure to do so "demonstrat[ed] poor judgment which merits an oral reprimand." Id.

As to Kempf, Crocker felt that no disciplinary action was warranted. While Kempf had also been involved in a "mooning" incident, Crocker noted that the incident had occurred at Kempf's own home, during a private party. Id. (AG 1009). Accordingly,

- 11 -

613

Crocker recommended that Kempf not be the recipient of
administrative discipline. Id.

On October 18, 1984, L. Clyde Groover, Jr., Assistant
Director ("AD"), Administrative Services Division ("ASD"), issued
letters of censure to Dillon and Bohle. The letters advised the
two men that they had "engaged in crude and unprofessional
behavior" at the 1983 Christmas party; that their conduct had
been "clearly inappropriate in an office setting;" that they had
fallen short of the "high standards of conduct" to which special
agents were held; and that their actions had been "indicative of
extremely poor judgment." Id. (AG 957, 958). In his letter to
Dillon, Groover also spoke of the "seriousness" with which he
viewed Dillon's "misconduct" and of his expectation that Dillon's
"behavior in the future" would be "beyond reproach so that
instances of this nature do not recur." Id. (AG 958). In
addition to the letters of censure, SSA Murphy also received an
oral reprimand for his failure to report the "mooning" incident.

    III.   The Initial Complaints of Racial Harassment: The
            Chicken-Bone and Other Incidents (August -
            November 1984).

    A.   The First Set of Allegations. As the foregoing
investigation was proceeding, SA Rochon began to complain of
racial harassment within the Chicago Field Office. At a meeting
held on August 1, 1984, he reported to two of the office's
leaders, SAC Edward D. Hegarty and ASAC Milt Ahlerich, that
certain acts of discrimination had recently occurred, including
the "leaving [of] chicken bones on his desk and [the] placing

- 12 -

614

Abbreviated List of Sources

Newspapers & Magazines

Associated Press
Chicago Tribune
Courier Mail (Queensland, Australia)
Daily Telegraph (Sydney, Australia)
Des Moines Register
Evening Standard (London)
Gentleman's Quarterly Magazine
Globe and Mail (Canada)
Guardian (London)
Lincoln Journal
Lincoln Journal-Star
Los Angeles Times
Metropolitan (Omaha)
New York Post
New York Times

Omaha Sun
Omaha Star
Omaha World-Herald
Orange County Register
St. Petersburg Times (Florida)
Sunday Times (London)
Tampa Tribune
Toronto Star
United Press International
US News & World Report
USA Today
Village Voice
Washington Post
Washington Times

Television & Video

Conspiracy of Silence, Yorkshire Television
FOX's America's Most Wanted
NBC Today Show
CBS 48 Hours
Lawrence King interview on Omaha's channel 7

Books & Journals

Becker, Thorsten, et al. "Researching for New Perspectives: Ritual Abuse/Ritual Violence as Ideologically Motivated Crime." In R. Norblitt and P. Norblitt (Eds.) *Ritual Abuse in the 21st Century: Psychological, Forensic, Social, and Political Considerations.* Bandon, OR: Robert D. Reed Publishers, 2008.

Becker, Thorsten, et al. "The Extreme Abuse Surveys: Preliminary Finding Regarding Dissociative Identity Disorder." In A. Sachs and G. Galton (Eds.) *Forensic Aspects of Dissociative Identity Disorder.* London: Karnac, 2008.

Colodny, Len and Robert Getlin. *Silent Coup: The Removal of a President.* New York: St. Martin's Press, 1991.

Collins, Leslie and Rita Collins, *The Say Book.* Boys Town: Boys Town Press, 1989.

Dallam, S.J. "Crisis or Creation: A systematic examination of false memory claims." *Journal of Child Sexual Abuse.* 2002 9 (3/4), 9-36.

DeCamp, John, *The Franklin Cover-Up.* Lincoln, Nebraska: ATW, 1992.

Mayer, Jane, and Jill Abramson, *Strange Justice: The Selling of Clarence Thomas.* New York: Houghton Mifflin Company, 1994.

Ross, Collin. *Bluebird: Deliberate Creation of Multiple Personality Disorder by Psychiatrists.* Richardson, TX: Manitou Communications, 2000.

Young, Walter C., et al. Patients reporting ritual abuse in childhood: a clinical syndrome. Report of 37 cases. *Child Abuse and Neglect.* 1991;15(3):181-9.

Government & Court Documents

Department of Treasury, United States Custom Service, Report of Investigation
Douglas County Grand Jury testimony
Nebraska State Patrol Investigative Reports
Omaha Police Department Investigative Reports
Omaha Police Department Inter-Office Communications
Notes of Dennis Carlson, Vice Chair of Foster Care Review Board
Nebraska Department of Social Services Reports
Nebraska Department of Social Services "Investigative Narrative" on Webb home
Foster Care Review Case Review Reports
Carol Stitt, Director of Foster Care Review Board, letter to Robert Spire, Nebraska Attorney General
Julie Walters, Boys Town youth worker, March 1986 interviews of Eulice and Tracy Washington
Results of Eulice Washington's polygraph by the Nebraska State Patrol
Nebraska's Washington County Sheriff's Reports
Foster Care Review Board's Stitt, Carlson, and Williams testifying before Unicameral's Executive Board
Nebraska Unicameral's Legislative Resolution 5
Nebraska Attorney General Robert Spire's petition for the formation of the Douglas County grand jury
Investigator Lowe's memo on meeting with Nebraska Attorney General's Office
Investigator Lowe's review of Nebraska Attorney General's Office Investigative Reports
Investigator Lowe's report on meeting with confidential informant
Investigator Lowe's report on interview of Patricia Flocken
Investigator Lowe's report on interviews with Shawneta Moore
Investigator Lowe's report on interview with OPD officer Irl Carmean
Investigator Lowe's report on meeting with Social Services Personnel
Investigator Lowe's report on interview with OPD Chief Robert Wadman
Investigator Lowe's report on interviews with the Washington sisters' relatives
6/29/89 Testimony of Carol Stitt and Dennis Carlson to Franklin Committee
6/29/89 Testimony of OPD officer Irl Carmean to Franklin Committee
6/29/89 Testimony of Assistant Attorney General William Howland to Franklin Committee
6/29/89 Testimony of Attorney General's Office investigator Thomas Vlahoulis to Franklin Committee
6/29/89 Testimony of Nebraska Attorney General Robert Spire to Franklin Committee
National Transportation Safety Board report on Gary Caradori's plane crash
Douglas County grand jury "Witness Schedule"
Douglas County grand jury "Exhibit Description"
Omaha Police Department catalogue of exhibits seized from Peter Citron's home during the execution of search warrant
FBI transcription of March 9, 1990 phone call between Troy Boner and Alisha Owen
Nebraska Center for Women at York: Visitor's Register
The Nebraska Center for Women at York: Phone Signup Sheets
Federal Search Warrant for Alisha Owen's cell at Nebraska Center for Women at York
Douglas County Judge's authorization for NSP Investigator Charles Phillips "to effect whatever detention is necessary" to obtain bloods sample from five-year-old Amanda Owen

Douglas County Grand Jury report

Edward Fogarty deposition of Pamela Vuchetich (State of Nebraska v. Alisha Owen)

State of Nebraska v. Alisha Owen trial transcripts

Nebraska Supreme Court, State of Nebraska, Appellee, v. Larry E. Packett, Appellant No. 42857

Federal "Conditional Non-Prosecution Agreement" of Alisha Owen

Federal "Conditional Non-Prosecution Agreement" of Troy Boner

Federal "Conditional Non-Prosecution Agreement" of Danny King

Amended Federal "Conditional Non-Prosecution Agreement" of Troy Boner

Amended Federal "Conditional Non-Prosecution Agreement" of Danny King

Alisha Owen correspondences at the Nebraska Center for Women at York

Federal subpoena of Pamela Vuchetich for Alisha Owen's "folder/notebook"

FBI debriefings (FD-302s)

FBI inter-office memorandums

Troy Boner's handwritten recantation of child-abuse allegations that was penned at Omaha's FBI Field Office on 3/20/90

City of Omaha, Nebraska Personnel Department Health Evaluation Report on Robert Wadman

State of Nebraska, Appellee, v. Martin L. Anderson, Appellant, Supreme Court of Nebraska Decision

Lancaster County, Nebraska Sheriff's Office Coroner Report on Aaron Owen

Office of Chief Medical Examiner, Tarrant County, Texas, Autopsy Report for Troy Boner

State of Nebraska, Appellee v. Alisha Owen, Appellant A-94-1147

State of Nebraska, Appellee v. Alisha Owen, Appellant A-92-0866

State of Nebraska, Appellee v. Alisha Owen, Appellant A-95-5072

State of Nebraska, Appellee v. Alisha Owen, Appellant A-91-0836

Nebraska Court of Appeals responses to appellant Alisha Owen

Nebraska Supreme Court response to appellant Alisha Owen

Opinion of the Nebraska Court of Appeals, State of Nebraska, Appellee v. Leslie E. Collins A-97-0984

Gary Caradori Documents

Investigator Caradori's daily logs of his Franklin investigation

Investigator Caradori's reports on meetings with confidential informants

Investigator Caradori's meetings with former Franklin Credit Union executives

7/12/90 Federal subpoena served on Caracorp

Investigator Caradori's correspondences throughout Franklin Investigation

Investigator Caradori's testimony to the Franklin Committee

Investigator Caradori's "Leads List"

Investigator Caradori's letters to alleged perpetrators

Investigator Caradori's videotaped interviews of Alisha Owen, Troy Boner, Danny King, Paul Bonacci, and a Franklin Credit Union security guard

Investigator Caradori's synopses of his videotaped interviews

Letter from Nebraska Secretary of State to Investigator Caradori

Letter from Investigator Caradori to Nebraska Secretary of State

Affidavit of Senator Loran Schmit's regarding FBI death threat to Alan Baer

Affidavit of Senator Loran Schmit's regarding Gary Caradori's life being endangered

Douglas County Grand Jury subpoena of Caracorp phone records
Caracorp phone records

Other Documents

1983 program of the Nebraska Frederick Douglas Republican Council reception honoring Lawrence King

Lawrence King's résumé

Internal Franklin Federal Credit Union documents

Lawrence King's Franklin Credit Union correspondences

Lists of the invitees for Lawrence King's Nebraska and Washington, DC parties

Letter written by Lawrence King in the capacity of Advisor, Youth Affairs Committee, National Black Republican Council

Richard Young Hospital's "Nurses Notes" on Shawneta Moore

Kirstin Hallberg's handwritten notes

Kathleen Sorenson's handwritten notes

Bonnie Cosentino affidavit alleging misconduct by Douglas County Grand Jury assistant prosecutor Terry Dougherty

Statement to Ernie Chambers of woman who alleged misconduct by Douglas County Grand Jury prosecutor Samuel Van Pelt

Omaha/Douglas County History Timeline

Nebraska Center for Women at York Superintendent's correspondences regarding Alisha Owen

The "DeCamp Memo"

Results of Karen Ormiston polygraph by Professional Security Consultants

Transcripts of phone call between John DeCamp and Rusty Nelson on 7/24/97

Pamela Vuchetich's correspondences regarding Alisha Owen

Pamela Vuchetich's phone records

Henry Rosenthal's subpoena of Pamela Vuchetich

Henry Rosenthal's correspondences regarding Alisha Owen

Henry Rosenthal deposition of Michael Flanagan (State of Nebraska v. Alisha Owen)

Lawyer Gerry Spence's deposition of Robert Wadman (Singer v. Wadman)

Affidavits from jurors in State of Nebraska v. Owen

7/29/92 Affidavit of Robert Janecek

5/23/92 Affidavit of Donna Owen

Aaron Owen "suicide letter"

John DeCamp's correspondences regarding Alisha Owen

John DeCamp's Petition for Writ of Habeas Corpus on behalf of Alisha Owen

Edward Fogarty's correspondences regarding Alisha Owen

1/5/2000 Henry Rosenthal Affidavit

Edward Fogarty's "Post Conviction Remedy" on behalf of Alisha Owen

Result of Donna Owen polygraph by Thomas J. Wheeler

1/30/2004 Report on the Investigation of Child-abuse Allegations at Father Flanagan's Boys' Home, James Martin Davis

Patrick Noaker's deposition of Father James Kelly (Rivers v. Boys Town)

Larry Walker's rental lease from Knudson Investment Co., Inc.

MK-ULTRA documentation

Index

O

P

R

Rama, Sri Swami 19
Randall, Gary 55, 56
Rather, Dan 152, 221, 428, 438
Reagan, Maureen 37, 510
Reagan, Nancy 37
Reagan, Ronald 34, 37, 39, 277, 282, 285, 288, 468
Republican National Committee 17, 38
Republican Party 17, 36, 38, 79
Richardson, Elliot 279, 617
Richard Young Hospital 63-66, 69, 72-76, 84, 85, 89, 90, 223, 224, 258, 259, 492, 620
Rivers, Todd 472, 473, 620
Road Less Traveled, The 201
Rodriguez, Paul 166, 170, 172, 275-279, 284, 287, 292, 298, 300, 302, 304, 309, 465, 468, 477, 486
Roethmeyer, Patricia 56
Rogers, Charlie 41-45, 100, 446, 447, 492
Rooney, Mickey 181
Rose, Charlie 14
Rosenthal, Henry 236, 240, 312, 322-330, 333-354, 357-386, 389-396, 398-417, 421, 427, 432-435, 441, 445, 453, 457-460, 485, 620

S

Safire, William 279
Saint Joseph's Hospital 113-115, 213, 256, 315, 354, 357, 373, 379, 435
Schmit, Loran 78-82, 95-100, 109, 127, 131, 134, 137-147, 162-166, 170-173, 176, 178, 217, 240-242, 254, 263-270, 273, 321, 383, 398-401, 408, 411, 412, 425, 438, 467, 492, 493, 499, 584
Sevareid, Eric 279
Shiina, Motoo 281-284, 292
Sigler, Bob 43, 44, 136, 138, 253, 446, 447, 450, 453, 456, 458, 492
Simpson, O.J. 453
Solberg, Steve 388, 391-395

Sorenson, Kathleen 53-55, 58, 60, 64, 224, 225, 256, 373, 492
Sorenson, Ronald 53
Southwick, Rick 391, 393, 395
Spence, Craig 166, 279-311, 465, 468, 480, 471, 477, 491, 493, 494
Spire, Robert 73, 74, 80, 87, 97, 98, 132, 133, 146, 217, 218, 492, 493, 618
Spitzer, Elliot 469
Staskiewicz, Ronald 137, 138, 217, 253, 335
Stephens, Jay 298, 301
Stitt, Carol 71-75, 79, 80, 97, 221-224, 227, 258, 259, 492, 618
Strange Justice: The Selling of Clarence Thomas 40, 617
Strasser, Alan 298-300
Swift, Gustavas 31, 33

T

Tate, Tim 16
Thalken, Thomas 141, 149, 438, 439
Thomas, Clarence 36, 39, 40, 617
Thompson, Hunter 484, 485
Thornburgh, Richard 308
Time for Burning, A 79
Today Show 38, 617
Tracy, Spencer 181
Tripp, Patrick 53-58, 221, 259
Tucker, Jerry 86
Turner, Damien 430, 431, 447
Turner, Maurice Jr. 13

U

Union Pacific Railroad 31-34, 361
University of Nebraska 18, 32, 71, 73, 78, 82, 146, 218, 240, 398
University of Utah 145
Urbom, Warren 27, 482, 483, 495
U.S. Customs Service (USCS) 10-15, 19, 473, 487, 498
US Medical Center for Federal Prisoners 134, 135, 136, 262
U.S. News & World Report 10, 13, 14, 468, 617
U.S. Secret Service 133, 276, 288, 289,